How the Sex-Drugs-and-
Rock'n'Roll Generation
Saved Hollywood

Peter Biskind

Simon & Schuster Paperbacks
New York   London   Toronto   Sydney

Easy Riders, Raging Bulls

Simon & Schuster Paperbacks
Rockefeller Center
1230 Avenue of the Americas
New York, NY 10020

SIMON & SCHUSTER PAPERBACKS and colophon are registered
trademarks of Simon & Schuster, Inc.

For information about special discounts for bulk purchases,
please contact Simon & Schuster Special Sales:
1-800-456-6798 or business@simonandschuster.com.

Designed by Karolina Harris
Photo Research by Natalie Goldstein

Manufactured in the United States of America

17 19 20 18

The Library of Congress has cataloged the
hardcover edition as follows:

Biskind, Peter.
Easy riders, raging bulls : how the sex-drugs-and-rock'n'roll
generation saved Hollywood / Peter Biskind.
p.   cm.
Filmography: p.
Includes bibliographical references and index.
1. Motion picture producers and directors—United States—
Biography. 2. Motion pictures—United States—History. I. Title.
PN1998.2.B56   1998
791.43'0233'092273—dc21
[B]   98-2919   CIP
ISBN-13: 978-0-684-80996-0
ISBN-10:   0-684-80996-6
ISBN-13: 978-0-684-85708-4 (Pbk)
ISBN-10:   0-684-85708-1 (Pbk)

Acknowledgments

HOLLYWOOD is a town of fabulators. The people who dwell there create fictions for a living, fictions that refuse tidily to confine themselves to the screen, but spill over into the daily lives of the men and women who regard themselves as stars in the movies of their own lives. Although this book tells readers altogether more than they may wish to know about the Hollywood of the '70s, I do not flatter myself that I have arrived at "the truth." At the end of this long, twisted road I am once again struck with the force of the old maxim, the more you know, the more you know what you don't know. This is particularly true in the case of Hollywood, where despite the reams of memos and contracts that now gather dust on the shelves of university libraries, very little of what really matters is committed to paper, so that an endeavor of this sort is dependent on memory — in this case of an era twenty or thirty years in the past. Not only is the terrain distant, but in this period memory has been enfeebled by booze and drugs.

In a town where credit grabbing is an art form, to say that memory is self-serving is to say that the sun rises in the east and sets in the west. Moreover, defect of memory is a shield that enables people to go to work in the morning, protecting them from the unspeakable behavior that is taken for granted there. As director Paul Schrader puts it, "In this business, you've got to have a selective memory. Otherwise, it's too painful." Kurosawa's *Rashomon* remains one of the truest movies about the movies and the people who make them.

In this maze of mirrors, lucky is the chronicler who does not lose his or her way in the infinity of reflections. So despite the wealth of bizarre and lurid detail to come, be assured that this book merely scratches the surface. The elusive "truth" is stranger still.

Many, many people in Hollywood were anxious to have the story of this decade told. As producer Harry Gittes puts it, "I want my children to know what I did." These were the best years of their lives, the years they did their finest work, and they were more than generous with their time and encouragement, always willing to make the phone calls that paved the way for yet more interviews. They know who they are, and I am infinitely grateful to all of them.

In addition, I wish to acknowledge the generous help and support of the current and previous staffs of *Premiere* magazine, where I happily worked while researching and writing this book, particularly the founding editor-in-chief, Susan Lyne, for giving me the freedom I needed, as well as Chris Connelly, for teaching me the importance of the *National Enquirer*, Corie Brown, Nancy Griffin, Cyndi Stivers, Rachel Abramowitz, Terri Minsky, Deborah Pines, Kristen O'Neil, Bruce Bibby, John Clark, Marc Malkin, Sean Smith, and the current editor, Jim Meigs. Many more helped me with research and transcribing, and among them I would like to thank John Housley, Josh Rottenberg, and Susanna Sonnenberg.

Michael Giltz fact-checked the book, and Natalie Goldstein researched the photographs. Sara Bershtel, Ron Yerxa, John Richardson, Howard Karren, and Susan Lyne read the lengthy manuscript and gave me invaluable editorial help, and in this regard I would particularly like to thank Lisa Chase and Susie Linfield. George Hodgman made this book happen when he was at Simon & Schuster, Alice Mayhew gave it her blessing, and Bob Bender, along with his assistant, Johanna Li, helped it to see the light of day. My agent, Kris Dahl, guided me through the shoals of writing and editing.

Finally, I would like to thank my wife, Elizabeth Hess, and daughter, Kate, for their unfailing patience and support.

For Betsy and Kate

Contents

Introduction:
Knockin' on Heaven's Door

"Some friends of mine were saying the '70s was the last Golden Age. I said, 'How can you say that?' They replied, 'Well, you had all these great directors making picture after picture. You had Altman, Coppola, Spielberg, Lucas. . . .'"

— MARTIN SCORSESE

February 9, 1971, 6:01 in the morning. A scattering of cars, headlights glowing fuzzily in the predawn gloom, had just begun to navigate the freeways as the first commuters sleepily sipped coffee out of Styrofoam cups and listened to the early morning news. A high of 71 degrees was expected. The Manson trial, now in the penalty phase, was still titillating the city of Los Angeles. Suddenly, the ground started to shake violently, not like the rolling, almost soothing motion of previous earthquakes. This was an abrupt heaving and falling that was terrifying in its intensity and duration, threatening to go on forever. For many, the 6.5 quake felt like the Big One. Manson's girls would claim later that Charlie himself had brought it down on the sinners tormenting him.

Over in Burbank, Martin Scorsese was jolted out of bed. He had just gotten a big break, an editing job at Warner Bros., and had arrived from New York a few weeks earlier. Marty was staying at the Toluca Motel, across the street from the lot. Dreaming of rare books when he heard a rumble, he imagined he was in the subway. "I jumped out of bed, looked out the window," he recalls. "Everything was shaking. Lightning was slashing across the sky — it was the electric wires from the telephone poles, falling down. It was terrifying. I thought, I gotta get outta here. By the time I pulled on my cowboy boots, got my money and the key to the motel room, and made it to the door, it was over. I went to the Copper Penny, and while I was having coffee, there was a big aftershock. I got up to run, and a guy looked at me and said, 'Where are you going to go?' I said, 'You're right. I'm stuck.'"

For Scorsese, there *was* nowhere to run. He had followed his dream to Hollywood, and if it was going to be a bumpier ride than he had imagined, he either had to stick it out or go back to New York, make industrials, live in the old neighborhood and eat cannoli, always knowing that he hadn't had the stomach for what it took to make it in the movies.

Before the dust settled, sixty-five souls had perished in the quake. None of the people who populate this book was among them. *Their* injuries would be self-inflicted.

FOR OUR PURPOSES, the earthquake of 1971 was supererogatory, unnecessary, gilding the lily, as Hollywood has always been wont to do. The real earthquake, the cultural convulsion that upended the film industry, began a decade earlier, when the tectonic plates beneath the back lots began to shift, shattering the verities of the Cold War—the universal fear of the Soviet Union, the paranoia of the Red Scare, the menace of the bomb—freeing a new generation of filmmakers frozen in the ice of '50s conformity. Then came, pell-mell, a series of premonitory shocks—the civil rights movement, the Beatles, the pill, Vietnam, and drugs—that combined to shake the studios badly, and send the demographic wave that was the baby boom crashing down about them.

Because movies are expensive and time-consuming to make, Hollywood is always the last to know, the slowest to respond, and in those years it was at least half a decade behind the other popular arts. So it was some time before the acrid odor of cannabis and tear gas wafted over the pools of Beverly Hills and the sounds of shouting reached the studio gates. But when flower power finally hit in the late '60s, it hit hard. As America burned, Hells Angels gunned their bikes down Sunset Boulevard, while girls danced topless in the street to the music of the Doors booming from the clubs that lined the Strip. "It was like the ground was in flames and tulips were coming up at the same time," recalls Peter Guber, then a trainee at Columbia and later head of Sony Pictures Entertainment. It was one long party. Everything old was bad, everything new was good. Nothing was sacred; everything was up for grabs. It was, in fact, a cultural revolution, American style.

By the late '60s and early '70s, if you were young, ambitious, and talented, there was no better place on earth to be than Hollywood. The buzz around movies attracted the best and the brightest of the boomers to the film schools. Everybody wanted to get in on the act. Norman Mailer wanted to make movies more than he wanted to write novels; Andy Warhol wanted to make movies more than he wanted to reproduce Campbell's soup cans. Rock stars like Bob Dylan, Mick Jagger, and the Beatles couldn't wait to get in front of and, in Dylan's case, behind the camera. As Steven Spielberg puts it, "The '70s was the first time that a kind of age restriction was lifted, and young people were allowed to come rushing in with all of their naïveté and their wisdom and all of the privileges of youth. It was just an avalanche of brave new ideas, which is why the '70s was such a watershed."

In 1967, two movies, *Bonnie and Clyde* and *The Graduate*, sent tremors through the industry. Others followed in quick succession: *2001: A Space Odyssey* and *Rosemary's Baby* in 1968, *The Wild Bunch, Midnight Cowboy,* and *Easy Rider* in 1969, *M*A*S*H* and *Five Easy Pieces* in 1970, *The French Connection, Carnal Knowledge, The Last Picture Show,* and *McCabe & Mrs. Miller* in 1971, and *The Godfather* in 1972. Before anyone realized it, there was a movement — instantly dubbed the New Hollywood in the press — led by a new generation of directors. This was to be a directors' decade if ever there was one. Directors as a group enjoyed more power, prestige, and wealth than they ever had before. The great directors of the studio era, like John Ford and Howard Hawks, regarded themselves as nothing more than hired help (over-) paid to manufacture entertainment, storytellers who shunned self-conscious style lest it interfere with the business at hand. New Hollywood directors, on the other hand, were unembarrassed — in many cases rightly so — to assume the mantle of the artist, nor did they shrink from developing personal styles that distinguished their work from that of other directors.

The first wave, comprised of white men born in the mid- to late '30s (occasionally earlier), included Peter Bogdanovich, Francis Coppola, Warren Beatty, Stanley Kubrick, Dennis Hopper, Mike Nichols, Woody Allen, Bob Fosse, Robert Benton, Arthur Penn, John Cassavetes, Alan Pakula, Paul Mazursky, Bob Rafelson, Hal Ashby, William Friedkin, Robert Altman, and Richard Lester. The second wave was made up of the early boomers, born during and (mostly) after World War II, the film school generation, the so-called movie brats. This group included Scorsese, Spielberg, George Lucas, John Milius, Paul Schrader, Brian De Palma, and Terrence Malick.

When all was said and done, these directors created a body of work that included, in addition to the titles mentioned above, *The Last Detail; Nashville; Faces; Shampoo; A Clockwork Orange; Reds; Paper Moon; The Exorcist; The Godfather, Part II; Mean Streets; Badlands; The Conversation; Taxi Driver; Raging Bull; Apocalypse Now; Jaws; Cabaret; Klute; Carnal Knowledge; American Graffiti; Days of Heaven; Blue Collar; All That Jazz; Annie Hall; Manhattan; Carrie; All the President's Men; Coming Home;* and *Star Wars.* So rich was the soil of this decade that it even produced a compelling body of secondary work, then regarded as aesthetically or commercially wanting, that nevertheless has considerable merit, including *Scarecrow; Payday; Night Moves; The King of Marvin Gardens; Next Stop, Greenwich Village; Straight Time; Diary of a Mad Housewife; Silent Running; Bad Company; Tracks; Performance; The Wind and the Lion;* and many of the films of Cassavetes. The revolution also facilitated ready access to Hollywood and/or studio distribution for Brits like John Schlesinger (*Midnight Cowboy*), John Boorman (*Deliverance*), Ken Russell

(*Women in Love*), and Nicholas Roeg (*Don't Look Now*). And Europeans like Milos Forman, who made *One Flew Over the Cuckoo's Nest*; Roman Polanski, who made *Rosemary's Baby* and *Chinatown*; Bernardo Bertolucci, who made *Last Tango in Paris* and *1900*; Louis Malle, who made *Pretty Baby* and *Atlantic City*; and Sergio Leone, who made *The Good, The Bad, and the Ugly* and *Once Upon a Time in the West*. As well as veterans like Don Siegel, Sam Peckinpah, and John Huston, who suddenly found the freedom to do some of their best work, pictures like *Dirty Harry*, *Straw Dogs*, *Pat Garrett and Billy the Kid*, *The Man Who Would Be King*, and *Fat City*. It brought out the best in journeyman directors like Sydney Pollack and Sidney Lumet, who respectively made *They Shoot Horses, Don't They?*, and *Serpico* and *Dog Day Afternoon*; and allowed an actor such as Clint Eastwood to develop a body of work as a director.

The new power of directors was legitimized by its own ideology, "auteurism." The auteur theory was an invention of French critics who maintained that directors are to movies what poets are to poems. The leading American proponent of the auteur theory was Andrew Sarris, who wrote for the *Village Voice*, and used this pulpit to promote the then novel idea that the director is the sole author of his work, regardless of whatever contribution the writers, producers, or actors may make. He ranked directors in hierarchies, which had an instant appeal for the passionate young cineastes who now knew that John Ford was better than William Wyler, and why. Recalls Benton, "Reading Sarris was like listening to Radio Free Europe."

The young directors employed a new group of actors — Jack Nicholson, Robert De Niro, Dustin Hoffman, Al Pacino, Gene Hackman, Richard Dreyfuss, James Caan, Robert Duvall, Harvey Keitel, and Elliott Gould — who banished the vanilla features of the Tabs and the Troys, and instead brought to the screen a gritty new realism and ethnicity. And the women — Barbra Streisand, Jane Fonda, Faye Dunaway, Jill Clayburgh, Ellen Burstyn, Dyan Cannon, Diane Keaton — were a far cry from the pert, snub-nosed Doris Days of the '50s. Most of these new faces were schooled in the Method by Lee Strasberg at the Actors Studio, or trained by the other celebrated New York teachers: Stella Adler, Sanford Meisner, or Uta Hagen. In fact, a lot of the energy that animated the New Hollywood came from New York; the '70s was the decade when New York swallowed Hollywood, when Hollywood was Gothamized.

By this time it has become a cliché to insist that this was, by any measure, a remarkable era, the likes of which we will very probably never see again. Every age gone by is lit up by a retrospective glow of nostalgia, and the specialness of the '70s was by no means evident at the time. As Scorsese puts it, "We were just guys who wanted to make movies, and we knew we could be cut down any second by these people at the studios." Certainly this period had its share of schlock. But *Airport*, *The Poseidon Adventure*, *Earthquake*, and *The Towering Inferno* to one side, the '70s was truly a golden age, "the last great time," in the words of Peter Bart, who was vice president of production at Paramount until mid-decade, "for pictures that expanded the idea of what could be done with movies." It was the last time Hollywood produced a body of risky, high-quality work — as opposed to the errant masterpiece — work that was character-, rather than plot-driven, that defied traditional narrative conventions, that challenged the tyranny of technical correctness, that broke the taboos of language and behavior, that dared to end unhappily. These were often films without heroes, without romance, without — in the lexicon of sports, which has colonized Hollywood — anyone to "root for." In a culture inured even to the shock of the new, in which today's news is tomorrow's history to be forgotten entirely or recycled in some unimaginably debased form, '70s movies retain their power to unsettle; time has not dulled their edge, and they are as provocative now as they were the day they were released. Just think of Regan stabbing her crotch with a crucifix in *The Exorcist* or Travis Bickle blowing his way through the ending of *Taxi Driver,* fingertips flying in all directions. The thirteen years between *Bonnie and Clyde* in 1967 and *Heaven's Gate* in 1980 marked the last time it was really exciting to make movies in Hollywood, the last time people could be consistently proud of the pictures they made, the last time the community as a whole encouraged good work, the last time there was an audience that could sustain it.

And it wasn't only the landmark movies that made the late '60s and '70s unique. This was a time when film culture permeated American life in a way that it never had before and never has since. In the words of Susan Sontag, "It was at this specific moment in the 100-year history of cinema that going to movies, thinking about movies, talking about movies became a passion among university students and other young people. You fell in love not just with actors but with cinema itself." Film was no less than a secular religion.

Finally, the dream of the New Hollywood transcended individual movies. At its most ambitious, the New Hollywood was a movement intended to cut film free of its evil twin, commerce, enabling it to fly high through the thin air of art. The filmmakers of the '70s hoped to overthrow the studio system, or at least render it irrelevant, by democratizing filmmaking, putting it into the hands of anyone with talent and determination. The avatars of the movement were "filmmakers," not "directors" or "editors" or "cinematographers"; they tried to break down the hierarchies that traditionally dominated the technical crafts. Indeed '70s people were the original "hyphenates," starting as writers, like Schrader, or editors, like Ashby, or actors, like Beatty, then moving into directing without necessarily giving up their original vocation.

The New Hollywood lasted barely a decade, but in addition to bequeathing a body of landmark films, it has a lot to teach us about the way Hollywood is run now, why today's pictures, with a few happy exceptions, are so unrelievedly awful, why Hollywood is in a perpetual state of crisis and self-loathing.

If this book had been written during the '70s, it would have focused exclusively on directors. It would have been a book about the art of the director, how director Y made X shot with Z lens because he was crafting a homage to *Citizen Kane* or *The Searchers*. Many excellent studies and innumerable biographies with exactly this approach already exist. If this book had been written in the '80s, when executives and producers became media darlings, it would have been about the film business. But written in the '90s, it tries to look at both sides of the equation, the business and the art, or more precisely, the businessman and the artist. This is a book about the people who made the movies of the '70s, and who more often than not destroyed themselves in the process. It tries to explain why the New Hollywood happened, and why it ended.

THE NEW HOLLYWOOD implies an Old Hollywood, of course. In the mid-'60s, when *Bonnie and Clyde* and *The Graduate* were gestating, the studios were still in the rigor-mortis-like grip of the generation that invented the movies. In 1965, Adolph Zukor at ninety-two, and the only slightly younger Barney Balaban, seventy-eight, were still on the board of Paramount; Jack Warner, seventy-three, ran Warner Bros. Darryl F. Zanuck, sixty-three, was firmly in command at 20th Century-Fox. "If you were these guys, you weren't going to give this up," says Ned Tanen, who at the time was a young man with the music division of MCA, and later headed motion pictures at Universal. "To do what, go sit at Hillcrest Country Club and play pinochle?"

In the palmy days of the old studios, there was something of an apprentice system that allowed the sons of union members to enter the industry. When the studios cut back in the '50s, these men, often veterans back from World War II, were last hired and the first to go. The day-to-day operations were still in the hands of the prewar generation of producers, directors, department heads, and crews who were in their fifties, sixties, and seventies. New Hollywood producer Irwin Winkler likes to tell the story of his first job as a young man, in 1966, at MGM. As a novice, Winkler got stuck with an Elvis Presley movie, *Double Trouble*. Having obviously read too much Sarris, he puzzled Presley's manager, the famously ill-humored Col. Tom Parker, by asking, "Please, sir, I'd like to meet the director." Parker replied, "You be in front of the Thalberg Building at eleven o'clock in the morning, your director will be there." Sure enough, at eleven o'clock in the morning a car pulled up, not a limousine, but a Chevy, with a black chauffeur. Next to the chauffeur was the man Winkler wanted to meet, an elderly gentleman named Norman Taurog, a Hollywood veteran best known for *Boys Town* with Spencer Tracy in 1938. He got out of the car with difficulty, tottered slowly up the steps, and extended a frail hand, covered with liver spots, as Winkler burbled, "Mr. Taurog, sir, great to meet you, isn't that nice you have a driver and all, that's wonderful." Taurog replied, "I like to drive myself, but I can't see very well."

"You can't see?"

"No, I'm blind in one eye, and the other eye is going real fast." Two years after Taurog completed *Double Trouble*, he lost his eyesight entirely.

In those days, there was apparently nothing anomalous about a blind director. Way back in the '30s and '40s, the producer on the studio payroll was the only person who would see a picture through from beginning to end. Directors, on salary, were there to make sure the actors hit their marks while the camera was running. They exited the production after the shooting phase was over. They were low on the totem pole, barely higher than writers. "Directors weren't even allowed in the room," says John Calley, who headed production at Warners throughout the '70s and now is president and COO of Sony Entertainment. "Warner would run the dailies, would tell the producer what he wanted — 'I want a close-up on Jimmy Cagney' — and the producer would tell the director, who only then was allowed to see the dailies."

There was only one maverick in this producer-dominated system: United Artists. This was a company that had empowered directors from its inception, back on January 15, 1919, when it was founded by Charlie Chaplin, Douglas Fairbanks, Mary Pickford, and D. W. Griffith. The idea was that the filmmakers would control their own destinies, cut out the middlemen, the meddling moguls who got rich off their labor. It seemed like a great idea, but it never quite worked the way it was supposed to, and by the end of the '40s, the company was losing $100,000 a week. The surviving owners, Chaplin and Pickford, were not speaking to each other, and in 1951 they sold the company to Arthur Krim and Bob Benjamin, two smart lawyers with some motion picture experience.

With the divorcement decrees of the late '40s separating the studios from their theater chains, the courts invalidating the old contract system with which the studios held the talent in veritable thralldom, and a growing number of stars participating in profits and starting their own production companies, Krim recognized, before anyone else, that the staggering investments in overhead — back lots with their wardrobe departments, acres of props, contract players, and so on — were a thing of the past. Krim understood that the only way for a motion picture company to prosper was to be run as a studio without a lot, that is, as a financing and distribution entity. What UA had to sell, the thing that would make the tiny company more desirable than its big brothers, was artistic freedom, and a bigger slice of the profits. By the mid-'60s, the upstart that no one would take seriously had become fat and saucy. UA prospered with the hugely successful James Bond pictures, the *Pink Panther* series, and Sergio Leone's spaghetti Westerns with Clint Eastwood. They even cornered the movie rights to the Beatles before anyone had ever heard of them, and would mint money with *A Hard Day's Night* and *Help!*

But even UA was a geriatracy. If you didn't know someone, didn't have an uncle in distribution or a cousin in costumes, it was almost impossible to crack the system, especially for directors. It was a catch-22 situation: you couldn't direct a picture unless you had already directed a picture. True, by the mid-'60s, the first students had entered what few film schools there were, but they were told they couldn't get there from here. Sound designer Walter Murch started at USC in 1965. He says, "The first day that we all got together, the head of the camera department surveyed us with a baleful eye, and said, 'My advice to you, is quit now. Get out fast. Don't continue with this because you all have expectations that are not going to be fulfilled.' "

"It was not like the older generation volunteered the baton," says Spielberg. "The younger generation had to wrest it away from them. There was a great deal of prejudice if you were a kid and ambitious. When I made my first professional TV show, *Night Gallery*, I had everybody on the set against me. The average age of the crew was sixty years old. When they saw me walk on the stage, looking younger than I really was, like a baby, everybody turned their backs on me, just walked away. I got the sense that I represented this threat to everyone's job."

Still, the studios, which seemed impregnable from afar, had been rotting from within since the late '40s, when the judgments against them had made the industry more vulnerable to the onslaught of television. The old men who ran the studios were increasingly out of touch with the vast baby boom audience that was coming of age in the '60s, an audience that was rapidly becoming radicalized and disaffected from its elders. The studios were still churning out formulaic genre pictures, an endless stream of Doris Day and Rock Hudson vehicles; big-budget epics, like *Hawaii*, *The Bible*, and *Krakatoa, East of Java*; war films, like *Tora! Tora! Tora!* and *D-Day the Sixth of June*. Even when a few of the expensive musicals, like *My Fair Lady* and *The Sound of Music*, did spectacular business in the mid-'60s, they spawned an orgy of imitations like *Camelot*, *Doctor Dolittle* and *Song of Norway*, whose budgets spiraled out of control. At the same time, the stars who ornamented these creaky vehicles were not drawing the way they used to. *The Sound of Music* represented the last gasp of family entertainment, and in the half decade that followed, the war in Vietnam grew from a blip on the map somewhere in Southeast Asia to a reality that might easily claim the life of the boy next door.

The net result was that by the late '60s, the studios were in dire financial shape. According to *Variety*, 1969 marked the beginning of a three-year slump. Attendances, which hit an all-time high of 78.2 million a week in 1946, plunged to a low of 15.8 million a week in 1971. Box office was down, inventories were up. Money was tight, therefore costly to borrow. According to Bart, "The movie industry was more on its ass than any time in its history, literally almost wiped off the face of the earth."

To change metaphors, the once proud studio system, already a leaky vessel, was listing badly, and the conglomerates were circling beneath the chop, looking for dinner. Although Hollywood watchers looked on gloomily as studio after studio became no more than an appetizer for some company whose primary business was insurance, zinc mining, or funeral homes, there was a ray of sunshine. The same upheavals that had left the studios bruised and battered made room for fresh blood in the executive suites.

Youthful veterans of the Golden Age of live television in the '50s joined the rebellious refugees from the New York theater and other mavericks to fashion a new kind of movie, light years ahead of the prevailing fare. In 1960, Cassavetes scraped together enough money to make a feature called *Shadows* in New York, entirely outside the system. Kubrick, working in England, made *Lolita* in 1962, and then followed it with *Dr. Strangelove* in 1964, a savage and scathingly funny demolition of Cold War culture. Lumet directed *The Pawnbroker* the following year, and the year after that, Mike Nichols made Edward Albee's scabrous *Who's Afraid of Virginia Woolf?* for Warners, which did for the family what *Strangelove* did for the arms race.

Still, the handful of daring American movies was nothing compared to what was going on in the rest of the world. Wherever you looked — Poland, Czechoslovakia, Yugoslavia, Sweden, Japan, Latin America — directors with unpronounceable names were making stunning movies. It was the Golden Age of postwar European and Japanese cinema, the era of the French New Wave, of Ingmar Bergman, of Akira Kurosawa, of Michelangelo Antonioni and Federico Fellini. Although these films were "foreign," they seemed more immediate, more "American" than anything Hollywood was turning out. They hit home with a shock of recognition. Sean Daniel, who grew up to become an executive at Universal and shepherded *National Lampoon's Animal House* to the screen, was an antiwar activist in high school in Manhattan in the '60s. He recalls, "You saw *The Battle of Algiers* ten times so you could memorize how to build the proper cell structure. I'll never forget seeing a platoon of Black Panthers, in matching black leather jackets and berets, sitting in front of me, taking notes during the show."

In America, real innovation was coming not so much from feature directors as from the practitioners of cinema verité like Richard Leacock, D. A. Pennebaker, and the Maysles brothers, who had developed cheap, lightweight equipment that enabled a whole generation to take to the streets to capture a reality that was rapidly becoming more fantastical than anything springing from the febrile brow of even the most inventive screenwriters. Assassinations, love-ins, prison breaks, bombings, airplane hijackings, hundreds of thousands of people flocking to Washington to levitate the Pentagon, dollar bills tumbling slowly through the air onto the floor of the New York Stock Exchange, were daily occurrences.

There were no maps to this wilderness of change. No one had blazed a trail. "When the movie factories were blown apart by television in the '50s, there weren't a bunch of people who said, 'This is where we go now,'" says Scorsese. "People had no idea. You pushed here, and if it gave there, you slipped in. And as all that pushing and shoving was going on, the equipment was changing, getting smaller and easier to use. Then the Europeans emerged. Combine all those elements together, and suddenly by the mid-'60s, you had a major explosion."

In the context of the financial hemorrhaging of the late '60s, the new group of young executives was considerably more inclined to take risks than its predecessors, especially if the risks were confined to picking up the occasional American independent or stray British or European art film, such as *Alfie*, *Georgy Girl*, or Antonioni's *Blow-Up*. Not only did Antonioni's picture afford the first glimpse of full frontal female nudity in the living memory of filmgoers, it also boasted of a meandering, opaque narrative structure that left most of the older executives scratching their heads. They didn't have a clue, but they knew it, and were flailing about for help. When neophyte director Paul Williams, then in his early twenties, went to MGM to pitch a project in 1967, he was told, " 'No, no, no, we want to make movies that aren't about anything. Like that *Blow-Up* picture.' " Williams adds, "*Blow-Up* had confused the hell out of them. People really started feeling they didn't know what was going on. It was much easier to get stuff going." While Winkler was making Presley movies, next door at the same studio British director John Boorman was making *Point Blank* (1967), a groundbreaking elliptical thriller bristling with sudden bursts of violence. "There was a complete loss of nerve by the American studios at that point," says Boorman. "They were so confused and so uncertain as to what to do, they were quite willing to cede power to the directors. London was this swinging place, and there was this desire to import British or European directors who would somehow have the answers."

Adds Paul Schrader, who was then the film critic for the major underground newspaper in L.A., the *Free Press*, "Because of the catastrophic crisis of '69, '70, and '71, when the industry imploded, the door was wide open and you could just waltz in and have these meetings and propose whatever. There was nothing that was too outrageous." Says Guber, "If you were young or you came out of film school, or you made a little experimental film up in San Francisco, *that* was the ticket into the system. It was like a petri dish with an enormous amount of agar, so that anything you dropped in there grew."

When the hippies finally did come knocking, in other words, the gates swung wide open, creating the illusion, as Milius puts it, that the citadel was empty. But this was only an illusion, and a dangerous one at that. The citadel was filled with land mines and booby traps. And although the decade of the '70s contains shining monuments to its great directors, the cultural revolution of that decade, like the political revolution of the '60s, ultimately failed. As writer-director Leonard Schrader, Paul's older brother, puts it, "This group of people started to make really interesting films, and then just took a toboggan ride into the gutter. How the hell did that ever happen?"

How indeed?

One:
Before the Revolution
1967

• *How Warren Beatty created a scandal with* **Bonnie and Clyde,** *while Pauline Kael made America safe for the New Hollywood, Francis Coppola blazed a trail for the movie brats, and Peter Fonda hatched trouble.*

"We're in the Vietnamese War, this film cannot be immaculate and sanitized and bang-bang. It's fucking bloody."

— ARTHUR PENN

Warren Beatty may well have been the first man to kiss Jack Warner's feet, certainly the last. The story goes, Beatty was trying to get Warner to finance *Bonnie and Clyde,* a movie Warner had no use for. Warner didn't like Beatty, his endless phone calls, his grousing and bitching. Not a day passed that Beatty didn't want something. So far as Warner was concerned, he was just another pretty face, on his way to blowing a promising career on a bunch of artsy-fartsy "films." Even Elia Kazan's *Splendor in the Grass,* his first picture, the one that put him on the map, never made any real money. Bill Orr, Warner's son-in-law, was right. He had fallen asleep at a screening. In fact, Beatty never had had a real hit. He thought he was too good for the pictures he was offered, and he even turned down the President of the United States. John F. Kennedy wanted the studio to turn *John F. Kennedy and PT-109* by John Tregaskis into a movie, wanted Fred Zinnemann to direct it, and Beatty to star in it. Not only did Beatty refuse to play Kennedy, he told Pierre Salinger to drop the project because the script "sucked." Warner was not used to being told his scripts sucked, and he kicked Beatty off the lot, shouting, "You'll never work in this town again," or something to that effect.

"He always hated me," Beatty recalls. "He said he was afraid to have a meeting with me alone because he thought that I would resort to some sort of physical violence." But getting physical was not Beatty's style. He was, after all, an actor. One day he cornered Warner in his office, fell to the floor, grabbed him around the knees: "Colonel!" — everyone called him "Colonel" — "I'll kiss your shoes here, I'll lick them."

"Yeah, yeah, get up, Warren."

"I've got Arthur Penn, a great script, I can make this movie for one six; if nothing else, it's a great gangster movie."

"Get up, get up!"

Warner was embarrassed. He barked, "What the fuck you doin'? Get OFF THE FUCKIN' FLOOR!"

"Not until you agree to make this movie."

"The answer is NO!" Warner paused, caught his breath. It was not much of a risk at $1.6 million, compared to, say, the $15 million he was spending on his pet project, *Camelot*. Besides, he was thinking about selling his stake in the studio, calling it a day. With any luck, by the time the picture came out, he'd be far away, in the south of France at his palace on the Riviera, far richer even than he was now. Why not indulge the meshuggener guy. He asked the star for a letter putting the budget in writing. He never got it, but Beatty got his deal.

Beatty insists none of this ever happened, but it's a story told over and over by people who swear they were in the room, witnessed it with their own eyes. It's one of those moments that should have happened, because it's so ripe with irony, bleeding with meaning, a genuflection at the feet of the Old Hollywood by a symbol of the New at a time, the mid-'60s, when no one had the foggiest notion that such a distinction would ever come to pass.

BEATTY NEEDED *Bonnie and Clyde*. After making a splash with *Splendor* in 1961, his career had indeed faltered, a result of poor choices and a youthful cynicism about Hollywood combined with certain romantic notions with regard to the women in his life, who perhaps absorbed more of his time than they should have, an attitude excusable in that this was not a glorious era in the business. The men Beatty admired, Kazan, George Stevens, Jean Renoir, Billy Wilder, were in decline. The old order was dying, but the new one had not yet been born. Beatty had spent the last three years with Leslie Caron, whom he had met in early 1963 at a dinner party thrown by her agent, Creative Management Associates (CMA) head Freddie Fields, at the Bistro, a popular Beverly Hills restaurant, to promote her Oscar prospects for *The L-Shaped Room*. Beatty had seen all her films — *An American in Paris*, *Lili*, and *Gigi* — and had a fan's crush on her. He asked her if he could see her home. At the time, Caron was married to Peter Hall, director of the Royal Shakespeare Company, but husbands were never much of an encumbrance in Hollywood, and she embarked on a discreet, but passionate affair with the charismatic young star.

Beatty had just finished *Mickey One*, an opaque and pretentious American "art" film with a European flavor directed by Arthur Penn. When it wrapped, he flew down to Jamaica to visit Caron, who was there shooting *Father Goose*, with Cary Grant. At night, in Caron's bungalow, she and Beatty discussed his career problems. He saw himself as an heir to James Dean, Marlon Brando, Montgomery Clift, but couldn't understand why they were taken seriously, while he was treated like a playboy.

Beatty began noodling around with a film that would eventually be titled *What's New, Pussycat?* — after his signature phone greeting to female friends. "I wanted to do a comedy about the plight of the compulsive Don Juan," he says. He got into business with a friend of his, an agent turned producer, Charles Feldman. Handsome and debonair, Feldman had founded Famous Artists and represented stars like Greta Garbo, Marlene Dietrich, and John Wayne. "Charlie taught Warren a lot, like you don't put anything in writing, you don't sign contracts, you can walk out at any time," says Richard Sylbert, whom Feldman also mentored. Sylbert was a young art director who, like Beatty, had begun his career with Kazan, designed *Splendor*, as well as *Baby Doll* and *A Face in the Crowd*, in addition to many of the most important pictures of the day, including *The Manchurian Candidate* and *The Pawnbroker*. Continues Sylbert, "Charlie would not be denied. He was a seducer, just like Warren. Warren would always say, 'You don't have any friends; just make the best deal you can.'"

Beatty intended to star in *What's New, Pussycat?* and wanted Feldman to produce it, but he stipulated a condition. Feldman was known for casting his girlfriends in his movies. His girlfriend of the moment was the French actress Capucine. Beatty wanted assurances that a Capucine-like character would not find its way into the script. "Fuck you," retorted Feldman, who did not relish being told what to do. But eventually he agreed, and work on the script proceeded.

Back in New York, Beatty and Feldman realized they needed a good joke writer, and one night they went to the Bitter End, a club in the Village owned by Fred Weintraub, to catch a comedian they heard was funny, Woody Allen. They liked what they saw, and Feldman offered Allen $30,000 to work on the script. Allen said, "I want forty." Feldman said, "Forget it." Woody replied, "Okay, I'll take thirty if I can be in the movie." Feldman gave in. So a movie that had once featured Warren Beatty, now featured Warren Beatty and Woody Allen. Allen went to work. But as draft followed draft, Beatty began to notice that the girl was taking on a European, specifically French cast; he could see Capucine coming over the brow of the hill. But worse, he noticed that his part was smaller, while Woody's was growing larger.

Feldman and Sylbert, who was associate producer, were staying at the Dorchester in London, when Beatty arrived for a meeting. He confronted Feldman, accused him of violating their agreement, creating a role for Capucine, letting Allen write him out of the script. Recalls Sylbert, "Warren said, 'Charlie, I'm not going to do it.' Charlie was in shock. Furious. He was not a man you do that to lightly." Adds Beatty, "I finally walked out in a huffing bluff or bluffing huff, thinking they wouldn't let me go. But they were only too happy to let me go." Continues Sylbert, "Warren went back to do a picture with some bimbo at Universal. I said 'Are you kidding me? You're gonna turn out to be George Hamilton when you grow up!' "

What's New, Pussycat? became a big hit, and a turning point for both Beatty and Allen. "Woody was very unhappy with the movie that was finally made," continues Beatty. "I was even unhappier, because I would have gotten rich off it. After that, Woody was always in control of whatever he did. And so was I."

Only one year shy of thirty, Beatty was looking for a project that would turn his career around. One evening, he and Caron had dinner with François Truffaut in Paris. Caron wanted him to direct her in the life of Edith Piaf. Truffaut wasn't interested, but he mentioned he had been sent a lively script called *Bonnie and Clyde*, which had a great role for Beatty. Truffaut said Beatty should get in touch with the writers, Robert Benton and David Newman.

THE *BONNIE AND CLYDE* light bulb had gone off in the heads of Benton and Newman two years earlier, in 1963, when both men were working at *Esquire* magazine. Like any reasonably hip young man or woman in the early '60s, they were less interested in magazines than they were in the movies. "All the time, everywhere we went, the only thing any of us talked about, was movies," recalls Benton. He and Newman had just seen Jean-Luc Godard's *Breathless*, and couldn't get it out of their heads. But most of all, they loved Truffaut. "Within two months, I saw *Jules and Jim* twelve times," recalls Benton. "You cannot see a movie that often without beginning to notice certain things about structure and form and character."

In the early '60s, film schools virtually did not exist. Benton and Newman educated themselves by simply going to the movies at the art houses (the Thalia on 95th Street and Dan Talbot's New Yorker on Broadway between 88th and 89th), the new New York Film Festival that burst onto the scene in 1963, and the Museum of Modern Art, where a kid named Peter Bogdanovich was programming retrospectives of Hollywood directors. "Bogdanovich did two brilliant monographs, one on Hitchcock and one on Hawks," continues Benton. "Those were the closest things we had to a textbook."

One day, Benton and Newman came across a book by John Toland called *The Dillinger Days*, which touched on the escapades of Bonnie Parker and Clyde Barrow, who cut a swath of bank robberies and mayhem across the Midwest and South in the early '30s. Benton was no stranger to the legend of the outlaw couple. He had grown up in East Texas. "Everyone knew somebody who had met them or seen them, and kids used to go to Halloween parties dressed up as Bonnie and Clyde," he recalls. "They were great, great folk heroes." Better, they spoke directly to the antiwar generation. Says Newman, "Being an outlaw was a great thing to want to be, whether it was Clyde Barrow or Abbie Hoffman. All the stuff we wrote had to do with *épater le bourgeois*, shaking society up, saying to all the squares, 'We don't do that, man, we do our thing.' But the thing we loved about Bonnie and Clyde wasn't that they were bank robbers, because they were lousy bank robbers. The thing about them that made them so appealing and relevant, and so threatening to society, was that they were aesthetic revolutionaries. In our view, what kills Bonnie and Clyde is not that they broke the law, because nobody liked the fucking banks — but that they put a tattoo on C. W. Moss. His father says, 'I can't believe that you let these people put pictures on your skin.' This is what the '60s turned out to be about."

Working at night, with the banjo picking of Lester Flatt and Earl Scruggs' "Foggy Mountain Breakdown" on a Mercury record blaring scratchily from the stereo, they wrote a treatment. With the nothing-to-lose bravado of neophytes, they set their sights on their patron saint, Truffaut, to direct it. After all, they felt they had written a European film. "The French New Wave allowed us to write with a more complex morality, more ambiguous characters, more sophisticated relationships," says Benton. Truffaut waltzed the two writers around the floor, dithering about his other commitments. After sending them to Godard, with whom they had a brief flirtation, Truffaut finally told them he would direct their movie. The script, with the director attached, went out to the studios, which worried that the main characters — killers, after all — were unappealing, and that Truffaut was ill-suited to direct this material. Their chances were not helped by the fact that their script featured a ménage à trois: Bonnie was in love with Clyde, and Clyde with Bonnie, but he needed the stimulus of C. W. Moss to get off. This was in keeping with their notion of Bonnie and Clyde's transgressive style, as well as the experimentation that was becoming a defining characteristic of the sexual revolution of the '60s. Benton and Newman got turned down all over town. They became afraid they were going to grow old and die peddling the script.

One cold and dismal Saturday morning in February 1966, Benton's phone rang. He picked it up. A voice said, "This is Warren Beatty." Benton, thinking it was a gag, said, "Who is this, really?" The voice replied, "This is really Warren Beatty." Beatty said he wanted to read the script, was coming over to pick it up. Benton thought "I'm coming over" meant sooner or later, a couple of days, maybe, a week, maybe never. But within twenty minutes, the bell rang. His wife, Sally, opened the door, and there was Beatty, who took the script and left. About a half hour later the actor called again and said, "I want to do it."

Benton was worried about the ménage à trois. He said, "Warren, what page are you on?"

"I'm on page twenty-five."

"Wait till you get to page forty, then call me back." Beatty called back an hour or so later, and he spoke words Benton had been waiting years to hear: "I've finished the script. I understand what you mean, but I still want to do it."

Beatty optioned the script for $7,500. Later, his company, Tatira (his mother, Kathlyn, was called "Tat" as a child; his father's name was Ira), paid Benton and Newman a writing fee of $75,000. Beatty was unsure whether he wanted to star in the film himself. The historical Clyde was very much a runt, and he imagined Bob Dylan in the role.

Having acted on impulse, Beatty started to worry he'd made a mistake — the story had been told before on film, the gangster genre was dead, etc. He returned to L.A., where he was living in the penthouse of the Beverly Wilshire Hotel. "He was walking around saying, 'Should I do it?' " says writer-director Robert Towne, then a close friend. "He asked everybody, including the operators at the Beverly Wilshire." Towne told him: "Go ahead."

In 1966, the way you controlled a picture was to produce it. After his experience with Feldman, Beatty was determined to do just that, even though he knew that there was little or no precedent for an actor actually producing a picture. But in this, as in other ways, he set a precedent. On March 14, 1966, he sent the writers a note, imploring them to cut the script down for the purpose of resubmitting it to the studios. "Some of these clowns may forget that they've already read it," he wrote. "Please make yourselves really unhappy. Cut off arms and legs, etc. . . . Pick an image of some executive that Lillian Ross might have written about and try to make him happy."

Director after director turned Beatty down. Temperamentally cautious in the extreme, Beatty did not feel he was ready to direct it himself, especially when he was starring in the picture. He needed someone smart and talented, but also someone he could work with. Benton and Newman finally suggested Arthur Penn. They had been impressed by *Mickey One*, appreciated that it was an attempt to do a "European-American film." According to Towne, "Penn was a court of last resort. Warren considered *Mickey One* highly affected and pretentious, but he thought quite rightly that Arthur was an immensely talented and intelligent man." Beatty went to Penn not once but twice. He told Benton and Newman, "I don't know if Arthur is going to want to work with me again, but I'm going to lock myself in a room with him and not let him out until he says yes."

ARTHUR PENN WAS VIRTUALLY in hiding when Beatty called him. A slightly built, forty-three-year-old man of serious mien, he had come up in '50s

live television, and had achieved considerable success in the theater. He first
went out to Hollywood in 1956, to Warners, where he made *The Left-Handed
Gun*, a Billy the Kid story with Paul Newman and a Freudian spin. It was a
dreadful experience for him. He recalls, "I finished shooting, they said,
'Goodbye!' " He turned his footage over to an editor, and the next time Penn
saw *The Left-Handed Gun* was months later on the bottom half of a double bill
in New York.

After *Mickey One* flopped in 1965, Penn's movie career spiraled downward.
Hollywood was not a place for intellectuals, no matter how talented, and Penn
suffered the kinds of humiliations routinely heaped on directors. First he was
brutally kicked off *The Train* by the star, Burt Lancaster. Then producer Sam
Spiegel took *The Chase* away from him in post-production and recut it.

Penn hit bottom, did nothing for a year and a half. It was at this moment
that Beatty came knocking with *Bonnie and Clyde*. Like Beatty, he was hungry.
"Beatty and I both had a sense that we were better than we had showed," said
Penn. Still, Penn did not much like the script. Beatty, however, would not be
denied, and dragging his feet, Penn finally agreed.

While Benton, Newman, and Penn were working on the script, Beatty made
a deal with production head Walter MacEwen at Warners. He said, "Look, just
give me $200,000, and I'll take a percentage of the gross." *

"How much?"

"Well, 40 percent."

"Fine."

Although the deal would be a disaster for the studio, it didn't look so bad at
the time. Modestly budgeted pictures like *Bonnie and Clyde* were breaking
even at about twice their cost. Warners didn't expect *Bonnie and Clyde* to do
very well, and according to their deal, Beatty wouldn't see any money until the
movie made almost three times the negative cost,† leaving a small cushion of
profit for Warners.

Benton and Newman, babes in toyland, went out to L.A. in July 1966 for ten
days to work on the script. They went up to Beatty's penthouse suite in the
Beverly Wilshire, aptly called El Escondido (the Hideaway), where he lived
alone. It was small, consisting of two rooms filled with a disorder of books,
scripts, records, half-eaten sandwiches, and a slew of room service trays piled

---

* The "gross" means the "adjusted" gross, which is the studio's share of the box office receipts,
called "rentals," minus certain costs, such as studio overhead. A percent of the gross is much more
lucrative than a percent of the net, which is the gross minus so many expenses besides studio
overhead that net participants usually get nothing at all.

† The negative cost is the cost of a picture from its inception through the completion of
post-production (editing, sound mixing, etc.). It excludes sums the studio charges for making
prints, overhead, distribution, advertising, and so on.

against the door or buried amid the debris of phone messages and crumpled typing paper, and a piano. Outside was a good-sized terrace covered with Astroturf on which he lay in the sun reading, or looking out over the shopping district of Beverly Hills and, on a clear day, the sprawling homes rising above Sunset Boulevard in the distance. Beatty drove them around in his black Lincoln Continental convertible with red leather upholstery, one of four cars with which the Ford Motor Company supplied him every year. Every time he turned on the radio, they'd hear "Guantanamera." At the time, Beatty was seeing Maya Plisetskaya, the Russian ballerina. She was older than he, and stunningly beautiful, great bone structure, no makeup, no jewelry, dressed simply and unpretentiously in plain blouses and slacks. As Stella Adler, Beatty's former acting teacher is reputed to have said, "They're madly in love, but of course neither can understand a word the other is saying."

Beatty shepherded Benton and Newman through their encounters with Mac-Ewen. "Warren said, 'He's going to say this, I'll say that, then he's gonna say this, then Arthur will say that,' " recalls Newman. "We went in, and it went exactly the way Warren said it was going to happen. It was like the Twilight Zone." But Warner tried to back out at the last minute. He was unhappy that Penn and Beatty had populated the cast with unknowns. He memoed Mac-Ewen, saying, "Who wants to see the rise and fall of a couple of rats. Am sorry I did not read the script before I said yes. . . . This era went out with Cagney." About a month before they were to begin production, Penn, too, tried to back out. He felt the script problems had not, could not, be solved. Beatty refused to let him go, and brought in Towne for a polish.

ROBERT TOWNE, three years Beatty's senior, was born Robert Schwartz in 1934, and spent his early years in San Pedro, just south of L.A., where his father, Lou, had a small ladies clothing store called the Towne Smart Shop. His mother, Helen, was a great beauty, something of a trophy wife. He had a brother, Roger, who was about six years younger. San Pedro, a blue-collar fishing port, was a romantic venue for someone like Towne, and years later in interviews he always gave the impression he grew up there, but in fact, his father, who changed the family name to Towne, had gotten into real estate and reinvented himself, becoming a successful developer. He moved the family to Rolling Hills, a gated community in the most affluent part of affluent Palos Verdes, where everyone had horses. Towne went to an exclusive private school, Chadwick, and then moved to Brentwood as a teenager. He grew up to be tall and athletic, but it took him a while to find his look. By the '60s, his hair had already begun to thin. He grew it long and brushed it to the side, concealing his receding hairline. Towne's melancholic, hang-dog expression and pale, feverish eyes, along with the Talmudic slope of his shoulders gave him a rabbinical cast he could never entirely shake.

Towne had an appealing personality. He was a sweet, gentle, self-effacing man. In a town full of dropouts, where few read books, he was unusually literate. He had a real feel for the fine points of plot, the nuances of dialogue, had the ability to explain and contextualize film in the body of Western drama and literature.

Before the '70s, screenwriters were disposable. If a project was going badly, the studio would throw another writer on the fire. Even they didn't take themselves seriously. Towne's was the first generation of Hollywood writers for whom scripts were ends in themselves, not way stations on the road to the great American novel. Towne's forte was dialogue. "He had this ability, in every page he wrote and rewrote, to leave a sense of moisture on the page, as if he just breathed on it in some way," says producer Gerald Ayres, who would hire him to write *The Last Detail.* "There was always something that jostled your sensibilities, that made the reading of the page not just a perception of plot, but the feeling that something accidental and true to the life of a human being had happened there."

Towne was a wonderful talker, but he could be didactic and long-winded, and many found him self-absorbed. Says David Geffen, who came to know Towne well, "Bob was a very talented writer, although an extraordinarily boring man. He always talked about himself. He used to go to Catalina to write, and he would describe to you in endless detail watching the cows shit."

Towne broke into the business writing for television, then wrote for Roger Corman, who was producing exploitation flicks for American International Pictures (AIP) and became celebrated for allowing many of the movie brats to pass through his shoot-today-edit-tomorrow low-budget motion picture academy. Towne claims he and Beatty, then in their twenties, first met as one was entering, the other leaving the office of Dr. Martin Grotjahn, their common psychoanalyst. Towne had a script, a Western called *The Long Ride Home* that Corman wanted to direct. Beatty happened to read it, thought about playing the lead. Recalls Towne, "He set up a meeting with Roger, which was unusual, because Roger was doing his quickies with five-day production schedules, and Warren had worked with Kazan. He asked to look at an example of Roger's work. Roger showed him *The Tomb of Ligeia* that I had written for him. This was not something that endeared Roger, as a director, to Warren. Warren said, 'Look, I feel like I'm about to get married, and the bride is just beautiful, but then I learn she's been a hooker for eight years.' " Beatty declined the picture, but liked Towne, and they came to be fast friends. They talked on the phone daily, sometimes more.

Both Towne and Beatty were great students of medicine, and Towne became a fast draw with the PDR (*Physicians' Desk Reference*), the bible of pharmaceuticals. At one point, the two men, along with Jack Nicholson, semiseriously entertained the notion of finding an outstanding premed student, putting him (even better, her) through medical school, and then maintaining him as their own personal doctor, always on call.

Famously hypochondriacal in later years, Towne was worrying about his health even then. He had backaches and allergies. When most people get a cold, they ignore it. Towne was at the doctor in a wink, before the phlegm surfaced at the back of his throat, worried that his sniffles might portend something worse, a cat's-paw for the murky nimbus of illness that he imagined surrounded him. His allergies were so debilitating he said they kept him script-doctoring, too weak to write originals. He was allergic to different things at different times. One day it would be molds and spores, then soy, the carpets in his home, an acacia tree in the backyard, which he insisted be chopped down. He thought he had a thyroid disorder. He was allergic to wine and cheese, even damp weather. Later he bought a special air filter, the kind hospitals use in burn rooms to keep out bacteria.

Towne started work on *Bonnie and Clyde,* and labored for three weeks during preproduction. "Both Warren and Arthur judged the script to be in trouble," he recalls. They objected to the ménage à trois. Beatty liked to play against his image, but he said, "Let me tell you one thing right now: I ain't gonna play no fag." He thought the audience wouldn't accept it. "They're going to piss all over my leg," he said, using one of his favorite expressions. Benton and Newman didn't get it. "We were trying to make a French movie, and those were issues that never bothered Truffaut," says Benton. But Penn told them, "You're making a mistake, guys, because these characters are out there far enough. They kill people and rob banks. If you want the audience to identify with them, you're going to lose that immediately if you say this guy is homosexual. It's going to destroy the movie." Benton and Newman came around, made Clyde impotent instead. Towne agreed. "None of us felt we had to avoid a taboo," he says. "We just felt we couldn't dramatically resolve relationships that complex, and still rob banks and kill people. You just run out of time. You look at *Jules and Jim,* and it takes a whole movie to go from Tinker to Evers to Chance. Without the action and the violence."

Towne's primary contribution was to move some scenes around. There's a pivotal moment in which the gang picks up an undertaker (Gene Wilder). They're all fooling around in the car, high on the excitement of robbing banks, until someone asks the man what he does. He tells them. The disclosure palpably dampens their spirits, underlined when Bonnie says, "Get him out of here." The scene originally appeared toward the end, after Bonnie visits her mother. Towne moved it up, to a point before she sees her mother, so that it emphasizes the dark cloud of doom that hovers over the gang, and makes the subsequent reunion with her family a bittersweet occasion, not a happy one, the way Benton and Newman had it. He also wrote a tag line for Bonnie's mother, a cold shower on the sentimentality of the sequence. After Bonnie expresses their desire to settle down nearby, Mother Parker says, "You try to live three miles from me, and you won't live long, honey."

Says Towne, "When I was a kid, I noticed four things about movies: the characters could always find parking spaces at every hour of the day and night, they never got change in restaurants, and husbands and wives never slept in the same bed. Women went to sleep with their makeup on and woke with it unmussed. I thought to myself, I'm never going to do that. In *Bonnie and Clyde* — although I don't think it was my doing — Bonnie counts out every penny of change, and C. W. gets stuck in a parking place and has a hard time making a getaway."

By the time they were ready to go on location, the script revisions were finished, and Towne's job was done. Beatty asked him if he had any ideas for new projects. Ever since *What's New, Pussycat?* got away from him, Beatty wanted to return to the same territory, the story of the compulsive Don Juan. Towne had been thinking about updating a Restoration comedy by William Wycherley called *The Country Wife*, which concerns a man who convinces his friends he's been rendered impotent by his doctor, so they trust him with their wives, foolishly, as it turns out. Towne had met a friend of a friend, a hairdresser who was heterosexual, shattering his preconceptions about hairdressers. What better way to update Wycherley than to make the character a hairdresser, whom everyone assumes is gay. Beatty liked Towne's idea, and hired him to write the script, for $25,000. Towne would accompany him to the set of *Bonnie and Clyde* in Dallas and write there. The working title was *Hair*. Later, it would become *Shampoo*.

Bonnie and Clyde was cast out of New York, the site of a revolution in casting almost single-handedly carried out by Marion Dougherty. When she started working, in the early '60s, casting was still in the dark ages. "It was like ordering Chinese dinner," says Dougherty. "They had all these people under contract, so you selected one from column A and one from column B." By the late '60s things weren't much better. Explains Nessa Hyams, who was trained by Dougherty, "Most of the casting people were in L.A., and were middle-aged, ex-service-men, functionaries. Their idea of casting was to call the agents, who brought all the kids in — they were very similar in look and style, sort of nondescript, blond hair, blue-eyed kind of thing. Marion went to the theater, so she always knew who the new up-and-coming people were. There were a lot of young actors running around New York not yet discovered."

Penn and Beatty didn't need Dougherty, because both had worked in the theater and live television — which became the gene pool for the New Holly-wood. The cast was filled with actors out of this milieu: Gene Hackman, Michael J. Pollard, and Estelle Parsons. Outside of Beatty and Faye Dunaway, who had been hired to play Bonnie, none of the cast remotely resembled movie stars. Hackman had an average, Midwestern look; Parsons was plain; and by conventional standards, the rubbery-featured, moon-faced Pollard looked like a sideshow attraction. In short, they resembled real people.

From a casting point of view, the other turning point, being prepped around the same time, was *The Graduate*. In the book, the Braddocks and their friends, including the notorious Mrs. Robinson, were WASPs. Director Mike Nichols had indeed tried to go that route, offering Mrs. Robinson to Doris Day, who turned it down, saying, "It offended my sense of values." He read Robert Redford and Candice Bergen. But Nichols's instincts told him there was something off. "When I saw his test, I told Redford that he could not, at that point in his life, play a loser like Benjamin, 'cause nobody would ever buy it. He said, 'I don't understand,' and I said, 'Well, let me put it to you another way: Have you ever struck out with a girl?' And he said, 'What do you mean?' It made my point." Nichols turned the families into Beverly Hills Jews, and gave the part to Dustin Hoffman instead. Choosing Hoffman over Redford was very bold indeed. The picture's huge success launched Hoffman's career, which in turn opened the floodgates for the ethnic actors from New York.

The most remarkable thing about the production of *Bonnie and Clyde* was that it was shot on location in Texas, far from the heavy hand of the studio, and Beatty had to fight for it. He wanted to know the whys and the wherefores of everything Penn did, and he had plenty of his own ideas as well. Says Parsons, "Warren and Arthur would argue about every shot. We used to go to our dressing rooms and wait and wait." Towne had become close to Penn as well as Beatty. "I was this sort of buffer between them," he says. "For example, Arthur had this scene that he wanted to do with Bonnie and Clyde, pretending what it would be like when they were dead. Warren came to me and said, 'You can't write that fuckin' scene, 'cause it's a fuckin' pretentious piece of shit.' I thought, Well, maybe I'll try and make it work; it's only paper. I kept trying to make it work, and it never looked particularly good, and Warren kept yelling at me about it. 'We can't pamper him! How can you do this?'

"My theory about that was — there's this joke about the guy who gets VD during the Korean War. The American doctor says, 'This particular form of VD is just untreatable, and the only thing we can do, 'cause you're going to get gangrene, is amputate it.' The guy says, 'You can't do that.' He hears about some strange medicine man in the hills. He finds the medicine man and shows him his problem. The medicine man says, 'The American doctors, they say cut?' He says, 'Yeah, yeah. No cut?' The medicine man says, 'No, no, wait two weeks, fall off by itself.' What I felt was, in two weeks it would fall off by itself. Once Arthur had a chance to see the dailies and gain some confidence, he would not want to shoot the scene. And he didn't."

When Beatty wasn't acting, producing, or arguing with Penn, he was in his Winnebago. Girls clambered in and out at all hours of the day and night. The cast and crew watched it rock back and forth like a ship upon the sea.

Beatty and Penn, Benton and Newman had all agreed that the violence should shock. The bullets should hurt not only the characters, but the audience as well. "It used to be that you couldn't shoot somebody and see them hit in the same frame; there had to be a cut," explains Penn. "We said, 'Let's not repeat what the studios have done for so long. It has to be in-your-face.' "

But at the end, Penn wanted a different effect. The idea of doing the controversial climax, wherein Bonnie and Clyde are mowed down by the law in a hail of bullets in slow motion like grotesquely tumbling marionettes, was Penn's. He explains, "Remember, this was the time of Marshall McLuhan. The idea was to use the medium as a narrative device. I wanted to take the film away from the relatively squalid quality of the story into something a little more balletic. I wanted closure." When a piece of Clyde's head is blown away by a bullet, Penn wanted it to remind audiences of the Kennedy assassination.

The production returned from location in the spring of 1967. By June, the cutting was nearly done, and Beatty showed it to Warner at the screening room in the mogul's palatial home on Angelo Drive. Warner wouldn't sit in a warm seat, so if the room were used before he used it, his chair was off limits. He was famous for his weak bladder. "I'll tell ya something right now," he said, turning to Penn. "If I have to go pee, the picture stinks." The movie was about two hours, ten minutes. They still needed to take about fifteen minutes out of it. The film started, and five or six minutes in, Warner excused himself. He returned to his seat for another reel, and then he relieved himself again. And again. Finally the lights went up, bathing the Renoirs and Monets hanging on the walls in a soft glow. There was a dead silence. "What the fuck is this?" asked Warner. Silence. "How long was that picture?" Son-in-law Bill Orr said, "Colonel, it was two hours and ten minutes." Replied Warner, "That's the longest two hours and ten minutes I ever spent. It's a three-piss picture!" Beatty and Penn didn't know whether to laugh or cry. Beatty tried to explain the picture to Warner. He spoke with painful deliberation, his sentences swallowed by the ominous silence that filled the room. Finally, grasping at straws, he said, "You know what, Jack? This is really kind of a homage to the Warner Brothers gangster films of the '30s, you know?" Warner replied, "What the fuck's a homage?"

They screened the film for Father Sullivan of the Catholic Legion of Decency. He swore Dunaway didn't have any panties on in the opening scene where she runs down the stairs. Recalled Beatty, "He kept running the film back and forth, saying, 'Oh no, that's her breast!' And we'd say, 'No, Father, it's just her dress, it's silk.' And he'd say, 'No, no, I see her breast! Wait, I think I see a nipple!' We'd say, 'No, no, that's just a button.' "

A few weeks later, Warner went to New York, where he announced the sale of his stake in the studio to Seven Arts Productions, a tiny film packager for television, for $183,942,000, a case of the minnow swallowing the whale. Warner personally cashed out with $32 million. Eliot Hyman became the new CEO; his son, Kenny, who produced *The Hill* and *The Dirty Dozen* for MGM,

became head of production, with a three-year contract. The new owners retained Benny Kalmenson, Warner's number two, as well as marketing executive
Richard Lederer and Joe Hyams, who worked for Lederer. Kenny Hyman
immediately announced he would woo directors by giving them more artistic
control. He picked up Sam Peckinpah for two films, *The Wild Bunch* and *The
Ballad of Cable Hogue*, after the director had been virtually blackballed for
drunkenness, disrespect, and other crimes against the studio system. And he
gave a young in-house writer a shot at directing a Fred Astaire musical, *Finian's
Rainbow*.

IF *BONNIE AND CLYDE* was one of the last pictures of the old Warner
regime, *Finian's Rainbow* was one of the first pictures of the new Hyman
regime. Just as Beatty was finishing up, Francis Ford Coppola, who had gone
to film school at UCLA, set to work. The year before, Coppola had directed
his first serious feature, *You're a Big Boy Now*, from his own script, adapted
from a novel by David Benedictus. Says John Ptak, who also went to UCLA
and became an agent, "Ninety percent of the directors started as writers because
there was no way that you were gonna be a director. Nothing. Nada. The only
thing that these guys really had was the ability to tell a story." *You're a Big Boy
Now* was regarded as nothing less than a miracle. "In those years, it was unheard
of for a young fellow to make a feature film," Coppola recalled. "I was the first
one!" Those who followed worshipped him. "Francis was our idol," says actress
Margot Kidder. "If we could meet Francis, that was as close to God as one
could get."

When Coppola had gone to UCLA in 1963, the film departments were
ghettos for slackers and shirkers. USC's was housed in an old stable; UCLA's
was quartered in Quonset huts left over from World War II. "It wasn't considered a serious major," recalls screenwriter Willard Huyck, who entered USC
in 1965. "You'd be walking by the film school, they'd grab you and say, 'You
want to be a filmmaker?' It was very easy to get into." The other motivating
factor was, of course, the Vietnam War. Explains sound designer Walter Murch,
"We had all gone to film school because we were interested in film, but it was
also this bubble of refuge from being drafted."

At the age of twenty-eight, Coppola was a hefty five foot eleven, bearded,
wore horn-rims with glass-brick lenses. He was terminally rumpled, as if he had
slept in his clothes. This was his Fidel Castro phase, and he generally wore
fatigues, boots, and a cap. He took *Finian's Rainbow*, which came with a
rock-bottom budget for a musical, a cast already in place, and a strong producer,
against his better judgment. He explained, "Musical comedy was something
that I had been raised with in my family, and I thought, frankly, that my father
would be impressed."

One day in the summer of 1967, he noticed a slight, reticent young man of twenty-three, also bearded, hanging about the edges of the set, watching the ancient crew totter about its job. He wore the same outfit every day: jeans and a white shirt with a button-down collar, tails out. George Lucas was the USC star whose student short, *THX:1138:4EB/*Electronic Labyrinth had taken first prize at the third National Student Film Festival in 1968, and whose Warners internship allowed him to do essentially whatever he wanted on the lot for six months. Lucas intended to apprentice in Warners' legendary animation department — Tex Avery, Chuck Jones — but like most everything else at the studio, it had been closed down, and he gravitated to Coppola's set, the only sign of life on the lot.

Lucas was almost pathologically shy — particularly with adults. When he began dating the woman he would eventually marry, Marcia Griffin, it was months before she could extract his place of birth. "It was really hard to get him to speak at all," she recalls. I used to say, 'Well, George, where'ya from?'

" 'Hmm. California.'

" 'Oh, okay, where in California?'

" 'Umm . . . Northern California.'

" 'Where in Northern California?'

" 'Just up north, the San Francisco area.' He would never volunteer anything about himself. Very private, very quiet." But with Coppola, Lucas could talk movies, and Francis recognized a kindred spirit. He was the only other "beard" on the lot, the only other film student, the only person under sixty — almost.

Lucas was thrilled to meet Coppola, who was already a legend among the USC film students. Says Murch, "Because of his personality he actually succeeded in getting his hand on the doorknob and flinging open the door, and suddenly there was a crack of light, and you could see that one of us, a film student without any connections to the film business, had put one foot in front of another and actually made the transition from being a film student to being somebody who made a feature film sponsored by one of the studios."

But after two weeks watching Coppola struggle with *Finian's Rainbow*, Lucas decided he'd seen enough. Coppola was annoyed: "What do you mean, you're leaving? Aren't I entertaining enough? Have you learned everything you're going to learn watching me direct?" He offered him a slot on the production. Lucas, too, fell under Coppola's spell.

However, Coppola was under the thumb of producer Joe Landon. The young director hated the idea of shooting on the lot, wanted to go on location in Kentucky where the story was set, but of course the studio refused, and unlike Beatty, he didn't have enough clout to get his way. Toward the end of production, he broke free, went up to the Bay Area with some actors, a skeleton crew, and shot guerrilla style.

Coppola's methods were so unorthodox, he always felt his days were numbered. Recalls Milius, "Francis had this closet in the producer's building. He was stealing film stock and equipment and putting them in there. He said, 'Someday when they finally throw me out of here, we'll have enough and we can make another film' "

BONNIE AND CLYDE was finished early in the summer of 1967. The studio guys had snickered through the screening of the rough cut, and Lederer knew they were going to bury it. It wasn't even on the schedule. The head of distribution was a man named Morey "Razz" Goldstein. Without having seen the picture, Goldstein decided to release it on September 22 at a drive-in in Denton, Texas. "September, in those days, was the worst time of the year to send out a picture," says Lederer. "It was just throwing it away." One day in New York, Lederer got a call from a guy who worked at the studio doing trailers for him. He said, "I just saw a rough cut of *Bonnie and Clyde*; it's dynamite, a special movie." Lederer went to Kalmenson, said, "Benny, listen. Don't lock in *Bonnie and Clyde* just yet. Let's take a look at it before we make our decision. There's a rough cut available. Warren will scream, but I can get it sneaked in overnight."

The next afternoon, Lederer screened the picture for himself and his staff. He was knocked out. He went over to Goldstein's office, found the four division managers in a meeting. Goldstein said, "Dick, we've seen the movie, and we're sticking with our original schedule. But I tell you what we'd like to do, one of those great country premieres in Denton. You get the old cars and raise hell, and you bring Warren, and Arthur and Faye, and we'll have a great time." Lederer was furious. He turned to the division managers and said, "Listen. No problem getting the old cars, but that's about all I can get. The only place Warren is gonna go when he hears what you're doing is into this office with a knife, to cut off your balls, one by one." He got up and walked out.

Meanwhile, the first public screening was held at the old Directors Guild building on Sunset. Beatty invited the giants of Hollywood, the men he had cultivated — Charlie Feldman, Sam Spiegel, Jean Renoir, George Stevens, Billy Wilder, Fred Zinnemann, Sam Goldwyn, Bill Goetz, and so on. It was a nervy thing to do, and his friends told him he was crazy because there was nothing this crowd liked more than sticking it to some poor schmuck who was starring in a movie he was producing — must be some kind of vanity thing. The day before, Rex Reed's nasty "Will the Real Warren Beatty Please Shut Up" had appeared in *Esquire*. Beatty was humiliated, and still depressed about the piece. He sat through the film out of sorts, barely looking at it. *Bonnie and Clyde* concluded with its balletic ambush. "In those days, people were not getting their heads blown off with hundreds of thousands of squibs in every scene," says Beatty. "It was as violent a piece of film as had ever been in movies." There was a long silence, which seemed to him like an eternity. Then the entire audience erupted in cheers. Ten rows behind him, somebody stood up and said, "Well, Warren Beatty just shoved it up our ass."

On the basis of this and other screenings, Beatty fought for better playdates. Goldstein was obdurate, said, "You guys are all crazy with this movie, give up on it already." But Beatty did not give up. Joe Hyams persuaded him and Penn that the Montreal Film Festival was the appropriate place for the premiere. "I remembered they had a picture called *Mickey One*, a piece of shit, and the only place in the world it succeeded was in Canada," recalls Hyams. "I said, '*That* picture made it in Canada! *This* picture can make it in Canada!' " *Bonnie and Clyde* premiered worldwide at the Montreal International Film Festival at Expo '67, on Friday, August 4.

"What a reaction. It was incredible," recalls Lederer. "There were fourteen curtain calls for the stars, there was a standing ovation. After it was all over, Warren was on the bed in his suite with a girl on either side, dressed, but cuddling up to him. There was this nice young French girl who was the macher of the film festival. Warren said to this girl, 'Listen, honey, where is the wildest spot in Montreal? I want to go there tonight.' She said, 'Mr. Beatty, *this* is the wildest spot in Montreal!' "

In New York, *Bonnie and Clyde* opened at the Murray Hill and the Forum, on 47th Street and Broadway, on August 13, right in the middle of the Summer of Love, a few weeks after riots leveled the ghettos of Detroit and Newark. Bosley Crowther had seen the picture in Montreal, and hated it. His review in the *New York Times* was devastating. He called it "a cheap piece of bald-faced slapstick that treats the hideous depredations of that sleazy, moronic pair as though they were as full of fun and frolic as the jazz-age cut-ups in *Thoroughly Modern Millie.*"

Print critics had considerably more influence then than they do now. Movies opened slowly, starting in New York and L.A. and moving outward to the hinterlands at a leisurely pace, like ripples in a pond, and therefore their success depended on reviews and word of mouth, as well as print ads. Still, movie reviewing was not taken seriously. It was a gentleman's sport, dominated by Crowther's middle-brow taste. A bad review from him could kill a picture. Lately he had been on a tear against violence in movies, slagging not only Robert Aldrich's *The Dirty Dozen*, but John Boorman's *Point Blank* for their lack of redeeming social value. Crowther repeated his attack on *Bonnie and Clyde* on two successive weekends in the Sunday Entertainment section. "I was scared to death of his power and the fact that his review made me look bad," says Lederer. "It really hurt me."

Benton and Newman and their families had rented a house in Bridgehampton for the summer. Benton told Sally, "Look, it's just another movie. It's been a big part of our lives, but you can't expect anything." Then he read Crowther's attack and thought, "It's not even going to last two weeks." The rest of the notices — especially the influential *Time* and *Newsweek* reviews — were nearly as savage as Crowther's. Joe Morgenstern, writing in *Newsweek*, called the film "a squalid shoot-'em-up for the moron trade." But the *Times* began to receive letters from people who had seen the film and liked it. What's more, Pauline Kael loved *Bonnie and Clyde*.

Kael was a tiny, birdlike woman, who looked like she might have been the registrar at a small New England college for women. Her unremarkable appearance belied a passion for disputation and a veritable genius for invective. Her writing fairly crackled with electricity, love of movies, and the excitement of discovery. Emerging in middle age from the shadows of Berkeley art houses where she wrote mimeographed program notes for a coterie of whey-faced devotees, Kael blinked in the glare of the New York media world, then went to work. She shunned politics, but something of a New Left agenda nevertheless found its way into her reviews. Her version of the antiwar movement's hatred of the "system" was a deep mistrust of the studios and a well-developed sense of Us versus Them. She wrote about the collision between the directors and the executives with the passion of Marx writing about class conflict.

Kael was very much the activist, very much the filmmakers' advocate. Like Sarris, she was not merely writing service pieces advising readers how to spend their Saturday nights. The two reviewers were waging war on "Crowtherism," as they called it, soldiers in a battle against Philistinism. At the same time, they would convince the intelligentsia that Hollywood "movies," which had always been déclassé — William Faulkner and F. Scott Fitzgerald had gone slumming when they went to Hollywood — could be art.

What Kael was saying was fundamentally sensible, but her sympathies left her vulnerable to the ballad of the helpless artist, a sad song that more than one director, hungry for a favorable review, was ready to sing. Says writer-actor Buck Henry, "Everyone knew that Kael was feedable, that if you sat next to her, got her drunk, and fed her some lines, you could get them replayed in some other form."

Kael saw right away that Warners was too hidebound to understand what they had in *Bonnie and Clyde*. It was a situation tailored to her talents. She weighed in with a nine-thousand-word review that *The New Republic*, for which she was writing at the time, refused to print. It ended up in *The New Yorker*, and secured her a regular spot there. In her review, she said that "*Bonnie and Clyde* is the most excitingly American American movie since *The Manchurian Candidate*. The audience is alive to it." But more than that, she conducted a campaign to rehabilitate the film. Kael had acolytes — critics who followed her lead and would later be dubbed "Paulettes" — and she mobilized the troops. Rumor had it that she persuaded Morgenstern to see the picture over again. A week later, he published an unprecedented recantation.

"The Pauline Kael review was the best thing that ever happened to Benton and myself," recalls Newman. "She put us on the map. This was a genre gangster film in its broad outline, not a highly respected genre. What she did was say to people, 'You can look at this seriously, it doesn't have to be an Antonioni film about alienated people walking on a beach in black and white for it to be a work of art.' " Adds Towne, "Without her, *Bonnie and Clyde* would have died the death of a fuckin' dog." Giving a major share of the credit to the writers, Kael slighted Beatty, dismissed him as a middling actor. He called Kael, charmed her. When she finally met him, some time later, at a screening of a documentary on Penn, she says "he came on very strong to my daughter, who was a teenager at the time."

Benny Kalmenson, a holdover from the Warners regime, was a former steelworker, a squat, heavyset man who, like many Warners executives, dressed like a mobster from one of the studio's famous gangster pictures. "He was always saying, fuckin' Warner this, fuckin' Warner that — every other word was fuck, fuck, fuck," recalls Lederer. "He was a streetfighter." When Kalmenson finally saw the picture, his reaction was simple, "It's a piece of fucking shit!" Furious, Beatty followed him into his office, said, "Let me pay you for this negative and I'll give you a profit." Kalmanson looked at him as if he were a termite, replied, "Ah, get the fuck outta here, Warren, where the fuck are you gonna get two fuckin' million dollars?" Beatty said, "I can get it, don't worry." Later, Beatty thought, They're beginning to take me seriously. They know they can get out of it if they want to.

But it didn't matter. *Bonnie and Clyde* opened in Denton, Texas, on September 13, went wide through the South and Southwest the next day. After two weeks, it was shoved aside by a high-profile Seven Arts production, *Reflections in a Golden Eye*, with Marlon Brando, that Seven Arts had booked into *Bonnie and Clyde*'s theaters before it had purchased Warners. (Coppola had worked on the script.) "In effect," says Beatty, "to have kept *Bonnie and Clyde* going would have lost them the theaters for *Reflections.*"

Bonnie and Clyde did no better than fair business in New York. Lederer went to Kalmanson, implored him to pull the rest of the September dates to give word of mouth time to build. "I really think this man was beginning to have an inkling that the business was passing him by," recalls Lederer. "This was a watershed movie for him, because he knew he blew it. But he was stubborn, a man of iron will. I thought he'd kill me. He cursed me — 'I don't want to hear any more about this fuckin' *Bonnie and Clyde*, I'm not taking anything out of release, I've got eighteen pictures to put out, it's gonna stay where it is, goddamn it!' And it did. And it died. It was finished by the end of October. I was discouraged by that September opening, after we'd broke our asses, so I gave up on the picture. I had done my best; I never felt it could be resurrected. I really didn't."

•

AROUND THIS TIME, Peter Fonda was in Toronto attending a Canadian exhibitors convention, doing his bit to flog his latest AIP picture, *The Trip*, from a script by Jack Nicholson. At the time, he was the John Wayne of biker flicks, having starred in AIP's biggest hit, *The Wild Angels*, which had pulled in a nice $10 million gross on a $360,000 budget. Fonda, looking elegant in a custom-made double-breasted suit, despite the conspicuous absence of socks and shoes, was seated next to Jacqueline Bisset. "I'd always wanted to fuck her," he says. "She asked me, with this devastating smile, 'Peter, how come you don't have any shoes or socks on?' I smiled back at her and said, 'It's because I can put my foot up under your dress, Jackie,' and my foot was on its way up her leg. 'Don't!' she shrieked. 'Stop it!' Then I heard, 'Gentlemen, Peter Fonda.' 'Excuse me, Jackie. That's me.'" Fonda made his way to the podium, made a few halfhearted remarks, accepted an engraved gold Zippo lighter, and retreated to his red-flocked room at the Lakeshore Motel to sign hundreds of glossies for the wives, children, and friends of the exhibitors.

"I was a little bit loaded, and I looked at . . . a photograph from *The Wild Angels* of me and Bruce Dern on a chop," he recalled. "Suddenly I thought, that's it, that's the modern Western; two cats just riding across the country . . . and maybe they make a big score, see, so they have a lot of money. And they're gonna cross the country and go retire to Florida . . . When a couple of duck poachers in a truck rip them off 'cause they don't like the way they look."

It was 4:30 in the morning, and the only person crazy enough to get the idea was Dennis Hopper. Although the two men often feuded, Fonda and Hopper were best of friends. It was 1:30 in the morning in L.A. Fonda called Hopper, woke him up. "Now listen to this, man . . ."

"Wow, that's a hell of a story. What are you going to do with it?"

"Well, I figure you direct it, I produce it, we'll both write it, and both star in it, save some money."

"You'd let me direct it, man?"

"Well, *I* surely am not ready to direct it and you want to direct and I like your energy, yeah, I want you to direct it."

According to Hopper, he and Peter had promised each other they would not become biker stars, were meant for better things, so he was not enthusiastic. But so far nothing better had presented itself, and this film was a lock, since Fonda had a three-picture deal at AIP. Dennis's response was, "Peter, did they say they'd give you the money?"

"Yeah."

"Then I think it's a great fuckin' idea!" They debated what the drug score should be. Hopper said, "Peter, we couldn't carry enough grass on bikes that's gonna make anybody able to retire. That's a stupid fucking score. It's got to be something else."

"What about heroin?"

"It's got a bad connotation. A terrible idea. Why not cocaine?" Cocaine it was. "I picked cocaine because it was the drug of kings," recalls Hopper. "I had gotten it from Benny Shapiro, the music promoter, who had gotten it from Duke Ellington." In those days, no one dreamed cocaine was habit forming. Since it wasn't available on the street, and it was very expensive, it was scarce. (In the movie, they used baking soda.)

Fonda's call couldn't have come at a better moment for Hopper. He had hit rock bottom. A wild and disheveled sometime actor, talented photographer, and pioneering collector of Pop Art, a former pal and acolyte of James Dean, whom he had met on the set of *Rebel Without a Cause*, Hopper had been blackballed for crossing swords with director Henry Hathaway. He was in the habit of buttonholing studio types at parties and hectoring them about the industry — it was rotting from within, it was dead — the Ancient Mariner on acid. He kept saying, "Heads are going to roll, the old order is going to fall, all you dinosaurs are going to die." He argued that Hollywood had to be run on socialist principles, that what was needed was an infusion of money channeled to young people like himself. He recalled, "I was desperate. I'd nail a producer in a corner and demand to know, 'Why am I not directing? Why am I not acting?' Who wants to deal with a maniac like that?" They smirked, moved away. "New York and Hollywood are hard for me, where you have to go and sit in a producer's lap at those parties," confessed Hopper. "I try to be polite and courteous, and then sure enough, I get pissed off and blow it. Let's face it, I can't stay on my best behavior for long. I don't have the social amenities to make it or enjoy it."

Hopper was living in L.A. with his wife, Brooke Hayward. Brooke was the daughter of agent-producer Leland Hayward and actress Margaret Sullavan — who had once been married to Henry Fonda. She was about as close as Hopper would ever get to Old Hollywood royalty. Brooke was in the middle of an affair with designer Richard Sylbert when she met Hopper while they were both acting in an off-Broadway show called *Mandingo* in 1961. Her stepmother of the moment, Pamela Churchill Hayward, later Pamela Harriman, was perennially matchmaking, trying to fix her up with eligible males, "the son of General Pershing, that kind of shit," says her brother, Bill. "I think Brooke brought Dennis around just to shock her." But she was in love. "He was an incredibly colorful character in those days," recalls Brooke, "a sweetheart."

The same year, the beauty and the beast got married and moved to L.A. Brooke had two children from a previous marriage, and in April 1962, they had a baby girl they named Marin. But the honeymoon was not to last. Even as a young man, Hopper had been a dedicated drinker, having developed a taste for beer at the tender age of twelve when he was out harvesting wheat on his grandfather's farm in Kansas. During the '60s, it got worse. Recalls Brooke, "We didn't have a lot of alcohol in the house, because if we did, Dennis would finish it off in minutes. He'd even drink the cooking sherry."

Brooke attributes the beginning of his decline to the first love-in in San

Francisco in 1966, where he got into acid in a big way. When he got back, she continues, "he had a three-day growth of beard, he was filthy, his hair was crazy —he'd started growing a ponytail—he had one of those horrible mandalas around his neck, and his eyes were blood red. Dennis was altered forever."

It was right after the love-in that he broke her nose, the first time he'd ever hit her. "It wasn't a big deal, but it did make me think twice about ever getting into an argument with him," says Brooke. "And after that, it was like opening the floodgates." One night, she drove from their home on North Crescent Heights down to a theater on La Cienega in her yellow Checker cab to watch Dennis rehearse his part in a Michael McClure play, *The Beard.* Hopper was playing Billy the Kid, who, in the words of Peter Fonda, "rips off Jean Harlow's panties and eats her out—in heaven." Hopper was nervous about performing in front of an audience. "He was completely crazy," Brooke recalls. "After the performance, I said, 'I've left the children alone, I've got to go home.' He said, 'No, I don't want you to leave.' I got back into the car, and he jumped on the hood, and kicked the windshield in, in front of about ten people. I was scared, and I had to drive home with no windshield." (Hopper says he doesn't recall the incident.)

Inclined toward paranoia to begin with, Hopper was becoming more so under the influence of alcohol and chemicals. He imagined himself persecuted like Jesus Christ, dying in his thirty-third year. Even his friends were afraid of him, thought he had a loose screw.

Needless to say, Dennis wasn't a barrel of fun to live with. He was extremely jealous, particularly of Sylbert. But Brooke was faithful, at least partly because, as she says, "I was scared to death of Dennis, it would have been suicidal, he would try to strangle me," and partly because she had her hands full taking care of her three kids. He would often fall asleep drunk with a lit cigarette between his fingers, starting fires. "One time I woke up, the room was full of smoke, there was Dennis lying in bed, and there were flames coming out all over," Brooke remembers. "I pushed him out of the bed so he didn't catch on fire. Sometimes I've regretted that, often wondered what would have happened if I hadn't."

Whiskey and drugs were part of Hopper's artistic program. He saw himself in the great tradition of boozing actors going back to the early days of film, John Barrymore and W. C. Fields. Dennis liked to quote Van Gogh saying he drank for a whole summer before he discovered his famous yellow pigment.

Hopper claims that Hayward was a manic-depressive. "It was hard. She would be up and talking at a party, performing, and the second the last person left, she would fall into this deep funk. I would try to talk to her, she would slam the door of her room, lock it, shut herself in there for days at a time. It was a nightmare. And she wasn't using drugs, and she wasn't drinking. She just had a major problem. I remember she took a bunch of pills. I think she tried [suicide] a couple of times. She ended up in Cedars." (Hayward denies that she tried to commit suicide.)

Brooke was by no stretch of the imagination a supportive person. She had a sharp tongue, and she applied this lash to Dennis, mocking him, putting him down, making sure he knew she thought he would never amount to anything. She had grown up with Fonda, seen it all — his mother's suicide, Peter shooting himself in the stomach when he was ten, the parade of stepmothers. To her, Peter and Dennis were a confederacy of losers. "Nobody took *Easy Rider* terribly seriously," she recalls. "Was this film really going to get made? If it got made, would it ever be seen?" Dennis complained, "The day I started *Easy Rider*, Brooke said, 'You are going after fool's gold.' You don't say that to me, man, about something I've waited fifteen years — no, all my life — to do."

Says Fonda, "My wife put the movie down too, but I didn't break her nose."

Hopper badly wanted to direct, and understood that *Easy Rider* might be the only shot he'd ever get. Fonda and Hopper lined up Terry Southern, who was a hot writer at the time, with *Dr. Strangelove*, *The Cincinnati Kid*, and *The Loved One* to his credit, to turn the story outline and their notes into a proper script, and produce it. The movie was then called *The Loners*. But suddenly, AIP head Sam Arkoff began coming up with objections. He didn't like the idea of the heroes dealing hard drugs. "The audience will never get over it," he said. Fonda replied, "What we're doing is fucking with the rules. There should be no rules, man. We're being honest to ourselves." Then AIP stipulated that if the movie fell behind, they had the right to take it away. Fonda said, "No, can't do that." He and Hopper were unhappy with AIP, but they had nowhere else to turn.

BONNIE AND CLYDE opened in London on September 15, became a hit, more than a hit, a phenomenon. The Bonnie beret was all the rage, hip, happening, but the groundswell that was building for the picture was too late to affect the bookings in the U.S.

Then, on December 8, weeks after it had closed, *Time* magazine put it on the cover — a silk screen by Robert Rauschenberg, yet — as the peg and prime example for a story bannered: "The New Cinema: Violence . . . Sex . . . Art," by Stefan Kanfer. In the body of the piece, Kanfer cited the lesbian scenes in *The Fox*, the jarring shock cuts in *Point Blank*, the violence of *Bonnie and Clyde*, and the experimentation of films like *Blow-Up* and *The Battle of Algiers* to argue that European innovation was entering mainstream American film-making. He defined the characteristics of the New Cinema: disregard for time-honored pieties of plot, chronology, and motivation; a promiscuous jumbling together of comedy and tragedy; ditto heroes and villains; sexual boldness; and a new, ironic distance that withholds obvious moral judgments. *Time* called *Bonnie and Clyde* "the best movie of the year," a "watershed picture," bracketing it with groundbreakers like *The Birth of a Nation* and *Citizen Kane*. Kanfer even compared the climactic ambush to Greek tragedy.

After *Time* hit the newsstands, Beatty paid a call on Eliot Hyman. He said, "We have to rethink this. The movie's been mishandled. I want you to re-release the picture." Hyman rolled his eyes. Nobody rereleased pictures. "There's a conflict of interest in your booking *Reflections in a Golden Eye*, a Seven Arts movie, and *Bonnie and Clyde*," continued Beatty. "I'm going to make trouble for you." Hyman refused again. He had been appalled when he discovered the size of Beatty's profit participation. In fact, the actor's slice was so large Hyman felt it didn't pay him to re-release the movie; the studio wouldn't make any money even if the picture did well. Finally, Hyman said, "I'll release the picture if you reduce the size of your cut."

Now it was Beatty's turn to refuse, and he did, saying, "I'm gonna sue you, Eliot." Hyman regarded him coldly, figuring the odds, as he nervously flipped his pencil up in the air, caught it, threaded it through his fingers.

"What the hell would you sue me for?"

Beatty was bluffing, didn't have the foggiest idea what he would sue him for, but vaguely familiar with Hyman's past, which he knew included some questionable associations, he thought, Eliot knows more than I could possibly dream of. So he looked him in the eye, and said, "I think you know." Within a couple of weeks Hyman had rebooked the picture. "With a man like Eliot, that was, of course, the best thing to say, because whatever it was he knew, it frightened him," says Beatty. The picture reopened on the day the Academy nominations were announced. *Bonnie and Clyde* got ten.

Bonnie and Clyde went back into twenty-five theaters, many the identical ones it originally played. The groundswell had been such that the same exhibitors that had had the film rammed down their throats the first time were now clamoring to get it back. On February 21, Warners released the movie in 340 theaters. In September, it had grossed $2,600 for a week at one theater in Cleveland; it played the same theater in February and grossed $26,000. "By the time it got back to the theaters, the studio could not get very good terms, because they had screwed the release up so badly," says Beatty. Still, the numbers were dramatic. By the end of 1967, the picture had netted $2.5 million in rentals. In 1968, when it was re-released, it netted $16.5 million in rentals, then making it one of the top twenty grossing pictures of all time.

Beatty had begun to see Julie Christie, whom he had first met in London in 1965 at a command performance for the Queen. "Julie was the most beautiful and at the same time the most nervous person I had ever met," he says. "She was deeply and authentically left-wing, and making this fuss over royalty did not amuse her. She could not contain her antipathy for this type of ceremony." She had grown up poor on a farm in Wales, and she was not impressed by the fact that Beatty was a movie star, in fact, held it against him. She indulged her profession only to support her myriad causes.

Nevertheless, they became seriously involved, and remained so for about four years. Christie had no trouble fitting into L.A.'s hip political scene. She shared his suite when she was in town, dashing through the lobby of the Beverly Wilshire Hotel in a diaphanous white cotton sari with little underneath. "If ever a movie star existed for whom stardom meant nothing, it was Julie," says Towne. "She was genuinely a blithe spirit." Five-figure residual checks would flutter from her handbag onto the floor of the hotel lobby as she rummaged around for her keys. One day she appalled Beatty by losing a $1,000 check in the street. But she was clear and uncompromising about her priorities, never stayed in Hollywood longer than she had to, and when she had made enough money, she would stop acting. By march of 1967, however much she disdained stardom, she had become a hot actress, having won an Oscar for *Darling*.

When Christie was elsewhere, Beatty indulged his singular form of recreation. He was always on the phone with women, rarely identifying himself, speaking in a soft, whispery voice, flattering in its assumption of intimacy, enormously appealing in its hesitancy and stumbling awkwardness. He told them that yes, he was in love with Julie, but he wanted to see them anyway. Not in the least put off, they appeared to find this reassuring. He explained his MO: "You get slapped a lot, but you get fucked a lot, too."

BONNIE AND CLYDE won awards from the New York Society of Film Critics, the National Society of Film Critics, and the Writers Guild. The Oscars were scheduled for April 8. On April 4, Martin Luther King, Jr., was assassinated. The denizens of Beverly Hills acknowledged the occasion by driving with their lights on. King's funeral was set for April 9, and five Academy participants — four of them black (Louis Armstrong, Diahann Carroll, Sammy Davis, Jr., and Sidney Poitier) plus Rod Steiger — threatened to withdraw if the show was not postponed. The Academy reluctantly agreed to reschedule it for April 10. The competition shaped up to be one between the Old Hollywood and the New. It was *Bonnie and Clyde* and *The Graduate* against two safe liberal films, *In the Heat of the Night* and *Guess Who's Coming to Dinner*, as well as a big musical, *Doctor Dolittle*, that had bombed at the box office, nearly finishing the job *Cleopatra* had started at Fox. Martha Raye read a letter from General William Westmoreland thanking Hollywood for raising the morale of U.S. troops in Vietnam through its work with the USO. The host was Bob Hope, who joked about Lyndon Johnson's recent decision not to seek reelection. The Old Hollywood laughed. The New Hollywood, including Beatty and Christie, Dustin Hoffman and his date, Eugene McCarthy's daughter Ellen, and Mike Nichols, sat stonefaced through Hope's patter. Nevertheless, the *Bonnie and Clyde* gang were confident, expecting to clean up. "We were so fucking sure we were going to win the Oscars," recalls Newman. "Ken Hyman came up to us in the lobby, and said, 'Got your speech ready, boys?' "

Benton and Newman lost. So did Penn, to Mike Nichols for *The Graduate*. *Bonnie and Clyde* lost Best Picture to *In the Heat of the Night*. After all the Sturm und Drang, it won only two awards, Estelle Parsons for Best Supporting Actress and Burnett Guffey for Best Cinematography — ironic, because Guffey hated the way he was forced to photograph the film and developed an ulcer during the shoot. "We're all disappointed," said Dunaway. "As a bunch of bankrobbers, we was robbed."

"There were people in Hollywood who just hated that movie," recalls Benton. "The thing that ticked off Crowther is that there was banjo music while they were shooting people. It was perceived to be a thumbing-your-nose attitude, a moral flipness, an arrogance, because nobody in this movie ever said, 'I'm sorry I've killed somebody.' "

Bonnie and Clyde was a watershed. "We didn't know what we were tapping into," said Penn. "The walls came tumbling down after *Bonnie and Clyde*. All the things that were in concrete began to just fall away."

If the '50s saw American culture turning away from Marx toward Freud, *Bonnie and Clyde* signifies not so much a return to Marx, as an escape from the insistent navel-gazing and psychologizing of Tennessee Williams and William Inge, a rebirth of interest in social relations. "The Freudian nature of their own relationship puts me to sleep," said Beatty, referring to the desperate couple. "I've seen too much of that." If Freud was dead, long live Wilhelm Reich. Not unlike *Splendor in the Grass*, *Bonnie and Clyde* carried a message of sexual liberation. In the picture's somewhat crude emotional economy, Clyde's gun does what his dick can't, and when his dick can, there's nothing left for his gun to do, so he dies. It was all summed up by that ubiquitous antiwar bumper sticker: Make Love, Not War.

Bonnie and Clyde came out in the middle of the sexual revolution, and its real originality lay in the fact that it recognized that in America fame and glamour are more potent than sex. "Andy Warhol was giving parties at the Factory with Viva, Edie, Cherry Vanilla, the fifteen minutes of fame bit," says Newman. "None of those people did anything; they just wanted to be celebrities. Likewise, our take on *Bonnie and Clyde* was that *they* wanted to be celebrities. They saw in each other the mirror of their own ambitions. Although they were both at the bottom of the shit heap, in each other they saw someone who validated an image of what they could be. He creates for her a vision of herself as a movie star, and from that moment on, even though he couldn't fuck her, he's got her."

Moreover, from the moment Clyde introduces himself and his partner, saying, "I'm Clyde Barrow and this is Miss Bonnie Parker. We rob banks," the movie brazenly romanticizes the outlaws — bank robbers and killers. In the crucible of the Vietnam War, and without the old Production Code to keep movies on the straight and narrow, the line between good guys and bad guys had become increasingly tenuous. In 1962, James Bond, with his "license to kill," coolly executed a larcenous metallurgist in *Dr. No*, even though he knew the man's gun was empty. But *Bonnie and Clyde* went considerably further, reversing the conventional moral polarities. The bad guys in this film were traditional authority figures: parents, sheriffs.

However, it is not only the violence of Bonnie and Clyde, not only their refusal to say they were sorry that antagonized "them"; it was the flair and energy with which the film pits the hip and the cool against the old, straight, and stuffy. It says "fuck you" not only to a generation of Americans who were on the wrong side of the generation gap, the wrong side of the war in Vietnam, but also a generation of Motion Picture Academy members that had hoped to go quietly, with dignity. *Bonnie and Clyde* made that impossible, brutally shoving them out the door, and the people of that generation understood perfectly. On some level, Crowther must have seen himself in Sheriff Hamer, and must have been angered by it. By doing it differently, and in most ways better, Beatty and Penn, Benton and Newman thumbed their noses at the people who had come before them. If the Bond films legitimized government violence, and the Leone films legitimized vigilante violence, *Bonnie and Clyde* legitimized violence against the establishment, the same violence that seethed in the hearts and minds of hundreds of thousands of frustrated opponents of the Vietnam War. Newman was right. *Bonnie and Clyde* was a movement movie; like *The Graduate*, young audiences recognized that it was "theirs."

AS A RESULT of *Bonnie and Clyde*, Beatty became, if not necessarily an auteur, one of the most powerful figures in the industry. He was sent every script in town. He rented a second suite in the Beverly Wilshire, and hired an assistant, Susanna Moore, a nineteen-year-old sometime model who grew up in Hawaii and later would become a novelist. She went up to see him, nervous, the phone ringing off the hook, Warren very flirtatious. At the end of the interview, as she was about to leave, he stopped her, walked over and said, "There's one last thing I haven't checked yet — I need to see your legs. Can you lift up your skirt?" Moore duly lifted her skirt. "Okay, you got the job."

Beatty used to go to parties at the Château Marmont, where Roman Polanski and his girlfriend, Sharon Tate, Dick Sylbert, and Paul, Dick's identical twin brother, also a production designer, and Paul's wife, Anthea, all had suites. Polanski, funny and elfin, loved to perform. He told stories that went on and on, twenty, thirty minutes. "You couldn't get a word in edgewise," recalls Dick, who designed *Rosemary's Baby*, which they had just finished. "The guy was like those kids who get up at bar mitzvahs and dance and sing. Drive people crazy. And competitive. You told a joke, he told a joke. But he was a sweetheart."

Polanski had a rather European attitude toward women. He always spoke to Sharon as if she were a child, insisting that she wait on him, rarely lifting a finger to help himself, as in, "Sha-ron, get more wheeskee for Deek." Recalls Sharmagne Leland-St. John, a sometimes actress and Playboy bunny who would later marry Dick, "Sharon was the sweetest creature I had ever met, very smart, but very stupid too. Once she was sitting on a chair, and watering this plant. She would empty a pitcher, and go for some more water, and do it again as we sat there wondering when it would occur to her that the water was going straight through the pot down onto the carpet."

Leland-St. John was then living at the Château with Harry Falk, formerly married to Patty Duke. "Sharon said to Harry, 'Roman wants to marry me, I don't know what to do.' Harry gave her some fatherly advice, and she said, 'Thank you, I really appreciate it, you saved my life, I'm not going to throw my life away by marrying this little putz,' and a couple of weeks later, there she was, getting married in London." But, according to writer Fiona Lewis, who knew them well, "They were crazy about each other. Roman worshipped her."

BONNIE AND CLYDE would go down as the first script Towne "saved," the first notch on his gun. He once said, "I don't know what would have happened if it had been arbitrated," implying he might have gotten a writing credit if he had tried. But he never demanded credit, he says, because Beatty asked him not to. Privately, Towne told at least one person he had written the movie, and he carefully nurtured a reputation as a script doctor. He worked behind the scenes like a shadow, careful not to leave footprints. It was by no means all calculation; he couldn't help himself. He was a born kibitzer. And he was generous. He mentored Jeremy Larner, who won an Oscar for writing *The Candidate*. "I couldn't have written it without him," says Larner.

Despite the sound and the fury over *Bonnie and Clyde*, Beatty and Towne found time to labor over the script of *Shampoo*. It was not a happy collaboration. Over the course of a few months in 1968 and 1969, they met repeatedly for lunch, usually at the Source or the Aware Inn, downing cup after cup of chamomile tea. After these sessions, Towne would go home and write. But it soon became evident to Beatty that something was wrong; the script wasn't happening. Towne suffered from writer's block. "Bob would love to work for money on rewrites on which he got no credit, and would do it quickly," says producer Jerry Ayres. "Over three weeks, he'd have a whole new script ready. But something that had his name on it would become all involved in the neurosis of completion and failure, and take forever." Paramount production head Robert Evans, who later hired him to write *Chinatown*, said, "Towne could talk to you about a screenplay he was going to write and tell you every page of it, and it never came out on paper. Never."

Towne had two weaknesses. He was poor at structure, a serious problem for a writer who would become notorious for his windy, 250-page scripts. And for all his facility with words, he was not a born storyteller. He had difficulty imagining the simplest plots, the most rudimentary sequence of events. He anguished over what he felt was his poverty of imagination. "Robert had written a script that was very good in atmosphere, and in dialogue, but very weak in story, and each day the story would go in whatever direction the wind was blowing," says Beatty. "He just never wound up with anything."

From Towne's point of view, Beatty was too linear. "He would not allow me to stop and think about everything and nothing," he says. "Nietzsche or Blake said, 'The straight roads are the roads of progress, the crooked roads are the roads of genius.' Warren will not knowingly go down a crooked road."

Finally, Beatty lost patience. He was tired of sitting around in restaurants, munching carrot sticks and tossing around ideas that came to nothing. He said to Towne, "Look, I don't wanna keep waiting for what you're gonna do. Finish by December 31, and show it to me. If you don't do it, let's forget it. I'm gonna do it myself." December 31 rolled around, and there was no script. Beatty was angry, and they didn't speak for months. Towne thought *Shampoo* would never be made. Eventually, Beatty decided to do another movie, *McCabe & Mrs. Miller*.

Two:
"Who Made Us Right?"
1969

- *How BBS kicked off a director's cinema in Hollywood with* **Easy Rider,** *while Dennis Hopper became a drug-crazed guru of the counterculture, and Bert Schneider the éminence grise of the American New Wave.*

"Nobody had ever seen themselves portrayed in a movie. At every love-in across the country people were smoking grass and dropping LSD, while audiences were still watching Doris Day and Rock Hudson!"

— DENNIS HOPPER

Bert Schneider and Bob Rafelson were strolling in Central Park. It was the early '60s, and both men were unhappy, for different reasons. Bert had risen quickly through the ranks of Screen Gems, the TV arm of his father's company, Columbia Pictures. At a tender age, he had reached the lofty perch of treasurer, and had been selected to head the division, but in a bit of reverse nepotism, his father blocked his further advance. Bert was frustrated and angry. Rafelson, meanwhile, had drifted from job to job. He felt he was too smart and hip for the work he had been doing, was cut out for better things.

Schneider and Rafelson were in the habit of getting together at lunchtime, bitching about their jobs and talking about their dreams. Rafelson's dream was a company of his own. "The problem in moviemaking," Bob told Bert, "is not that we don't have talented people; we don't have people with the talent to recognize talent. Take France, with the New Wave, or England, with Tony Richardson's company, Woodfall, the neorealist films of the Italians — these people exist here as well, but the system for allowing them to flourish doesn't exist, there's no encouragement for them. What this business needs is not better directors, but better *producers* who are willing to give directors with the ideas a chance to do films their own way. It's not just final cut, it's final *everything.*"

Bob liked Bert precisely because he had short hair, didn't smoke dope, and knew the business end of the business. He listened to Bert complain about the management of his own company, then said, "Why don't you quit?"

"And do what?"

"Start a company with me."

Schneider did quit Screen Gems, in 1965, and joined Rafelson in L.A., where they did form a tiny company, Raybert — later renamed BBS with the addition of Schneider's friend Steve Blauner — that transformed the industry.

IN THE BEGINNING, Rafelson was the one with the ideas. He was the one who haunted the Thalia and the New Yorker, the one who was a cousin of the legendary Samson Raphaelson, writer of Ernst Lubitsch's comedies. With his older brother, Donald, he grew up at 110 Riverside Drive, on 81st Street. The family was comfortably middle-class. Bob's father manufactured hats. Bob went to private school, Horace Mann, and his parents belonged to a country club in Westchester.

Toby Carr had her first date with Bob when she was thirteen. He took her to "the house of a friend of his where there was a girl he was interested in," she recalls. "He and the girl wound up necking on the couch all night, while I stood by his friend's piano and listened to him play *Rhapsody in Blue* over and over again. At the end of the evening, when I got out of the cab, I mouthed these polite words, like 'Thank you very much, I had a very good time,' which of course wasn't true, and he just kind of leaned over and pulled the cab door closed and sped off. Like, 'Yeah,' slam. I should have known something right then. When I look back on that night, it was all so obvious. I was definitely looking for trouble."

Rafelson's mother liked to drink. She went on alcoholic binges, holed up in her room for days on end. She was alternately abusive and seductive. "Bob was sort of like that too," says Toby. "He could lead you along a path, thinking one thing, and then he'd do a 180 on you, leaving you unhappy or mad or hurt, betrayed, like he was playing with your mind. I think he learned that from her."

Bob was supposed to go into the family business, but he despised hats and desperately wanted to get away. When he graduated from high school, he went to Dartmouth College. It was the '50s, and he wore black turtlenecks, read Samuel Beckett, Jean-Paul Sartre, and Jack Kerouac. He was handsome in the Jewish way, a shock of dark brown hair over a high forehead, rosebud lips frozen in a permanent pout under a fighter's battered nose. He was tall, thin, and powerfully built, coiled so tight he seemed to vibrate with an electric charge. He was invested in being hip, looked to black people — both male and female — for validation, the kind of person for whom Mailer's "White Negro" was written. There was an intense, brooding quality about Bob, and a cruel, predatory streak that could be attractive, although years later, when his prospects had dimmed and his career was nowhere, he just seemed depressed.

While Bob was at Dartmouth, Toby was at Bennington College. Despite their unpromising first date, through a series of fluky circumstances right out of *Carnal Knowledge*, they ended up as a couple. "He had that kind of vitality, the ability to take you on his trip, turn you on, which was very compelling," says Toby. "He was kind of a bad boy, a troublemaker, which, combined with his storytelling talents that probably came from a need to escape his own reality, made him extremely provocative."

Bob and Toby were married in the mid-'50s, had a son named Peter. In New York, they were friends with Buck Henry, who had been a couple of years ahead of Rafelson at Dartmouth. "Bucky was incredibly funny, very repressed, very prurient, almost like an adolescent," recalls Toby. "He was always interested in fringe people, strippers and weirdos." He lived in a hole-in-the-wall basement apartment on 10th Street in the Village. There was a life-sized stuffed gorilla seated on the living room floor. Buck never took off his pajamas. When he went out, he simply flung his street clothes over them.

Rafelson, meanwhile, in his early twenties, got a job through friends of his parents from the country club at Channel 13's *Play of the Week* where he wrote additional dialogue for Shakespeare, Giraudoux, Ibsen, Shaw, and so on. In June 1962, the Rafelsons made their way to Hollywood, where Toby gave birth to her second child, a daughter named Julie. Bob and Toby blossomed in the California sun, he tall and muscular, she pert and raven-haired. Bob landed a job at Revue Productions. Revue was the TV arm of Universal, which had just been taken over by MCA, run by Lew Wasserman and Jules Stein.

Rafelson was assigned to a show called *Channing*, set on a college campus, for which he hired playwrights like Edward Albee and Jack Richardson, a mischievous move a little bit akin to hiring Norman Mailer to write *The Flying Nun*. He finally collided with Wasserman over an episode in which he wanted to hire an actor named Michael Parks to play opposite Peter Fonda. Parks had less than perfect skin, and Wasserman, a tall and intimidating man, took exception to him. Given to volcanic rages he telegraphed by tapping a dagger-sharp letter opener on the mirror finish of his desktop, Wasserman had a large, wedge-shaped head under a shock of prematurely white hair. His nose seemed slightly out of focus, a protuberant smudge perched above thin lips compressed in a line of anger. He wore heavy, oversized glasses that gave him the look of a malevolent owl. He fixed Rafelson with a glare, his eyes swimming behind the lenses, and bellowed, "I don't want to see these degenerate stories anymore, and I *never* want to see an actor who has pimples on the back of his neck. What the hell does that got to do with anything real?"

"*This* is real?" exploded Rafelson, wrathful in the righteousness of his convictions, pointing to the awards, medallions, souvenir ashtrays, and other tchotchkes on the vast expanse of Wasserman's desk. "What's this fuckin' bull-shit?" he roared back, leaning over and sweeping them onto the floor with his arm. "Don't hire an actor with pimples? Jesus fucking God!" Wasserman uncharacteristically put a fatherly arm around his shoulders, escorted him out of his office and off the lot. Once he cooled down, Rafelson realized that his brilliant career might very well be over. He found a bathroom and threw up.

BERT SCHNEIDER WAS the young businessman with the house in the 'burbs, the wife and kids. Born in 1933 in the lap of luxury, he was sandwiched between two brothers, Stanley, the elder, and Harold, the younger. His father, Abe, was reputed to have started at Columbia Pictures sweeping floors. When the beastly Harry Cohn died, he ascended the throne, with Leo Jaffe as his lieutenant. Abe was a magisterial presence. He was tall, spoke in measured tones that appeared to convey great wisdom.

Stanley was stolid and unimaginative, a conventional soul who would lead a conventional life. Harold was angry and volatile like Sonny Corleone, and wounded and resentful like Fredo. In fact, "it was all like *The Godfather*, very dynastic, very Mafioso-like," says someone who knew them well. "It was almost like you mingled your blood with Bert when you were his friend or business associate. He'd do anything for you if you were in trouble, but if you made any mistakes, you were dead."

Bert was raised in New Rochelle. He was tall, six foot four, and skinny, which accentuated his height. Strikingly handsome, with high cheekbones, icy blue eyes that conveyed a sly, faintly amused look which said he knew more than anybody else in the room, full, sensual lips, and a long, narrow face topped by a tangle of blond hair, he affected a languid air, laid-back and cool. Nothing got to Bert. When he sat down, he spilled into a chair like a rag doll, no sharp angles or joints. Director Henry Jaglom remembers him from Camp Kohut, for Jewish kids in Oxford, Maine, where he was Jaglom's counselor: "He was the All-Star, Mr. America, the blond, baseball-playing, heroic kid that everybody either wanted to grow up and be like, or have as their big brother."

Bert's best friend and main man was Steve Blauner. When Steve arrived on the scene, Harold became the odd boy out. "Steve *was* Harold," as Bert would say later, explaining a lot of things about his relationship with his younger brother. As teenagers, Bert and Steve would steal away from their comfortable homes and hang out at the Italian bookie joints in White Plains. One after-noon, when Steve was seventeen, he was watching a tennis match from the umpire's chair at the club, when he spied a stunning girl in a cute white outfit and flaming red hair walk onto the court behind him. She had perfect features — big brown eyes, freckles, small, regular teeth, and a full, ripe figure. "I kept turning around so much I was embarrassed, so I got off the stand, and went down and sat behind the courts so nobody would know who I was looking at," he recalls. "Afterward, I asked, 'Who's that girl?' Somebody said, 'That's the girl we're trying to get Bert to take out.' So I ran over to Bert and said, 'You gotta get a look at this girl!' "

Judy Feinberg, who grew up in neighboring Scarsdale, and went to Fieldston, was quite the catch. Her family was even wealthier than the Schneiders. Judy first met Bert when she was fifteen, on a double date at his fraternity, while he was home from Cornell for Christmas. She had a curfew, Bert had the car and was upstairs necking with his date. When it came time for her to leave, her date was afraid to interrupt Bert, so she marched upstairs and did it herself. "I wasn't going to be grounded and have my Christmas vacation ruined," she says. "I guess Bert was fascinated by that." They got married on Christmas Day 1954, while she was a student at Sarah Lawrence. He was twenty-one, she eighteen.

Bert was expelled from Cornell for gambling, girls, and bad grades. But it didn't much matter, because there was always the family business. He started at Screen Gems in 1953 at the bottom, schlepping cans of films around the city. Bert and Judy's life together was '50s picture postcard perfect. They had two children, two years apart, a boy named Jeffrey and a girl named Audrey (after Judy's favorite actress, Audrey Hepburn). Bert looked and behaved like a Young Republican. He held relatively commonplace views on most things, and could look forward to a bright and uncomplicated future. "I was into the American dream," he said. "I pushed my political instincts into the background. I wanted a family, career, money, the whole bit."

Says Toby, "Bert and Judy went out to L.A. in this splendid decade of hope, found the great house in Beverly Hills, the wonderful schools for the kids. They were blessed, these people. It was like the Garden of the Finzi-Continis. Bert, and his princess Judy, were truly Jewish royalty. Then slowly we all began getting into all these strange self-destructive, quirky, unpredictable areas of life, that ultimately destroyed everyone, destroyed the fabric of what was."

Buck Henry recalls a celebratory dinner, held just before they left New York. It was small, just three couples, Bert and Judy, Bob and Toby, Buck and his wife, Sally, whom he had met when she was Mike Nichols's secretary. They went to a club. Buck was watching Bert do the twist, chuckling to himself over how geeky he looked, thinking, Gee, there's an awful lot of noise coming from Bert's pockets. He's gonna have to learn to take the keys and the change out before he starts to really swing in L.A. "Within three or four years, Bert, who I don't think had ever smoked a joint at that time, knew more about exotic drugs than any human being who had ever walked the earth," says Henry. "For the nice Jewish boys from New York, going to L.A. was like going to the New World. They stepped off that plane and put on funny suits, and bought funny cigarettes, and found very young blond girls. It was a comic version of the guys who came out here originally and made the business."

But there was nothing funny about what Bert and Bob did when they got there; they made money, lots of it. One day, Bob walked into Blauner's office and said, "I want to make *Hard Day's Night* as a TV show." He and Bert persuaded Screen Gems to back it. They put together an ersatz group called the Monkees. The show was an immediate, if unlikely, hit. Rafelson taught himself how to direct simply by doing it. It seemed for a while that the Monkees might be a training ground for other young directors. Martin Scorsese came by, William Friedkin, but neither connected. Friedkin, who was not to be outdone in the hip department, told Rafelson and Schneider, "This is lame, nothing more than a Beatles ripoff, four bourgeois guys running around, chasing their wallets."

The Monkees introduced Schneider and Rafelson to the fast-lane music scene. Schneider acted as though he was born to it. He grew a beard, let his hair fill out until it became a dramatic, curly blond mane, which stood in striking contrast to his richly colored velvet suits, black and dark green. When Bert made an entrance, it changed the chemistry of the room. He had the charisma of a movie star, but it was not just looks; he was possessed of extraordinary personal authority. Ostentatious about smoking pot, he puffed away with the zeal of a recent convert, as if he had personally discovered marijuana. He is said to have even passed out joints at a Columbia board meeting.

Jaglom, who had traveled west from New York in 1965, became fast friends with Jack Nicholson, and fell in with Rafelson, was astonished to hear that Bob's partner was his old camp counselor. He became both Bert's court jester and one of a series of younger brothers or wayward sons Bert attracted. Jaglom favored long scarves dramatically flung over his shoulder, as well as extravagant, floppy hats. He also befriended Orson Welles, a vast, damaged vessel adrift in a hostile sea, perennially in search of a safe harbor. Welles was venerated by the New Hollywood, and the wreckage of his career was regarded with horror and indignation as the most egregious example of how the town destroyed the auteur.

Jaglom used to hang out at the house of Donna Greenberg and her millionaire husband on La Costa beach in the Malibu Colony. Donna wasn't in the business, but she was clever, wealthy, attractive, and had a wonderful home, with rooms and more rooms for guests, a swimming pool on the beach, and an expansive patio. Donna used to have the Rafelsons over regularly, along with Buck and Sally, and John Calley, who had just come to Warners to head production. Julie Payne, daughter of actor John Payne and child actress Ann Shirley, dropped by too. Julie, a Hollywood brat, knew everyone. She had a perfect American body, sinewy and tanned. High cheekbones and eyes at a slight slant gave her an exotic look. Julie was fierce and wild, chain-smoked cigarettes, drank a lot, was apt to burst into Donna's house at 1:00 A.M., screaming, "I want to use your swimming pool to have a good fuck." Rafelson was very much the alley cat, tried to nail anything that moved. Even Julie was shocked. "He was always pawing me," she recalls. "I was in the pool, three feet from where Toby was sitting, and he paddled up to me and grabbed my breast. Nobody had ever done that to me before. I certainly wasn't going to scream, right there in Toby's hearing. I couldn't believe that he had done that, it was so gross."

Rafelson and Schneider considered themselves, and indeed behaved like, sexual outlaws, for whom nothing was taboo, nothing too flagrant. When Toby had to leave a party early to relieve the baby-sitter, Bob would call a girlfriend, who would invariably arrive moments later to seat herself in Toby's chair, still warm. He had innumerable affairs, and one relationship with a black woman named Paula Strachan that must have lasted nearly half a decade. Bob met Paula, who was nineteen, when he and Jack were auditioning dancers for Bob's first feature, *Head*. "They were princes," says Strachan. "I was very young and very stupid." Says a friend from those days, "Bob was a role model for drug taking and promiscuity. He had a group of young people who adored him. I think a lot of young lives were harmed by Bob Rafelson."

"These were people who didn't feel authentic," adds Toby. "Artists suffer, and upper-middle-class Jewish boys from New York didn't feel they had, at least not in the same way. They'd missed the civil rights movement because they hadn't gotten to the point where self-indulgence was less important than putting yourself on the line. By the '70s, we were still trying to act like the adolescents we had never been, when we were in our thirties."

Schneider doubtless began his strange voyage merely enjoying the advantages nature had so lavishly bestowed upon him — his looks, his intelligence, his charisma — all gilded by wealth and an innate sense of privilege, unclouded by self-doubt, a dynastic assurance that everything he did was right. Bert was so relentless that he came on to almost every pretty woman who came his way, like Linda Jones, wife of Monkee Davy Jones. One affair, with Toni Stern, was serious and lengthy. (Bert hooked her up with Carole King, and she wrote King's big hit, "It's Too Late." She refused to comment.) Nicholson is said to have once warned a friend, "*Never* bring a woman that you're serious about around Bert or Bob." Or, as Bert's brother Harold put it more succinctly, "Bert would fuck a snake."

Judy Schneider was a class act. Jaglom, who had dated Natalie Wood and was close friends with Candice Bergen, thought she was the most beautiful woman he had ever seen. But as Bert embarked on the '60s trip, he began to make fun of Judy's bourgeois refinement, liked to rattle her cage with real and contrived vulgarities. He had the ability to fart at will, and did so at inopportune moments, never failing to upset her. He would try to shock her by introducing locker room language into conversation. Money — how much who was getting paid for what — was a private affair, but sex was a publicly traded commodity among the Raybert guys, sexual exploits a variation on who could piss further. No one would hesitate for a moment before discussing the texture and flavor of his wife's or girlfriend's vagina; Bert's favorite term for it was "poozle." The BBS house style of discourse was brutal. Half playful, half hostile, the guys routinely traded extravagantly nasty epithets. Bert in particular had a gift for nailing people at their weakest points, and he would take no prisoners. If they failed to respond in kind, showed fear or anger, or worse, were intimidated into silence, they were "lame-o's" (Nicholson's phrase), as in, "get this lame-o away from me." It was as if they were re-creating the high school locker rooms they were never in.

As the '60s progressed, Bert went far beyond cuckolding his friends, which presented, after all, little challenge, and helped himself freely to the decade's smorgasbord of liberation theologies, spiritual and corporeal, developing a highly evolved ideology of promiscuity to justify his behavior, not that it needed much justification in the days of free love.

Despite the counterculture's official ideology of love, things were getting weird. Donna Greenberg's house was always open to anyone who dropped by. "One beautiful, sunny Sunday morning, I was having breakfast on the patio with my four-year-old, the nanny, my husband, and our oldest son, who was thirteen or fourteen," she recalls. "We had just had a paint-in, painting our seawall with peace signs, graffiti, that sort of thing. Suddenly, the most frightening group of hippies walked onto our patio, stood around and stared at us, wandered through our house. I was petrified, but I didn't know what to say, and it was also the '60s, being nice to people who wore lots of beads and jewels and bandannas. There was a piano covered with all the pictures one collects of children and family and loved ones and everyone I knew. In little silver frames. They gathered around the piano and looked at the pictures. Then they walked out, leaving us shaken. They got down to the end of the beach, but they couldn't get out, and a police car came, and I found myself walking down there and telling the police to let them go, they were my guests. Don't ask me what the impulse was. It was the Manson family."

THE WILD SUCCESS of the Monkees was making everybody connected with them rich. Bob and Toby bought a Spanish-style home on Sierra Alta above Sunset, near Graystone, the old Doheny mansion leased by the American Film Institute (AFI), then in its infancy. The Rafelsons' house was a corner of New York in L.A., stuffed with African artifacts, glossy coffee-table books on Japanese printmaking, photography, antiques. It became a hangout for an odd assortment of New Hollywood kids: Dennis and Brooke, Bert and Judy, Buck Henry, and Jack Nicholson and his girlfriend, Mimi Machu. Toby was the den mother. She filled the house with candles, supplied sweets and good dope, made sure everybody was happy. Rafelson, always in search of *la différence*, had come across some welding glasses with small dark lenses and flaps on the sides that became a permanent feature of his face. He sat on the floor, listening to jazz, smoking "jayskis," as he called them, maybe dropping some acid in the Jacuzzi behind the house, maybe eating a few mushrooms, taking a little mescaline or hash.

Despite his success, Rafelson was dissatisfied. After two seasons, word was out that the "Prefab Four" didn't play their own songs on their recordings. The phenomenon was pretty much over, and the truth was, the Monkees had become an embarrassment. As a sometimes musician, self-proclaimed hipster, and professional outsider, he hated everything they stood for. Friedkin was right. As someone said, if whitebread could sing, it would have sounded like the Monkees. Besides, Rafelson was tired of television; he wanted to direct features. Why not turn them inside out, show the world that they, and more important he, was in on the joke, nay, had authored the joke. "I think that repudiating the very thing the Monkees stood for, using them in order to do this, which he didn't mind doing, shows you what his colors were, which was that his own image of himself was more important than the product," says Toby. "I think the need to feel cool, in the minds of guys like Bob and Bert, was terribly, terribly important."

The film was *Head*. Like nearly every other aspiring young director, Rafelson fancied himself a European auteur; with characteristic arrogance, *Head* was to be his 8½, the summation of his career and his meditation on his art. Unlike Fellini, however, there was nothing to sum up, it being his first feature. Rafelson asked Nicholson to write it. At this point, Nicholson's acting career appeared to be over. After a decade of B pictures, he had barely made a dent. Jack used to hang out at the Raybert offices, had become good friends with Bert. They went to Lakers games together, where Bert had expensive, courtside seats, and ostentatiously sat through the National Anthem. So Jack and Bob fired up some joints, dropped acid, took a walk on the beach, and came up with the novel idea of deconstructing the Monkees in a mélange of music, Vietnam footage, and kitschy pop culture artifacts.

While Rafelson and Nicholson were shooting, Schneider was watching Walter Cronkite on CBS news. It was not a pretty picture. The conflict in Vietnam, the so-called living room war had taken up residence in the place where people lived, and seemed like it was going to go on forever.

Up north, in Oakland, a Black Panther named Huey Newton got into a scuffle with a couple of cops in October of 1967. Police officer John Frey ended up dead, and Newton was arrested on a murder charge. The Panthers, who advocated armed self-defense, had become the darlings of the white New Left a few months before by descending on the statehouse in Sacramento dressed in black berets and black leather jackets, armed to the teeth. After

Newton was jailed, brightly colored orange buttons featuring a black panther and the words "Free Huey" blossomed on dashikis and tie-dyed shirts all over California. On September 10, a jury found Newton guilty of voluntary man-slaughter and remanded him to the Men's Colony in San Luis Obispo for two to fifteen years.

Schneider appeared to be increasingly uncomfortable over what the Weath-ermen would later call "white skin privilege," a common ailment in the movie industry where the rain of money took its toll. Says Buck Henry, "A lot of that stuff came out of middle-class guilt: 'How come we're rich, and maybe a little bit famous, when our grandfathers had to struggle so much, and how come we're telling people what to do all the time, when we just came over on the boat.' " Years later, after the South Central riots of 1992, while his contemporar-ies were buying guns to protect their Bel Air mansions, Schneider is said to have told a friend, "I wish they'd come up here and burn my house down."

ONE DAY, Hopper, Fonda, and playwright Michael McClure dropped into the Raybert offices to pitch an idea. AIP was dragging its feet on *Easy Rider*, and nobody else in his right mind would put up hard cash for bad-boy Hopper to direct. "You know Dennis," laughed Nicholson. "You don't exactly just turn over some money to him and say, 'No problem,' you know what I mean?"

Rafelson had met Hopper in New York, through Buck Henry. Bob had literally tripped over him on the floor at a party at Buck's girlfriend's apartment in the East Village. Hopper was pitching Rafelson McClure's play *The Queen*, which featured the principals of the Lyndon Johnson administration — Johnson, McGeorge Bundy, Dean Rusk, and Robert McNamara — in white, off-the-shoulder beaded gowns, eating lobster and planning the assassination of JFK. Schneider limped in, his leg in a cast, and sat down at a desk in the back. Fonda and Hopper were about to go into Nicholson's office to smoke a joint, but Rafelson introduced them to Schneider, saying of Hopper, "This guy is fucking crazy, but I totally believe in him, and I think he'd make a brilliant film for us." Schneider looked them over — Hopper, short and dark, in his filthy jeans, denim jacket, beard, ponytail, headband, his darting eyes shining with a paranoid glitter, a furrow slicing his brow like a knife; Fonda, tall and storklike, strikingly like his father, except for the long blond hair, fringed jacket, and rawhide moccasins — and listened to their rap. *The Queen* seemed a little much, even for Bert and Bob, and when Hopper asked for $60,000, Rafelson changed the subject, asked, "How's your bike movie coming?" Fonda replied, "Oh, AIP is just dickin' us around, man, puttin' all these restrictions on us, it don't look too good there."

"Get the fuck outta my office and talk to Bert." They did, and Bert agreed to finance *The Loners*, as it was then called, to the tune of $360,000. He did not have a studio lined up to distribute the movie, and he was using his own money to back Dennis and Peter, neither of whom had a track record directing or producing, but did have reputations as trouble. In other words, based on little more than a hunch, he was crawling very far out on an extremely thin limb. Moreover, he promised not to interfere. The idea behind Raybert, after all, was to enfranchise directors. Later, even when Bert disagreed with the casting of his movies, he backed down, saying, "What makes us right?"

With eleven points* each (Southern may or may not have had the other eleven), and Schneider the rest, Fonda and Hopper were ready to go. Bert wrote them a personal check for $40,000 so that Hopper could film somes scenes at Mardi Gras. It was sort of a test; if he passed, he could go ahead. But Fonda got the dates wrong. They thought they had a month to prepare; suddenly they realized they only had a week. Hopper scrambled to gather friends who had 16mm cameras. They also realized they needed a proper producer, preferably someone who knew his way around Hollywood. Paranoid as always, Hopper wanted to surround himself with relatives and friends. He called his brother-in-law Bill Hayward, and hired him for $150 a week. They quickly assembled a crew. There was a production meeting in Hayward's office the night before they were set to leave. Everyone had long hair, was sitting on the floor. The meeting was very loose, very casual, very '60s. At one point, toward the end of the meeting, Hopper said, "All right, man, we don't have a gaffer. Who wants to be the gaffer, man?" like he needed a blackboard monitor. Recalls Hayward, "Some broad says, 'I'll be the gaffer!' She was a girl that had been sent out from New York to do still photography. Dennis said, 'Fine. You want to do that? I can dig it. You'll light the picture.'

"I knew then there would be trouble, because being a lighting gaffer is a real honest-to-God fucking job that requires some expertise," continues Hayward. "Having a meeting for Dennis was like having an audience. There was no way he was going to listen to anybody else. It was all about his speeches. So when they get to New Orleans, there was war. Lots of people have never spoken to each other again, lots of hard feelings. And it was much worse than anybody thought it was going to be."

Brooke Hayward drove Dennis to the airport. She said, "You're making a big mistake, this is never going to work, Peter can't act. I've known him since I was a child. You're just going to make a fool out of yourself."

"You've never wanted me to succeed, you should be encouraging me, instead of telling me I'm going to fail. I want a divorce."

"Fine."

According to Hopper, "That was it, I never saw her again."

Mardi Gras lasted five days. There was no script. Peter and Dennis knew the

---

* A point is short for a percentage point of the profits.

names of the two main characters, Billy, after Billy the Kid, played by Hopper, and Wyatt, after Wyatt Earp (aka Captain America), played by Fonda. They also knew they wanted to shoot an acid trip, but didn't know much else. The three cameramen, Barry Feinstein, Baird Bryant, who had shot for New York underground filmmaker Adolfas Mekas, and Les Blank, later celebrated for his whimsical ethnographic documentaries, stumbled about in confusion. Hopper had told each one that he was the first camera. Recalls Peter Pilafian, Bryant's soundman, "There was disagreement as to what the larger movie was, and what stage things would be at when the characters got to Mardi Gras. Dennis was this semipsychotic maniac. There would be a couple of handguns, loaded, on the table. He liked that kind of atmosphere." Adds Bill Hayward, "He went right off the rails down there, just completely fucking lost it."

From Hopper's point of view, there were too many chiefs, not enough braves. "Every one of them wanted to be a director," Hopper recalls. "I didn't want anybody shooting any film unless I told them to. But every time I turned around, they'd be shooting."

The first morning, Friday, February 23, 1968, Hopper gathered the cast and crew in the parking lot of the airport Hilton at 6:30 in the morning. "I was really keyed up," he says. "As far as I was concerned, I was the greatest fuckin' film director that had ever been in America." He appeared to be in the grip of full-blown paranoia and, remembers Bryant, "he just started haranguing us about how he'd heard a lot about how many creative people there were on this crew, but there is only one creative person here, and that's me. The rest of you are all just hired hands, slaves. He was totally out of his mind. He was just raving; probably he had some combination of drugs and alcohol." According to Fonda, he raged at each astonished person in turn, "This is MY fucking movie! And nobody's going to take MY fucking movie away from me!" until he shouted himself hoarse. Southern listened to Dennis's performance, and made motions as if he were jacking off an enormous dick. He knew, as everybody did, that James Dean was Dennis's guru. When Dennis came out with something particularly nutty, he'd say, "Jimmy wouldn't appreciate that, Dennis." Fonda was looking at his watch, thinking, "This is un-fucking-believable. We missed the start of the parade." He continues, "Everybody was looking at me because I'm the producer, and all I could think of was, Oh, shit! I'm fucked. It's my twenty-eighth birthday. What a fucking present I've given myself—this little fascist blowin' us all off, absolutely going nuts." Fonda asked Pilafian and the other soundmen to record surreptitiously Hopper's ranting. He thought it might come in handy.

People started quitting. On the final day, Hopper shot the acid trip in the graveyard with Fonda and actresses Karen Black and Toni Basil. "I showed up with my camera, and nobody else was there," says Bryant. "The whole crew had just had it. Dennis bullied Toni to take her clothes off and crawl into one of those graves with the skeletons." The cemetery sequence was the pièce de résistance of the Mardi Gras shoot. It only took a day and a half, but Dennis and Peter had a serious falling out. Hopper was trying to get Fonda to bring up his feelings about his mother—who had committed suicide—for a scene in which he mumbles reproaches to a statue of the Madonna. "Here's what I want you to do, man," said Hopper, who by that time, late in the day, had had a generous helping of speed, wine, and weed. "I want you to get up there, man, I want you to sit on that, that's the Italian statue of liberty, man, I want you to go up and sit on her lap, man, I want you to ask your mother why she copped out on you."

"Hoppy, you can't do that. You're taking advantage. Just because you're part of the family because of Brooke, that doesn't give you the right to make me go public with it like this. Captain America don't have no fuckin' parents, man. He just sprung forth, just the way you see him. I'm not takin' Peter Fonda's mother complex and puttin' it up there on the screen."

"Nobody's gonna know, man. You gotta do it, man."

"Everybody's gonna know, they all know what happened." Although it was Fonda who was angry and upset, it was Hopper who was unaccountably close to tears. Fonda finally climbed up on the Madonna, and squeezed out, "You're such a fool, mother, I hate you so much," while Hopper watched, tears running down his cheeks. "That was the first time I'd ever vocalized any of that stuff," says Fonda. "I actually started breaking down myself. I was sobbing."

Reflects Hayward, "It may not sound like a big deal to most people, but it was an actor trusting a director and him going outside the bounds of what he was supposed to know. Peter never got over that. They developed a rift in their relationship that never recovered. I don't know quite why it's as bad as Peter— I mean, it kind of worked!"

Paranoid to the end, Hopper demanded Feinstein's exposed stock, saying, "I don't trust you—gimme all your film, I want it in my room!" Feinstein started throwing the film cans at him, whereupon Dennis jumped him, kicked and pummeled him. They went flying through a door into the room shared by Basil and Black. According to Dennis, Peter was in bed with both women. The two men paused for a second to contemplate this spectacle, and then Feinstein heaved a television set at Dennis. (Says Black, "I was never in bed with Peter Fonda, believe me.")

As they were wrapping up in New Orleans, Peter called Brooke back in L.A. in the middle of the night. He said, she recalls, "We're finished. Dennis is coming back tomorrow. I think you ought to take the children and get out of the house. Dennis has gone berserk."

"Well, I've certainly seen—"

"No, this is much worse. And the footage is going to be dreadful, the whole thing is awful, it's a disaster, I can't work with him, I'm going to have to fire him." She thought, I could take the children, but where am I going to go, and besides which, is that a good thing to do? Is it a nice thing to do? Is it the correct thing to do? A few hours later, she got a phone call from Southern that disturbed her more. He said, "You gotta get out of the house. We've all seen Dennis misbehave in the most terrible ways thousands of times in your living room, as you know better than anyone, but this time it's really serious. This guy's around the bend." She was nervous, thought to herself, If Dennis knows he's going to be fired, that's going to make it trickier. He's going to be under a lot of pressure. It could happen that he would strangle me to death, and not even know it. And then what would happen when the children found me in the morning? She decided to stand her ground.

When Hopper returned, he took to bed for three or four days, his custom when bad things happened, as they did all too frequently. "The dying swan," as Brooke calls him, held court in the bedroom. Hopper finally got up to attend a screening of the Mardi Gras dailies for Schneider, Rafelson, and other interested parties. Recalls Bill Hayward, "It was just an endless parade of shit." Brooke, who went with Dennis, says, "It was just dreadful stuff, murky, the camerawork wasn't any good. The talent I knew Dennis had, and Peter knew Dennis had, that we'd seen in the second unit stuff for *The Trip* that he'd shot, none of that was there. There was a terrible silence in that screening room." Several days went by, with Peter presumably trying to find a replacement for Dennis, who was getting increasingly edgy. Remembers Brooke, "He was now drinking a great deal, and doing a lot of different drugs, which did not help his state of mind, and he was under the gun. He was violent, and dangerous. Exceedingly dangerous."

Hopper claims he was unaware that Fonda wanted to replace him until Bert told him later that Peter had played the tapes of his tantrums in New Orleans for him and Nicholson. Bert said, he recalls, "I want to tell you about your friend Peter Fonda. He told me, 'Hopper's lost his mind, he's obviously crazy.' Peter and your brother-in-law Bill Hayward tried to get you fired. So you're not confused about who your friends are." Fonda handed Bert a check for $40,000, saying, "This is not going to work. When Hopper gets on the set, he loses it. I think he's absolutely blown away that I'm the producer."

"Well, don't you want to make the movie?"

"Hell, yes."

"Let's find a way of doing it. I don't think Dennis had the proper preparation, he doesn't have the right crew, that'll make a difference."

One night, as Brooke prepared hot dogs and beans for the children, Dennis came striding into the house accompanied by underground filmmaker Bruce Conner, best known for a montage film called *Cosmic Ray*. Conner sat down at the Victorian organ, and started to play. According to Brooke, Dennis was incensed because the children had eaten all the food, leaving nothing for his dinner. He threatened her. She says that her little son Jeffrey stood in front of her with his arms crossed, saying, "Don't you get near my mother." With Conner still pounding at the organ like a mad Phantom of the Opera, refusing to look up, Marin began to scream, and Brooke thought, These children have already seen too much. If he gets any worse than he is right now, I won't be able to handle it. I've got to get out of here. She took Conner aside, and pleaded, "Bruce, I want you to get Dennis out of here now, far away." He replied, "I don't want to get into the middle of this." She hissed, "I'm not asking you to get in the middle of this. I want you to get him out of the house. On some excuse, go down to Malibu, go see Dean Stockwell, so I can get myself together." Hopper and Conner left, Brooke packed up the children, and spent a week out in a shack where her friend Jill Schary lived in Santa Monica with *her* alcoholic husband. They slept on the floor in sleeping bags. "I went underground," continues Brooke. "Dennis did not know where I was. I got a divorce lawyer, who said, 'We've got to have a restraining order, but as long as he's in the house — you gotta get him outta the house.' Then my brother called me, said, 'You're not going to believe this, but Dennis has just been arrested for smoking dope on the Strip, and he's in jail.' "

As Hopper recalled the incident, "They stopped me only because my hair was somewhat long, and I was driving an old car. They said I'd thrown a roach out of the car, which I had *not*. Well, I did have this roach in my *pocket*. Then, in court, they produce as evidence not *my* roach, which was wrapped in *white* paper, but somebody else's roach, which was wrapped in *black* paper. How ludicrous, man! It was dark. They couldn't have even *seen* a *black* roach."

Continues Brooke, "I called my lawyer, said, 'Dennis is in jail.'

" 'Great. Go back to the house.' That's what did it. Dennis being in jail speeded up the restraining order. Bert bailed him out, and got Dennis out of town on a lengthy location scout. So that's how I survived. It was just luck. If Dennis had been replaced, I'm sure he would have killed me." Dennis and his close friend, production manager Paul Lewis, later broke into the house to get the art Dennis said was his, but they say Brooke had removed it. She adds, "When we did get divorced, I probably could have gone for half of his cut from *Easy Rider*, but I refused to take a nickel from him, because I didn't want him coming after me with a shotgun and shooting me."

WHILE HOPPER AND FONDA were going at it in New Orleans, Schneider had convinced Columbia to distribute the picture. Although Raybert was on the Columbia lot, it might well have been on a different planet. The management of Columbia was relatively stable, but it was a stodgy, conservative studio almost totally out of step with the emerging counterculture. Throughout the '60s, while the other studios were bottoming out, the company had been doing well with *Lawrence of Arabia*, *Ship of Fools*, *Funny Girl*, and *A Man for All Seasons*, insulating it from the changes around it. But by the late '60s it was starting its downward slide. Columbia president Leo Jaffe once torpedoed a deal for *Hair* that was at the signing stage, saying, "As long as I am president of this company, I cannot have a film that says 'fuck' in it." Bert hated the studios, and Columbia's evident disdain for this project confirmed his antipathies. He wouldn't even show them the dailies.

Stanley Schneider ran the studio out of New York. He was turning out to be a major disappointment. By all accounts a decent and loyal man, he was in every way the opposite of Bert: cautious, conservative in his tastes, without "a creative bone in his body," according to Robert Lovenheim, a junior executive. Stanley passed on *The Sting*, Stanley passed on *Blazing Saddles*, because he was offended by the farting. When he would smoke the occasional joint, an assistant would put his palm under the tip to catch the ash. Lovenheim and Guber once asked him to look at *M*A*S*H* because Robert Altman was desperate to get away from Fox and looking for a place to set up his next picture. He refused, saying, "A Schneider does not go and see a picture on the Fox lot!"

Leo and Stanley didn't know what to make of Dennis. Jerry Ayres, who was then an executive, was present at one meeting between the three. "There was Dennis, with the spinach hanging down and the leather hat, and in the middle of the meeting, he got up and stuck his finger up my nose." But if Bert wanted to mind him, keep him away from the front office, that was fine.

Hopper and Lewis, whom Bert had hired as the production manager, traveled all over the South, a seriously risky trip in those days, when longhairs — Hopper's was down to his shoulders — were being threatened and beaten.

According to Hopper, he called Peter from New Orleans and said, "How's the script going?"

"Oh, we haven't started writing yet."

"What the fuck're you talking about? That's really nuts. We've already got all the locations, we know exactly what we want to shoot, and we don't have a fuckin' script?" Hopper flew to New York, went to the Fonda town house on East 74th Street, and discovered that Peter, Southern, and Rip Torn, who had been cast as Hanson, the ACLU lawyer who joins the trip, had gone out to dinner with a few girls to Serendipity, a hip restaurant in the East 60s. Like Southern, Torn was a big name. He had appeared in numerous films, including *Baby Doll*, *A Face in the Crowd*, and *Sweet Bird of Youth*. Hopper burst in upon the revelers, who were all drinking wine and having a fine time of it, and shouted, "What the fuck is happening, Peter, why aren't you guys writing?" Having gotten their attention, he continued, "Things are so rough out there I couldn't even stop in Texas, they're cutting dudes' hair with rusty razors." Torn, who hailed from Texas, recalls he tried to calm Hopper down, saying, "Aw, take it easy, not everyone from Texas is an a-hole," and stood up, extending his hand, but Hopper batted it away, pushed him, saying something like, "Sit down, you motherfucker." Then, says Torn, Hopper grabbed a steak knife off the table and threatened him with it, placing the point between his eyes, about five inches away. Torn, who had been a military policeman in the army, disarmed Hopper, reversing the knife and putting it on his chest. According to writer Don Carpenter, who was also there, Hopper jumped backward, bumping into Fonda, knocking him down. Hopper exclaimed, "I've got a buck knife. You wanna have a knife fight?" Torn replied, "I'll wait for you in the street. Bring your guns. Bring your knives. Bring your pals, and we'll find out in about three seconds who the punk is." He walked outside. "I knew he had a buck knife, but I had to consider what would happen if he did have a gun," adds Torn, "so I stood between two cars with a trashcan lid I was going to sail at him and run like hell. But he never came out." Torn, who had a conflicting commitment, could not get Raybert to pay him what he wanted, and never did play Hanson.*

The search was on for someone to replace Torn. "Bert was a little bit nervous that between Fonda and Hopper and this notion that we were not going to be on the set, we would never get a film," recalls Rafelson. He persuaded Dennis to accept Nicholson, who would be his eyes and ears, or, as Jack put it, to stop Dennis and Peter from killing each other.

At that point, Hopper claims he shut himself in Southern's office for two weeks and wrote the script himself. Hopper had already tried to get rid of Southern, but Bert refused, saying, "You don't have any names in this, he's a big name." Says Hopper, "Terry never wrote one fucking word, not one line of dialogue."

According to both Hopper and Fonda, after supplying the title *Easy Rider*, Southern left the picture. Southern always maintained that he wrote the entire script. Indeed, there exists a full script with Southern's name on it, covered with his handwriting. In a 1969 interview, Nicholson said, "There was a pretty firm script, but we worked to get that feeling — so it would seem improvised." Southern also claimed, shortly before his death, that the famous ending was his as well. He says Hopper and Fonda wanted the characters to go off into the sunset. "Dennis Hopper didn't have a clue as to what the film was about," he asserted. "When Dennis read it, he said, 'Are you kidding? Are you going to kill off *both* of them?" He continued, "In my mind, the ending was to be an indictment of blue-collar America, the people I thought were responsible for the Vietnam War."

Southern said Fonda and Hopper only got script credit because he did them

---

* Hopper went on *The Tonight Show* in 1994 and claimed that he had fired Torn because Torn pulled a knife on him. Torn won a $475,000 judgment against Hopper for defamation. The judge ruled that Hopper was not a credible witness.

a favor, called the Writers Guild and pleaded with them to add their names. "Neither of them are writers," he said. "They can't even write a fucking letter." He never received a penny more than the $3,500 he was owed for the script. "It was supposed to be a third, a third, a third," he added. "I would write, Peter would produce, and Dennis would direct." The evidence is hopelessly contradictory, but Southern did maintain, "They ignored our agreement."

Torn believes Hopper simply got rid of him and Southern after using their names to get the ball rolling. He says, "You have a director who's in your face all the time, doesn't want you there, does that mean that you dropped out or that you were driven out? I've never understood why it was necessary to attempt to destroy a man that only helped the project. Terry died penniless. Let's give the guy his due."

In any event, Peter gave half of the newly available points to Bill Hayward, and put the other half into Pando, his production company. When Hopper found out, he confronted them. He was so angry he wanted to push Fonda and Hayward out the window. "We're supposed to have an equal split," shouted Hopper. "What the fuck are you doing?"

"Then you quit, you quit?" Fonda bellowed in reply.

"No, man, I'll see you on the set." According to Hopper, "From that point on, Peter was so paranoid he got bodyguards. Paul Lewis said, 'Keep him in the fuckin' trailer.' So we locked him in his trailer. He screamed and cried and belched, 'I've been shot in the stomach, I'm in the middle of the desert, I'm dying, I can't work, I need a sandwich,' it was fucking unbelievable. This complaining, bitching, crying wimp just went on and on. If you could have done anything to try to sabotage the movie, Peter Fonda did it." (Fonda denies he hired a bodyguard, and Lewis has no recollection of locking him in his trailer.)

Fonda and Hopper's relationship remained tense throughout the shoot. "I was never afraid of him," says Fonda. "I was wearing a belt, the primary chain from the motorcycle, chrome. When you're belted in the face with that motherfucker, you find that's a skull crusher. At dinner someplace during the shooting Dennis was getting out of line, and I just said, 'Well, at least I don't hit women.' He looked at me and didn't say anything, because I knew he'd slugged Brooke."

The production, which traveled to several locations in California and the South, was conducted on a considerably more professional basis than the Mardi Gras circus. Still, Hopper and Fonda broke a lot of rules, used real people picked up along the way, improvised much of the dialogue. If it was cloudy one day and sunny the next, they shot anyway, ignoring the mismatches. If some of the raw film stock had chemical stains on it, no matter. Fonda called it "cinema verité in allegory terms."

Ironically, Hopper didn't like bikes. "I can't stand the goddamn things," he said. "I was *terrified* of that bike. I once hit an oil slick on Sunset Boulevard with a chick on the back, and I was in the hospital for ten days. So when I made the movie, every time a shot was done, that bike went right back on the truck."

Legend has it Nicholson smoked a prodigious number of joints during the shooting of the campfire scene when the three men discuss the prospects of a Venusian invasion. He boasted that he had smoked dope every day for fifteen years, said it slowed down the tempo of his acting.

The film took a little over seven weeks to shoot. Just as they were finishing up, all their motorcycles were stolen from their mechanic's garage in Simi Valley. They were so out of it that they had the wrap party, and then realized they had forgotten to shoot the second campfire scene, where Captain America says, famously, "We blew it," so they had to shoot it later. Fonda stared at the fire, thinking, What's my motivation? My motivation is 'Hello, you fascist fuck, you've blown our big chance.' "

In the editing room, Hopper continued to follow his vision. The French New Wave directors had dispensed with traditional optical effects like dissolves, fades, and so on, because they couldn't afford them, but their absence created a different aesthetic, gave their films a documentary flavor and speeded up the pacing. Hopper liked that, and he was also influenced by the American underground filmmakers. He refused to discard technical "imperfections" like lens flair* that had always ended up on the cutting room floor, which also lent the film a homemade, amateur look. "It was Bruce Conner's influence on Dennis that got him to cut as wildly as he did, which was totally against the principles we all had studied, and it seemed free-form and abstract," says Fonda. "I liked that. One of the reasons I called Hopper from fuckin' Toronto was that I knew he had the gift, he had the knowledge and ability and I didn't."

Some of his ideas were just nutty, Brecht on acid. For example, he wanted to run the credit sequence upside down. According to Bill Hayward, Hopper's knowledge of editing came from the hot splicing days, where you cut into a frame every time you make a splice, losing the frame in the process. In the '60s, film editors developed butt splicing, cutting between frames. Consequently he would never cut anything. One day, Hayward asked him to take out a scene: "If we hate it, we'll stick it back in." But Hopper stared at him blankly. "Dennis believed," he continues, "and this was a revelation after we found it out, because he cut for months under this misapprehension — that once you made a cut you couldn't put anything back. It was absolutely stunning. He was the worst editor that's ever been." Worse still, a prestigious French director attended

---

* Lens flair, a spiral-like reflection, occurs when the axis of the lens comes too close to the sun and the light bounces around the elements of the lens.

a screening, told Hopper he had created a masterpiece, not to lose a frame. Hopper dug in his heels.

"Every day there was a screening," recalls Rafelson. "There was an enormous amount of dope floating around, and not very much progress by way of, I'm going to take this out, I'm going to reshape this. It was sort of like, he loved it. Well, the reason he loved it at that length was because everybody who came to those screenings was doped up." The cut he loved best was four and a half hours long, without the 16mm footage. Hopper was convinced that it should play as a road show, with an intermission, high-priced tickets, reserved seats. "Dennis, there is no fucking way Columbia is going to go for that," said Hayward. "This is not *Lawrence of Arabia!* We gotta get this film cut down to a normal length."

Months and months dragged by, with the film no nearer to completion. Fonda complained to Schneider that Hopper was cutting him out of the movie: "What we have here is a movie called Billy and his friend, Captain America." Hopper went way past his deadline getting the picture to Pando. Pando was late delivering the picture to Raybert. Raybert was later still getting the film to Columbia. Schneider kept asking, "Where's the picture? Where's the picture?" Hayward told him, "Listen, we can't do any better than this without getting rid of Dennis, because Dennis is still jerking off in the editing room."

Nobody wanted to be the one to tell Hopper to leave. Says Fonda, "I wasn't going to, because I was sure that he would try to kill me. And as I refused to pack a pistol just because of Dennis Hopper, I was defenseless against him. He could jump out at me anyplace, get me with a bottle or a knife." Once again, it was Schneider who made the call. After a year, he finally told Dennis, "The film's too long, we're not going to destroy your movie, but I want you to take a holiday." Like everyone else, Hopper found it hard to say no to Bert, and allowed himself to be persuaded to go to Taos for Christmas while they reedited the movie. Bert bought Dennis and his girlfriend, Felicia, first-class tickets to Taos. He told Hopper to work on the fifteen hours of footage from Mardi Gras. "Dennis could go dick with this stuff, fuck around with it forever, think he was doing something, and we could go on and finish the movie," says Hayward. Adds Brooke, "Bert was the heroic savior of that movie. Without him, there never would have been an *Easy Rider.*"

Finally, the moment of truth arrived. Hopper was summoned from Taos to view the cut. Hayward ran the picture for him. "I was just horrified by this idea," he recalls. "I had always managed to somehow avoid Dennis's horrible temper. But I never wanted to be on the downside of it. We cut the shit out of the movie, from like four hours to ninety-four minutes or whatever. We had seen it in the intervening stages, but he hadn't. I knew that when the lights came up, he would be pissed; everybody was going to get it, but I would be the principal recipient." When the screening was over, and Hayward asked, tremulously, "Do you see anything wrong with it?" Hopper screamed, "You ruined my film. You've made a TV show out of it." But he eventually accepted it.

There was a lot of residual ill-feeling. Fonda had told Hopper they'd divvy up the profits, but now Fonda and his company had fifteen and a half points or so, and Hopper only had eleven. Just before they shot the credits, Fonda says Schneider called him into his office. Schneider said, "Hopper wants to take your name off the writing credits." Fonda thought, Jesus, Dennis, how 'bout that I just dreamt I was a part of the film and you acted my part too? You know, let's get serious." Fonda wanted to just get the film out, was willing to appease Hopper. He said, "I'll think about it overnight." The next day he went into Bert's office and said, "Okay, Bert, you know what I did, Rafelson knows what I did, Nicholson knows, I mean the people who made the movie know. So fuck it, you know. Let him have the credit, just say it's based on an original story by Peter Fonda, even though I was involved in the entire writing process. Just get him out of my life." The next day, Bert told him, "He won't go for it."

"He won't go for what?"

"For based on your story."

"Did he say it was his story?"

"He was yelling a lot about it was all his ideas and his things."

"I don't understand. Why can't he make the compromise if I'm willing to make the compromise?"

"Well, then he wouldn't be able to be nominated for Best Original Screenplay because it would be screenplay based on a previous story."

"Fuck him! Shoot the credit like it is in the contract." The credit reads, "Screenplay by Dennis Hopper, Peter Fonda, and Terry Southern." Hopper then sued Fonda for what he considered his rightful share of the points, but the suit was thrown out of court. Says Fonda, "Hopper will forever believe that I've cheated him and that he was the only person who wrote *Easy Rider*. Dennis has always resented the fact that I hired him, that it wasn't his own original idea."

Peter got the new supergroup that had just recorded its first album, Crosby, Stills & Nash, to do the score, and Bert made the deal. But any friend of Peter's was an enemy of Dennis's. "I sabotaged that," Hopper says. "They picked me up in a limo at Columbia, and drove me over, played the music, I told Steve Stills, 'Look, you guys are really good musicians, but very honestly, anybody who rides in a limo can't comprehend my movie, so I'm gonna have to say no to this, and if you guys try to get in the studio again, I may have to cause you some bodily harm." As if that weren't enough, the group hired a new manager, an ex-agent from William Morris whom Schneider allegedly referred to as "the little asshole." One day, at the recording studio, David Crosby introduced the manager to Schneider: "This is Bert Schneider. Bert's the guy who thinks you're an asshole." That was it. There was no way Crosby, Stills & Nash's music was going on the track of *Easy Rider*. The manager's name was David Geffen.*

For the most part, Hopper and Fonda just used the music from the temporary soundtrack. This was one of the first times a movie was yoked to the driving power of '60s rock 'n' roll, and in the future, rock music would become a major element in films like *American Graffiti, Mean Streets*, and *Apocalypse Now*.

BBS screened *Easy Rider* for the Columbia brass, many of whom had come from New York to see it. After three or four reels, most of them walked out. Blauner, who was still at Screen Gems, went out to dinner at Don the Beach-comber's, with his boss, Jerry Heims. "He was sitting there like somebody had died, and he smiled like his lips were gonna crack and he was gonna start to bleed," recalls Blauner. "What's Bert doin' to his father?" Heims asked Blauner.

"What's Bert doin' to his father? Don't you understand what you got here?"

"What're you talkin' about?"

"Look, the worst you got is a bike movie, which you paid half a million dollars for. Which will gross $8 to $10 million."

Columbia may not have known what to make of *Easy Rider*, but within the counterculture, word began to build. Actor Bruce Dern knew Nicholson from the old days, and was just finishing *They Shoot Horses, Don't They?* with Jane Fonda. One day, Jane said to him, "Wait'll you see Peter's movie, you're gonna freak out, 'cause there's a guy in that movie who is so fantastic, somebody has finally made a good biker movie."

"Whaddya mean, a biker movie. We made all the biker movies. I did eleven of them. It's over for biker movies."

"No, this one's different."

"Who's in it?"

"Dennis, and this guy Jack Nicholson."

"Jack Nicholson? I gotta pay attention to Jack fuckin' Nicholson, he's gonna be a movie star? Sure enough, six months later, he was."

Bert insisted the picture go to Cannes, where it won an award for the best movie by a new director. Fonda wore the uniform of a Union cavalry general and a bushy fake beard to the premiere. The symbolism was evident to him, if nobody else; it was meant to suggest that he and his generation were engaged in the second Civil War. When it became clear that the movie might be a hit, he quipped that the Columbia executives stopped shaking their heads in incomprehension, and began nodding their heads in incomprehension.

Easy Rider opened on July 14, 1969, at the Beekman, then on Third Avenue and 58th Street in New York. As Blauner recalls, "The management of the Beekman had never seen people like this on the East Side. They were sitting

---

* Geffen says this never happened.

on the sidewalk, no shoes. They had to take the doors off the stalls in the men's room because people were in there smoking pot." *Easy Rider* stunned the counterculture with a shock of recognition.

According to Bill Hayward, the picture cost $501,000. It took in $19.1 million in rentals, a phenomenal return on the investment. Said Hopper happily, "We made all of our money back the first week. In one theater."

Like *Bonnie and Clyde*, *Easy Rider* portrayed rebels, outlaws, and, by extension, the counterculture as a whole, as victims; they were extinguished by the straight world, by LBJ, by Richard Nixon's silent majority or their surrogates. *Easy Rider* also shared *Bonnie and Clyde*'s Oedipal anger at authority in general and parents in particular, most evident in the cemetery sequence. But, also like *Bonnie and Clyde*, a certain darkness, a premonition of disaster hovered around the edges of the story. There was a spirited debate in the press over what Captain America actually meant when he said, "We blew it."

The impact of *Easy Rider*, both on the filmmakers and the industry as a whole, was no less than seismic. Hopper was catapulted into the pantheon of countercultural celebrities that included John Lennon, Abbie Hoffman, and Timothy Leary. He was surrounded by groupies and acolytes. He may have started down the slippery slope to megalomania and grandiloquence on his own, but he had plenty of help. *Life* magazine called him "Hollywood's hottest director." He was credited with single-handedly creating "a style of a New Hollywood in which producers wear love beads instead of diamond stickpins and blow grass when they used to chew Coronas." Along with Southern and Fonda, he was nominated for an Oscar for Best Screenplay. Hopper himself credits the picture with putting cocaine on the hippie map. "The cocaine problem in the United States is really because of me," he says. "There was no cocaine before *Easy Rider* on the street. After *Easy Rider* it was everywhere."

Hopper was only too happy to discourse on the significance of *Easy Rider* to anybody who would listen, which was just about everyone. "When we were making the movie, we could feel the whole country burning up — Negroes, hippies, students," he said. "I meant to work this feeling into the symbols in the movie, like Captain America's Great Chrome Bike — that beautiful machine covered with stars and stripes with all the money in the gas tank is America — and that any moment we can be shot off it — BOOM — explosion — that's the end. At the start of the movie, Peter and I do a very American thing — we commit a crime, we go for the easy money. That's one of the big problems with the country right now: everybody's going for the easy money. Not just obvious, simple crimes, but big corporations committing corporate crimes."

To the Hollywood old guard, the good news was that after nearly a decade of floundering, the movies had finally *connected*, found a new audience. The bad news was that *Easy Rider* was another slap in the face, more punishing even than *Bonnie and Clyde*. Unlike Beatty, who was an insider, Hopper and Fonda were renegades, Hollywood-bashers, the Vietcong of Beverly Hills. To them, it was vindication, beating Hollywood at its own game, proof that you could get high, express yourself, and make money all at the same time. In a certain sense, as Buck Henry puts it, *Easy Rider* was authorless, the automatic handwriting of the counterculture. He says, "Nobody knew who wrote it, nobody knew who directed it, nobody knew who edited it, Rip was supposed to be in it, Jack was in it instead, it looks like a couple of hundred outtakes from several other films all strung together with the soundtrack of the best of the '60s. But it opened up a path. Now the children of Dylan were in control."

Hopper and his friends were seized with a millennialism that seemed to be sweeping everything before it. As he put it, "I want to make movies about us. We're a new kind of human being. In a spiritual way, we may be the most creative generation in the last nineteen centuries. . . . We want to make little, personal, honest movies. . . . The studio is a thing of the past, and they are very smart if they just concentrate on becoming distributing companies for independent producers."

It wasn't only the feverish, drug-crazed Hopper, high on his success, who was talking like his. He was the collective voice of the new generation. No one could have been less like Hopper than George Lucas, but Lucas said, "The studio system is dead. It died . . . when the corporations took over and the studio heads suddenly became agents and lawyers and accountants. The power is with the people now. The workers have the means of production!"

Recalls Peter Guber, who was then rising fast through the ranks at Columbia, "Everything seemed different after *Easy Rider*. The executives were anxious, frightened because they didn't have the answers any longer. You couldn't imitate or mimic quite as easily, churn them out like eggs from a chicken. Every day, there was a new person being fired. If you watched where the furniture truck stopped, in front of some producer's building, or some executive's office, you knew before he knew that he was dead. My inexperience, lack of contacts and relationships were not handicaps. Because of my youth, people asked, 'Well, what do you think?' "

Perhaps the most concrete result of *Easy Rider*'s success was the legitimation of the Raybert idea, and the transformation of the company into a significant cultural force. It not only made a big movie, it defined a sensibility, opened Hollywood to the counterculture. As Schrader, who lost his job at the *Free Press* by panning *Easy Rider*, summed it up, "BBS fired a cannon shot across the bow. Coppola and Lucas would sink the ship."

Shortly before the picture was released, Raybert became BBS (Bert, Bob, and Steve), with the addition of Blauner. Blauner had become an enormous, intimidating three-hundred-pound bear of a man, bluff and plainspoken, with a bushy red beard. As an executive at Screen Gems, he favored expensive, flashy suits. After he joined BBS, he was said to have taken the suits out and burned them, become a hippie, wearing beads and ripped clothes.

With Rafelson doing the negotiating because Schneider hated Columbia so much he couldn't bear to do it himself, BBS concluded a deal that allowed it to produce six films without interference, so long as each cost under $1 million. BBS had final cut, but final cut came with a price. Schneider, Rafelson, and Blauner personally guaranteed the cost of the negatives. If the picture went over, the money came out of their pockets. BBS and Columbia went 50-50 on the net. "Normally, net means nothing," says Blauner, "but we came from the counting rooms, so it was, 'Don't fuck with us.' " BBS realized it had a good thing in Nicholson, who was the de facto fourth partner, and he was automatically considered for every project.

Harold Schneider would be the unit production manager on all the BBS pictures. Harold was the mad dog in Bert's basement, the Doberman, as he was called. If Bert was ice, Harold was fire. He flew into rages, screamed, blustered, and threatened, growing red in the face, the veins in his neck popping out like ropes, a fine plume of saliva erupting from his mouth. With Harold, there was no middle ground between normal conversation and apoplectic rage. Harold was jealous of Bert, and the two men didn't get along well, but Bert trusted him — he was family — and knew he would keep the budgets under control. Harold could glance at a scene on the page and tell what it was going to cost to within a penny. He already had plenty of experience; he had worked on, and been fired from, more pictures than he could count.

Under the BBS umbrella, Bert, Bob, and Steve decided to move off the lot. Columbia bought them a four-story building at 933 North La Brea. On the top floor were the executive offices, each decorated by the respective wives. Bert's office was vast, as intimidating as the most conventional executive office at the most conventional studio, one difference being the secretaries spent a good deal of their time rolling joints for the guys. The office contained a pool table, a huge desk, a 1948 Wurlitzer juke box on loan from Jaglom, and a Tiffany chandelier. Bert could press a button on his desk and his door would swing open or closed. There was a sauna and a shower in the little hallway between his office and Bob's — which contained an antique piano. Silver trays with bowls of pot on them sat on tables. Almost any young, attractive woman who went up to the offices would get hit on. They kept score.

BBS quickly became a hangout for a rag-tag band of filmmakers and radicals of various stripes. There was no hipper place in Hollywood, no hipper place anywhere. Sitting in the BBS screening room watching Alejandro Jodorowsky's *El Topo*, the wild, surreal cult film that ran as a midnight movie in New York and Berkeley throughout the '60s, and smoking a joint with Bert and Bob, Dennis and Jack was the ultimate high. Schneider stayed very much in the background, but he was in many ways the Godfather. "Bert brought Columbia very successful product, with the music end of things, the Monkees, and then

Easy Rider," says Jacob Brackman, a screenwriter who worked with BBS. "People thought he really had taste and integrity and energy and was making very creative kinds of deals. His reputation was basically, he'll take care of you. All these people got little pieces of *Easy Rider,* down to the secretaries. It was almost unheard of. People really looked up to him. He could do just what he wanted."

Adds Jaglom, "Orson [Welles] always said that Hollywood had been ruined by Thalberg, who invented this idea of the creative producer, the producer who told the director what to do. That lasted from the '30s to the '60s. Bert reversed that. It was going to be a Hollywood Nouvelle Vague. The choice was no longer between doing it their way or not doing it at all. The possibility opened up that you could really do serious and interesting work, and survive commercially. We wanted to have film reflect our lives, the anxiety that was going on as a result of the war, the cultural changes that we were all products of," he continues. "The original idea of BBS was that we were all hyphenates. We were all writers, directors, and actors, and we would work on each other's movies, giving people points, making movies inexpensively, with everybody working at scale, everybody participating. We were all running in and out of each other's offices, reading each other things that we had just written. Anybody who was eccentric and strange enough, people said, 'Okay, what do you want to do?' And it all came out of a sensibility that nobody was supposed to exploit anybody else, we were all supposed to be sharing, working collectively. But make no mistake, there was one person who was in charge, that was Bert Schneider."

Still, there was a contradiction at the heart of BBS; it walked the line between being a countercultural powerhouse and a conventional production company. Says Jim McBride, an underground filmmaker known for a film called *David Holzman's Diary,* who admittedly had a bad experience with BBS, "The truth is, they were very schizophrenic. We used to call them the 'Hollywood sperm,' because they were all children of successful Hollywood people. They had beards, but in other ways, they didn't seem all that different. These were very rich guys who were playing at being hippies. But Bob sure had great dope."

WHATEVER WYATT MEANT when he told Billy, "We blew it," the words would shadow the decade. Indeed, those with an ear for such things had no trouble hearing the ominous minor chord behind the '60s Top Ten score of *Easy Rider.* In her essay "The White Album," Joan Didion, describing the ambience of the late '60s, writes: "I recall a time when the dogs barked every night and the moon was always full."

In the wee hours of Saturday morning, August 9, 1969, with *Easy Rider* in theaters for less than a month, Charles Manson's gang ventured forth from the

Spahn Ranch and murdered Sharon Tate, eight months pregnant, in a Benedict Canyon house at 10050 Cielo Drive she and Roman Polanski had rented after it had been vacated by Candice Bergen and her companion at the time, Terry Melcher. Four other people were killed as well, including the hairdresser Jay Sebring, and two friends of Polanski's, Abigail Folger and Voytek Frykowski.

A pervasive sense of dread and paranoia settled over the town like smog, shot through with sharp currents of shock and unease. "On August 9," writes Didion, "I was sitting in the shallow end of my sister-in-law's swimming pool in Beverly Hills when she received a telephone call from a friend who had just heard about the murders at Sharon Tate Polanski's home. . . . I also remember this, and I wish I did not: I remember that no one was surprised."

Despite the relative obscurity of the victims, the murders hit home. No one was untouched. Everybody knew them. They had had their hair done by Sebring, like Beatty and Towne, or had been invited up that night and had begged off because they were too tired, too stoned, or had something better to do, like Bob Evans. The sense that "it could have been me," haunted the hills. Just a few months earlier Polanski had tried to get Beatty to take over his lease. Beatty recalls, "I went up to look at the house, and thought, Yeah, I'll stay here for a while, because I wanted to get out of the hotel, but then Abigail and Voytek walked out from another part of the house, and said that Roman had told them to take the house. They said, 'There's plenty of room for everybody,' but I thought, No, I don't want to be in a house with other people." Towne, whose Hutton Drive home was near Cielo Drive, and remotely situated at the end of a long driveway, locked it up and moved elsewhere. Rumors flew that Manson had a celebrity hit list which included the names of Elizabeth Taylor and Steve McQueen.

Polanski was in Europe scouting locations for *Day of the Dolphins*, which he was supposed to direct. A few days before the murders he was in Paris at a club called Circus, in high spirits, rating women with a friend, as in "I just saw an 8," "No, she's a 6." He and Sharon were not getting along particularly well. Roman wasn't about to let marriage curtail his sex life. He had lately slept with Michelle Phillips, of the Mamas and the Papas. Sharon knew that he was fooling around. The day of the killings, he was in London with Beatty and Sylbert. He got on the next flight back to Los Angeles. "Roman was sitting on my lap on the way there, crying," says Sylbert. The police assigned two cops to guard him, and gave the director no peace, questioned him relentlessly. Even though he was in London when it happened, he felt they suspected him. "*He* suspected a lot of his friends," says Sylbert. "He had either fucked their girl-friends or their wives." Polanski wondered about Papa John Phillips, Michelle's husband, who, according to Phillips, threatened him with a meat cleaver.

"Roman was a brilliant man, the best read, most cultured director I have ever met in my life," says Paramount's Peter Bart, who worked with him on

Rosemary's Baby. "But in those days, people who were close to Roman had a tendency to die. He was always at the edge of the flame." At Rafelson's, Buck Henry entertained Nicholson, Schneider, Hopper, et al. with a ghoulishly embroidered account of what the police had found. "The breast was in the breadbox, the cock was in the glove compartment of Sebring's car . . ." There was a brisk sale in pistols and guard dogs. Intimidating automatic gates that had heretofore been beneath contempt in the Age of Aquarius, became de rigueur.

People scrambled to get on the I-almost-got-killed bandwagon. "If half the people who were supposed to have been there that night, had been there, it would have rivaled Jonestown," says Henry. It was as if people wanted to have been part of it, slaughtered like animals for some dark purpose of their own. This wasn't death at the hands of the "pigs," as *Bonnie and Clyde, The Wild Bunch, Butch Cassidy,* and *Easy Rider* had fantasized it, it was a much better, more frightening, more compelling script: Manson was themselves, a hippie, the essence of the '60s. If Hollywood was the forbidden planet, he was the monster from the id. "It was, 'I'm famous, I'm a celebrity, I don't deserve it, somebody's going to kill me, or my wife or my family,'" continues Henry. "To me, it was the defining event of our time. It affected everybody's work, it affected the way people thought about other people."

Manson wanted Hopper to star in the film version of his life. Hopper didn't want to meet him, because Sebring was a good friend of his, but curiosity finally triumphed over scruple. "I walked up to the courthouse, where he was in a cell, and all the little girls were camping in tents outside," he recalls. "He'd cut himself, a cross on his forehead. I asked him why. 'Don't you read the newspapers, man, all my followers have cut themselves like this so when the black revolution comes, they'll know which ones are mine.' I figured he wanted me 'cause he'd seen *Easy Rider,* but he proceeded to tell me, he'd seen me on a TV show, *The Defenders,* where I killed my father, 'cause my father had brutalized my mother." Manson missed his calling. It was inspired casting—he should have been a producer—but Hopper never did do the movie.

The great irony, of course, was that the murders happened a brief two years after the Summer of Love, a week before Woodstock, the celebration of all that was supposed to be best about the '60s. It was as if, at the moment of ripeness, the dark blossoms of decay were already unfolding. Psychedelics were on their way out, acid had been laced with speed to make a paranoia-inducing drug called STP. Haight-Ashbury was already being decimated by speed and smack, and Hollywood was getting ready to take a fast ride down the cocaine highway. There was a sense of closure, that an era was over, that people had gotten away with a lot for a while and, for the more apocalyptically minded, that the Grim Reaper was going to cut them all down. "It was the end of the '60s," says Sylbert. "All over town you could hear the toilets flushing."

But despite the moral and metaphysical aftershocks from the Manson killings, which lasted well into the next year as the trial dragged on and on, Hollywood returned to normal. Beatty held a small wake for Sharon in his penthouse apartment. After the funerals, the bizarreness of the murders gave way to the quotidian, the reassuring. The reception was at Bob Evans's house, a barbecue. He served hot dogs. As the police searched for the Tate killers, *Easy Rider* roared across America's screens through the long, hot summer of 1969, through the fall, and into the new year, the new decade. And what a wild ride it would be. The Manson murders may have been a sign, but most people would be too busy making movies, doing drugs, having sex, and spending money to heed it.

Three:
Exile on Main Street
1971

• *How Robert Altman butted heads with Beatty on*
McCabe & Mrs. Miller, while John Calley revived Warners,
and Coppola presided over the rise and fall of American
Zoetrope.

"Suddenly there was a moment, when it seemed as if the pictures you wanted to
make, they wanted to make."

— ROBERT ALTMAN

In the final throes of post-production on his eagerly awaited new picture, *Catch-22*, Mike Nichols and his producer, John Calley, decided to check out the competition, a picture Robert Altman had just finished that sounded a bit like their own. The two men sank into the plush seats of the screening room. That *M*A*S*H* represented a serious threat to *Catch-22* was the furthest thing from their minds. Nichols, after all, coming off *Who's Afraid of Virginia Woolf?* and *The Graduate*, was America's hottest director.

Right away, however, Nichols got a tight feeling in his chest as Altman's darkly comic vision played out in front of him, recognizing that he had been blindsided. "We were waylaid by *M*A*S*H*, which was much fresher and more alive, improvisational, and funnier than *Catch-22*," he says. "It just cut us off at the knees." So it came as no surprise to Nichols that *M*A*S*H* became a huge hit. Nor to Altman either, who was acutely aware that he was chasing Nichols's tail. He had a banner up in his office that said, "Caught-22."

Meanwhile, Beatty, tired of waiting for Towne's draft of *Shampoo*, said to his agent, Stan Kamen, "Let's find a picture I can do with Julie." Kamen replied, "What about Robert Altman? He's got a script called *McCabe & Mrs. Miller*." Beatty had never heard of Altman, but he screened *M*A*S*H*, and appreciated Altman's antic style. Like Arthur Penn, Altman was interested in the relation between the medium and the message, but whereas Penn could often be portentous, Altman was playful, favoring narrative and visual puns. He was always reminding the audience it was watching a movie. Best of all, like *Bonnie and Clyde*, *M*A*S*H* was a "fuck you" from the cool to the uncool.

Beatty read the *McCabe* script, liked it well enough, but thought to himself, I just don't know if Julie will want to do this. It's an American woman, and really isn't anything at all like her. "Julie never wanted to do anything," he recalls. "She was the most selective actress I've ever met. She tested for *Doctor Zhivago* in a five-day screen test. She was totally unknown, they gave her the picture and initially she turned it down. So I had to really push her into doing this, because I thought she could be very funny in it."

Beatty called Altman from New York, where he was staying at the Delmonico on 57th Street, then flew to L.A. to meet the director, after which he agreed to do the picture. Altman was paid $350,000 to direct. The business was in such bad shape, that even though Beatty was in great demand, he had to forgo his customary salary up front in lieu of a cut of the back-end gross. The picture was financed by Warners.

McCABE WAS NOT the sort of project Jack Warner would have liked. Nor was the rambunctious Altman the kind of director he appreciated. But Jack Warner wasn't at the studio anymore, nor were Eliot and Kenny Hyman. In 1969, Kinney National Service — a company that got its start in funeral homes and parking lots — bought Warner Bros.–Seven Arts. Kinney's Steve Ross did not directly involve himself in the operations of the studio. He hired agent Ted Ashley, forty-seven, to replace Eliot Hyman. Ashley had been head of the powerful Ashley-Famous agency that Kinney had acquired two years earlier. He was the first of a long line of agents who would abandon the agencies in the coming decade in favor of the studios or producing.

Ashley was born in a tenement in Brooklyn, and worked his way up from the William Morris mailroom. "Ted is ruthless, but he simulates niceness better than any person I have ever known," said an executive at another studio. "With Teddy, the operative phrase is, 'Love me or I'll kill you.'" At five foot four and 138 pounds, Ashley was a gnome of a man, but he had a reputation as a serious stud. He was, as producer Don Simpson, who started his career at Warners, puts it, "the pussy freak of all time."

Ashley didn't waste any time before he cleaned house. Of the Hymans' twenty-one top executives, he fired eighteen, and put together his own team. Calley, thirty-nine years old, was on the set of *Catch-22*, having breakfast with Tony Perkins, one of the featured actors in the film. They were in the middle of the eggs, when he got the call. He took it, returned to the table. "I just got the weirdest call."

"What was it?" wondered Perkins.

"It was Ted Ashley, asked me if I wanted to be head of production at Warners."

"What did you say?"

"I said I just can't imagine myself doing that." In his mind's eye, Calley saw middle-aged men in beautifully tailored suits easing their custom-bodied Bentleys into their own parking space surrounded by guards. "I just can't make the connection. I said I'd think about it overnight."

"Don't be an asshole. How many guys get a chance to be head of production? What's the worst thing that can happen?"

"I can fuck up."

"So what else is new? They all fuck up. Harry Cohn? Look at the shit he made. You gotta do it."

"Yes, of course, you're right. What a schmuck I'd be not to have that experience." Calley called Ashley back, said, "I'd love to."

The young production head had learned how to make deals at the knee of his father, a car dealer-salesman-hustler. As a youth, Calley had few expectations. He talked his way into a job as a messenger at NBC, and then climbed up through the ranks. By 1969, he was a producing veteran, having been in charge of films like *The Loved One*, *The Cincinnati Kid*, and *The Americanization of Emily* for Martin Ransohoff's Filmways.

Calley got romantically involved with Elaine May, and through her he met Mike Nichols. Calley and Nichols became the best of friends, which is how Calley brought *Catch-22* to Filmways, and produced it. The story goes that Ransohoff loved Calley like a son. When he realized that Calley had signed a contract barring him from the set, he went berserk and fired him.

Ashley also hired Frank Wells, a Rhodes scholar and Clint Eastwood's attorney, to head business affairs. Nessa Hyams, out from New York, headed casting. Tony Bill was the in-house producer. Ashley held on to Warners veterans Dick Lederer, who was upped to vice president of production, and Joe Hyams, who in turn hired Simpson, a kid from Alaska, of all places. Calley hired two more young story editors, first Barry Beckerman, twenty-three, and then Jeff Sanford, twenty-five. Ashley also threw in a wild card, music entrepreneur Fred Weintraub, forty-one, making him VP of creative services, based in New York.

Under Calley, Warners became the class act in town. Urbane and witty, he gave the impression that he was somehow above it all, slumming in the Hollywood cesspool. As one wag put it, he was the blue in the toilet bowl. Calley immediately bought the guest house of the old Barrymore estate, with its heated kennels and Renaissance sundial in the pool. He was so hip he didn't even have a desk in his office, just a big coffee table covered with snacks, carrot sticks, hardboiled eggs, and candy. Lots of antiques. His style was English gentleman. He had a green thumb with money, played the gold market, loved to buy and sell expensive cars and boats. His deal gave him a new car every year, and he bought the most expensive ones. He had half a dozen Mercedes Gullwings in storage as an investment. "He knew where every yacht of any size in the world was, what its tonnage was," says Buck Henry. "He never bought anything he didn't sell for more money than he bought it for."

Calley created an atmosphere congenial to '60s-going-on-'70s filmmakers. The production executives put in long hours, but they dressed in work shirts and jeans instead of suits. Even Wells wore jeans. Sanford wore sandals, and fixed his long hair in a ponytail. "You went to Universal and they all looked like cutouts," recalls Nessa Hyams. "Once you got to Warners, you were in the middle of Woodstock. Five o'clock in the afternoon, instead of the clinking of ice in a glass would be the aroma of marijuana wafting down the first floor." Adds Sanford, "It was sort of an asset to be into pot and acid. We were all hippies."

Every day, after lunch, the Warners executives screened "art" films. They watched all the Kurosawa they could get their hands on, as well as Fellini, Truffaut, Renoir, Ermanno Olmi, René Clair. Brand-new prints. Ross had given Ashley a free hand. Ashley did the same for Calley, who says, "If McQueen and Streisand had walked into Ted's office and said, 'Here's our script, we'll work for nothing, Barbra sings twenty-five songs, we'll take off all our clothes, da-da-da,' he would say, 'I'm thrilled, but you gotta go see John Calley.' He franchised me."

Ashley had hired Calley at least in part because of his relationships with directors, and it was to them that Calley turned. "We started doing pictures without producers almost immediately," he says. "The studios felt directors were madmen. When we made the deal with Kubrick for *Clockwork Orange*, everyone was excited about getting him, but then the panic set in: 'How can we control him?' The studio would buy somebody because of his gifts and then make it impossible for him to use those gifts. I never felt that. I was the only person in a position of power at a studio that had ever worked on a film. I was really comfortable with directors. If this is the guy who is looking through the camera, and evaluating the lines, he better be in charge. We started doing pictures without producers almost immediately. Directors had to run the fucker."

Calley drew up a list of twenty or so directors with whom he wanted to be in business. Kubrick and Nichols were at the top, but there were also Sydney Pollack, Mark Rydell, and Billy Friedkin. Then there were the Brits, John Boorman, Tony Richardson, Lindsay Anderson, and Jack Clayton. Calley inherited Sam Peckinpah and Luchino Visconti from the Seven Arts regime.

Practically the first thing he did when he got to the studio was call Arthur Penn and say, "Listen, Arthur, I'd like you to reconstitute *Left-Handed Gun*. It's a tragedy and it should never have been —" Penn said, "Great!" Calley called

Rudy Fehr, the elderly head of editing who had been at the studio as long as anyone could remember. He said, "I want the outtakes from *Left-Handed Gun* because Arthur is going to recut it." Fehr said blithely, "Oh, ve vere able to throw avtervards out all dat shit!"

Calley and Wells made the perfect good guy–bad guy team. Wells was a hardnose, very careful with the nickels and dimes. Calley would always say, "If it was me, I would back your project, but Frank, or Ted, he just doesn't like it." Says an executive who worked with him, "Calley is a genius at being on the side of whoever it is he's talking to, and the other guys are the bad guys." Often it was true. Calley brought the talent in, and Wells drove it out.

The new regime's first hit, *Woodstock*, was brought in by Weintraub. Fred was a large, jovial man, who wore his hair long, in a ponytail, topped with a soft, blue John Lennon–style hat with the short bill. He was a colorful character who owned the Bitter End Coffeehouse in the Village, where Beatty and Charlie Feldman saw Woody Allen, and Bob Dylan played. Ashley and Weintraub had become tight when Ashley was still an agent.

"Nobody supported me," recalls Weintraub. "They sat me down, said, 'There's been twelve festival films, all of them were bombs, why do you want to do another bomb? Calley did not want to do *Woodstock*. I said, 'I'm gonna quit unless you guys do it.' " Calley thought, There's so little money involved here, they could turn the film stock into guitar picks if the film were no good. He gave in. *Woodstock*, which cost Warners a ridiculously small sum, took in $16.4 million in domestic rentals when it was released in 1970. Ashley rewarded Weintraub by bringing him out to L.A. Fred's new office looked like an ashram, complete with a beaded curtain in the doorway, incense, and, of course, the odor of grass. *Woodstock* gave Weintraub considerable clout at the studio, where he seemed to be the executive in charge of alternative lifestyle.

Warners' next hit was *Summer of '42*, which took in $14 million in rentals. Wells, their Eastwood connection, brought the star over from Universal for *Dirty Harry*. Kubrick came aboard, and made *A Clockwork Orange*. Pollack made *Jeremiah Johnson*. Alan Pakula made *Klute*. Friedkin would make *The Exorcist*. Truffaut directed *Day for Night*, and Visconti, *The Damned* and *Death in Venice*. Warners picked up an independent production called *Billy Jack* which became a money cow, and also grabbed a film by Scorsese called *Mean Streets* that no one else would touch. Some of the projects, like *Deliverance*, directed by Boorman, surprised even them. Barry Beckerman urged Calley to buy it, but his colleagues thought he was crazy, said, "Wait a minute. Three guys with canoes go into the country for the weekend, and a brain-damaged boy plays a banjo solo on a bridge and then one of them gets fucked in the ass — you think that's a movie?" Calley was ready to flush it, but Beckerman came into his office, said, "You asshole, you gotta do this movie." Calley said, "You're right, I'm being a schmuck. I'm not trusting my instincts."

Prior to *Deliverance*, Boorman had made *Hell in the Pacific* for ABC Films in 1968, and the producers had changed the ending without telling him. "It was so traumatic that I vowed I would never make a picture again without having final cut." A year or so later, everything had changed. Recalls Boorman, "I worked with James Dickey on the script, gave it to Calley, and he said, 'Okay.' There were no notes, just a general conversation. The director was in charge." Calley also allowed Boorman to produce, which gave him a further measure of protection. Throughout the decade, producing credit would become de rigueur for successful directors. It was at once an expression and a guarantor of their power.

Calley had hardly forgotten that M*A*S*H had buried *Catch-22*, so he put Altman high on his wish list of directors. Which is why, when he had the opportunity to finance a picture directed by Altman with Beatty and Julie Christie, he jumped.

A LAPSED CATHOLIC, Robert Altman had been a rebel from the word go. He was born into a prominent Kansas City family on February 20, 1925. Bob was the oldest child, the only son, with two sisters. His father, B.C., sold insurance, and cut quite a figure, gambling, whoring, and drinking. The family was comfortable; there was always a safety net, which may have fueled the financial and emotional brinkmanship Altman practiced in later life. Altman enlisted in the air force at the age of nineteen, and served as a co-pilot flying B-24s against Japan during the final days of World War II.

He married LaVonne Elmer. Right before the wedding, the lovebirds had a bad car accident. Her jaws were wired shut, and during the ceremony, she had to mutter her wedding vows through clenched teeth. Altman walked away unscathed, which would become the story of his life. The couple moved to L.A., where he tried to scrape together a living. He had a variety of odd jobs, including tattooing identification numbers on dogs. He relaxed by going to the movies. He saw David Lean's *Brief Encounter* and Vittorio De Sica's *The Bicycle Thief*, which awakened in him an interest in pictures. He started writing scripts and stories. But Bob just couldn't seem to take hold. He separated from LaVonne and moved back to Kansas City, where he got a job working on industrials at the Calvin Company.

L.A. had given him a taste for glamour and glitz. He sent his favorite leather jacket there to be cleaned, and he contrived to approximate what he imagined to be a Hollywood lifestyle in Kansas City — no mean trick — with generous portions of girls, gambling, and booze. During lunch he would repair to the home of a hooker for a quick $2 blowjob. "Altman had this idea that was a very Hollywood thing to do," said Richard Peabody, the friend who accompanied him, "to get your cock sucked on your lunch hour."

In 1954, Altman met and married his second wife, Lotus Corelli, a former model. This marriage lasted three years, and the Altmans had two boys, Michael and Stephen. A year later, he made a low-budget feature, *The Delinquents*, that was financed by a small Midwest exhibitor. He was determined to edit the picture in L.A. The exhibitor refused to pay his airfare, so in the last week of August 1956, he dumped the dailies into a '56 Thunderbird that he had finessed from the production, and headed west, accompanied by an Iranian friend, Reza Badiyi. Altman turned his back on Kansas City for good, leaving behind two marriages, a couple of kids, his parents, and his sisters. During the trip, they listened to the Republican convention, which nominated Eisenhower and Nixon. Altman was a Democrat, supported Adlai Stevenson.

The following year he landed a job working for *Alfred Hitchcock Presents*. This would be the beginning of a decade's worth of television work, which repeatedly saw him make his mark with innovative methods. He would antagonize whoever there was to antagonize, and in high dudgeon, move on to something else. Along the way, like a snowball rolling downhill, he picked up people who would become part of his creative team. Among them was Tommy Thompson, whose claim to fame was that he had, in 1946 while working for the Armed Forces Radio Services in Tokyo, reported that Japan had been invaded by a Godzilla-like sea monster. This prank was something Altman could appreciate, and the two men became fast friends. Thompson began working regularly for Altman as his first assistant director (1st AD). He used to pick him up from his apartment in a grand old building on the northwest corner of Fountain and La Cienega in West Hollywood, to take him to work. Often, he'd knock on the door, no answer. He'd walk in and find Bob, passed out, an unfinished drink by his side. "He was like this big Pillsbury Dough Boy," Thompson recalls. "I'd get him in the shower, dressed, down to the car, and we'd get out on the location. He sat in a high director's chair, while I stood behind him. As they'd rehearse, he'd nod off, and I'd kind of poke him, and he'd wake up and say, 'How was it?' I'd say, 'Run it again,' and he'd say, 'All right, let's run it again.' And he'd go back to sleep, I'd punch him, say, 'Say, "Cut!" ' 'Cut! How was it?' 'Tell 'em to go faster.' 'Speed it up a little, guys.' We'd run through the whole day like that."

In 1959, at Desilu Productions, where he worked on a series called *The Whirlybirds*, he met Kathryn Reed, who would become his third wife. She was an extra, playing a nurse. It was a hot day, and he had a wet rag over his hair, which was thinning. He said his hair was in a race between turning gray and going bald. As Reed got off the bus, he asked, "How are your morals?" "A little shaky," she replied, and walked away, over to the coffee machine. He followed her, said, "If you mix coffee with hot chocolate, it kinda comes out like cappuccino." She thought, This guy's really been around. He gave her a ride in a helicopter, and that was it. Both were in the middle of divorces. They got married in Mexico, and when their divorces became final, about a year later, they remarried in California. She had a daughter named Connie from a previous marriage. The three moved into an apartment in Brentwood. Two years later, they moved into a house in Mandeville Canyon, up above the chic section, in what Kathryn called the "Malibu slums," where they lived for nine years.

Altman fought his way from producer to producer, series to series, eventually ending up at Warners, directing shows like *Hawaiian Eye* and *Maverick*, as well as *Bonanza*, shot on the lot, all the while complaining he was being cannibalized by his ex-wives for child support and alimony. He'd get calls on the set, and scream into the phone, "All right, put me in jail, will that do any good?"

After a stint directing *Combat*, a down-and-dirty, handheld, documentary-flavored war-is-hell series (Manson family member Sandra Goode once cited it as her favorite show), Altman left for the *Kraft Suspense Theater*, at Universal. As usual, Altman fell out with his boss, and was promptly fired. In September 1963, in a typical display of suicidal bravado, he gave an interview to *Variety* in which he called Kraft's show "as bland as its cheese."

It was at this juncture, when Altman was looking for a new agent, that George Litto entered his life. Litto was pugnacious, volatile, and funny, with the large ego of a short man. He was Sicilian, one of those guys who is always right, knows the best restaurants, makes the best deals. "I couldn't fathom why the hell he was calling me, except that I guess everybody else was afraid to represent him," Litto says. "We were from the same school, that Hemingway, Hammett, Chandler, hard-drinking, hard-talking, take-no-shit thing. John Huston was our hero. But I also wanted to be involved with people who were going to do outstanding things."

Litto took him on. "The truth of the matter is, he was a lousy business investment," he continues. "He took up an awful lot of my time and I didn't make that much money with him. But I enjoyed it because he was this bombastic-rebel, bomb-thrower, crazy son of a bitch. He was confrontational. He would get in your face and tell you to fuck off. He didn't suck up. He could be a miserable prick. Bob could be whatever he felt like being, and as a matter of fact you almost couldn't tell what he was going to be at any given meeting, which was the most engaging part."

In 1963, Altman set up shop on the other side of town from BBS. Lion's Gate, at 1334 Westwood Boulevard, was housed in an old Tudor two-story building two blocks south of Wilshire. The offices became a hangout for his crowd. There was the obligatory pool table, pinball machines, and barber's chair. Two wooden spiral staircases led to the second floor. There was a courtyard in the back, and eventually Bob bought the upstairs on the other side, and turned it into an apartment. A bar was built into the wall of his office.

Bob liked to do things in style; no one ever drank out of paper cups, always crystal. He never imbibed during the day. He was strictly an "Is it five o'clock yet?" kind of guy. In fact, the crew always knew they were on the last shot of the afternoon when he sent a prop man for his first glass of Cutty Sark. Altman could be a mean drunk. "Bob had a black side when he drank," says Thompson. "He'd be in his cups, sitting around, telling stories, having a wonderful time, and all of a sudden the booze'd hit him, and he'd go after you — he'd kill you, across a room, he could just say, 'Let me tell you something about yourself. . . . Your fucking personality is just . . .' and you'd be in tears and leave. It got to the point where when I'd fix him a drink, I'd fill the glass with water, and then float a little scotch on the top, and very carefully take it over to him, so when he'd drink it, he'd think it was solid scotch." Adds Litto, "Whatever you could say about Bob's high life and fast living, I've never seen his lifestyle interfere with his work during that period. At five in the morning he was sobered up, at his office at six."

Altman loved to gamble and would often take off for Las Vegas on the spur of the moment. On one trip he was accompanied by a pal and his female companion. The friend entered Altman's room at the Sands to find the director cavorting among $100 bills scattered about the rug. He had just won $5,000. According to the friend, Bob said, "I'll give you one of these for your girl."

"What the hell are you talking about? You're not getting her!"

"I'll give you two!"

Altman took to grass like a guernsey. Thompson and his other friends were relieved. He'd get a relaxing high off weed without the nastiness that surfaced with booze. Altman flung himself headlong into the '60s. He let his hair — what there was of it — go long, grew a beard, wore turtlenecks, caftans, ankhs, and beads.

Despite the fact that he was set up in his own offices, the late '60s was a dark time for Altman. He refused to do any more TV, determined to hold out for a feature. Meanwhile, he'd sit around with his pals watching old *Combat* episodes and guzzling Cutty Sark. He was gambling, trying to make enough off the track to get along, living off Kathryn's child support payments. His drinking got worse. He would pass out in restaurants and have to be carried home.

In 1968, Altman got *That Cold Day in the Park* through Litto. It was tough going. Says Litto, "Nobody wanted to make a picture with Bob Altman." Finally, the agent corraled Donald Factor, heir to the cosmetic fortune, to finance it. Nicholson wanted to play the lead, but the director thought he was too old. Harold Schneider was the assistant director (Altman couldn't stand him, fired him right away), and the picture was shot in Vancouver. Bob couldn't help directing off the set, plucking the wings off the people around him. According to one source, he liked to play mind games. He was the kind of person who liked to stir the pot, betray a confidence to get a reaction, tell someone what someone else had said behind her back — making it up if necessary — just for the fun of it.

ABOUT A WEEK after Calley took his new position, he got a telegram from San Francisco that said, "Shape up or ship out." It was signed, "Francis Ford Coppola, American Zoetrope." Coppola had a long-standing relationship with Warners, for whom he had done *Finian's Rainbow*. It had been a disaster, and worse, a detour away from Coppola's vision of himself as an auteur. He was determined to get back on track, get away from the back lot and make his own films his own way. When he was a child, his mother once disappeared after a quarrel with his father and spent two days alone in a motel. This incident became the kernel of *The Rain People*, which he wrote while he was working on *Finian's Rainbow*, and directed in the summer of 1968. Coppola always believed in forcing the studio's hand by spending as much of its money as he could until it had no choice but to commit. It worked with *The Rain People*, although in this case he used his own money to prime the pump. "To have had the guts to have plunked down $20,000 of his own was astonishing," says Walter Murch. "That has been part of Francis's genius all along, to walk not only out on the gangplank, but off the edge of it and seemingly not fall down but sort of hang there in space while the sharks are nipping at his heels, and he's saying, 'Come on out, it's great.'" Eventually Coppola persuaded Warner–Seven Arts to back it. "Francis could sell ice to the Eskimos," Lucas said admiringly. "He has charisma beyond logic. I can see now what kind of men the great Caesars of history were, their magnetism."

Like *Easy Rider*, *The Rain People* chronicled a cross-country trek, albeit in the opposite direction, from east to west. Like Hopper and Fonda, Coppola and Lucas realized movies no longer had to be shot and edited in Hollywood. The new, lightweight equipment meant that they could just get on the road and look for the "real" America, shooting real stories about real people. (Coppola was careful to refer to *The Rain People* as a documentary so he wouldn't have to use a union crew.) The crew, no more than twenty-odd people, bundled themselves into vans and headed out of New York. Among them was a skinny teenager named Melissa Mathison, who would go on to marry Harrison Ford and be nominated for an Oscar for writing *E.T.* Melissa had been baby-sitting the Coppolas' kids since she was twelve, and was busy arranging three-legged races while the guys talked film.

In the documentary Lucas shot about the making of *The Rain People*, he catches Francis on the phone to the studio, screaming, à la Hopper, "The system will fall by its own weight! It can't fail to!"

On the road, Coppola and Lucas had conversations that sounded not too different from those between Schneider and Rafelson. "Francis saw Zoetrope as a sort of alternative *Easy Rider* studio where he could get a lot of young talent for nothing, make these movies, hope that one of them would be a hit, and eventually build a studio that way," said Lucas. "It was very rebellious. We had very off-the-wall ideas that never would have been allowed to infiltrate the studios. Zoetrope was a break away from Hollywood. It was a way of saying, 'We don't want to be part of the Establishment, we don't want to make their kind of movies, we want to do something completely different.' To us, movies are what counts, not deals and making commercial films." Added John Milius, who stayed in L.A. but would revolve around the gravitational field of Zoetrope, "Francis was going to become the emperor of the new order, but it wasn't going to be like the old order. It was going to be the rule of the artist."

After he wrapped *The Rain People*, Coppola took off for Denmark, where he visited a company, Laterna Films, housed in a mansion by the beach, filled with state-of-the-art equipment and stunning girls. His fate was sealed. At a trade fair in Cologne, he made an impulse purchase of new, flatbed KEM editing consoles and sound mixers for $80,000. He had no money to pay for them and no place to put them.

Coppola's wife Eleanor did not want to raise her kids in the Hollywood lifestyle; Francis didn't want to live in the shadow of the studios, and was particularly unhappy with their lock on post-production sound. He had an intuition that in the hands of creative people, sound could make a much greater contribution to filmmaking. They chose San Francisco. "I think Francis left L.A. because he didn't want to be a small fish in a big pond," says Marcia Lucas, who moved up north with George to take part in the experiment. "I think he wanted to be a big fish in a small pond." In any event, Francis set up the temporary headquarters of American Zoetrope in the fall of 1969 in two floors of a warehouse at 827 Folsom Street. They hired hippie carpenters to frame the walls who were so stoned on acid that the next day the Sheetrock had to be ripped out because it was off plumb. Ellie chose orange cloth to cover the walls and royal blue for the furniture. There were transparent inflatable plastic couches she had purchased in Europe. Coppola installed a pool table and an espresso machine. Antique zoetropes (primitive viewing devices) were tastefully displayed in Mylar cases behind the receptionist. Francis's office was decorated in Swedish modern — Eames chairs on a gold-colored rug. There were editing rooms, and space for an art department, wardrobe, props, and sound dubbing. The core group, all of whom moved up from L.A. with their families, included Lucas, who was vice president, and Murch. As flamboyant as Coppola was, there was one rule at Zoetrope — no drugs — which distinguished the company from the weed-wacked BBS.

Coppola continued to dazzle the young filmmakers he had gathered around him. Murch sound-mixed *The Rain People* at Folsom Street on the new German machine. Something went wrong with it, and after they all stood around for a while scratching their heads, Francis said, "I betcha it's the capacitor. Gimme a soldering iron." To Murch's astonishment, Coppola dropped to his hands and knees and crawled under the mixing console, took out one of the capacitors, and soldered on a new one. Says Murch, "He was not somebody who said, 'Let's bring in an expert to fix it.' You had to admire a guy who not only wrote, produced, directed, but was able to figure out what was wrong and patch it up, which was beyond my ability, even though I was the sound mixer."

Francis had a serious impact on Lucas, always telling him he was a genius, building his ego. According to Marcia Lucas, "George was not a writer, and it was Francis who made him write, said, 'If you're gonna be a filmmaker, you have to write.' He practically handcuffed George to the desk." Francis was always after him, insisting he would have to learn how to talk to actors. But it soon became clear that George's and Francis's notions of what the new company should be differed radically. If Francis wanted to create a countercultural MGM, all George wanted was a roof over his head where he could gather his friends and re-create the USC experience. Their clashing styles were a source of friction. "My life is a kind of reaction against Francis's life," Lucas explained. "I'm his antithesis." Francis was large and bulky, Lucas small and frail. Francis was emotional, George, reserved. Francis was reckless, George, cautious. Francis was collaborative to a fault. Lucas had a vision he defended fiercely. Where Francis would delegate, Lucas was a control freak, would have done everything — write, shoot, direct, produce, and edit — himself. No matter how little money Francis had, he always acted like a man with more. No matter how much money George had, he always acted like a man with none. Coppola referred to him disparagingly as the "seventy-year-old kid." Countered George, "All directors have egos and are insecure. But of all the people I know, Francis has the biggest ego and the biggest insecurities." Still, Francis was probably the best friend the shy and socially maladroit Lucas would ever have.

AFTER CALLEY RECEIVED Coppola's telegram, he called Francis, asked him what he was up to. The director explained that he had gathered a bunch of talented former USC and UCLA students in a new company. He particularly talked up Lucas, told Calley he was a "gigantic talent," and pitched THX 1138, a feature based on Lucas's student short that Francis had promised to produce. "George was like a younger brother to me," says Coppola. "I loved him. Where I went, he went." Coppola persuaded Calley to give him $300,000 for developing ten or so screenplays that he referred to as his "multipicpac," which included his own script for The Conversation, and others by his film school pals Willard Huyck, Carroll Ballard, Matthew Robbins, Hal Barwood, and so on. He also convinced Calley to back THX, and give him another $300,000, to finance the start-up of Zoetrope. (In addition, he tossed into the pot a John Milius script called *Apocalypse Now* that he had absolutely no relationship to, except that Lucas, who was attached as director, had told him about it.) He assured Warners that he would take responsibility for the financial controls, be the daddy, the big brother, the bridge between the studio and the kids who trusted him but would not have anything to do with the studio.

Barry Beckerman was assigned to baby-sit Coppola for Warners, but such was Francis's personal charm that Beckerman went over to the other side. "Francis had this Mansonesque effect on all of us," he recalls. "If he'd told me to stab Ashley, I probably would've stabbed Ashley." The one thing Coppola knew how to do really well, right from the beginning, was spend money. Adds Beckerman, "As Francis always said, it takes no imagination to live within your means."

Coppola told Warners he wanted to do personal films, like Fellini and Antonioni. He submitted an autobiographical script, but Warners was not impressed. "Frankly, it was puerile, just boring," says an executive who read it. "It was not Antonioni, it was Anthony Quinn, and made me feel that he wasn't terribly interesting as a person making films about himself. He was a wonderful filmmaker, but not an auteur."

The Zoetropeans couldn't live by dreams alone, and they had to struggle to stay alive. It wasn't long before the experiment began to turn sour. Equipment disappeared. The company was often unable to meet payroll. Much to Coppola's chagrin, some of the employees tried to unionize. Coppola was not sympathetic. "The feeling from working for Francis is tough shit if you don't think you're getting paid enough or if you don't think your working conditions are good enough," said Deborah Fine, a former Zoetrope librarian. "There's a million people out there that would kiss the ground to work for him for nothing."

ONE DAY, when Altman was hanging out in Litto's office, the agent handed him a screenplay, saying, "This is written in a style that might appeal to you. Read it." It was *M*A*S*H*. The writer, Ring Lardner, Jr., was just emerging from the shadow of the blacklist. Litto saw a similarity between the feel of the piece and the material Altman liked to do. Altman called a day or so later and said, "This is great. Can you get me the job?" Litto replied, "I don't know. Probably not." Fox was an old-line studio that still liked to work with producers. Ingo Preminger had a deal there, and Richard Zanuck had given him the green light on *M*A*S*H*. Lots of directors, including Friedkin, had turned it down. Litto showed Preminger some of Altman's work. Preminger liked what he saw, and decided to take a flier on the director. Litto negotiated the deal, $125,000, and 5 percent of the picture. But when Fox heard that Preminger wanted to hire Altman, they went through the roof. He was still infamous for a TV show he did nearly a decade earlier that had gotten the studio into hot water. One of the Fox executives expressed the general feeling at the studio: "You're making a deal with trouble!" Owen McLean, Zanuck's business affairs guy, was a tough nut. McLean called Litto, said, "George, I have a memo here that Ingo, without authorization, made a deal with you for Bob Altman. We cannot stand behind this because Ingo was not — "

"All I know is I made the deal, Owen. I'm just a humble agent. Just tell me what you have to say and I'll transmit your proposal to my client."

"You're full of shit, George, but here's the deal: $75,000 cash, take it or leave it. Don't come back and try to negotiate with me. That's what he gets if he wants to do the picture."

Litto called Preminger, said, "McLean is trying to provoke me. He doesn't want Bob to do the picture."

"What are you going to do, George?"

"I'm going to make the deal, and if the picture's great, I'm depending on you to fix it later." Litto called Altman, told him the terms. Altman was furious. Litto said, "Bob, you really want to fuck 'em?"

"I'd love to fuck 'em."

"Okay, take the deal. You'll make a great picture. I'll make you rich on the next one, all right?" The director acquiesced. Litto never did make Altman rich. But he came close, and would have succeeded had Altman not indulged in his propensity to shoot himself in the foot.

Altman had a deal. But Lewis "Doc" Merman, head of physical production, was going to make sure Altman knew his place. He said, "This guy's not gonna run roughshod over us." Despite the inroads New Hollywood directors were making in the front office, the heads of physical production, as well as the department heads — camera, lighting, sound, editing, and so on — were old-line veterans set in their ways. They insisted that movies be shot the way they had always been shot, which meant with studio equipment, no matter how obsolete or ungainly, operated by union crews. They didn't care that movies could now be produced cheaper and faster with small, often local crews and lightweight equipment. In fact, inexpensive methods threatened their turf. Hopper was right when he said that pictures that cost under a million dollars undermined the whole system. Angry, Altman scrawled a note that read, "M*A*S*H is *not* going to be directed by Robert Altman," and stuck it to his bathroom wall. One night, Kathryn called Litto's home in Benedict Canyon. "I have terrible news," she said. "Bob was up all night. He's not going to do the picture."

"What are you talking about?"

"He's on his way to see you right now to tell you he's not going to do the picture. I don't know what we're going to do. We're so far in debt."

"Kathryn, relax. He's going to do the picture."

"How do you know he's going to do the picture?"

"Because he owes me too much fucking money not to do the picture."

Altman pulled up in the driveway, walked in the door. "George, I don't want to do the picture. First it's sixty-five days, now it's forty-five days. Boy, I can't stand this shitheel Merman. He wants me to start a shot here, as the guy walks out the door. I cut, and three weeks later I shoot the other piece. I had a great time making *Cold Day in the Park*, no fucking bosses around."

"I know you really liked that. But Don Factor still don't have his money back, and it was only five hundred fucking grand."

"But he won't let me make the movie the way I want to make it. I've gotta pick my own cameraman. I need my own art director. I want to shoot off the lot in England, Seattle, or — "

"Fox's Malibu Ranch. It's off the lot."

"Okay, the Malibu Ranch."

"You know what? You haven't said anything here that I think is unreasonable or outrageous. Why do you think they won't give you this?"

"Doc fucking Merman . . ."

"Doc fucking Merman is not your producer. You have to talk to Ingo." Preminger saw to it that Altman got what he wanted.

Casting *M*A*S*H*, Altman avoided stars, save for his two leads, Elliott Gould, coming off an Oscar nomination for Paul Mazursky's *Bob & Carol & Ted & Alice*, and Donald Sutherland, both of whom were basically character actors. As Altman puts it, "It was more exciting to work with an unknown cast than it was to do a picture with whomever the reigning stars were at that time. Because then you're just taking orders." Of the twenty-eight speaking parts, only half the actors had had previous screen experience. Like other New Hollywood directors, for Altman the picture was the star, which is another way of saying, the director was the star. Many '70s directors (Altman, Scorsese, Woody Allen) developed, in effect, repertory companies.

Altman created a casual, low-key environment that most of the actors loved. Dailies, to which everyone was invited, were run in a party atmosphere, with cast and crew unwinding from the day, drinking, and smoking pot. Still, some of the actors didn't trust him. "I love his work, but he can be pretty mean and cruel and manipulative," recalls comedy writer and performer Carl Gottlieb, who had a small role as Ugly John, the anesthesiologist. "And contrary to popular belief, he hates actors. He doesn't pay them — everybody works for scale — and he doesn't allow them a complete performance. He always breaks it off."

On the thirty-ninth day of the shoot, Litto came to the set, said to Altman, "Another week, you'll be finished here."

"I'll be finished in two days."

"What?"

"I can't wait to get the fuck outta this fucking studio."

Altman's problems with the hidebound Fox bureaucracy continued into the post-production. One day, Altman was in the editing room with his editor, Danford Greene. The head of post-production walked in, saw Altman, and said, "Get away from the Moviola. You can't touch that machine, you're not an editor." Altman retorted, "I can touch any goddamned machine I please," and continued running film. Altman and Greene had some pinups on the wall, and the next day they got a memo that required all pictures of naked women be removed from the editing room walls of 20th Century-Fox, effective immediately. Altman marched into the recording studio, put the memo on tape, and used it in the movie in the form of a loudspeaker announcement: "Attention, attention. Please remove all pictures . . . by order of the commandant. Thank you."

There were a lot of other things in M*A*S*H for the Fox executives to hate. The two producers were looking at the dailies the same time they were watching the rushes from *Patton*. It was a long way from George C. Scott to Gould and Sutherland. M*A*S*H was the anti-*Patton*. Zanuck and Brown sat in the back of the screening room, looked at each other, and groaned. They were appalled by the fuzzy focus, the raw language, the nudity, and the rivers of gore that flowed through the operating room sequences. "It was the first time you saw guys during an operation covered with blood saying, 'Nurse, get your tits out of the way,' " says Litto. It was the first major studio movie in which "fuck" was used.

"Zanuck had a list of thirty notes, cuts, and changes," continues Litto. "He practically wanted to reedit the picture." The executive wanted to go up to the Bay Area for a Stanford game, so Preminger convinced Zanuck to do a preview in San Francisco. Continues Litto, "I was sitting behind Dick and David Brown. It was all very strained, because they were saying, 'When this screening's over, we're going to cut this picture up.' *Butch Cassidy and the Sundance Kid* went on first. Then we went on, and during the operation that opens the movie, like five people walked out, and then in a few more minutes another five, and then about twenty people more. I was sinking down in my seat and I had this pain in my stomach. I said to myself, 'Jesus Christ, I thought this picture was great. Why are they all walking out?' Finally there's the scene where they steal the jeep, and the audience loved it. Big applause. Then something else, more applause. Then at a certain point there was practically a standing ovation and the audience just went wild. About twenty minutes into the picture, Dick turned around and he said, 'George, we've got a hit.' I got back up in my seat and I said, 'All right fucker, now pay that percentage.' "

Some of the Fox executives thought Altman had packed the house with friends, so there was another screening in New York for Zanuck, père. Recalls Altman, "Darryl Zanuck had these two young girls with him, these two bimbos over from France, in their twenties. And he said, 'Oh, you've got to cut all this,' and they said, 'No, this is a great picture,' and that is how M*A*S*H was allowed to be released the way it was."

Pauline Kael loved M*A*S*H, inaugurated a half-decade-long critical love affair with Altman, calling it "the best American war comedy since sound came in." She lobbied the critics within her orbit to give it good reviews. Kael became good friends with Bob and Kathryn. She would hang around his offices when she was in L.A., go out to eat with him. "They were very thick," says Thompson. "She loved Bob, Bob adored her. She was one of the gang." Concurs Joan Tewkesbury, "Bob would cultivate her. She would come to the sets."

M*A*S*H pulled in $36.7 million in rentals, putting it third for 1970, behind *Love Story* and *Airport*. It got five Oscar nominations, including Best Picture and Best Director, and did especially well in Europe, where it fed off anti-American sentiment. Despite the fact that it was set in the Korean War, it was perceived as a slap at U.S. involvement in Vietnam.

Preminger only produced one more movie. The business was changing, and now it would be the directors who selected their producers, not the other way around. Indeed, M*A*S*H was a full-fledged "Altman" film, announcing the director as an "auteur," in the French sense, not all that surprising since he had been experimenting and refining his approach in television for over a decade. There were the themes, the "anti-s": militarism, clericalism, authoritarianism. (The *New York Times* noted that it was "the first American movie openly to ridicule belief in God.") There was the improvisation, the ensemble acting, the self-consciousness that drew attention to the filmmaking, the loose-knit narratives that dispensed with the traditional beginning, middle, and end, where the energy of the individual sequences carried the piece. And finally, there was the layered soundtrack with overlapping dialogue. Hopper had liberated *Easy Rider* from the prettifying aesthetic of technical excellence, but until now, nobody had done the same for sound. Based on M*A*S*H and the films that followed, Altman became the quintessential New Hollywood director. The irony, of course, was that he was a good twenty years older than, say, George Lucas.

In the heady atmosphere of a smash hit, Altman took the opportunity to rewrite some history. If he was truly going to be an auteur, he had to write the script as well or, since he wasn't a writer, at least derogate the contribution of the writer. True, a screenplay for Altman was generally no more than a point of departure. But even though the actual dialogue rarely corresponded to the script, the writers created the characters which the actors inhabited, providing them with a basis for improvisation. Although he had initially praised Lardner's script in interviews, Altman now implied that he had discarded it and started from scratch. "Bob was never one to acknowledge a writer's contribution," says Litto. "The movie was 90 percent Ring Lardner's script, but Bob started saying he improvised the movie. I said, 'Bob, Ring Lardner gave you the best opportunity you had in your life. He'd been blacklisted for years. What you're doing is very unfair to him and you ought to stop it.' "

Litto went to Zanuck to get his points back, said, "Dick, we got screwed. Come on, you guys, we had 5 percent, we had a deal. Listen, you can't penalize me or Bob for being smart enough to do this picture. We should all enjoy the benefits now, you can't keep all the money."

"I understand what you're saying," Zanuck replied. "I'm not saying no. Let me talk to Ingo, and we'll see what we can do." Litto thought Bob was going to get his five points, which would have set him up for life, even at the rate Altman flushed money. Meanwhile, the director, convinced he had been cheated, excoriated the studio at every opportunity. One day, Zanuck sent Litto the headline of an interview Altman had done with a note on it. The headline was a quote, attributed to Bob: "Fox is going broke and I'm glad." The note said, "Thank Bob Altman for this and forget about the percentage." Litto called Altman, said, "Bob, do you realize how much fucking money you just cost me and you?" Without missing a beat, Altman snapped back, "Fuck him and the studio and the horse he rode in on." Then Altman went off to shoot *Brewster McCloud* in Houston.

WARNERS HATED LUCAS'S FIRST FEATURE, *THX 1138*. It pictures a bleak futuristic landscape in which people are admonished to "work hard, increase production, prevent accidents, and be happy."

THX had worried the studio. For one thing, Coppola insisted on keeping Warners and Lucas apart. He would be the go-between. Francis told Warners, "You've got to understand something, I can't get Lucas involved in working with a studio about developing a script. He trusts me, we can do it together, he and I, it'll be great, but stay out of it. We'll bring you the finished film."

Lucas shot the film on a shoestring, edited it in the attic of his home in Mill Valley. The picture was screened on the Warners lot in May 1970. At the screening was the gang from the studio — Ashley, Calley, Wells, Lederer, Beckerman — and Coppola. One executive was appalled. He said, "Wait a minute, Francis, what's going on? This is not the screenplay we said we were going to do. This isn't a commercial movie." Francis appeared to be as shocked as the executive, replying, "I don't know what the fuck this is." This was about as apologetic as Francis got.

Coppola had seen a few reels the night before, while Murch was mixing the track, and he didn't quite know what to make of it. He told Murch, "This is either going to be a masterpiece, or a masturbation." But he wasn't worried about the screening for the studio. All along he had reassured Lucas, saying, "Listen, George, we're making the film for so little money, one of the luxuries that gives us is the ability to tinker with the editing. This is your first film, we're all learning, we're trying something new here, it would be crazy to think we're going to hit the bull's-eye the first time." Both men regarded it as a work-in-progress. This was a miscalculation. The new Warners regime, having thrown out all its inventory, had something to prove, and quickly. The feeling was, Wait a minute, this film finished shooting in December and here it is five months later, we should be looking at a locked cut. These guys have been jerking off up there. Coppola was supposed to have supervised the production and he hadn't even bothered to see the movie! Wells was outraged. It was clear to Warners that Francis had been telling the studio what he knew they wanted to hear — "I'm going to supervise him," etc. — while telling Lucas what he wanted to hear — "Do your own thing, it's gonna be great, they'll love it." Lucas must have suspected that THX would have an unfriendly reception, because, paranoid as always, he asked Murch, Robbins, and Caleb Deschanel, another pal from USC, to sneak onto the lot, saying: "You guys, wait near the base of the water tower, and as soon as the screening is done, go up to the booth, tell them you're from the editorial department, and take the work print, so Warners can't get it." They did, keeping their eye on Theater A until they saw Wells and company filing out, at which point they grabbed the print, threw it into Robbins's VW bus, and drove off.

Warners claimed, as Ashley puts it, "We weren't in the editing business. We didn't automatically run for a pair of scissors and start cutting up people's movies." Nevertheless, after the May disaster, the studio took the film away from Lucas. "Wells could never let anything go — he was a good soldier, he had to make it work somehow," says a source. "He talked to Fred Weintraub, who said, 'I know exactly what to do with this fucking thing, you take this out and you take out that, and we put in this, and then it will work.' Fred was always saying, 'We're taking it over, I can fix it, trust me.' He was a bull in a china shop. The next thing I knew, they were recutting the film, really pissing George off." As Lucas put it, "They were cutting off the fingers of my baby."

The thing Weintraub liked about THX was what he called the freaks, the hairy dwarfs who appear at the end, and later were transformed into the Wookiees of Star Wars. He told Lucas, "Listen, if you hook the audience in the first ten minutes, they'll forgive anything. You gotta put your best stuff up front, so what I want you to do, George, is put the freaks up front, the end at the beginning."

"Put the freaks up front" became the shorthand Lucas would use derisively to refer to the studio's stupidity, turning everything upside down in the interests of making a buck. For him, the "freaks" were the executives. Dealing with Weintraub was Lucas's first exposure to the studio, unmediated by Coppola. "He had to sit in the same room as one of the monsters, one of the freaks, who had the power to tell him what to do," says Murch. It was an experience Lucas never forgot. But it could have been worse. Weintraub never did succeed in making Lucas put the freaks up front. "George knows how to fight," continues Murch. "He's a Taurus, and he has that stubborn thumping his head against the obstacle, digging in his heels, becoming uncommunicative, 'I will not do this,' and it works. It does intimidate people."

Coppola took off for Europe, while Rudy Fehr, Warners head cutter, snipped four minutes out of the film. *THX*, which had been shot in 1969, cut and recut in 1970, finally opened—and closed—in the spring of 1971. Even Lucas's wife, Marcia, didn't think much of it. "I like to become emotionally involved in a movie," she says. "I want to be scared, I want to cry, and I never cared for *THX* because it left me cold. When the studio didn't like the film, I wasn't surprised. But George just said to me, I was stupid and knew nothing. Because I was just a Valley Girl. He was the intellectual."

THX was the death knell for the Zoetrope deal. The scripts Coppola was supposed to be delivering weren't being delivered, and those that were, outside of *Apocalypse Now*, the studio didn't much like. "Coppola was developing this screenplay, *The Conversation*," recalls Jeff Sanford. "We read it, and we told him that we didn't want to do it. I remember him turning to me, because I was the only one in the room his age, and I had a ponytail, a beard, and I was wearing sandals. He said, 'Jeff, you don't like this?' It was one of those historic moments. 'I must tell you,' I said, 'I don't think this is going to be an interesting movie.' "

Warners was still trying to get on its feet, and Wells was ranting and raving about overages. According to a source, the conversations with Francis went this way: Warners said, "Okay, we have a deal, you're running Zoetrope?"

"Yeah, I'm running it."

"But you're fucking up."

"I'm an artist."

"But you said you were the executive."

"What are you talking about, I'm a fucking artist, you're Philistines!"

"You're humping us . . ."

Adds the source, "It was an old tune, but Francis played it more than most. He was the victim of a curious split—between an enormous gift and wild incompetence, the kind of incompetence informed by a sort of megalomania from one realm that so infected the other that it fucked him up. It gave him the confidence to do things that he should never have done. He wanted to be Harry Cohn, on some level, but he didn't know how to do it."

At the same time Coppola wanted to tear down the studio system, he wanted to be a mogul. He was fascinated by the studio politics that his friends didn't understand and couldn't have cared less about. He used to say, "I'm not the oldest of the young guys, I'm the youngest of the old guys."

On Thursday, November 19, 1970, there was a final meeting among Coppola, Ashley, and Wells, which became legendary in Zoetrope lore as Black

Thursday. Willard Huyck picked up Francis at the Burbank airport, because the director's back was out. Francis was carrying his scripts fitted neatly into seven black boxes (one for each person at the meeting) whose spines were embossed with the American Zoetrope logo. Huyck and a few others waited down the hall in Beckerman's office. When Francis came out of the meeting, he was ashen. "Calley and Ashley had decided that they didn't want to be in business with Coppola," says Sanford. Adds Lucas, "They saw *THX*, went ballistic, and a couple of days later, they said, 'We don't want any of these scripts. And besides that, we want our money back.' That's when the shit hit the fan. We were rising, and suddenly it was the crash of '29."

The collapse of the deal was bad enough, but from Zoetrope's point of view, what really rankled was the $300,000 loan Warners demanded that Coppola pay back. According to the source, "Wells was calling those shots. If he had said, 'Let 'em go, and fuck it if we made a bad deal,' that would have been fine. But what happened was, Wells felt there was a deal, he wanted back what was owed, and he busted Coppola's balls to get it. It was chickenshit; they were talking about a couple of hundred thousand dollars at the most. But that's the way Wells looked at things. What I thought was creepy was I thought they had gotten on the wrong side of somebody who turned out to be a wonderful filmmaker."

Indeed, it was a colossal blunder on the part of Ashley, Calley, and Wells. As Coppola put it with only slight exaggeration, "They had turned down what became the whole '70s cinema movement. They had the option for everybody, and they gave us this vote of no confidence." Lucas was furious, and didn't speak to Ashley for over a decade. He believed that Warners bad-mouthed him around town, made it harder for him to set up his next movie, *American Graffiti*. Years later, in order to bid on *Raiders of the Lost Ark*, Ashley had to apologize to Lucas, and then Warners didn't get the film anyway. In fact, Coppola and Lucas only rarely worked for Warners again.

When Warners turned off the tap, the studio's checks for $2,500 a month stopped, and Zoetrope faced imminent bankruptcy. Francis, on the other hand, blithely continued to pirouette over the void. He always had a cavalier attitude toward money, other people's as well as his own. Haskell Wexler gave him $27,000 to buy him a KEM. It never arrived, and when Wexler demanded his money back, Coppola just shrugged. Says Wexler, "Francis was a gonif." On the verge of bankruptcy, Coppola sent out elegant invitations on heavy bond paper to the 1970 San Francisco Film Festival. On the bottom of Lucas's was a note: "This invitation cost $3 to print, type, and send to you." Coppola's flamboyant *après moi le déluge* gesture upset Lucas even more. Says Coppola, "George became very discouraged by my 'bohemian' administration."

The bad taste left by the aftermath of the *THX* fiasco worked like a slow poison on the friendship between Francis and George. Lucas felt Coppola had let him down, wasn't there to help him fend off Warners. He also felt that Francis had charged Zoetrope expenses against the *THX* budget, all the more galling because it was the kind of thing that studios routinely did. As Zoetrope wound down, Lucas was often on the phone, hustling editing gigs for his wife, Marcia, and laying the groundwork for his next movie, *American Graffiti*. One day, Coppola's majordomo, Mona Skager, opened the phone bill and flipped out. She confronted Lucas, saying, "You've run up an $1,800 bill with all these calls, and none of them are about Zoetrope business." George was angry and humiliated. He had to go to his father—surely no easy task, since he was a conservative businessman and disapproved of his son's choice of career. Marcia came in and gave Skager a check. When Coppola found out about it afterward, he was furious. "It's not my style," he says. "I would have never done that to a friend, Mona was way out of line. I always believed that that incident was one of the things that pissed George off and caused a breach."

"I needed to go and develop another project, I couldn't rely on Zoetrope to do that for me," says Lucas. "It fell apart." Coppola was both heartbroken and angry. "I had always regarded George as my heir apparent. He'd take over Zoetrope for me while I went out and did my personal films. Everybody utilized Zoetrope to get going, but nobody wanted to stick with it." For all intents and purposes, Zoetrope was dead.

Just when Zoetrope's prospects looked gloomiest, Coppola got a message from Paramount. They wanted him to direct a picture based on a book by Mario Puzo called *The Godfather*.

THE *McCABE* CAST and crew flew up to Vancouver in mid-October of 1970. Beatty and Christie rented a beautiful glass house up above the bay. Altman found a nice home for himself as well, which became the focal point for endless parties. He loved to bet on football and bought three or four TV sets so he could watch several games at once.

Altman had never worked with a star like Beatty, who wasn't like Sutherland and Gould. They complained and bitched, but finally did what they were told. Beatty wasn't about to do anything he didn't want to do. He was used to controlling the production. As Towne put it, "If the director was indecisive, Warren would absolutely destroy him. He'd ask so many questions—and he can ask more questions than any three-year-old—that the director didn't know whether he was coming or going." On the other hand, Beatty had never worked with a director quite like Altman before, freewheeling and irreverent, also used to getting his own way, and moreover enjoying the confidence of coming off a huge hit. But the two men liked, or at least respected, each other, agreed on an approach to the material, and the odds were even they could get through the production without killing each other.

"We had a director who was at the top of his form and a really good cast," says Beatty. "But there was one problem: there was no script." Based on a novel by Edmund Naughton, the script, by Altman pal Brian McKay, was very much a conventional Western, the story of of a mysterious stranger riding into a godforsaken turn-of-the-century town in the Northwest, a gunslinger with a past.

Altman too was unhappy with the script, as he was unhappy with most scripts. "It was one of the worst Western stories you've ever heard," he said. "It had all the clichés. This guy was a gambler, and she was a whore with a heart of gold, the three heavies were the giant and the half-breed and the kid. . . . I said, 'You really wanna make this film?' " Continues Beatty, "So we started frenetically taking it apart scene by scene, and I realized that Altman just wanted us to improvise this movie. I believe in improvising, but I don't believe in improvising from nothing, and I just wasn't going to do it. So I had to write a script. I had to go down into the basement of this house, where I worked to make sure there was something we could say to each other every day. I worked quite a bit more on the script than he did. I think Altman was much more happy with a kind of hit-or-miss approach. My approach was more linear."

In the hands of Altman and Beatty, any resemblance to a traditional Western ended the moment McCabe rides through a drenching rain into the town of Presbyterian Church. The character became a flummoxed antihero, in keeping with both Altman's cinema of helplessness and Beatty's inclination to play with and subvert his own star persona. Clyde Barrow and McCabe "shared a sort of foolishness," explains Beatty. "They were not heroes. I found that to be funny, and Altman found it to be funny; we really agreed on that." What they didn't agree on was credit. Altman took a writing credit on the picture, after apparently trying to get his friend McKay's credit removed. Says Thompson, "Bob didn't want to split the credit with the writer. He wanted to be the auteur."

Altman always hated beginning a picture, kept postponing the start date. Wednesday became Thursday, Thursday became Friday, and then it was, "Let's get a fresh start on Monday." Even then, he might throw away the first day's shooting: "Let's shoot the second day, and go back and reshoot the other stuff."

The town became a character in its own right. Altman had the cast and crew live in the settlement in which the drama would unfold as it was being built. Says Beatty, "Bob had a talent for making the background come into the foreground and the foreground go into the background, which made the story seem a lot less linear than it actually was."

To the new bag of camera tricks Beatty and Penn, Hopper and Fonda brought to *Bonnie and Clyde* and *Easy Rider*, Altman added the zoom lens, an affront to Old Hollywood cameramen, because focus is always at risk. Actors don't like it much either. They regulate their performance according to how far they are from the camera, but the director would stage a master shot packed with people, and then would reach through the crowd with the zoom for close-ups so that the actors were unsure if they were one face among twenty, or all alone. But under the influence of the verité documentarians, the street style of filmmakers like Godard, and the low-budget resourcefulness of Cassavetes, a technique like zooming was becoming more acceptable. It was key to Altman's innovative style, an unusual melding of fiction and documentary, lending his films an unprecedented sense of life.

Another Altman touch was the film's mellow yellow hue. He says, "One of the big problems was that the lenses were so sharp, and the stock was so good, that it was going to look like a Christmas card unless I worked constantly on how to achieve a look that fit the subject, and if working on the film stock was the way to do that, that's what I had to do. I was trying to make a painting that didn't look like somebody else's painting." He used to walk around the set with an enormous Polaroid Land camera, wearing an old yellow velour sweatshirt. One day he pointed the camera toward his stomach, snapped a picture, then took another of the set, creating a double exposure with a yellowish cast. He went to the director of photography (DP), Vilmos Zsigmond and said, "This is what I want the film to look like, and we can achieve this by flashing the film."* Says Beatty, "It was considered a very bold thing to do. You flash the positive, but you don't flash the negative, because then you can't do anything about it if it's fucked up."

As the production proceeded, the relationship between Altman and Beatty began to fray. Altman complained of Beatty's "nit-picking, the way he pushed and bugged me." Beatty wanted to know the purpose of every setup, of every camera move, entrance, and bit of dialogue. The two men had radically different ways of working. Beatty was meticulous. As Nicholson put it, "He'll chew something till the cows come home." He was used to big-budget productions where money was no object. He invariably did take after take, slowly working his way into his performance. Altman, who never had any money and came up doing industrials and television, liked to shoot and run. Often, he did no more than one or two takes. He believed that too many takes spoiled the spontaneity of the performance.

According to Altman, the problems had to do with Beatty's and Christie's contrasting work methods. He says, "Warren wouldn't start rehearsing until the camera was rolling on take four or five. Julie was always the best on her very first take, and after a while, she started losing interest, and you could see it. So I had one actor who was getting better, and another who was getting worse. So finally I tried to put the camera on her first, and then try to get him in.

"Warren was great in the film, and there were no bad relations, but it was a touchy situation. He once said, 'Tell anybody this and I'll call you a liar, but

* Flashing means preexposing the raw film stock to low-level light.

this picture is about me as a movie star and Julie second, and then all the rest of the people in this picture, who don't count.' And he was a little upset that I was spending so much time building up an atmosphere. Because he had never made films that way. Warren is basically a control freak. He wants to run the show."

Eventually, Altman learned to run around Beatty, rather than through him. There is a brief scene in which the actor is sitting in his office drinking, nothing complicated. As he reaches for the bottle, he knocks it over, catches it, and pours himself a drink. As Tommy Thompson recalls it, "We shot it once, we shot it again, we shot it about eight or nine times. After take ten, Bob said, 'That's good for me, print two, five, ten.' Everybody was ready to go, it was one in the morning, and Warren said, 'Wait, wait, wait a minute. I'm not happy with it.' Bob said, 'No, no, it's fine.' Warren said, 'I want another one.' Bob said, 'Okay.' Did another one. 'You happy with that, Warren?' 'No, I want another one.' " Adds Jim Margellos, the production manager, "It was like a test of wills. There was so much tension between the two of them you could cut it with a knife." Continues Thompson, "Finally, Bob said, 'Look, I'm tired, and I can't tell the difference anymore. Tommy will stay here with you, and you can shoot until you're happy with it. Good night, guys, I'll see you tomorrow morning,' and he left. I don't know how many we did, thirty, forty, till Warren finally said, 'two, five, ten, eighteen, twenty-seven, thirty-four, and forty,' and we wrapped. It was four in the morning, but Warren was happy and Bob was happy." Adds Joan Tewkesbury, who was the script supervisor, "The path to success is sometimes the one of least resistance: " 'You want to shoot the Taj Mahal? Fine. I don't give a shit!' "

For his part, Beatty says, "A lot of times, Bob would wonder why I was working so hard. I'm just a person that thinks, when you go to all that trouble to set up a movie and build a set and get dressed and go there, I don't see any harm in doing a number of takes."

Altman got his revenge in the scene that ends the movie. McCabe, pursued through a blizzard by the company's hired gunslingers, is fatally wounded and falls into a snowdrift. Recalls Margellos, "Warren was buried up to his ears, with snow blasting into his face from the wind machine. It was colder than hell. Bob kept saying, 'Okay, one more time.' They dug Warren out, put him back, and did it again. He must have done it twenty-five times." As the film would evolve in the editing, Altman underlined his message. He cuts away from McCabe to the townies frantically trying to save the burning church, and to Mrs. Miller stoned on opium. As the wind howls and snowflakes slowly cover McCabe's fallen figure to the mournful sounds of Leonard Cohen on the soundtrack, they are all oblivious to the drama of his death. The crosscutting at once makes a bleak commentary on the empty pretensions of heroism, and underlines Altman's contempt for stars.

Before the shoot finally wrapped at the end of January 1971, Kael visited the set, had a couple of dinners with Bob.

McCABE HAD BEEN a physically exhausting shoot. Altman fled to Paris for R&R. Beatty went off on Sam Spiegel's boat, where he began his own draft of *Shampoo*. Towne had finally turned in his draft the previous January. Reading it over, Beatty felt it was still shapeless. "Towne's script didn't have the structure it needed, so I put one in," he says. "Now there were two versions of *Shampoo*."

During the period in which Towne was working on *Shampoo*, and shortly thereafter, he formed an attachment to a woman and a dog, not necessarily in that order. Towne had started seeing Julie Payne when he returned to L.A. after a stint in London in 1969. She moved into the Hutton Drive house with him. While Towne was sitting at the typewriter, enveloped in a cloud of cigar smoke, she was out in the yard digging up stumps and transplanting rose bushes. Towne used to call her Mammy Yokum, because of her powerful wallop.

In the panic that followed the Manson murders, the writer acquired a large Hungarian sheep dog, named Pannonia's Hira Vasak. Hira was a huge slobbering beast with matted dreadlocks. It looked like a dirty mop on legs. It was a perfect animal for him, a one-man dog that growled menacingly at other people, acting out the anger Towne was so good at concealing. It was a rare breed, a Komondor; there were not many in this country, and he loved to lecture people on its fine points. But he was devoted to the dog, and once he leapt into a neighbor's cesspool to save Hira's "fiancée," who had fallen in. He emerged covered with shit; it was no small feat for someone so in love with cleanliness as Towne. Says Jerry Ayres, "Hira was so big he couldn't get into the back of his car, so Bob sat it next to him in the front seat, while Julie sat in the back." To Ayres, that seemed to sum up the relationship.

When Beatty got back, he took his script to Towne, and said, "I'm gonna make this picture whether you like it or not, do you wanna do it?" Towne read it, agreed to come back on board. The two men patched up their differences and resumed their close relationship. Although Towne was far too politic to crow about his friendships with Beatty and Nicholson, and later with Paramount production head Robert Evans, he couldn't resist dropping names. He had an ego to feed and care for, and was never entirely successful in submerging it in the sea of his ambition. Says Beatty, quoting Elia Kazan, "Never underestimate the narcissism of a writer." Towne aspired to be treated as an equal by his movie star pals, and he was eager to show he could hold his own. He'd disappear for a week, then confide in a conspiratorial tone, "Don't tell anybody, but I was in a hotel room in Houston rewriting Beatty's picture." The implication was, he was indispensable to Beatty. Says Evans, "Bob claims to have done a lot more writing for Warren than Warren says he did. If I had to bet, I'd bet on Warren. He has a clearer head."

Although Towne would rarely talk about Beatty, he occasionally let others overhear his end of a phone conversation with the actor, in which he made it clear Beatty couldn't push him around. He would say, "You cunt . . . you're just being a cunt . . . that's more cunt stuff," and so on for half an hour. Says screenwriter Jeremy Larner, whom Towne let listen to him talking to the star, "Towne was tremendously turned on by the conversations with Beatty. He had a certain relish for dealing with him. His attitude toward Nicholson was that Jack was this brilliant boy who you had to let indulge himself any way he wanted to, but with Beatty, here was somebody who was capable of being crafty, somebody more worthy of Towne's mettle. Towne probably thought a lot more about Beatty than he did about Jack. He was more in love with Beatty. Most guys in Hollywood are more turned on by each other than they are by the women they fuck." According to Evans, "Towne treated Jack as an equal, but looked up to Warren as a messiah."

Towne would very occasionally complain about how difficult Beatty was, but in fact, he was growing to resemble Beatty more and more. When Beatty grew a beard, Towne grew a beard. Their voices sounded alike, the syntax and emphases were the same. Like Beatty, he would call in the wee hours without identifying himself, just start talking in a barely audible whisper. They sounded so alike on the phone that Beatty would call Julie pretending to be Towne.

"Towne was like this shadow image of Warren," says Buck Henry, except he was "someone the girls just got away from, they went to the wrong restaurant." The word around Hollywood was "Towne is Warren's nigger." He did some work on almost every picture Beatty did, sometimes without money or credit, and he didn't even get to brag about it. Beatty is said to have induced Towne to work on the script of *The Parallax View* during the writers' strike in the spring of 1973, an infraction that would have blackened Towne's name within the writing community had anyone known about it, and could have earned him a sizable fine, not to mention a suspension. Towne used to joke about his dependent position, called Beatty "Badge," as in, "Badge can get me into the A-list parties," and referred to himself as "Sharecropper." But he resented it. "I always felt like one of those parrots at Hefner's," he says. "They would clip their wings, so they could fly a little, but not beyond the grounds of the Playboy Mansion." In his mind, Beatty owed him an enormous debt.

SINCE BEATTY had been away during the post-production of *McCabe*, Altman screened it for him when he got back. "I couldn't hear what people were saying," recalls Beatty. "The sound in the first couple of reels, in which one would ordinarily expect that the exposition would be laid down and had to be clear, was not clear." Beatty was upset, not to say furious, over the muddy track.

Why the track was so indistinct has always been a bit of a mystery. The weather had been terrible in Vancouver, where it snowed, rained, and the winds blew. The sound mixer had a tough time getting a clean recording. Not only did Altman dislike retakes, he also disliked looping the sound later in a studio. Altman thought the sound was fine, he'd gotten just what he intended, and dismissed Beatty's complaints as the grumbling of a star. Says Thompson, "The principals thought every word out of their mouths was a pearl, and they didn't want music, let alone other dialogue, obscuring it."

Altman shrugged off Beatty's objections, saying, "Warren was infuriated, he is still infuriated, and he'll just have to stay infuriated."

But it wasn't only Beatty who couldn't hear it. One weekend, during the shoot, editor Lou Lombardo came up. According to Litto, "Bob had a lot of guys that just said yes. Lou had no fear. When Bob did something he didn't like, Lou would say, 'It's shit.' " Lombardo edited for Sam Peckinpah as well as Altman, and once when he was being interviewed by a pert, fresh-faced young entertainment reporter who asked him to compare the two directors, he leaned back as if to deliver a profundity, and said, "Sam Peckinpah is a prick, and Robert Altman is a cunt!" Altman showed him some rushes, asked him how he liked them. Lombardo loved what he saw, but hated what he heard; the sound, he said, was "fucked." Altman blew up. "He stormed off into his bedroom, slammed the door, and never came out," recalled Lombardo. "I was trying to tell him the fucking sound is bad, and it still is bad. . . . He never changed it. I think he accomplished what he wanted to do with sound in M*A*S*H — where it was audible but it was overlapped. . . . But on *McCabe*, it was recorded in there — a dirty track, a muddy track. It was like trying to get an out-of-focus picture in focus."

Beatty complained about the track to the studio, but didn't get much satisfaction. The new Warners regime had very little product, and was anxious to get the film out. Besides, it considered itself helpless before the new power of the Auteur. Says Ashley, "You think we could've gotten them to redo it? This was an individual who presumed himself to be an artist." Adds Beatty, "Things had progressed to such anarchy in the studio system, and filmmakers were treated with so much respect, if we had photographed the movie in darkness, they would have thought that was an interesting approach, and hoped they could exploit it in the marketing." The star had to be satisfied with looping some of his lines, which didn't make the track any more audible and irritated Altman. "I can hear it every time I see the picture," he says. Nobody was happy.

The press screenings in New York and L.A. on June 22, 1971, at the Criterion and the Academy theaters were a disaster. Recalls Altman, "When the picture opened in New York, there was a big preview at one of those huge Broadway houses for all the critics. And there was something wrong with the soundtrack. It wasn't checked by my editor and I was told that it had been checked. And so that bad soundtrack, on top of the design of the sound, really made it impossible to hear. I screamed, 'You've got to shut it off, there's something wrong with the soundtrack.' They said, 'Oh, that's the way you did it.' Well, it wasn't the way I did it. I left the goddamned theater and went someplace and had a steak. I was ready to get on a plane and go to Alaska."

Kael quite rightly raved, called it "a beautiful pipe dream of a movie," went on *The Dick Cavett Show* and talked it up. But the daily critics were less enthusiastic, and Beatty's efforts to revive it, as he did *Bonnie and Clyde*, failed. *McCabe* was a much different, more difficult picture. For all the scandal it created, *Bonnie and Clyde* was still a star vehicle, with a conventional, if episodic narrative. The love story was a little bent, but it was still a love story. Although *McCabe* shares *Bonnie and Clyde*'s distaste for authority and cynical mistrust of the "system," de rigueur for any New Hollywood movie, it went further than *Bonnie and Clyde* in undermining the traditional romance, and boasted of an unabashedly unhappy anticlimax photographed in cold long shots. Like Hopper, Altman was going down the road of genre deconstruction, which, it seemed, the box office would not support. Says Altman, "It still hasn't grossed a million dollars. And it was the last time I worked for Warner Brothers."*

Altman felt Beatty stabbed him in the back. "He was really a bit of an asshole," he says. "He was quite brutal about it when it came out, and of course blamed me for its defects. Warren is a very self-oriented person. Many people think it's his best film, but it didn't succeed, so he didn't like it. He'll never mention it."

For his part, Beatty blamed the bad sound for the picture's failure to perform. "It prevented it from having a tremendous commercial potential because the audience was confused," he says. "If it hadn't had to meet a certain date in the summer, it would have been remedied by Altman. I don't think he intended to screw it up." But once again, Beatty paid a price for not producing. As he puts it, "Had I been the producer I would have killed Robert Altman."

Despite the strains in the Beatty-Altman marriage, the two men, different as they were, exerted a certain amount of influence on each other. A few years after *McCabe*, Altman made his own *Bonnie and Clyde — Thieves Like Us*. *McCabe*, in turn, had a significant impact on *Shampoo*, which is much more an ensemble piece than Beatty had ever made before, and much more episodic.

McCabe's indifferent performance, coming right after *Brewster McCloud*, tarnished the golden reputation Altman had earned with *M*A*S*H*, and did little to help him get his next film launched. *Images*, an impenetrable, dreamy excursion into what Altman imagined the female mind to be like, flopped as well. But Litto managed to get him a three-picture deal at United Artists. Altman made two of the pictures, *The Long Goodbye*, and *Thieves*. The orphan of the three would turn out to be, if not his most successful, his best film, the fullest realization of this talent: *Nashville*.

* As of 1997, the picture had netted $4.1 million in rentals.

Four:
The Moviegoer
1971

- *How* **The Last Picture Show** *became another jewel in the BBS crown and anointed Peter Bogdanovich, while Bob Rafelson scored with* **Five Easy Pieces,** *and* **The Last Movie** *destroyed Hopper and his hopes.*

"Bogdanovich was arrogant, but he was talented, smart, a very good director. He knew what to say and when to say it. He had the world by a string. Nothing bad had happened yet."

— ELLEN BURSTYN

One hot, airless night in August 1968, around the time of the Democratic convention in Chicago, Bob Rafelson saw *Targets*. He told Bert Schneider, "I just saw a movie that sucks, but the guy who made it knows how to make movies, get him in here." Henry Jaglom heard Peter Bogdanovich's name mentioned, perked up, said, "Hey, I know that guy from New York, I'll call him," and did. Bert got on the phone to Peter, said, "We really loved your picture, man, let's find something each of us likes." Peter sent a book called *The Looters*. They read it, but Bert was unenthusiastic. "I don't think this is really something that you're dying to do," he said.

"Yeah, it is."

"Naah, it's not really something we wanna do with you. Somethin' else. You'll like somethin' else. You don't wanna do this kind of thing, a thriller."

One night, Peter and his wife, Polly Platt, were over at Bert and Judy's for a small dinner party. Their house on Palm Drive, in the flats of Beverly Hills, was not cool and hip like Toby and Bob's; Judy had "decorated" it — Westchester cum Beverly Hills — with cut flowers in the bathrooms, fresh bars of soap, neatly folded guest towels. Despite what he said to Bogdanovich, Bert was unsure about Peter. He worried that the director was too straight to fit into the hip, counterculture atmosphere of the company. "I don't want to work with

Bags," he had complained to Rafelson, using Nicholson's nickname for Bogdanovich.

"Why?"

"He's boring. He's boring."

"Ain't we had enough tsuris with all these crazos we've been working with?"
replied Rafelson, alluding to Dennis Hopper. "Why can't we make one film
with one guy who will actually go out there and make the thing without driving
us crazy?"

Bogdanovich was annoyed that Bert had dismissed *The Looters*. Respectful
of directors to a fault, he thought producers were the scum of the earth. Bert
wondered if Peter had any other ideas. Polly piped up: "There's Larry McMurtry's novel *The Last Picture Show*." Bert asked Peter to get it for him; Peter told
Bert to go buy it. Arrogant himself, Bert respected arrogance in others. Far from
put off, he called Peter about a week and a half later, said, "Ya know, it wasn't
easy to get a copy of that book. 'Go buy it.' I did."

"Well?"

"It's very good. Let's make it."

Schneider proceeded to explain the BBS idea to Peter: Bert would retain
final cut, but there would be no interference, no visits to the set. He told Peter
there would not be a lot of money up front, only $75,000, but he would give
him a fat chunk of the back end, 21 percent of the net. He asked him to make
sure there was some nudity in the script. Peter had to use Harold Schneider as
his line producer, had to hold the budget under $1 million, and stay within an
eight-week shooting schedule. Peter agreed to the terms. *The Last Picture Show*
was a go project.

PETER BOGDANOVICH was born on July 30, 1939, in Kingston, New York.
His father, Borislav, was a Serb immigrant and a talented pianist. In Yugoslavia
he was forced to take students to make ends meet. One of them was a thirteen-
year-old girl named Herma, from a wealthy Jewish family that had fled Austria
a step ahead of the Nazis. Borislav and Herma married, then left for America
in 1938. Herma was pregnant with Peter.

It was a truly eccentric family. Borislav turned to painting, and covered the
walls of their dark, cavernous apartment on Riverside Drive and 90th Street in
Manhattan — a few blocks uptown from Rafelson's building — with his gloomy
canvases. He loved the colors of decaying fruit, and the rooms were filled with
mildewed oranges and pears spotted with patches of fuzzy mold he used for his
still lifes. Borislav's room was painted red; he always wore pajamas while he
worked, and a hat with the crown cut out that allowed his frizzy hair to stand
straight up on end, like a cartoon character. He was sensitive about his hair;
Herma was not allowed to touch it, and in the course of their marriage never

did, not even when they made love. He cut his hair himself, and kept it in the bottom drawer of his dresser.

Peter was a bookish boy who had to be prodded to come out of his room. His father generally ignored him, but Peter was the focus of his mother's disappointments and thwarted ambitions. Herma had given birth to another son, Antony, who died the year before Peter was born. She had accidentally spilled boiling soup all over him. Borislav and Herma rarely spoke of it, and Borislav never forgave Herma her carelessness. Nor did she forgive herself. For Borislav, Peter could never replace Antony; for Herma, on the other hand, Peter had no alternative.

Precocious in the extreme, young Bogdanovich took acting lessons with Stella Adler when he was fifteen. Some kids collect baseball cards, Peter accumulated 3 x 5 index cards recording the vital statistics — along with his own impressions — of every film he saw. He went to six or eight movies a week, and liked to claim that between the ages of twelve, when he started the cards, and thirty, when he stopped, he put away 5,316 in all. Later, Peter would boast to Bob Benton, among others, "I've seen every American film worth seeing." His favorites — *Red River, Citizen Kane, Rio Bravo* — he saw over and over again. It was *Citizen Kane*, he said, that made him want to become a director.

In his early twenties, Bogdanovich got a job programming films at the New Yorker Theater. He recalls, "One of the first movies we booked was John Cassavetes' *Shadows*, which played on a double bill with *The Magnificent Ambersons*. We had lines around the block. *Shadows* was the beginning of the New Hollywood."

One day in January 1961, Bogdanovich was holed up in his tiny, windowless third-floor office above the theater writing notes for *The Forgotten Film* series. He had that film nerd's sallow complexion, but with his thick dark hair, regular features, and obvious intelligence, he was not unappealing. It was a time when most American cineastes, like Benton and Newman, were sitting at the feet of the French New Wave directors, but on the wall, underground filmmaker Jonas Mekas had scrawled a defiant aphorism of Peter's: "The best movies are made in Hollywood."

Bogdanovich was in a particularly good mood. One of his programming coups, *Freaks*, was playing that night, and the Museum of Modern Art had just called, asking him to do a monograph on one of his heroes, Orson Welles. He looked up from his desk to see in the doorway a lively face framed by bleached blond hair, almost white. The face said, "Mr. McDonovich?"

Polly Platt was an army brat, and on her mother's side, a descendant of American bluebloods. She had had a difficult childhood. Her parents were both alcoholics, and her mother, who suffered from bouts of mental illness, knocked her around. Her father was Dutch, and she grew up in the shadow of one of those dreary, repressive Protestant religions. Her first husband was killed in a car accident after they'd had a fight. At Carnegie-Mellon University in Pittsburgh, she decided she wanted to study scenic design for the theater. She was told, "You're a woman and you cannot study scenic design. Design costumes instead." She did, and introduced herself to Bogdanovich as someone who was going to work with him in summer stock that June.

Although not a great beauty, Polly could make a striking impression. Having lived in Arizona, she favored clothes from the Southwest — concho belts, knee-high Navajo kaibab boots made of rawhide with silver buttons up the sides — that made her decidedly exotic among the Jackie Kennedy look-alikes in New York. Displaying a bohemian disregard for convention, she liked to go without shoes and underwear. Bras and panties were just two more things to wash, and she felt sexier without them.

Peter certainly thought so. He courted her with lines from Clifford Odets, speeches from *Cyrano de Bergerac*, diverted her with his appalling impressions of Jerry Lewis. He initiated her into the mysteries of the cinema. For her part, widely traveled and already a veteran of one marriage, she opened up the world of the senses to a young man who was still living with his parents and had spent nearly all his life in dark theaters watching shadows on a screen.

But despite Platt's bohemian attire, she and Peter were boringly straight. They didn't smoke, didn't drink, didn't do drugs. They were the prince and princess of the movie nerds, perfect for each other. Benton called them Mr. & Mrs. Right. Peter liked Howard Hawks, Polly liked John Ford. Their worst fights were over who was the better director.

Bogdanovich was wildly ambitious. "Peter's father was a manic-depressive and a failure," says Platt. "I think Peter's drive must have come out of that — 'I can't be like him.' " He worried his name was too long to fit on a marquee. He envied Wyler, Ford, and Hawks their no-nonsense Anglo surnames, and thought of shortening his to Bogdan. Polly consoled him by reciting the polysyllabic names of the great European and faux-European directors: Erich von Stroheim, Josef von Sternberg, Otto Preminger. They talked about the kinds of pictures they wanted to see, wanted to make. Platt continues, "I knew I didn't want to see women wake up in bed with their lipstick and hair in place, and I didn't want to see movies where I could tell way in advance how they were going to end."

Peter and Polly got married at City Hall, a year after they met, in 1962, when each was twenty-three. Their apartment, near his parents, was crammed with a motley mix of hand-me-downs from both sides. She did some costume designing, but he became sulky when his dinner wasn't on the table, so she stopped, and began translating and typing up articles on Hawks, Ford, and Frank Tashlin by Godard and Truffaut from the French bible of auteurism, *Cahiers du Cinéma*. She helped him interview directors, who would be impressed and flat-

tered by their preternatural familiarity with their films. They could recite all
the credits, recall each cut and camera move.

They would go down to Times Square and see five movies a day at 50 cents
a pop. Polly carried a long hatpin with which she picked her teeth and warded
off gropers. At night, they stayed home, watching movies on *The Late Show*.
They lived on Fudgsicles, dropping the sticks behind the red velvet camelback
couch. He drank Canada Dry ginger ale by the gallon, and developed a perfora-
ted ulcer, so serious he vomited blood and nearly bled to death. He gained
prodigious quantities of weight as the doctors fed him milk, butter, and ice
cream for his stomach. Later, he would become fussy and obsessive about food.

Soon, cracks appeared in the facade. He recalls, "Polly could be very abrasive. Very loud. Jumping in with her opinions when they weren't asked for,
alienating people. There were a lot of dark areas in Polly's life that I really
didn't understand. It was never a very romantic relationship. It was more that
we enjoyed working together. I was very young, didn't really know the difference between love, in love, sympathy, compatibility. I don't think I knew what
I was getting into."

Peter and Polly met *Esquire*'s Harold Hayes at a dinner party in New Rochelle. Hayes was impressed by Peter's passion for movies. He asked him to
cover Hollywood for the magazine. "I watched Hawks do *El Dorado*, Hitchcock
do *The Birds*," says Bogdanovich. "There weren't any film schools at that point;
I learned how to direct by watching these guys. I saw a preview of *The Man
Who Shot Liberty Valance*, and I knew I was seeing the last great movie of
Hollywood's Golden Age. When that train goes away, I thought, that's really it,
isn't it, the end of Ford. And the end of Ford was really the end of that era."

Bogdanovich and Platt went to Monument Valley to do a story on Ford, who
was shooting *Cheyenne Autumn*. On the set, they got close to Sal Mineo, who
was the only person their own age. Mineo gave Polly a trashy-looking paperback
by Larry McMurtry whose cover pictured a shirtless stud bestriding a scantily
clad woman lying in the middle of a road. It was *The Last Picture Show*, and
Mineo wanted to make it, starring himself. Polly read it, agreed that it would
make a wonderful movie.

Despite his rapid progress as a writer about film, Peter was not getting any
closer to making them. They realized they had to move to L.A. Owing back
rent, they filled a shopping cart with books and sneaked them into the service
elevator in the dead of night, and then into their car, an old, yellow, 1951 Ford
convertible which they naturally called "John Ford." They hit the road in June
of 1964, with all of $200 in their pockets, her one-eyed spaniel, and their black
and white TV set in the back seat. Once they got to L.A., they found a rental
in the Valley, in Van Nuys, best known as the place where Robert Redford
grew up.

Peter dogged publicists for invitations to screenings, especially when they were accompanied by food. He would come back for seconds and thirds at Directors Guild of America buffets, and stuff his pockets with rolls. But they knew a lot of people, mostly the Old Hollywood directors who appreciated their admiration. Peter wore Jerry Lewis's cast-off suits, and Lewis even gave him one of the Mustangs in his fleet, saying, "Take the one without the phone; you don't need a phone." Director Fritz Lang invited them for breakfast every Sunday morning, told Polly that Peter was not to be trusted, that eventually he'd leave her. They saw Hawks and Ford regularly. Predictably, Hawks liked Peter; Ford liked Polly. When their friends went away, they house-sat. Like X-rated Goldilockses they went through the closets of Beverly Hills mansions trying on clothes and fucking in every bedroom.

Platt felt threatened by the Hollywood beauties on every corner. She and Peter were at dinner one night at the Flying Tiger on Ventura Boulevard with Hawks and Sherry Lansing (now chairman of the motion picture group at Paramount), then a drop-dead gorgeous starlet who played the love interest in *Rio Lobo*, when Hawks leaned across Polly toward Peter, and shooting a glance at Sherry, said, "If you really want to be a director, this is the kind of girl you should be with." Peter nodded sagely. It didn't do much for Polly's disposition. Once during a fight, Peter got so angry he put his fist through a plasterboard wall.

One day, Bogdanovich went to a screening of Jacques Demy's *Bay of Angels* in Hollywood. Roger Corman was sitting behind him. Someone made introductions. Corman knew his byline from *Esquire*, asked him if he would be interested in writing for the movies. Bogdanovich was, and Corman hired him as his assistant director on *The Wild Angels*, the picture that made Peter Fonda a star, of sorts. Bogdanovich recalled, "I went from getting the laundry to directing the picture in three weeks. Altogether, I worked 22 weeks — preproduction, shooting, second unit, cutting, dubbing — I haven't learned as much since."

Corman was pleased with his work. "Do you want to direct your own picture?" he asked. Bogdanovich replied, "Are you kidding?" *Targets* was a sniper story loosely based on the recent rash of mass murders, like the one of August 1966 in which Charles Whitman perched on top of a tower on the campus of the University of Texas, and picked off students with a high-powered Remington rifle. The budget was a mere $125,000. Corman instructed the young director, "You know how Hitchcock shoots, don't you? Plans every shot, totally prepared. You know how Hawks shoots, don't you? Doesn't plan anything. Rewrites on the set."

"Right."

"Well, on this picture, I want you to be Hitchcock."

Targets was shot in April 1967, in twenty-three days. Bogdanovich got a lot of help from his friends. Director Sam Fuller told him to pinch his pennies and spend them all on a big ending. He did, using ideas he had soaked up from other movies. "The ending of *Targets* was based on *Bonnie and Clyde*," says Bogdanovich. "Except that we didn't have them shot up." Peter and Polly collaborated on the script and editing, which was done in the kitchen of their home on Saticoy Street. She designed the costumes and sets, wrote the checks. They were a great team. He was the enthusiast, she the critic. He thought they were succeeding; she thought they were failing. He was verbal, she was visual. He typed, she talked; then he talked, and she typed. "He's the locomotive, I'm the tracks," is how she put it.

"Polly was a very strong driving force behind Peter," says Paul Lewis, the unit production manager. "She did not let his ego get in the way as it later did. She would say, 'Don't be an asshole about things,' and he would respect and listen to her. He would listen to anybody in those days."

Peter and Polly continued to socialize. They would invite Hawks, Ford, Renoir, Welles, Odets, Cary Grant, Don Siegel, Irene Selznick, and others to dinner, which they would consume under the walnut tree in their small backyard. Hawks had little sympathy for the antiwar demonstrators battling police in the streets of Chicago. "If I was in charge," he said, "I'd arrest them all, cut their hair off. Shoot 'em!" Platt, who opposed the war, was appalled: "You know, Howard, they have a point. We have no business in Vietnam." She looked at Peter, across the table, his face in his hands. He had no political convictions to speak of. He always said, "It has nothing to do with us. We're artists." She thought, You won't support me. You have to become your own man, you can't just be a carbon copy of Howard. He'd be impressed if you stood up to him. But you won't; you're a coward. Later she would say, "I think that was the day I stopped loving Peter."

Platt gave birth to their first child, a girl named Antonia, after Peter's dead brother, Antony. *Targets* was released in the summer of 1968, and flopped. Bogdanovich always thought it was a victim of Martin Luther King's assassination, which made people leery of sniper films. Meanwhile, Peter watched his peers pull in front of him. "Coppola was ahead of us," says Platt. "Peter didn't know him yet, but he was ferociously competitive, and we were very jealous of the fact that he got to make *Finian's Rainbow* and *Rain People* before us, while we were floundering around trying to get a foothold."

BBS, MEANWHILE, was raking in money from *Easy Rider*, and moving quickly into its next production, *Five Easy Pieces*, directed by Rafelson and featuring Nicholson, who was fast becoming BBS's most valuable asset. "I thought I was real lucky," says Rafelson. "I had bagged into a guy who didn't even know he was a fuckin' actor." Bert treated him like a star, lent him money to buy an $80,000 house up on Mulholland. They had dinner together at least twice a week, and Bert was the one who got Jack into the position where he got points. "They were close like brothers," says James Nelson, who did post-production for all the BBS pictures. "They'd fly together to Lakers games."

Jack wanted to direct, and Bert made it happen for him, acquiring *Drive, He Said*, based on a novel by Jeremy Larner, about college basketball '60s-style. Jack was a sociable guy who'd been around the Hollywood block, and he trailed in his wake a coterie of old friends he had collected from earlier projects, acting classes, even high school. Bert didn't want anyone whispering in Jack's ear but him. His attitude was, "Jack has outgrown you, get outta here," and he had no use for people like Fred Roos and Harry Gittes, whom he considered among Jack's "lame-o" pals. Roos was an inspired casting director, the Marion Dougherty of the West Coast, who had produced a couple of Nicholson's B movies in the mid-'60s and really put *Drive, He Said* together, a fact Bert refused to acknowledge. Gittes enjoyed the distinction of being the best of Jack's best friends — there were many. When Jack became a star, Gittes was his reality check, the one who could say things to Jack that nobody else could. Nicholson would later borrow his name for the character he played in *Chinatown*, Jake Gittes. Harry had known Jack since the early '60s, when Harry was enjoying a successful career on Madison Avenue producing commercials and Jack was a struggling actor. Both men grew up without fathers, and recognized each other as damaged people. "All we had was terrible memories of no one being there," says Gittes. "The pain of the handicapped overwhelms everything else. They've got it all, you've got nuthin.' Jack was full of rage all the time."

Bert Schneider was getting the reputation for being a killer negotiator, with ice water in his veins. He loved to read contracts, would sit at his desk with his arms folded across his chest, a hand on each shoulder, scanning the pages like a juicy novel. Occasionally, Gittes found himself in the unenviable position of having to negotiate with Bert. "I always felt it was a cat and a mouse," he says. "Bert was the cat and I was the mouse. These BBS guys beat the living shit outta me. They were the meanest people I'd ever met in my life, brutal, inhumane inflicters. Respect and loyalty, that was the way BBS operated. They had a gangster mentality. This was the Jewish, Bugsy Siegel type of hipness — 'We are not the soft Jews.' And believe me, these *were not* the soft Jews. These were the coldest, toughest Jews I'd ever met in my life. To another Jew! I said, 'Landsman!' They said, 'Get lost!' Whatever your weakness was, Bert would be on it like stink on shit."

Jack resisted Bert's efforts to separate him from his old friends. He was loyal, to a point. Continues Gittes, "I would've thought that Jack would've been watching out for me a lot more than he did. I don't blame Jack, though, 'cause Jack got the living shit beat out of him when he was starting out. But I have never forgiven Jack for getting involved with these guys. BBS brought out his mean side, the hardball side of Jack."

Larner often found himself at odds with Nicholson over *Drive, He Said.* "What was secretly true about Bert and Bob, and overtly true about Jack, was that they were comparing themselves to every other cock in town," he says. "Bert would always line up behind Jack. He told me, 'My job is to keep Jack happy. Jack wants to rewrite your script, I gotta support him; Jack wants to fire you, I gotta support him.' " (In fact, Nicholson did not fire Larner.)

Bert didn't have a very high opinion of writers, had absorbed more of the studio attitude from his father than he would have probably cared to admit. During the editing of *Easy Rider,* he'd walked with Hopper past the writers' offices on the way to Abe's private dining room at Columbia, and amused himself by pounding on the doors, roaring, "Get out from under your desk, motherfucker, I know you're in there. Why don't you write something, turn something in, you jerk-off."

Indeed, Bert and Jack were well matched. When they were together, which was often, it was simple. Bert gave, and Jack took. For Jack, success meant never having to pay for yourself. He never picked up a check if he could possibly avoid it. His home was filled with freebies he'd hustled, or which had just appeared, unsolicited, manna from movie star heaven — bags of expensive golf clubs, heaps of fine Italian shoes. But Bert, who had a more highly evolved sense of power, paid for everyone, entangling his friends and acquaintances in a sticky web of indebtedness. Years later, when Jack became a superstar, and the power relationship between the two men shifted dramatically, Bert called in some of his notes. He tried to take, but Jack wouldn't give.

Five Easy Pieces was a small, personal film, European in sensibility, character-, rather than plot-driven. It focuses on a downwardly mobile pianist named Bobby Dupea (Nicholson), from a comfortable WASP family of musicians who is discovered at the beginning working on an oil rig. Stanley Schneider begged Bert not to let Rafelson do it because *Head* had flopped. But to Bert, this was just fuel for the fire. In the fall of 1969, Rafelson started on preproduction. The writer was Carole Eastman.

Nicholson prided himself on his eye for talent, and Eastman was one of his discoveries. She broke in as an actress, then turned to writing, making a specialty of working-class characters. She had a great ear for the lilt and humor of blue-collar dialogue. A sensitive soul, nerves very close to the surface, she was striking to look at — tall, blond, rail thin, with a long neck, a skittish bird apt to take flight at the rustle of a leaf. Except that she had a fear of flying. "She wouldn't step on a plane if you put a gun to her head," recalls Buck Henry. "She was born to be an eccentric old lady." Carole was a bit of an agoraphobe, wouldn't leave Los Angeles, wouldn't ride in someone else's car unless she drove. She was phobic about having her picture taken, obsessive about food at the same time that she coughed continuously from chain-smoking. Even in L.A., she rarely went to places with which she was not already familiar. Her sexual orientation was a matter of endless debate; men hit on her all the time, but she never seemed to have a lover, of either sex.

Rafelson was a bully, the kind of person who brought all sorts of things to bear on a situation to get what he wanted, threatened and badgered, bellowing, "You owe me!," then proceeding to enumerate all the things he'd done for you. He was not about to take a back seat to Eastman, however talented she might be. Even though Rafelson had done little of note up to that point, it was an affront to his vanity if his name did not appear at least once among the screenwriting credits. Later on, he insisted to an interviewer, "No film that I have directed . . . started with material outside myself," and modestly compared his style to that of the severe, minimalist aesthetic of the much admired Japanese director Yasujiro Ozu. He knew everything; no one else knew anything. He was famous for once lecturing Ingmar Bergman's legendary DP, Sven Nykvist, on lighting. Writers felt that, like other directors who didn't write (as well as some who did), he would poach on their turf. Says Walon Green, who wrote *The Wild Bunch* (with Sam Peckinpah) and adapted *At Play in the Fields of the Lord* for Rafelson some years later, "If he wrote ten words, he'd say he wrote the whole thing."

Rafelson told Eastman his ideas, and she went off for six weeks with Richard Wechsler, an old New York friend of the Rafelsons. He baby-sat her until she came up with a script, whereupon she would have nothing to do with Rafelson. "She felt she would become polluted if she had to talk to the director," says Wechsler. Rafelson made some script changes, and took co-story credit on the same card as Eastman. She was furious. Concludes Buck Henry, "If he could rewrite Shakespeare, it was nothing to ask a Carole Eastman for credit."

Rafelson would never discuss credit or money. He'd say, "Talk to Bert." Bert would say, "You know Bob; I think he's gonna lose his enthusiasm for the project, he's not gonna wanna do the picture if he's not the auteur. Between you and me, I'll make it worth your while, you share the credit with him."

Still, "a lot of the ideas were Bob's," says Toby Rafelson. "The notion of a talented guy who rebels, and in a way wastes his talents until he's left with nothing, had a lot to do with him and his perception of the people around him." Indeed, the fantasy of downward mobility was entertained by Rafelson himself, and to some extent Schneider and Blauner, who affected the speech habits of truck drivers, and fancied themselves somehow of the street.

Five Easy Pieces was shot on the BBS budget, forty-one days beginning in early winter 1969, spilling over into January, for $876,000. Rafelson tried to control the pacing of Nicholson's performance by manipulating his drug intake. "He'd say, 'Do you think we should give Jack some grass or some hash for this scene?'" recalls Wechsler. Bob and Jack had brutal fights, but when they were over, they were over.

Toby still had no idea that Bob was fooling around. "He covered his tracks very, very well," she says. "I couldn't have realized it consciously, or I wouldn't have stayed with him." Although there may have been an element of willful blindness on her part. She once said, "In Hollywood, if you're married to a powerful guy, you don't ask them if they're cheating on you because they are, and if you can't take it, you shouldn't be there." She had a recurrent nightmare, in which they were together with a group of people in a house of many rooms, or riding on a swiftly moving train. One moment he was at her side, but the next he would be gone. She anxiously made her way down the long hallways or corridors looking for him, throwing open doors, and invariably discovered him in bed with someone. They left her feeling miserable, but after all, they were only dreams.

Rafelson, always a director first, producer second, was already growing uncomfortable in his role at BBS, worried he was spending too much time looking for new talent, digging up projects, helping to cast other people's pictures. Indeed, he had suggested Ellen Burstyn to Bogdanovich. He envied Bogdanovich, thought, Why aren't I making *The Last Picture Show*? It's the perfect Bob Rafelson movie. Later, he would say, "I think it's the best movie we ever made."

NOW THAT *THE LAST PICTURE SHOW* was happening, Bogdanovich finally got around to reading the book. He realized, to his chagrin, that it had less to do with the last picture show, or the end of movies, than with coming of age in the early '50s — in a godforsaken, desolate Texas town, yet. The story revolved around the friendship between two young men, Duane, a charming roughneck from the wrong side of the tracks, and Sonny, the good boy trying to find his place in the world, and the damage inflicted on both of them by the rich, bored, Anarene femme fatale, Jacy Farrow. Thrown into this mix is Sam the Lion, the elderly proprietor of the pool hall and run-down movie theater. Sam, rolling cigarettes and telling stories, is the sole repository of decency in the town, and when he dies, suddenly, of a stroke, it all goes to hell. As Sonny puts it, "Nothing's really been right since Sam the Lion died."

Peter was in a funk. He was a New York boy; what did he know from small towns in Texas? Polly liked the book because it could have been her, had she grown up in the Midwest instead of Europe. "There were all these movies about this, but they were all fake," she says. "Everything that's in the book, the taking off of the bra, hanging it on the car mirror, the hands that were cold and the girl who would only let him touch her tits, just barely getting your hand up this girl's leg, were experiences I'd had as a young woman. There were parts of a woman's body that were completely off limits in America. These were things that it was just impossible to show in Hollywood films, whereas in European films, like *Blow-Up*, you saw pubic hair."

Just as Beatty and Penn, Benton and Newman saw *Bonnie and Clyde* as a

French treatment of American themes, Peter and Polly saw that by 1969, in Polly's words, at last it might be possible to "make the book in America the way the French would have made it, where these weird American sexual mores could be investigated."

Bogdanovich wanted to shoot in black and white, thought it would convey period better than color, but it was unheard of. Finally, he asked Bert. The whole idea of BBS was to empower directors, and Bert was as good as his word, said yes. "Don't forget, at that point *Easy Rider* was still the success story of the hour," says Bogdanovich. "If we said we wanted to shoot in 16mm and blow it up, they would have let us."

Once again, Peter and Polly collaborated closely. She would design the sets, supervise the costumes. They huddled with McMurtry in their house in Van Nuys and hammered out a script. Bogdanovich got his best ideas while shaving, and one day it occurred to him to cast John Ford stalwart Ben Johnson for the role of Sam the Lion, the owner of the Royal. Johnson didn't want to do it. He didn't like talking about the clap, which the script required him to do. "I've never had to say words like that," he complained to Peter. "My mother's gonna see the movie." Bogdanovich called Ford. "Jack? Ben doesn't want to do it. He says it's too many words."

"Oh, Sheesus, Ben always says that. He always worried about words. Lemme phone old Ben."

Half an hour later Ford called back. "Peter, he'll do it."

"Well Jesus, whaddya say to him?"

"I says, 'Ben? D'ya wanna be Duke's sidekick for the rest of your life?' "

With Johnson on board, Peter attended to his novice cast. He had seen scores of young actresses for the role of Jacy Farrow. No one seemed right. Like Altman, Peter and Polly were not looking for stars. One day, while they were standing on the checkout line of a supermarket near their house, Polly pointed to a face staring at them from the cover of *Glamour*. "She had funny little spit curls, she was very impertinent, and Southern-looking, blue eyes," recalls Platt. "She looked like she had a sexual chip on her shoulder, as if she were daring you to try something."

Peter asked Marion Dougherty, who was casting the film, to find her. He met Cybill Shepherd at the Essex House on Central Park South in New York. She was big (five foot nine) and robust, radiating health and wholesomeness. With blond hair, pert nose, and creamy complexion, she was stunningly beautiful. Casually dressed in bleached jeans, a matching jacket, clogs, and no makeup save for the pale blue eye shadow that set off her china blue eyes, she had an unspoiled, coltish look. Bogdanovich was entranced. She sat on the floor, told him she was reading Dostoyevsky, but when he asked her which book, she couldn't remember the title. As she searched her memory, he couldn't help but notice that she was toying with one of those flowers that come in the small vase with breakfast. "There was something so casually destructive about it," he decided later. "It seemed to imply the kind of woman who doesn't mean to be cruel to men, but who is."

Peter asked Dougherty to call her in again, said, "You've got to see her nude. I have to see if she has any stretch marks or anything because there's nudity involved."

"She doesn't have any stretch marks, for chrissakes. She's seventeen or eighteen."

"Have her come in with the tiniest bikini you can find."

Says Dougherty, "He was falling in love with Cybill, and Polly was having a baby. You could feel the vibes."

The BBS guys were dubious; after all, Shepherd had never acted before. Nicholson was delighted. He hit on her at every opportunity. Platt had intimations of trouble. Pregnant with her second child, Alexandra (Sashy), she threw herself into preproduction in L.A. Cybill had a boyfriend back in New York who tried to talk her out of doing the nude scenes. He called constantly, torturing her over the phone. One night, after a particularly painful argument, Peter offered to drive Cybill home. "I knew," says Polly. "The tone of his voice, it was familiar, and I just knew."

"Polly accused me of being crazy about Cybill the day we arrived on location, before it even occurred to me," says Bogdanovich. "It irritated me enormously." He turned to Polly, snapped, "That's ridiculous. I'm not infatuated. She's funny, I like her. She's an actress in the picture. She's never acted before. I'm helping her. What *is* the problem here?" Cybill was flattered by his attentions. "Peter made making movies seem to be the most exciting activity in the world," she said. "A lot of people thought I had to be dumb. I had an agent who would slow his speech when he spoke to me. Peter didn't. He never talked down to me."

Timothy Bottoms, a rising young star who would years later distinguish himself by peeing on Dino De Laurentiis's shoes during the production of *Hurricane*, had a crush on Cybill, and couldn't understand why Peter, who already had a wife and children, was hitting on her. They fought throughout the production, and eventually, Bottoms got his revenge: he gave Cybill a novel by Henry James called *Daisy Miller*.

BOGDANOVICH AND PLATT took time out from preproduction on *The Last Picture Show* to watch the 1969 Oscars, which fell on April 7, 1970. The big studio musicals that year—Universal's *Sweet Charity*, Paramount's *Paint Your Wagon*, and Fox's *Hello, Dolly!*—had all bombed, although one, *Hello, Dolly!* was improbably nominated for Best Picture, along with *Anne of the Thousand Days*, *Z*, and *Butch Cassidy and the Sundance Kid*. New Hollywood films like

Easy Rider and *The Wild Bunch* were largely ignored; only *Midnight Cowboy* got a Best Picture nomination. The fault lines were most apparent in the contrast between two of the nominees for Best Actor, John Wayne, for *True Grit*, and Dustin Hoffman, for *Midnight Cowboy*. (Jon Voight was nominated as well, for the same film.)

Peter and Polly were rooting for Wayne and *True Grit*; they had no use for Hopper, who had been nominated, along with Fonda and Southern, for Best Original Screenplay. One evening, a few months earlier, Danny Selznick had invited them to dinner at the house of his father, David O. Selznick, and his wife, Jennifer Jones. The other guests included Dennis and Brooke, and George Cukor. Dennis, drunk and pugnacious as usual, turned to Cukor, poked a finger in his chest, and started on his usual refrain, saying, "We're going to bury you. We're gonna take over. You're finished." Cukor, considerably better bred than Hopper, politely murmured, "Well, well, yes, yes, that's very possible, yes, yes."

Peter and Polly were mortified. Says Polly, "We never forgave him for it. He disrespected one of our heroes."

By the time the ceremony came around, Hopper had forgotten all about the awards, and had to be reminded to show up. *Midnight Cowboy* won Best Picture, but Hopper et al. lost, as did Peter's sister, Jane, who had been nominated for *They Shoot Horses, Don't They?* (Jane flashed a clenched fist to the crowds on her way in.) Wayne beat out Hoffman and Voight. Hopper, who had played a bad guy in *True Grit*, went over to congratulate him. He was Wayne's in-house communist. Whenever some dramatic antiwar action occurred, Wayne would hold him responsible, and come looking for him. When the two were working on *True Grit*, Wayne once flew his helicopter in from the minesweeper he kept at Newport Beach, landed on the Paramount lot, swaggered onto the soundstage with his .45 hanging from his belt, and bellowed, "Where's that pinko Hopper? That goddamn Eldridge Cleaver's out there at UCLA saying 'shit' and 'cocksucker' in front of my sweet daughters. I want that red motherfucker. Where is that commie hiding?" Hopper concealed himself in Glen Campbell's trailer until Wayne gave up.

Toward the end of that same month, Nixon invaded Cambodia, and four students were shot to death on May 4 by the National Guard on the campus of Kent State, in Ohio. On May 29, the Appellate Court of California ordered a new trial for Huey Newton, and on August 5, he was released on bail. Bert met Huey for the first time in September. The producer knew a star when he saw one, and Huey was a star. Brackman recalls, "Huey was beautiful like the way Belafonte was beautiful. He was a fantastic specimen of health and clarity and physical and personal power."

Bert was mesmerized by Huey. Ironically, while his friends and protégés looked to him for support, regarded him as a guru, he himself hungered for someone to follow. After he met Huey, he explained, with the disarming naïveté of a bedazzled teenager, "How can I put it? He's my hero. If he's not Mao, I'll eat it."

Hopper assumed that BBS would finance his next movie. But he was so difficult, even Rafelson wasn't interested. Bert too was wary. "He just had this instinct that after the success of *Easy Rider*, Dennis's ego would be so inflated that it would be completely uncontrollable, and he was right," says Richard Wechsler. Only Blauner was eager, thought they would be crazy not to.

The Last Movie was an inspired Pirandellian meditation on Westerns, colonialism, and death. It focused on "a stunt man in a lousy Western," as Dennis explained it: "When his movie unit goes back to the States, he stays on in Peru to develop a location for other Westerns. He's Mr. Middle America. He dreams of big cars, swimming pools, gorgeous girls. . . . But the Indians . . . see the lousy Western for what it really was, a tragic legend of greed and violence in which everybody died at the end. So they build a camera out of junk and reenact the movie as a religious rite. To play the victim in the ceremony, they pick the stunt man. . . ." In Hopper's mind, it was a "story about America and how it's destroying itself." As in *Bonnie and Clyde* and *Easy Rider*, the doomed "hero" meets a dire end, expires in a flash of violence.

Hopper had once intended *The Last Movie* for Montgomery Clift, but by this time Clift was dead. He started testing people for the lead. One day, he walked into BBS, announced, "I can't find anybody, I gotta play the part myself." Blauner exploded, "Kiss my François Truffaut, motherfucker." Blauner buttonholed Bert: "The only way the picture works is the way it's written. This is a guy when it's over for him, he's a broken-up stunt man, it's Joel McCrea or somebody, but it's not Dennis, some young guy that you can't feel sorry for him, so go getta job. Dennis wants to play it? It'll ruin the picture." Bert, from his producer's perch, agreed. "When we got involved in making the movie to begin with, it was with the understanding that he was not going to try to do both jobs," he has said. "When Dennis came in and said he really couldn't do it without playing the part, I gave him a big hug and a kiss. I didn't want to deal with the heartache."

BBS passed, and Hopper had to look to the studios for a deal. To Calley, at Warners, life was too short; Dennis was simply a wacko. Not even Columbia was interested. Their deal was with Bert, whom they saw as the creative force behind *Easy Rider*. They regarded it as a movie waiting to happen. "If Hopper hadn't done it, *Easy Rider* would have happened a minute later or an hour later or a day later with some other film," says Peter Guber.

Hopper had once dated Jules Stein's daughter Susan — every father's nightmare — but Stein had handled it with equanimity. Universal was an unlikely home for Hopper. By the end of the decade, it was a studio that was making millions churning out television product, but its movies were a joke. "It was a miserable place to be," says Tony Bill, who produced *The Sting* at Universal. "It was the coldest and most impersonal experience I've ever had in the business. They gave a giant victory party for *The Sting*, and told me I couldn't bring my children. I refused to go."

Wasserman couldn't figure out why *Easy Rider* and *The Graduate* had become hits. "It was frightening," says production executive Ned Tanen. "These were aging gentlemen who did not remotely understand where their audience had gone. They looked at a movie like *Easy Rider*, and they said, 'What in the hell is this?' It's against everything they thought was a value in this country; they were still worshipping the grand ol' flag. But suddenly they were looking at these movies where everybody was dropping acid, was fucking in the park. Even I, who was much younger, didn't know who was a star anymore. Robert Redford made movies that worked and movies that didn't."

Recalls Danny Selznick, who worked for Tanen, "Wasserman said, 'We've got to find out.' And indeed, research proved there was a new generation of young people that didn't care who was in movies, that seemed to want movies about real people and real situations. In fact, if you had a star in a movie, it might hurt the picture, because it would make it not very credible. You saw Gregory Peck in a movie, you thought it was Gregory Peck."

Wasserman may have been out of touch, but he was smart enough to know it, and in 1969, he started a new unit, a youth division, making Tanen its chief. Like Schneider, Tanen was a maverick. A native Californian, he had a filial love-hate relationship with Wasserman, with whom he shared a hair-trigger temper. Along with MCA, TV executive Sidney Sheinberg, whom Tanen did not like, Wasserman was grooming him as his successor. Tanen was given to wild mood swings; when he was down, he was very, very down, everything was awful, his movies, his job, his life, life on earth. He was the original guy with the dark cloud over his head. Says Don Simpson, "He was clinically manic-depressive." But Tanen was smart and, according to Steven Spielberg, who didn't have much use for him, "Like Sid, he was one of the few people in Hollywood who was not afraid to speak his mind."

Borrowing a leaf from Schneider's book, the idea was to produce films for under $1 million, preferably $750,000. "For $5 million they could have five pictures, five chances at a breakthrough," says Selznick. The talent would be paid scale, but they would be given a hefty chunk of the back end, as much as 50 percent. Universal offered final cut, an extremity from which even BBS shrank.

"When the companies started making these movies, they didn't go gently into them," explains Tanen. "They said to kids who could not have gotten an appointment on the lot two weeks earlier, 'It's your movie, don't come back to us with your problems, we don't even want to know about them.' These were not movies where the studios were dealing with someone they trusted. They were dealing with kids whom they didn't trust, didn't like their arrogant behavior, didn't like the way they dressed, didn't want to see ponytails and sandals in the commissary while they were eating. They viewed them with absolute dread. Beyond dread. It was like they just wanted to send them to a concentration camp. But the studio left them alone because they thought they'd screw it up if they interfered, and the movies didn't cost anything. They realized that here was a fountain of talent. That's how, in the late '60s, early '70s, it became a director's medium."

The first two films out of the gate from Tanen's unit were *Diary of a Mad Housewife*, directed by Frank Perry, and *Taking Off*, directed by Milos Forman, and starring Buck Henry. They were critical, if not commercial successes. Tanen also financed Peter Fonda to direct *The Hired Hand*, and Monte Hellman to do *Two-Lane Blacktop*. Later there were Cassavetes's *Minnie and Moskowitz*, Douglas Trumbull's *Silent Running*, and Lucas's *American Graffiti*.

But urged on by Stein, the first picture Tanen actually signed up was *The Last Movie*. Tanen had heard all the Hopper stories, and thought to himself, I know the studio is having a rough time, but this ridiculous person is going to save us with *The Last Movie*? He asked Stein, "Are you sure you want to get us into this? We're going to have terrible problems here. Dennis may be gifted, but he's not really there all the time. He's erratic, unreliable, and he seems to have a problem editing, he can't put a movie together. Who knows what we could end up making?" But Tanen thought, The whole world is waiting for Dennis's next picture. Who are we to turn it down? This is where we start. He put up $850,000. Hopper got the *Bonnie and Clyde* contract, which is to say, he shared the risk with the studio. He was paid a pittance, $500 a week, but got 50 percent of the gross and total control over the movie.

The BBS folks were tickled by the idea of Dennis at Universal. "I just was laughing," says Rafelson. "Uh huh, I wanna see this work out. A lot of people who were at the studios were not interested in discovering talent. They were attracted to the success they thought the talent might bring. Let's get anybody who worked at BBS and hire them, because it's obvious they know who's wired. Some executive called me after Dennis made the deal and said, 'How do I talk to this guy?' My answer was, 'Are you crazy? Don't. Do what we did. Give 'em the money and let 'em go shoot the movie.'"

When Hopper, now thirty-four, decided to play the lead in *The Last Movie* himself, he shed thirty pounds, cut off his mustache and shoulder-length hair. It was Christmas. He sent a package done up with bright holiday wrapping to his daughter, Marin. She excitedly tore off the ribbons and colored paper to find an old Polaroid box filled with a hank of her father's hair.

The Last Movie was shot in Peru. Peter Fonda, Jaglom, and Michelle Phillips all had small roles. Sam Fuller played the director. At that time, Peru was the cocaine capital of the world, and every cokehead in L.A. wanted to work on the picture in order to smuggle drugs back up north. Hopper repeatedly got himself into scrapes with the Peruvian authorities. But he finally finished, informed Universal that he would need a year to edit the film (three months was standard), and he was going to do it in Taos.

PRINCIPAL PHOTOGRAPHY on *The Last Picture Show* commenced in October 1970, in Archer City, Texas, just three weeks after Platt gave birth to Sashy. Orson Welles was the baby's godfather. Archer City was where McMurtry had grown up; it even boasted of a yellow-brick hotel in which Bonnie and Clyde once took refuge.

Now a fastidious dresser, Bogdanovich self-consciously played the director. He wore horn-rimmed glasses, bell bottoms, and turned up his shirt collars, with the wings folded over like a paper airplane, Elvis-style. Trying to stop smoking, he always had a toothpick in his mouth, nervously broke the old one, inserted a new one. Platt, staring through large, oval shades with blue lenses, sat next to him behind the camera. They discussed every shot. Later, some people, including Ben Johnson, would whisper that she directed the movie as much as he did.

Back on La Brea, Bert and Steve were not happy with the dailies. "We felt we had made a mistake with the subject matter, we should've had Peter do a caper movie, because this picture was too somber, too dark, too down," says Blauner. They also couldn't help but notice the absence of master shots,* and Bert was worried that the dailies wouldn't cut together. He asked Rafelson to look at them, saying, "I can't understand this fuckin' stuff, man, what is this?" Rafelson checked out the dailies, told Schneider, "He knows exactly what he's doing, it will cut like butter, and don't bring me in here again." Peter edited in his head, in the camera.

Post-production head Jim Nelson says, "Peter was the only director I've ever worked with, you could send his trims† off to Bekins in an envelope."

The entire cast and crew was staying at the Ramada Inn, a tacky motel with a lobby out of *The Best Little Whorehouse in Texas*. The floor was planted with a blood red rug; painted gold banisters flanked the stairs going up to Peter and Polly's two-bedroom suite. Midway into the picture, Peter recognized he was falling hard for Cybill, said something like, "I'm not sure who I'm more attracted to, you or [the character] Jacy." She broke off with Jeff Bridges, with whom she was having a production fling, and the romance blossomed. Peter

* A master shot is a long shot of an entire scene that is photographed first and then broken down into subsequent medium shots and close-ups.
† Outtakes.

returned from the set later and later each night. One night he did not come back at all, and Polly realized she could no longer deny to herself that the relationship between Peter and Cybill had become sexual. She confronted him, hysterical. Peter apologized, claimed he couldn't help it, that he had never had a cover girl before, that he was in the throes of a sexual obsession. He said he felt old, and she made him feel young. "We thought it was just going to be for the picture," says Bogdanovich. Polly tried to see it from his point of view, but it made her furious, anyway. Especially when he said, "I don't know if I want to have a wife and children."

"Yeah, well, we exist," she retorted. "We're alive, we're here, there's nothing you can do about it. What do you want to do, kill us?"

She moved into the other bedroom. She didn't want to lie there counting the minutes until he came home. They managed to compartmentalize their emotions to avoid disrupting the movie. In the morning, they drove to the set together, discussed the day's setups as if nothing were happening. In the evening, she retired to her own room. "It was hideous," she says. The fights got uglier. He screamed, "If you're so unhappy, why don't you go home."

"Go home to what? Go home to think about you fucking Cybill? It's my movie as much as yours. You can only feel for people on celluloid. You have no concept what it's like in real life to feel grief. Picture it in a movie, Peter, and maybe you'll get it."

One day Polly found herself speeding down a stretch of arrow-straight Texas highway between Archer City and Wichita Falls in a rented Ford station wagon, with Peter next to her. She was again hysterical, screaming that without him, she didn't want to live. She was driving fast, edging past seventy-five. Suddenly, she swerved off the road into a rutted, newly plowed field. "I'm going to kill us both," she shrieked, as the car bounced over the furrows, ka-boom, ka-boom, ka-boom, until the hood flew up, and the car bottomed out in a cloud of red dust. They both burst out laughing.

But soon the laughing stopped. By the end of the shoot, Peter and Polly's marriage, like a vehicle in a slow-motion traffic accident, was wrecked beyond repair. Their friends looked on, aghast. "They were like this extraordinary couple," recalls Benton. "It was like watching an amoeba split." Says Bogdanovich, "I felt terribly guilty. My parents had been married for years, and the idea of divorce was alien to me. I regretted what happened with Polly. She suffered, and the kids suffered, and the kids suffered because of Polly's suffering. I'm sorry for the pain, the kids, more than anything. But I also never felt about anybody quite the way I felt about Cybill. It was one of those times when life just takes over, and you don't really have control. I don't regret what I did, in the sense that I wouldn't have done it if it happened again, 'cause it wasn't just a movie thing, it was real."

•

IN THE FALL OF 1970, just before Bogdanovich left for location, *Five Easy Pieces* had opened to rave reviews and more than respectable box office. It won the New York Film Critics Award for best picture. Rafelson won best director, Karen Black best supporting actress, and it confirmed the promise Nicholson had shown in *Easy Rider*. Once again, Bert shared the profits, sent day players* four-figure checks. Nobody in Hollywood did that. *Five Easy Pieces* was the second BBS triumph in a row. The company was batting 1.000. But the same could not be said for Bert's relationship with his wife, Judy. Throughout the winter, the two had been moving further and further apart. Judy was uncomfortable with the new sexual mores, so different from the ones she had grown up with.

In all fairness, Bert could hardly exclude his wife from the bountiful garden of his sexual Rousseauism. His attitude was, Judy is too uptight, too possessive. He encouraged her to sleep around, the only restriction being she tell him all about it. Bert knew that she might do as he suggested, if only to get back at him, and he tried to fix her up with his friends, thereby gaining a measure of control over her and them in the process. According to one friend, he told him, "My wife really likes you, I'm going out of town, why don't you take her out to dinner." He encouraged another to sleep with Judy. The friend didn't understand it, felt like a pawn in a '70s version of *Les Liaisons Dangereuses*. There was a sentimental side to Bert; he wanted everybody he loved to love one another, get in bed togther, a pansexuality that was probably enhanced by acid and MDA, the so-called love drug.

Incited by the very '60s conviction that Americans were wallowing in a sea of false consciousness and hypocrisy, Jaglom embarked on a campaign of truth telling. He, Bert, and Judy, sat by the side of Bert's pool, lit up joints and interrogated one another: What do you really feel? Do we really love each other? Do we want to fuck anybody else besides each other? Finally, Bert confessed his affairs to Judy. But these were casual encounters. Worse, from Judy's point of view, was the lengthy relationship with Toni Stern. Nor was she pleased to hear that everyone in their circle knew about it except her. On several occasions Jaglom and Blauner had even acted as beards.

After one bad fight on February 8, 1971, Judy kicked Bert out. Devastated, he took refuge in Jaglom's bachelor pad in the Hollywood Hills. He expected her to call, but she didn't. Bert couldn't believe it. "Anyone who can have me and doesn't want me is insane," he told Jaglom. Finally Jaglom fell into a fitful sleep after an all-night session of soul searching that ended at 4:00 A.M. Two hours later, he was rudely awakened. The house was swaying so violently he thought, Oh my God, Bert, what are you doing? He imagined that Schneider, stricken with grief, was shaking the house to its very foundation. It was the earthquake. Jaglom ran to the room where Bert was sleeping, but the bed was

---

* Actors paid by the day.

empty. Worried his kids would discover he hadn't spent the night at home, Schneider wanted to be there when they woke up. Bert and Judy agreed to spend the summer apart. They never got back together.

Bert rented a home in Benedict Canyon above the Beverly Hills Hotel that looked like it might have belonged to Dean Martin. It was a one-story, rambling house with a pool table, wood floors, a zebra rug, suede sofas, yellow and black swirly wallpaper in the bedroom. Across a shallow ravine, some two hundred yards away, was the old Barrymore estate, where Calley lived, and where Candice Bergen looked down on Bert's place from a tower called "the Aviary." Bert and Candy knew each other slightly, but Jaglom, who was friends with both, played Cupid, convincing them they were right for what ailed each other.

Bergen was primed for a relationship like this one. Like Shepherd, she had been a successful model, but knew there must be more to life. She had always been uneasy in her skin, resented the fact that she was regarded as little more than a pretty face, a dilettante photographer and journalist. Bergen was deeply sympathetic to the antiwar movement, embarrassed by her father, Edgar Bergen's, friendship with the Old Hollywood right — Ronald Reagan, Bob Hope, Charlton Heston, as well as the fact that he had made his living throwing his voice into wooden dummies. She had recently been acclaimed in *Carnal Knowledge*, yet was insecure about her acting abilities. In short, she had something to prove.

Bergen became a regular visitor at Schneider's home. Like Cybill to Peter's Pygmalion, Bergen was the perfect fellow traveler for Schneider's political and spiritual journey. She presented a surface that was as brittle, burnished, and impenetrable as one of her father's polished dolls. Bert, a man for whom the term "mindfucker" was invented, urged her to loosen up, get in closer touch with her feelings, drop some acid. As he had with the younger men around him, he easily fell into the role of mentor. He cajoled, lectured, railed against her personality "flaws." But she proved a fractious student. She found him infuriatingly smug and patronizing. Nevertheless, by mid-summer, they were deeply in love, an established couple. "Bert and Candy" replaced "Bert and Judy."

Bert became known for his parties. The house was always filled with a yeasty mix of stars, Black Panthers, antiwar activists, and hangers-on of various stripes. One regular was Bert's close friend Artie Ross, nearly ten years his junior. Artie was born into a well-to-do Jewish family in Harrison, New York. His mother's best friend was Judy's mother. His parents and Bert's parents belonged to the same country club. Ross felt suffocated by the privileged Westchester private schools he was sent to, and was more than ready for the '60s. When college rolled around in 1965, he lit out for Berkeley. Artie's mother was leery, but she comforted herself with the idea that Bert and Judy were in California, and they would look after him. When Bert moved to L.A., Artie sought him out. In photographs taken at the time, Bert has his arm around Artie. Artie was another kid brother.

There was a lot of semipublic sex at Bert's parties and, of course, drugs. The latest treat was nitrous oxide, which people did in combination with MDA. They filled inflatable pool toys with the gas — beach balls, inner tubes, often a big, blue plastic dolphin — pulled the plugs and inhaled until the toys were empty. "You could go very far out very fast with it, and then you came back almost all the way within a couple of minutes with every breath of oxygen you took," says Brackman. "It was a very radical change of consciousness. It was like the brain went into *Star Wars* land, leaving the body behind."

Eventually, Brackman acquired a tank of nitrous oxide that he kept in a closet of his girlfriend's apartment. It was unusually large, about six feet high, a month's supply. Brackman had bought it with his MasterCard using a prescription written by Andrew Weil, a Harvard M.D. who had done some pioneering drug research in the '70s. (Weil later went on to write best-sellers about natural healing.) Brackman deducted the nitrous as a medical expense. He explains, "Once you got it, you could call them up, they'd come and pick up your old tank and give you a new one, just like a bottled water supplier, no questions asked."

MEANWHILE, *Picture Show* was burning up the Bel Air screening circuit. It is easy to see why people were impressed. In an era of gaudy color, it was shot in a restrained black and white, had a spare, dusty look, Dorothea Lange or Walker Evans set in motion, or better, from Peter's point of view, Ford in his *Grapes of Wrath* period. And yet, as Platt intended, it delivered a European frankness that was new to the American screen and even more unusual in this Dustbowl setting: Sonny and his girlfriend listlessly making out in the front seat of a truck, her bra hanging from the rearview mirror, a casual shot of her bare breasts just there, a fact of life, like the dry tumbleweed visible through the windshield. In another scene, the kids casually discuss the virtues of making it with a heifer compared to a hooker, and at a swimming party at a rich kid's home, we see full frontal female nudity with pubic hair.

But *Picture Show* has a lot more to offer than mere titillation. Everything works, looks, and sounds just right. Tim Bottoms is splendid as Sonny, tentative and goofy-looking, fumbling through the last years of adolescence toward adulthood, eyes sorrowful beneath a mop of tangled hair and blinking as if he's just been hatched, trying to navigate the strange world of adults. Ditto Shepherd, as Bogdanovich instantly understood, perfect at tearing the wings off the boys, self-absorbed, thoughtless, and tempting, a blond lollipop. And the others, Burstyn as her bored mother, trapped in an unfulfilling marriage having once traded wealth for happiness, overwhelmed by melancholy, the feeling of life passing her by. And Cloris Leachman as the coach's lonely wife, reduced to having an affair with Sonny. And Ben Johnson, of course, carrying with him the moral authority of the Old Hollywood, all those years working for Ford. The only misstep is Bridges, too Hollywood handsome to convince anyone he's a redneck. When the Royal, the only theater in town, does close, someone says, "Nobody wants to come no more. Baseball in the summer, TV all the time." Sonny and Duane catch the last show, Hawks's *Red River*, watch John Wayne and Montgomery Clift saddle up for the cattle drive to Missouri. The last shot is the one that remains in memory: the desolate main street of Anarene, emptied of people, the wind howling, leaves and bits of debris whipped through the air. It's as powerful an image of alienation and loss as anything in Antonioni.

Picture Show hadn't even opened yet and Peter was being fought over by two of the biggest stars in Hollywood, Steve McQueen and Barbra Streisand. According to Platt, Peter took entire credit for the picture, rarely acknowledging her. It's like I died, she thought. She couldn't get work. She fantasized about shooting him with her father's .45.

Peter's agent was Sue Mengers. Short and zoftig, she wore muumuus and rose-tinted, oversized glasses, was loud, abrasive, and very funny. When Sharon Tate was murdered, she famously reassured Streisand, also a client, "Don't worry, honey, they're not murdering stars, only featured players." She once said, "I'm so driven I would have signed Martin Bormann." Ali MacGraw called her a female Billy Wilder. Although her list was comprised mostly of stars, she began to represent directors as well. After all, they were becoming stars. She wouldn't say, "You want to direct? Go back to the theater." Instead, it was, "Oh, you underpriced baby. Stan Kamen is keeping you down. I'll get your mil, honey."

Mengers too became known for the parties she threw at her house on Dawn Ridge Drive. If you were happening, or hoped to happen, attendance was de rigueur. They were business occasions more than anything else: Ann-Margret met Mike Nichols at Sue's and got *Carnal Knowledge*. Burt Reynolds would meet Alan Pakula and get *Starting Over*. Lauren Hutton would connect with Paul Schrader and get *American Gigolo*. Paul Newman and Joanne Woodward were frequent guests. Woodward always sat in a chair, knitting. As soon as someone lit up a joint, they left. The atmosphere was so heady that Cybill was scared to go. Peter had to drag her down the driveway by the arm.

Bert wouldn't let Mengers see the picture. He didn't like agents, wouldn't deal with them, thought she had a big mouth, which was true. If he knew he was going to lose Peter he didn't care. Peter was into Barbra by then, and Bert didn't hold opinions on people, didn't try to force them to work for BBS if they didn't want to. Bert did show the film to Streisand, who was moved to tears, and wanted Peter to direct her in something "significant," something that would showcase her acting, as well as her voice.

But Peter had promised McQueen to do *The Getaway* next. When McQueen took another film instead, Peter had a way out, and one day found himself in Calley's office. Calley asked him what he wanted to do next. "I sort of would like to do a screwball comedy," said Bogdanovich, tentatively.

"Well, do that."

"Something like *Bringing Up Baby*, kind of an uptight professor and a screwy girl, a wacky dame."

"Fine, do that."

"Just like that?"

"Yeah."

He walked out of Calley's office thinking, This Hollywood thing isn't so hard.

Calley agreed to pay Bogdanovich $125,000 to direct his screwball comedy, plus 8 percent of the net. Peter hired Ryan O'Neal, with whom Barbra was involved, for the male lead. The picture was called *What's Up, Doc?*

WHEN HOPPER GOT BACK to native soil, he announced his engagement to Michelle Phillips. He himself was not into marriage, he explained to his friends, but "she *just won't have it any other way!*" Said one friend, "Dennis falls in love . . . [with] any girl who stands in front of him. Michelle doesn't know that yet." They got married, appropriately enough, on Halloween. The marriage lasted about a week. John Phillips called it the "Six Days' War." Michelle — now known as "Holly Hopper" — told him Hopper terrified her and her daughter Chynna by firing guns in the house, and handcuffing her to prevent her from running away, saying he thought she was a witch. He hit her, the way he hit Brooke — "one shot," he admits. One morning, when he woke up, she was gone. Michelle told John that Hopper chased her to the airport in his pickup when he discovered she had left, drove out onto the runway in an attempt to stop the plane from taking off. Later, she called him. Hopper said, "I love you; I need you." She replied, "Have you ever thought of suicide?"

The editing of *The Last Movie* dragged on, as it did with *Easy Rider*. "Dennis would run it over and over again for every hippie who would come through Taos," Tanen recalls. "They would tell him, 'Hey, man, you should put more into it.' Every time I would go to Taos, it would be twenty minutes longer; it kept growing, like a malignancy." Rafelson rode into town to help him. "Dennis never showed up," he recalls. "For the first day or two he was swacked all the time. He would get violent and weird and crazy." The story went that Hopper invited Alejandro Jodorowsky (*El Topo*). He had finally come up with a presentable cut that had a beginning, middle, and an end, and showed it to Jodorowsky. Jodorowsky told him he'd failed, had merely made a conventional Hollywood movie. Hopper was stung. He tore the film to pieces, started over from scratch, throwing out the narrative. Hopper denies it. "Nobody influenced me. I was a fucking stubborn, dogmatic dictator, that nobody could penetrate," he says. "They could take it away and cut it, but there wasn't any way of reaching me."

Meanwhile, back at Universal, Tanen waited, biting his nails and worrying about his job. *The Last Movie* was the flagship of his boutique operation, and there was a lot riding on it. "The editors would come back and tell me, there's no footage, there's nothing to cut to, there literally are scenes missing," he recalls. There was a film within a film, which Tanen derisively called "a film without a film." He continues, "The pressure from Universal about this movie was nightmarish. Wasserman wasn't the easiest guy in the world when things were going well, and this little operation was not going well. The studio was not doing well." He paid Hopper another of his periodic visits. Kit Carson and Larry Schiller were making a documentary about the director called *American Dreamer*. They had persuaded Hopper to walk naked through downtown Los Alamos for the delectation of their camera. In return, they had agreed to fulfill a Hopper fantasy, in this case, produce fifty beautiful girls at his house for a "consciousness-raising session."

In the middle of this scene, Tanen arrived in his limo. "I was wearing my MCA suit, there on business to talk to him about this movie," he recalls. "I walked in, and this enormous orgy was going on — I mean, full-blown. My God, I couldn't even imagine how many people. Buttocks and boobs going in all directions." Schiller, an overweight, slovenly young man with greasy black hair, was shooting the party. "I went to Dennis and said, 'Can I talk to you?' " continues Tanen. "Dennis was out of his bird, totally gone. In the corner of my eye, I saw this guy pointing a camera at us. I said to him, 'Would you please not do that?' He kept going. I said, 'Listen, I don't want to have to ask you again.' He ignored me. I said, 'Please, I'm going to ask you one more time.' He was still doing it, so I grabbed the camera, threw it through the window and grabbed him, this enormous fat man, and I said, 'You fuck, I'll kill you, fucker!' Dennis said, 'Man, get me a camera! I want to shoot this!' The tits and asses were still going in all directions, and I was thinking, What can I do to get out of this business? Although that picture almost put me out of the business."

Hopper was still a celebrity. He was on the cover of *Life* June 19, 1970. The intense aura of expectancy that surrounded *The Last Movie* had reached a fever pitch. Tanen knew the truth. He had screened the movie with Dennis and Julie Stein at the executive screening room at the top of the Black Tower, that housed the executive offices at Universal. When the movie was over, there was dead silence. The two executives were in shock. Then, through the wall, clear as a bell, they heard the projectionist say, "They sure named this movie right, because this is gonna be the last movie this guy ever makes." Recalls Tanen, "We had a thing called catastrophe — not disaster — catastrophe. This was a full-blown earthquake on the nine level and there was nothing you could do.

You couldn't cut it, you couldn't add to it. This was what the movie was, there was nowhere to run."

Universal was gingerly conducting test screenings on campuses where *The Last Movie* could be expected to find its audience, if audience there was. The film was screened at the University of Iowa at nine o'clock in the morning. "I figured, Well, how much trouble can we get into? Who'll be awake?" recalls Tanen. They took a United Airlines flight to Iowa City. "As we were landing, Dennis was flushing drugs down the toilet on the plane," Tanen continues. They arrived at a theater near the campus. Tanen feared they'd draw a hayseed crowd, and was pleased to see an audience of freaks. He thought, This might be okay. But after the screening, Hopper got up to talk to the audience. Tanen recalls, "They were throwing things, screaming abuse at him — 'It's the worst piece of shit . . .' This wasn't just hostility. I was getting really uncomfortable feelings, something could happen here that's not going to be good, like this could be *Suddenly, Last Summer*. So I finally dragged him from the theater, and we were going through the lobby, where there was one of these old-fashioned popcorn machines, and the most beautiful eighteen- or nineteen-year-old girl sitting behind it. Adorable. Classy, Midwest. 'Mr. Hopper,' she said. I looked at her and thought, Oh Jesus! If only we can get to our car. Dennis said, 'Yes, my dear?' She answered, 'Can I talk to you? Did you make this film?' He said, 'Yes.' He was being very flirtatious, very charming. She hauled back and popped him from about six inches away, right in the nose. Blood started streaming out and she started screaming at him, 'You sexist fucking pig!' I grabbed him. I said, 'They're going to eat us, they're going to devour us and we're never going to be seen again!'

"I got him to the airport. I had to call Wasserman, who was waiting for a report on the preview. I called him from this phone booth, thinking my life was over. He picked up, said, 'Well, how did it go?' I'm looking out the window and there was Dennis holding his nose, blood all over his shirt. I said, 'Well, Lew, we have a little work to do!' "

The Last Movie won the Critics Prize at the Venice Film Festival, and Universal opened it at the Cinema 1 in New York. It was roasted by the reviewers; no one went, and after two weeks, it died. Hopper thought the studio had dumped it. He was bitter. "I won the Venice Film Festival, and they say, 'Recut it!' " he complained. "I overestimated my audience. I'd gone around to universities selling *Easy Rider*, and everybody was saying, 'We want new movies.' I said, 'Boy, have I got a movie for you.' In point of fact, what they really wanted was 1940-opiate kind of movies where they didn't have to do a whole lot of thinking — what Spielberg and Lucas came up with."

Reflecting on Hopper's experience, Nicholson, who was now seeing Michelle Phillips, was also disillusioned. Corman once told him that European movies only became voguish because of their sexual explicitness, and that when

American movies caught up, the European pictures would fade away. Now Jack had come to the conclusion that Corman was right: "All the American audience's supposed greater education, through *Jules and Jim*, *8½*, and so on, to more sophisticated formal approaches to viewing narrative, character, observations about humanity, seems to have evaporated. It now seems that the reason for the success of *Blow-Up* was that it included the first beaver shot in a conventional theater. It's a success such as Antonioni had never had before and hasn't had since."

The Last Picture Show was about the end of an era of motion pictures; *The Last Movie* was much more thematically ambitious and apocalyptic. Hopper, inflated by the sense of destiny that fueled the counterculture, was making a statement about the death of the Western, of national expansionism and spiritual expansiveness, and therefore of the American Dream. But it turned out to signify the end of his own career, instead. It was a devastating personal defeat from which he didn't begin to recover for two decades. Says Hopper, "I was there before everybody. I saw Lucas come and Lucas go, Spielberg come and Spielberg go, Scorsese come and Scorsese go. There were seventeen years when I couldn't do anything. I was stopped from making movies." Like a firefly, Hopper flashed brightly for a brief three years, then went dark.

Although Hopper didn't direct again for over a decade, he did do some acting, and directors learned to work around the drugs. One director wouldn't use him after lunch, when the alcohol kicked in. Another knew that Dennis would grab whatever was around — uppers, downers, what have you — and worried that, say, if Dennis took one drug during a long shot in the morning and a different one during a close-up in the afternoon, the energy levels would be different, making it impossible to cut them together. The two men went through the script and agreed on what drug Dennis would use in each of his scenes. When Hopper got the next day's call sheet, there was a notation at the bottom indicating the appropriate drug.

The failure of *The Last Movie* was also a blow to the kinds of films people like Hopper and Nicholson hoped to make. In fact, Tanen's whole slate suffered, particularly in light of other New Hollywood pictures that flopped, like Coppola's *The Rain People*, and the success of Old Hollywood formula films like Universal's own *Airport*, which had been a top grosser the year before. Rudy Wurlitzer's script for *Two-Lane Blacktop* had been hailed on the cover of *Esquire* as the best script of the year, and Universal agreed to let Wurlitzer direct a film in India. He went over there to scout locations. When he returned, *The Last Movie* lay in ruins. "There was no way they were going to do this crazy movie with a first-time director in India after they'd gone through the Hopper fiasco in Peru," he says. "You felt that there'd been a big shift. They weren't going to take those kinds of chances anymore. For three or four years there was a kind of romance going on that quickly led to disillusionment and cynicism." Or, as Hopper's line producer Paul Lewis puts it, "The freedom that we were allowed was over with *The Last Movie, The Hired Hand,* and *Two-Lane Blacktop.* The end of the '70s began at the beginning of the '70s." Adds Oliver Stone, who was just coming out of NYU Film School in 1971, "The *Easy Rider* period was over. You couldn't make those films anymore. They really nailed us."

In fact, none of Tanen's pictures did any business. There was a fatal flaw in the whole idea. The pictures may in fact have had audiences, but they never had a chance to find them. They were released through the studio's marketing and distribution divisions, which, like the departments of physical production, were still in the dark ages, geared to big-budget mainstream movies. The fifty-something executives didn't have the foggiest idea how to market pictures like Hopper's, and worse, didn't care.

"I saw coming events casting their shadow when Ned decided to do Robert Aldrich's *Ulzana's Raid,* with Burt Lancaster," says Selznick. "It wasn't what our unit was all about."

" 'Don't you understand? Our films aren't working, Danny, with no filmmakers and no stars. I'm gonna be hung in effigy in the public square.' "

" 'I'm sympathetic, but if we make a violent picture with Burt Lancaster and Robert Aldrich, the unit is dead.' "

" 'It *is* dead. You might as well face it.' "

" 'Look, we still have *Graffiti* in the can, it isn't out yet.' "

" 'Do you really think the fortunes of this unit are gonna be changed by a little picture called *American Graffiti*? The verdict on this unit is in, and Lew Wasserman's made it.' "

IN THE SPRING OF 1971, Bogdanovich called Benton and Newman in New York. He told them he wanted to do a modern version of Hawks's *Bringing Up Baby*. Thrilled, they flew out to Hollywood to start work on *What's Up, Doc?* They called Peter and Cybill at their apartment in Sunset Towers, a posh address in a deco building on Sunset Boulevard where George Stevens lived. "We had seen *The Last Picture Show,* so we knew Cybill was this great dish," says Newman. "And she *was* great to look at, a vanilla ice cream sundae. She came out of the bedroom, sat on Peter's lap. Peter goes, 'Hi, honey,' nuzzling, while Benton and I sat there." Peter marked up *TV Guide,* indicating the movies she should watch. She bought popcorn and candy, pizza and Coke, and they trooped over to the Warners lot where Peter could arrange screenings of anything he wanted. Continues Newman, "She was being tutored to be a Peter Bogdanovich girlfriend. She said, 'I'm going off to UCLA to see — ' She opened the schedule. '. . . there's an Allan Dwan at three o'clock, and at five-thirty, should I stay and see that Frank Borzage?' She came up with her little reports on these different auteur films. Once in a while he'd go out of the room and she'd roll her eyes, and go, 'He just wants me to know everything about the movies.' "

As the start date for *Doc* rolled around, Calley was growing increasingly nervous. He recalls, "We were pay-or-play with everybody. I mean we had Barbra, we had Ryan, big numbers. It was a nightmare." The script, in Calley's opinion, was "a terrible piece of shit. We were supposed to start in three weeks. I was sitting by my pool reading it on a Saturday. I wanted to blow my brains out, it was just awful." He called Buck Henry, asked him to rewrite it. But Calley still had to convince Bogdanovich to go along with the idea. "Bogdanovich's arrogance was monstrous," says Calley. "He had *Last Picture Show* about to come out, so he was unbearable." Peter told Calley to relax, he'd make it up as he went along. "I'll be the conductor," he said. Calley responded, "Forget it. This is dreck, you've been developing it for six months, we can't make it, and you're going to have to work with Buck." Henry rewrote the script in two weeks. "It was not the greatest comedy ever made, but it worked," Calley adds, "and we were able to make some dough with it."

Peter was a little bit in awe of Streisand, so he held himself in check. *Doc* was filled with wonderful New York character actors supplied by Nessa Hyams. "Using New York actors appealed to Peter's ego," she says. "It was a thing in the '70s to discover new people. After *Midnight Cowboy*, it was like, 'Get me another Jon Voight. Make me another movie star.' "

Altman wanted to use one of Peter's actors, Michael Murphy, in *Images*, his next picture after *McCabe*. But Bogdanovich refused to release him. "He kept him for one scene, to stand on the street with a suitcase for a long shot," Altman recalls. Altman never forgave him, and thereafter referred to him as the "Xerox" director, alluding to his irritating practice of speaking of each of his films in terms of the great directors, as in, "*Picture Show* was my Ford picture, *What's Up, Doc?* was Hawks." Said Altman, "I can pretty much do without Peter Bogdanovich. . . . I've never seen a film of his that was passable."

But Bogdanovich was not losing much sleep worrying about Altman's opinion of his films. *The Last Picture Show* premiered at the New York Film Festival in the fall of 1971. The festival also showed Bogdanovich's AFI documentary, *Directed By John Ford*. Peter flew in from the set of *Doc* to attend, with Cybill. Afterward, he and Cybill, Bert and Candice, Jack, Bob and Toby et al. ate Italian at Elaine's to celebrate the film's success. Bert, confided, smiling, "I slipped another one by them."

Bogdanovich flew back to the set of *Doc*. He was in his dressing room on a stage at Warners, shooting the banquet sequence when Bert called: "Are you sitting down?"

"I am now."

"I'm gonna read you the opening sentence from *Newsweek*. . . . 'The Last

Picture Show is a masterpiece. . . . It is the most impressive work by a young American director since *Citizen Kane!*' Are you there, Peter?"

"Are you making this up?"

" '. . . it is the finest film of an otherwise dreary season. . . .' "

"Jesus Christ."

Irritating Cybill, Bogdanovich took Polly to the L.A. premiere at Filmex. He had managed to have an affair with his estranged wife during the production of *Doc,* while Cybill was in New York, shooting commercials.

The Last Picture Show was a hit, and a critics' darling as well. As Peter sensed when he approached the project, coming of age in a small town in Texas was not something he knew much about. Not only had he grown up in New York, he had never even come of age, being one of those children who struck people as premature adults. But he had succeeded in making the material his own, if only by throwing himself headlong into an adolescent affair with Cybill that provoked the jealousy of Bottoms and Bridges, mimicking the mechanics of the plot. As Schneider and Rafelson had recognized, Bogdanovich was aesthetically, at least, quite conservative. Scorsese puts it this way: "The last person to make classical American cinema was Peter. To really utilize the wide frame and the use of the deep focal length. He really understood it." In contrast to authority-bashing, adult-baiting pictures like *Bonnie and Clyde, Easy Rider,* and *M*A*S*H, The Last Picture Show* is reverential toward its patriarch, Ben Johnson's Sam the Lion, who is the film's teacher, law-giver, fount of values. When he dies, an era ends, just as surely as it does in Ford's elegiac *Liberty Valance.*

Riding the *Picture Show* wave, Warners decided to go up against *The Godfather,* releasing *Doc* at Radio City Music Hall at Easter 1972. Streisand and Mengers saw it together at the first screening. They both thought it was a disaster. Barbra's manager, Marty Ehrlichman, blamed Mengers. As they were leaving the screening, he hissed, "Are you satisfied? You've ruined her career!" Weeks later, Calley called Mengers at Klosters, in Switzerland, where she was vacationing. He said, "It's a hit. It's a smash." After *The Godfather,* which broke every record, *Doc* would be the third highest grossing movie of 1972, $28 million in rentals against a budget of $4 million.

When Bogdanovich returned to New York, his hometown, he felt like a conquering hero: "I grew up in Manhattan, and to come back at the age of thirty-one or thirty-two was exhilarating. *Picture Show,* which was being compared to *Citizen Kane,* was still playing on the East Side in one theater when *Doc* opened on the West Side in March. And it was being compared to *Bringing Up Baby.* I had it all at that moment. We broke the Music Hall house record the first and second weekend, a thirty-year record. I was at the top of the *Variety* charts with two pictures for most of that year, and the Oscars had just been announced, and *Picture Show* got eight nominations, including two for me.

The biggest kick I got was seeing my name on the marquee when I hadn't even asked for them to put it there. *My* name circled the marquee: PETER BOGDANOVICH'S COMEDY. It was the peak of my career. It was worth a lot of the shit that followed."

Five:
The Man Who Would Be King
1972

• *How* **The Godfather** *made Francis Coppola the first superstar director, while Paramount's Bob Evans saved the studio, and Robert Towne and Roman Polanski fought over* **Chinatown.**

"We were going to be the new Godards and Kurosawas. Francis was gonna lead us. He wanted to ride in the car, but he still was at the head of the parade."

— JOHN MILIUS

During the summer of 1972, agent Freddie Fields had a party attended by Bogdanovich, Friedkin, and Coppola. Francis and Billy, accompanied by Ellen Burstyn, who was about to star in Friedkin's *The Exorcist,* left the party in the new Mercedes 600 stretch limo Francis had won in a bet with Paramount when *The Godfather* hit $50 million. Francis had a bottle of champagne which he spritzed over the car, christening it. They were all well lubricated, driving along Sunset on their way to an "in" diner downtown, singing "Hooray for Hollywood." Peter had left at the same time, in a Volvo station wagon driven by Polly. By happenstance, the two vehicles pulled up alongside each other at a red light on the Strip. Billy stood up and poked his head through the sun roof. Seeing Bogdanovich, he shouted, "The most exciting American film in twenty-five years!" quoting a review of his own picture, *The French Connection.* Holding up five fingers, he added, "Eight nominations and five Oscars, including Best Picture!"

Not to be outdone, Bogdanovich poked his head out the window of the Volvo, recited a line from one of his reviews which he had apparently committed to memory: "*The Last Picture Show,* a film that will revolutionize film history," adding, "Eight nominations, and my movie's better than yours." Francis, large and bearded, thrust himself through the sun roof and bellowed, "*The Godfather,* a hundred and fifty million dollars!" Platt thought, These three guys know they're being assholes, but it's all in fun. This is the way Hollywood is supposed to be.

IN MARCH OF 1968, Paramount found itself with the opportunity to become the proud owner of the option on a 150-page manuscript by Mario Puzo called *The Mafia*, if only it could beat out Universal. Puzo waited uneasily in the outer office of Robert Evans, the studio's head of production. Puzo was a fat man with a passion for gambling and good cigars. As Evans recalls it, Puzo said, "I owe eleven Gs bad. If I don't come up with it, I'll have a broken arm.' I didn't even want to read it. I said, 'Here's twelve thousand five hundred, write the fuckin' thing.' "*

Puzo never heard from Paramount again. Evans, according to his number two, Peter Bart, "idolized gangsters, but he was fascinated with Jewish gangsters — Bugsy Siegel — not Italian ones." Moreover, distribution had turned thumbs-down. The *Brotherhood*, a Paramount mob picture with Kirk Douglas, had bombed in 1968. "There was no great enthusiasm for making *The Godfather*," recalls Albert S. Ruddy, who would become the producer. "That was the year they lost about $65, $70 million, which today would be like $250 million." Then *The Godfather* became a best-seller. Paramount perked up, but still wanted to do the movie on a small budget, $2, $3 million. Continues Ruddy, "I do believe they would not have been unhappy if the book had dropped off the best-seller list. But it wouldn't go away." When Universal offered Paramount $1 million for the option, Evans and company realized they might have something, and decided to go forward. Puzo was asked to write a script that updated the story, fill it with hippies and other contemporary references.

Director after director turned it down, including Bogdanovich. Evans and Bart screened mob movies, realized that they had all been written and directed by Jews. Evans concluded he needed an Italian if he were going to "smell the spaghetti," as he put it. Bart suggested Coppola, whom Bart had written about when he worked for the *New York Times* in the mid-'60s. "That's your esoteric bullshit coming out," snapped Evans. "The guy made three pictures: *You're a Big Boy Now*, artsy-fartsy, no business, *Finian's Rainbow*, a top Broadway musical he made into a disaster, and *Rain People*, which everyone rained on." But for Evans, the fact that Coppola was Italian was a big plus, and despite his reservations, he told Bart to go ahead.

Ironically, as much as Bart was finding it difficult to persuade Evans to hire Coppola, he was having as much trouble persuading Coppola to take the assignment. The director thought of himself as an artist. *The Godfather* was *Finian's Rainbow* all over again: a big best-seller, somebody else's material, and

* Puzo says this meeting never took place.

worse, material that was beneath him. Recalls Coppola, "I was into the New Wave and Fellini and, like all the kids of my age, we wanted to make those kinds of films. So the book represented the whole kind of idea I was trying to avoid in my life." Bart hammered him about his debts. He still owed $300,000 to Warners. "Francis, you're just a kid," he said. "You can't live your life this way. This could be a commercial movie. It'd be irresponsible of you not to do it." Coppola got angry, became more intransigent. Evans couldn't believe it: "He can't get a cartoon made in this town, yet he doesn't want to make *The Godfather*."

But Bart was right; the debt to Warners hung heavily upon the young director. And he owed money elsewhere, to Roger Corman and others. Coppola was in the editing room where Lucas was recutting *THX* when the call came from Paramount. While he was waiting for Evans to come on the line, he turned to his friend and asked, "Should I do this?"

"I don't see any choice here, Francis," Lucas replied. "We're in debt, Warners wants their money back, you need a job. I think you should do it. Survival is the key thing here." Adds Lucas now, "For him, it wasn't really, Should I do this movie? It was, Can I really accept the fact that the dream of Zoetrope, of this alternative studio, all this stuff we'd been talking about for the last two years—failed? Because at that point, Zoetrope fell apart."

But Evans and Bart still had to sell Coppola to their boss, Gulf + Western head Charles Bluhdorn, and Stanley Jaffe, president of the company, who was the son of Columbia president Leo Jaffe. Evans called Bluhdorn in New York. "Look, this kid is coming east, just listen to him for half an hour."

"Vat is dis fucking guy, vaddid he do in his last fucking picture?" screamed Charlie, an Austrian immigrant.

"His last picture was *Finian's Rainbow*."

"How dare you zend me *Phhinian's* fucking *Rainbow!* Id vas disgusting piece of shit."

Francis went to New York, talked to Bluhdorn. Two days later, Bart got the call. "Da kid's a brilliant kid, he talked great line, but can he direct?" asked Bluhdorn.

"Trust me, Charlie; he can direct."

UNLIKE STEVE ROSS at Warners, Charlie Bluhdorn soon took a very personal interest in the studio Gulf + Western had acquired back in the fall of 1966. He was thirty-nine when he replaced Paramount chairman Adolph Zukor. (Mel Brooks would refer to the corporate mother ship as Engulf and Devour.) Bluhdorn was a balding, choleric man who wore Wasserman-like Groucho glasses clamped down on a broad nose. His mouth was filled with large, square teeth, like Scrabble tiles. Everyone who worked for him was certain he was Jewish, but if so he took great pains to conceal it. Mob lawyer Sidney Korshak told Evans that his sister went to synagogue with Bluhdorn in Chicago, but the Gulf + Western chief always professed ignorance of Jewish holidays.

Bluhdorn was a brilliant financier who played the commodities market like a violin. After a meeting, he would pound the table, announce, "Vile ve've been zidding here, I made more money on sugar dan Paramount made all year." He had an infectious laugh, and could be extremely charming when he wanted to be, but mostly he screamed in a guttural accent, terrifying his minions. They took pleasure in mimicking his Hitlerian inflections, referring to him as "Mein Führer" behind his back. One executive recalls that when his boss lost his temper, which was often, "these little white foamy stalagmite, stalactite type things appeared on both sides of his mouth. I thought, Does he have rabies?"

Bluhdorn had vast holdings in sugar and cattle in the Dominican Republic, where he reigned like a medieval lord. He had his own landing strip, where the company Gulfstream would sit in readiness, and where his own armed guards patrolled. When Gulf + Western acquired South Puerto Rican Sugar, Bluhdorn got a resort, Casa de Campo, along with it. Later in the decade, Barry Diller, who would head Paramount, encouraged him to develop it. Bluhdorn built an elaborate guest compound for the studio's use, called Casa de Paramount. When visitors arrived, a phalanx of maids, gardeners, and guards dressed in white posted themselves around the circular driveway to greet them. Don Simpson, who became head of production in the late '70s, recalls traveling down there with Bluhdorn. He says, "Charlie had these black slaves in white linen uniforms with gold braid serving him drinks. It was evident that they wanted to slit his throat. I tried to make friends with the servants, like, 'By the way I'm not with him. When the revolution comes, spare me; I'm poor.'"

The Gulf + Western chief was a man about whom it was impossible to be neutral, and reactions to him ran the gamut from devotion to fear and loathing. Evans swore by him, but to Peter Bart, "He was a thug, a terrible person, an absolutely unmitigated awful human being." And Simpson says, "He was a mean, despicable, unethical, evil man, who lived too long. He was scary because he always had a sharp stick and unless you batted it away and said, 'Fuck you,' he'd poke you until you bled to death. He was a man who clearly had a chemical imbalance. He had no problem breaking the law. He was a criminal." Simpson apparently kept his feelings to himself while Bluhdorn was alive. He was respectful to a fault in Bluhdorn's presence. Indeed, there was a rank smell about Paramount in those days; it was better not to know too much. Bluhdorn seemed to have few qualms about turning to gray money. He was under investigation by the SEC throughout the '70s, and he was close to Korshak, the real Godfather of Hollywood.

Bluhdorn's head of distribution was Frank Yablans. Yablans had earned a reputation as someone who could squeeze a profit out of the worst clinkers Paramount released, and when he had something to work with, he made miracles. He had gotten a lot of the credit for *Love Story*, with its gnomic, but effective tag line: "Love means never having to say you're sorry."

Yablans was the son of an immigrant Brooklyn cabbie who was still plying his trade while Frank was climbing the Paramount ladder. Frank liked to say he graduated from the "Brooklyn Street Corner School of Economics." He was short and tough, a street kid quick on his feet with a wicked sense of humor he used as a bludgeon. He had an enormous ego. Says Friedkin, who got to know him later, "Frank had the biggest Napoleonic complex of anyone short of Napoleon." As Al Ruddy puts it, he was "a bully, crass, corny, and loud, just trying to beat the shit out of everybody. Frank was truly, 'It's me baby, I can write, produce, direct, I know more than anyone in the history of Hollywood.' He believed everyone was full of shit but him."

To compensate for his diminutive stature, Yablans turned his office in the Gulf + Western Building on Columbus Circle into a split-level affair. Staring down from the platform on which his desk sat, he had a six-inch advantage on people sitting on the other side. In the days before the women's movement, Yablans would think nothing of walking past one of his female employees saying, "Nice tits today, honey." But he was liked because he was forthright and direct, you knew where you stood. He ran things like a family business, was "Frank" to the troops, knew everyone by their first names. He was always accessible, always open to ideas.

Predictably enough, beneath Yablans's bluster was a man filled with self-loathing. Bart recalls, "We were in London together, going out for dinner. I picked up Frank in his room. He was finished dressing, looking at himself in the mirror, and he said, 'You know, I'm a really ugly man, I'm a homely fat Jewish man.' He was furious at Evans because he was a great-looking guy and all the girls were buzzing around him."

Bluhdorn liked Yablans. They were cut from the same cloth, both willing to go for the jugular. It was management by fear and testosterone. The two men would trade extravagant insults, no holds barred. Yablans would think nothing of calling his boss a Nazi. He says, "Charlie was a very sinister, Machiavellian kind of guy. You went along with him, or you fought him. I chose to fight him, because if I didn't, he'd run amok. But either way you lost." After one particularly vitriolic exchange, Bluhdorn sent Yablans a case of mouthwash.

The fights were often over money. Yablans says, "Me and Evans had a father-son relationship with him. But he had that Eastern European mentality: 'I'll pay your rent, I'll buy you a car, anything you want, so long as you're under my thumb.' The minute you try to break free, he'd turn on you like a jackal. Had we done for Steve Ross what we did for Charlie Bluhdorn, we'd be worth together a billion dollars today. Charlie was so cheap, I said, 'Charlie, your logo should be two pushcarts, crossed. You're a peddler, that's all you are.' "

As his head of production, Bluhdorn, in a typically impulsive move, hired Evans, a failed actor (his claim to fame was the role of a matador in *The Sun Also Rises* and a featured part in *The Fiend Who Walked the West*), totally devoid of qualifications. According to Howard Koch, Sr., whom Evans replaced in 1966, Evans had cozied up to Bluhdorn's French wife, Yvette, who told her husband, "He's gorgeous. We've got to get a good-looking guy, real sexy, to run the company." Possibly, Bluhdorn hired Evans because he didn't care very much what happened to the studio, which accounted for no more than 5 percent of Gulf + Western's revenues. In any event, he was a gambling man, and he gambled on Evans, telling him, "The Paramount caca in charge there now is ninety years old. He saw *Alfie* and couldn't even hear it." People in the business regarded Evans's appointment as bizarre, even by Hollywood standards. "What a joke," said BBS's Steve Blauner. "I figured he was fucking Bluhdorn or something."

Evans was one of the great crash-and-burn stories of the '70s, but then he was only thirty-six, brash and ambitious, and indeed strikingly good-looking, in a Robert Wagner sort of way, a permanent tan, dazzling white teeth, hair slicked back, and later, long and casually tangled. The son of a Riverside Drive dentist (he grew up in the same building as Rafelson), Evans was born on June 29, 1930, and had been in the clothing business with his brother, Charles. (When Bluhdorn was angry, he used to refer to Evans as "that pants cutter.") Evans was very much the ladies' man, a sharp dresser given to sartorial clichés like suede jeans and gold chains. Had he not had the good fortune to meet Bluhdorn, he might well have spent his youth as a gigolo, squiring dowagers around the spas of Europe. His voice was hoarse and gravelly, sounded like he had swallowed ground glass, and he mumbled.

Evans evinced a peculiar mixture of treacly Hallmark Card sentimentality that would flower in his romance with Ali MacGraw, and a self-destructive darkness that would lead him into murky waters way over his head. A natural-born patsy, he was a mob groupie, proud of his close friendship with Korshak, who was his lawyer. But for all his vanity and foolishness, Evans was a warm, loyal, and generous man. Says Ruddy, "Bob wasn't egocentric in the way Frank was egocentric. Bob wanted to be seen with beautiful women, had wall-to-wall pictures of himself with every actor who ever came to town. But there was a softness to Bob. He was basically a gentle person." Evans got away with a lot because he was never threatening to those above him. He had a real talent, often exercised, for eating crow. When Evans did damage, it was more often to himself.

For $290,000 or so Paramount bought Evans a sixteen-room Regency house with an egg-shaped pool protected by one-hundred-foot eucalyptus trees and high walls in Beverly Hills. Out front stood a two-hundred-year-old sycamore, and a thousand ornamental rose bushes sprouted from beds around the house. He called it Woodland, and it became his pride and joy. At the high tide of his success, he played tennis with Nicholson, Dustin Hoffman, Henry Kissinger, Ted Kennedy, John Tunney and his other trophy friends. He attracted players like Jimmy Connors and Pancho González, who teamed up with him in doubles. He would bet on the matches, but he still had to serve every fourth time, and always lost.

Evans had a genius for self-promotion. Joyce Haber had replaced Hedda Hopper at the *Los Angeles Times*. Evans provided paragraphs of material for her column to her over the phone. She was a regular at his dinner table. He practically turned the studio publicity head into his own personal press agent. Whenever he visited the set of one of his pictures, he brought the production to a halt so he could pose with the stars.

Most of all, Evans liked the company of women, especially models, actresses, and hookers. When he woke up in the morning, he could never remember their names. He had a housekeeper who brought him breakfast in bed — black coffee and a piece of cheesecake. Under the cake dish she put a piece of paper with the name of the girl. It is said he gave away his pajamas to the girls as souvenirs. Everyone suspected that Evans supplied Bluhdorn with women. Says an executive who worked at the studio in those days, "At Bob's house there was pussy all around the place. Bluhdorn bought Paramount 'cause he figured it was an easy way to get laid."

On October 24, 1969, Evans wedded Ali MacGraw, whom *Love Story* would make into a star. Bart didn't like her. "Ali was one of these people who felt like she had to decorate herself like a '60s person," he says. "She was about as much a '60s person as Leona Helmsley. She was materialistic, self-aggrandizing, and basically would fuck any actor she played opposite of." But on the surface it was one of those storybook marriages that the press loves. Evans seemed to have it all.

In the light of later events, particularly his addiction to cocaine, it is easy to underestimate Evans, but he was an extremely effective executive for nearly a decade and presided over Paramount's renaissance. "You have no idea what a great mind Evans was in those days," says Friedkin. "Sharp, attentive. The drugs have just destroyed it." Evans was a great packager, a great stroker of talent. He gave his actors, writers, and directors parties when they got married or divorced, he got them lawyers, got them laid, babied them, solved their problems. "You were dealing with a guy who was swimming in the same pool, and it gave you a sense of community," says Buck Henry. "Calley was the same way. Those guys didn't seem to be at the service of Wall Street. They seemed to be in the service of the filmmaker, and it made a huge difference."

Bluhdorn's penchant for making deals personally was making a mess of things, and Paramount had something like $100 million tied up in five or six productions, movies like *Darling Lili*, *Catch-22*, and *The Molly Maguires*, all of which bombed. To save money, the executive offices were moved to a modest building at 202 North Canon Drive in Beverly Hills. Evans wanted to be near his favorite restaurant, the Bistro, in which Korshak held a major interest.

Evans and Bart began to sing the same song as Calley and Co.; they began to put their money on directors. "Everybody was looking for an answer," says Bart. "One answer seemed to be, if you found a brilliant young director with a vision, go with him. It was Kubrick, more than anybody, that had an impact on us."

After the move to Canon Drive, the studio's luck changed. With Bluhdorn chastened, the run of flops became a run of hits: *Romeo and Juliet*, *The Odd Couple*, *Plaza Suite*, *Rosemary's Baby*, *Love Story*. Between Bluhdorn, Jaffe, Yablans, and Evans, Paramount was a loony bin of big personalities, egos, and tempers. The studio worker bees used to refer to them as "the Manson family." It was amazing any pictures got made at all, but they were smart and they all loved movies. By 1971, Paramount was head of the studio class.

COPPOLA AND BOGDANOVICH were the same age. Francis was born on April 7, 1939, in Detroit, while dad Carmine was playing the flute on the *Ford Sunday Evening Hour* radio show; thus his middle name. He was sandwiched between his older brother, August, who was brilliant and handsome, the Renaissance prince, and young Talia, his father's favorite. Francis recalled that his mother would say, " 'Augie's the bright one, Tallie's the beautiful one, Francie's the affectionate one.' And it was true."

Carmine had been a child prodigy, whose instrument was the flute. He hit his peak in his twenties, and went downhill from there, once bottoming out by playing the piccolo at the track with a Nedick's hat on his head. Like many people who flee from what they're best at, Carmine took his talent for the flute for granted, and longed to spread his wings, compose symphonies or conduct opera.

Carmine was the "maestro," and his wife, Italia, catered to his every whim. The emotional life of his family turned on what Francis later called the "tragedy" of his father's career. Coppola once said of his father, he was "a frustrated man who hated anybody who was successful." Remembers Talia, "All of us felt guilty, about being young, about having our own lives. I thought, How can I go to school, how can I be happy, how can I be anything, with my poor father not doing well. It's a terrible thing when you feel that your success is occurring when someone close to you is experiencing failure."

Carmine and Italia did not want any of their children to go into the arts.

"For my generation, the biggest thing for Italians was to be a doctor, a lawyer, an engineer, get married," says Tallie. "In high school, when Francis wanted money to direct a film with a little Kodak camera, my mother wouldn't give it to him, and I went to the janitor, who gave me a quarter to help him."

Because the family moved from city to city, Coppola was the perennial new kid in class, with a girl's name, yet, the class donkey. Truly an unprepossessing adolescent, he was skinny and graceless, with floppy ears, a cleft chin, and glasses. He compared himself to Ichabod Crane, was eaten up with self-loathing, mortified by an imagined physical anomaly. "I used to go into school with my glasses off and face covered, I was so embarrassed about my lower lip," he said. "My mother wanted me to get a lip job to make my lips skinny."

When he was eight or nine and living in Jamaica, Queens, Francis was struck by polio. He spent nearly a year in bed with his legs paralyzed, in quarantine. Polio was a killer, and none of his friends could or would visit him. Tallie remembers them crossing the street to avoid her. "All the kids just vanished," Francis recalls. "I basically didn't see a kid for a year and a half." The family was terrified. "I remember my mother and father crying," he continues. "I had never seen my father cry before. I was shocked when I tried to stand up and I couldn't. They sent me off to some hospital in Jamaica. The kids were three high in beds in the hallways and the bathrooms. My doctor said, 'You know, you're a young soldier, and you have to understand that you're not going to be able to walk again.' "

Francis recovered from his illness, but he never regained his agility. One leg was shorter than the other, and he felt branded. He says, "A lot of my getting into the movie business stems from me feeling this isolation, and since I wasn't good at sports anymore, I gravitated to the theater, because theater, like athletics, is something that you do after school and you make friends and you have parties."

Coppola graduated from Hofstra College at the end of the '50s, and enrolled in UCLA Film School. In 1963 he wrote and directed *Dementia 13* for Roger Corman in Ireland. Even then, before the '60s really took hold, his friends at UCLA were scandalized. "I was called a cop-out because I was willing to compromise," he remembered. On the set, he ran into a friend of a friend, Eleanor Neil, an artist and a tapestry-maker. With a pale, WASPy look and long brown hair parted in the middle, she was a bit of a hippie, wore a leather Eisenhower jacket, beads, and long skirts with odd combinations of color, purples and oranges. She was everything he was not, the porcelain Polly Platt to his olive-skinned Bogdanovich, and he hired her as the art director. He was three years her junior. They were married in February 1963.

The same year, producer Ray Stark hired Coppola, then twenty-four, to rewrite *Reflections in a Golden Eye*. He quickly became the house writer for Seven Arts, working on scripts for pictures like *This Property Is Condemned*, and *Is Paris Burning?* He was filled with dreams, but with an ambivalence that would run through his career, he expressed a qualified willingness to work within the system. "The way to come to power is not always to merely challenge the establishment, but first to make a place in it and then challenge and double-cross the establishment," he said. "You have to set your sights and be unscrupulous."

In 1966, he began working on a script for a movie of his own, *You're a Big Boy Now.* Bored with the hack work he was doing for Seven Arts, he quit. Using the tricks he had learned from Corman, and breaking all the rules, Coppola shot *You're a Big Boy Now* the same year at the tender age of twenty-seven. Like the Monkees, it was either a homage to, or rip-off of, Richard Lester's *A Hard Day's Night,* depending on your point of view. After he had finished, Coppola walked the streets of New York with his head high and chest out, feeling pretty good about himself. Then, someone told him, "There's another young director who's made a feature, and he's only twenty-six." "What?" screamed Francis in dismay. "I was so shocked. It was Willie Friedkin." When Coppola's film opened in March of 1967, the *L.A. Times*'s Charles Champlin wrote words that expressed Coppola's innermost longings: *You're a Big Boy Now* "is one of those rare American things, what the Europeans call an *auteur* film."

Coppola installed himself and Eleanor in an A frame in Mandeville Canyon, and bought a Jaguar. Friedkin was a frequent visitor, and Francis tried to fix him up with Tallie. Recalls Friedkin, "Francis was always the first to hear about a new piece of equipment. He bought a new lightweight Arriflex, said, 'Look at this, this is what Godard uses and this is how we're all gonna make films someday, and all this big shit is gonna disappear and we're gonna be free to tell our stories in the street.' "

In the fall of 1970, Coppola met Martin Scorsese at the Sorrento Film Festival. Scorsese was an intense kid from New York who had an encyclopedic knowledge of film and spit out his words like machine-gun bullets. He was small, bearded, and long-haired. Francis — large, bearded, long-haired, and also from New York — looked like his older brother. The two men became fast friends.

WOODSTOCK, released in 1970, had become such a big hit for the new Warners management that Fred Weintraub tried to repeat the trick by dropping a million or so dollars on a bunch of hippie rockers to drive across the country in a caravan of buses, giving free concerts and generally doing their thing, while a crew filmed their antics. The first editor had mucked it up, and Weintraub summoned Scorsese, whom he had met when the young film school graduate from New York was editing *Woodstock,* to recut it.

When he arrived in January 1971, Scorsese came down with a serious case of culture shock. "I had a really hard time adjusting to L.A.," he recalls. "Even living by myself. I was basically a kid, very sheltered. Food, I had no idea. Driving, forget it." The freeways terrified him. He drove his 1960 white Corvette on local streets only. His asthma got worse. He was in and out of the hospital, couldn't go into a room in which someone was smoking, kept an oxygen tank by his bed. "I never really got much sleep at night because of waking up coughing," he recalls. "I had mounds of tissues around the bed in the morning. By the time I got past an attack in the middle of the night, took an asthma pill and fell into a really deep, peaceful sleep, it was time to get up again. So I was always a little cranky, never quite all there. Wherever I went, I was always late."

Scorsese medicated himself with an inhaler, and he gained a lot of weight as a result of the junk food he was eating and the cortisone he was taking. Says Don Simpson, who met him on the Warners lot, "What he was taking was basically speed. Marty was always saying, 'Here, you want a hit of this?' One hit, you were just flying. I finally realized why he was so hyper, because he had the inhaler to his nose day and night, which is why he could stay up for days on end talking about movies and music, more about music than movies. He had this rock'n'roll head, knew every lyric and every title. He understood that the music was really a critical aspect of the zeitgeist of the times."

The only two people Scorsese knew in L.A. were John Cassavetes and Brian De Palma. Scorsese had met De Palma at NYU, the summer of 1965, the year *The Sound of Music* cleaned up at the box office. The two men had adjacent editing stalls. De Palma was already a legend for the struggling filmmakers in New York. He had several independent features under his belt — *Greetings* and *Hi, Mom!*, featuring a very young Robert De Niro. When Weintraub called him in the spring of 1970 and asked him to direct a picture for Warners called *Get to Know Your Rabbit*, the director joined the exodus to L.A. He dropped in on Jennifer Salt, a young actress and friend he had used in a couple of movies. (She was the daughter of blacklisted screenwriter Waldo Salt, who wrote *Midnight Cowboy*.) Salt was staying with actress Jill Clayburgh, who was in town from New York doing *Othello* at the Mark Taper Forum. Salt recalls, "We were all sitting on the beach, and I said, 'I'm going to move out here.' Brian said, 'Me too. Come on, let's take this town by storm.' The feeling was, we were kids and we were going to take over Hollywood."

Get to Know Your Rabbit starred Tommy Smothers. It was alike in spirit to *Greetings*, another installment in the mini-cycle of dropout films that included *A Thousand Clowns* and *The Trip*, and seemed to suit De Palma's temperament. But the New Hollywood directors were not proving so easy for the studios to assimilate. Brian knew *Rabbit* wasn't working, wanted another week to shoot. Warners said, "You've had your time, forget it." De Palma wanted to innovate, use 16mm footage. Warners told him he was crazy, "We don't do things that way here." Recalls Scorsese, who was on the lot at the same time, "We were fighting to open up the form. Our idea was, the lighter the camera the better. You could move faster, break down a location faster, get the lights off the ceiling faster. We weren't equipped to shoot in studios, didn't come from the studio tradition."

Warners was not sympathetic. "Brian De Palma was a monster," says Calley. He threw him off the picture, and it was recut and released, just barely, in 1972. Says De Palma, "I always felt Warners had a certain kind of elitist arrogance to it that started with Calley and Ashley—these guys were somewhere in the ether. They talked to Stanley Kubrick and Mike Nichols, and we were obviously not important."

THE DAY AFTER Bluhdorn hired Coppola to direct *The Godfather* in 1970, the director and family celebrated by sailing for Europe on the *Michelangelo* with no more than $400 and a bunch of credit cards belonging to his assistant, Mona Skager. He commandeered the bar on the ship as his office, broke down the book, and pasted the pages all over the windows.

The studio had assigned the film to Al Ruddy, who, with his associate producer, Gray Frederickson, a bluff, fun-loving Oklahoman, had done another *Easy Rider* rip-off, *Little Fauss and Big Halsy*, the only movie Paramount had produced in recent memory that had come in under budget. Ruddy discovered that Coppola was not so pliable as the studio had assumed. The young director fought for period setting (the '40s, which was the time frame in the novel), fought to shoot in New York, fought for a larger budget—and won. His stubborn refusal to cave in to Paramount's demands, together with the book's long-term lease on the best-seller list, brought the studio around, transformed the film from a low-budget quickie into something very different.

After hitting a wall with BBS, Fred Roos had gravitated to Coppola, whom he helped with the casting. Roos had a positive genius for matching the right face in the right role, and he too planned to draw heavily on the pool of New York theater– and TV-trained ethnic actors for *The Godfather*. He and Coppola used a lot of nonactors as well, just because they looked right, like a former wrestler, Lenny Montana, known as the Zebra Kid, just out of New York's Rikers Island prison, who played Luca Brasi. Coppola, like Altman, like Bogdanovich, like the other New Hollywood kids, didn't care about marquee names. "I was not looking for stars," he says. "I was looking for people who would be believable to me as real Italian-Americans, who don't talka lika Luigi, and have New York accents as opposed to Italian accents."

Evans, who was a celebrity himself, did believe in stars, and as *The Godfather*'s profile rose, he took a sudden interest in the casting. After all, this was a studio picture, Coppola was a nobody, a pisher, and Evans expected to call the shots the same way he had on *Love Story* and his other movies. But even so, such was the sense of entitlement enjoyed by the directors of this generation, that Evans was unable to impose his whim even on someone as powerless as Coppola. The casting of *The Godfather* was a battle between the Old Hollywood approach of Evans, and the New Hollywood ideas of Coppola. Everyone had a candidate for every part, and no one seemed to have the ultimate authority.

According to James Caan, who had appeared in *The Rain People*, Coppola's initial wish list consisted of himself for Sonny, Robert Duvall for Hagen, and Al Pacino for Michael. Pacino in particular was anathema to Evans. Although *The Godfather* was written as an ensemble piece, it was Michael who was going to have to carry the picture, and Evans worried that Pacino couldn't do it. He was unknown, short, and looked no more like a movie star than Michael J. Pollard or Gene Hackman. Evans suggested Redford, Beatty, Nicholson, even his pal Alain Delon, and kept referring to Pacino as "that little dwarf." Recalls Coppola, "They told me Al was too scruffy and looked too much like a gutter rat to play a college boy." Every time Coppola finished a conversation with Evans, he hammered the phone, smashing it with the receiver. Pacino did little to help his own cause. Indeed, the young actor impressed nobody but Francis. While Pacino waited to see the director at the Zoetrope offices on Folsom Street, he wore a groove in the carpet nervously pacing around the pool table. He refused to look anyone in the eye, keeping his gaze cast down at the floor.

Meanwhile, Coppola began scouting locations. He ate pasta at the table of Scorsese's mother and father in Little Italy. "He recorded my father's voice to listen to the accent," Marty recalled. "My mother was constantly giving him casting suggestions. One night at dinner she told him she wanted Richard Conte in the picture, and he put him in. Another time, she asked him how many days he had to shoot, and he said, 'A hundred days.' She said, 'That's not enough.' I said. 'Mom, don't get him terrified!' "

But the casting problems wouldn't go away. Decisions were made and unmade. Who would play the Don himself? Coppola wanted Marlon Brando, but Brando was out of favor. His antics in *Mutiny on the Bounty* were legendary —he was reputed to have given the clap to half the women on Tahiti, where the film was shot. He was hugely overweight, and worse, his most recent picture, Gillo Pontecorvo's *Burn!*, had flopped.

Undismayed, Coppola tried to sell Brando to the Paramount executives at a fractious meeting at the headquarters of Gulf + Western in New York. When he brought up Brando's name, Stanley Jaffe, prematurely bald and pugnacious, slammed his fist on the table and announced that the actor would never play the Don as long as he was head of Paramount Pictures. Whereupon the director appeared to have an epileptic fit, and dramatically collapsed in a heap on the floor, as if rendered senseless by the stupidity of Jaffe's diktat.

Shaken, Jaffe gave in. Coppola videotaped Brando transforming himself into

Don Corleone by putting Kleenex in his mouth and shoe polish on his hair. "I knew it was a waste of energy to talk to Ruddy, even Evans, and that it was Bluhdorn who didn't want him, so I went to New York," the director recalls. He set up a half-inch videotape playback machine on Bluhdorn's conference room table and went into his office and said, "Could I just see Mr. Bluhdorn a minute?"

"Francis, vat are you dooink?" Bluhdorn poked his head into the conference room and looked at the video screen, saw Brando putting up his blond hair, and barked, "No! No! Absolutely not, I don't vant a crazy guy!" and started to leave the room. But he turned back for a moment, just when Brando began to shrink in his skin like a deflated balloon. He gasped, "Who are ve vatchink? Who is dis olt guinea? Dat's terr-iff-ic!" Coppola got his man.

Francis and George Lucas discussed the pressures that the studio was exerting on Francis. George said, "Don't try to make this into one of your films. Just roll over and let them do it to you. Trying to win a game of poker with the devil, they'll crush you, and you won't get the money you need to make the films we want." But it was too late. Coppola was deeply immersed in Mafia lore, had scouted locations, had made the picture his own. And then there was the biggest incentive: to fuck Evans. According to Roos, "Early on, Francis said about Evans, 'This guy's an idiot. Ninety percent of what he says is stupid.' He handled him. Tolerated him."

Eventually, Evans gave in. "Four months later, after all this tension, I ended up with my cast, Brando and Pacino," Coppola says. "If I hadn't've fought, I would have made a movie with Ernest Borgnine and Ryan O'Neal set in the '70s." But Coppola was exhausted. Recalls Bart, "Evans made Francis's life miserable. Bob took his preparation time shooting fucking tests. Francis didn't have time to think about the movie, the locations."

Paramount was still fighting to keep the budget low. The lead actors were paid only $35,000 each. Brando, who was desperate for the role, was paid $50,000, with some net points thrown in. Coppola only received $110,000 and six points (6 percent of the net).

Ellie, pregnant with Sophia, her third child, relocated to New York to be with Francis in a tiny apartment on West End Avenue. Coppola sat down with Dean Tavoularis and Gordon Willis, the DP, to plan the visual style of the picture which, they decided, would be classic in its simplicity. "There weren't a lot of contemporary mechanics introduced, like helicopters and zoom lenses," says Willis. "It was a tableau form of moviemaking, where the actors move in and out of frame, very straightforward. It was supposed to feel like a period piece." The director recalls, "We talked about the contrast of good and evil, light and dark, how we'd start out with a black sheet of paper and paint in the light. The camera would never move unless the people were moving."

But the dark, underlit look of the film was daring and unconventional. The wisdom of the day at the studios was that every picture had to be brightly lit. As Willis put it, "Screens were so blitzed with light that you could see into every corner of every toilet and closet on the set," adding, "I'd always hear, 'They have to be able to see it in the drive-ins.'" But Willis was going to do it differently. He insists, "There was no discussion of lighting. I just did what I felt like doing. The design came out of the juxtaposition of the bright, cheerful garden party wedding that was going on outside, and the underbelly in this dark house. I used overhead lighting because the Don was the personification of evil, and I didn't always want the audience to look into his eyes, see what he was thinking. I just wanted to keep him dark."

The Godfather began production on March 29, 1971, while Bogdanovich was editing *Picture Show*, and Altman was finishing up *McCabe*. To all appearances, Coppola did not have much going for him. "Francis's credentials at that point, as a director, were zip," recalls Steve Kesten, the first AD, who was later let go, a victim of palace intrigue. "He was at the bottom of the abyss." The tough New York crew was used to working down and dirty for the likes of Kazan, Lumet, and Penn. Coppola struck them as indecisive. "Running a set means you gotta be the guy that makes it go forward," continues Kesten. "And it just wasn't happening. Nothing got done. Francis was always having to be nudged along." One day they were location scouting on lower Fifth Avenue. Suddenly Francis disappeared into Polk's, a famous hobby store, and spent the afternoon buying toys with money he didn't have. Every morning he would close the set and rehearse the actors till noon, leaving the crew sitting around cleaning their nails. This left only half a day for the actual shooting.

Pacino twisted his ankle during the scene where Michael shoots Sollazzo, and by the end of the first week, Coppola was already behind. He was rewriting the script at night, sometimes during the day between setups, creating chaos with the production schedule. Actors showed up who had been written out of scenes and never notified. Coppola recalls, "It had gone terribly, and I was like in deep, deep, deep trouble because I hadn't finished the hospital scene where McCluskey punches Michael. And they didn't like the rushes."

Indeed, as Willis puts it, "When that dark stuff started to appear on the screen, it seemed a little scary to people who were used to looking at Doris Day movies." The dailies were so dark the Paramount execs could make out nothing more than silhouettes. No one had ever sent in rushes like this before. Says Coppola's sister, Talia Shire, who played Connie Corleone, "They were black, looked like shit." Evans asked Bart, "What's on the screen? Do I have my shades on?"

Brando arrived at the beginning of the second week. Continues Coppola, "They hated Brando, said they couldn't understand him." Evans asked, "Is this movie gonna have subtitles?" Recalls producer Gray Frederickson, "The scene when Brando sees the body of Sonny Corleone, says, 'Look what they've done to my boy,' Evans told Ruddy, 'This kid's an imbecile, he can't even get a performance out of Marlon Brando, that's the most overacted, worst played scene I've ever seen.'"

Most films used professional extras; the same faces would turn up again and again, looking like cookie cutouts. Francis didn't want to use professionals, because he didn't want *The Godfather* to look like other movies. He wanted the faces to look authentic, so he spent a lot of time casting the extras. Says Frederickson, "That was not the way Hollywood had ever done things before, and it freaked them out. Extras were extras. To the studio, it was just time wasted." The day they shot Clemenza with the cannoli, Jack Ballard, Paramount's head of physical production, told Francis, "If you don't finish on time today, you're not gonna come to work tomorrow." Rumors flew that, indeed, Coppola was going to be fired.

Al Ruddy was staying at Frederickson's apartment in New York, and Frederickson overheard his conversations with Evans. He warned Coppola that he was about to be replaced. Francis won a few days' respite, because nobody — not Evans, not Ruddy, not Jaffe — wanted to be the one to fire him. He had just won an Oscar for writing *Patton*, and somehow he managed to hang on to his job.

Nevertheless, his problems continued. Coppola clashed repeatedly with his DP. He created so much turmoil and chaos on the set that strong-willed individuals were always tempted to step in to make sure the picture got made. Willis was a formidable presence, a man used to getting his own way, and like many cinematographers, wanted to be a director — the so-called DP disease. He shared the widely held conviction that Coppola did not know what he was doing. "It was hard for Francis because everybody was trying to pull his pants off," says Willis. "He was not well schooled in that kind of moviemaking. He had only done some kind of on-the-road running-around kind of stuff." He adds, "I was like Hitler. If anybody was doing the right thing to get this movie made from day to day, it was me." He insisted that the actors make their marks, because the light levels were so low that if they missed them, they'd be out of focus, even invisible. Willis accused Coppola of abandoning the careful preparations they had agreed on and tossing up the deck every morning when he came to the set to see where the cards would fall. "I like to lay out a thing and make it work, with discipline," he said. "Francis's attitude is more like, 'I'll set my clothes on fire — if I can make it to the other side of the room it'll be spectacular.' You can't shoot a whole movie hoping for happy accidents. What you get is one big bad accident."

Willis worked slowly and meticulously, which Francis, who was under brutal pressure from the studio to make up for lost time, found infuriating. He had grown up in the theater, and he liked and cosseted actors, was not going to straitjacket them to please the DP. Willis "hates and misuses actors," he complained. "I said 'They're not mechanics, they're artists.' Gordy acted like a football player stuck with a bunch of fag actors."

Scorsese dropped by the set when Coppola was shooting the funeral of the Don. He recalls, "Francis just sat down on one of the tombstones in the graveyard and started crying." Things came to a head with Willis one day when Pacino took a wrong (unrehearsed) turn off a corridor in the Corleone house and blundered into darkness, a portion of the set that had not been lit. Francis wanted to know why not, why his actors couldn't have the freedom to go wherever they wanted.

Willis said, "Okay, but I'll have to relight, it'll take a while." Coppola shouted, "I want to shoot now." Willis stalked off the set, went to his trailer, and refused to come out. Francis, looking for the camera operator, Michael Chapman, bellowed, "I want somebody to operate right away." Chapman ran into the bathroom and locked the door. Realizing he couldn't get any of Willis's crew to lift a finger, Coppola screamed, "Why won't they let me make my movie?" and marched up to his office. Finding the door open, he slammed it closed, and then proceeded to pound his way through it with his feet and fists. The blows sounded like gunshots, and Fred Gallo, the AD, thought, Ohmigod, he's shot himself.

In this case, the old cliché turned out to be true. The tension between Coppola and Willis proved creative. Coppola relied on his DP to frame the shots. Coppola's strengths were writing dialogue, storytelling, and working with actors, not visual composition. Willis achieved a unique look — rich earth colors, buttery yellows and browns — that would go down in cinema history.

On top of everything else, the production had all kinds of problems with the Mafia. The Italian-American Friendship Association, headed by Mafia boss Joe Colombo, Sr., made life miserable for Coppola by blocking his access to key locations. Recalls Ruddy, "When I was in New York, I got the call from Evans to go see Colombo. He was hysterical: 'This guy called me up, he was threatening me, I told him *you* were producing the movie. He said, "When we go after a fish we cut off its head." You gotta go see this guy.' Evans hid out on the whole fuckin' movie. He went to Bermuda with Ali."

The Godfather wrapped in September 1971, after six months of shooting.

COPPOLA WAS ANXIOUS to funnel the post-production money into his ailing company; he convinced Paramount to let him edit in San Francisco. The day arrived when Francis had to screen his cut for Paramount in L.A. Evans had a bad back, and he had begun taking painkillers and other drugs to alleviate his distress. "He had a guy come in every day, one of these Dr. Feelgood guys, who gave him an injection, a vitamin shot — who knows what it was," says Bart. "I didn't believe they were vitamins, I believed they were amphetamines." Evans's butler, David Gilruth, wheeled him into the Paramount screening room on a hospital bed. He wore fine black silk pajamas and black velvet slippers with gold foxes brocaded on the toes. Coppola could tell when he was bored by what he was seeing, because he'd hear the buzz of the motor as the producer lowered the bed to take a nap.

Francis had brought his people — Murch, Roos, Frederickson — as well as Towne, who had helped him by providing — in a fine example of his allusive style — the key scene in which Don Corleone cedes power to Michael and the two men declare their love for each other while never directly mentioning it. Coppola paid Towne $3,000. He asked, "Do you want credit?" Towne joked, "Don't be ridiculous. I only wrote a couple of fuckin' scenes. If you win an Oscar, thank me."

Towne did not then know Evans. He took in the spectacle — the bed, the tassles, the black silk pajamas — thought, Do I really want to hear what this guy has to say? Evans started to hum, hummed for about three minutes, and then, as the lights went down, put his thumb into his mouth, where it remained for the next two hours and twenty-five minutes. Towne thought, If this man is running a studio, this industry must be in big trouble.

There are as many versions of what happened in that screening room as there were people there, proving the adage that success has many fathers, failure, none. According to Evans, he met with Francis after the screening, alone. "The picture stinks," Evans told him. "You shot a great film, where the fuck is it, in the kitchen with your spaghetti?"

Evans claims that against Coppola's wishes, he told Bluhdorn not to expect the picture for Christmas because it needed reediting. "I bent over too many times on this flick, Charlie, to take any more shit," he said. "The fat fuck shot a great film, but it ain't on the screen." According to Evans, Coppola went back to the editing room, complaining bitterly: "You're making this picture so long, Evans, half the people will be asleep before it's all over."

Coppola believed Evans was just waiting for an excuse to take the picture away from him. "The deal was, I was going to edit the movie in San Francisco, at Zoetrope," he says. "But he warned me that if it was more than two hours and fifteen minutes, he was going to yank the film to L.A. and cut it there, which I dreaded. So when we finished the film — it was about two hours and fifty minutes — I said, 'Let's cut it down as best we can.' So we lifted out the nonplot stuff and got it down to around two-twenty. When Evans saw it, he said, 'Where's all that stuff that makes it so great? I'm yanking the film to L.A.' So it was clear they were going to take the film to L.A. either way. We got to L.A. and we put all the footage back. I said, 'See? Isn't that better?' And he said, 'Yes, that's better.' "

"Evans felt that he was a filmmaker," says Calley. "His fantasy was him on a hospital bed in a projection room running reels of *The Godfather*, repairing the chaos that Francis had dropped on the world. It was stuff out of his fantasies of what Thalberg was like." But most of the people who were involved agree that Evans did support a long, three-hour version, and did lobby Yablans, who by now had succeeded Jaffe and become head of the studio, into postponing the release date, no small accomplishment.

But almost nobody agrees that Coppola preferred the short version. Says Yablans, "Evans behaved very badly. He had everybody believing Coppola had nothing to do with the movie! He created a myth that he produced *The Godfather*. Evans did not save *The Godfather*, Evans did not make *The Godfather*. That is a total figment of his imagination."

Evans's claims infuriated Francis, and would continue to rankle over the years. In 1983, when the two men were quarreling over *The Cotton Club*, Francis sent Evans a telegram Evans framed, in a red Lucite heart he hung in his bathroom. It read, in part: "Dear Bob Evans: I've been a real gentleman regarding your claims of involvement in *The Godfather*. I've never talked about you throwing out the Nino Rota music, your barring the casting of Pacino and Brando, etc., but continually your stupid blabbing about cutting *The Godfather* comes back to me and angers me for its ridiculous pomposity. You did nothing on *The Godfather* other than annoy me and slow it down."

Up to the end, Coppola believed he had a flop. He was living in Jimmy Caan's tiny maid's room in L.A. like an immigrant, sending his per diem back to his family in San Francisco. One day he went to see *The French Connection*, directed by his pal Friedkin, which had just opened with a big splash. He was accompanied by one of his assistant editors. On their way out of the theater, the assistant was raving about the movie. Coppola said, "Well, I guess I failed. I took a popular, pulpy, salacious novel, and turned it into a bunch'a guys sitting around in dark rooms talking." The assistant replied, "Yeah, I guess you did."

The Godfather was shown to exhibitors in New York, who were not happy about a three-hour movie. Its lengthy running time would halve the number of screenings per night and reduce their profits proportionately. Predictably, the screening went badly. On his way out of the theater, an old-timer turned to Francis, who was standing by the door and said, "Well, it ain't no *Love Story*." It was the darkness before the dawn. When the picture was shown again, only a week and a half later, Ruddy came out of a screening wreathed in smiles, saying, "Through the roof, baby, it's gonna be a monster hit!"

Meanwhile, strains were showing in the Evans-MacGraw marriage. Evans used to say, "I had a great sex life with Ali until I married her, and I couldn't fuck her once after our marriage. Couldn't get it up." Evans was afraid that MacGraw had been off screen too long, and he pressured her into doing *The Getaway*, to be directed by Sam Peckinpah. She was reluctant, preferring, claims Evans, to spend her time pressing flowers and writing poetry at Woodland. *The Getaway* started production in mid-January 1972, while Bob and Francis were still going at it.

Later he would claim that the time he was required to spend in the editing room cost him his marriage because he didn't have a chance to visit the set of the *The Getaway* where the flirtation between MacGraw and McQueen blossomed into a full-blown love affair and a seven-year relationship. Scoffs Yablans, "Evans pushed them together. He created the breakup with Ali, the public cuckolding. 'Bob, you're gonna lose your wife. These two are going at it hot and heavy.' 'It's just a passing thing—' He didn't give a shit. It didn't matter to him. He's a very strange man. He couldn't be married, couldn't live a normal, sane life. He drove her out."

EVANS'S EAGERNESS to claim credit for *The Godfather* reflected his growing unhappiness with his deal at Paramount. He had turned the studio around, he felt, and had not been properly rewarded. Didn't MGM give Thalberg a percentage of every film he made? More, he itched to see his name on the screen. Korshak negotiated a deal that gave Evans the right to produce a couple of pictures a year under his own name. And he would have points, a cut of the profits. Evans had no doubt which project would kick off his new deal: a phone-book-thick script he couldn't make heads or tails of, *Chinatown*.

Towne had conceived the idea, tailored to Nicholson and Jane Fonda, on the set of *Drive, He Said*. In the form of a Raymond Chandleresque detective story, it told the tale of how unscrupulous developers had made L.A. a boomtown by stealing water from powerless farmers. One day, during post-production on *The Godfather*, Evans called him. Over a meal at Dominick's he told Evans about the script he was working on. He had appropriated the title, *Chinatown*, from a chance remark made by a friend of his, a cop. "The one place I never really worked," said the cop, "was Chinatown. They really run their own culture."

Sketchy as it was, Evans loved it, particularly the title, which he thought was commercial, and the idea of Ali—forget Jane—starring opposite Nicholson. He offered him $25,000 to develop it. When *Chinatown* became a go project, Towne was paid $250,000 and 5 percent of the gross, a sweet deal for a writer, one of the reasons people liked Evans; he made them rich.

Evans wanted Roman Polanski to direct it. It had been three years since the Manson family had murdered Sharon Tate, but Polanski was still in the twilight zone. When he traveled, he carried a pair of Sharon's panties with him in his bag. He was living comfortably in Rome and less than eager to return to the scene of his wife's murder. "It was just bad memories," says Polanski. But Evans, assisted by Nicholson, Towne, and Dick Sylbert persisted, and he finally agreed.

Meanwhile, Evans was battling with his own studio. Bluhdorn and Yablans thought he was crazy to take on *Chinatown*, an elaborate, labyrinthine story. Bart reminded him, "I went through a picture with Bob Towne, *The Parallax View*, and it was a nightmare getting him to write. He's the most anal man who ever lived." But, he adds, "It was typical of Evans to bring the elements together and to get Towne to finish the fucking script. I certainly have to hand it him." Evans was dazzled by Towne's talent, or rather, what he perceived as his friends' high regard for Towne's talent. "I was star fucking," Evans confesses. "I believed there was some magic, if Jack liked it." Yablans may have thought Evans was crazy, but not so crazy that he didn't demand half of Evans's points. Or so Evans claims. (Yablans denies it.)

As usual, Towne was taking his time getting a completed script to Paramount. He came to Bart with the idea for a Tarzan story from the gorillas' point of view. Bart thought it was just a delaying tactic, and said, "I don't want to hear about it. Just finish *Chinatown*." So Towne called Calley, to whom he was very close, and set up the Tarzan project at Warners.

The script Towne finally handed in told a long, intricate tale, teeming with characters and scenes, chock-full of detail and small touches that limned the texture of America in the '30s. It contained a startling subplot, in which the theft of water and the rape of the land were mirrored by an unspeakable family crime, incest between Noah Cross, a rapacious developer, and his daughter, Evelyn. In the portrait of Cross, Towne may have been settling some family scores. Cross displayed a passing resemblance to Towne's own father, Lou. Both were developers. According to Towne's wife, Julie Payne, "Lou wanted him to go into the building business, which neither Robert nor his brother, Roger, had any interest in. I think his father hated Robert. He didn't pay any attention to him until he became successful."

Polanski finally arrived in L.A., and began house hunting. A friend found him one at the top of Benedict Canyon that required he drive past the Cielo Drive house with its split-rail fence still decorated with Christmas lights. Polanski had blocked it out, didn't even notice. Eventually, he rented George Montgomery's home in Beverly Hills.

According to Evans, Polanski's first reaction to the script was dismay. He exclaimed, "What kind of script is this? I should've stayed in Poland." He and Sylbert, who was slated to design the production, met with Towne at Nate 'n Al's, a delicatessen in Beverly Hills. "We said the script needed an enormous amount of work," recalls Polanski. "It was terribly long and convoluted, it had too many characters, it had a lot of episodic scenes which were not essential and were making it more confused. Bob was a little bit depressed after that."

THE BUZZ AROUND THE RELEASE of *The Godfather* was fierce. The film opened in New York in an unseasonably late snowstorm on March 15, 1972. The lines were six abreast, blocks long. Evans had been counting on Brando's appearance at the premiere to make it an event, but Brando ducked out at the last minute. Evans plugged the hole with Henry Kissinger, who flew up from

Washington. Ali flew in from the set of *The Getaway* in El Paso. As he waltzed MacGraw around the floor of the St. Regis roof, Evans was blissfully unaware of her affair with McQueen. "This was the best time of my life, but it was all a fraud," he says. "My wife was fucking another guy, and I had no idea. She had as much interest in being with me as being with a leper. She was looking at me and thinking of Steve McQueen's cock."

Coppola, his sense of himself as an artist deeply compromised by the very fact that he had agreed to direct this film in the first place, the feeling of violation compounded by his conviction that the movie was going to be a flop anyway, and still nursing the wounds inflicted by the struggle to bring the film to the screen, fled to Paris, where he wrote a script. His friends called, saying, "*The Godfather*'s a huge hit." He'd answer, "Oh, yeah, great," and turn back to his work.

The marketing campaign for *The Godfather* was traditional; the money was spent on print ads. The exhibition pattern, however, broke new ground, would change the way movies were distributed, paving the way for the ultimate destruction of the New Hollywood. Prior to *The Godfather*, pictures played first runs for a specified number of weeks before they went into their second and third runs. During the first run, they opened at one A screen in every market. The A screen had "clearance" over other A theaters in the vicinity, which meant that if a picture played a prime location, say, the National in Westwood, no other theater within a fifty-mile radius could book it for the length of the first run, which could last for a year or more. Then the picture worked its way down to the second- and third-run theaters. Moviegoers in Hollywood or the San Fernando Valley were expected to make the trek to Westwood. This was a good system from the director's point of view — the movies had plenty of time to find their audiences — but was less than desirable from the studio point of view. For one thing, the ad dollars were expended on the first run when the picture was playing a relatively small number of theaters, so by the time it got to the thousands of second- and third-run theaters, there was no advertising support. For another, the revenue from exhibitors trickled in slowly, over months, sometimes years. To Yablans's way of thinking, the studios were risking huge amounts of money, and in effect subsidizing the construction of new theaters with money that properly belonged to them and could have been collecting interest. He not only bullied the exhibitors into paying substantial amounts up front, often more than covering the costs of production, he also got a better split. In the case of *The Godfather*, Yablans says he got an unprecedented $25 to $30 million from the chains before the picture even opened, and a 90/10 split (in favor of Paramount) for the first twelve weeks, after which the percentages became more equitable. As Ruddy put it, Yablans made the exhibitors an offer they couldn't refuse: "It was the start of the blockbuster mentality. Paramount had the locomotive, and fuckin' killed them. You want *The Godfather*? You owe us $80,000. We want the money, now!"

But what Yablans really wanted to do was to break the exhibitors' clearance policy. Because of its three-hour running time, if he couldn't book it into multiple theaters in a single market, he would never get the kinds of profits he anticipated. Gene Klein was the owner of National General, which controlled Westwood, among other locations. Yablans brought him to Evans's home, where he took everyone he wanted to impress, and they got drunk and stayed up all night. Yablans hammered Klein until he gave in.

In New York City, *The Godfather* opened in five first-run theaters, with playtimes staggered. Nationally, *The Godfather* made what was then an unusually wide break, going to 316 theaters, adding another fifty-odd over the course of the next few weeks. The cumulative result of Yablans's methods — the money up front, the favorable splits, the massive release — resulted in a dramatic, not to say revolutionary, transformation of Paramount's cash flow. Money poured through the pipeline, faster and in vastly greater volume than ever before in the history of the movie business, a million dollars a day by mid-April. In mid-September, only six months after it had opened, the film became the biggest grosser of all time, surpassing *Gone With the Wind*, which took thirty-three years and numerous re-releases to set its record. By the time its first run was concluded, *The Godfather* netted $86.2 million in domestic rentals. Not only did *The Godfather* revive Paramount, which owned an unprecedented 84 of the 100 points, it was like a jolt of electricity for the industry, which was still awakening from the half-decade-long coma that began after *The Sound of Music*.

At a meeting, some months earlier, Coppola, joking with Evans and Ruddy, had asked for a Mercedes 600, the big stretch limo, if the picture hit $15 million. Evans replied, "No problem at $50 million." Recalls Coppola, "When the picture had done $100 million, George Lucas and I walked into the Mercedes dealership in San Francisco and I said, 'We want to see the Mercedes 600.' " They were custom-made, very expensive and hard to get. The Pope had one, so did Francisco Franco. "The salesmen kept passing us along to other salesmen, because we looked like slobs, and had driven up in a Honda. They showed us a few sedans, and we kept saying, 'No, no! We want the one with the six doors.' So finally some young salesman who didn't know any better took the order. I said, 'Send the bill to Paramount Pictures,' and they did."

The Mercedes was nice, but money alone would not salve Coppola's wounds. He would never be satisfied merely with a commercial hit, not even one with the elephantine proportions of *The Godfather*. It was the reviews that were the sweet revenge. Kael (sometime later), called it "the best gangster film ever made in this country."

The Godfather hit a cultural nerve. It was all things to all people, which is perhaps, as marketers would soon realize, a sine qua non for blockbusters. On the one hand, it is very much a film of the '60s. Released just before Watergate, the brilliant opening scene in which the massive head of Brando gradually emerges from the darkness as the camera slowly pulls back, while Bonasera the baker petitions the Godfather to avenge his violated daughter, establishes the premise that the American dream has failed, the melting pot is an illusion, and the ethnic poor are trapped at the bottom of an unjust system. The Mafia provides what the government does not: simple justice, and a version of welfare for the underclass, an Old World system of values that cushions the shock of capitalism. Like *Bonnie and Clyde* and *Easy Rider*, *The Godfather* was critical of the values of the generation of the father. Coppola compared Michael Corleone to Nixon; he began as an idealist, distancing himself from the Family, and ended up by embracing and replicating its values.

On the other hand, despite Coppola's schoolboy Marxism (he always equated the mob with capitalism), *The Godfather* looked forward to the conservative family values of the Reagan era. In judging how far *The Godfather* was from some of the generation gap films that preceded it, it is only necessary to compare the scene Towne wrote in which a dying Don Corleone and Michael reach an understanding, to the scene in *Five Easy Pieces* in which Bobby Dupea and his father, symbolically mute and crippled, do not. In its emphasis on generational reconciliation, on ethnicity, and on the Mafia as, in effect, a privatized government of organized vigilantes that performs functions the government can't or won't, it foreshadows the Reagan right's attack on the Washington establishment in the next decade. "In the seventies, we felt families were disintegrating, and our national family, led by the family in the White House, was full of backstabbing," said Towne, referring, of course, to the Nixon gang. "Here was this role model of a family who stuck together, who'd die for one another. . . . It was really kind of reactionary in that sense—a perverse expression of a desirable and lost cultural tradition."

Finally, unlike the antigenre exercises of Hopper and Altman, Coppola, like Bogdanovich with *What's Up, Doc?*, breathed life into a dead formula, looking forward to the genre gentrification of Lucas and Spielberg to come.

Ironically, although Warners executives dismissed Coppola as a wannabe auteur, he connected to the themes of *The Godfather* (and its sequel) in a profound way. The issues of power, sibling rivalry, masculinity, and patriarchy hit home as they never would again in any other film he would ever make. Coppola obviously identified with Michael, the prodigal son, and in Michael's pact with the devil lies the tale of Coppola's uneasy relationship with the studios, and his brave, if stumbling attempts to build his own independent power base. The *Godfathers* would be the most personal films Coppola would ever make.

THE OSCARS THAT YEAR fell on April 10. *The Last Picture Show* was up against *The French Connection, A Clockwork Orange, Fiddler on the Roof,* and

Nicholas and Alexandra. The Academy awarded Charlie Chaplin an honorary Oscar, which he traveled from his home in Vevey, Switzerland, to accept. It was the first time he had set foot on American soil since 1952, when he left under the shadow of the House Un-American Activities Committee investigations. The hand of Bert Schneider was evident; it was a BBS family affair. He had orchestrated the rehabilitation of Chaplin, produced a documentary on him that Artie Ross put together, and asked Bogdanovich to select the sequences from Chaplin's work to show on Oscar night. Candy Bergen shot his picture for the cover of *Life.*

Obviously identifying with Chaplin, who was persecuted in his adopted country, and still smarting from the pain of *The Godfather* production despite the picture's success, Coppola was feeling sorry for himself. He thought, Charlie Chaplin, man, I can't believe he's accepting an Oscar. They called him a communist, and now that he's an old man and no longer a threat, who wants it then? When I'm eighty years old they're not gonna trudge me out and give me some humanitarian award. I want it now, when I'm young and have ideas, can do something with it. But nobody's rooting for me.

The French Connection beat out *The Last Picture Show,* winning five Oscars, including Best Picture, Best Actor (Gene Hackman), and Best Director. Clutching his Oscar, Friedkin rushed up to Bogdanovich.

"Congratulations, Billy."

"Peter, Peter, Peter . . . "

"Billy, what? What?"

"You know? You're gonna get a dozen of these." He threw his arms around Bogdanovich, hugged him close, and in the process thumped him hard on the forehead with his Oscar. Bogdanovich — who never would win an Oscar — thought, Jesus, you already won the fuckin' Oscar, now you've clobbered me on the head with it.

Towne and Polanski worked on the *Chinatown* script at Polanski's house for two months or so in the spring and summer of 1973. It was hot and dry, the revisions went slowly. Towne didn't think the script needed a lot of work and put small effort into doing any. He arrived every morning around eleven with his dog, Hira, took and placed phone calls, knocked the ashes out of his pipe, relit it.

"The goddamn dog would lie on my feet in this hot room and drool," says Polanski. "Bob would fill his pipe and smoke, and this smoke filled up the room — it was really a hard experience for eight weeks of that. Bob would fight for every word, for every line of the dialogue as if it was carved in marble." Polanski would give an impassioned speech about why this scene should be changed in such and such a way, and then Bob would kind of nod his head and say, "I've got to take Hira out now for a piss."

"We fought, every day, over everything," Towne confirms. "Names. 'What's her name?' 'No, it can't be that, it's too Jewish.' 'Who says it's Jewish?' Over the teenyboppers that Roman would run out and take Polaroid pictures of diving off the fucking diving board without tops on. Which was distracting. With braces."

Nowhere in the script was there a literal Chinatown. Towne thought that was fine; he was a writer, and for him, it was metaphor. But Polanski, the director, wanted something concrete, felt strongly there had to be a scene set in Chinatown. They went back and forth. At one point, Sylbert quipped, "Maybe it's enough if they eat Chinese food."

Then there was the ending, a famous locus of dispute that quickly deterio-rated into mutual abuse. "I went to art school in Poland — "

"A Polish art school's a contradiction in terms, you fuckin' asshole," Towne interrupted.

"A guy would draw an arm and he didn't want to change it because he didn't think he could draw another one."

"Roman, if you think you're talking about me, you're fuckin' full'a shit. I can draw as many arms as you want. I just think it's bullshit to rewrite this."

In Towne's original script, Evelyn Mulwray kills her venal father, Noah Cross. In other words, a happy ending in which innocence defiled is avenged and evil is punished. For Polanski, the world was a darker place. He felt Cross should live, get control of the child he incestuously fathered, while Evelyn should die. The detective, Jake Gittes, can do no more than look on, helplessly. "I thought it was a serious movie, not an adventure story for the kids," says Polanski. Concludes Towne, "Roman's argument was, That's life. Beautiful blondes die in Los Angeles. Sharon had."

COPPOLA WAS GRADUALLY LEARNING to enjoy his success. Truly the ugly duckling transformed into a swan, when he went down to L.A., he would sample the favors of women, courtesy of Frederickson. "For a long time I didn't want to be alone," he recalled. "The romances . . . were pretty conventional, schoolboy kind of romances. I had a couple of romances that were sort of the-most-beautiful-girl-you-ever-saw kind of things, which all of us, when we're young, have that fantasy."

Back in San Francisco, he began getting million-dollar checks in the mail from Paramount, anointing the new aesthetic and moral legitimacy of the director with enormous economic power. "I was . . . one of the first young people to become rich overnight," he said. Francis started to think of himself as Don Corleone. Still, he was nagged by the feeling that he had taken a momentous misstep from which he would never recover. "In some ways it did ruin me," he complained. "It just made my whole career go this way instead of the way I really wanted it to go, which was into doing original work as a writer-director. Basically, *The Godfather* made me violate a lot of the hopes I had for myself at that age."

For a dreamer like Francis, sudden riches were a mixed blessing. He was like a boy sitting at a table loaded with sweets; he couldn't decide what to eat first, and characteristically, he ate them all. The rush of power distracted him. "It just inflamed so many other desires," he explained, adding, "I think I was just running away from being alone with myself as I had been forced to be when I was sick as a kid. I didn't want to be in a room alone with no friends."

Coppola spent his money on real estate and toys. He bought a robin's egg blue twenty-eight-room Queen Anne row house at 2207 Broadway (near Fillmore) in San Francisco's posh Pacific Heights with a breathtaking view of the Golden Gate Bridge. One room was devoted solely to electric trains. His friends referred to him as "F. A. O. Coppola." Another contained a Wurlitzer juke box full of rare Enrico Caruso 78s. A ballroom was turned into a projection room, replete with a Moog synthesizer and a harpsichord, and a collection of roller skates left over from *You're a Big Boy Now*. He greeted guests wearing a caftan. Like a newborn porpoise, he cavorted in a small, clover-shaped Moorish-style swimming pool. A Warhol Mao print hung on the wall in the dining room, and the furniture was Italian modern, leather belted on chrome. There was a brass bed in the master bedroom. A few years later, at the end of Coppola's buying spree, when he had homes in San Francisco, Napa Valley, Los Angeles, New York, and a temporary one in Manila where he was shooting *Apocalypse Now*, Ellie realized she was responsible for twenty-seven bathrooms.

Coppola had no interest in reviving Zoetrope in its old, collective form. Instead, he re-created it as a more traditional production company, housed in the Little Fox Theater and the Sentinel Building, a landmark seven-story flat-iron building that had survived the 1906 earthquake. Francis bought it from the Kingston Trio. Faced with cream color tile and copper molding, it was nestled at the corner of Columbus and Kearny among the strip joints and peep shows of North Beach, within spitting distance of City Lights Booksellers and Tosca, a trendy bar. He restored it with tender loving care and lots of money. His own offices, on the top floor, designed by Dean Tavoularis, were fit for a Renaissance prince. There were windows on three sides, intricate handcrafted white-oak paneling and inlay in the art deco style, brass fixtures polished to a high sheen, and a cupola girdled by a 360 degree diorama depicting scenes from his pictures under a deep azure sky painted by Dean's brother, Alex.

He plowed ahead with new, and characteristically grandiose plans. He bought a radio station, *City* magazine, a Jet Ranger helicopter, and a half interest in a Mitsubishi MU2L turboprop, which he shared with financier George Gund. The aircraft were referred to within the company as *Air Francis*. Later he bought part ownership in a chain of theaters, Don Rugoff's Cinema 5 in New York, which would take care of his exhibition needs (he had three films slated for production — *Apocalypse Now, Tucker,* and *The Black Stallion),* one very important brick in the edifice he hoped would eventually see him independent of Hollywood. "My motive has been to bypass the kinds of deals filmmakers have to make . . . deals in which the filmmaker has to totally surrender ownership, final cut, any say in how the film is released, in order to get the dollars up front to make a movie." He even induced Rugoff to change the name to Cinema 7. April 7 was his birthday, and 7 was his lucky number.

There were a lot of strange people flitting about Zoetrope, attracted by Coppola's success. One was a girl nicknamed Sunshine, more for the substance (a kind of acid), than for the light. She was the kind of person who would slip a psychedelic in your drink and disappear with Pigpen of the Grateful Dead. She was gifted at reading people; whatever it was you were most insecure about, she would divine it in a second, and then she'd nail you. Francis had a blackboard in his office. One day, when he wasn't there, she waltzed in and wrote across the top, "When You're Rich, You Never Have to Say You're Sorry." In subsequent months, Francis covered the blackboard with writing, erased it, covered it again, erased it. But he never erased Sunshine's message.

Six:
Like a Rolling Stone
1973

• *How Hal Ashby made* **The Last Detail** *over Columbia's nearly dead body, while Beatty launched* **Shampoo,** *BBS got an ugly dose of reality, and Faye Dunaway nearly pissed away* **Chinatown!**

"Ashby was the most American of those directors and was the most unique talent. He was a victim of Hollywood, the great Hollywood tragic story."

— PETER BART

Hal Ashby was scouting locations for *The Last Detail* in Canada, accompanied by casting director Lynn Stalmaster. Charles Mulvehill, his line producer, was supposed to meet his flight at LAX. He arrived a few minutes late. There was Stallmaster, but no Ashby.

"Where's Hal?"

"The strangest thing happened. We got to the gate in Toronto, they stopped Hal, and they searched him, and they led him off."

"Led him off where?"

"I don't know. To jail, I guess."

"Didn't you get off the plane?"

"Hell no! I thought I should come home." Says Mulvehill, "We all carried dope at that point. Hal had just enough on him for a joint, maybe a little hash. It wasn't anything we considered heavy narcotics." Ashby lamely told the inspectors he was carrying herbs. "Hal sometimes had a tenuous grip on reality," says Jerry Ayres, who was producing the picture for Columbia. "The Canadian authorities, seeing this man who looked like a Vietnamese farmer, with his mosslike beard hanging down, well, who else would they search? Hal would be the first person you would stop. You wouldn't even need the dogs to sniff him out. He just had a sign on him, 'I'm a drugged-out hippie.' "

Mulvehill phoned Ayres at the studio, said, "Hal's in jail. Do something."

Ayres called the Columbia lawyers, while Mulvehill hopped a plane to Toronto to bring him back. "I got off the plane and walked into the main airport area, and there was Hal, going through his suitcase, trying to repack it. Today, we would look at him as a bag man, a street person.

" 'Hal, you're out!'

" 'Yeah, I'm out.' "

The studio lawyers had freed him. Ashby and Mulvehill got on a plane to L.A. Ashby, very unhappy, was cursing the "motherfucking" customs inspectors, and how unfair the laws were. Just after touchdown, as the plane was taxiing to the gate, there was an announcement over the loudspeaker: "Is there a Hal Ashby on board?" Mulvehill thought, Okay, the juice is finally starting to flow, now we're going to get the red carpet treatment from Columbia. He waved his hand, said, "I'm with him, he's on board, and I'm with him." The next thing they knew they were both in a holding area at airport security up against the wall being strip-searched. Hal said, "Really guys, you don't think that I'd be stupid enough to carry some shit after having gone through what I just went through, do you?" He was angry, but he was quiet, polite. "On one level," says Mulvehill, "Hal hated authority. But on another level, he was afraid of it." The search concluded, Ashby and Mulvehill jumped into the Columbia limo that was indeed waiting for them, and were whisked away to Appian Way, in Laurel Canyon, where Hal lived. Three or four years later, the lawyers got the arrest stricken from his record.

THERE'S NO WORSE CAREER MOVE in Hollywood than dying. Hal Ashby is now largely forgotten because he had the misfortune to die at the end of the '80s, but he had the most remarkable run of any '70s director. After *The Landlord*, in 1970, he made *Harold and Maude, The Last Detail, Shampoo, Bound for Glory, Coming Home,* and *Being There,* in 1979, before his career disappeared into the dark tunnel of post-'70's, Me Decade drugs and paranoia.

Ashby was exactly ten years older than Coppola and Bogdanovich, born into a Mormon family in Ogden, Utah, in 1929. He was the youngest of four kids. His parents divorced when he was five or six. His father lost his dairy farm because he refused to allow his milk to be pasteurized. In 1941, he stuck a gun under his chin and pulled the trigger. Hal discovered the body in the barn. He was twelve.

As a teenager, Ashby was rebellious and independent. He dropped out of high school, and was married and divorced by the time he was seventeen. He worked at a variety of odd jobs. One day he was repairing a concrete railroad bridge in Wyoming, when he had an epiphany. It was only September, and already the water in the cup he was holding had acquired a brittle crust of ice. He poked his finger through it, took a drink, and turned to a friend, said, "I'm goin' to California and live off the fruit of the land."

It was 1950. Ashby was broke. After three weeks of pounding the pavements, he called his mother collect to ask for help. She accepted the call, but refused to help. With literally his last dime, he bought a Powerhouse candy bar that he made last for three days. On the fourth day, he went to the California Board of Unemployment and asked them to find him a job at a studio. They found one: operating a Multilith at Universal. Ashby married and divorced again by the time he was twenty-one, in 1950. The following year, he became an apprentice editor at Republic, then at Disney. He and Nicholson both worked at Metro in 1956 and 1957. Hal was an assistant editor.

Early on, Ashby developed a social conscience. He got involved in the civil rights movement, went on some freedom marches. Later, he gave money to the striking farmworkers, hosted meetings at his home, and visited Cesar Chávez, their charismatic leader, up in Delano. He was deeply opposed to the war in Vietnam. On the other hand, as soon as he had some money, he bought a Cadillac convertible, which he proudly drove onto the lot. He hated the system with a passion, but part of him very much wanted to succeed in establishment terms.

Eventually, Ashby found his way to Robert Swink, a first-rate editor who worked for William Wyler and George Stevens. Ashby was his assistant on several Wyler and Stevens films, *The Big Country*, *The Diary of Anne Frank*, and *The Greatest Story Ever Told*. Hal hated working for Stevens. He had to do all the shitwork, taking the thousands upon thousands of feet that Stevens shot, and cataloguing the frames at the head and tail of every shot. But he worked his way up and did the first cut on Tony Richardson's *The Loved One* in 1965, which Calley produced. Ashby quickly earned the reputation for being one of the best editors in the business. For the generation that preceded him, cutting was just a job. Editors left the cutting room at 5:30, went home to their families. For Hal, it was a passion. He thought nothing of working twenty-four hours at a stretch, spending the night in front of the Moviola, chain-smoking cigarette after cigarette, head nodding over the screen. He was an insomniac, never seemed to need sleep, nor for that matter, food. He never needed to go to the bathroom. Hal had a remarkable memory; after seeing a piece of film once, he would never forget it, and he made it his business to have total recall of every take, every trim. If he were asked for a shot, he knew exactly where it was. But Hal drank heavily, went on binges where he disappeared for days at a time. In 1966, he went on the wagon, except for the occasional glass of wine, and switched over to grass.

In the mid-'60s, Ashby hooked up with director Norman Jewison. The two men became extremely close; friends thought Ashby saw in Norman the father he missed. Jewison took care of him, let him sleep on the couch in his office during Hal's divorce from his third wife, Shirley. Ashby worked on several of Jewison's best pictures, including *The Cincinnati Kid* (1965) and *The Thomas Crown Affair* (1968). In fact, says cinematographer Haskell Wexler, who shot some of these films, "I saw what a force Hal was, making Norman's creativity blossom. They were a good combo, and I don't think Norman's made as good pictures since he and Hal were partners."

The climax of Ashby's editing career came in 1967, when he beat out Bob Jones *(Guess Who's Coming to Dinner)* to win an Oscar for *In the Heat of the Night*. He created a flurry of controversy by telling the press he was going to use his Oscar as a doorstop. By that time he had had it. "I'd been working seventeen hours a day, seven days a week for ten years," he said. "I'd wake up at three A.M. and go to work. I'd try to leave the studio at six, and still be there at nine. I'd gotten better and better at my work, meanwhile wrecking [my] . . . marriages. Suddenly, I was tired. I'd become a film editor because everyone said it was the best training for a director. But suddenly I was almost forty, and I no longer had the energy to pursue it. So I stopped."

By the time Ashby was editing Jewison's *The Russians Are Coming! The Russians are Coming!* at the Mirisch Company for UA on the old Goldwyn lot, Mulvehill, who was only a kid, was head of production. Harold Mirisch was considered the only one of the Mirisch brothers with any brains. When he died suddenly, the bottom dropped out of the company. "There was nothin' going on," says Mulvehill. "I was the head of nothin' going on."

Mulvehill hung out with Ashby, smoked grass, and talked about the kinds of films they wanted to make. "We would have philosophical discussions about how fucked up everything was," he recalls. Ashby would say he wanted to make films about the "human condition." Like the other New Hollywood directors, he "was anti-star," continues Mulvehill. "At the time, I took that at face value, thought that was his philosophy of filmmaking, but now that I look back, it was ego. He felt the picture should be the star, not the actor, which meant, ultimately, the star was the director, Hal Ashby."

Hal was the quintessential flower child, even though in 1967 he was thirty-eight. He looked like a tall, hip Ho Chi Minh, with oversized, rose-tinted glasses in wire frames, his face hidden by blond, going-on-white hair parted in the middle that cascaded over his forehead and descended on either side into a wispy white beard he never trimmed. (It covered a weak chin.) Ashby favored bell bottom jeans or threadbare corduroy pants, sandals, and beads. He had neglected his teeth, and eventually spent a lot of time and money at the periodontist having his gums pared back. But he was clean to the point of fastidiousness. He smoked dope, all day long, on the job and off. Hal had a motorcycle, and was heavily into the music scene, especially the Rolling Stones. In another life, he would have loved to have been Mick Jagger. Ashby gave out mellow, laid-back vibes. But as with many such people, appearances were deceptive. Says Mulvehill, "He had a lot of anger and a lot of rage that he didn't know how to handle and never dealt with."

Jewison gave Hal his shot at directing. He had acquired a book called *The*

Landlord, which he was too busy to do himself. He turned it over to Ashby. It was produced by the Mirisches for UA. As would be his wont, Hal cast *The Landlord* without stars. On the set, in the middle of the production, he married Joan Marshall, a tall blonde, his fourth wife. Jewison and Ashby, mentor and protégé, fell out over the ending of *The Landlord*. Creative differences. For Hal, it was probably a case of the son freeing himself from the father.

Peter Bart saw *The Landlord*, liked it, and sent Ashby *Harold and Maude*. This was an oddball script, a black comedy featuring a young man who repeatedly tries to commit suicide until he forms a redeeming attachment to an eccentric woman old enough to be his grandmother. Says Bart, "To me, *Harold and Maude* was a symbol of that era. It would have been unthinkable in the '80s or '90s. In those days [late '60s] people would walk in, wacked out, with the most mind-bending, innovative, and brilliant ideas for movies. *Harold and Maude* was written by a pool cleaner."

For Ashby, it was the perfect script, as loony as he could hope for. He cast Ruth Gordon, an elderly Broadway actress who had scored with a bit part in *Rosemary's Baby*, and actor Bud Cort. Ashby blocked the studio's attempt to impose a producer of its own, and instead asked Mulvehill to work on it as his producer, even though Mulvehill had little idea what a producer did. He resigned from Mirisch to embark on a new career. The two of them went into a meeting with Paramount, where they were forced to go over the budget line by line when they were so stoned they could barely read the numbers, and managed to get the studio to approve $1.2 million.

The picture wrapped in late February, early March of 1971, right around the time *The Godfather* started up. Hal edited up at his Appian Way house. He rented, because he was paying so much alimony he was afraid to own anything. In those days, Laurel Canyon was a hippie community. The houses were cheap, and they were filled with struggling artists, musicians, and actors. Carole King lived next door to Ashby, pounding on her piano. Spielberg lived there, across the street from Don Simpson, who was sharing a house with Jerry Bruckheimer. Alice Cooper had a house nearby, so did Mickey Dolenz of the Monkees. Fleetwood Mac lived behind it. Hal's was a funky, two-story, Spanish-style affair, with arched doorways between the rooms, each painted a different pastel color. He lived in one large room upstairs, where there was a bed, a pool table, and a big Advent TV. He lived sparsely, as if unwilling to make any place home, unwilling to undertake the obligation of being there. His Oscar was nowhere in sight.

The studio was high on *Harold and Maude*, and the buzz was good, so much so, in fact, that Ashby and Mulvehill figured they had it made. "We felt it was going to be the best film of the year, it was gonna knock 'em dead," recalls Mulvehill. "We were gonna have control over what we were gonna do." They started a film company called DFF, Dumb Fuck Films.

Ashby's marriage to Joan fell apart just as the production began. He started seeing a girl who was a stand-in for Ruth Gordon. She lived in a van, had a diamond drilled into one of her front teeth. But after four divorces, Ashby had learned not to marry again. He liked tall, thin, athletic girls built like boys and, as Wexler puts it, "they'd usually end up with a Mercedes, if nothing else." When he was bored with a girl, he would ignore her, spend all day watching TV and then tell her to get out. According to his close friend Bob Downey, Sr., he used to say, "When one's gone, you just open the window, there's another one climbing right in." At one screening, Ashby asked if he could invite a few of his ex-wives. Recalls Bart, "There was this whole row of them, big blond girls who all looked like they were born in Utah."

The picture opened at Christmas 1971, in time for Oscar consideration, although, as it turned out, it didn't get much consideration. The reviews were scathing. In the very first one, A. D. Murphy wrote in *Variety* that the film was about as funny as a burning orphanage. Paramount cut it loose without another word. Even though *Harold and Maude* would eventually become a cult classic, it closed in a week. "You couldn't drag people in," says Mulvehill. "The idea of a twenty-year-old boy with an eighty-year-old woman just made people want to vomit. If you asked people what it was about, ultimately it became a boy who was fucking his grandmother. We were devastated, couldn't believe it, and the scripts and phone calls that had been coming in just stopped. It was as though somebody had taken an ax to the phone lines. It was really a rude awakening. It was a big, big shock to Hal." After *Harold and Maude*, Ashby dissolved DFF.

Then the phone rang. It was Ayres, asking Hal if he'd gotten Robert Towne's script for *The Last Detail*. When Towne returned from the set of *Drive, He Said*, he plunged into the task of adapting Darryl Ponicsan's novel. Ayres had convinced Columbia to give him the shot on the basis of his consultant's credit on *Bonnie and Clyde*. Ponicsan's novel was another exercise in '60s-style anti-authoritarianism. It presents two navy lifers, "Bad Ass" Buddusky and "Mule" Mulhall, whose job it is to escort a third sailor, Meadows, from a base in Norfolk, Virginia, to the Portsmouth, New Hampshire, Naval Prison to serve eight years for the crime of attempting to lift a polio donation can. The novel ends in true '60s fashion with the two escorts going AWOL in disgust. Towne put a more pessimistic spin on it. The lifers merely do their duty as charged. "I didn't want Buddusky and Mulhall to feel overly guilty about transporting Meadows to jail," he explained. "I wanted to imply that we're all lifers in the Navy, and everybody hides behind doing a job, whether it's massacring in My Lai, or taking a kid to jail."

The script was tailored for Nicholson (Buddusky), and Rupert Crosse, a talented black actor whom Towne had met. Ayres started looking for a director. He sent the script to Altman, and then to Ashby. "I thought this was a picture that required a skewed perspective, and that's what Hal had" says Ayres. "He felt to me like a brother in the fraternity of the self-styled underground of the early '70s. He was distrustful of people from the studios he considered bombastic or authoritarian. But if somebody came to the door and said, 'I've been driving a bus, and I've got a great idea for a scene,' he'd say, 'Okay, do it.' "

At first, Ashby turned it down, muttered, "Oh yeah, white sailor, black failure." But after reading the script a second time, he changed his mind. Studios distrusted Ashby for the very same reasons Ayres liked him. He was barely verbal, never made much effort to communicate with the executives who hired him. He made Columbia nervous. Still, the budget was so low it was barely a blip on the screen. The studio approved him.

The project was considered a daring one for Columbia, and the studio was balking at the torrent of obscenities in the script (unlike the novel), which contained lines like, "I *am* the motherfucking shore patrol, motherfucker." It refused to commit until Towne cleaned it up. Recalls Guber, "The first seven minutes, there were 342 'fucks.' At Columbia, you couldn't have language, couldn't have sex. If you made love, it had to be at 300 yards distance, no tongues." Says Towne, "Now that movies were opening up, this was an opportunity to write navy guys like they really talked. The head of the studio sat me down and said, 'Bob, wouldn't twenty "motherfuckers" be more effective than forty "motherfuckers?" ' I said, 'No.' This is the way people talk when they're powerless to act; they bitch." Towne refused to change a comma, and Nicholson backed him up.

The project languished for eighteen months waiting for Nicholson, who wouldn't be available until he finished his latest picture for BBS, *The King of Marvin Gardens*. Guber told Ayres, "I can get Burt Reynolds, Jim Brown, David Cassidy, and a new writer, since this Towne won't clean up the screenplay. We'll give approval for production right away." Ayres demurred, and Columbia, after some grumbling, agreed to wait. Says Guber, "They were afraid that the film would go somewhere else, to another studio, and they had already suffered that fate with *Young Frankenstein* and other films." Ashby's bust didn't help. Continues Guber, "If it had emerged more publicly in the press, it would have really injured the company and they might have closed the picture down. Nicholson's fierce loyalty to Hal made a big difference."

THE KING OF MARVIN GARDENS featured, in addition to Nicholson, Ellen Burstyn and Bruce Dern. Bob Rafelson directed, from a script by Jake Brackman. It told the story of two brothers, the older one a flamboyant confidence man with an eye to the pot of gold at the end of the rainbow, full of scams and tricks. The younger one, quieter, more introverted, earned his living as a Jean Shepherd–style late-night radio DJ who soliloquizes into the wee hours, getting lost in the tangle of his own memories.

It was a powerful script, and there was every reason to believe it would yield another triumph for BBS. Nicholson was loyal to Rafelson, and chose his projects based on the director. He considered Rafelson, with some reason, to be an auteur. So did Rafelson. After *Five Easy Pieces*, "Bob certainly saw himself as heading for that international pantheon," says Brackman, "creating a legend for himself à la John Huston."

Nor had the double success of *Five Easy Pieces* and Bogdanovich's *Last Picture Show* done anything to moderate Rafelson's confidence in his casting instincts, which knew no bounds. Initially, Nicholson was to play the older brother, Dern the younger, but Rafelson immediately realized that the more surprising, original way to go would be to cast Jack in the quiet role of the DJ, and Dern as the flamboyant con man, let him, in effect, play Jack. His theory was, as he puts it, "take away the audience's presuppositions, their props, so that violence becomes more violent, beauty becomes more beautiful, sex becomes more sexy. Everything gets amped." Burstyn played Dern's lover, and Julie Robinson her companion, a girl young enough to be her daughter.

Robinson had a lovely, pale face, ethereal and vulnerable, a real heartbreaker. "She was luminous," recalls Burstyn. "You looked in her face you felt you could fall into her eyes." She had a major drug habit, had been on the Magic Bus with Ken Kesey, and she had had a small part — and brief affair with Jaglom — in his first film, *A Safe Place*, also produced by BBS. But she was a terrible actress, stiff and halting. According to Dern, Rafelson became infatuated with her. "It was open adoration, very definitely the whole syndrome of, I'm making a movie star — a director takes an unknown and she blossoms under his tutelage," says Dern. "It was just the way he touched her, the way he moved her around, like she was a possession. Toby was standing there every day, and he would just carry on as if it were OK. Bob truly loved her. I think it destroyed his marriage." (According to Rafelson, they did not have an affair. Robinson later died in a fire.)

"Nobody wanted him to cast Julie," says Brackman. "Bob had a wild hair up his ass, an instinct that he was going to go with. He had a hard time acknowledging that his instinct was incorrect. Bob did have a thing for her, but her performance destroyed it. By the time he was seeing the dailies, he was no longer in love — if you could call it that — with Julie. Bob was realizing that he, the great caster, had made a mistake, which was horrendous to him. He felt like she'd tricked him. He was overreaching and overestimating himself." At the same time, he continued his affair with Paula Strachan. Everyone knew about it but Toby. Says Brackman, "Toby would fly in and Paula would be flown out."

Principal photography began around Thanksgiving 1971 and spilled over into the winter of 1972. Bob was almost as much into the idea of being a director as he was into directing itself. Very much the poseur, he strode onto the set with a viewfinder dangling from his neck, surveying his domain. "Bob was a very cerebral director," says Burstyn. "He had a lot going on in his head.

On the set he was remote, aloof. He was more result-oriented than Bogdano-vich, who was involved in the process of acting, the nuts and bolts. Bob told you where he wanted you to get to; he didn't care so much how you got there."

Marvin Gardens got a tepid reception at the New York Film Festival, and was perfunctorily released by Columbia in the fall of 1972. Nicholson even had a hard time getting a limo to take him from interview to interview. Colum-bia was having a very bad year. Ironically, it was still putting out the kinds of big-budget trash the other studios had abandoned after *Easy Rider*, and in 1972, it lost millions on *1776*, *Nicholas and Alexandra*, *Oklahoma Crude*, and *Lost Horizon*. It was on the brink of financial disaster.

Nor was BBS still cruising from hit to hit. Jaglom's *A Safe Place*, *Drive, He Said*, and *Marvin Gardens* had flopped, and a Jim McBride project, *Gone Beaver*, had aborted one day before the beginning of principal photography. It was clear that Bert Schneider's heart was no longer in the company. Says Brackman, "On *Marvin Gardens*, he basically was as completely removed from everything as somebody at a studio. I doubt if he ever read the script." Adds Dern, "I was watching a company start to come apart. It appeared to me it was through a lack of interest. That's what shocked me. Bert didn't give a shit." Schneider decided to take a sabbatical from the picture business.

BBS was starting to feel more like an albatross than the creative haven it once was. "At one point Bert turned to me and said, 'You collect the rent, I'm tired of this shit,'" recalls Rafelson. "We encouraged people to come and camp out, weird documentaries were being made, strange directors. Any time some Japanese or Indian or Yugoslav director came to America the first place he would arrive was there. We didn't give a fuck-all; we'd let anybody have a screening. People were getting shot in the building because of the politics, the Black Panther stuff, busts and cops and God knows what. I didn't know who the fuck was in that building. None of them could pay. I didn't want to produce anymore. I felt I was burned out. I rather suspected by this point that I was famous enough that I could get a gig just by walking in the door of a studio. Boy, was I in for a rude awakening! It didn't work that way, and it happened within weeks of the decline of BBS."

Schneider was spending more and more time and resources on the Black Panthers, who were moving away from confrontation toward a more realistic appreciation of what was possible. They organized a Survival Conference at which they gave away food and shoes. Bert footed the bill, to the tune of $300,000. Ashby put some money in as well.

On June 13, 1971, the *New York Times* had published *The Pentagon Papers*, a devastating internal history of the government's conduct of the war leaked by a former Defense Department analyst named Daniel Ellsberg. Nixon decided to prosecute Ellsberg, and Schneider had become deeply involved in his de-fense effort, called the Pentagon Papers Peace Project. "That was a major turning point," he said. "I had been involved with the peace movement for a long time, but that finally pushed me over the edge."

In addition to Bert's other problems, his relationship with Candy Bergen had fallen on hard times. It had been frozen into a form that would destroy it: Bert the teacher, Candy the student. Bert built her up, Bert tore her down. Candy was closed, uptight. Bert was open, in touch with his feelings. He talked more and more about "sexual nonexclusivity."

"What do you mean by that, exactly?" asked Candy.

"Where two people feel secure enough and free enough to explore sexually with other people."

"What do you mean, explore sexually?"

"I'm sorry it's so threatening to you, Bergen, but you have to understand that I'm a love object for every woman who walks into my office. . . . Start dealing with that. It's time you began growing up."

Partly as a result of his activities with the Pentagon Papers Peace Project, Schneider decided that what the country needed was a really good documentary on the war. Rafelson suggested Peter Davis, who had made a name for himself with a CBS documentary called *The Selling of the Pentagon*. The new film would be called *Hearts and Minds*.

JUST AS *The Last Detail* was about to go into production, Rupert Crosse was diagnosed with terminal cancer. Ashby postponed the shoot, waited for him to decide whether he wanted to do the film or not. "Most movie companies drive the wagons right over the grave," said Nicholson. "Hal delayed the start of *The Last Detail* for a week so an actor could come to terms with the knowledge that he had a terminal illness." When it became clear he didn't want to do the picture, he was replaced with Otis Young. The ever-geeky Randy Quaid, looking like a cartoon character, a pasty-faced doll awkwardly fashioned out of soft cheese, was perfectly cast as the kid, Meadows.

Haskell Wexler was slated to shoot it, but he couldn't get a union card for an East Coast production, and Ashby upped Michael Chapman from camera operator to DP, in the same way he had made Mulvehill a producer on *Harold and Maude,* and would later turn his editor, Bob Jones, into a writer. His approach was in keeping with the '60s distaste for the rigid hierarchy and pigeonholing that characterized an industry in which someone might be an assistant director his whole life, never a director.

Like other New Hollywood directors, Ashby was getting a reputation for being a producer killer. "A lot of times producers never even showed up," says Mulvehill. "Hal wouldn't deal with them. So after a while, they said, 'Fuck it.' He particularly disliked the creative producers who brought scripts to him. It really frustrated him that he couldn't originate material. By getting rid of them, he could assert authorship over the project." Ayres, who was an acquired taste anyway, was no exception. You loved him or hated him. The first time he met Mulvehill he extended his hand, said, "Hi my name is Jerry Ayres, and I'm an alcoholic bisexual." Mulvehill wondered, Is this a proposition, or what?

The Last Detail finally began principal photography in November 1972. Actors, at least those who didn't much like to be directed, loved Ashby. Nicholson called him one of the greatest "nondirectors" of all time. "He would become their dad," says Mulvehill. "He'd stroke them, he'd try things, he'd let them try things, he created an atmosphere that was totally permissive — and yet he was no fool, he knew when something wasn't working, he'd move it along as well." He'd let them try almost anything they wanted, saying, "I can get behind that."

Ayres had recommended his pal Bob Jones as an editor. His father had edited *Gentleman's Agreement, Panic in the Streets,* and some other films for Kazan, and Jones had edited *Cisco Pike.* Initially, he didn't want to work for Ashby. "I'd heard what a crazy man he was, worked twenty-five hours a day, worked in his house," says Jones. But they hit it off, and Jones took the job.

By the time they were ready to wrap, Ashby and Mulvehill were barely speaking. "Chuck took a lot of crap from Hal," says Jones. "He bore the brunt of much of Hal's craziness. At the end of the shoot, Chuck said, 'Never again.' " Ashby was rarely angry in public, but by himself, it was another story. "He would come to a slow boil, get back to some private space — a car, and fucking explode, start cursing. He could be mean, sarcastic," says Mulvehill, who lived by Hal's suffrance. Although Ashby had made him a producer on *Harold and Maude,* he hadn't been able to get into the Producers Guild, and what Ashby gave, Ashby could take away. "I didn't have any other relationship, I didn't have anywhere else to go," Mulvehill says. "I was in a totally vulnerable position. I was doing what I was doing because of my relationship with Hal, and he knew that.

"After his father killed himself, Hal never worked through it," he adds. "The end result was that he tried to keep himself from being rejected. He was always doing the rejecting, always ending relationships. You could predict when the girlfriends would come into his life, and when they were going to leave his life. When he was in post-production, getting rid of a movie, he would be getting rid of his relationships. His old friend or girlfriend would be leaving, and he would have struck up a relationship with somebody new. Hal was passive-aggressive. He would not confront you — Hal hated confrontations — and at that time I didn't want to confront anything, either."

Once again, Ashby edited at home, on Appian Way. He sat in front of the KEM with preternatural concentration, lighting up joint after joint, sometimes with a roach stuck to his lower lip, chewing sugarless gum and snacking on dried figs, nuts, small bowls of rice, running the footage, back and forth, back and forth. He had been a vegetarian since 1968. When he had been a kid on the farm, he had observed the routine cruelty inflicted on animals by the farmhands. He was tormented by dreams in which cows and hogs were slaughtered for food. The editing took forever, as was usual with Hal, as he slowly sifted through the footage. The studio would call, and he would lock himself in the bedroom and refuse to come to the phone. At one point, he flew to London. The very next day, the head of editing called Jones, said, "We're coming up to take the film."

"What do you mean, coming to take the film?" replied Jones, incredulous.

"It's a corporate decision, we're coming up to take the film."

"You can't do that."

Gradually, the calls would come from executives higher and higher in the Columbia food chain, until John Vietch, head of physical production, got on the line: "You don't have any choice. We're taking it."

"I do have a choice, I have the key to the house. I'm locking it up, and sending everybody home. If you want to take it, you're breaking and entering."

Jones made good on his threat, called Hal in London, who in turn made Columbia call off the wolves.

Towne dropped in periodically while Ashby and Jones were editing. He didn't like what he saw, didn't like Hal's pacing. "The good news about Hal was that he would never allow a dishonest moment between people," says Towne. "But gentle soul that he was, he almost considered it a moral imperative never to interfere with the actors. He would never pressure the performers, provoke a clash on the set. He left his dramatizing to the editing room, and the effect was a thinning out of the script."

Ayres was still tight with Towne. The producer had left his wife, Ann, two children, and a Frank Lloyd Wright house to move in with his male companion, Nick Kudla. "Bob Towne has always been a very cool character, very politically astute, very careful in his moves," says Ayres. "He was always lecturing me, because I'm an impetuous person, 'Jerry, be the last one to stick your head aboveground.' Well, I was always the first one to stick my head aboveground, and he was always the last." One day, Towne came over with his dog, Hira, to see Ayres. "He came in, I said, 'This is Nick . . .' 'Oh hi, Nick,' I showed him around the place, 'This is my work room,' and he saw the room had no bed in it. He noticed the other room had one double bed in it, and I saw as clearly as a shoe dropping, his mind going click, click, click.

"About a week later, Bob said to me, 'Jerry, just one thing about this coming-out-of-the-closet thing, you know, these guys won't understand this, it will ruin your reputation,' and so on, and I said, 'Bob, I don't want to live in shame anymore, you know?' I got furious at him. He and Warren were so intimate, they were twisted together like a knot, so I said, 'Listen, you and Warren squabble on the phone every day like a couple of lovers, go all over the world fucking the same women in the same room. If you two guys aren't lovers you're the next thing to it.' He got furious at me, and we didn't see each other for years."

THE OSCARS WERE HELD on March 27, 1973. *The Godfather*, which had been nominated for ten Oscars, won only a disappointing three: Best Picture, Best Actor (Brando), and Best Adapted Screenplay (Coppola and Puzo). Coppola lost Best Director to Bob Fosse, with *Cabaret*. Brando scandalized the audience by sending Sacheen Littlefeather, on behalf of an organization called the National Native American Affirmative Image Committee (which he appeared to have made up) to decline his Oscar, in the name of Wounded Knee.

Sporting a blue velvet dinner jacket, Coppola was profuse in his thanks to everyone but Evans, whom he "forgot." He even remembered to thank Towne. There was a dinner afterward in the ballroom of the Beverly Hills Hotel. Frank Wells was sitting at the Warners table with Dick Lederer and a couple of other executives. Getting up from his seat, he said, "Let's go over and congratulate Francis." Lederer said, "Don't Frank, don't. He's a Sicilian, he will not shake hands with you." Wells walked over anyway. Coppola spotted him when he was about ten feet away, shook his head, and said. "No. No. I'm not shaking hands with you."

Evans was furious at Coppola's snub, but he had other things on his mind. He was getting deeper into drugs. According to Nicholson, cocaine really took hold around 1972, having burned through the music crowd into the film community. One of the reasons it took hold, he claimed, was that it was a sexual aid. Nicholson had had a problem with premature ejaculation, a fact he generously shared with his fans via *Playboy*. "Cocaine is 'in' now," he said, "because chicks dig it sexually. While it numbs some areas, it inflames the mucous membranes such as those in a lady's genital region. If you put a numbing tip of cocaine on the end of your cock because you're quick on the trigger and need to cut down on the sensation, I guess it could be considered a sexual aid. And it's an upper, so you've got added energy."

Cocaine was a drug well suited to the driven, megalomaniacal, macho lifestyle of Hollywood, much more so than grass, which had a mellow, laid-back effect, or psychedelics, which facilitated self-exploration. "In your brain, you're bulletproof, you're the happiest guy in the room," says Dick Sylbert. "You can write, you can direct, you can act. A couple of toots, there's nothing you can't do."

What was sauce for Nicholson was poison for Evans. "What started as a fuck drug all but ruined my life of fucking," he wrote in his book, *The Kid Stays in the Picture*. "A snort of . . . coke stops the rush of blood from brain to tool.

Coming up short is your cock. Coming up long is dialogue and energy." Evans's habit wasn't evident immediately; at meetings, Paramount executives wondered why he kept putting his hand in his pocket and rubbing his index finger along his gums. Eventually, Evans stopped coming to the office, took to working out of his bed at home, in his pajamas.

According to Dick Sylbert, "The studio was falling apart, Bob wouldn't have a meeting with anybody. He had his phones and his grapefruit in the morning and he had Peter Bart. The phone would ring, Bob would pick it up. Somebody would say, 'Bob, what time is it?' Bob would have to call Peter and say, 'Peter, what time is it?'"

"I felt that he was abusing himself, and losing it," recalls Bart. "The amphetamines were getting to him, or whatever it was that he was into, sleeping pills, uppers, downers. They were making him extraordinarily nervous and jumpy. He was very bitter about Ali MacGraw, and he was becoming somewhat unstable. Since there was just him and me, I was being put in a position of approving things because I couldn't find him. I was making decisions that a vice president for production shouldn't make. There were too many crises taking place."

One of the most pressing problems was the matter of a sequel to *The Godfather*. Paramount had Puzo working on a script right away, but Coppola refused to direct it. Bluhdorn did his best. He never tired of repeating that Francis possessed something more valuable than the formula for Coca-Cola.

With Evans preoccupied with *Chinatown* and his personal life, and barely speaking to Coppola anyway, it fell to Bart to corral the director. Coppola was adamant. Too many talented people had had their hands in *The Godfather* — Brando, Willis, Puzo — for him to be secure in calling it his own. Doing another one might undo everything. "If it bombs, then people will look at the first *Godfather* and say it was all Brando, or whatever," said Coppola. "If I took my career to an insurance actuary, he'd tell me to lay off the sequels if I wanted to stay healthy."

Bluhdorn persuaded him to produce it, to supervise it, if he didn't want to direct it. He would let him select the director. Three months later, Coppola called Evans, said, "I got the guy to do it."

"Who is it?"

"Martin Scorsese."

"Absolutely not! Marty Scorsese is a horrible choice. Over my dead body."

Coppola went back to Bluhdorn, said, "I can't work with these guys. They say no to everything and they exhaust me."

"Vell den, do it yourzelf."

One morning, Coppola sat down to breakfast with Bart. "I have no interest in the *Godfather* movies," he told Bart. "I want to go and do my own work, even if I have to make it on Super 8. To try to get back into that family again is gonna be a dry heave. The idea of having to work on what is gonna be a big expensive film with a lotta pressure, a lotta people telling me what to do, just sounds like two years of misery."

"This will make it so you can do your own work," said Bart. But Coppola, still bitter about Evans and having found this theme, was on a roll. "I'm tired of—I do something that people want, that they love, they beg me to do it, and then they start attacking me, second-guessing me. That's why I like to cook. You work hard in the kitchen, you come out, and usually people say, 'Ummm, that was good,' not, 'There's mildew on the rigatoni.' "

"Look, who was the star of *The Godfather*?" continued Bart, patiently, laying it on thick. "Brando? Pacino? . . . No, it was you. What does a star get?"

"A million dollars," replied Coppola.

"If I can get you a million dollars to write and direct, will you do it?"

"Okay, you got a deal." Bart's argument made sense. Coppola realized that if *Godfather, Part II* were successful, it would give him the kind of independence he needed to do his own films. Coppola stipulated that none of the executives and producers who were involved with *The Godfather* could be involved with the sequel. Evans was not allowed to put a foot on the set. He also secured a commitment from Paramount to finance *The Conversation*. Bart called Bluhdorn, told him the good news. Bluhdorn started yelling, " 'Yes, yes, close da deal. Vhere are da papers? Do it! Do it!' I think this was one of the times we couldn't find Bob. There was no one minding the store."

The deal was signed on June 22, 1972. This was the first time a director had been paid $1 million up front, in addition to gross participation. It was the beginning of a new era for directors, and Yablans, for one, saw the handwriting on the wall. "We paid Francis $60,000 to make *The Godfather*," he says. "When you get into these big numbers, the directors have contempt. They're not gonna listen to you telling them they can't shoot this or they can't do that. They're gonna look at you and say, 'The schmuck.' " As soon as the news got out, Frank Wells demanded that Coppola pay back the $300,000 he still owed Warners for development at Zoetrope. "Warners hurt me in many ways," says Coppola. "They threatened to put a 'cloud' over *Godfather II* unless they had their development money returned to them. They truly acted like an 'Evil Empire.' "

WHEN ASHBY WAS FINISHED EDITING *The Last Detail*, there was more trouble with Columbia. The executives hated the jump cuts he had lifted from Godard. The release was delayed six months while they again fought over the profanity. Ayres finally persuaded the studio to submit it to Cannes. Columbia refused to throw the obligatory party. But after Nicholson won Best Actor, it would have been extremely embarrassing for Columbia to keep the picture on the shelf.

During the summer of 1973, while Ashby and Ayres were wrangling with Columbia, the banks stepped in to stop production and acquisitions. Under the Schneiders, the studio had wracked up a pretax loss of $72.5 million, and an after-tax loss of $50 million, the third highest annual loss in Columbia's history. The stock fell from a high of $30 a share in 1971 to $2 a share in 1973. Columbia was facing bankruptcy. Allen and Co., the investment firm that was a major stockholder, engineered a coup. Bert's father, Abe, was elevated to the post of honorary chairman at $300,000 a year. Stanley Schneider cashed out in June. Alan J. Hirschfeld became CEO of the corporation, backed by Herbert Allen. Agent David Begelman, late of CMA, became president.

Begelman kept Peter Guber as his number two. Although unfortunate in the light of hindsight, at the time the Begelman appointment seemed like good news for Columbia stockholders. The studio was belatedly getting the benefit of the broom that swept the others clean in the late '60s. But it was not good news for the Schneiders. Bert had gone on a trip to China with Candy for three weeks in April 1973, sponsored by *The Guardian*, a left-wing newspaper. He wrote postcards with the half-jokey salutation, "Dear Fellow Cultural Worker." They returned on May 9, her twenty-seventh birthday. Some friends gave her a party. Bert refused to go. She stayed late. At 1:30, he called the party, snapped, "Get home immediately." When she got back to his house, he was sitting on the bed, voice shaking with anger. He had the tape recorder out, so she could play the tape back later and benefit from his analysis. "It was four A.M., and he was still going; when was I going to get in touch with my behavior? . . . I was irresponsible and cruel. He was screaming. . . . Suddenly, he picked up the television at the foot of the bed and hurled it into the next room, where it shattered on the brick floor." Now they fought constantly. The patio furniture ended up at the bottom of the pool. Carpenters were on daily call to repair the damage.

When Bert returned from China, he found that the family business had turned into a company of strangers. "I knew Begelman from the days he was robbing Judy Garland," says Blauner. "He was always a thief. But I had a nice relationship with him." Begelman couldn't have been more eager to renew the deal with BBS. "He would have made a deal with our receptionist, with our janitor," continues Blauner. At about the same time, however, Bert had dropped by the Columbia offices at 711 Fifth Avenue in New York. He had finished his business, was trying to leave, when the Columbia executives insisted he meet Alan Hirschfeld. Bert didn't want to meet Hirschfeld, but he had no choice. He had never told Columbia a thing about *Hearts and Minds*; it was none of their business, and all they knew was the title. The two men exchanged pleasantries, and as Bert was leaving, Hirschfeld said, "Well, I can't wait to see *Hearts and Minds*."

Bert said, "Ya know, it's not the normal kind of picture."

"Whaddya mean?"

"It's a documentary."

Hirschfield wouldn't have known a documentary if he'd tripped over it. "They shit," says Blauner. "This wasn't going to satisfy them, they figured Bert had gone around the bend, so get outta the deal." Adds Rafelson, "Bert's way of dealing with things was to say, 'This *is* a picture. It doesn't *say* I can't make a documentary. So fuck you!'" In December, BBS got a letter canceling the sixth picture. Columbia was playing hardball, withholding money due Schneider from his previous films.

But if you wanted to win a game of hardball with Bert, you had to have balls of steel. As Rafelson put it, "Who gave a shit about the lawsuits? That was the attitude of everybody who ever worked at BBS. That's what we prided ourselves on, that we were a company of fuck-you, in-your-face guys who could get along together." The feeling around BBS was that the fact that *Hearts and Minds* was a documentary was just an excuse to take another shot at the Schneiders. Columbia just wanted to get rid of all vestiges of the family, Bert included, lest it wrest control of the studio from its new bosses.

Nevertheless, the parties at Bert's continued. Sidney Prince, Bert's shrink, conducted informal group therapy sessions in the hot tub that included Calley, who had fallen hard for a Czech bombshell introduced to him by Milos Forman. She was a stunning, statuesque blonde, a former Miss Czechoslovakia, named Olinka. He hired her as his housekeeper, and took in her daughter as well, her daughter's father (he had been a Mr. Universe), and her parents. None of them spoke any English. "All these people would walk around his house speaking Czech, not interacting in any way with the English speakers, not a word, not yes, not no," recalls Buck Henry, who was around a lot. "John never learned a word of Czech. We'd say, 'John, do you know what they're talking about?' He'd say, 'No, thank God I don't. I'll be upstairs reading.'" Calley eventually married her, and then paid her what in his book was the highest compliment: he named his sixty-five-foot yawl after her. The happy couple spent their honeymoon on the boat in the Aegean, accompanied by Sue Mengers and her husband. Mengers recalls, "Olinka would get up every morning looking like what she was, Miss Czechoslovakia, the most gorgeous girl, in this little bikini. She'd say, 'Good morning,' and jump off the boat and swim, while I'd be huddled there wrapped in a towel. My husband would look at Olinka, and then he'd look at me, just like Chuck Grodin. I was Jeannie Berlin, the heartbreak kid, I swear to God."

If Bert and Candice were becoming unglued, Bert and Huey Newton were getting tighter and tighter. Huey spent more and more time at Bert's home.

"Huey was pretty coked up most of the time," recalls Brackman. "He was a mad rapper." Cocaine was becoming a fixture at parties, sitting out on coffee tables in crystal dishes and bowls. Says Brackman, "It was so widespread that weenie straight people — even they did an occasional toot."

Some Panthers up in Oakland thought Huey had gone Hollywood, that his easy access to Schneider's money and cocaine were distracting him from the struggle. Conversely, it was easy to see Schneider's infatuation with Huey as the worst form of radical chic. "I've always thought left-wing politics in and out of Hollywood was about pussy and/or drugs," says Buck Henry. "The first time I saw Huey, I thought, This is really bad news, people being seduced into sexual and drug behavior that they might not have indulged in had they not been involved with the movement. And a lot of lives were left behind. Huey served the sense of these guys' embarrassment about where they came from and what kind of privilege they received, and in return he got a lot of cute white girls laid at his feet. He also laid down a dose of clap and syphilis that went through an awful lot of people."

But in Bert's case it was more than radical chic. If the bottom line in Hollywood was money, Schneider was serious. His checkbook was always open. He would walk into Panther headquarters in Oakland and write a check for $100,000 without blinking an eye. "Bert really put his money where his mouth was," say Toby Rafelson. "He was very much a mensch, very courageous, very willing to give away money in order to do the right thing."

For nearly two years, Bert had been taking care of Susan Branaman, who was dying of cancer. She was a Mack, of the Mack truck family, had been to Radcliffe College but had dropped out, gotten involved with a painter and poet in North Beach, and had become a hooker to support her heroin habit. When she died, Bert held a wake for her. Her body had been cremated, and her remains set out in bowls. The bereaved guests snorted the ashes, like they snorted coke.

Bob Rafelson too was floundering. Columbia asked him to do a picture, wanted him to come over to the lot for a meeting. As always his own worst enemy, he replied, "I'm not going over to Columbia Pictures. You come to my office." The president and the chairman made the trek to La Brea. "It was fucking unbelievable," he continues. "I didn't know that I was being arrogant. I didn't know what the rules were." Rafelson acted out the movie he wanted to do next. They said, "This is great, we're going to do it."

Then Rafelson added, "Terrific, but there's one more thing, we've got to get things solved with this documentary problem. You guys aren't accepting the movie, we got to get it resolved."

"Of course, we'll take care of it." Recalls Rafelson, "I never heard from them again. I couldn't understand it. I couldn't find a powerful enough person to find out why I couldn't find out. They seemed so enthusiastic and so reassuring.

And I wasn't even out of the office yet. I found out, man, this is a nasty business out there." Rafelson had developed a reputation of being hard to work with, belligerent and insistent on his own way.

In August 1973, while Bob and Toby were at their house in Aspen, a propane stove exploded, injuring their daughter Julie, who was about to turn eleven. Julie was very much the apple of Bob's eye, and equally as precious to her mother. They rushed her to the hospital in Denver, but she was badly burned and an infection set in. Bert and Judy, who were barely speaking to each other, flew out to be with Julie and her parents. Julie died. Says Henry, "Nobody ever recovers from that, and it affected everything Bob ever did after that." Toby had found out about her husband's infidelities, including his affair with Paula Strachan. (Paula was shortly to marry and later divorce Bob's older brother, Don.) Toby learned that many of her good friends had slept with him, so that all her relationships were compromised. She was the proverbial last to know.

Toby was going through what Judy had endured three years before. "None of the women I knew, who were the female sides of all these couples, were as irresponsible as the men, nor did they have the same urge to rebel as the men did," says Toby. "I let Bob go his way, but I wasn't going to participate. Once in a while I would do a drug trip with him, but rarely, because I never really trusted that he would be there for me. But when you're with somebody who's experimenting and feeling his oats, whether he's screwing around or taking drugs or talking in certain ways that you don't particularly approve of, it's very hard to hold a marriage and a house and a life together, and continually put that person down or disapprove of them." Toby and Bob had always bantered, exchanged playful barbs. But now it turned vicious. Then Toby was diagnosed with cancer. Her friends felt he was not there for her.

The spring and summer of 1974 were hard for Bert and his friends. The trouble was bad, and came often. Peter Davis's wife, Josie Mankiewicz, was killed by a taxi cab in New York as their young son watched. Relations between Schneider and the new regime at Columbia continued to deteriorate. Begelman agreed to take *Hearts and Minds* to Cannes in 1974. He asked for a copy of the rough cut to screen for the board of directors. Schneider refused. He thought the request was "weird." Begelman saw the film for the first time in the spring and reversed himself, refused to send it to Cannes. Schneider ignored him, continued his preparations. Begelman demanded that the Columbia logo be removed. BBS sued Columbia for various monies allegedly owed, and to force Begelman to release *Hearts and Minds*. Eventually, Jaglom ponied up $1 million, which he and his partner, Zack Norman, had laboriously raised from dentists and plastic surgeons over the course of five years to produce his own Vietnam-themed picture, *Tracks*, to star Dennis Hopper. He bought *Hearts and Minds* from Columbia, then turned around and entered into a distribution deal with Calley, who released the film in December 1974, in time to qualify for the Oscars.

Bergen got two writing assignments that took her to Africa, where she was rumored to have had an affair with William Holden. She and Bert were having so much trouble, she dreaded coming back. She kept the alleged affair secret, and when she did finally return, things seemed better. They dropped acid, joked about getting old together, her pushing his wheelchair. But Holden apparently plied her with cables and gifts, and Bert couldn't help but recognize something had happened between them. He was angry and bitter. He said it wasn't the infidelity that bothered him, he could even dig it, so much as the lying. In March, he kicked her out. (Bergen refused to comment.)

Still, Schneider was devastated. Bert played a piece of music Chaplin had written for his documentary, a lush, sentimental composition, fantasized about marrying Candice on Chaplin's vast lawn at Vevey, and wept. He started seeing a teenager from his daughter's school who says she was "sixteen years old" at the time. She adds, "There was a twenty-five-year age difference between us." They met in a movie line, a Marx brothers film. "It was exciting, glamorous, kind of forbidden," she says. "It wasn't forbidden, but it probably should have been."

CHINATOWN went into production in the fall of 1973. The relationship between Polanski and Towne had deteriorated to the point where Towne knew he was unwelcome on the set. He watched dailies at night with Evans in his screening room, after Evans had watched them with Polanski. The first day, Evans was driven to the location — an orange grove — flat on his back in a station wagon. Polanski, stressed out and feeling sick, lay beside him. When they arrived at the set, Nicholson and Dick Sylbert were leaning against a tree, waiting for them. Polanski got out of the car, walked over to them, and threw up. "That was the beginning of the movie," says Sylbert. "We went downhill from there."

The actors were used to the American warm bath school of directing, which is to say, a collaborative approach, with lots of tender loving care from the director. That was not Polanski's way. "Roman is Napoleon with actors, 'They do what I tell them to do,' " says Evans. "He'd say, 'In Poland, I could just go make my fucking movies.' " He was dictatorial and controlling. He gave Nicholson so many line readings that Anthea Sylbert, who was the costume designer, half expected him to begin speaking with a Polish accent.

But Nicholson and Polanski were good friends, and Nicholson was more often than not amused by Polanski's eccentricities. Says Anthea, "Jack was always amused." Dunaway, on the contrary, was decidedly not. Cast as Evelyn Mulwray, she considered herself a "star," and did not go out of her way to ingratiate herself with the director or the crew. The actors had small dressing rooms on the set, as well as trailers. According to several sources, Dunaway was in the habit of peeing in wastebaskets rather than take the walk to her trailer. (Dunaway, when asked about her urinary habits, said she has "no recollection" of such behavior.) When she did use the john in her Winnebago, she did not deign to flush it, calling for a teamster instead. Several teamsters quit.

Dunaway was puzzled about her character's motivation and, by all accounts, got little guidance from Polanski. He would shout, "Say the fucking words. Your salary is your motivation." She was obsessed with her look. Indeed, with her trapezoidal cheekbones, alabaster skin, marcelled, honey-colored hair, and blood red lipstick, she looked stunning. Recalls Polanski, "Every time I shouted cut, first there had to be Blistex and lipstick, and then the powder. Right after the clapper board, she would start all over again." Things came to a head while they were shooting a scene at the end of the second week in the Windsor restaurant behind the old Ambassador Hotel where Robert Kennedy had been shot. Dunaway and Nicholson are seated on a red-leather banquette in a two shot favoring Dunaway. According to Polanski, "There was one hair that would stick out from her hairdo and catch the light and I was trying to get rid of it, trying to flatten it and it would not stay." Polanski walked around behind her and plucked the hair. Dunaway screamed, "That motherfucker plucked my hair!" or something very much like it, and stormed off the set. Polanski did the same.

Evans arranged a truce between the director and his leading lady, but it didn't last long. "There was a scene where she gets in the car after seeing her daughter, and Jack is in the car waiting for her and scares the shit out of her," recalls John Alonzo, the DP. "She kept saying to Roman, 'Roman, I have to pee. I have to pee.' 'No. No. You stay there. Johnny, you ready?' I said, 'I'm ready.' 'You stay there. We shoot, we shoot.' And then he said, 'Roll the window down. I got to talk to you. You're turning too far right. Don't look at Jack, just look ahead.' Then she threw a coffee-cup full of liquid in Roman's face. He said, 'You cunt, that's piss!' And she said, 'Yes, you little putz,' and rolled the window up. We were all speculating that maybe Jack peed in the cup for her. [Or maybe] she had a small bladder or something."

The picture finally wrapped in early 1974. The crew fabricated a huge tube of Blistex, and presented it to Dunaway as a going-away present.

SINCE THE DAYS of *Bonnie and Clyde*, Beatty had operated as an independent producer on his personal projects. He realized that if he used his own money to develop his films and hire the talent, he could both maintain control over them and get a better deal from the studios by playing them off against one another. "He was so courageous at what he did, taking these tremendous risks," says Dick Sylbert. "He could've really come a cropper, and he almost went into the shithouse on *Shampoo*. He nearly outsmarted himself."

According to Towne, one morning, over breakfast, Beatty casually asked for a co-screenwriting credit. He felt he had been screwed out of one by Altman on *McCabe*. Without missing a beat, Towne said, "Okay." A friend, to whom Towne told the story, was outraged, asked him, "Did Warren really write any of it?" Towne replied something like, "Naa, ya know, what he did was cross out a lot of stuff that I wrote, and he told me to do this and that, and we usually fought about it, and sometimes he really fucked things up."

"How could you let him get away with that?"

"Oh, you know Warren. Unless you do things like that, you're not going to get the other stuff you can get from Warren."

Beatty had already hired key members of the cast—Julie Christie, Goldie Hawn, Lee Grant, and Jack Warden, who plays a wealthy businessman—and the key below-the-line people, Dick Sylbert, Anthea Sylbert, and the DP, Laszlo Kovacs. He was in for a million dollars of his own money before he had a deal, and he stood to lose a lot of money if the production didn't start on schedule. Although Towne was again on board, he was still dragging his feet, and Beatty was getting impatient. "Robert's failure to deliver on time kept a host of highly paid people on contract waiting," he says.

By that time, the relationship between Beatty and Christie had ended, although they remained good friends. She had called him at his Beverly Wilshire suite one night, and said it was over. He hung up the phone, thought, She's with somebody, I can tell, and said out loud, mournfully, "They've all dumped me." As Beatty wryly put it, "She thinks I'm Jack Warden."

Shampoo was a hard sell, and Beatty was having a difficult time setting it up. Lester "the Investor" Persky was putting together a package of films he intended to finance for Columbia. He says, "It was very hard-hitting, and the studios didn't think a film named *Shampoo* about a hairdresser who was pretending to be gay, and was making out like a bandit with all the wives and girlfriends of his friends, was a sympathetic character, or believable. They thought it was awful." Evans, on the other hand, would have bought used toilet paper from Beatty and Towne, and Beatty knew it. So he took it to Paramount first. Evans was staying at the Carlyle Hotel in New York. Beatty flew in with the script, sat there while he read it. Evans was desperate to do it, and made him an offer. But Beatty had no intention of taking the first offer he got. He took the project to Warners, where he already had a deal for *Heaven Can Wait*, with Muhammad Ali attached. He talked numbers with Frank Wells, who topped Evans. Meanwhile, Yablans overruled Evans. Beatty went to Begelman at Columbia, who was desperate for product. According to Evans, Beatty said, "Look Bob, I'm bringing it to David, and I want to tell him that you want it. He offered me three million four. I want to tell him that you offered four million." Evans says he resisted.

"I can't do that Warren, because we have a deal amongst the guys that we can't lie —"

"Hey, come on, Bob, it's me. Begelman calls you, I want you to tell him you're offering four million for it."

Indeed, Evans was a star-fucker before he was anything else and says he gave in. Begelman made an extremely sweet offer, almost twice as much as Warners, way more than was prudent, given Columbia's parlous financial condition, and given the fact that Begelman hated the script, thought it was cynical and offensive. But it *was* Beatty, and if Columbia didn't produce it, somebody else would. Beatty went with Columbia. But by this time, Begelman had come to his senses, and welshed on the deal. "People thought Columbia was going into Chapter 11 at that point, and he simply reneged on it, because the deal was bigger than he should have offered," says Beatty. "When he reneged, I went back to Warners." But Wells played hardball. He asked Beatty, "Warren, what were those numbers we talked about back then?" Warren said, "Here they are." Wells looked at them, raised his head to look Beatty in the eye and said, "No, no, I think they were half that much."

Beatty was fucked, not to put too fine a point on it; as Dick Sylbert said, he had nearly outsmarted himself. But he had an ace up his sleeve, Carole Eastman's script for *The Fortune*, which, according to Mike Medavoy, who was Eastman's agent, Beatty had bought for $350,000. With Nicholson attached, himself opposite Nicholson, and Mike Nichols directing, it was about as close to a guaranteed hit as you could get in the mid-'70s. If Begelman wanted *The Fortune*, he would have to take *Shampoo* too. (Beatty denies he bought *The Fortune*, denies he yoked it with *Shampoo*.)

Beatty collared Begelman at a political fund-raiser. The Columbia executive knew what Wells had done, knew Beatty had already spent a lot of his own money, knew he had the upper hand. He said, "I never made you any promises." Beatty poked his finger into Begelman's chest, hard, backing him across the room, saying in a loud voice, "You're a liar. I know you're a liar and you know I know you're a liar, but we're gonna forget that, and we're gonna do this deal. You have nothing, you need this picture. Just match my original deal with Warners." Begelman, who was nothing if not self-possessed, was nevertheless getting red in the face, flustered, and finally gave in. Beatty had his deal, but it was for only half of what Columbia originally offered, approximately equal to the original Warners deal. According to Beatty, he couldn't even get first dollar gross, and had to settle for a cut of the "rolling gross."* Still,

---

* Rolling gross or rolling break-even was a novel idea that rendered gross profits — not to mention net profits — worthless. Essentially, it meant that distribution and other costs would be added on to the negative cost even while a film was in release, so that the break-even point kept rolling, or increasing. As some wag put it, "the break always rolled away from the filmmakers."

once the profits of *Shampoo* reached a certain level, Beatty's participation hit 40 percent.

In a move of what turned out in hindsight to be stunning stupidity, Begelman laid *Shampoo* off on Persky. The deal made Persky a very rich man. Begelman retained the lion's share of the profits of *The Fortune*, which was going to be a resounding flop. Beatty only made one mistake. Although he may have genuinely wanted to work with Nicholson, *The Fortune* script was essentially a pawn on the *Shampoo* chessboard, so he didn't bother to read it.

Jack didn't need to read it. As Harry Gittes puts it, "Jack was always wild about Carole. She was the first person to understand how brilliant he was, and write a character for him — a blue-collar intellectual, which is what he is — and he never, ever forgot that."

All that remained was for Beatty to hire a director for *Shampoo*. He knew Ashby, and liked him, offered him $750,000. Beatty says Towne objected. "He felt that Hal was a little lax," says Beatty. "Hal was never a person to fight to get it right, exactly the way it was on the page. Towne said, 'I implore you not to use Hal Ashby, use Mark Rydell.' I said, 'I'm using Hal Ashby.'"

Ashby had gotten close to Nicholson in the course of *The Last Detail*. He hung out with him, went to Lakers games with him and Bert. Like Rafelson, Mike Nichols, and a few other directors, Ashby tried to hitch himself to Nicholson's star. He wanted Jack for every new project he announced. But he had a difficult time getting anything off the ground. He tried to set up two films that later became big hits with other directors. Ironically, both would be produced by Saul Zaentz. He wanted to direct *One Flew Over the Cuckoo's Nest*, and had talks with Zaentz and co-producer Michael Douglas. But Zaentz was the kind of creative producer Ashby hated. The director was too withdrawn and suspicious, refused to say how he would approach the book, so they walked away, found Milos Forman. The film was shot in the Oregon State Hospital in Salem, not a fun place to spend a lot of time. The unpleasantness index was so high that cast and crew were spending their off hours hanging out on street corners trying to score lids of grass from local dealers, mountain men with buds in their beards. This was good for the local economy, but embarrassing for the film, so the production office used petty cash to make bulk, shopping-bag-sized purchases. One of the production assistants occupied himself with breaking down the bricks and selling baggies to the actors for the same price they were paying on the street.

Later, after Forman and Zaentz won Oscars for the film, Ashby was bitter. He also wanted to direct *Hair* for Zaentz, but that also went to Forman. It was a frustrating time for the director. On the one hand, he had nothing but contempt for the studio system, and was looking to get out. He even talked of starting a film collective. "Basically it would have been a fucking dictatorship, and he would have been in charge," says Mulvehill. On the other hand, Ashby

Gene Hackman looks on as Arthur Penn and Warren Beatty shed blood over Bonnie and Clyde.

1

2

Dennis Hopper "was violent and dangerous," says Brooke Hayward. "When [I got] divorced, I probably could have gone for half his cut from Easy Rider . . . [but I didn't] *because I didn't want him coming after me with a shotgun."*

3

4

Peter Fonda in his den. "When Easy Rider came out, everyone debated the meaning of Wyatt's famous line, 'We blew it,'" says Fonda. "My motivation was 'Hello, [Dennis], you fascist fuck, you've blown our big chance.'"

The Easy Rider gang (from left: Hopper, Fonda, Jack Nicholson) goes to Cannes in 1969. When it became clear that the movie might be a hit, Fonda quipped that the Columbia executives stopped shaking their heads in incomprehension and began nodding their heads in incomprehension.

Michelle Phillips (right, with Nicholson and Hopper) suggested Hopper commit suicide after their week-long marriage ended.

6

George Lucas, c. 1971. He never forgave Warner Bros. for trimming THX: 1138. He said, "They were cutting off the fingers of my baby."

Beatty dressed as McCabe (of McCabe & Mrs. Miller) and director Robert Altman dressed as Timothy Leary. Beatty says, "Had I been the producer I would have killed Robert Altman."

8

Beatty and Christie (above) at a 1971 American Film Institute benefit in New York City, and (at right) at the L.A. Forum for a McGovern rally on April 15, 1972. "If ever a movie star existed for whom stardom meant nothing, it was Julie," says Robert Towne. One day she appalled her lover and McCabe & Mrs. Miller *and* Shampoo *co-star Warren Beatty by losing a $1,000 check in the street.*

It was "this splendid decade of hope," says Toby Rafelson, shown here with husband Bob Rafelson soon after they moved to L.A. in the early '60s. "Then slowly we all began getting into these strange self-destructive, quirky, unpredictable areas of life that ultimately destroyed everyone."

11

Before: "[Wife] Polly accused me of being crazy about [Cybill Shepherd] the day we arrived on location" for The Last Picture Show, says Peter Bogdanovich, shown here with Platt several years later. "It irritated me enormously." After: "I never felt about anybody quite the way I felt about Cybill. It was one of those times when life just takes over, and you don't really have control."

13

14

"*I thought Marty [Scorsese] was just the cutest thing I had ever seen,*" recalls girlfriend Sandy Weintraub. "*He was chubby and he had long hair and no neck, and was shorter than me.*"

Bert Schneider and Candice Bergen enjoy a day at the races. Schneider urged her to loosen up, get in closer touch with her feelings, drop some acid.

Upon meeting Huey Newton for the first time, Schneider said, "If he's not Mao, I'll eat it."

16

*Bob Evans, Charlie Bluhdorn, and Frank Yablans, Paramount's "Manson family,"
enjoy a rare moment of levity.*

Evans and wife Ali MacGraw at the premiere party for The
Godfather. *Says Evans, "She was looking at me and thinking
of Steve McQueen's cock."*

19

Bogdanovich directs Shepherd in Daisy Miller. *Says his agent, Sue Mengers, "Peter always protected himself against attractive leading men opposite Cybill, with actors he could feel superior to."*

20

Francophile Billy Friedkin dug his own grave when he inexplicably remade Wages of Fear *as* Sorcerer.

Too much of a good thing: Francis Coppola clutches three Oscars for The Godfather, Part II.

Beatty takes a bite out of Carrie Fisher on the set of Shampoo. *(Below)* He talks, while *Shampoo co-writer Robert Towne listens. Towne, who did a lot of work for Beatty, used to refer to himself as the "sharecropper." (Bottom) Towne's companion, Julie Payne, at the* Shampoo *premiere with David Geffen.*

22

23

24

Schneider and Hearts and Minds *director Peter Davis, with their Oscars on April 8, 1975. Bert holds the telegram from the Provisional Revolutionary Government of Vietnam that scandalized the audience.*

25

Scorsese on the set of Taxi Driver, *flanked, from left to right, by Shepherd, Jodie Foster, and Albert Brooks.*

26

27

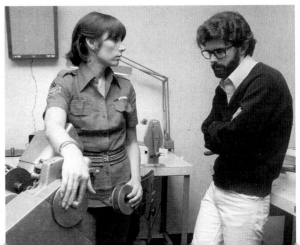

Marcia and George Lucas in the editing room. According to Marcia, George always said, "Emotionally involving the audience is easy. Anybody can do it blindfolded, get a little kitten and have some guy wring its neck."

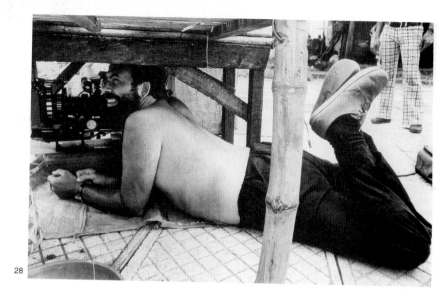

28

Coppola's "personality had changed," says the script supervisor of Apocalypse Now. "He was no longer bound by any normal conventions. Francis would tread on anyone he could tread on."

29

1 EACH
BUFFALO, WATER
U.S. ARMY

30

Marlon Brando disliked Hopper so much he wouldn't do any of their scenes in
Apocalypse Now *together.* (Below) *Coppola with Bunnies Cyndi Wood, Linda*
Carpenter, and Colleen Camp on December 3, 1976.

31

32

Scorsese enjoys a night out with wife Julia Cameron and mistress Liza Minnelli. (Right) Scorsese with Robbie Robertson. "It was a shame that Marty wasn't gay," says former girlfriend Weintraub. "The best relationship he ever had was probably with Robbie."

33

Steven Spielberg and Amy Irving. Although several of his friends thought she was using him, she recognized the limitations of the movies Spielberg and his friends were making. She said, "I'm glad I didn't do Star Wars because it was a nothing part. I would not want to get famous because of that movie."

34

The three musketeers: Brian De Palma, Spielberg, and Scorsese.

35

A boy and his gun: Paul Schrader poses with a familiar prop. (Below) Schrader and Nastassja Kinski on the set of Cat People. *According to director John Milius, she said, "Paul, I always fuck my directors. And with you it was difficult."*

36

Towne and Payne with their newborn, Katharine, in July 1978. (Below) *Also in 1978, Towne with Olympic Amazons, some to appear in* Personal Best. *Says Payne,* "*He abandoned everything for* Personal Best, *and went off on this wild journey that never ended.*"

Says actor Bruce Dern, "What happened to Hal Ashby, both what he did to himself, and they did to him, is as repulsive to me as anything I've seen in my forty years in the industry."

badly wanted a hit, badly enough to overcome his disdain for stars and star vehicles. He wanted it badly enough to direct a Warren Beatty project, which he knew, or should have known, would mean giving up a large measure of control to Beatty. Continues Mulvehill, "Hal was on a certain level very pragmatic. He had not used stars in any of his pictures, and they both flopped." The studio wouldn't even open *Detail*. Adds Jerome Hellman, who produced *Midnight Cowboy*, and would shortly do the same for one of Ashby's most successful pictures, *Coming Home*, "Warren was a giant star, and Hal looked up to and cherished his friendship with Warren. I think for him to do *Shampoo* was like a validation, because as complicated as Hal was, and as quixotic as he was, he didn't want to fail, he wanted to be on the A list." Concludes Mulvehill, "Hal admired the way Warren dealt with his success, he admired his control, his power. Warren massaged the system. Hal didn't play it that way." So when Beatty offered him *Shampoo*, he was ready.

The new regime at Columbia, which still had *The Last Detail* on the shelf, finally agreed to preview it in San Francisco. It was a huge success. Begelman was finally embarrassed into releasing the picture in December 1973 at the Bruin in Westwood, in time for Academy consideration. It did well, but then, making a serious miscalculation, he pulled it after only a week, thinking he would re-release it right before the Oscars, by which time word of mouth and Academy nominations would build it into a hit.

At the same time, in December 1973, Beatty, Ashby, and Towne sat down for a week or so of intensive work—they started at 9:00 in the morning and worked till 11:00 at night—in Beatty's suite at the Beverly Wilshire. They were under heavy pressure, because in order to hold the actors, they had to begin shooting in six weeks, by the end of January. They talked through the scenes, then Towne went into the next room to write. His control over the script considerably diluted, Towne was unhappy. He says, "Both Warren and Jack in differing ways used their political power to control creative situations."

Shampoo went into production in January 1974. If *Shampoo* had an auteur, it was probably Beatty. From the start, Ashby was at a disadvantage. Beatty had filled the key production slots with his own people, and Hal had no allies, except for editor Bob Jones. "Hal hated authority, and on that picture, Warren represented authority," says Mulvehill. "It was his film. Hal was a control freak without any control."

Adds Jones, "It was tough for him. I'd go on the set, and Warren and Towne would be off whispering in the corner. Hal would be sitting in the other corner." Haskell Wexler was a good friend of Hal's. "I visited the set a number of times," he says. "Hal was like an office boy on that, and he wasn't used to being that way. Warren chewed Hal up and spit him out."

One day, Dick Sylbert was standing outside the studio. "Hal walked up to

me and said, 'I can't take it anymore. These guys won't let me alone.' He hated
it, because we'd have meetings, and we'd go, 'All right Hal, this is what we're
gonna do.' We beat the shit out of him, had him boxed in—Warren, Towne,
myself, and Anthea. Actor, script, set, and costumes. They'd make him reshoot,
do takes he didn't want to do, coverage he felt he didn't need. But generally he
was smart enough to just go with the flow. He was the best person they could
have hired, because Ashby's feelings about people were very good. He was a
sweetheart of a man, and a wonderful director. To do that movie, you couldn't
be mean, you couldn't do an Altman."

The situation was delicate, with Beatty trying to get the best out of Hal, but
also directing through him. Anthea Sylbert puts it this way: "It was a collaborative effort, with Warren at the helm. One day, Warren said to me, 'I want you
to watch that scene there.' So I watched it. Then he came to me and he said,
'Well, how was it?' 'Just okay.' He said, 'Go tell Hal.' I said, 'I'm not telling Hal
anything. You go tell Hal.' "

Towne rewrote as they went along. "There were three of us behind the
camera," he says. "If one of us wasn't satisfied with a take, it was done over. In
the celebrated scene between Warren and Goldie where she asks, 'Were there
other women?' and he replies, 'Well, there were a few times at the shop—let's
face it, I fucked them all . . .' Originally he said, 'Grow up, everybody fucks
everybody.' Warren was towering over Goldie, so it seemed like he fucked
everybody and then was lecturing her about it. I called for a reshoot. Hal
thought it was okay, and Warren, being the prudent producer, was reluctant,
but I insisted, and then he got mad at me for not having realized that it was
fucked up before we shot it. I went for a walk with my dog, Hira, and realized
that Warren had to be sitting down and Goldie towering over him, and that
this speech had to be personal. It had to be torn out of him, so I did a rewrite."

Beatty was leery about starting *The Fortune* without a break, thought he
might be making a mistake, but Nichols reassured him, told him it would be
all right, *he* would make it all right. But Eastman's script had no third act.
When Jack returned from shooting *The Passenger* in Spain, the reality sank in.
Not only was the 240-page script unfinished, it never would be. Eastman
refused to rewrite, refused to touch a word. She had an extremely high opinion
of her abilities, regarded herself as a Virginia Woolf. She didn't like Nichols
any more than she liked Rafelson. As Hank Moonjean, the line producer, puts
it, "If the director had been Jesus Christ, I don't think she would have been
pleased." They tried to hammer her, said, "You're being completely unprofes-
sional, Carole." But she wouldn't give an inch, shot back, "I like being an
amateur, I don't want to be a professional." Nichols panicked, tried to get Jack
to lean on Carole, but it was no go, she would not write an ending. Nichols
said, "We're never going to have a complete script, we're going to start anyway."

The only thing Nichols could do was try to reduce the length. He had hired

Polly Platt to design the production, and she was in on the meetings between Nichols and Eastman at the Beverly Hills Hotel. "He kept cutting all the good stuff out of the movie," recalls Platt, who took Eastman's side. "She would suffer over it, but she couldn't do anything about it. She had this curious habit of putting both of her hands inside of her T-shirt and grabbing each of her tits, like she was protecting herself. Mike was trying to make the movie for a price — he'd gone very far over budget on those other movies, and they were flops — so this time he was going to prove to the studio that he could bring it in on budget." Platt argued with Nichols, as was her way, and he fired her, hired Dick Sylbert.

Nicholson had broken up with Michelle Phillips. "Jack always has the same dynamic with women," says Gittes, "tremendous push-pull. He was pulling away for the first three fourths of the time. Then eventually the girlfriends pull away — who can have a relationship with an actor who goes on location with beautiful women, wanna fuck 'im? — and he started chasing them. The key word is control. As soon as he lost control of his women, he went out of his mind." He liked to sleep with women, but he didn't like them. After *Shampoo*, Beatty began seeing Michelle, who had a cameo in one of the party scenes. During the production of *The Fortune*, she hung around the set, "didn't know whose lap to sit on," as Dick Sylbert puts it. Beatty and Phillips were not well matched. She was in many ways the opposite of Christie, used to living the high life, going to Aspen for Christmas. He had never taken a vacation in his life. She allowed Beatty to gratify several interests at once, one day letting him accompany her on a visit to her gynecologist. The doctor obligingly let him share the view.

TRUE TO FORM, as *Shampoo* was coming to a close, Ashby dumped Dyan Cannon, whom he had been seeing, and got involved with one of Nicholson's exes, Mimi Machu, whom Hal had met at the *Chinatown* wrap party. Mimi was house-sitting for Nicholson; she and Hal spent a lot of time there, drove to the beach together in Mimi's battered U.S. mail truck. He plunged quickly into *Bound for Glory*, a biopic based on the life of Woody Guthrie, for UA.

When *Glory* fell into his lap, Ashby related to it right away. Having grown up on a farm in the '30s, he felt a real kinship with Guthrie. "He loved that sense of freedom that Woody Guthrie had, never tied down to anything," says Machu. "He loved to roam." *Shampoo* had taught Hal the virtues of surrounding himself with allies, and he persuaded Mulvehill to work with him again on *Glory*. "It'll be just like old times," he said. Mulvehill agreed, but right away noticed a difference. The success of *Shampoo* made Hal much more sure of himself, much more confrontational. According to Mulvehill, "Hal said, 'Fuck you, this is what I'm gonna do, if you don't like it, stick it in your ear.'

He was also more into publicity for himself, his image as a filmmaker." He went way over budget, from $4 million to $7 million. The shoot was scheduled for seventy days, and went to 118. "We shot and shot and shot," says Mulvehill. "Frankly, it was the start of Hal's inability to deal with his success."

Ashby had neglected his health. "Hal's lungs were very weak," says Machu. "He was asthmatic from years of smoking." He was still smoking a couple of packs of long, thin Shermans every day, as well as vast numbers of joints. He was also doing a lot of coke. His behavior became increasingly erratic, gentle and soft-spoken one minute, loud and abusive the next. Haskell Wexler was the DP. He was Ashby's favorite DP—they did four films together. Wexler shot what he called "dirty" films, films that had a gritty look. But he was getting tired of dealing with Hal's mood swings. "Hal was snorting," says Wexler. "He fired me, for no reason. All of a sudden he said, 'You're fired.' 'Whaddya mean I'm fired?' 'You're fired.' Then he started to scream and stomp. I went to Hal and I said, 'You're not the Hal Ashby I love and respect. You're the Hal Ashby who's doing something to himself up his nose, and I'm not going to accept it.' I really chewed him out for being a doper, and he backed off."

Finally, Hal came down with a bad, raspy cough that got worse and worse as the production progressed. The doctors thought he had lung cancer, and it gave him a bad scare. He gave up the Shermans, started on four- and five-day fasts to purify his system.

The Last Detail received three Oscar nominations, Randy Quaid for Best Supporting Actor, Towne for Screenplay, and Nicholson for Best Actor, as Begelman anticipated. But by the time he re-released the picture in the spring of 1974 to take advantage of them, whatever heat it had generated during its initial release in December had dissipated. It was a shame, because it is a marvelous movie, full of the kind of funny, raunchy throwaway lines only Towne could write, and only Nicholson could say. Watching Nicholson talking Towne was like listening to Bob Dylan playing with the Band. There were a million ways to have ruined this picture, by patronizing or sentimentalizing the not very bright working-class characters, by shedding tears over Meadows's fate, by overemphasizing the fleeting moments when the movie's themes crystallize, before dissolving again into the blurred gray landscapes glimpsed through the windows of fast-moving trains, but Ashby's touch is delicate and sure.

Ashby was good at putting trouble, both personal and professional, behind him. He had moved on to *Shampoo* and then to *Glory* without looking back, and when *The Last Detail* died, he hardly seemed to notice.

Seven:
Sympathy for the Devil
1973

- *How bad boy William Friedkin made* **The Exorcist,** *joined Coppola and Bogdanovich in the Directors Company trying to take over the world, while Altman got himself in trouble.*

"There's a darkness in my soul, a profound darkness that is with me every waking moment."

— BILLY FRIEDKIN

On December 8, 1969, a scant four months after the Manson murders, twenty-three miles east of San Francisco at the Altamont Speedway in the white trash town of Livermore, Alameda County, 400,000-plus long-haired flower children gathered on a chilly fall afternoon to hear the Rolling Stones in the West Coast's answer to Woodstock. Security was augmented by a couple of hundred Hells Angels, who were accustomed to performing such chores for Bay Area bands like the Grateful Dead in exchange for free beer. They came rolling in on their chrome Harleys like squat toads atop gleaming steeds, accompanied by the loud thrum of the three-stroke engines and the smell of gasoline. They were accessorized with brass knuckles, knives, and leaded pool cues. The crowd, having sat through sets by the Jefferson Airplane and watched the Angels beat up Marty Balin, was growing impatient for the featured act. Finally, Mick Jagger burst upon the stage wearing gold, skintight velvet pants, thigh-high red boots, and a red and black ruffled shirt with flowery sleeves. The band broke into "Sympathy for the Devil," shortly to be celebrated for cineastes by Jean-Luc Godard, in his film of the same name. Suddenly there was a commotion at the foot of the stage. Then, as the band played "Under My Thumb," a young black man in a Day-Glo green jacket made the mistake of leaning against one of the choppers. As a pack of Angels surrounded him, he incautiously brandished a .38. Three Angels jumped him, and then he was dead, knifed in the back,

neck, and face. It was all caught on film, of course, immortalized in the
Maysles brothers' documentary *Gimme Shelter*. The '60s had ended again, and
again badly. By the time William Peter Blatty's novel *The Exorcist*, based on an
ostensibly true story, appeared in bookstores two years later, Americans were
ready for a creepy tale of demonic possession and pure evil, especially after
the bloodletting of Vietnam, Kent State, and Manson. It became an instant
bestseller.

WARNERS WAS LOOKING for someone to direct *The Exorcist*. Calley had
lined up the usual suspects, but every one of them had a reason why he didn't
want to bring the novel to the screen. He asked Mike Nichols, who said,
"I'm not going to stake my career and the picture's success or failure on the
performance of a twelve-year-old girl." He asked Arthur Penn, who was teaching
at Yale and declined. He approached John Boorman, who didn't like the novel,
thought it was a story about torturing a child. Blatty, who wrote the script, and
was also a producer on the movie, sent a copy to Bogdanovich. Flattering the
powerful director, he wrote an inscription on the flyleaf: "If you don't make
this movie, nobody will." But it wasn't Peter's kind of picture, and he turned it
down, naively thinking Blatty meant what he said, that therefore it would never
be made. Then Blatty remembered William Friedkin, whom he had met some
years earlier when the director had called a TV script of his "the worst piece of
shit I ever read in my life." Blatty laughed, thinking, This guys got balls.

Since then Friedkin had developed a reputation. As one producer put it,
"Billy was a tough critter. He didn't give a fuck about anybody else that walked
the face of the earth. He was a guy, you'd known him for thirty years, saved his
ass by putting together the deal, he'd turn to you and say, 'Get off the set.' "
Blatty didn't know anything about this, just recalled that Friedkin was somehow
unfettered by the usual Hollywood inhibitions, and willingly jeopardizing
his chances to direct by speaking his mind. I can trust him, he thought. He
also recalled that Friedkin was known for his documentaries. "Someone who
could give the film a sense of reality was what the fantasy absolutely needed,"
he says.

Blatty sent Friedkin a copy of the novel with the same inscription he had
used for Bogdanovich. Unlike the others, Friedkin jumped. "A good part of my
motivation was to make a better film than Francis," he explains. "We were
ambitious and competitive. Someone would always raise the ante." At the
time, *The Exorcist* seemed impossible to make, the special effects — levitation,
possession, poltergeists — were way beyond the state of the art. Blatty says, "It
was all very well for the reader's imagination when it's on the page, but to have
it mashed into your face like a custard pie on the big screen and say, 'This is
it,' I mean, it could have been ludicrous. He could have been a laughingstock.
But nothing daunted him."

Friedkin received $325,000 for directing. Blatty gave him five points from his share; Warners gave him another five. Friedkin says he had final cut. He hated Blatty's 226-page first draft, complained the writer had strayed too far from his own book. There were lots of flashbacks and flashforwards. Friedkin accused Blatty of doing to himself what his own worst enemy wouldn't. He said, "I just want you to tell a straight story from beginning to end, with no craperoo." Blatty listened, and started over.

The director and the writer hit it off immediately. Friedkin found Blatty to be a nervous guy with a facial tic, jet black hair, and olive coloring. He had such a Levantine cast, that when he first came to Hollywood he passed himself off as a Saudi prince. The two men had in common an inordinate attachment to their mothers. Both had recently died, and Blatty was writing a book about his. "My grief could be described by an outside observer as neurotic, overdrawn, and one might describe Billy's reaction as the same as mine," said Blatty. "Who knows what deep psychic effect it had on both of us."

For his part, Blatty found Friedkin immensely charming and entertaining. "There was a certain element of danger about him," he says. "Billy was extremely fluent socially. He knew something about everything, especially the film business. He had a hale, convivial presence that I enjoyed immensely." Friedkin surrounded himself with characters out of Damon Runyon, cops and gangsters he met through Jimmy Breslin.

Blatty wanted Brando for Father Karras, but the director vetoed him. Recalls Blatty, "His reason was that if he cast Brando, it would be Brando's picture." He had seen what had happened to Coppola, and did not want to share the limelight. He turned down Nicholson as well, eventually settling on a cast of solid, but not flashy actors, including Ellen Burstyn, fresh from *Marvin Gardens*, for the mother, Chris MacNeil.

Casting the part of Regan, the possessed girl, was harder. At the time she was interviewed, Linda Blair was twelve. Friedkin needed to make sure she could deal with the more outré requirements of the role. He asked her, "Did you read *The Exorcist*?"

"Yes."

"What's it about?"

"It's about a little girl who gets possessed by the devil and does a lot of bad things."

"What sort of bad things?"

"She pushes a guy out a window and masturbates with a crucifix and — "

"What does that mean?"

"It's like jerking off, isn't it?"

"Yeah, do you know about jerking off?"

"Oh, sure."

"Do you do that?"

"Yeah, don't you?"

She got the role.

Once Friedkin started to work, he was demanding and autocratic. He had a furious temper that left him literally foaming at the mouth with saliva spewing from his lips. He threw phones, stamped his feet. "He never threw anything lethal," says Evan Lottman, who was one of the editors on *The Exorcist.* "It was all calculated to terrorize and subdue." A few days before he was scheduled to begin principal photography, he discovered that the set was not to his liking. Without a second thought, he fired his production designer, John Robert Lloyd, who had worked on several films with him, and ordered the set rebuilt, delaying the start date six weeks. The buzz on the set was that this was only a pretext, because Friedkin wasn't ready, needed more time. He called Burstyn into his office to inform her that the start date was going to be pushed back. While they were talking, Billy's secretary buzzed him, said, "Charlie Greenlaw's on the phone." He was Warners' head of physical production. Despite the so-called greening of the studios, most of the young directors still saw them as the enemy, and Friedkin was not about to take any mouth from the front office. He says, "A lot of the guys running studios, they had never made a picture, they'd never written a film, produced, photographed, tapdanced in a movie, let alone directed one, and I thought, These guys really don't know what they're talking about." Billy knew exactly what Greenlaw wanted. Without breaking his stride, he said, "Tell him if he's calling to fire me, I'll take the call, otherwise I'm speaking to Miss Burstyn," and went right on talking.

FRIEDKIN WAS BORN in Chicago on August 29, 1935. (He always managed to give the impression he was four years younger than he was.) He came from the kind of lower-middle-class family Rafelson wished he'd come from. "It was a fucking slum," said Friedkin, referring to the old neighborhood and, as usual, scarcely bothering to mince words.

The Friedkins lived in a one-bedroom apartment. His mother Raechael (Rae), was an operating room nurse. "My mother was a saint," he says. "I never heard her say one negative thing about anyone. She was like Florence Nightingale." He fell in with a bad crowd, and credits her with saving him from the eventual fate of his companions — drugs, jail, death — by returning him to the straight and narrow after he had been arrested for armed robbery.

Louis Friedkin, his father, had been a merchant seaman and semipro softball player who ended up working for his older brothers in a chain of discount men's clothing stores on the South Side of Chicago. Entirely devoid of ambition, Louis never made more than $50 a week, and was out of work for the last two years of his life. He died, indigent, on a gurney in a hallway in Cook County Hospital. Friedkin viewed his father with a mixture of affection and contempt for not making more of himself.

Despite the fact that he was only five foot eleven, Billy was a decent basket-ball player, a good shooter, dreamed of being All-Pro, another white hope like Bob Cousy. As a teenager, he started going to movies. *Diabolique* and *The Wages of Fear* made a big impression. He saw *Psycho* over and over, studied it. Television documentaries like *Harvest of Shame*, for *CBS Reports*, also made an impact. After he finished high school, his parents couldn't afford to send him to college, and he got a job in the mailroom at WGN-TV in Chicago. He saw *Citizen Kane* at the Surf movie theater on the Near North Side. Like so many others, he said it changed his life, made him want to become a director. "He had Welles posters on his wall," recalled Wilmer (Bill) Butler, a cinematographer who knew him well in those days, and would later work for Coppola, Spielberg, and Forman. "He admired his style, the way he held himself above everyone else. Welles didn't have much time for fools. And Billy didn't either."

Friedkin claims he directed his first live television when he was twenty-two, for which he earned $33 a week. A year later he was directing regularly. He got fired from every station in town, but over the next several years, he somehow managed to direct, he says, over two thousand shows, including a dozen documentaries. With local TV in its embryonic stage, it was a great time to be young and ambitious. Friedkin and Butler were too green to know what they couldn't do. "We were having a ball, walking down the street, blowing ideas out of our heads, and then we went out and did them," says Butler.

Friedkin was fearless. "Chicago had a black South Side that white people didn't go into if they had any sense," continues Butler. "We were there in the middle of the night, just walking into these nightclubs and shooting film, no permission. How do you keep from getting killed doing that? I don't know what you'd call it—madness. He was just driven. To get a film done, nothing would stand in the way."

Even then he had a reputation for being difficult and abrasive. Says Butler, "Billy had this fantastic ability to see through people. Between the time you came through the door and the time you got to his desk, he had you made. If Billy wanted to tell you what you were really like, he was going to destroy you. It was like a psychiatrist going right inside your head and unhooking the wires."

In the early '60s, Friedkin made a documentary called *The People Versus Paul Crump*. Crump was a black man who may or may not have killed a guard in the course of a holdup at a baby food factory. He professed his innocence; the film would be a plea to spare his life. *The People Versus Paul Crump* won the Golden Gate Award at the San Francisco Film Festival in 1962. David Wolper saw it—it beat a couple of his own entries—and offered Friedkin a job. But he wasn't ready to leave Chicago, and turned it down.

Chicago in those days was bubbling with talent. Haskell Wexler was making documentaries. Every Friday night, Friedkin played poker with Studs Terkel and Nelson Algren. "I remember the day I decided to leave Chicago," he says.

"It was one of the few nights that I lost at poker. The game lasted till Saturday morning. Studs lost too, and we got outside, there was a massive snowstorm that we weren't aware of, three, four feet of snow, below-zero weather, the wind screaming off the fucking lake, and my car wouldn't start. We started to walk home, which in my case was about seventy-five blocks. It was like through the steppes. Studs would say, 'Ah, there's the hotel that my old man used to run.' I didn't give a shit, I was freezing, and on that walk, I said to myself, 'I gotta get the fuck outta here.' " Like Bogdanovich, Billy headed west in 1965, in an old Ford.

Friedkin joined Wolper but soon left him to take a job directing episodes of *Alfred Hitchcock Presents* for television. On Friedkin's first day of shooting, Hitchcock came to the set to film his introduction to the series. His only words to the young director were, "Mr. Friedkin, you're not wearing a tie." Friedkin thought he was joking; he wasn't. Always the take-no-prisoners iconoclast, Friedkin said later, "I don't give a flying fuck about him, and I'm not a worshiper of his, nor have I ever set out to emulate him." He added, "But I'm glad that people deify directors because I make more money that way." Five or six years later, he ran into Hitchcock at a DGA awards ceremony for *The French Connection*. He walked up to the great man's table, snapped his bow tie in front of his nose, and said, "How'd'ya like the tie, Hitch?" Of course, Hitchcock didn't remember the incident, but Friedkin never forgot, or forgave, a slight.

Once Friedkin broke into features, he made four in quick succession. The first was *Good Times*, with Sonny and Cher, released in 1967, another attempt, like the Monkees, to rip off *A Hard Day's Night* and *Help!* *Good Times* flopped, and Friedkin realized he didn't like any of the scripts he was looking at. He announced to *Variety* in April 1967, when *Good Times* came out, that "the plotted film is on the way out and is no longer of interest to a serious director. . . . A new theater audience, I'm told, is under thirty and largely interested in abstract experience. . . . I defy anyone to tell me what *Blow-Up, Juliet of the Spirits, La Guerre Est Finie*, and the Beatles films are about." He attacked the industry for its big-budget productions, and swore he would keep the budgets of his own films down to a million or under.

No sooner were the words out of his mouth, however, than he plunged into a $5 million film, *The Night They Raided Minsky's* for UA, from a script co-written by Norman Lear. Ralph Rosenblum, who later cut for Woody Allen and edited *Minsky's*, was annoyed and puzzled by the director's "aggressiveness and rank-pulling." But Rosenblum felt the studios had brought it on themselves. "Hollywood was in its down-on-your-knee-to-youth phase at the time," he wrote in his book (with Robert Karen), *When the Shooting Stops*. "The studio executives had billed Billy as a prodigy — who could be surprised if he behaved as if he were on an altar?"

Friedkin moved his mother out to L.A. that same year, installed her in a big house he was renting in the flats of Beverly Hills, between Sunset and Santa Monica, that used to belong to Mickey Rooney. Referring to his obsession with his mother, Friedkin's enemies — and there were many already — used to refer to the house as the Bates Motel.

After *The Birthday Party*, an adaptation of a Harold Pinter play which did no business at all, Friedkin made *The Boys in the Band*, which was released in 1970. The script was written by Mart Crowley, who also produced, and was based on Crowley's play of the same title. Crowley introduced Friedkin to Kitty Hawks, daughter of Howard Hawks and Slim Keith. Keith had been married briefly to Leland Hayward, which made Kitty Brooke Hayward's half-sister for a Hollywood moment. Kitty was a stylish, beautiful, and very well connected rather neurotic woman who had a famously bad relationship with her legendary father. She was working at an ad agency and did some modeling. She and Friedkin started seeing a lot of each other during the production of *Boys*, and he moved into her apartment in New York at 1049 Park Avenue.

One day, she got a letter from her father, then in his seventies, whom she had not seen in almost two decades, asking to meet her. He had seen her picture on the cover of *Vogue*. Billy and Kitty flew out to L.A., met him at Chianti Ristorante on Melrose. When they arrived, he was already there, bald as an egg, eyebrows like little puffs of cotton, looking like a newborn baby. He pushed a brown paper grocery bag at her, saying, "I've got something for you." Overcome, tears welling up in her eyes, she opened the bag — and inside were two men's shirts, unwrapped, from the May Company he had bought and tossed into the bag. *Boys* had just come out. Hawks said, "That's about those queer fellows."

"Yeah," replied Friedkin.

"I don't know why you'd want to make a picture like that. People don't want stories about somebody's problems or any of that psychological shit. What they want is action stories. Every time I made a film like that, with a lotta good guys against bad guys, it had a lotta success, if that matters to you."

When they returned to their hotel, she burst into tears. Friedkin got the shirts.

Hawks's words did matter to Friedkin. "They really stayed with me," he recalls. "I would have embarked on a course of having made obscure Miramax type films before Miramax. But I had this epiphany that what we were doing wasn't making fucking films to hang in the Louvre. We were making films to entertain people and if they didn't do that first they didn't fulfill their primary purpose. It's like somebody gives you a key and you didn't even know there was a lock; it led to *The French Connection*." Later, Friedkin would say he was making pictures for his uncle in Chicago who worked in a deli — "Therefore I have my finger on the pulse of America."

On the basis of his last two pictures, Friedkin had gotten the reputation for being an art film director, the kiss of death. He was depressed, afraid he would never work again. He almost took a job as an editor at Random House. Afraid that he was becoming unemployable, he did an abrupt about face, planted some quotes in *Variety* that placed him firmly in the Hollywood mainstream. "American films of the '30s and '40s had clear story lines and strong characters," he said. "The New Wave of European filmmakers took over and we all went out and copied Godard and Fellini, forgetting where our roots were."

The French Connection was a fact-based thriller about a drug ring busted up by the New York police department adapted from a novel by Robin Moore. It had been a best-seller, but the project had nevertheless been turned down all over town. Phil D'Antoni, who produced *Bullitt* at Warner–Seven Arts, was attached as producer. On the basis of *The People Versus Paul Crump*, he approached Friedkin. Just before Dick Zanuck left Fox, he said, "I got an extra two million dollars in a drawer here, if you guys can do the picture for that, I'll make the thing." He also warned them: "If you muck it up, it'll just be another episode on *Naked City*." "Zanuck was right," said Friedkin. He thought to himself, I gotta put a cop up there like they've never seen before, a cop who's good and evil, as much victim as victimizer. You don't see that on *Naked City*.

Slim Keith was putting a lot of pressure on Kitty and Billy to get married. But Billy wasn't the marrying kind, at least not then. Women found Friedkin fascinating. Susanna Moore met him before she became Beatty's assistant. She says, "Billy had a kind of stream-of-consciousness way of thinking and speaking where the unconscious is very close to the surface that was irresistible, and there was a kind of playfulness and surrealism and brilliance." He had a series of one-night or one-week stands with "a lot of girls with big tits who gave great head," as he puts it.

"The first sex I had was with a black hooker, five bucks a pop, and for years I would just see hookers," he recalls. "I don't know that I had the most healthy sexual upbringing. I was really a scoundrel. All I was interested in doing was getting laid. We were shooting *The French Connection* on Madison Avenue and 69th Street, in front of the Westbury Hotel, Gene Hackman running down the street after some French guy, and a girl with blond hair walked right through the shot. I said to my AD, 'Get somebody out there, bring her back,' and I wound up fucking her for six months. That's all Francis ever cared about, and Bogdanovich — his muse was his cock." Meanwhile, according to Howard Rosenman, a bright kid from Far Rockaway who was producing commercials, Kitty began an affair with him. (Hawks refused to comment.)

The French Connection was shot in New York for five weeks through the winter of 1970 and 1971. Producer Philip D'Antoni felt that the reason *Bullitt* had done so well was because of the hair-raising car chase through the streets of San Francisco, and he insisted there be one in this film as well. Friedkin obliged, shooting a stomach-churning chase, featuring a car and an elevated subway for which *The French Connection* became duly famous. It was a hard shoot, and Friedkin was often moody and depressed.

Friedkin took a traditional approach to *The French Connection.* "I came back to clarity of presentation," he said, meaning he abandoned the New Hollywood mannerisms of his early work. Later, he would say that what he cut in the editing were the scenes that made the characters more complex, but retarded the action. In two short years, as if heeding Hawks's chance remark, Friedkin had reversed course.

Still, increasingly conservative though Friedkin sounded, *The French Connection* was far from a conventional picture. He was comfortable with the documentary idiom and used it, giving the film a loose, handheld feel that anticipated *Hill Street Blues* by a decade. Often, he wouldn't bother to block a scene, just told the cameraman to follow the actors. Moreover, the moral landscape of the film was dark, complicated, and European. "In those days, Coppola and I and other guys, we'd sit around and talk about which way film was heading," he recalls. "You know, Godard or Fellini, documentary and street reality, or formalism and works of the imagination. They were not, it seemed to me, diametrically opposed. I had seen Z by Costa-Gavras. It made me realize you could take an actual story and make it as exciting as good fiction. I thought, I know how to do that. Fuck, that's like introducing documentary technique. It was a big influence on *The French Connection.*"

Pace Hawks, there were no clear-cut heroes and villains. *The French Connection* was cynical and hard-edged. Friedkin resisted Hackman's inclination to sentimentalize his character, the "hero," Popeye Doyle. In one scene, Doyle shoots an unarmed man in the back who is running away from him. The villain, the French connection (aka "Frog One"), escapes, and at the end, Doyle shoots and kills an FBI agent. Like Altman, Friedkin dismissed the script (for which Ernest Tidyman won an Oscar). From his point of view, the dialogue was ad-libbed and improvised.

By June, the engagement to Kitty was off. "My career has ruined every personal relationship I've ever had," Friedkin complained, "and there's nothing I can do about it. In order to make a relationship work, both parties have to be concerned about what's right for *us*. But if *us* is ever at odds with what is right for *me* and *my picture*, there's no contest. Maybe it's a cavalier coldness on my part—I just don't know myself that well."

The French Connection, which cost $1.8 million, was released in New York on October 7, 1971. Friedkin was on the phone to the studio the night it opened, asking for the numbers, how many people attended the first show, the second show. He hung up, a big grin wreathing his face. "I'm a millionaire," he announced happily. Indeed, *The French Connection* was a huge hit, reaping $26.3 million in domestic rentals before it played out, plus $12 million foreign

and a $2 million TV sale. It turned Friedkin into a bankable director. His first
check totaled $643,000. He started taking tennis lessons with pro Alex Olmedo
at the Beverly Hills Hotel.

After Friedkin won his Oscar, he was battered by feelings of inadequacy.
"The next day was the only time I ever went to see a psychiatrist," he recalls. "I
was profoundly unhappy. I told him I won an Oscar and didn't think I deserved
it. It was not so much unworthiness I felt, as much as I had a perspective: the
Shostakovich 7th Symphony, the Beethoven 5th Symphony, I've never done
anything like that. He never said a word, just kept writing, voluminous notes
on a yellow lined pad. The hour was up, and I left."

Still, Friedkin's foray into commercial filmmaking had paid off. For the
moment, anyway, he relinquished whatever thoughts he had of turning his
considerable talents to anything other than making money. "I have no image
of myself as an artist," he boasted in the press. "I'm making commercial films,
I'm making a product designed to have people buy it."

IN EARLY SUMMER Coppola called Bogdanovich, told him that Bluhdorn
had suggested starting a company. "We'd get a bunch of directors in, make
pictures with complete autonomy, and eventually take the company public,"
recalls Bogdanovich. "That's how we were going to make a lot of money." The
idea was based on First Artists, an actors' company that included Barbra Streisand, Paul Newman, and Sidney Poitier—only with directors. In many ways, it
marked the zenith of directors' power in the '70s, and its fate prefigured their
fall from grace. Coppola and Bogdanovich, along with Friedkin, flew to New
York to meet with Bluhdorn. During the flight, they played poker. Bogdanovich won $100 from Francis, and on the return trip, $100 from Friedkin,
playing blackjack.

Friedkin, who had never met Bluhdorn, was the first one to arrive at his
suite in the Essex House. Bluhdorn opened the door, leaned over and sniffed
Friedkin's neck, asking, "Friedkin, vat's dat shit you're verink?"

"Guerlain."

"Guerlain? Come here!" He led Friedkin to his bathroom, where he had
every aftershave in the world, including a cut glass Baccarat bottle of Guerlain.
He opened it up, saying, "Dis is vat I do to Guerlain," and poured it on his
shoes. "That was my introduction to Charlie Bluhdorn, and he never got any
saner as long as I knew him," Friedkin recalls. "Then he launched into a long
speech about how years earlier he had been a doorman at the Essex House,
saying, 'Now I own dis fuckink tink. Dat's vhy I invited you so you learn how
to be smart and make money like me.'"

When Coppola and Bogdanovich arrived, Bluhdorn laid out his idea. They
could make any picture they wanted under $3 million without submitting

anything to Paramount. The studio agreed to capitalize the company to the tune of $31.5 million. Quipped Billy Wilder at the time, "This deal should win an Oscar." To Bluhdorn, it seemed like an inspired scheme, a way to corral the three hottest directors on the planet. But that was only the beginning. Bluhdorn envisioned raiding all the other studios, especially Warners, where he hoped to grab Kubrick and Nichols. This in particular appealed to Coppola, who was still livid at Wells for trying to extract his pound of flesh. "Part of my desire to get involved with [Friedkin and Bogdanovich] is revenge," he said at the time, "for lots of vindictive, Mafia-like reasons — because I'm so mad at Warner Brothers."

Bluhdorn, still very much the loose cannon, had cooked up the idea without telling Yablans. Five minutes before a second meeting at the Gulf + Western Building on Columbus Circle, Bluhdorn called the Paramount head. "You von't belief vat I've done, an impossible dream, an impossible dream," he barked into the phone.

"Tell me, Charlie, what have you done? What's the impossible dream?"

"I put togedder a company, a director's company, vid Francis and Friedkin, and Bogdanovich."

"Oh, that's great, that's great, Charlie, have a good time with it."

"Vaddya mean? It's goink to be part of you."

"It's not gonna be part of me. I don't even know what's it's about, don't tell me it's gonna be part of me."

"Well, come on up here." Yablans went upstairs to find Bluhdorn with the three directors in the conference room. Smiling broadly, teeth flashing like Chiclets, Bluhdorn said, "Vaddya think of dat, Frank? Is dis a great idea or vat?"

Yablans replied, "I think it's shit. I think it's the worst, stupidest, dumbest idea I ever heard in my life. And I'm not gonna have any part of it. Why don't you just give 'em the company, Charlie? What the fuck are you paying me for?"

"Frank, vaddya talkink about?"

"You guys are on an ego trip, you're gonna make a bunch of crap, you're not exclusive, you're gonna go off and do films for other people, and we'll get the dregs."

"Don't be like dis, Frank, don't be like dis. Be nice."

At this point Friedkin, who was getting increasingly agitated, leaped up and yelled, "Frank, you're really full of shit. You're a fucking asshole, as a matter of fact, and I don't know what we're doing sitting here talking to you about this anyway." Bluhdorn pleaded with him to stay. Friedkin replied, "Fuck both you guys," and stalked out.

Despite this inauspicious beginning, the three directors were intrigued enough — both with the artistic freedom and with the promise of big profits down the road—to proceed, provided Evans, whom Coppola detested, was kept in his cage. Yablans was still opposed. The last thing he needed was a satellite company siphoning money out of his budget to produce pictures over which he had no control. He blamed the whole thing on Francis. "Coppola was playing Charlie like a Stradivarius," he says. "Forty percent of the whole idea was probably his. He was passing himself off as, Poor little me, all I wanna do is make my films, walking around in Puma sneakers and a corduroy suit, while he was flying in on Learjets and using stretch limos. He was a true Mercedes Marxist." But Yablans went along with it, thinking, There is no way this can work, they'll eat each other alive. They're the Arab League, a company built on egos. Give a director the power to go off and do anything he wants to do with absolute impunity, you'll get nothing but garbage. "I wasn't going to allow it to happen," he says. "But it was clear to me, if it was going to fail, it had to come from them. It had to implode." So he sat back and watched the fun.

Coppola invited Bogdanovich and Friedkin up to San Francisco, hosted dinners for them at his Broadway home. Friedkin says, improbably, that Lucas served the food while the three directors talked among themselves: "He was still Francis's assistant, one of those guys hanging around him for scraps." Coppola presided over the tiny filmmaking community in San Francisco more like Louis XIV than the Godfather. No hiding behind walled compounds for him. He was much too flamboyant. Coppola was the sun that lit the sky and made the grass grow. He was the source of all work, the source of all pleasure. Tom Luddy was his Talleyrand. He ran the Pacific Film Archive, which allowed him to pass prints to Francis for private viewings in Coppola's screening room, to parade a glittering array of celebrity foreign directors through Zoetrope to pay their respects to the king. Every night there was a dinner, a screening, an event. Luddy was seeing Alice Waters, whose innovative restaurant, Chez Panisse, became the Zoetrope commissary. Francis's home was the site of a nonstop party. Young women were asked if they wanted to join Francis. "It was no secret that Francis was a major pussy hound," says Marcia Lucas. "Ellie used to be around for half an hour or so, and then she'd disappear, go upstairs with the kids, and Francis would be feeling up some babe in the pool. I was hurt and embarrassed for Ellie, and I thought Francis was pretty disgusting, the way he treated his wife." Ellie had become Kay Corleone. Coppola always wanted Friedkin to move up to the Bay Area and work with him. Says Billy, "I loved Francis, but the very thought of getting closer to him or being a part of his circle was repellent to me."

Friedkin was already involved with *The Exorcist*, but promised to do his next picture for the Directors Company. Peter Bart suggested Bogdanovich do a project he had developed called *Addie Pray* (the title was eventually changed to *Paper Moon*), as his first picture. The story was set in the Depression, and turned on the prickly relationship between an itinerant con man and his precocious daughter.

Unlike the other new Hollywood directors, Bogdanovich was very much at home in Hollywood, very much embraced his celebrity. He was riding high, busy — although he was too intoxicated with himself to realize it — sowing the seeds of his own destruction. Almost everyone who met him detested him. He was an inveterate name dropper. When he opened his mouth, it was "Orson" this and "Howard" that, "John" something else. He liked to parade his erudition, and had a bad habit of lecturing instead of conversing. As one junior executive put it, "The first time I met him, it was as if I were in the presence of God. I had to go up to him and introduce myself, and he wasn't about to reciprocate and say his name, because that might indicate that there was some doubt as to who he was." Preening like a peacock, he told the *New York Times* in words that would come back to haunt him, "I don't judge myself on the basis of my contemporaries. . . . I judge myself against the directors I admire — Hawks, Lubitsch, Buster Keaton, Welles, Ford, Renoir, Hitchcock." Modesty required a demurral: "I certainly don't think I'm anywhere near as good as they are, but," he couldn't help adding, "I think I'm pretty good."

When Peter talked about Cybill, he patronized her. "Cybill started out as a whim, an instinct, a little voice in my ear that I listened to. I had an itch, and I scratched it. . . . She's very malleable. You can bend her in any direction. She does what she's told." It became impossible to pick up a magazine without seeing the two of them beaming toothily from the cover, winsome and smug, as if to say, We're Peter and Cybill, and you're not. Cary Grant told him to shut up. "Will you stop telling people you're in love. Stop telling people you're happy."

"Why?"

"Because they're not in love and they're not happy. And they don't want to hear it."

"But Cary, I thought all the world loves a lover."

"Don't you believe it. It isn't true. Just remember one thing, Peter, people do not like beautiful people."

Adds Bogdanovich, now chastened, "And so, an enormous amount of envy and jealousy and shit hit the fan."

When they were not sitting for photographers, the couple haunted the talk shows, appearing regularly on Johnny Carson, for whom Peter became an occasional replacement. He had become a bit of a dandy, wearing candy-striped shirts with white collars, occasionally improved by an ascot. He sported a gold signet ring with his initials on it. He relished invitations to the White House, didn't mind a bit that it was Nixon who was doing the inviting.

Bogdanovich shopped around for a home at an address suitable for his new station in the community. With income from *Doc*, he and Cybill set up housekeeping in a seven-thousand-square-foot Spanish-style hacienda built in 1928 on Copa de Oro in Bel Air, across the street from John Ford's home. The windows were shaded by picturesque green and white striped awnings that looked out onto a courtyard with a fountain in the center, surrounded by flowers. It was furnished with white couches and heavy European pieces made out of dark wood. The walls were covered by his father's gloomy paintings, in the heavy gilt frames made by his mother. The hedges were neatly clipped, the pool crystalline, the Rolls-Royce Silver Cloud lustrous in the garage, along with his four other vehicles. He still hated to drive, got lost on the UCLA campus every time he left the house if he were behind the wheel himself. "I don't drive unless I have to. I'm driven," he said, smiling at his own cleverness. He was said to have nineteen servants. Still, life was not perfect. He complained about the help to visiting journalists, said the grounds weren't picked up properly. He had always worn glasses, he worried that the pink spots they left on the bridge of his nose might show up in his press photos. Orson Welles was living in a bedroom off Peter's study. He turned it into a toxic waste dump full of half-eaten dinners and redolent cigar butts. Cybill couldn't stand having him around.

Bogdanovich was determined not to do *Addie Pray*. He saw it as another *Picture Show*, a period piece, thought he'd be repeating himself. He had been trying to get a Western off the ground at Warners written by Larry McMurtry, a script that would eventually become *Lonesome Dove*. He wanted John Wayne, Jimmy Stewart, and Henry Fonda. Stewart and Fonda committed, Wayne refused. "Naw, it's kindofa end-of-the-West Western, Pete. I'm not ready to hang up the spurs yet." Bogdanovich believed Ford sabotaged it, told Wayne not to do it. "It was one thing for me to write a book about him, make a film about him, another thing for me to take three of his stars and make a really great Western," he says. "It was too much."

A couple of months later, Yablans says he got a call from Bogdanovich, who was in New York at the Plaza. "Frank, it's Peter. I'm sick, you gotta get me the company doctor."

"How sick are you?"

"Very sick, 105, 106, something like that."

"God, Peter, if it goes any higher, you could die."

"Yeah, that's why I'm calling you. You have to get me a doctor."

"Are you going to do *Paper Moon*?"

"What! What kind of a question is that to ask me now?"

"Are you going to do *Paper Moon*? Because if you don't give it to me, I don't give a fuck if you live or die! You can find your own doctor."

"You can't be serious about this."

"I'm very serious."

"I can't believe that you're this cruel."

"I'm this cruel, Peter." (Bogdanovich has no recollection of this exchange.)

Peter gave *Paper Moon* to Platt, asked her to come up with one reason why he should do it. She liked it, reminded him that he was the father of two daughters, and suggested Tatum O'Neal for the girl. Bogdanovich came back with Ryan for her dad. They got excited, but realized that Evans would never go for it because of O'Neal's affair with MacGraw during *Love Story*. But Bogdanovich called Evans anyway. As they suspected, Evans wouldn't have anything to do with Ryan, came up with his usual names, Beatty and Nicholson. Eventually, he changed his mind, but now it was Polly who didn't want to work on the picture. She thought, Everybody is going to be staring at me, wondering how I'm dealing with it. It's going to be humiliating. Turning to her estranged husband she said, "Well, I'll do it if I don't have to look at Cybill. She can't come on the set." Peter agreed.

Coppola's first film for the Directors Company was to be *The Conversation*, from his old script about a detective who uses high-tech sound equipment to do his work and eventually falls into a paranoid funk and autodestructs. Friedkin wasn't happy about it. "*The Conversation* was a very obscure rip-off of Antonioni's *Blow-Up* but with sound," he says. Peter didn't like it any more than Friedkin did: "Francis said it was gonna be a Hitchcock kind of movie, but it didn't end up being a Hitchcock kind of movie," he grumbles. But they were not allowed to veto one another's pictures.

At a gala press luncheon at "21" in New York, on August 20, Paramount launched the company. Yablans announced, a bit prematurely, as it turned out, "They've gone through their growth period. Coppola isn't interested in filming a pomegranate growing in the desert. They're all very commercial now."

The Conversation wrapped in March, and several weeks later, Friedkin saw a cut at Francis's home in Napa Valley. He recalls, "I thought it was like watching paint dry or listening to hair grow, and immediately when the lights went up, Francis went around the room and asked each of the hangers-on how much they thought the film was gonna do, and he got all these ludicrous estimates.' Then he got to me, and I said, 'Francis, we'll be lucky to get $500,000 on this picture. I think it's unintelligible, it's ridiculous.' He said, 'It's a first cut.' I said, 'Whatever it is, you're asking me, I'm telling you. There's no story, no nothing. It's just a collection of shots. I really hated it.' He said, 'Well, I hope you're wrong,' and I said, 'So do I.'"

Paper Moon opened in New York on May 16, 1973, to rave reviews and long lines at the box office. It made $16.5 million in rentals. Bogdanovich was going from hit to hit, critical triumph to critical triumph. It wasn't doing much for his people skills. If possible, he was becoming even more insufferable. He carried the reviews around with him in his pocket.

According to the bylaws of the company, each director was entitled to a cut

of the others' pictures. Coppola took $300,000 out of *Paper Moon's* profits, and
so did Friedkin, who had still directed nothing. Yablans saw this as an opportunity to cause some trouble. "Once they took Peter's money, it was over," he
says. "I constantly called Peter, said, 'When are these guys going to make a
movie, Peter? Christ! They have your money, what's going on here?'" It
worked; Bogdanovich was furious. "Francis always said he felt he owed it to
me," says Peter. "I kept saying, 'Could I get it now?' He never had money again.
Billy didn't feel he owed me anything."

Peter was looking for projects to do with Cybill. Ever since Tim Bottoms had
given her a copy of the Henry James novella *Daisy Miller* on the set of *The
Last Picture Show*, she had had her heart set on doing it. Bogdanovich was now
ready. "She's so right for it — as though Henry James had her in mind when he
wrote it," he said, with typical modesty. Woody Allen had lunch with Bogdanovich shortly after it wrapped. Peter spent the whole meal agonizing over
whether the credits should read, A Peter Bogdanovich Film of Henry James's
Novella; or Henry James's Novella Directed by Peter Bogdanovich; or Henry
James's *Daisy Miller*, a Film by Peter Bogdanovich; or Peter Bogdanovich's
Daisy Miller, from Henry James's Novella.

But the picture created more friction among the three directors. "The next
thing I knew was that Peter was making *Daisy Miller*, starring his girlfriend
who had no discernible acting ability whatsoever," says Friedkin. "He never
talked to me about it. I only got the script because it was contractual. I looked
at this thing and I thought, What the fuck is going on around here? Peter was
pussy-struck. He could not see that Cybill was not a great actress. He was just
using this company as a vanity press. I reminded him that we all had an
agreement that we weren't going to take projects like that, that no other studio
would make with us and dump them into this company.

"The Directors Company was an amazing thing and it was ultimately destroyed in a Machiavellian way by Yablans," Friedkin continues. "He even let
Cybill do a record album called *Cybill Does It to Cole Porter*, and he put up a
gigantic billboard for it on the Sunset Strip, all of which was part of his design
to undo the company. After all, this was not Barbra Streisand. This was a
woman who had never sung professionally, never released a record. Frank knew
that if he encouraged Peter along that path . . ."

Meanwhile, Peter marched blithely ahead. He was feeling generous toward
Polly. "I'll give you a job anytime you want." But she didn't want to work with
him anymore. *Paper Moon* was also his last hit. Bogdanovich and Platt had
made a singularly creative team, and when she withdrew, Bogdanovich lost, at
the very least, a person who could say no. Despite protestations to the contrary,
he surrounded himself with yes-men. Says Paul Lewis, who had worked with
him on *Doc*, "I don't think it had to do with Polly, I think it had to do with his
own ego. He believed that he became Orson Welles. And he wasn't."

When *Daisy Miller,* his second picture for the Directors Company, came out in New York on May 22, 1974, Bogdanovich got his first bad reviews. Bad wasn't the word for it; the film got killed by the very same critics who had hailed him as a genius a year earlier for *Paper Moon.* The hammer fell hard on Shepherd. One critic wrote that she was considered "a no-talent dame with nice boobs and a toothpaste smile and all the star quality of a dead hamster." Said Shepherd: "After *Daisy,* I could walk in a room and feel a concentrated hatred."

Bogdanovich was stung by the notices: "When someone yells, 'You're a motherfucker!' right in your face, you don't forget it. . . . You stop reading them. Then some of it gets back to you anyway — friends tell you the meanest parts." One of the reasons the picture flopped was because both male leads were so unappealing. It was no accident. "I begged him, said, 'Peter, this is a romance,' " recalls Sue Mengers. "But he resisted. He always protected himself against attractive leading men opposite Cybill, with actors he could feel superior to unless he could make them look like him, the way he put glasses and a hat on Ryan in *What's Up, Doc?*" Still, the picture was a respectable failure with classy and difficult material. It would get worse.

Daisy Miller was, however, the last straw for the Directors Company. After the two flops, "Billy said he wanted out," says Bogdanovich. "We said, 'You haven't even made a picture.' He said, 'Well, I can get more money elsewhere.' He chose the cash over the freedom. The company didn't work because Billy didn't want it to go on." Says Friedkin, "I could see what Frank was doing in letting these vanity projects go forward, and I was not gonna put my next picture through a company that had a management that was trying to sabotage the company. I withdrew."

From the outside, it looked like three brats fighting over the spoils. Says Bob Rafelson, "They all wanted to do BBS again. But that was gone. This wasn't young guys trying to fight for a statement. These guys were trying to fight for 10 percent of the gross from first dollar, and were pissed off that the other guy didn't make a hit film."

AFTER *PAPER MOON,* Platt got a call from Altman. He asked her to design *Thieves Like Us.* She had just done the '30s in *Paper Moon,* she was tired, she wanted to spend time with her girls. But she also wanted to meet him. She flew to New York, stayed at the Pierre. "He was not in good shape," she recalls. "He liked me because he couldn't seduce me. He tried in every way. He and his wife were right next door to me, and the minute she left he came on to me. He said he had affairs with all the women he worked with."

As a result of his string of flops, Altman had a hard time setting up *Thieves,* which, like most of his movies, had an unhappy ending. Even though George

Litto had made a three-picture deal with UA, David Picker, who ran production, balked at *Thieves*. By 1973, UA was a company in trouble. Arthur Krim
and Bob Benjamin had sold it in 1967, when it was churning out hit after hit,
to a conglomerate called Transamerica. Financially, the two men did very well
for themselves and retained effective control over day-to-day operations, but
the hot streak turned cold. Christopher Mankiewicz, son of Joe, nephew of
Herman, worked there in the '60s, and again in 1978. From Transamerica's
point of view, he says, "there was a lot of resentment, because UA had had
twelve, fifteen years of success, then the Jews had taken the goys for a fortune,
and suddenly UA stopped being successful." In 1974, Krim tried to buy the
studio back. Transamerica chairman John Beckett not only turned him down,
he put someone over Krim, effectively demoting him to number two in the
company he had built. The Krim team found the new management guidelines
intolerable. Transamerica challenged Mike Medavoy, who became head of
West Coast production in 1974, on his company car, a Mercedes, de rigueur
for someone in Medavoy's position in Hollywood, but unthinkable in the
culture of a corporation that only allowed Fords and Chevys to senior VPs of
its subsidiaries.

There was bad blood between UA and Altman. When *The Long Goodbye*,
the first film in his UA deal, opened weakly, the company pulled the film and
redesigned the marketing campaign, in an unusual effort to give it a second
chance. But regardless, Altman denounced UA to the *New York Times*. "When
he went to the press and shit all over us and took credit for getting us to do
something that we had volunteered to do, I was totally offended by it," says
Picker. Confrontational as ever, Altman was doing himself no favors.

Picker wanted Altman to direct a film about Nashville, based on a script they
owned adapted from a book called *The Great Southern Amusement Company*.
Altman didn't like the script, said, "I won't do this, but I'll make you a Nashville
movie if you'll finance *Thieves*." Picker agreed, but according to Litto, refused
to pay Altman, who was broke, until the film was delivered. When Altman and
script supervisor Joan Tewkesbury arrived at the airport near the location in
Jackson, Mississippi, they learned that the deal had fallen through. Picker
had taken exception to Altman's budget, $1.3 million, slashed it by $500,000.
Tewkesbury looked at Bob, and said, "Yeah, but we're all here. We have to
continue." Bob agreed. He was already financing preproduction out of his own
pocket. "Bob always did that," says Litto. "Get them a little bit pregnant; he
intimidated them into going ahead." Litto had to kick in some of his money to
make up the difference. Picker's behavior left a bad taste. There wasn't even
any money for dressing rooms. The production assistants had to go from door
to door, offering locals $5, $10 for use of their bathrooms so the stars could
change into their costumes.

Louise Fletcher had a major role in *Thieves*, which her husband, Jerry Bick, was producing. They and the Altmans were close. Fletcher hadn't acted in over a decade, and Altman persuaded her to take the role of Mattie. "There was this wonderful atmosphere on the set," says Fletcher. "He did everything possible for an actor to find the truth. But he had a split personality, fucked you after it was over. You don't exist anymore, you're dead. Bob insisted on getting his going rate, but asked everyone else to sacrifice and take scale. He rails against this industry, like in *The Player*, but he's part of it. Like a lot of directors, they have their eye on the prize." Adds Tommy Thompson, Altman's AD for a decade, "He'd always position himself for his money. Look at him now, a lot of failures, but he's always done fine."

Altman treated Bick badly. He had the typical New Hollywood director's attitude toward producers: he wanted to do it himself, and he did. Says Thompson, "Jerry was desperately trying to produce, trying to have some say, and Bob didn't want it. It was just an annoyance to him."

It was on *Thieves* that Bob first hired Scott Bushnell, who eventually came between him and his most loyal collaborators. She came from the American Conservatory Theater (ACT) in San Francisco. Bushnell was a woman of medium height, thin, with shoulder-length black hair, black eyes, and long yellow nails who wore hippie-ish granny dresses. She didn't like to have her picture taken. Scottie was widely disliked. Behind her back, people called her a witch.

While Altman was still in Mississippi, he asked Tewkesbury to go to Nashville and keep a diary that would be the basis for a script. Months afterward, Altman himself visited Nashville, along with Tewkesbury and Platt, whom he had asked to work on the picture. The Watergate hearings were on television and Bob, who was obsessed with and detested Nixon, would not leave his room.

When Altman submitted Tewkesbury's script, which had nothing to do with the book, Picker wrote him a note that said, "This is not a script." Recalls the director, "He hated it, so they threw it out." Altman, who was still aggravated by what he considered to be the slipshod marketing campaign the company had done for *The Long Goodbye*, had yet another reason to be angry. UA had just brought Eric Pleskow over from European distribution and made him president of UA. The company threw a big bash for him at Chasen's, to which were invited all the UA brass, plus their stars and directors, including Altman and Sam Peckinpah. Peckinpah had too much to drink, as usual, and took a swing at producer Jerry Briskin, against whom he had apparently nursed a grudge for a decade, over *Major Dundee*. Not to be outdone, and similarly well lubricated, Altman got into an argument with Picker. Picker said, "Fuck you," Altman said, "Fuck you too," and the upshot was, Altman was free to take *Nashville* elsewhere, which he did, to Jerry Weintraub at ABC Pictures. (Picker has no recollection of this confrontation.)

The Lily Tomlin character, Linnea Reese, was based on Fletcher, whose parents were deaf, and Fletcher was supposed to play it. "*Nashville* was in development, and my parents came from Birmingham to visit the set of *Thieves*," says Fletcher. "He witnessed Jerry not being able to communicate with them, and I was sort of the go-between, the interpreter for them with everybody. He got this idea to write a character who has a deaf child, and the father isn't able to communicate with the child, and that was going to be my part. So, one day, when we were back in L.A., Bob's wife, Kathryn, called me on the phone, and said, 'Guess who came into the office today? Lily Tomlin.' I said, 'Oh, great. What part's she going to play?' There was a silence. She said, 'Bob hasn't called you?' I said, 'No, Bob hasn't called me.' It turned out that it was my part. He took my family identity, then to treat me in that way. I stopped speaking to him, because he hurt me so bad.

"That was the same year I made *Cuckoo's Nest*," continues Fletcher. "One morning, I was at the Sherry Netherland being interviewed by Aljean Harmetz from the *New York Times* in the coffee shop, and Bob was in another booth. I didn't know it, until he verbally attacked me, in a loud voice, saying, 'You don't speak to me, after all I did for you. You don't speak to me.' That was the last straw. Jerry had already produced two of his movies, and he was like a broken man over working with Bob. Kathryn picked up the pieces. People work for him for a certain amount of time, and then they say, 'I can't.' "

Platt never did do *Nashville*. "I hated the way Bob treated his wife. He infuriated me, kind of reminded me of Peter."

PRINCIPAL PHOTOGRAPHY began on *The Exorcist* on August 14, 1972, in New York, where Friedkin still had his apartment and was at a safe distance from the studio. The schedule called for 105 days of shooting. Two hundred days later, in March 1973, when Coppola had already wrapped *The Conversation*, they were still shooting.

Wells tried to dissuade Blatty from hanging around the set "producing," but Blatty, who wanted to learn the business, wouldn't listen. Almost immediately, he collided with his new best friend. "I didn't know what a producer was supposed to do, but I knew one thing, I was supposed to watch the budget," he recalls. The budget was of more than academic interest to Blatty, because after a certain point, he would begin to see dollars. If the budget grew too large, his cut would recede, become smaller and harder to see. "Then one day I was in the production office, when the phone rang," he continues. "One of the production assistants puts her hand over the mouthpiece and looked around. There was no one else there. No production manager, no Friedkin, just me. I was the producer, so she looked to me to produce." She said, "Mr. Blatty, Ellen Burstyn is calling from the airport. She doesn't want to take a taxi. She wants a limo. But Mr. Friedkin said no limos for anybody. What should I do?"

"He said no limos for anybody? Well, no limos for anybody. And I have to go. I have an appointment."

The next day, Friedkin and Blatty had lunch at the Carnegie Deli, stuffed themselves with pastrami sandwiches, then ambled down Seventh Avenue. Friedkin started in on how badly and undiplomatically Blatty had handled Burstyn. Blatty defended himself. They had stopped at the corner waiting for the light, when Friedkin said, "Bill, if you don't like it, why don't you just fire me." Blatty called him, replied, "Okay, you're fired." Friedkin turned on his heel, and strode away. "My intention was very simple," recalls Blatty. "I was stupidly trying to do what I assumed a producer should do. I thought, Monday morning, Billy and I will patch it up and we won't have any more of these ambiguities about who's running what. But Monday morning, the studio sent in a team of seven attorneys for Billy, plus his agent, to hold his hand and assure him I had no legal right to fire him. I was defeated. I went to the Sherry Netherland where Billy was staying. If Billy didn't want to cope, suddenly his throat was too sore and inflamed. He got psychosomatically ill, couldn't talk. We patched it up, interspersed with spritzes of medicine from his spray bottle. I told Warners, 'From this point on I am not responsible.' And of course from that point on the budget went from four million two to twelve million something."

Right from the start, Friedkin raised the bar for himself. On the cloth back of his director's chair to the left of his name was stenciled "An Oscar for *The French Connection*." To the right of his name was the outline of another Oscar, with a question mark inside it. It also became clear that this would not be an easy shoot. The first shot inside the 20th Century-Fox soundstage on West 54th Street was a close-up of bacon cooking on a griddle. The scene called for the camera to dolly back, but there was a wall in the way, and everything ground to a halt on the newly built set until the problem was solved. Then Billy decided he didn't like the way the bacon was curling. Once again, the production stopped while the prop master searched the city for preservative-free bacon (hard to find in 1972) that would presumably remain flat while it cooked. Friedkin was moving so slowly that when one of the crew returned to the set after being out sick for three days, the director was still on the same shot.

Billy had a short fuse. He fired people in the morning, and rehired them in the afternoon. If he came up to someone and said, "Have you got a minute?" it was a sign that something unspeakable was going to happen. He would turn on anyone for anything at any time. Says one crew member, "He's the only guy I ever saw shake hands with someone with gusto and a smile, and then turn as he was exiting past that person, and say, 'Get this guy outta here.' " On the set he was known as "Wacky Willy."

Friedkin was a technical director, very involved with the lenses and the effects. He was not particularly good with actors, nor did he like them. He used to say, "I'd rather work with tree stumps than actors." (He got his wish, in 1990, with *The Guardian*.) Or he'd scream, "You're putting me in the toilet, in the fucking toilet!" He was fond of shooting guns to scare the actors, or playing tapes at high volume, anything from the soundtrack of *Psycho* to South American tree frogs. He often turned the camera on without telling the actors. He was ruthless and would do anything to get what he wanted. At the end of the film, as Father Karras is about to die, a priest gives him absolution. The director used a real priest, Father William O'Malley. O'Malley did take after take. Unsatisfied, Friedkin finally said, "Bill, you're doing it by the numbers."

"Billy, I've just given my best friend his last rites fifteen times, and it's two-thirty in the morning."

"I understand that. Do you trust me?"

"Of course I trust you," O'Malley replied.

Billy belted him across the face with his open hand. It may not have been Stanislavsky, and it scandalized the Catholics among the crew, but it worked.

"When I did the next take, my hand was shaking," says O'Malley. "Sheer adrenalin."

Recalls Burstyn, "He liked to manipulate actors, he liked tricks. But he was always great with me, except when he permanently injured my spine." At the climax of the scene where Regan, kneeling on her bed, her face and nightgown splattered with blood, jabs the crucifix into her vagina as a raspy voice speaking through her croaks, "Let Jesus fuck you!" and "Lick Me!" as she pulls her mother's head toward her crotch, she wallops MacNeill in the face, knocking her off the bed and against the wall while a dresser lurches menacingly toward her. Burstyn had a rig around her midriff with a wire coming out of the back so the stuntman could jerk her off the bed onto the floor. They did one take, but Friedkin wasn't satisfied. Ditto take two. The third time, Burstyn said to Friedkin, "Billy, he's pulling too hard, ask him to lighten up."

"Well, it has to look real."

"I know it has to look real, but I'm telling you I could get hurt. He's pulling me too hard." Billy looked at the stuntman and said, "Okay, don't pull her so hard." Then she turned away, and out of the corner of her eye, she caught him shaking his head, instructing the stuntman to ignore what he had just said. This time when she was yanked to the floor she landed on her coccyx. She was in unbearable pain, and let out a bloodcurdling scream. Billy just moved the camera in on her. "I was furious when he did that, exploiting the pain I was feeling," she says. "Since then I've always had trouble with my back."

While they were shooting in Washington, D.C., Bob Fosse's *Pippin* opened at the Kennedy Center, on its way to New York. Friedkin and Blatty caught one of the performances. In the cast was a ravishing young dancer with magnificent legs named Jennifer Nairn-Smith. She had been a member of Balanchine's New York City Ballet. By the time she had her fifteen minutes of fame in *Pippin*, Nairn-Smith had been involved with Fosse, who in turn was seeing another of his dancers, Anne Reinking. Jennifer was from Australia. After leaving home at seventeen, she had studied with the Royal Ballet in London, and had a role as a snake dancer in the ill-fated Burton-Taylor *Cleopatra*. John Calley was in Rome producing a picture called *Hemingway's Adventures of a Young Man*. He sent her a telegram asking her to star in a movie. "I grew up in the '50s, in the bush, all I knew was small towns and cattle," she recalls. "My mother said to me, 'Don't go out with any dirty old Hollywood producers.' So I wouldn't let him touch me — it was a neck up and knees down kind of thing. He would say, 'I've given up a weekend in Monaco with Betsy Drake and Princess Grace and you won't let me touch you.' " According to one story, he told her he was dying of cancer, only had six weeks to live. "He pursued and pursued, and I finally went to bed with him years later in the Mayfair Hotel in London where they starched the sheets," continues Nairn-Smith. "I finally gave my precious body to this person with the whole expectation of what that entails, and then he disappeared."

"Jennifer was stunningly beautiful," says Blatty. "I had to meet her." He called her, complained to Louis DiGiaimo, who cast *The Exorcist*, "Lou, she doesn't know who I am." DiGiaimo said, "Bill, who the fuck do you think you are? Frank Sinatra?" Blatty asked him to phone her. She didn't return his call. Not only did she have Fosse, she was being stalked by someone who had threatened to kill the director, and she was seeing Raul Julia, Barry Bostwick, and several other men as well. When *Pippin* opened in New York, DiGiaimo phoned again, said, "Bill Blatty wants to meet you. Have breakfast with him." This time she agreed, and met him at the Palm Court at the Plaza. "He was morose, crying about his mother," she recalls. He asked her if she would accompany him to a sound studio where he was trying to contact her spirit on the other side. She had never been able to resist serious weirdness, and she agreed to go. Blatty had read a book called *Breakthrough: Electronic Communication with the Dead*, by a Latvian psychologist, and thought he was having some success recording the disembodied voices of the dead on blank tape. Over at F&B Ceco, a production house on the West Side, a technician rolled tape. Blatty called, "Mother. Mother, if you're there, come."

While Blatty was thus preoccupied, Friedkin sneaked into the hen house. He too thought she was a magnificent creature, and pursued her avidly, apparently turned on by the fact that she was in such demand. She had been warned against him, but it didn't matter. "I partly went with him to get away from my stalker," she continues. "But he was captivating, magnetic. He would seduce you with his ideas. He said every single thing I thought I wanted to hear. He had just won an Academy Award and was successful and famous, and he had a great mind. When he put his attention on me there was nothing like it." She says Friedkin bought her a diamond engagement ring from Tiffany. It was tear shaped, with a diamond on each side mounted in gold. They went to the Algonquin to celebrate.

Friedkin consumed culture with the voracious appetite of the autodidact. He took her to museums and concerts. But she could never get him to talk about his childhood. "William denied his whole background," she says. "He hated being Jewish. Think Yiddish, dress British." Adds Blatty, "My theory is that Bill was wounded over his Jewishness when he was young, because that would tend to foster an 'it's me against the world' kind of an attitude, and therefore 'anything's fair for me to do, because they all really hate me and they're my enemy.' "

For Nairn-Smith, the relationship was a head trip, as they liked to say in the '60s. For all his passion for basketball, physically, she found Friedkin lacking. "He loved junk food, loved hamburgers and hot dogs," she recalls. "He had a terrible body, this horrible fat stomach and wide hips and spindly legs. He'd go to the gym and get a rubdown. That was the extent of the workout." His hair was long, like everybody else's, and he wore lightly tinted aviator glasses, because, says Jennifer, "he had these small, beady little eyes."

Billy had to go to Iraq to shoot the top of *The Exorcist*. He pressured her to quit *Pippin* and visit her parents in Tasmania while he was in Iraq. Two of Friedkin's circle of familiars, Jerry Murphy and Fat Thomas, who had scared off her stalker, collected her in a bullet-riddled Cadillac and drove her to the airport.

With Jennifer now in his possession, the chase was over, and abruptly, the romance ended. The other men were no longer aphrodisiacs, but annoyances. "There were people still buzzing around," she continues. "He was upset at that, banned it all. He started intimidating me. He was a monster. Once he raised his hand, and I said, 'If you ever do that, I'll be gone in three seconds flat.' But he came down on me very heavily. He pushed a button in the insecure part of myself. You know these women who get beaten? They can't stand up, lose all self-respect, self-control, self-everything. It's pretty terrible. I was like putty, totally retreated and withdrew."

Meanwhile, the production was falling further and further behind. Christmas 1972 found Friedkin still shooting at Fox in New York. An enormous table was put out on the stage laden with holiday food. Friedkin got drunk and tried to do the tablecloth trick, but only succeeded in sending the dishes flying.

The rushes were scary, but the overruns were scarier. "Billy was really bad, he wasn't controllable, and fighting," says Warners' Joe Hyams. Adds executive Dick Lederer, "The movie was running way over. He was driving them crazy, because he was absolutely intent on getting it exactly the way he wanted, and there were terrible technical problems, to freeze the set so that icicles would form, cost a fortune in air conditioning. Until he got it he wouldn't quit. The cost was going up and up. It was scary."

Wells wanted to move it to L.A. where they could exercise more control over Friedkin. But once Friedkin got some film in the can, the studio was helpless. Every time a suit would indicate concern over the budget, Billy would say, "So fire me." Of course, he knew they couldn't. Recalls Friedkin, "I'm sure they were sticking pins in a Bill Friedkin doll. But I made as though I was working on the Sistine Chapel, and they never really bothered me." Adds Blatty, "They had the tiger by the tail. The head of physical production, Charlie Greenlaw, would fly in once a week. He would come through the door of the soundstage about two feet but no further, and after twenty minutes he'd say, 'Well, I've got to catch my flight back.' and he'd be in a cab back to Kennedy."

Ultimately, it was the rushes that made the difference. According to Calley, "There was a lot of newspaper stuff about, it's a runaway, the company is going to lose its ass on this picture, and Friedkin is running amok. Everybody was afraid of *Cleopatra*, that almost brought down Fox. A $7 million budget blew up to a $30 million budget. It was like when Stanley Kubrick took *2001* to Wasserman, Lew said, 'Kid, you don't spend over a million dollars on science fiction movies. You just don't do that.' And this was about, you don't spend over a million bucks on a horror movie. But Billy was an angel. He was extraordinary and he would come up every day and say, 'You've seen the dailies, are they okay?' I'd say, 'Billy, I can see the wires. When she does the head thing. It's a bad joke.' He said, 'Look, I don't want to bury you. Maybe I can cut it.' I said, 'No, we gotta do it again. The whole point of this is, it has to be perfect.' " But perfect or not, Friedkin was setting a precedent that would come back to haunt him. He was acting as his own producer.

WARNERS WAS DETERMINED to open *The Exorcist* at Christmas 1973, and tried to rush the picture through post-production, but there were new delays. With most films, the editor is at work assembling a rough cut while the director is still shooting. But Friedkin was so determined to control every aspect of the production that he hired an editor with no feature experience and refused to cut film during the eight- or nine-month production. It wasn't until Friedkin wrapped that he hired a veteran editor, Evan Lottman, who had to begin from scratch. Says Lottman, "It was all about power. He wanted to be in control of the film."

The score was written by Lalo Schifrin, an Oscar-nominated composer. The time came for Friedkin to hear the score, played by a hundred musicians on a studio stage. Billy leaned over and said, "Sounds like fuckin' Mexican marimba music. I hate fuckin' Mexican music." And he threw it all out. Six weeks later on a dubbing stage at Todd-AO, he needed a piece of music. He said, "I remember something that Lalo did that maybe we can use here." The techie put the reel on, Friedkin listened to it and hated it so much he went back in the machine room, grabbed the reel, ran out the front door and threw it as far as he could into the parking lot across the street, saying, "That's where that fuckin' marimba music belongs."

Friedkin talked Nairn-Smith into going to L.A. with him. They rented a place on Sunset Plaza Drive, behaved as if they were married. Their friends referred to them as "the Friedkins." They wore wedding bands from Cartier. He wore his on his pinkie, would get upset if she weren't wearing hers. He forbade her to dance. She told him, "If I can't dance, I've got to do something. I can't be just having facials and doing my nails." He was obdurate. She said, "Okay, if I can't dance, I want a baby."

"Okay, you can have a baby," she says he said. Some weeks later she ventured, "You know what? We're pregnant."

"No, you can't have it."

"Oh, but you said . . ." Friedkin wasn't happy. "He screamed and foamed at the mouth and intimidated me into an abortion," she says. "Then I got pregnant again and they were twins and then there was another abortion. From then on, my life stopped."

The sound mixing took four months, went down to the wire. Like Coppola, Friedkin would solicit opinions from anyone who was around, the more déclassé, the better. He used to ask the janitor to look at a reel, and if he understood it, that was good enough for him, and he'd put it to bed. Jennifer was helping with the looping. "She was a wonderful girl, and Billy treated her like a dog," says Jim Nelson, who was hired at the last minute to supervise the mix. "He screamed and yelled at people, he was the worst. I went from a seven-year contract as his associate producer to the guy he hated most in the world — in two minutes. We were right up against the release date, and Calley called on Friday, said, 'Are you guys gonna be done?' I said, 'Basically we're finished.' Billy heard me on the phone, and he said, 'We're not finished until I tell you we're finished. You have betrayed me, blah blah blah,' and that ended it. He made Rafelson look like Donna Reed. Bob wanted his own way, but he wasn't vicious. Billy was vicious."

Usually, when studio executives screen a picture, they exit without comment. After Ashley, Calley, and Wells saw *The Exorcist* for the first time, they just sat there, dumbfounded. Calley asked, rhetorically, "What in the fuck did we just see?" They loved it, but did not know what they had, and decided to release it in no more than thirty theaters, where it was to play exclusively for six months, a terrible release pattern for a potential blockbuster, as *The Godfather* had shown. Nor did Warners preview the picture. They were afraid to. Says Friedkin, "If *The Exorcist* had previewed it would never have come out. 'Cause people would have written on cards, 'This is terrible, you have a little girl masturbating with a crucifix, you dirty Jew bastard.' Those were the kind of notes we got anyway, afterward. But if we'd gotten them before, they would have died."

The Exorcist was trade-screened on December 21, and opened on December 26. Burstyn was in her kitchen, watching the TV. "There was a shot of people in Montreal standing in line from four o'clock in the morning waiting for the movie theater to open up, and it was like forty degrees below zero or something. I thought, How can a movie have that kind of impact before it even opens? I just couldn't believe it."

The Exorcist was strong medicine. People collapsed, fainted, reportedly broke into hysterics. The exhibitors were ready with kitty litter for those who couldn't keep their dinners down. Moviegoers who were convinced that they or loved ones were possessed by the devil besieged the Catholic Church with requests for exorcisms. An official of the Church of Scotland wrote that he'd "rather take a bath in pig manure than see the film." Reviewers were divided. Kael hated the movie, made fun of Blatty talking about communicating with his dead mother, scoffed at his serious claims for the movie, quoted Friedkin at his most Goebbels-like: "If it's a film *by* somebody instead of *for* somebody, I smell art."

It is easy to see why people, especially women, detested the picture. It presents a male nightmare of female puberty. Emergent female sexuality is equated with demonic possession, and the men in the picture—almost all celibate priests—unite to abuse and torture Regan, as John Boorman recognized, in their efforts to return her to a presexual innocence. Having Regan jam a crucifix into her vagina is intended to be a sensational and fiendishly inventive bit of sacrilege, but it is also a powerful image of self-inflicted abortion, whether the tool is a crucifix or a coathanger. Both Friedkin and Blatty were fixated on their saintly mothers; the scenes between Karras and his dying mother were obviously heartfelt for both men, and in the repressive sexual economy of the film, Regan's whore is the flip side of the Madonna. *The Exorcist* is filled with disgust toward female bodily functions; it is perhaps not too much of a stretch to see the famously gross scene in which Blair vomits pea soup as a metaphor, Carrie-like, for menstruation. Indeed, *The Exorcist* is drenched in a kind of menstrual panic.

But for most people, the picture worked. It was terrifying. Like *Bonnie and Clyde* and other New Hollywood pictures, *The Exorcist* turned its back on the liberal therapeutic framework of the postwar period. (The psychiatrist in the movie is just befuddled, clearly inadequate to the task, and Burstyn has no choice but to call upon the Church.) In exchange, the picture substituted a kind of born-again medievalism. Like *The Godfather*, *The Exorcist* looked ahead to the coming Manichaean revolution of the right, to Reagan nattering about the godless Evil Empire. Satan is the bad dad who takes up residence in the household of the divorced MacNeil in the stead of the absent father-husband. Families who pray together and stay together don't have unseemly encounters with the devil.

Friedkin was upset by the conservative release pattern. He says, "They didn't see this thing coming. They didn't see *Star Wars* coming. These were things that happened to them. They didn't make them happen. Imagine what *The Exorcist* would have done had it opened like *The Godfather*, or *Jaws* a couple of years later." Despite the fact that Warners had mucked up the distribution, *The Exorcist* grossed about $160 million ($89 million in rentals), in the days of $3 tickets, before it played out.

Indeed, the numbers were astounding. *The Exorcist* accounted for 15 percent of key market grosses in February 1974. When the box office numbers started coming in, Dick Lederer walked into Barry Beckerman's office at Warners, threw them on his desk, and said, "Kid, the fun is over. There are guys in New York looking at these figures, saying, 'This is the kind of money you can make in the movie business?' We've been having a good time out here and been very successful, but it's gonna get real serious after this." Like *The Godfather* the year before, *The Exorcist* changed the business.

THE NIGHT *THE EXORCIST* opened in Paris, Friedkin wanted to meet French filmmakers, and with the help of Joe Hyams and the French Film Office had dinner with Henri-Georges Clouzot, Claude Berri, François Truffaut and a few other French directors upstairs at Fouquets. It was a love fest. They all adored *The French Connection*, and as the red wine flowed, the French were fulsome in their praise of the American. Likewise, to meet the cream of France's Nouvelle Vague was any American cineaste's dream, and Friedkin was excessively deferential. He proceeded to confess that he'd stolen from all of them, and he particularized, going through their films scene by scene, explaining how he adapted them to his own. They were dumbfounded. Clouzot asked, "How could you keep all that shit in your head?" Clouzot's films had a big impact on Friedkin as a young man, and he repeatedly addressed him as "maestro." Clouzot asked Friedkin what he was going to do next. "I want to do your picture," replied Friedkin in all innocence. *"Wages of Fear."*

"Why?"

"I want to do it. It's a masterpiece."

"Billy, you're being foolish. You're a bright young guy, what do you want to do this old tired shit for?"

"Please, maestro, let me do it."

Flattered, Clouzot gave him the rights, which Billy discovered later he didn't own. As he was leaving, Billy joked, "I promise you I will not do it as well as you did."

Eight:
The Gospel According to
St. Martin
1973

- *How Martin Scorsese made* **Mean Streets,** *Lucas proved* **he could kill kittens with** **American Graffiti,** *while* **Nicholas Beach became the movie brat Malibu.**

"In the trades I see, 'This picture will be helmed by veteran director Martin Scorsese.' It seems like only yesterday I was a 'new young filmmaker.'"

— MARTIN SCORSESE

In the summer of 1973, Martin Scorsese and producer Jonathan Taplin were making the rounds, looking for a studio to distribute *Mean Streets*. Scorsese thought he had an in at Paramount. After all, his good friend Francis had directed the movie that saved the studio, that made Italians-with-guns a hot item. Marty had a meeting, came away elated. He didn't yet know that rarely in Hollywood did anyone ever say no. He thought, Oh my God, they love me! They're going to take the picture. The next morning, he and Taplin were going to screen the film for Peter Bart, and later that afternoon, for Warners. Scorsese asked Taplin, "Warners is bidding for it?"

"Yeah . . ."

"Paramount's going to take it, so do you want to cancel the Warners appointment?"

"Well, maybe we shouldn't. Maybe we should go just in case, just to see. Maybe they can have a little bidding war between them."

"That would be great." They were confident that when Bart and his assistant, Ronda Gomez, saw it, they would close the deal at Paramount. But Bart was in a bad mood, made worse by the spectacle of Marty's friends — his agent, Harry Ufland, his writing partner, Mardik Martin, Taplin, and a few others — lounging around the screening room when he had been assured Scorsese would be there alone. Marty popped a Valium, trying to calm himself down. No more than ten minutes in, Bart leaned over the telephone console, called the projectionist on the intercom, and the lights went on. He stood up and announced, "Don't waste my time, go sell it to John Calley, I'm not interested," and walked out. "We were shocked," says Scorsese. "It was like a slap." Quips Bart, "I really felt the courteous thing for the studio to do was give a quick answer. They didn't take it that way. It was a quicker answer than they wanted."

Taplin took Scorsese to a Turkish bath. "We had the film with us in huge 35 mm cans, walking around like beggars with this movie," recalls Scorsese. "We sat in the bath laughing, from the unexpectedness of it, and saying, 'Thank God we didn't blow off Warners.'"

That afternoon, they drove out to Burbank, screened it for Calley, and Leo Greenfield, head of distribution, both of whom had lived in New York. Scorsese was in a state of high anxiety as the film began, the lovely shots of the corridor of lights arching over the crowded streets of the San Gennaro festival sparkling against the night blackness of the city, dying as each frame went through the projector. Calley and Greenfield had ordered lunch, and just when De Niro began his brilliantly incoherent improv with Keitel in the back room of the club, nervously explaining in insanely intricate detail why he hadn't been making the payments on the money he owed, a waiter walked through the door of the screening room, stood right in front of the screen, and asked loudly, "Who's got the tuna on rye?" Somebody said, "Shhh," and Scorsese breathed a sigh of relief. He felt it had kicked in.

Calley and Greenfield were getting excited, pointing at the screen exclaiming, "Hey, I remember that place." "I used to hang around with a guy just like that." Calley said, "Wait till Ted Ashley sees this. He used to live right around the corner." They cracked up when Sandy Weintraub and her sister Barbara appeared in one scene, and De Niro said, "Which one do you want, the Weintraub broad?" By the picture's climax, a hush had fallen over the screening room, as the executives watched and heard the swerving car and the squeal of brakes, the shots, the crash, De Niro covered with blood, holding his neck, staggering past the geyser of water from the broken hydrant, and then it was over. No one said a word. Walking out, Marty joked that Calley had liked the picture because the Weintraub girls were treated like pieces of meat, and he couldn't stand their father, Fred, his former bête noir at Warners. Whatever the reason, they had sold *Mean Streets* to Warners.

FOR SCORSESE, *Mean Streets* meant a return to the old neighborhood, the place in which he had grown up. An insular, devoutly Catholic ethnic subculture, Little Italy on New York's Lower East Side might just as well have been another planet. Scorsese was born on November 17, 1942, in Flushing, Queens, where his barely upwardly mobile parents, like other children of immigrants, fled the tenements. Five years later, for reasons the young boy never fully understood, his family moved back to a fourth-floor walk-up on Elizabeth Street, his father's old block. Charlie Scorsese was a pants presser and tailor, his mother a seamstress. They were hardworking union people, only a generation removed from the Old Country. "I lived in a Sicilian village most of my life," says Scorsese. "There was Us, and there was the world. You could feel palpable tension, always on the verge of violence."

The younger of two boys by seven years, Marty grew up among priests and gangsters — and flickering images on the screen. "When you go to the movies as a child, you don't know there's anybody behind the camera," he says. "You just think the actors do it. Then you realize, 'Wait a second. That looks beautiful. This name seems to be appearing a great deal. These films all have something to do with the cavalry, or family life, like *How Green Was My Valley. The Informer. The Grapes of Wrath.* The images, the darkness of the clouds, silhouettes against the hills, and the music — what you're noticing, I guess, is poetry. Coming from a family that didn't have any books in the house, I had to discover it all myself."

Scorsese rarely ventured outside the neighborhood. He was short, frail, and sickly, a momma's boy. He was so allergic to animals he was taking his life in his hands if he petted a dog. His older brother, Frank, was jealous of the attention he got, used to beat him up. "Marty is basically a coward," says friend Mardik Martin. "In *Mean Streets*, the mook scene, you see Marty in the corner running — that's him. He would always hide." In later life he would go to great lengths to avoid conflict, learning to let other people do his fighting for him, his agent, his pals. He would express his anger in his films. He lived most happily in his own imagination.

After high school, Scorsese went to the seminary, studied for the priesthood. But driven by a single-minded passion to make movies, he entered NYU in 1960 as an undergraduate. It was a new world. "As somebody coming from the Lower East Side where my father couldn't even afford an 8mm camera, I couldn't make pictures like other kids, who had 16mm cameras, did their own little movies in their country homes. But I actually wanted to say something on film and I was able to get my hands on the equipment."

At NYU, he fell under the spell of Haig Manoogian. Manoogian taught his students to make films about their own lives, what they knew. He'd say, "Suppose what you know is eating an apple. Try to make a five- to six-minute picture on that. Very hard to do." Influenced by Italian neorealism and the American documentary movement of the '30s, he taught the films of Paul Strand, Leo Hurwitz, and Pare Lorentz. These directors all prettified their images, were believers in immaculate composition and lighting, but Scorsese also absorbed the filming-on-the-fly flavor of the new cinema verité movement pioneered by Donn Pennebaker and Ricky Leacock that was going on around him. The slice-of-life influence would show up in his student films, then in *Woodstock*, and later in the grittiness of *Mean Streets*, *Taxi Driver*, and *Raging Bull*. Manoogian hammered away at his students with his anti-Hollywood aesthetic. "Don't reach for the revolver right away," he repeated again and again. "That's melodrama. If you want to do that, go work in television, go out to L.A. We're not making that kind of cinema." Manoogian's classes were filled with middle-class kids; he had never had a student like Scorsese. Guns *were* what he knew. "Every day I grew up in the Lower East Side somebody had a gun," he says. "It was like second nature to me."

Marty was the star. Recalls director Jim McBride, "He was on a whole other level from the rest of us. He could quote films to you, describe them shot by shot. While we were humping around, trying to find the right exposure, he was making these little gems."

Like (almost) everyone else, the film that made him want to be a filmmaker was *Citizen Kane*. But there were other influences as well. At the 8th Street Playhouse in 1960, he saw *Shadows*. "It had an emotional truth to it, power," he continues. "It made me realize that *I* could make a movie." He adds, "All my life I've been bouncing back and forth between *Shadows* and *Kane*." And then there was Roger Corman. "Every morning at NYU we had to light a candle to Ingmar Bergman," he recalled. "They made us study *Wild Strawberries*." But Scorsese preferred *The Wild Angels*: "It was Corman's movies we studied in those strange dives all over New York." But unlike, say, Bogdanovich, Scorsese was also inspired by the Europeans, films like *Before the Revolution* and *Accatone*, directors like Truffaut and Godard. "What Godard was showing was new ways to use images to tell a story, new ways to shoot, to cut," he says. "In *Vivre Sa Vie*, when the guy comes into the record store where Anna Karina works, says, 'I want some Judy Garland,' the camera tracks her all the way across the store as she goes and takes an album out of the top shelf and then goes all the way back. Little things like that suddenly opened up your mind to other ways of doing things, not two people in a frame talking. There was a kind of joy that burst into me when I saw the movies by these guys."

Despite his passion and obvious talent, Scorsese had few prospects. "All I could realistically hope for," he continues, "was to make a short film and maybe work for the USIA. But I was determined to make features, personal movies, something about my life."

Scorsese met Mardik Martin at NYU in 1961. Martin was an Armenian, born in Iran and raised in Iraq. His family was wealthy, but he fled Iraq to avoid the draft, and ended up in New York, penniless, washing dishes in restaurants to earn his way through school. He could barely speak English, and Scorsese was the only kid who would talk to him. They were both short and manic — outsiders. Scorsese was still living in a cramped room in his parents' apartment. They became friends. Scorsese didn't drive, couldn't afford a car.

Martin drove him around in his ancient red Valiant, a junker, took him to Barneys in the days before it went upscale. His father's son, Marty lived and breathed clothes. He was a snappy dresser. Everything had to be just so, the shirts with French cuffs, the starched collars, the slacks with creases like razor blades.

Working with Martin, Scorsese made a couple of award-winning shorts, among them *It's Not Just You, Murray*, in 1964. Scorsese won a Screen Producers Guild Award, and in 1966, he went out to L.A. for a week to work on a Monkees episode for Rafelson, but he couldn't bring himself to do television, didn't understand it, didn't like it. Manoogian's words rang in his ears.

While he was working on *It's Not Just You, Murray*, he met an actress in the NYU program named Larraine Marie Brennan. She was "black" Irish, a bit of a kook, into numerology, the I Ching. They got married in 1965, and Marty finally left his parents' home, moved into a flat in Jersey City with Larraine. "Our wives hated us," Martin recalls. " 'Why don't you guys give up and get a decent job. What are you talking about, films?' We couldn't go home because they would pick on us." Scorsese was working on a loosely autobiographical script with Martin that drew, as Manoogian never tired of repeating, on what he knew. It was called *Season of the Witch*. They had contempt for Puzo's *The Godfather*, then a best-seller, which Scorsese knew bore no relation to the truth. He would tell it like it was. The two young men sat in Martin's Valiant and wrote. In the winter, in the cold and snow. "We were used to that," Scorsese says. "We were film students. Film students write anywhere."

He was also struggling with a film called *Who's That Knocking at My Door?*, and had shot seventy-odd minutes of it that summer. Featuring Harvey Keitel, who eked out a living as a court stenographer during the day, it took four years to complete. The delays made filming almost impossible. "It was all stopping and starting," he recalled. "You started shooting a scene, then two months later when you wanted to reshoot, the actors had cut their hair, or had another job and couldn't work. It was a nightmare."

Scorsese's parents supported his filmmaking efforts; his father paid the lab bill for *Who's That Knocking* out of his own pocket. After Marty finally completed it, he had to insert a nude scene to attract a distributor. He picked up his agent, Harry Ufland, who worked for William Morris. Scorsese met Jay Cocks in 1968, when Cocks was researching a story on student filmmakers for *Time*. Later, Cocks got Scorsese and his friends into press screenings at the New York Film Festival, and persuaded Cassavetes to look at *Who's That Knocking*. "This movie is as good as *Citizen Kane*," exclaimed Cassavetes. "No, it's better than *Citizen Kane*, it's got more heart." Marty almost fainted. "He couldn't believe this guy was saying this stuff," recalls Cocks. "And John meant it, and from that day on, he loved Marty like a son."

Woodstock was Scorsese's introduction to the '60s. He joined the 500,000-

odd mud-covered hippies like a visitor from another planet, nattily attired in a blue blazer over a shirt with French cuffs.

Meanwhile, Marty's marriage was coming apart. He and Laraine had a baby girl named Catherine, after his mother, whom he regarded as a saint. Marty would get up with the baby in the middle of the night, watch *Psycho* on TV. With the baby came increased pressure from Laraine to earn a living. "Before they split up, they were fighting all the time," recalls Martin. "Once, my wife and I drove all the way to Jersey City from Queens where we lived to have dinner with them. I could hear them yelling and screaming inside. Marty opened the door, said, 'Yeah, look, we can't make it for dinner, I'm sorry.' " For Scorsese, with his Catholic background, the decision to leave his young wife with a newborn was torture, but it was that or give up his dream of becoming a filmmaker, and in the interest of his career, he was ruthless.

Scorsese made the move to L.A. in early 1971 to edit *Medicine Ball Caravan*. Fred Weintraub used to have an open house every Sunday, where he entertained nubile Hollywood hopefuls around his oversized waterbed. Brian De Palma went, Marty went, and a few months after the earthquake, Marty ran into Sandy Weintraub. She was, as Don Simpson put it, one of Fred's "two big-titted daughters." Sandy was a nineteen-year-old hippie with no idea what she wanted to do with her life. She had just come out from New York to visit her father. "I thought Marty was just the cutest thing I had ever seen," she recalls. "He was chubby and he had long hair and no neck, and was shorter than me. I walked over to where he was, and sat down on the floor. I looked up at him, and I said, 'If I borrow some money from my father, will you let me take you out to dinner.' And he went like, 'Wow, okay.' It was the '60s, and I didn't have anything to wear except the jeans I came out with, and a couple of T-shirts. But I wanted to wear a dress. So I went to a fabric store and I bought a yard of cloth and tied it around my body, sort of toga style. That was our first date." They went to a movie, of course—*Shaft*.

Marty and Sandy became an item, and lived together for four years, well into *Taxi Driver*. (They would be creative partners as well; she would have an associate producer credit on *Alice Doesn't Live Here Anymore*.) "Marty was tempestuous, volatile, passionate about his life," she adds. "We went to everything that came out. We went to double bills, triple bills. We never ever looked at a movie and thought, Oh wow, what a great career move for him. He breathed, ate, and shat movies. I would tell him about my dreams, and he would tell me about the movie he had seen on TV the day before. He just loved the work. If he had any fear, it was that someday he wouldn't be able to do that anymore."

WHEN SCORSESE MOVED TO L.A., Brian De Palma introduced him to actress Jennifer Salt, who was making the rounds, looking for work and a place to live. One day she tested for John Huston, who was directing *Fat City*. All the actresses wore the same dress, and when Salt pulled it over her head, the armpits were still moist from the woman who read before her. Her name was Margot Kidder. "It was so tacky," recalls Salt. But each had heard of the other.

Kidder was staying at the Sunset Marquis while she looked for work. She and Salt decided to find a share. Donald Sutherland, whom Kidder knew from Canada, turned them on to a $400-a-month house on Nicholas Beach.

Kidder and Salt's lopsided A-frame was unfashionably far from the action, up the Pacific Coast Highway past Malibu where the Old Hollywood lived. Tom Pollock, an attorney, had a shack there, actress Blythe Danner and producer Bruce Paltrow lived nearby. Producers Michael and Julia Phillips would soon move in next door, and writers John Gregory Dunne and Joan Didion lived up the hill. The Salt-Kidder house, not to mention Salt and Kidder themselves, became a magnet for young Hollywood, a place where the wannabes could take a few tokes, drink red wine, trade John Ford stories, and stare at Salt, Kidder, and Salt's old school chum, actress Janet Margolin, sunbathing topless.

The house had a big living room flanked by benches along the walls with an open brick fireplace in the center surrounded by ugly wall-to-wall carpeting. On the second floor were two bedrooms, Margot's in front, on the ocean, and Jennifer's in back. Out in front was a flagpole that proudly flew the Salt-Kidder colors, a tie-dyed flag.

Salt and Kidder were an odd couple, the Lady and the Tramp. Salt was the princess from Sarah Lawrence. Kidder, from a blue-collar family, was raised in trailers and motel rooms, or nearly so. She was cute and scrappy, funny, a tomboy, and enormously bright. Salt taught her how to dress; she taught Salt how to hotwire cars, as it were. Kidder was sexually aggressive, not to say ravenous, slept with nearly every man who crossed the threshold. She acted impulsively with little thought for consequence, moved from crisis to crisis enveloped by dark clouds of Sturm und Drang. She broke hearts and sued producers. Kidder was heavily into the movement, and struck her friends as not altogether stable. She had a Frances Farmer quality about her. And of course she took drugs like they were going out of style, always the first on her block to smoke, snort, or swallow the pill du jour.

One day at the beach, Eve bit into the apple. It was inevitable. Actor Peter Boyle brought over a vial of coke. Everyone was still on pot and psychedelics, so it was show-and-tell time. "Our attitude about drugs was, they're mind-expanding, something we do to push the envelope, so, no problem," recalls Kidder. They considered themselves revolutionaries, and drugs were a tool. She continues, "The only question was, 'Well, how do you do it?' Me, of course, being me, went, 'Oh, of course I'll try it,' because I didn't have the same amount of sensible paranoia that other people had. I stuck a straw in the coke and just went, 'Pphhhht!' sucking in half the vial, freezing my lungs and making me unable to breathe. I was gasping, shaking in my boots for thirty seconds. That was my introduction to cocaine.

"Out of the drug taking came a lot of swampy ideas, but also a lot of creative thinking and, most importantly, breaking down of personal barriers and that ridiculousness of pride and holding oneself to oneself and having a phony social persona. If that hadn't been the case, none of us would have developed our talents. But Steven Spielberg didn't take drugs, Brian didn't, Marty didn't, until later when he got into trouble with coke. The directors who ended up successful were very protective of their own brains."

Margot started seeing De Palma. They were passionately in heat, making it anywhere and everywhere, once in a closet at Taplin's house, during a party. At the time, Bobby Fischer was challenging Boris Spassky, and a chess craze had swept the beach. Brian taught Margie how to play, upset the board onto her lap when she made a dumb move. She played and played until the day she beat him, then lost interest.

De Palma had a sarcastic wit and a positive genius for saying the wrong thing at the wrong time. He invariably antagonized people who didn't know him, but his friends were amused. He had been so traumatized by the *Get to Know Your Rabbit* debacle, it took him a while to shake the experience. Professionally, Margot and Jennifer weren't doing well either. By the end of 1971, both had been out of work for some time. But Brian had a surprise for them. Under the Christmas tree that year, wrapped in gift paper, was a script for Jennifer, and a script for Margot. It was *Sisters*, one of two scripts Brian had ready to go. (The other was *Phantom of the Paradise*.)

Brian brought his friends over, and others came as well. On any given weekend, Salt found herself cooking for De Palma, Spielberg, Boyle, Brackman, John Milius, Richard Dreyfuss, director Walter Hill, Bruce Dern, writer David Ward, and so on. Even Rafelson occasionally came to the beach. They grilled steaks, ate spaghetti, tossed salads. Recalls Salt, "I was always thinking, Should it be chili and the three-bean salad and the cheesecake, or should we barbecue chicken — Oh, Steven doesn't like it when I cut up zucchini in the salad, Marty likes the chili — that was where I was at. I cooked for these boys, gave lots of parties, made them take drugs and take their pants off and get down." Adds Kidder, "The reality was that we always got the drugs and we always got the food and we basically served our guys, the whole time putting down the notion that we as women would do that. There was a real contradiction in what we perceived ourselves to be doing and what in fact we were doing."

The guys were high on themselves, on their budding careers, the sense of unlimited possibility. "The goal of all these people was to make their first movie before they were thirty, because that was what the French New Wave had done," recalls actor Kit Carson. "We were the generation that was never going to get old," says Kidder. "We were not going to be the establishment, we were going to do films that made statements, whether they were personal ones or political ones."

Marty and Sandy would make the drive up the Pacific Coast Highway almost every weekend. Sandy wasn't crazy about going, but Marty said it was important for his career. Nicholas Beach was isolated; the only rules were the ones they made for themselves. Like, if you wanted to be cool, and of course everybody did, you had to go skinny-dipping, which was especially hard on Marty, because the cortisone he took for his asthma made his body blow up. He wouldn't even go near the water, sat on the sand fully dressed. Spielberg, who didn't much like the water himself would say, "C'mon, let's go in the ocean."

"No, no, no, it's very bad, it's evil. There's things out there you don't even want to know about."

"You afraid of jellyfish? There's no jellyfish out there."

"No, no, no, things with teeth." He paused, added, "I don't do water." Milius, meanwhile, surfed happily off the beach in front of the house.

Marty had a sweet, Old World courtliness about him that endeared him to Kidder and Salt. One day he appeared in an immaculate white suit with a bouquet of flowers for each of them. Says Kidder, "Marty seemed wildly dedicated to creating a new kind of film, a film of substance, to putting his personal vision on film, to marrying his confusion at being a Catholic boy and the intensity of his own spirit with film itself. He loved people trying new things, he loved bravery of personal expression, and he talked about it a lot, very eloquently, albeit very quickly. I don't remember many silly talks with Marty about nothing."

Recalls Scorsese, "The period from '71 to '76 was the best period, because we were just starting out. We couldn't wait for our friends' next pictures, Brian's next picture, Francis's next picture, to see what they were doing. Dinners in Chinese restaurants midday in L.A. with Spielberg and Lucas. My daughter named one of Steven's movies *Watch the Skies*, although he renamed it *Close Encounters* after that."

ONE OF THE BOYS on the beach was Paul Schrader. When Schrader got to UCLA in 1968, he spent a year making up for lost time, watching the films his fundamentalist parents wouldn't let him see as a kid, crisscrossing the city, scuttling from one film society to another. "People today complain about watching a movie on tape," he says. "Did you ever watch an 8mm print of *Nosferatu* on a sheet?" Everyone was under the sway of Bernardo Bertolucci's *The Conformist*. Continues Schrader: "You looked at Bertolucci, it was just like he took Godard and Antonioni, put them in bed together, held a gun to their heads, and said, 'You guys fuck or I'll shoot you.'" He didn't do particularly well at

UCLA. Recalls screenwriter Gloria Katz, "He failed production, and was crying in the halls trying to get us to sign a petition so he could continue, and they spun him off into film history."

Like Scorsese and others who were culturally and emotionally sandbagged by the '50s, Schrader was a bomb waiting to go off. By the time he got to L.A., he was seriously deranged, although he massaged his reputation as a wild man when he realized he could make it work for him. He adopted the standard garb of the Vietnam generation: an army surplus jacket and combat boots. After a couple of years in L.A., Schrader left his wife, Jeanine Oppewall, and took up with Beverly Walker, a successful publicist who handled New Hollywood films like *Zabriskie Point*, *Two-Lane Blacktop*, and *Marvin Gardens*. Schrader was a proponent of what he called "fucking up," that is, forming attachments to those above him in the food chain. Since he was a bottom feeder at the time, almost anyone, even a publicist, qualified, but it was a shrewd move, because Walker was well connected and highly regarded. In addition to a love and a publicist, he also found a cheerleader, in-house agent, and editorial consultant.

In this sea of nerds, Schrader was the nerdiest. Short, with greasy black hair, a broad, fleshy nose, and geeky, Groucho Marx glasses, he carried all his childhood frailties with him into young adulthood. He suffered from nervous tics, ulcers, and asthma. A speech impediment made him mumble self-consciously, eyes cast down, staring at his feet. He was even claustrophobic.

But Schrader had a formidable intelligence, and the ability to reinvent himself again and again. He was funny, fierce, and ambitious, and Walker liked him. When he took her to see movies at UCLA, he drove like a maniac up on the sidewalk to outflank the traffic. But soon she turned wary. "What I couldn't stand about him was that he used me so relentlessly," she says. "I knew a lot of people who were very successful. He didn't know any of them, and wanted to meet them. Then he would try to exclude me and develop his own relationships with them, so he could forward his own career."

Walker had had a desultory romance with Clint Eastwood. "In Hollywood, men put enormous pressure on women to fuck them, even if it's only once," she says. "It's like the dog that pisses on the lamppost. They want that kind of connection to you, and then maybe they can relax." Eastwood and Walker had remained friends, and Paul knew it. "What kind of a relationship can you have with someone when you fuck them, and then you turn over, and they're asking you to give a script to Clint Eastwood?" she asks. Almost immediately, Beverly and Paul started to sour as he would rifle her Rolodex for contacts. "I really think he would steal his own mother's diary if he could," she says. "He had absolutely no conscience, no moral scruples." His brother, Leonard, recalls, "I used to say to him, 'Paul, how can you use people like that, who are your friends.' He gave me a puzzled look and said, 'What else are friends for?' He knew it was shitty, but so what? 'You want to make it, or what?'"

Eventually, Walker left Schrader, temporarily relocating to Northern California, in June 1972, where she worked as an assistant to the producers of *American Graffiti*. She recalls, "Paul was calling me every night, begging to come up, but I would never let him, because I knew he just wanted to meet George, and from there, Francis and all these people who lived up there whom I knew. He was practically having a nervous breakdown, sobbing and threatening to commit suicide."

AFTER THE *THX* FIASCO, Lucas found himself at a crossroads. His reaction was not unlike Hopper's reaction to the failure of *The Last Movie*. "George thought not only had he managed to make a movie which was visually exciting, but it was really about something," recalls screenwriter and friend Matthew Robbins. "He was disappointed that there was no audience for American art films."

Francis told George, "Don't be so weird, try to do something that's human. Don't do these abstract things. All you do is science fiction. Everyone thinks you're a cold fish, but you can be a warm and funny guy, make a warm and funny movie." Marcia was on his case as well. "After *THX* went down the toilet, I never said, 'I told you so,' but I reminded George that I warned him it hadn't involved the audience emotionally," she recalls. "He always said, 'Emotionally involving the audience is easy. Anybody can do it blindfolded, get a little kitten and have some guy wring its neck.' All he wanted to do was abstract filmmaking, tone poems, collections of images. So finally, George said to me, 'I'm gonna show you how easy it is. I'll make a film that emotionally involves the audience.'"

Lucas was bitter that he had been forced into making a commercial movie, but it was also a challenge. He recognized that Hollywood was ignoring a big part of its potential audience, one that was tiring of the steady diet of sex, violence, and pessimism doled out by the New Hollywood, and was nostalgic for the upbeat values of the Old Hollywood. "Before *American Graffiti*, I was working on basically negative movies—*Apocalypse Now* and *THX*, both very angry," he said. "We all know, as every movie in the last ten years has pointed out, how terrible we are, how wrong we were in Vietnam, how we have ruined the world, what schmucks we are and how rotten everything is. It had become depressing to go to the movies. I decided it was time to make a movie where people felt better coming out of the theater than when they went in. I became really aware of the fact that the kids were really lost, the sort of heritage we built up since the war [World War II] had been wiped out by the '60s, and it wasn't groovy to act that way anymore, now you just sort of sat there and got stoned. I wanted to preserve what a certain generation of Americans thought being a teenager was really about—from about 1945 to 1962." He wanted to make a film about something he knew intimately, teenage rites of passage in a small town in the '50s—the hotrods, the top ten musical wallpaper that formed the background for everything from drag racing to heavy petting, the drinking, the girls, the anxieties generated by leaving home. He set the plot in the early '60s, on the eve of the Vietnam War, so that the story had a little more resonance, became an elegy for American innocence.

Graffiti was a difficult idea to make work on paper. It was an ensemble piece focusing on four young men with separate stories, and there was precious little in the way of plot. When Lucas's agent, Jeff Berg, sent his script to the studios, most of them turned it down. Bart was one of the executives underimpressed by Lucas. He thought, I can't imagine George directing a movie because he's so noncommunicative, the ultimate passive-aggressive. You'd have to grab him by the throat and shake him to get a word out of him. Finally, Universal showed a flicker of interest. Ned Tanen had grown up in the cruising culture of Southern California. He loved cars, and was intrigued by Lucas's tale of nerds on wheels. *Graffiti* became the last film in his group of low-budget pictures.

Tanen knew he needed a good producer to work with Lucas. Coppola, whom only yesterday Tanen had ridiculed as a clown, "Francis the Mad," was now the salvation of the industry, and so was the logical choice. Tanen gave Lucas a list of producers to choose from. George immediately put a check next to Francis's name. He wasn't too happy about it; he had been determined to go out on his own after *THX*, but now it seemed all roads led back to Francis. Coppola agreed immediately, saying, "Yeah, sure, great. But ya know, *we* should be doing this picture. Let's get it out of Universal, I'll finance it myself." Lucas gulped, thought, Oh my God, what's gonna happen here? Francis is going to fuck up my deal with his grandiose ideas. But Universal was not about to bow out, especially now that someone else was interested.

According to Coppola, there was no deal with Universal when he first went to City Bank in Beverly Hills, and secured a $700,000 loan against his cut of *The Godfather*. But Sidney Korshak dissuaded him, explaining that if *Graffiti* flopped, which was likely, his children would lose their annuity, that is, their future income from *The Godfather*. At the same time, Ellie Coppola, who did not particularly like the *Graffiti* script, convinced her husband that the time to borrow against *The Godfather* was when he would have to finance his own personal project that no studio would back. So he gave up his efforts to find financing.

Coppola got $25,000 and 10 percent of the net from Universal, and another 15 percent from Lucas. Tanen offered Lucas a budget of $600,000, including the music rights. Berg got it up to $750,000, still humiliating for Lucas, who had spent $1.2 million for *THX*. He was going backward. Still, it was something, with $20,000 for himself, and twenty-five points.

Coppola persuaded Willard Huyck and Gloria Katz to work on the script. From their point of view, "Francis got the movie made," says Huyck. "George would be at the airport, and he'd see two guys arguing, and he'd say, 'They're the exact people I want for my movie,' so he'd bring them in for a reading, and Francis would say, 'George, I think we need real actors.' " *Graffiti*, more than most, was a movie made in the casting, and once again it was Fred Roos who selected future stars like Richard Dreyfuss, Harrison Ford, and Cindy Williams.

Graffiti was shot in twenty-eight days, starting in the last week of June 1972. It was a tough shoot, no money, no time. Lucas was worried about directing the actors, never his strong suit. He hadn't the foggiest idea what to say to them, and he liked to say that actors are irrelevant. He believed that the most important parts of a film are the first five minutes and the last twenty. Everything in between is filler, and if there is enough action, no one will notice that the characters aren't particularly complex, or that the acting is wooden. He hired a drama coach to work with the actors, while he confined himself to presiding over the camera. Says Coppola, "George was given this cast, and he had to shoot so fast that there wasn't any time for any directing. He stood 'em up and shot 'em, and they were so talented, they — It was just lucky."

Tanen, fixated on one of his big productions, *Jesus Christ Superstar,* drove George crazy. George could never get him on the phone. On the other hand, when Tanen made one of his infrequent visits to the set, Lucas ignored him. "George has no social graces," says Katz. "And in his psychology, the suits had no business other than writing the checks. He didn't want to hear what they said, he didn't respect them, nothing. The idea that the suits actually made a profit on his movie was just appalling to him. And Ned was very combative. George did not appreciate that."

Tanen put Verna Fields on the movie, to edit it, assisted by Marcia. Fields had made a name for herself working for Bogdanovich on *Targets, What's Up, Doc?,* and *Paper Moon.* She was a large, warm woman with short brown hair and half glasses, hung on a string, perched on the tip of her nose. She was like a Jewish aunt, except that instead of talking gefilte fish recipes, she talked editing. They called her "Mother Cutter," and listened raptly as she dispensed Verna-isms, like "If you can't solve it, dissolve it."

In fact, Marcia first met and fell in love with George when Fields hired them both in the late '60s to help file and cut footage of LBJ's trips to the Far East for the U.S. Information Agency in her tract house in the Valley. Born in Modesto in 1947, Marcia Griffin was an air force brat. Her parents divorced when she was an infant, and she was raised by her mother in straitened circumstances in North Hollywood. Marcia was as outgoing as George was reserved. She was sunny, George dark. Like Bogdanovich and Platt, they complemented each other. They married in February 1969. When they moved to the Bay Area to participate in the Zoetrope experiment, they rented a house in Mill Valley, just north of San Francisco.

Verna and Marcia and George cut *Graffiti* in the garage of a house Coppola owned in Mill Valley that had been converted to editing rooms. On the

Moviola, Francis had taped Xeroxes of checks made out to him from Paramount for *The Godfather* for millions of dollars.

MEANWHILE SCORSESE was still struggling. He and Sandy went to parties, hung out. It was fun, but for the young wannabe director, they were always work. "I was an opportunist," he says. "I went to every party, talked to everybody I could to get a picture made. I looked at people in terms of whether they could help me. I'd find things out about them, or ways that I could see them and find their ideas tolerable — even if they weren't very likable. I had my own agenda. I was obsessive, relentless, ruthless." As Schrader puts it, "No one succeeds in film if he's not hustling. The first thing you think of when you wake up in the morning is, Who can I hustle? and the last thing you think of before you go to bed is, Who can I hustle?"

There was nobody he exploited more than Sandy. She took care of him, helped him with his scripts, nursed and mothered him as well as loved him. "He needed a lot of attention," says Weintraub. "We went to buy Marty clothes. We went to buy Marty a car. He had a little Lotus. It was so cute because he was so tiny and he had this tiny car." When it got to be too much, she used to complain he sucked her dry, like a vampire. Indeed, he was known as "Dracula" because of his nocturnal habits.

Scorsese was filled with phobias and anxieties, and he began to see a therapist. He hated to fly, and during takeoff gripped a crucifix in his fist until his knuckles turned white. He was beset by superstitions, a melding of Catholicism and some arcana of his own making, forebodings drawn from dreams, signs and portents of various kinds. He had an unlucky number, 11. They lived in a building with numbered parking spaces. When the digits on a space added up to 11, he would walk around it. He wouldn't travel on the 11th of the month, avoided flights in which the numbers added up to 11, and wouldn't take a room on the 11th floor of a hotel. He had a gold amulet to ward off evil spirits, and wore a pouch around his neck filled with lucky charms. On one occasion, he lost the pouch, freaked. Sandy had to run out, buy more charms, fill a new pouch with them.

"Marty had a kind of Rimbaud philosophy," says Taplin. "He said to me one time, 'I won't live past forty.' He really had this live hard, do your work, and die young philosophy. It wasn't that he was self-destructive, he just had a morbid feeling that he was going to die, either through an airplane crash, or his health was going to give out, and so he had to get as much in as possible."

Marty needed Sandy, but at the same time resented the tender loving care she lavished on him. Says Taplin, "She was very mothering, and he didn't want to be mothered sometimes." She was young and self-righteous, thought she knew everything. He had a bad temper, and although he was circumspect and indirect with men, with women he gave it full rein. The two fought constantly. "He got angry once and swept off the table with his arms and a glass went flying, and I was naked and I got some glass in my back. He never attacked me or hit me, but he was a wall puncher. And a phone thrower. We could not keep a phone in the house. One time I was on the phone with Taplin, angry about something. Marty grabbed it out of my hand, yelled at Taplin, threw the phone and broke it. Then he went down in the elevator, put a dime in a pay phone on the street, and continued to yell at Taplin."

As Marty became more successful, women who previously wouldn't have given him the time of day suddenly became available. This too was hard on their relationship. "You watched somebody who was not very physically fit, who never got the women, who was never considered handsome and attractive, all of a sudden go from being a little sort of overweight nebbishy nothing, to famous and rich," recalls Weintraub. "It had this enormous effect on you. It was like that beautiful cool blonde you wanted all your life, that shiksa, she was throwing herself at you and I was supposed to say no? It was the '70s, open relationships and stuff. I used to explain this to him, which would drive him nuts. I guess he felt like I didn't care. You lost either way."

Much of Scorsese's passion came from anger. Weintraub thinks the rage came from his father: "I remember his parents coming to visit, and his father leaned over and said kind of quietly, 'Are you still seeing that funny doctor,' the therapist. And Marty said, 'Yeah, it's really helping me.' His father turned around and his face got all distorted, really red and angry, and he said, 'When are you gonna grow up and be a man?' "

Toward the middle of 1971, Corman offered Marty *Boxcar Bertha* to direct. It was a variation on the theme of *Bonnie and Clyde,* a Depression-era drama about a persecuted union organizer (David Carradine), and a boxcar-riding hobo bimbo (Barbara Seagull, then Hershey), just the kind of tabloid melding of politics and sex that Corman loved. Says Simpson, "Roger, I swear, didn't know what picture Marty was making. All he cared about was, 'Is Barbara gonna, like, show tits in *Boxcar?*' "

Bertha opened on a double bill with *1000 Convicts and a Woman.* Scorsese was embarrassed by the film. He showed it to Cassavetes, who gave voice to what Scorsese himself had been thinking. "Nice work, but don't fucking ever do something like this again," said Cassavetes. "Why don't you make a movie about something you really care about." Scorsese turned down Corman's next assignment to make *Mean Streets.*

THE NEW HOLLYWOOD was a small town where everyone knew everyone, and eventually Schrader met Scorsese. But in those days, Scorsese hadn't yet made it, and Schrader, with his career always at the front of his mind, gravitated to the more successful members of the group. He had been introduced to De Palma by the ubiquitous Jay Cocks at the Fox screening room in New York, a magnificent CinemaScope theater called the Scheherazade, way over on the West Side. Schrader had recently given a favorable review to De Palma's film *Sisters*, featuring Kidder and Salt, in *LA*. Later, De Palma brought Schrader home to the Salt-Kidder house where he was living with Kidder. "This odd little character arrived at ten in the morning, banging on the door, and woke us up with a large bottle of scotch, which he slammed on the table, and then proceeded to follow Brian around like a lapdog," she remembers. "I thought he was pretty weird. I couldn't stand having him around, hated him. I wanted to be with Brian and there would be Schrader, smitten. He was someone who didn't like women. Brian was the guy all the guys wanted to be."

Schrader understood immediately that he was in his element. He says, "I'm basically depressive, cynical, prone to intellectualization. Therefore I got along with Marty and Brian perfectly." He was drawn to those like himself: displaced New Yorkers, crazies, artists. As producer Howard Rosenman puts it, "Paul was never a friend of the ordinary. He was attracted to neurotic, guilt-ridden Catholics, Jews — and Japanese." Schrader had written an impenetrable book about Ozu, Dreyer, and Bresson (later he would get a vanity license plate that said "OZU"), and was regarded, along with De Palma, as the intellectual of the group.

Schrader also attached himself to John Milius, who was the most successful of the regulars at the beach. After *Apocalypse Now*, he had written *Jeremiah Johnson*, *The Life and Times of Judge Roy Bean*, and a draft of *Dirty Harry*. He had also done a creditable job directing his first feature, *Dillinger*, although the picture had flopped. He valiantly flaunted his right-wing credentials, and did what he could to *épater les* movie brats. Milius, like Schrader, was a guys' guy; women found him hard to take. "It was impossible to relate to John, because he was this enormous blowhard," says Gloria Katz. "So unless you were gonna sit there and be enthralled by him for hours and hours on end, it was incredibly boring."

Says Rosenman, "Schrader was attracted to that male energy, Hemingway-esque thing of Milius's, as well as that self-destructive, killing himself, writer thing." Adds Kit Carson, "Schrader was in love with Milius, no two ways about it. He imitated Milius's behavior, the idea being, if you acted crazy, it scared people and they would respect you."

Women didn't like Schrader, didn't appreciate his finer points. He had a crush on Kidder. One night, the two of them were driving along Sunset in his car to meet Brian at a screening. "Kiss me! Kiss me!" he implored, out of the blue. She pulled away, said, "I'm not going to kiss you, are you crazy?" Paul was crushed, felt like he must display the mark of Cain. She slept with everything in pants — except him. He slammed on the brakes and put the car into a 360 spin. "He scared the wits out of me," says Kidder. "I pecked him on the cheek, he pulled the car out of the spin and drove to the screening."

Like Kidder, Sandy Weintraub couldn't stand Schrader: "Paul was a very messed up human being. When he left his apartment, he went to a bar and sat there and drank all night."

The feeling was mutual. "I didn't see what Marty saw in her," says Schrader. "She wasn't really attractive, and she wasn't funny, and she couldn't keep up with the conversation when the film references started flying back and forth. Those were my criteria for having someone around. But Marty was a man who needed a woman, and he would rather be with someone he was in trouble with, or not getting along with, than be alone. So he was always going immediately on to the next."

MEAN STREETS, which Scorsese's agent, Harry Ufland, was still shopping around (eventually, it would go through something like twenty-seven drafts), was still called *Season of the Witch*. Cocks renamed it, borrowing a phrase from Raymond Chandler. Corman offered Scorsese $150,000 toward shooting *Mean Streets*, but only if he agreed to rewrite the script for a black cast, so the picture could exploit the popularity of *Shaft* and its spin-offs. Scorsese refused. Cocks's wife, Verna Bloom, an actress who was featured in *The Hired Hand* and Wexler's *Medium Cool*, had introduced Scorsese to Taplin, an ex–road manager for Bob Dylan and the Band. Taplin wanted to get into films and told Scorsese he could raise the money to produce *Mean Streets*. The script had two meaty roles, Charlie, the Marty surrogate, written for Keitel, and Johnny Boy, the loudmouth pal with the loose screws.

Marty had also met Robert De Niro through Bloom, who had acted with her in a Jack Gelber play. Both men were invited to a dinner party at Jay and Verna's home on East 70th Street, decorated with a collection of Indian baskets from the Southwest that Bloom had collected during the shoot of *The Hired Hand*. Scorsese and De Niro had grown up within a few blocks of each other, but they were barely acquainted, probably because De Niro, the son of an artist, was raised in a middle-class, bohemian home. Although De Niro and Scorsese were poles apart, each wanted what the other had, and they hit it off immediately. Says Cocks, "Bob's way of rebelling was by getting into this heavy street thing, and Marty couldn't believe the kind of life Bob was raised in that put such an emphasis on creativity — it was like paradise, like liberation."

De Niro was very serious about acting, didn't hang out, didn't make small talk. In fact, he didn't talk at all. He was so shy he was next door to autistic, which made it hard for him to get work. "You couldn't get De Niro arrested," recalls casting director Nessa Hyams. "We schlepped him into every reading for every director we could, and he wouldn't talk, and we'd go, 'But he's so talented,' and the director would go, 'Thank you, next!' " Says Sandy Weintraub, "Communicating with Bob involved a lot of gestures and touching, very few words. He used to sit on a couch at parties and fall asleep."

De Niro read the script, turned down the role of Johnny Boy, the out-of-control, "funny in the head" neighborhood nut. He said he wanted to play Charlie, torn between the church and the mob. (The backers wanted a star — Jon Voight — for the role, but Voight wasn't interested.) Scorsese held fast to Keitel. De Niro changed his mind, agreed to do Johnny Boy.

The budget for *Mean Streets* was in the neighborhood of $600,000. Most of the movie — the interiors — were shot in L.A. in the fall of 1972. "In order to get the picture made I had to learn how to make a movie," says Scorsese. "I didn't learn how to make a movie in film school. What you learned in film school was to express yourself with pictures and sound. But learning to make a movie is totally different. That's the people with the production board, the schedule. That means you gotta get up at five in order to be there, you gotta feed the people."

Before going to L.A., Scorsese shot six days and nights in New York, the exteriors and some of the key interiors, the staircases in the tenements of Little Italy, the cemetery at Old St. Patrick's Cathedral that could not be replicated in L.A. There was virtually no money. Scorsese raised a crew of NYU students. "The kids were quite young," he continues. "The scene with the two gay guys in the car, two whole setups were lost, including Bob's close-up, because one of the assistant cameramen just forgot where he had put the film. Then he left. 'Forget it, I'm too tired. I want to go home.' I had to piece the whole thing together. Bobby fires a gun off the roof toward the Empire State Building, but the window that the bullet hits was in Los Angeles." Scorsese was so tense he wore white gloves throughout the shoot to stop himself from biting his nails.

Scorsese did not get much help from people in the old neighborhood. "It was easier for Francis to come into my neighborhood and shoot than it was for me. They were very paranoid. 'Who does he think he is? He's one of us. We don't want cameras here.' It was a very, very closed society. You had to make deals with everybody. By the end of it, when my father heard about it, he came to me and said, 'You should have talked to me. I could have spoken to so-and-so and so-and-so. And then he would have talked to so-and-so's father. And we could have made a deal with such-and-such.' I said, 'No, I didn't want to get you involved with it.' When they sent the bill, it was $5,000. So I asked Francis, and he gave me the $5,000. As soon as the picture was picked up, I paid Francis back."

After a screening of the rough cut of *Mean Streets*, Weintraub, Scorsese, De Niro, and a few others repaired to a restaurant for what Weintraub assumed would be a group dissection of the film, except that De Niro and Scorsese disappeared into the men's room for two and a half hours and hashed it out between themselves. Says Weintraub, "What Marty and Bob did together, they did in private. Definitely no women allowed."

Helping one another was a deeply ingrained habit among the New Hollywood filmmakers. Nevertheless, the flames of competitiveness burned hot and deep, if not always visibly. As Scorsese puts it, "There was always a fine line, where maybe one person was getting more attention than the other. But if the person who's getting less attention sees your rough cut, he could steer you in a negative way on purpose. Without evening realizing it. Because of the jealousy. It was very difficult." Adds George Litto, who produced for De Palma later in the decade, "Brian never believed he was as successful as Marty, Francis, or George. That made him very uncomfortable." De Palma advised him to get rid of one of the best scenes in the movie, the improv between De Niro and Keitel in the back room of the club that would get Calley's attention. He said, "It's just wasting time. Take it out." Scorsese did, but luckily Cocks told him to put it back, and he did that too. "Brian was more in the mainstream," adds Scorsese. "He was the one who talked very often about what would work in the marketplace. And like fools we thought *Mean Streets* would work in the marketplace. But we were making a different kind of film. We just didn't know that."

GRAFFITI PREVIEWED IN Lucas territory, at the Northpoint Theater in San Francisco on January 28, 1973. Tanen flew in on a commercial airline, the same flight as Hal Barwood, Matthew Robbins, and Jeff Berg. He was in one of his black moods. "Ned wouldn't sit with us on the airplane and he wouldn't share a cab to the theater," said Robbins. "He was furious before he even saw the movie."

It was a dream screening. Recalls Marcia, "The movie started, and the minute "Rock Around the Clock" came on, people just started whooping and hollering, and when Charlie Martin Smith drives in on a Vespa and bangs into the wall, the audience laughed! They were with the film all the way, and at the end, they were on their feet and applauded. Francis and George and I were all euphoric. We were in the back row, and suddenly this man stood up and said, very loudly and very clearly, 'This film is unreleasable.' I was in a state of shock."

Tanen discounted the audience response, thought to himself, This place is filled with George's friends. He cornered producer Gary Kurtz in the lobby: "This is in no shape to show to an audience. You should have shown it to us first. I went to bat for you, and you let me down." Wheeling around to face Coppola, who had just parted the sea of people surrounding him and Kurtz, he continued, angrily, "I'm very disturbed, we really have to get together, we have a lot to do." Coppola looked at George, thought, He's cowering on the side, sort of hiding. Scared. It's up to me.

"What are you talking about?" Coppola demanded, his voice shaking with anger. "You were just in the theater for the last two hours, didn't you just see and hear what we all just saw and heard? What about the laughter?"

"I've got notes. We'll have to see if we can release it."

"You'll see if you can *release* it?" roared Coppola, apoplectic. "You should go down on your knees and thank George for saving your job. This kid has killed himself to make this movie for you. He brought it in on time and on schedule. The least you can do is thank him for that." Francis whipped out a checkbook, and offered to buy the picture from Universal on the spot, saying, "If you hate it that much, let it go, we'll set it up someplace else, and get you all your money back." Tanen abruptly dashed to his limo and left for the airport. He thought Coppola was grandstanding. "Francis, who would have rather not even been involved with the movie, suddenly decided to become the godfather," he says. Tanen and Coppola didn't speak again for twenty years.

After it was all over, George called Willard and Gloria, devastated. He said, "I don't know what to do, this picture — people are responding off the wall, and they keep telling me they're going to put it on television." But he was pleased with Francis. He says now, "Francis really stood up to Ned. I had given him a bad time when the Warners thing came down over *THX*, I really held that against him — 'You're gonna let them cut it, you're not gonna go down there and stop 'em?' and when *Graffiti* came along, I said, 'Here we go again,' but Francis did what he was supposed to do. I was pretty proud of him."

ONE DAY, while Paul Schrader was playing chess with De Palma, he casually mentioned that he had written a script called *Taxi Driver*. It follows the nocturnal wanderings of a cabbie — a violent, alienated Vietnam vet — through Times Square as he encounters a variety of human offal and routinely cleans the blood and come off his back seat. He gets a crush on a blond campaign worker, and his attention wanders between her and Iris, a twelve-year-old hooker. The story climaxes in a bloodbath, as he blows away Iris's pimp and johns in an attempt to redeem her.

"I read the whole thing out loud to Jennifer and Jill Clayburgh one morning on Trancas beach," says De Palma. "I thought it was unbelievable, great writing, a great fucking script, but I couldn't see how to direct it. I said, 'Who is *ever* going to go see this? This is so crazy.' "

De Palma passed the *Taxi Driver* script to producer Michael Phillips, who lived with his wife, Julia, in a big, sprawling four-bedroom house on the bluff just down the beach from Margot and Jennifer. They, along with Tony Bill, had just finished *Steelyard Blues*, produced by Richard Zanuck and David

Brown for Warners, and were prepping *The Sting*, also produced by Zanuck and Brown, now at Universal. Both films were written by David Ward.

People drifted over from the Salt-Kidder house enveloped in a haze of marijuana smoke. Julia's office wardrobe was much the same as her beach wardrobe: jeans and a T-shirt. She wore her hair cropped short, making her look all of seventeen. But when she opened her mouth it was a different story. She swore like a stevedore. Director John Landis, who had just come to Hollywood and was in his early twenties, remembers her working the phone: "It was like, 'Tell him I'll rip his cock off and shove it up his fucking ass, you motherfucker,' language that was just Satanic in its profanity." Says Salt, "Julia had a real eye for spotting talent, and she would throw herself bodily upon it. In truth, though, I was a little bit contemptuous of Julia, because she was on the other side: to me, she was a business lady, she was management. I didn't understand why anybody was so intrigued by numbers and deals and phone calls, it was Redford this, and Begelman that. I was sort of a '60s queen, and she liked people that I couldn't fathom, people that to me were the sleaziest of sleaze."

Adds Kidder, "In those days, of course, agents were people that you looked down on and you didn't have anything to do with. Once Janet Margolin brought Freddie Fields up to the house. He arrived in a Rolls-Royce with a driver. We were just disgusted at this overt display of *nouveau riche* capitalism. He saw our bottles of Almaden and Red Mountain and promptly announced that he would send his driver back for some better wine. We were just horrified. We ostracized the poor girl and made fun of her for weeks. There was a code of what you did and didn't do. And you certainly didn't date an agent. And you didn't flash wealth, you didn't care about it, you didn't do things for money. You did things because you felt artistically compelled to do them.

"The secret that we all held in our hearts that no one revealed to each other was how ragingly ambitious we all were. That was the sense of recognition, like when dogs sniff each other out, recognition of a fellow traveler, someone who was going down the path toward success, not ruthlessly, the way these young, poof-dried agents did, but with some integrity, but still determined to get there. So for any of us to have posed, which we did, as hippies, political activists, or all-the-way spiritual beings seeking Babaramboooo or whatever, a higher life, was nonsensical."

Salt was right about Julia. She was ruthless, knew what she wanted, and let nothing stand in her way. One time she went to New York with Don Simpson to supervise the trailer for *Steelyard Blues*. Both were staying at the Sherry Netherland. "Julia 'Yes, I am a genius' Phillips blackmailed me," says Simpson. "We were at the hotel, in the elevator. She said, 'If you don't come to my room and fuck me, I will get on the phone tomorrow and get you fired.' I thought, No, I'm not. A) I don't want to fuck you. B) You're married to a man I really like, Michael Phillips. I said, 'I don't do that.' Homey don't play that. I went to my room and she called me. Called me, called me, called me. Finally I went upstairs. She was smoking a huge joint. I saw my opportunity, figured maybe if I could get high with her, it'd take her mind off it. So I did a couple of hits. Boom, boom. I managed to eat pussy rather than fuck her, much to my credit, and got her off. I gave my body for my career. Thank you, Anita Hill."

Says Julia, "It's not true. I would never have fired anyone over sexual favors. I didn't care enough about sex."

Michael Phillips loved *Taxi Driver*, and passed it along to Julia and Tony Bill. They optioned it for $1,000. (Later, they would reward De Palma with a point, as a finder's fee.) But within a few months, Bill and the Phillipses came to a parting of the ways. "The partnership foundered on what I later discovered to be Julia's drug use," says Bill. "She was very bright and could verbally wrestle to the ground anyone who she felt was standing in her way. She would yell, ride roughshod over people. I couldn't stand to be partners with someone for whom I had to apologize so often to so many people." They divided up their projects. *Taxi Driver* stayed with the Phillipses.

Scorsese wanted to direct *Taxi Driver*, but when he showed *Boxcar Bertha* to Schrader, Paul just rolled his eyes. "Paul was never really gracious to me at all, he was abrasive," recalls Scorsese. Marty had wanted to direct *The Yakuza* as well, a script Paul had just sold, but Schrader scoffed, insisted he wanted a "Tiffany" director. Says Schrader, "I was blind to the value around me. I took people for granted. I don't think I was as impressed by Marty as I was by Brian, 'cause Brian was more outgoing. Marty is extraordinarily secretive about his true feelings." Scorsese was hurt, furious.

Michael and Julia were no more impressed with Scorsese than Schrader was. But he hung in, reminding Julia, "Don't forget, I want to do *Taxi Driver*." She replied, "Come back when you've done something besides *Boxcar Bertha*." Not that it made much difference. It was still impossible to get a studio to commit to this dark, violent, uncommercial script. None of the principals had enough clout. Michael and Julia had nothing to show for themselves. *Steelyard Blues* flopped without honor, failing even to generate reviews. *The Sting* had yet to open. The *Taxi Driver* script scared everyone. "It hung in limbo for two, three years," Paul remembers. "Every studio said, 'This is a great script, and somebody should make it — but not us.'"

AFTER *MEAN STREETS* was completed, Marty got on a plane and went up to San Francisco and showed Coppola the print in his screening room. "That's when Francis first saw De Niro," he recalls. "And immediately, he put him in *Godfather II*." Marty found Francis enveloped in a cloud of sycophants who were fiercely jealous of outsiders. One, says Weintraub, particularly attentive, would follow him into the bathroom two steps behind him. "I don't think

Francis could fart without him catching it." On one occasion, he slammed the door of Francis's limo in Marty's face. "He treated us like dirt," says Weintraub. "When all of a sudden Marty's career was on the rise, he became Mr. Wonderful." Marty and Sandy slept in the attic of Coppola's Victorian. Recalls Scorsese, "Francis woke us up in the morning, blowing a trumpet, with his robe open."

Scorsese and Taplin took *Mean Streets* to Cannes in May. "Marty, Bobby, and I were introduced to Fellini," recalls Taplin. "When his distributor came into the room to pay homage to the maestro, Fellini said, 'Ah, you should buy his film, it's the greatest American film in the last ten years.' He hadn't even seen it."

With a foreign sale, Taplin was in an expansive mood. He invited everyone for lunch to Le Moulin de Mougins, a four-star restaurant in the hills above Cannes. De Niro was there with his female companion of the moment. "Bobby always had girlfriend trouble," says Taplin. "He picked these incredibly strong girls, top chicks, always black, and then he'd fight with them all the time. They would always be in tears the next morning, and he would buy them some perfume."

Marty, Sandy, De Niro, and the others were in the middle of an extraordinary meal when a bee the size of a small hummingbird buzzed the table. Sandy tried to ignore it, but it was making her nervous, and finally she called the waiter over, said, "This bee is bothering me," asked him to do something about it. The waiter took his towel off his arm and flicked it at the bee, which dropped stone dead into De Niro's girlfriend's water glass. She became hysterical, exclaiming loudly, "He killed the bee! A living thing! I can't believe this guy killed the bee!"

"Will you can it?" said De Niro, annoyed.

"What do you mean? You're gonna just let him kill this bee?"

"It's just a fucking bee!" They were starting to attract the attention of the other guests. De Niro was getting angrier, said loudly, "Will you shut the fuck up?"

"Why are you talking to me like that?"

They started screaming at each other, until De Niro said, "Why don't you take a fucking hike?"

"Goddamn right I will!" She stormed out of the restaurant.

Le Moulin de Mougins is twenty miles from nowhere. De Niro turned to Marty and the others and said, "Ahh, let her fucking walk, she'll come back." They finished their meal, called a cab, and sure enough, about five miles down the road, there she was, walking back to Cannes. De Niro said to her, "Get in." They sulked all the way back. The next morning he bought her a big bottle of perfume.

Mean Streets premiered at the New York Film Festival in the fall of 1973. "We were broke, beyond broke, really busted," remembers Sandy. "Harry

Ufland gave me his credit card so I could buy one dress for the interviews, and I had to wash it every night, iron it on the floor. The night it opened was one of the most exciting events of my life. They laughed where they were supposed to laugh, gasped where they were supposed to gasp. At the end of the movie, they shined a light on the box. Marty got a standing ovation. The *New York Times* gave it a rave. When we got back to the hotel, there was a stack of messages a foot high from people wanting Marty to direct their pictures."

A few nights later, they were at a Critics Award dinner at the Ginger Man, down the street from Lincoln Center. De Niro brought Diahnne Abbott, whom he had been seeing for some time. "Diahnne was in a conversation with François Truffaut," recalls Sandy. "Bobby was very jealous. He saw them talking and put a chair down behind Truffaut and straddled it. Truffaut finally realized that there was somebody behind him, and got up and said, 'Excuse me' and left. Bobby jumped up and said, 'What did he want? What did he *want?*' I was thinking, That was Truffaut. Who cares what he wanted? We're just punk kids here. You should be very happy."

SISTERS HAD BEEN PRODUCED by Ed Pressman. Extremely close to his mother, Pressman was using money from the family toy business to produce. He was short and socially maladroit. Stories about his faux pas abounded. One night, at a party, he was holding a glass of scotch in his hand when actor John Lithgow asked him the time. He instantly turned his wrist, dumping the scotch into his lap. It was easy not to take Ed seriously, and most people didn't. Says Salt, "Ed was totally spaced out, it appeared he had no idea what he was doing. We all felt the boys brought him along for the ride because he was a rich boy and his mother would bail them out of any trouble that they got into, so they played movies." Brian used to call him "Sparky" behind his back. Pressman was extremely tight with money, and when Brian had to sue him for dollars owed on *Sisters*, he stopped calling him "Sparky," and started referring to him as "the weasel." *Sisters* generally got good reviews, and it made its money back on the TV sale alone. Brian was on his way.

Jake Brackman introduced Pressman to Terry Malick, his dear friend and classmate at Harvard. A burly young man, barrel-chested and bearded, Malick looked a little like Peter Boyle with hair. He was shy and introverted, said very little. Malick came from Texas. His father was an executive with Phillips Petroleum, and he had two younger brothers, Chris and Larry. Larry went to Spain to study guitar with Segovia, a taskmaster of legendary proportions. In the summer of 1968, Terry learned that his brother had broken his own hands, apparently distraught over his studies. Terry's father asked him to go over to Spain to help Larry. Terry refused. The father went himself, and returned with

Larry's body. He had apparently committed suicide. Terry, as the eldest son, had inherited the birthright. He was the one who went to Harvard and became the Rhodes Scholar, and now when his youngest brother needed him most, he hadn't been there. He always bore a heavy burden of guilt.

Malick had written a script called *Badlands*. He wanted Pressman to finance it. Brian had studied Pressman with the intensity of a zoologist, and gave Malick some advice. Pressman's unprepossessing manner seemed to invite cudgeling from the boys in the upper form, as it were, and De Palma suggested alternating flattery with abuse. Malick, who was twice Pressman's size, was reputed to have once pulled himself out of a chair by grabbing Pressman's ear and hauling himself up with it.

Malick persuaded Pressman to finance *Badlands*, based on the story of the 1958 Midwest killing-spree of Charlie Starkweather, and his girlfriend, fourteen-year-old Caril Ann Fugate, starring Martin Sheen and Sissy Spacek. It was shot on a shoestring, $350,000 in out-of-pocket costs in Colorado. They didn't even have enough money to see dailies. This was Malick's first time out as a director, but he was determined to do it his way. One time, he said to a crew member, "I'll put [the actor] in front of the window so when it gets dark you can continue shooting, you'll have more light."

"Terry, you can put him wherever you want, we'll light it."

"Don't tell me, I've made two 8mm films."

In the script, the couple burns the girl's parents' home to the ground. The crew guy spread highly flammable glue all over the set, which may not have been properly ventilated, allowing fumes to accumulate. An assistant lit the match too soon, creating an inferno. The crew guy ran through the flames across the set to get out as the small-town fire department watched the flames, mesmerized, instead of starting the pumper engine. Hiring a Learjet with a doctor and nurse to fly him to a burn center in Southern California cost around $3,000. Jill Jakes, Malick's wife, allegedly refused to sign a check, ostensibly saying, "We're way over budget. We don't have money for that." Lou Stroller, the production manager, said to her, "If you were a fucking man, I'd put you right through that plate glass window." He paid for the plane out of his own money. (Jakes's recollection of the event is not clear, but she says, "I would never have said, 'No, that man is not going on a plane to a hospital.' ")

Malick was obsessed with the movie. Eventually running out of money, he continued shooting pickup scenes himself with the help of a couple of locals.

When it was finished, Pressman auctioned the film. It cost about $450,000, excluding $500,000 or so in deferred salaries. Brackman introduced Malick to Bert Schneider, who made some key calls, coached them on how to proceed. He felt they could have gotten more: "They didn't listen, didn't have the courage to walk out of the office." Calley bought it for $1.1 million, which just about covered the budget.

•

TAPLIN, buoyed by the reception of *Mean Streets* at the New York Film Festival, wanted to open it right away, in twenty-five cities, the same release pattern as *Five Easy Pieces* and *The Last Picture Show*, which had also been launched by the festival. He went to Bert for advice. Bert said, "Do it, because there's nothing opening in October except *The Way We Were*, and that isn't going to make a cent." Luckily, Taplin ignored him, but it didn't make much difference. It was released in late fall to critical raves. Kael was enthusiastic in *The New Yorker*, which instantly established Scorsese as a major talent. "Martin Scorsese's *Mean Streets* is a true original of our period, a triumph of personal filmmaking," she wrote, and later called it "the best American movie of 1973."

Recalls Taplin, "She'd never written a review like that in her life. It was amazing. There were lines around the Cinema I the next day. Kael made *Mean Streets*, made Marty, no ifs, ands, or buts about it. Studio executives liked to get their hip card punched too, so if Pauline said that this was great, it was great for them as well. They could take that around, because in those days they weren't having dick-measuring contests with the box office numbers on Monday mornings; they were more into like, Who's got the hot film? Who's got the film that everybody's talking about?"

In fact, *Mean Streets* was one of a kind, a bravura directorial performance. Nothing quite like it had ever been seen before. Scorsese had taken Manoogian's admonishments to heart. From the opening home movie credit sequence to the shaky handheld camera scenes of Charlie in bed to the wild "This guy is a fuckin' mook" brawl in the club done in one, long, breathtaking shot, Scorsese recorded life as he knew it. *Mean Streets* veers between a sense of raw documentary authenticity and a hallucinatory feverishness. If Bogdanovich gave us a coming-of-age story as John Ford might have done it, Scorsese gave us one as the Maysles brothers might have done it, *and* Sam Fuller — lurid and violent. If *Mean Streets* is a gangster film, a genre film, it is so in name only. Altman overturned genres by mocking and ironizing them; Scorsese did it by injecting them with so much intensity that the traditional conventions are split asunder, revealed for what they were: artificial formulas with little claim on our attention. If Bogdanovich and Platt thought they were introducing a new realism to their coming-of-age story — and they were — *Mean Streets* put *Picture Show* in a new light, no lesser for it, but different, making Bogdanovich's film look more stylized and elegiac. Just consider how *Picture Show* sentimentalizes the relationship between Sonny and the simple-minded Billy to score easy points for Sonny, while *Mean Streets* has no illusions about Johnny Boy, particularly in the extraordinary scene where he cruelly asks Charlie, "What happens when she comes?" — because his girlfriend is an epileptic — as Charlie beats his head against a wall.

The redemptive quality of mercy is all the more powerful in Scorsese's film because Johnny Boy is undeserving. The bloody climax makes the bittersweet conclusion of *Picture Show* comforting by comparison. Whereas Sonny leaves town, then comes back to face the woman he injured, finding solace and a measure of maturity in her forgiveness, Charlie flees the neighborhood to save Johnny Boy, but is wounded too, dragged down with him, and fails to escape, to transcend the limitations of his condition.

Johnny Boy, wearing his porkpie hat, liver-colored fake leather jacket, with an idiot's grin plastered on his face, the holy fool, is the free spirit that Charlie denies within himself, a sketch for *Taxi Driver's* Travis Bickle, who is a darker, more sinister version of the same character. De Niro allowed Scorsese to express his dark side. As Spielberg perceptively put it, Marty "lets Bobby go over the top and lose control so that Marty can remain in control. I think Bobby is just wonderful as a sort of extension of what Marty might have been if he hadn't been a filmmaker." Indeed, in *Mean Streets*, Scorsese plays the hit man in the back seat of the car who takes out Johnny Boy, just as he plays a man with a gun in the back seat of Bickle's cab in *Taxi Driver*. It is a fantasy of the director —the man in the shadows pulling the strings—as killer. "I was raised with them, the gangsters and the priests," as Scorsese himself put it. "And now, as an artist, in a way, I'm both a gangster and a priest."

Ironically, Scorsese's homage to his childhood, his neighborhood, cut him off from his past. A lot of the people in Little Italy didn't like *Mean Streets*. "It's pretty tough stuff, real life," he says. "It's not like some movie where everybody's singing and dancing and drinking bottles of Chianti." He couldn't, or wouldn't, go home again. Several years later, on the night of the premiere of *New York, New York*, there was a lavish party at Studio 54. Scorsese's brother, Frank, showed up. "He started an argument with Marty," recalls Mardik Martin. "It really got nasty. He was a little drunk too, so we had to take him outside. He was yelling at Marty, 'You don't do nuthin' for me, you're selfish . . .' Marty shouted back, 'What the hell am I gonna do for you?' His brother was jealous, no question about it." Scorsese rarely talked about him. He said only, "He's a different person. We don't see things the same way." Schrader, for one, never knew Scorsese had a brother. But Scorsese remained close to his parents, whom he moved out of the neighborhood and installed in a high rise near Gramercy Park in 1977.

Despite the glowing reviews, *Mean Streets* didn't exactly burn up the box office. Instead of bumping up against *The Way We Were*, they were run over by *The Exorcist*, from the same studio. "We thought the New York Film Festival meant something in L.A.," says Scorsese. "But nobody even knew about the picture." Adds Taplin, "At Warners, we were competing with *Deliverance*, *Clockwork Orange*, and *The Exorcist*. *The Exorcist* came out the week before or after *Mean Streets*, and it changed everything for us, because their attention went right to *The Exorcist*, and we were the poor cousin. Warners did a terrible job distributing *Mean Streets*. They didn't know what to do, sold it as a gangster movie. We made bubkes."

ON DECEMBER 23, three days before the release of *The Exorcist*, the Phillipses' world turned upside down. *The Sting* opened at 220 theaters. It was a huge hit, taking in $78 million in rentals. The Phillipses had a New Year's Eve party at their house, invited the gang. Milius fired his shotgun off the deck out over the water to welcome in the new year.

When the Oscar nominations were announced, *The Sting* was nominated for ten, including Best Picture. *The Exorcist* got ten, also including Best Picture, along with *American Graffiti*, *Cries and Whispers*, and *A Touch of Class*. *Last Tango in Paris*, *Serpico*, and *The Last Detail*, among others, were passed over. Ellen Burstyn was nominated for Best Actress. On April 2, 1974, *The Sting* won seven Oscars, among them Best Picture, making Julia Phillips the first (and only) woman to win an Oscar for producing. Cybill Shepherd was a presenter. According to *People* magazine, she "coyly botched film titles to plug Bogdanovich's *Paper Moon*, as well as their own *Last Picture Show*." *The Exorcist* only won two Oscars (Sound and Best Adapted Screenplay). Friedkin believed he was the victim of a vocal campaign by George Cukor against the movie, which the older man felt did not reflect well on the Academy.

Burstyn lost for Best Actress, but that made little difference to Calley, with whom she had become friendly. One day he called her, asked her to make another film at Warners. He sent her scripts. "In every one, the woman was either the victim, running from a pursuer, or she was a prostitute, and there just wasn't anything that interested me," she recalls. Finally, her agent found her a Robert Getchell script called *Alice Doesn't Live Here Anymore*. She sent it to Calley, who said, "Fine, let's make it. Who do you want to direct it?" Burstyn replied, "I'd like somebody young and exciting and new, somebody who's just coming up." She called Coppola, who said, "Look at a movie called *Mean Streets*." She did, and thought, "Yeah, that's the guy. Whoever this director is, he knows how to allow actors to be real. That's what I want for this movie, to have a sense of real life about it. What this script needs is the opposite of a polish. It needs roughing up. It was written like a Rock Hudson–Doris Day movie."

Scorsese and Burstyn met in Calley's office. If everything worked out, this would be Marty's first studio picture, and he was nervous, trembling like a leaf. He said, "I don't know anything about women." Sandy, pushing him into it, piped up, "Women are just people." She and Marty both felt that Bogdanovich had made a brilliant choice in following *The Last Picture Show* with *What's Up, Doc?* They were afraid that unless Marty took *Alice*, the studios would typecast him as a director of Italian gangster pictures. Marty accepted the assignment, went into preproduction. Soon thereafter, Burstyn ran into Peter at the studio, and told him about *Alice*. He said, "Great, who'd you get to direct it?"

"Marty Scorsese."

"Tell him not to move his camera so much."

Recalls Burstyn, "I did not relay that to Marty." (Bogdanovich and George Cukor signed his card so he could get into the Directors Guild.)

Burstyn was excited; as *Alice* went through a series of rewrites, it was fast becoming a very un-Hollywood film about a blue-collar woman whose loutish husband dies, allowing her to take her kid and follow her dream to become a singer. At the end, she meets a prosperous rancher (Kris Kristofferson), who falls in love with her. Burstyn was awash in the feminist tide of the early '70s. "I wanted her to leave the Kristofferson character and go on to Monterey, where she had a singing gig," she recalls. "Calley said, 'No, she has to end up with a man.'"

Burstyn argued with Calley, but he would not budge on the ending. Scorsese hired a lot of women to work on the picture. Toby Rafelson, who had only worked on her husband's movies, was the production designer. Her daughter's death was still an open wound, and she thought the work might distract her. "Toby took care of the aesthetics in Bob's movies, as Polly did on Peter's," says Burstyn. "They both had an incredible eye for detail, from the right doorknob on the door to the clothes. They were the eyes." Marcia Lucas was hired to edit. "We knew her, and we liked her, and she was in the union," recalls Sandy. "It was good for her to get away from George and his house. Here she was, a wonderful editor working on her husband's films. I don't think she got taken seriously." Recalls Marcia, "Marty called, and asked if I would do his first studio feature. He was terrified of the studio executives, that Warners was going to give him some old fuddy-duddy editor or a spy—the studios were known for having spies on projects. Marty liked to edit, and I felt like I was being hired to cut a movie so I wouldn't cut it, so I'd let the director cut it. But I thought, If I'm ever going to get any real credit, I'm going to have to cut a movie for somebody besides George. 'Cause if I'm cutting for my husband, they're going to think, George lets his wife play around in the cutting room. George agreed with that." Ultimately, Marcia gained Marty's confidence, and he let her cut the movie.

Scorsese was touchy around Burstyn. Although she didn't take anything but acting credit, it was her project, she had hired him. "I know I stepped on his toes a few times, and he said ouch. Kris wasn't experienced as an actor, was having trouble. I made a couple of suggestions to him. The next day, Marty said, 'I didn't know you were giving him directions between shots. We're gonna reshoot that whole scene.'"

One day, De Niro visited the set. He gave Marty a book he liked by Peter Savage and Joseph Carter called *Raging Bull*. It was the ghosted autobiography of a middleweight fighter, Jake La Motta. He thought there might be a movie in it, but Scorsese had more immediate things on his mind. The ending of *Alice* was still a problem. Was Alice going to settle down with Kristofferson and be a housewife, as Calley insisted, or was she going to have a career, a theme that Scorsese had struggled with in his own life and would examine again in *New York, New York.* "Warners was concerned about the fact that for a lot of the young directors, every ending had to be unhappy, because it was fashionable," recalls Scorsese. " 'I'm an artist — I'm gonna have an unhappy ending.' " Marty was upset, but he rationalized away his anger. He told himself, It's not Antonioni, it's not *Red Desert*. Just try to keep it true to its nature." Finally, they reached a compromise. Alice says, "I wanna go to Monterey, I wanna be a singer," and Kristofferson's character replies, "Come on, I'll take you to Monterey, I don't give a damn about the ranch or anything else. Whatever you want." The two ride away happily into the sunset. Then Marty changed his mind, tore it up. Recalls Weintraub, "He had a tremendous fear that he was never going to make a financial success, but that the critics loved him, so it became increasingly important to him to satisfy the critics. He was about to show it to Jay Cocks, and he was afraid that Jay was going to laugh at the soapy ending, so he chopped it all up. He almost ruined his movie because of his fear that the critics wouldn't like it. Marcia and I said, 'You've got to put it back.' "

But Scorsese had his own way of dealing with it. Says Burstyn, "Marty wanted the people in the café to applaud when Kris made his offer, because he always felt the ending was theatrical, not real, and the applause would underline that. He felt we should admit it. Then when it was all put together, the studio wanted to take off the opening section of Alice as a little girl. They felt it was artsy. Marty said if they did, he'd have to take his name off the picture. 'That's why I did the film, to do that, blah, blah.' They backed off."

Scorsese showed Burstyn a cut. He was nervous about the picture, touchy and quick to take offense. She recalls, "I didn't praise the film first and then tell him what I objected to, I just went right to my objections. And he said, 'I will never allow an actor in my editing room again.' "

No matter how *Alice* did, *Mean Streets* had moved Scorsese's career a giant step forward. Schrader had seen a rough cut and had changed his mind about Scorsese directing *Taxi Driver*. The Phillipses, too, went to a screening, and by the third reel they made their decision — on the condition he could deliver De Niro as well. No slouch in the paranoia department himself, Scorsese got angry when he heard there were strings attached. Keitel was his leading man, not De Niro. "All I could think of is how was I gonna trust her and Michael too, you know? But there was something about Julia that was tenacious. I knew she was gonna fight like I was gonna fight."

Nine:
The Revenge of the Nerd
1975

• *How Steven Spielberg's* **Jaws** *made the world safe for blockbusters, BBS enjoyed its last hurrah, while Bogdanovich's bubble burst, and Paramount and Warners turned over, slamming the door on the New Hollywood.*

"Jaws *was devastating to making artistic, smaller films. They forgot how to do it. They're no longer interested.*"

— PETER BOGDANOVICH

Steven Spielberg had taken his friends Scorsese, Lucas, and Milius to see the shark in the hangar in North Hollywood where it was being built. When he agreed to do *Jaws*, Spielberg thought he could just hire a shark wrangler to make a great white do a few pirouettes in the water, like a dolphin jumping through hoops. That proved to be wishful thinking, to say the least, and the result was in front of them, dubbed "Bruce," after Spielberg's lawyer, Bruce Ramer. There was nobody around. The polyethylene cast was half done, unpainted, just a gray, submarine-sized phallic thing with patches on the side, about twenty-five feet long. It was so large that Milius said, "They're overdoing it." Steven replied, "No, they aren't, the ichthyologist said this is exactly what it would look like." Milius got excited, said Steven was making the ultimate aquatic samurai film. Lucas regarded the storyboard, looked up at the big shark, and said to Spielberg, "If you can get half of this on film you're gonna have the biggest hit of all time." Spielberg, meanwhile, grabbed the controls, made the enormous mouth open and shut with a grinding noise, like an outsized bear trap. Lucas climbed the ladder, waited for the jaws to part, and stuck his head inside to see how it worked. Spielberg closed it on him. Milius thought, My God, we're like human tacos compared to that thing. Spielberg tried to open the mouth, but it was stuck, a premonition of things to come. After Lucas managed to extricate himself, the filmmakers jumped into the car and split. They knew they had broken something that had cost a lot of money.

STEVEN SPIELBERG WAS BORN in Cincinnati, on December 18, 1946, which was the year of birth on his driver's license. But there were rumors he had shaved two or three years off his real age in an effort to burnish his reputation as a wunderkind, and in interviews he created the impression he was younger than he actually was. Coppola had been twenty-six when he directed *You're a Big Boy Now*. Spielberg's ambition was to direct his first feature before he was twenty-one, but he didn't get *The Sugarland Express* until he was likewise twenty-six.

Spielberg had three younger sisters. His father, Arnold, worked in electronics for RCA, Burroughs, and IBM. His mother, Leah, was a frustrated concert pianist, now a housewife. The family moved to New Jersey, then to Phoenix in 1955. Like so many of the movie brats, Spielberg was a nerd. He referred to his childhood as the "wimpy years," described himself as "the weird, skinny kid with acne." He had a crew cut and large ears that stood out on either side of his head, like Dumbo. "I was a loner and very lonely. I was the only Jewish kid in school, and I was very shy and uncertain," he said. "I had friends who were all like me." Skinny wrists and glasses. We were all just trying to make it through the year without getting our faces pushed into the drinking fountain." Doubtless reflecting his parents' anxieties at the time (Leah started calling herself Lee), he wanted to be gentile. He experienced his family as "bohemian," and he desperately wanted to be "normal," to pass.

Spielberg even had a mild speech defect, a lateral lisp, and, like Schrader and Scorsese, lots of phobias, fears of elevators, roller coasters, airplanes, and so on. If anyone looked at him sideways, he got a nosebleed. You name it, he was afraid of it. His personal connection to some of the films for which he became famous, *Close Encounters of the Third Kind* (CE3K) and *E.T., The Extra-Terrestrial*, is obvious. His childhood was a time when he must have felt like an "alien" from planet Israel, plopped down among the earthlings, the middle-American population of Phoenix.

Spielberg's father buried himself in his work, and was usually absent. He clashed with Steven over his son's indifferent performance in school. Steven was an underachiever. He hated reading, watched TV instead, became, along with Lucas, one of the first directors of the TV generation. His great love was movies, and he occupied himself making elaborate productions in Super-8 — sci-fi and World War II pictures — using his classmates and contriving elaborate and resourceful do-it-yourself special effects.

In 1963, Spielberg persuaded his parents to let him spend the summer with an uncle in Canoga Park, outside of L.A. The following year, his parents moved from Phoenix to Saratoga, California, and divorced. He was classified 1A, and had to choose between Vietnam and college. The choice was obvious, but with his mediocre grades, the best he could do was California State at Long Beach. In 1968, he ran into Dennis Hoffman, a young man who owned an optical house but wanted to produce, and better, was willing to part with some money to do so. Hoffman lent him $10,000. He used it to make a 35mm featurette called *Amblin'*, the story of two hitchhikers who meet, fall in love, and separate. He showed it around, and in December of that year, Sid Sheinberg, head of Universal television, saw it. The next day, Sheinberg called him. "You should be a director," he said. Spielberg replied, "I think so too." Sheinberg offered him a seven-year contract. Spielberg was uncertain. He hadn't yet finished college. Sheinberg asked him, "Do you want to graduate college, or do you want to be a film director?" A week later, Spielberg signed the contract.

The first show he directed was the middle segment of a three-part pilot for Rod Serling's *Night Gallery*, starring Joan Crawford. He went over to her apartment to meet her. She was cordial, but didn't want to be seen in public with him. As reported later in *People*, he was two months shy of twenty-one (he was actually a few months shy of twenty-two), and she was afraid that people would think he was her son.

The *Night Gallery* segment did not do much for Spielberg's career. "I didn't work for almost a year and a half after that," he says. "I was a pariah in Hollywood because it got bad reviews, even though it got good ratings. They thought I was a white elephant, and I couldn't get a TV show, I couldn't get a feature, I couldn't even get a meeting. I sat around for a long time in my little apartment waiting for the phone to ring. I would have been much better advised not to have done that show and to have gone out on my own and made little films like Scorsese and gotten my start that way."

Spielberg found a psychiatrist who got him out of the draft, whereupon he lost whatever concern he had over the Vietnam War. He had no interest in anything but movies, not art, books, music, politics. Kit Carson ran into him at a party in the fall of 1968 right after the Democratic convention. "Everybody was up, the revolution was about to happen — burn it all down — that sort of thing," he remembers. "All Steve was interested in was trying to figure a way to throw a camera off a building and rig it with gyroscopes so that it wouldn't spin out of control as it went down, so it could give you some kind of a coherent picture, and then as it hit the ground, have a spring in it that would burst the film out so it would be safely contained. I said, 'This kid's like, fucked. He's completely lost in the ozone, talking about the Twilight Zone.' "

Spielberg spent several years directing TV: *Marcus Welby, M.D.*, *The Name of the Game*, *Columbo*. Russell Metty, a curmudgeonly Hollywood veteran in his sixties and the DP on his *Columbo* segment, gave him a hard time, because he was so young, complained, "He's a kid. Does he get a milk and cookie break? Is the diaper truck going to interfere with my generator?" But Spielberg was more like Metty than he was his contemporaries. "When I first heard about him he was already a Hollywood guy, absolutely part of the system without even a second thought, not a drop of rebellion in him," says Robbins, who became a close friend. "The sensibility of the work was always the most conservative. One of the things he made was a rip-off of *THX*, all these people running around in white pajamas in tunnels through a long lens. George Lucas used to grump about the fact that some Hollywood slickie had ripped him off for a TV show. We were all appalled. Who could it be? It was Steven! Who had this low-grade history at Long Beach State, wasn't even one of the guys."

When Spielberg finally got some money, he got a car, an Arizona teenager's idea of a cool car, an orange Pontiac Trans Am. It took him about two months to realize that everybody on the lot owned a BMW or Mercedes, so he got rid of it and acquired a green Mercedes convertible, but that brought with it its own baggage. "There was gossip about that Mercedes," continues Robbins. "How could anybody our age, in their twenties, drive a Mercedes! It was unthinkable. He had even decided he wanted to have a charity he would give to, like his parents would have instructed him. It was like he was walking around in daddy's shoes, scuffing around the carpet. But when I finally met Steven, it was like an instant click, in spite of all that."

Spielberg fell in with the USC crowd, Milius and company. He sat in on a course taught by Jerry Lewis. Spielberg had been introduced to Lucas in 1967, and a few years later, during the *THX* period, Lucas took him over to Coppola's office at Warners. Spielberg traveled up to Zoetrope, showed *Amblin'*. "I saw in Francis's eyes somebody who did not distinguish between old and young, simply between talented and not," Spielberg recalls. "He was producing for George, and to be in his circle meant a chance to direct a movie. You thought, Maybe here's somebody who's going to open it up for all of us. But he only opened it up for George. I wasn't really in Francis's circle, I was an outsider, I was the establishment, I was being raised and nurtured at Universal Studios, a very conservative company, and in his eyes, and also in George's eyes, I was working inside the system."

Spielberg directed *Duel*, a movie of the week for Barry Diller at ABC, in which a driver is stalked by a malevolent truck. It aired November 13, 1971. *Duel* got a lot of notice, and was released as a feature in Europe and Japan. Spielberg became a darling of the French critics. Recalls Simpson, "The media were saying all these things about this kid who made *Duel*, and then Marty and Brian would say, 'Well, what he did wasn't so extraordinary.' There was a little bit of envy."

Then Spielberg started *The Sugarland Express*, with Goldie Hawn. It was based on a news item Spielberg had clipped out of the paper about a convict fresh out of prison, on his way to see his kids, who abducted a cop and was followed through the back roads of Texas by a caravan of highway patrolmen. Lew Wasserman was skeptical, thought the *Easy Rider* days were over, but allowed Zanuck and Brown, who were the producers, to go ahead anyway. Spielberg enlisted Robbins and Hal Barwood to write the script. Goldie Hawn plays the con's wife and partner in crime. It was shot in the winter and spring of 1973, when Friedkin was shooting *The Exorcist,* Coppola *The Conversation,* and Bogdanovich *Paper Moon.* Instead of the producer pressuring the director to make the movie more commercial, with Spielberg, it was the other way around. He thought *Sugarland* might do better if the couple survived. He had to be restrained by Zanuck, who urged him to stick to the original concept.

After *Duel,* Michael Phillips, who was on the lot doing *The Sting,* invited him out to Nicholas Beach. "I worked really hard during the week and looked forward to those weekends," he recalls. "Sometimes everybody slept in sleeping bags on the floor, or on the beach on warm nights. It was as if a kind of movie brat wave was starting to amass out at sea. One day I got there late, walked onto the beach, and everybody was buried in the sand, just these heads sticking out. It was like they had become future lobby cards, head shots."

Spielberg gawked at the topless trio — Salt, Kidder, and Margolin. "I had never seen anything like that before," he continues. "I was raised at home in a very modest family. Even my sisters covered up. When it came time to take off the pants or talk about sex, we all became little boys looking for our moms to protect us. I had missed the entire era of hippies, right over my head. I was too busy making movies. This was a little bit of Woodstock on Nicholas Beach Road. It was the first time I really felt connected with the flower child generation."

Spielberg, who was emotionally still a teenager (he subsisted on Twinkies and Oreo cookies, slept in white crew socks and white T-shirts), fell under the spell of Margot Kidder, although he wasn't quite prepared for the whole package. "We were out at Stanley Donen's beach house, and Steve showed up with Margot," recalls screenwriter Willard Huyck. "She was wearing this white flowing dress. We looked over, and she was lying next to him on the sand, but she had pulled the dress all the way up so she could tan herself. She didn't have any underpants on. Steve went beet red. He went, 'Margot!' He was really embarrassed. Then, later at lunch, she was just really outrageous — it was like this kid from Arizona had met this bimbo — she was sitting there with her legs spread apart, eating her chili."

Kidder introduced Spielberg to De Palma, to whom he immediately attached himself. The older man was a ladykiller and had attitude to spare, both things Spielberg appreciated. Spielberg started wearing a safari jacket, De Palma's trademark garb. Eventually, he moved on to Marty, listening to him with the same rapt attention with which he absorbed De Palma's opinions.

Auteurism was foreign territory to him; the idea of movies as personal expression was novel. Says Kidder, "Steven loved movies, but this gang of guys who were going to put how they saw life onto film not only knew about film, but knew an extra element, which was artistic; they were going to be artists." Spielberg never considered himself a "real" filmmaker. "He didn't want to be the son of Jean-Luc Godard," recalls Carson. "He wanted to be the son of Sid Sheinberg. He was just so different from Coppola and Scorsese and Schrader." Added Milius, "Steven was the one who ran out to buy the trade papers. He was always talking about grosses."

Continues Kidder, "That was why Steven was in awe of them. He was more innocent of spirit and less complicated than Brian or Marty, and that's obviously reflected in his movies. He was much more normal than we were, in the sense of having our neuroses get in the way of our professional lives. Whatever trauma he went through because his parents got divorced he adjusted well to. He was never addicted or excessive. With Steven, what you saw was what you got." He didn't even do drugs. "I never took LSD, mescaline, coke, or anything like that," he said. "But I went through the entire drug period, several of my friends were heavily into it. I would sit in a room and watch TV while people climbed the walls."

Kidder tried to see to it that Spielberg didn't embarrass himself, but it was difficult. He had no sense of style, was just desperate to be cool like everyone else, but he didn't know how. He was short, so he bought cowboy boots to make himself seem taller. He was the kind of guy who wore bell bottom blue jeans with a crease. "They had thousands of zippers on them, and must have cost God knows what," recalls Huyck. "They were the most ridiculous-looking pants I had ever seen."

Spielberg dedicated himself to parsing the culture. "Every month he read all the magazines from *Tiger Beat* to *Esquire* to *Time* to *Playboy*," says Milius. "He wanted to become an expert on what was hip, how people were thinking."

Spielberg had little experience with women, and was extremely awkward and uncomfortable around them. He had a crush on Janet Margolin, but she never reciprocated. When he finally got a girlfriend, a stewardess he met while he was doing *Sugarland Express* and brought back from Texas with him, Kidder taught him about the birds and the bees: "Basically I was a Henry Higgins for him. I sat him down and went, 'Okay, Steven, here's how you do it — You don't wear your socks and your T-shirt to bed, get something besides the Twinkies in the fridge, and read her Dylan Thomas,' and he'd listen — 'Okay, okay' — 'and you'll win this girl's heart.' "

One day, Spielberg and comedy writer Carl Gottlieb, an old friend, were having lunch in the Universal commissary, when Victoria Principal, then a starlet with a tiny role in *Earthquake*, plopped down in the seat next to Steven and stuck her chest in his face. According to Gottlieb, she said, "I'd like to get to know you better." To him, her body language said, "If you want to fuck me you can, if I can be in a movie." She had reached under the table and grabbed his crotch. (Principal says they were just friends.) "Steven briefly brought out Victoria Principal to the beach, which was a stunner for all of us," says Kidder. "We prided ourselves on not being bimbos, and here was a bimbo with our beloved Steven. It was like, what? We tried to discourage that."

WHILE *THE CONVERSATION* was in post, Coppola left the Bay Area to begin *Godfather II*, which commenced principal photography on October 23, 1973, in Lake Tahoe. Again, he was working with Gordon Willis. Willis still had the bitter taste of *The Godfather* in his mouth. He initially refused the film, but as he explained to Michael Chapman, Paramount backed a dump truck of money up to his door, and he couldn't turn it down. Francis was besieged by hordes of groupies. As Ellie put it, a "fresh crop of adoring young protégées [was always] waiting in the wings." Coppola hired Melissa Mathison, his former baby-sitter, as his assistant. He had watched her grow up into a tall girl — about five foot eight — with sandy hair. She was thin and flat-chested, flashed a lot of gum when she smiled, and would never quite pass for beautiful, especially compared with some of the busty bimbos with whom Francis was seen, but she was bright, droll, and self-assured. Like Ellie, she was WASPy-looking, but more than a decade younger. She engaged Francis on an intellectual level, and best of all, she adored him. Melissa favored long dresses and skirts, hippie-style, and rarely wore a bra. He had been using her for odd jobs. She helped get the Broadway house ready for occupancy, cleaning the toilets. Now she answered phones and kept the fridge supplied with grape juice. Francis used to say, "She's the greatest thing in bed I've ever had. She fulfills all my fantasies." The liaison displeased Francis's parents, who were often on the set. When the production got to New York, in January 1974, 6th Street between Avenues A and B was dressed to look like the '20s. Francis wanted to be able to, say, talk to Willis three blocks away, so he had the street wired for sound. One day, according to Gray Frederickson, he got into a fight with his parents over Melissa. "You're a good Catholic boy. What do you mean carrying on with that girl?" yelled Italia. "I'll carry on with anyone I want to carry on with," retorted Francis, furious. "It's none of your business. I'm a grown man!" The sounds of this battle were carried over the speakers, to the amusement of the crew. Coppola, who had just shot a film about the morality of surveillance, had managed to bug himself. The shoot was an ordeal for Eleanor; she cried a lot.

•

IN THE FALL OF 1973, while *The Sting* was in post-production, and Spielberg was working on *The Sugarland Express*, Michael Phillips and Spielberg met for lunch in the Universal commissary and talked about their mutual nostalgia for '50s science fiction films. Spielberg had been gestating an idea about the first contact with aliens for a long time. To some degree, it was a remake of a film he had made as a teenager called *Firelight*. He told Michael he had an idea that concerned UFOs, Watergate, and a government cover-up. They made a deal to do *Project Blue Book* (later, *Close Encounters of the Third Kind*) as his next film. They set it up with Begelman at Columbia.

The Phillipses convinced Spielberg to hire Schrader to write the script, as bizarre a pairing as one could imagine. Spielberg came over to the house Schrader shared with his brother, Leonard, and laid out his ideas. All he had was an ending, and a series of images. "There's a horizon line right across the middle of the screen," he said excitedly, waving his arms around, painting a picture. "You're looking into infinity, it's night, the sky is black and full of stars, and you see these UFOs, these spaceships, and some of them are really big, and this spacecraft is coming in and it fills up almost 25 percent of the screen. And then from below the horizon, there's one that's bigger, and it fills a third of the screen, and then you realize that that's just the turret, this spaceship goes right off the frame on both sides, it must be five miles wide. And the red lights would come this way, the blue lights would be back here . . ." Paul and Leonard sat there, mesmerized. Leonard turned to Steven, said, "Look, what would this feel like if this ever happened? If there's a precursor, it's like Cortés and Montezuma meeting, two people who have no idea the other existed." They agreed that the issues raised by this encounter were spiritual: Who are we? Why are we here? How should we relate with each other?

"Why don't you do the life of Saint Paul?" Leonard asked Steven.

"Who's Saint Paul?"

"You know, Saint Paul was the guy who persecuted the Christians, the number one persecutor, until one night he saw the light on the road. And then he becomes the number one Christian. Take a guy whose job it is to hunt all those people spotting UFOs, a scientist, works for the Pentagon. Until one night, he sees one. He says, 'I have to be the first guy to make contact with them.' He discovers there is a whole program . . ."

Paul signed on in December 1973, and wrote a script about a UFO that crashes at the North Pole, pillaging Howard Hawks's *The Thing*. The story focused on the army's attempts to keep it secret. It was called *Kingdom Come*. Steven didn't like it. He said, "I want these people to be people from the suburbs, just like people I grew up with, who want to get on the spaceship at the end." Schrader had spent his life getting away from average Americans, couldn't have cared less about Spielberg's John Does. The argument grew heated. "If somebody's going to represent me and the human race to get on a spaceship, I don't want my representative to be a guy who eats all his meals at McDonald's," Schrader yelled at Spielberg.

"That's exactly what I *do* want!"

"If you don't want to do it my way, go find another writer."

Says Robbins, "Steven didn't like Schrader's work, and he didn't like Schrader." Spielberg later referred to Schrader's script as "one of the most embarrassing screenplays ever professionally turned in to a major studio or director."

In 1973, Richard Zanuck and David Brown had paid $175,000 — prepublication — for the movie rights to *Jaws*, a novel by Peter Benchley. The story was set in the summer tourist season on a fictional island called Amity, somewhat of a misnomer, as it would turn out. Zanuck and Brown knew they had to start principal photography in the spring of 1974. If they didn't, they would have to wait till the following summer, by which time the book's sales would presumably have waned. To make matters worse, in response to a threatened actors' strike, the studios were refusing to start pictures that could not be finished by June 30, when the SAG contract expired.

Unable to come up with a workable script for *Close Encounters* and unsure of his financing, Spielberg was looking for something to do, hanging out in his producers' office one day in the third week of June. As Spielberg has told the story, "[I] swiped a copy of *Jaws* in galley form, took it home, read it over the weekend, and asked to do it." But after Zanuck and Brown gave him the nod, he developed reservations, which he expressed at a dinner with Brown and his wife, *Cosmopolitan* editor Helen Gurley Brown, at the Spanish Pavilion in New York. He was worried that the project was too commercial. As Spielberg recalls, "I didn't know who I was. I wanted to make a movie that left its mark, not at the box office, but on people's consciousness. I wanted to be Antonioni, Bob Rafelson. Hal Ashby. Marty Scorsese. I wanted to be everybody but myself." He thought, Who wants to be known as a shark-and-truck director? "There are two categories, films and movies," he explained to the producer. "I want to make films." Brown replied, using the same argument Bluhdorn used with Coppola, "Well, this is a big movie, a big movie. This will enable you to make all the films you want!"

Spielberg knew that at worst, *Jaws* would be a tired exercise in an Old Hollywood genre, but at best, like *The Godfather* and *The Exorcist*, it might be reanimated by a New Hollywood approach. "I was hell bent on shooting on the open sea, and if they insisted I shoot it in the tank, I was absolutely going to quit the movie," he says. "That piece of polyethylene and floating timber and steel was not going to scare anybody, unless they believed it was real. The '70s was a time when the environment was crucial to the storytelling."

When *Sugarland* finally came out in April of 1974 (it was moved back to avoid *The Sting* and *The Exorcist*), the reviewers were enthusiastic. Kael, eerily dead-on about Spielberg, called him "that rarity among directors — a born entertainer," and described *Sugarland* as "one of the most phenomenal debut films in the history of movies." It became a bit of a cult film, but it flopped at the box office. Whereas *Bonnie and Clyde* had skillfully blended disparate emotional tonalities, *Sugarland's* audience was put off by the fact that what appeared at first to be a light romp suddenly plunged into tragedy. Spielberg concluded that it was too much of a New Hollywood downer for the audience to swallow. He had arrived at the same point in his career that Coppola had after *The Rain People* when he was debating whether or not to do *The Godfather*, and Lucas had after *THX*, gestating *Graffiti*. Much as Spielberg wanted to be Rafelson or Scorsese, he also wanted a hit. Brown's argument made sense. He changed his mind.

SPIELBERG DIDN'T MUCH LIKE Benchley's script for *Jaws*. None of the characters were likable, and he said that when he read the book, he rooted for the shark. There had to be *people* to root for. He asked John Byrum, a kid who had just gotten into town, to do a rewrite. Byrum went to his office. He recalls, "Steven was sitting on the floor of his bungalow playing with a toy plastic helicopter. Battery-operated. It flew around in circles. I start telling him my notions about the script, and he said, 'Oh, great idea!' Like a twelve-year-old. Then he said, 'I gotta have my think music on,' so he put on this James Bond album soundtrack." Byrum, who had an offer to write *Mahogany*, thought to himself, Do I want to spend a year with this guy, or do I want to be in San Tropez with Tony Richardson and Diana Ross. So he declined.

Pulitzer Prize–winning playwright Howard Sackler *(The Great White Hope)* wrote a draft that solved some problems, but by no means all, and the beginning of principal photography was only weeks away. Spielberg persuaded Zanuck and Brown to hire scriptwriter Carl Gottlieb. Robbins and Barwood also pitched in, uncredited.

Robbins introduced Spielberg to Verna Fields. They connected immediately, and he hired her as editor. She was a great favorite of Tanen's, and Spielberg, recalling what had happened to *American Graffiti*, perhaps thought she would buy him some insurance, protect him from Tanen, whom he didn't like. Tanen and Sheinberg were rivals. Spielberg was Sheinberg's protégé and worse, a pal of Lucas's, who still hated Tanen for "mutilating" *Graffiti*. Spielberg was not above such calculations. He had already hired Lorraine Gary, Sheinberg's wife, to fill a small part, a bold move, politically, that could have backfired. Fields turned down Bogdanovich's *At Long Last Love* to do *Jaws*. When Verna told him the bad news, Peter is reputed to have burst into tears.

Although Spielberg had welcomed the addition of Goldie Hawn to *Sugarland*, she hadn't been much help at the box office, and this time he resisted when the studio suggested Charlton Heston and Jan Michael Vincent, Universal's idea of square-jawed he-men for a man-against-the-sea saga, which is the way they imagined *Jaws*. "My goal was to find someone who had never been on the cover of *Rolling Stone*," said Spielberg. He adds, "I wanted somewhat anonymous actors to be in it so you would believe this was happening to people like you and me. Stars bring a lot of memories along with them, and those memories can sometimes, at least in the first ten minutes of the movie, corrupt the story." He would also, like Coppola, cast as many amateurs as he could, people who might have trouble reading lines, but nevertheless looked right. Zanuck and Brown suggested Robert Shaw, who had played in *The Sting*, for Quint. Richard Dreyfuss, then a struggling actor who is reputed to have carried a much abused scrap of lined yellow note paper in his back pocket with the names of all the casting directors who ever rejected him for a role, turned down *Jaws* three times. He didn't like the script, didn't like his character, whose main function appeared to be exposition. He was just there to dispense shark facts. "Then I saw *The Apprenticeship of Duddy Kravitz*, and I was just so freaked out, I thought my performance was so terrible, that I called Steven and begged for the job. I went with the fish movie. We started the film without a script, without a cast, and without a shark."

After six months in preproduction on *Jaws*, Spielberg was again ready to pull out. It was clear to him that Sheinberg indeed regarded the picture as little more than *Duel* with a shark. Spielberg was convinced, as he recalls, "that it was just an exploitation movie, *Moby-Dick* without Melville, without the eloquence. I was just making a Roger Corman movie. I stayed up at night fantasizing about how I could get myself off this picture short of dying, how I could frag myself, break my leg or shoot myself in the foot, fall down a flight of stairs and hurt my arm and maybe feign, Oh, I can't direct this movie, my arm doesn't work. I was out of my mind for a while. So I went to Sheinberg, and Zanuck and Brown, and said, 'Let me out of this film.' Dick pulled me aside and called me a knucklehead, said, 'This is an opportunity of a lifetime. Don't fuck it up.' And Sid said, 'We don't make art films at Universal, we make films like *Jaws*. If you don't want to make *Jaws*, you should work somewhere else.' Thank God, the three of them said 'No, you're stuck with us, and we're stuck with you.' Because it wound up being my ticket to freedom."

On May 2, Spielberg was at last ready to begin what would turn out to be an exquisitely difficult and costly production, with a raft of technical problems threatening the projected ten-week shooting schedule. The budget going in was $3.5 million. Zanuck and Brown had little idea how risky was the enterprise upon which they were embarking. No one had ever shot on the ocean in a small boat with a mechanical shark before. Then again, they had little idea how fortunate they would be in the outcome.

Watching the first day's rushes was "like a wake," recalled De Palma, who was visiting the set. "Bruce's eyes crossed, and his jaws wouldn't close right." On the third day, one of the three sharks sank. The crew took to referring to the movie as *Flaws*. The production shut down several times to accommodate repairs on the sharks. Delay followed delay. Spielberg worked slowly, was lucky if he got one shot in the morning and another in the afternoon. As they passed the June 30 deadline, hotel rates tripled for the summer season.

The delays began to drive the actors crazy. Their ill-humor was compounded by the fact that none of them thought the film would amount to anything. "*Jaws* was not a novel," Shaw told *Time*. "It was a story written by committee, a piece of shit." Dreyfuss likewise told the magazine he thought it would turn out to be the "turkey of the year."

The script was still a mess. Recalled Spielberg, "I knew what I needed to do was . . . something that was very frightening to me, which I understand Bob Altman does quite a lot, you subjugate absolute control to meaningful collaboration. Everybody gets into a room to determine jointly what kind of movie we are going to make here." As Scheider puts it, "Because we had nothing to shoot, we had so much time that we became a little repertory company. You had a receptive director, and three ambitious, inventive actors. Dreyfuss, Shaw, and myself would go up to Steven's house, have dinner, and improvise scenes. Gottlieb would write them down, and the next day we would shoot. So in a strange way, the inability of the shark to function was a bonus. We seized this occasion to elevate the material into marvelous scenes among these three guys."

Spielberg was under an enormous amount of pressure. He brought his own pillow with him from home, and put celery in it, a smell he found comforting. He had no time for anything but work. A female friend of a friend was brought out from L.A. for recreational sex. She slept with him, and left.

It felt like the production would never end. Sitting on the boat, waiting for a shot, Spielberg thought, I'm never going to finish this movie. This can't be done. It was stupid to begin it. No one is ever going to see this picture, and I'm never going to work in this town again. Spielberg's virtues, his energy and inventiveness, were getting him into trouble. "He would jump on an idea with great enthusiasm and take it a little step further until it became unreal," said Zanuck. "If you said, 'I think the family should have a dog,' next day you'd see *three* dogs there." For the final shot of the picture, after Bruce had been blown to smithereens, Spielberg had the darkly funny idea of showing a school of shark fins on the horizon. Zanuck and Brown talked him out of it.

As Spielberg fell further and further behind, the budget kept creeping up. Worse, the studio was unhappy with the dailies. Fields told him, "Steven, where is the action? They're waiting for the action." He replied, "I know, we're getting to it." There was talk of pulling the plug or going to the Bahamas to shoot in quieter waters. One executive suggested they could recoup their investment in eighteen months by showing the shark on the Universal Tour and charging an extra nickel. Spielberg believed it was Tanen who wanted to get rid of him. "Everywhere we went, people treated us with sympathy, like we had some kind of illness," said Brown. Spielberg was acutely aware that Zanuck had kicked Akira Kurosawa off *Tora! Tora! Tora!*

One day, Sheinberg arrived at the location from L.A. He had dinner at Steven's house, and afterward, the director excused himself and went off into a corner with Gottlieb, who was sharing the house with him, to work on the script for the next day's shoot. Sheinberg thought to himself, My God! This is the way this is being done? We may have footage that we will never be able to assemble into a movie.

The next day, Sheinberg went to the location, watched Spielberg shoot. During a break, they sat down on the wooden steps of the Kelly House, the cast and crew hotel where the executive was staying. Sheinberg said, "You know, this would be a lot faster and cheaper to shoot in a tank."

"Well, I want to shoot this in the ocean for reality," replied Spielberg.

"Your 'reality' is costing us a lot of money."

"I understand that, but I really believe in this movie."

"Well, I believe in you. I will back you in [either of] two decisions. If you want to quit now, we will find a way to make our money back. If you want to stay and finish the movie, you can do that."

"I want to stay and finish the movie."

"Fine."

But the real hero of this episode was Bill Gilmore, Zanuck and Brown's line producer who was in charge of the numbers. According to Gottlieb, "The week before [Sheinberg's visit], Gilmore had calculated the cost-to-date and cost-to-complete, and the picture was over, but not horrendously so. In the intervening week, apparently some stuff came to light, and it was obvious the picture was deeply in trouble. Probably with Steven's connivance, Bill locked the new budget in his desk, wouldn't give it to anybody, didn't let on that it existed. He could have been fired for that. The following week when that budget came out, the brass had already been there and approved, so they couldn't very well say no, so the picture went on."

The shooting on the Vineyard ended on September 17, 1974. The original fifty-five-day schedule having metastasized into 159 days, five and one half months. They were 104 days behind schedule. The final budge was about $10 million, an overage of almost 300 percent. Spielberg was humiliated: "It was a *shonda*, a scandal for the neighbors, meaning Mr. Sheinberg and Mr. Wasserman. Making a movie is like getting on a stagecoach, to paraphrase Truffaut. At first you're hoping for a pleasant journey. After a while you're just praying you get there. That's what *Jaws* was all about."

Spielberg spent the night in Boston waiting for his morning flight back to L.A. He thought his career was over. He recalled, "That night I had a full-blown anxiety attack, something that I had staved off for eight or nine months. I thought I was going crazy. . . . I was lying in bed alone in this hotel room, sweating, heart palpitations. I couldn't get out of the room. If I got out of bed, I'd pass out. I was too afraid to reach for the phone. I was a complete wreck. . . . In a way I could really relate when Francis made *Apocalypse Now*. When Hollywood was calling Francis self-indulgent, I was just looking at Francis and saying, Well he's just a human being going through what we went through on *Jaws*."

BY THE SPRING OF 1974, *Chinatown* had reached the final stages of editing. Towne, who had been frozen out of the production, boasted that he was getting his way in the editing room with Evans in the absence of Polanski, who had left to direct an opera in Spoleto. "Towne hated it," recalls Evans. "He criticized everything. 'Don't release it.'" He even contemplated taking his name off it. Says Beatty, "Towne has this whole technique whereby if it did well, he was part of it; if it didn't, he separated himself from it."

Paramount screened the picture at the Directors Guild screening room in June. Barry Diller was in the audience, sitting next to Towne, whom he had known since they were both kids, neighbors in Brentwood growing up, both sons of developers. The devastating last scene was unfolding before their eyes: Dunaway's creamy Packard halfway down the street in the middle distance, the gunshot, the car horn shrieking as Dunaway's head hit the steering wheel, the inevitable close-up — the actress sliding off the seat as the door opened, eye staring, blond tresses spilling out onto the running board, her daughter screaming, Huston enveloping her in a vast paw, Nicholson helpless and numb, as his guy says, "Forget it, Jake. It's Chinatown." The camera cranes up and back, the credits roll. Diller turned to Towne and said, "This is a great fucking movie." Robert thought, This guy's full of shit, he'll say anything. There was no applause. You could hear a pin drop. "The first person who walked up was Sue Mengers," recalls Evans. "She said, 'What kind of dreck is this shit?' The next morning the reviews broke, and chicken shit became chicken salad."

Evans could indeed be justly proud of himself for getting *Chinatown* to the screen, but he was not to reap the rewards. Something was rotten in Bluhdorn's kingdom. Bluhdorn and Yablans had not been getting along for over a year. There was no more socializing between the thirtieth and forty-second floors. But after the premiere, Charlie, Bob, and Frank went to dinner at Pietro's Steak House in New York to celebrate. Charlie toasted the picture, toasted themselves, the great team, the partnership. This was too much for Yablans. While Evans watched in horror, he lashed out, bellowing, "Charlie, we're not a partnership! I'm an employee, and Evans is an employee, even though Evans won't open his mouth 'cause he ain't got the balls to open his mouth. There are haves and have-nots in this world. You're a have, and I'm a have-not. So don't give me this partnership shit." Says Yablans, "That dinner was the beginning of the end."

Recalls Bart, "It is indescribable how bad the relations were at that company. Everybody was breaking down emotionally, it was an absolute disaster." Yablans, living with his wife in Westchester, was jealous of Evans's celebrity, and Evans believed Yablans was trying to undermine his position. Typical was a fight between Evans and Yablans over *Time* magazine's plan to put Evans on the cover. According to Evans, Yablans browbeat him, yelling, "If you're on the cover of *Time* magazine without me, I will make each hour of each day of each week that you're here so miserable, you'll be sorry you're alive." Evans was so intimidated, he said, "Fuck it, it ain't worth it." Moreover, Evans's production deal was making waves with many of the directors, like Beatty and Sidney Lumet, who had pictures at Paramount. Says Yablans, "They totally resented that Evans was using his position to pick off the best projects. And put his name on them." Beatty felt his *Parallax View* was not getting the full attention of distribution and marketing. Worse, it was released only two weeks before *Chinatown*. The two pictures played side by side at New York's prime site, the East 60s. Alan Pakula, who directed *Parallax View*, was furious. "How could they?" he asked, almost in tears, taking his umbrella and smashing it against the wall of his suite at the Sherry Netherland so hard the shaft broke. "We're doomed, absolutely doomed."

Beatty complained to Bluhdorn. Evans, and possibly Yablans, had a direct, vested interest in a competing picture. Bluhdorn wasn't aware that Evans had given Yablans half his points, if in fact he did. When he found out, he hit the ceiling, called Evans in, told him it wasn't working out, that either he had to revert to his previous arrangement, or exit the executive suite with a production deal. Evans protested. Bluhdorn said, "Legally you're right. . . . But do you want to be put in the closet for the next five years?" Evans felt Beatty had stabbed him in the back. He says, "My closest friend, he tried to kill me on it."

In October, Bluhdorn installed Diller over Yablans and Evans. Diller had been a film buyer at ABC and had done a lot of business with Paramount. He was credited with inventing the *Movie of the Week*, but the appointment raised eyebrows, even though it was evident that Yablans was on the way out.

Yablans made no secret of his hatred for Diller. Says producer Al Ruddy, "He tried to embarrass him and humiliate him." Shortly after his appointment, Diller came out to the West Coast, called a meeting of the department heads for nine o'clock in the morning. Yablans was conspicuously late, finally strolling in around 10:00. He sat down, listened to Diller drone on, thought, This guy has exactly six days of experience, and he's coming on very pompously. "I gotta tell what happened last night, Barry," he broke in, and proceeded with a lengthy, spectacularly vulgar, graphic, and — he claims — fictional account of his exploits the previous night, as only Yablans could do, complete with slapped rumps and pendulous breasts. "Even I was getting disgusted," Yablans recalls. Diller tried to laugh it off, but as Yablans ran on, undeterred, he started to get red in the face, said, "That's the most disgusting thing I ever heard in my life."

"If you think that's disgusting, wait till I tell you—"

"I'm asexual, this doesn't interest me at all," interrupted Diller, standing up. "I think it's time to end this meeting." It was a cruel joke, calculated to embarrass Diller, who was widely suspected of being gay. Recalls Yablans, "I knew it would torture Diller, who was trying to palm himself off as some very proper person. I didn't care. I wanted outta there so badly it was ridiculous. I didn't want to be part of Charlie, and I sure as hell didn't want to be part of Diller."

Shortly thereafter, Yablans got his wish. He left with the customary producing deal at Paramount, but some people suspected it was really a form of hush money. The studio was under investigation by the SEC, and Yablans was in a position to drop the boom on Bluhdorn.

Evans quickly followed Yablans out the door. Says Yablans, "When I left, Bob lost his bulletproof vest, and there was no way he could survive under Diller." But Evans made the best of it, took a production deal, and replaced himself with Dick Sylbert, the first time, so far as anyone could remember, a production designer had become head of production. Sylbert hired an impoverished Don Simpson as his assistant. Simpson, who had been hustling tennis games at a city court to make ends meet, had to borrow a sports jacket and a car for the meeting with Sylbert.

One of the first things Sylbert did was pick up Altman's *Nashville* for distribution. Kael created something of a scandal by accepting the director's invitation to a screening of the rough cut, reviewing the picture off that screening, thereby jumping the release date—and all the other reviewers—by months. It was a typical Kael move, calculated to prevent Paramount from recutting the movie and to goad the studio into putting some marketing muscle behind it. Her piece was full of the excitement of discovering a great work. She called it "an orgy for movie-lovers," and wrote, "I sat there smiling at the screen, in complete happiness." *Nashville* was Altman's best film, and the studio had high hopes for it. With its large, ensemble cast of character actors, wandering narrative, and refusal of genre, it was an echt New Hollywood creation. Its failure to perform at the box office, despite the blitz of good press, was not only another indication that the passions that animated the first half of the decade were on the wane, it also underlined the limits of Kael's power. When Altman was asked why it hadn't done better, he said, "Because we didn't have King Kong or a shark."

•

DREYFUSS, who avoided the war by working as an orderly in the L.A. County Hospital as a conscientious objector in 1972, was good friends with Abbie Hoffman. (He later played a detective in the Abbie-based movie *The Big Fix*, directed by Jeremy Kagan.) In April 1974, Abbie had gone underground to avoid doing time for selling three grams of coke to a narc. Bert Schneider gave him aid and comfort, as he continued to do with Huey Newton. On July 30 of the same year, Huey and his bodyguard, Big Man (six foot eight) Bob Heard, were allegedly assaulted by two cops in a bar in Oakland. Huey was arrested and released on $5,000 bond. Six days later, he apparently shot and killed a seventeen-year-old prostitute. He jumped bail, headed south, and ended up hiding out with Steve Blauner. Blauner lived in a big, gated home in Bel Air. The two men were an unlikely pair, but they hit it off. Huey was the godfather of Blauner's second child. But baby-sitting Huey was like tending a time bomb. "When he walked in the house he had a gun," says Blauner. "I said, 'Gimme the gun. My house, my ground rules.' He handed me the gun. I took the bullets out, I gave it back to him, empty. After a week in the house, twenty-four hours a day, he wanted to go to a movie, I figured I could disguise him, pull a hat down low, and I said, 'Whaddya wanna see?' He said, 'The most violent picture playing.' There was one of those make-my-day pictures — *Magnum Force* — that's what we ended up seeing."

When it looked like the charge against him might be taken care of, Newton returned to Oakland. But he was immediately slapped with more charges. On August 23, he failed to show up for a court appearance. The stakes were going up; like Abbie, Huey went underground. He made his way to Big Sur, stayed with Bert's friend Artie Ross and some others. They buried the car that brought him from Oakland with a bulldozer. Then he went south.

Huey's L.A. friends tried to come up with a way to get Huey out of the country to Cuba — by plane, by boat, by automobile. Life was imitating art in a serious way. The whole enterprise was referred to as "the movie." The principals adopted code names, like the Jew (Benny Shapiro, the music promoter pal of Bert's who had first turned Hopper onto coke), the Star (Huey), the Baby-Sitter (Artie). The goal? The Star (aka the Package) had to make it to the Big Cigar (Cuba), or go directly to jail. Darkly anticipating some such outcome, the conspirators referred to themselves as the Beverly Hills 7. On some level, it was all a game, but a deadly game. One night, Huey, his signature Afro in corn rows in a stab at a disguise, was at the Rafelsons' for a fried chicken dinner. Bob was very nervous, didn't want to have anything to do with him, kept making promises to Bert he'd do this and that to help out, but never came through.

At the same time, this being Hollywood, albeit counterculture Hollywood, Artie and director Paul Williams would begin a script based on the adventure. It was art imitating life imitating art.

Artie was part owner of a trimaran, which was then in Miami, in need of refitting. Bert reportedly paid for the latest radar and sonar equipment. The plan was to sail through the Panama Canal, pick Huey up in Mexico, and take him to Cuba by boat. Artie and a pal stayed with Artie's uncle Charlie Goldstein, who lived on a houseboat in Miami. After the work was finished, they took the trimaran on a shakedown cruise. The story—too good to be true —goes that the bottom snagged on an underwater Jesus in one of those snorkeling attractions off Key West, and the boat was badly damaged. Artie had to swim ashore. Soaking wet, he called Bert from a pay phone by the road. "Uh, Bert, we have a problem . . . !"

With the trimaran scuttled, they scrambled for a plan. According to an *Esquire* piece on Bert, "a Cuban exile, hired to fly Huey to Havana, trie[d] to sell the information to the Mafia." It was a crazy time. Someone took a shot at Huey, whereupon a squad of Oakland Panthers came down to protect him. Finally, Steve and Benny Shapiro simply drove Huey down to Mexico. "I did everything I had ever seen in any of those movies," recalls Blauner. "I stopped and got gas, used cash so there'd be no paper trail. I was gambling in those days, betting on ball games. I called the bookmaker from a pay phone like it was a normal Sunday, so that he'd think I was home betting. Benny was riding shotgun. When I got him across the border, he got on a plane to go down to Mexico City, and then he disappeared into the hills, waiting for Artie. I cried when I saw Huey get on the plane, 'cause I figured I'd never see him again.

"When I got back across the border from Mexico, I pulled over to the side of the road, and stopped. I looked at Benny, and I just felt thirty thousand feet high. 'Cause this was the first thing that I could think of that I had ever done under conditions of life and death—I could've gotten shot—for only one reason, the love of another human being. Totally without a reward. It had no bearing whether it was right or wrong, it was the fact that I had done this incredible thing, put my life on the line, for a loved one."

Artie minded Huey at Benny and Bert's hideaway in Jalapa. Jalapa was an inaccessible jungle compound on the west coast of Mexico that Bert, Benny, and a few others bought in 1968 when they thought fascism was riding the coattails of the new Nixon presidency. Artie had no illusions about Huey. "Artie's take on Huey Newton was that he was a crazy person who had killed all the people he said he had killed," says his sister, Dorien Ross. "Artie felt that he was in the midst of an insane thing, because this guy was off the wall, seriously paranoid, got in fights wherever they went. Artie wasn't political. He did it for Bert."

Finally, Goldstein says, Bert called him, asked him to find someone to sail Huey to Cuba. Goldstein found a captian, aka "Pirate," who had a lot of experience going back and forth to Colombia—presumably smuggling narcotics—to take Huey and his wife, Gwen Fontaine, on his boat from Acapulco.

According to Goldstein, Bert agreed to stand good for the boat if it was confiscated. When they were in Cuban waters, the captain lowered a dinghy, Huey and Gwen aimed themselves at the beach. The dinghy capsized. Huey didn't know how to swim and Gwen saved his life, dragging him onto the beach. They were immediately arrested by the Cuban authorities. Nevertheless, Huey had been successfully smuggled out of the country. In some sense, it was BBS's biggest production.

It had been three years since *Marvin Gardens*, and Rafelson finally got a project set up, *Stay Hungry*, with Jeff Bridges, Sally Field, and an unknown Arnold Schwarzenegger. Toby did the production design. Bob's longtime girlfriend Paula (now Toby's sister-in-law) visited the set, and he also managed to sleep with Field a couple of times. Coming off *The Flying Nun*, she was insecure about her sexuality, worried about her small breasts. Bob instructed Toby to supervise her look, make sure she was sexy. Toby was in the same bizarre position as Polly Platt, having to beautify the woman her husband was sleeping with. She finally left him. "It wasn't out of jealousy," she says. "I just developed a contempt for him, and a feeling of — if not compassion — at least a feeling of kinship with these other women. I thought, These are my sisters. I felt he was using women to feel more powerful, more loved, more studlike. It destroyed my respect for Bob. I lost patience with bullshit." She continues, "He was devastated — or so it seemed. His marriage was important to him. Not because he loved me so much, but because he wanted that structure. It legitimized him in some way. It anchored him." She stayed at the Château Marmont until he moved out of the house on Sierra Alta. Rafelson never again made a good movie. As Burstyn puts it, "In both Bob's and Peter Bogdanovich's cases, their best movies were made in partnership with their wives. And when the marriages ended, their work was not ever up to that same level."

On January 17, 1975, the cops raided Bert's home. His kids and their friends were having a wrap party for the school play. The neighbors called the cops, who handcuffed twenty-six-odd kids in a circle in the living room before taking them, along with Bert, to the station house where they were booked. The cops grabbed pot, hash, and three amphetamine pills.

On January 22, Stanley Schneider, working on *Three Days of the Condor*, ate some ice cream, lay down on the couch in his office, and died of a heart attack. Openly weeping, Bert was incoherent with grief over Stanley's death and Huey's disappearance. Friends thought that he was close to a nervous breakdown. A few weeks later, Bert copped a plea, and the drug charges were dropped.

COPPOLA INSISTED that *The Conversation* be released on his birthday, April 7, 1974. It was well reviewed, but did disappointing business. Post-production of *Godfather II* was affected by the love-hate relationship between Coppola and Evans. Evans claims he called him, begged him to rescue it. As Sylbert puts it, "At first, Francis told Bob Evans, 'Don't ever darken my toilet paper again.' But Francis is very good at collecting it, not very good at putting it all together. He got scared. Bob had to go up there." They previewed the film in San Francisco at the Coronet Theater in November 1974. Says Evans, "When Francis walked in, everybody stood up like he was a king. By the time the picture was over, three quarters of the audience had walked out. Why? He didn't use any of the Havana sequences. He cut out the best part of the fuckin' picture. I had to help him reedit *Godfather II* totally."

According to Coppola, "It was in my deal that Evans have nothing to do with it, and he didn't. He wasn't involved one iota in *Godfather II*."

At the beginning of the new year, Coppola became the first director ever nominated for two pictures by the Directors Guild. In February, *Godfather II* got eleven Oscar nominations and *The Conversation* received three. Both films had been nominated for Best Picture, along with *Chinatown*, *Lenny*, and *The Towering Inferno*, and Francis found himself in the enviable position of competing against himself. He personally received five nominations, and two other members of the Coppola clan, his father, Carmine, and sister, Talia Shire, were nominated as well. *Hearts and Minds* was nominated for Best Documentary, and Burstyn got her second nomination for Best Actress in a row, for *Alice*. Paramount, which had had a record year, dominated the Oscars with an astonishing number of nominations, including eleven for *Chinatown*. Yablans was quoted as saying the studio's motto should be, "If you don't like it, fuck you!"

Coppola had expected *The Godfather* to clean up two years before, and was keenly disappointed when he lost Best Director to Bob Fosse. Now he worried that *The Conversation* would split the Coppola vote, throwing the Oscar to Polanski, his main competition. He thought *Godfather II*, with its convoluted flashback structure, was too innovative and demanding to win Best Picture. When the ceremony came around on April 8, Coppola swept the awards. He won three Oscars himself. *Godfather II* won six, including one for De Niro, Best Supporting Actor. Burstyn took Best Actress. *Chinatown* had to make do with one, Towne's, for Best Original Screenplay. This would mark the high point of Towne's career. He wrote like an angel, but he wasn't satisfied; he wanted to direct.

Francis thanked everyone on earth, except Evans. Evans went over to congratulate him, and he said, "Jesus, Bob, I'm so sorry, I can't believe what an idiot I am, I forgot to thank you again." For Coppola, the icing on the cake was the Oscar for Carmine, who won (with Nino Rota) for Best Original Score. "After I'd spent a lifetime with a frustrated and often unemployed man who hated anybody who was successful, to see him get an Oscar, it added twenty years to his lifetime," Coppola said. On his way back to his seat, Carmine dropped the Oscar, and it shattered.

Despite his personal triumph, Francis was upstaged by Bert Schneider. *Hearts and Minds* won Best Documentary, capping the producer's career in film. When he walked up to the podium to accept, resplendent in an immaculate white tux, he stunned the glittering array of celebrities and millions of TV viewers by conveying "greetings of friendship to all American people" from Ambassador Dinh Ba Thi, chief of the Provisional Revolutionary Government delegation to the Paris peace talks. There was a moment of shocked silence, then a burst of applause, punctuated by scattered hisses. Coppola, who was still contemplating a picture about Vietnam, *Apocalypse Now*, seconded Schneider's gesture. He said, "Imagine, in 1975, getting a telegram from a so-called enemy extending friendship to the American people. After what we did to the Vietnamese people, you'd think they wouldn't forgive us for 300 years! Getting this positive, human, optimistic message was such a beautiful idea to me — it was overwhelming. Sinatra and Hope are too old to understand a message like that." Three weeks later, on the morning of April 29, with Saigon surrounded by North Vietnamese troops, South Vietnamese general Duong Van "Big" Minh surrendered. That day the last American was airlifted by helicopter off the roof of the American embassy. The war was over.

AFTER THE DEMISE of the Directors Company and the *Daisy Miller* disaster, Bogdanovich set up *At Long Last Love* (named after a Cole Porter song), at Fox. Mengers got him $600,000 to write, direct, and produce, plus 25 percent of the profits. The picture cost $5.5 million, and starred Cybill, Burt Reynolds, Madeline Kahn, and Eileen Brennan, not a bad cast. It was a period piece set in the '30s, about two couples who keep falling in love with the wrong people. "This movie was a fantasy of my divorce," said Bogdanovich. "Everyone ends up best friends," which was hardly the case in real life. It was a musical, with a dozen or so Porter songs. The only problem was, nobody in the cast could sing.

Mengers was with Peter at an out-of-town preview. "The audience was silent," she recalls. "Afterward, we went up to Peter's suite, and everyone was telling him how well it went. He said, 'Yeah, did you hear them laughing?' It was like the emperor's new clothes. I said, 'Peter, that audience was not laughing.' He became really angry at me, so angry that I left. By that point, Peter didn't want to hear the truth. You couldn't talk to him, he was beyond communicating, he was in a world where he only wanted to talk to people who agreed with him and told him how great he was. As with all really talented successful people, there weren't many who said to him, 'You're wrong.' " Says Bogdanovich, "It was just the opposite. We fucked it up by listening to everybody."

At Long Last Love premiered on March 1, 1975. "It was the most disastrous premiere, and the best party ever," says Ronda Gomez, who had left Paramount for an executive job at Fox. "People walked out of the theater onto a red carpet leading to the soundstage decorated like the '20s. But nobody said a word about the movie. Complete silence. They were shell-shocked."

"People loathed Peter," says writer David Newman. "His ego was just so monstrous. He was the great I Am, the Second Coming. This screening was a *disaster*, a *cataclysm*." The word on the street was that Platt had been the power behind the throne, and without her, he was nothing. He suspected her of abetting this spin. "She wanted to create the impression that she had invented me," he says. "That worked for a lot of people who were annoyed that I was doing so well, and helped her in her career." But he didn't need Platt to sabotage his reputation. He was so universally detested that Billy Wilder is supposed to have said that after news of the screening spread, you could hear the champagne corks popping all over town. Complained Bogdanovich, "It was treated as if we had committed one of the most heinous crimes ever, including child-murdering and rape." Thereafter, Bogdanovich and Shepherd archly referred to the film as "the debacle."

Mengers told Shepherd that she had to work with other directors. "Because whenever there might be a possibility of a movie, Peter would always say, 'No, no, no, I'm getting ready to start mine next week.' Not that there was a big demand for her. She probably wouldn't have done *Taxi Driver* three years earlier. Peter and Cybill were rude, cavalier toward people, insulted them. People take anything when you're hot; when you stop being hot, they pay you back."

Platt took the girls to see the picture in one of those grand old theaters on Hollywood Boulevard. They got there early, before the previous show ended, and they could hear the Porter tunes swelling in volume as the picture ended. "Then the ushers flung open the doors, with the red-leather padding, and not one person came out," she recalls. "We sat down, ten minutes later the movie started, and we were the only people there. The theater was empty. I felt so badly for Peter, I thought I was going to die."

WHEN SPIELBERG RETURNED from Martha's Vineyard to L.A., he knew he was in trouble. He had run 300 percent over budget, and had precious little to show for it. The first cut was a mess. None of the shots matched. Recalls producer Rob Cohen, "There would be a shot in the sun, a shot with rain, a shot with clouds, a shot with gray sky, blue sky. It was very hard to watch." Worse, the shark looked ridiculous. In Cohen's words, it "resembled a big phony rubber thing." The decision was made to downplay the shark, in effect, to edit around it, to postpone the first revealing of the shark until the third act. According to Cohen, this was Fields's idea. "Verna was the key figure in what happened in post," he says. He says Spielberg was going to remedy the failure of the mechanical sharks by interpolating documentary shark footage. But "she began to realize that what you could imagine was worse than what you could see," continues Cohen. "She did a clip job on it, threw out all the shark stuff, and just showed the results, the reactions. It was much more electric." But Spielberg later claimed that he realized this would be necessary when he was still in production. "The effects didn't work, so I had to think fast and make a movie that didn't rely on the effects to tell the story," he says. "I threw out most of my storyboards and just suggested the shark. My movie went from William Castle to Alfred Hitchcock." Gottlieb agrees. "That decision was collaborative, with Steven leading the way. Early on, one of our models was *The Thing*, a great horror picture where you didn't see the creature until the last reel. We said, 'Let's do that.' " Adds Michael Chapman, who was the camera operator on *Jaws*, "It was definitely Steven's film. He's an idiot savant, and the savant part is absolutely as real as the idiot part. He was a master of laying out shots that told a story elegantly and efficiently. I knew I could learn something just by watching his setups."

Jaws began to preview in spring 1975. Spielberg took Valium to get through the screenings. It sneaked in Dallas on March 26, at the Medallion Theater, after *Towering Inferno*. Spielberg was standing in the back, by the door, nervously flicking his eyes between the screen and the audience. The scene in the beginning when the boy on the raft is killed had just gone by when a man in the front row got up and broke into a run, heading toward the director. Alarmed, Spielberg thought to himself, My walk-out has become a run-out! He must really hate it. The man reached the lobby, and threw up all over the carpet, went to the bathroom, and returned to his seat! Said the director, "That's when I knew we had a hit."

TV advertising was in its infancy; television was still regarded as a rival medium, not an adjunct to movie promotion. Back in 1973, Lester Persky, who had a background in advertising, had convinced Columbia to do TV spots in a local market for a B movie called *The Golden Voyage of Sinbad*, and it worked. Two years later, Persky and Columbia found themselves with another potential disaster, a Charles Bronson prison picture called *Breakout*, and they tried television advertising again, this time nationally, over the networks. The effect was dramatic. *Breakout* made its costs back in its first few weeks. The other studios were monitoring Columbia's experiment, and when *Jaws* came along shortly afterward, Universal applied the same strategy. The studio spent over $700,000 — a staggering amount at the time — for half-minute spots in prime-time shows. If there were any doubt left about the effectiveness of TV advertising, the movie's success dispelled it.

Really wide breaks of several hundred theaters or more were reserved for stinkers, enabling studios to recoup their expenses before the picture died. But

Universal opened *Jaws* in 409 theaters, about the same number as *The Godfa-ther*, on June 20. "My secretary handed me this piece of paper . . . and said 'Here's the opening figures.' And I just stared at this number," recalled Spiel-berg. "Then I kept waiting for the next weekend to drop off and it didn't, it went up and it went up." Before they played out, *The Godfather* had racked up $86 million in rentals and *The Exorcist* $89 million. *Jaws* beat them both with $129 million, a record that stood for two years, until *Star Wars*. Spielberg had a tiny slice of the net, two and a half points, worth about $4 million, nothing compared to the forty-odd points shared by Brown and Zanuck. The latter said he earned more off *Jaws* than his father, Darryl, had made in his whole career.

Jaws changed the business forever, as the studios discovered the value of wide breaks — the number of theaters would rise to one thousand, two thousand, and more by the next decade — and massive TV advertising, both of which in-creased the costs of marketing and distribution, diminishing the importance of print reviews, making it virtually impossible for a film to build slowly, find-ing its audience by dint of mere quality. As costs mounted, the willingness to take risks diminished proportionately. Moreover, *Jaws* whet corporate appetites for big profits quickly, which is to say, studios wanted every film to be *Jaws*.

In a sense, Spielberg was the Trojan horse through which the studios began to reassert their power. As Spielberg admits, "My influences, in a very perverse way, were executives like Sid Sheinberg, and producers like Zanuck and Brown, rather than my contemporaries in my circle in the '70s. I was truly more of a child of the establishment than I was a product of USC or NYU or the Francis Coppola protégé clique."

While Spielberg was shooting in the Vineyard, he got into a contretemps with the novel's author, Peter Benchley, who took a swipe at him in the *Los Angeles Times*, saying, Spielberg "has no knowledge of reality but the movies. He is B-movie literate. . . . [He] will one day be known as the greatest second unit director in America." In one obvious way, Benchley was completely wrong, Spielberg having become probably the most celebrated director in America. But in another way, he was right; Spielberg is the greatest second unit director in America. What he could not have foreseen, however, was that such was Spielberg's (and Lucas's) influence, that every studio movie became a B movie, and at least for the big action blockbusters that dominate the studios' slates, second unit has replaced first unit.

By the '80s, Roger Corman, who gave so many New Hollywood directors their start, would begin to complain that he was having a hard time because movies he would make for peanuts with one of the Carradine brothers in the lead were starting to be made by the studios for $20 and $30 million, with big stars. *Death Race 2000* would become *Days of Thunder*, with Tom Cruise.

Like *The Godfather*, *Jaws* was very much a picture of its time, a post-Watergate look at corrupt authority. The Amity power structure, save for the chief of police, is united in wanting to cover up the shark attack to protect the almighty dollar, in the form of tourism. The picture's only villain, outside of the shark, is the mayor, an elected official, a politician. But *Jaws* was a film of the political center: of the three men who take on the shark, Quint, the macho man of the right is killed, while Hooper, the intellectual Jew of the left, is marginalized, leaving Brody, the everyman cop, the Jerry Ford, the familymanregularguy who was president when the picture came out, to dispatch the shark.

Moreover, although *Jaws* deftly uses the Us/Them formula deployed by films like *Bonnie and Clyde*, *Easy Rider*, and *M*A*S*H*, "Us" is no longer narrowly and tendentiously defined as the hip counterculture, but is expansive and inclusive, a new community comprised of just about everyone—all food, so far as the shark is concerned. It transcended the political and demographic divisions between the *Easy Rider* counterculture audience and Nixon's *Towering Inferno* middle-Americans.

Basking in the glow of his huge hit, Spielberg was enjoying himself for the first time in his life. "The summer of '75, I was feeling really good about myself and my career," he said. "I was at peace with the movie universe. I was in my car and I decided to treat myself to an ice cream cone. So I pulled into 31 Flavors on Melrose. There was a line when I walked in, and they were all talking about *Jaws*. They were saying, 'God, it is the most frightening film I ever saw. I've seen it six times.' It was just like the whole 31 Flavors was talking about it. I got my ice cream cone, pistachio, that's my favorite kind, and I got back in my car and I drove home. I turned on the TV set, and there was this story about the *Jaws* phenomenon on network news. And I realized—the whole country is watching this! That was the first time it really hit me that it was a phenomenon. I thought, This is what a hit feels like. It feels like your own child that you have put up for adoption, and millions of people have decided to adopt it all at once, and you're the proud ex-parent. And now it belongs to others. That felt very good."

ON JUNE 20, the same day *Jaws* made motion picture history, Artie Ross was invited to dinner at Judy Schneider's home on Palm Drive. She had sold the house, and, in her words, "I was giving a dinner for all the people who had participated in our lives there." Artie had been working for producer Ed Pressman, traveling through the South promoting *Sisters*. He had just returned to L.A., where he was living in the producer's old house in the Hollywood Hills. Artie had inherited Brackman's tank of nitrous oxide when Jake returned to New York, and was using it regularly. The idea was, the more gas you inhaled, the better the high. Most people held the black rubber mask over their noses, so it would just drop away if they passed out. But Artie was in the habit of strapping the mask over his face. He had put the tank at the top of the landing, so that if he did lose consciousness, he would fall down the stairs, and the mask would be ripped off. "People had been warning him about putting on this mask when he was alone, that it was very uncool," says Brackman. The night before, Artie had shown up at Bert's with a large purple bruise on his forehead, claiming he had just seen the white light, just seen God.

Bert was about to leave for Havana to visit Huey. In the early evening, Blauner stopped by Artie's, unannounced, intending to bring him to Judy's for dinner. "I knocked on the door and there was no answer," he recalls. "The door was ajar, so I pushed it open, I saw somebody's legs sticking out from around the corner, so I thought, Why's somebody hiding from me? I went around the corner, and there was a guy, slumped forward, on his knees. I pulled up the head, and there was this gas mask looking at me. I pulled it off, and it was Artie. He had died from an overdose of nitrous oxide. One eye was sort of open, there were gurgling noises, he had thrown up. I didn't know if he was dead, and I didn't know the address, so I ran up to the street, got the address, ran back, called emergency. By then I'd forgotten the address, so I ran back and forth again. I was blaming myself, but he'd been dead for hours, and I didn't know it."

Artie's death should have given pause, interrupted the headlong rush from grass to acid to coke to freebasing at the end of the decade. It was an intimation of John Belushi's death to come. But Bert and his circle shrugged it off. "It may have been the end of the nitrous fad, but Bert instituted an annual Artie Party on the anniversary of his death where people would get together and take a lot of drugs," says Brackman. "He did one the following year in Jalapa in which [writer] Michael O'Donoghue, on acid, took a swan dive into a patio and busted his front teeth." Reflects Salt, "There was such a devotion to drugs that everybody had to do a little dance around it. There had to be a way that it was cool, like, 'We'll meet you there soon, Artie.' Nobody dealt with it like it was — utterly pitiful."

HOLLYWOOD WAS THRIVING. Driven by *The Exorcist* and *The Sting*, the 1974 grosses were the highest since the peak of the postwar boom, in 1946. With *Jaws* leaving those movies in the dust, 1975 looked to be another record year. The Vietnam War, which had been a permanent fixture of the American landscape for a decade, was finally over, the despised Nixon licking his wounds in disgrace. It seemed as if the antiwar movement had won.

But changes were afoot. At about the same time Diller presided over the departures of Yablans and Evans from Paramount, Ashley and Calley left Warners. They would both eventually return, but the studio would never be the same. Calley was replaced by Spielberg's agent, Guy McElwaine, who joined Warners after his agency, CMA, the third largest in the business, merged with IFA, the second largest agency, to form a behemoth, International Creative Management (ICM) in January of 1975. The consolidation accelerated the flight of agents to the studios. In an eighteen-month period from roughly 1974 to 1976, something like fifteen to twenty people deserted CMA or ICM, including Freddie Fields, Mike Medavoy, and John Ptak. The agency business had never looked so dismal. So when five Young Turks left the largest agency, William Morris, to strike out on their own, no one on the outside took much notice. They called their new company Creative Artists Agency (CAA).

CAA mushroomed seemingly overnight to become the dominant institution in the industry. According to Yablans, "During my era in the early '70s at Paramount, we didn't have packages. You got a script, you hired a director, you hired the actors, you made a movie. Now they did it backward. The package was put together before the movie was ready to get made, so the script became the slave to the process, rather than the other way around. It was a lazy man's way of making movies." With the executive ranks less stable, novice production heads, often from the agencies, would become almost totally dependent on CAA for their product.

With BBS moribund, the changing of the guard at Warners and Paramount, the two studios responsible for most of the key pictures of the decade, and the birth of CAA, 1975 has to be regarded as something of a watershed year. Not only had *Jaws* whetted studio appetites for blockbusters and introduced expensive TV promotion, but some of the biggest directors of the early '70s went down in flames. The Bogdanovich bubble finally burst with *At Long Last Love*; *The Fortune* was Mike Nichols's third flop in his last four outings; while the mediocre performance of *Nashville*, along with Arthur Penn's *Night Moves*, suggested the dangers of the deconstructive, anti-genre road down which Penn and Altman were traveling, and served as a reminder that the audience for New Hollywood films might be considerably smaller than these directors supposed.

Precious few spied the dark clouds on the horizon. One was Kael. Always the Eeyore, she wrote a prescient piece in August 1974, in which she warned that television was debasing audience taste. "There's no audience for new work," she charged. Railing against "the bosses," their failure to push pictures like *The Conversation* and *Mean Streets*, and the revival of the star system, she recognized that the studios had recovered from the seismic dislocations of the late '60s. Ironically, the very success of the New Hollywood, rather than rendering the studio system obsolete, as Hopper and Penn had imagined, had merely reinvigorated it. She wrote, "These men were shaken for a few years; they didn't understand what made a film a counterculture hit. They're happy to be back on firm ground . . . ." Voicing the utopianism of an earlier decade that still echoed faintly through the self-satisfaction of the mid-'70s, and no doubt thinking about Scorsese and Altman, she called on directors to drop out, raise money outside the system. She warned, Cassandra-like, of the death of movies.

LIKE *THE GODFATHER,* *Jaws* was such a phenomenon that the director almost got lost in the shuffle. Some of Spielberg's friends derided his success, told him it was just luck, being in the right place at the right time, and that he would never repeat the trick. The picture was only nominated because of its grosses. Like *Easy Rider,* it seemed like a product of cultural automatic handwriting. Indeed, its lively script, strong in story and colorful character development, was a serendipitous accident, entirely uncharacteristic of Spielberg's subsequent work. Ironically, one of his greatest gifts may very well have been his recognition of his own limitations, his talent for playing the perfect audience to his inspired collaborators, and his spongelike ability to soak up their contributions.

Spielberg was so sure he was going to be nominated for an Academy Award that he invited a TV camera crew to his office to film his reaction to the good news. Only there wasn't any. *Jaws* was nominated for Best Picture, but the director was slighted. Instead, the Academy selected Altman for *Nashville,* Milos Forman for *Cuckoo's Nest,* Stanley Kubrick for *Barry Lyndon,* Sidney Lumet for *Dog Day Afternoon,* and Federico Fellini for *Amarcord* — a splendid array of directors and pictures for this pivotal year. Complained Spielberg, as the camera caught him with his face in his hands, "I can't believe it. They went for Fellini instead of me!" Nominating the picture and not the director was a real slap in the face.

Says Leonard Schrader, "In the early '70s, when I heard Scorsese talk for hours with my brother, with De Palma, with Spielberg, about how to play the power game, the assumption, never questioned, was that power was a means, not an end. We wanted to make great films, we wanted to be artists, we were going to discover the limits of our talent. Now what was left was power for its own sake, not as a means, but as an end. This generation started out as believers. They behaved as if filmmaking were a religion. But they lost their faith."

Spielberg was consumed by anxiety and self-doubt. Although friends had pitched in all along the way, when credit time came, Spielberg felt that some members of the team were getting too big for their britches. The camaraderie that bound the movie brats was fraying around the edges. Even getting too much press attention was dangerous, getting nominated for an Oscar when the director wasn't was asking for it, and winning when the director didn't (or even when he did) could be fatal. Often, directors broke up a winning team, as was the case with *Jaws*. Says one person who worked for Spielberg, "The number of times he wanted his name on the screen was an embarrassment. If he could have written, 'Hair Styled by Steven Spielberg,' he would have."

When Verna Fields later won an Oscar for editing *Jaws* (she died of cancer in 1982), Spielberg took umbrage at her words to the press, which indeed were pointedly ambiguous, much like Towne's comments on *Bonnie and Clyde*. She said, "I got a lot of credit for *Jaws*, rightly or wrongly." (Marcia Lucas always felt she took too much credit for *Graffiti*.) Fields was slated to edit *Close Encounters*, as well as get a producer's credit. But, according to Julia Phillips, who would later be thrown off *Close Encounters* because of her drug habit, and therefore had reason to dislike Spielberg, "Steven started to resent all the credit she was giving herself for its success and asked me to kill her off." When Fields was to be featured in a Kodak ad celebrating women in the industry, she claims he asked her to have her replaced by Marcia Lucas.

Spielberg was particularly sensitive about the writing credit, which went to Gottlieb and Benchley. Gottlieb says, simply, "Spielberg didn't write it." Gottlieb had fashioned an account of the production called *The Jaws Log*, which he showed to Spielberg in typescript. "I didn't want to say anything that would piss him off," he continues. "When the book came out, I sent him a copy. He looked through it and hurled it across the room in disgust. The reason he did that, the reason he was miffed that Verna got an Oscar and he was overlooked, was that it troubled him that there was anyone else who could have a public and legitimate collaborative claim. Not even an authorship claim, but merely a collaborator's troubled him. He always liked to have collaboration on his terms. You collaborated with Steven at your peril. It wasn't enough to be the wunderkind, to the point where he took a year off his age. In those days, there were real auteurs around, and Steven was not going to be one of those guys, much as he wanted to be. Because his film was so wildly popular, he was always denied that recognition. It was not perceived of as art, but entertainment. With each successive film, he was more and more careful to maintain that position as the auteur."

Spielberg took steps to make sure credit would not be an issue on *Close Encounters*. Julia Phillips said he "made me pressure every writer who made a contribution to the script." She told Schrader that none of his work was left in the shooting script, and that Spielberg wanted sole writing credit. Paul agreed not to contest it. "Steve felt he hadn't been given enough credit for the *Jaws* script, he was going to make sure that didn't happen again," recalls Schrader. "My office was right next to Michael and Julia's at Columbia, and I thought we were all friends. But this credit thing left a pretty sour taste." He added, Spielberg "seemed to resent the fact that *anyone* has ever helped him, whether they be Verna Fields, Zanuck and Brown, Peter Benchley, Carl Gottlieb, Mike and Julia Phillips. That's Steve's problem." For his part, Spielberg commented,

"It surprises me that Schrader would slink after someone else's success by vividly inflating his imagined contributions."

Schrader was not the only writer who did uncredited work on *Close Encounters*. Jerry Belson did some writing, so did John Hill. Finally, Spielberg tried to do it himself. Like Lucas, he was not a facile writer, and once again, his friends rescued him. "Steven started cutting and pasting and writing his own stuff," recalls Robbins. "Hal Barwood and I were really upset by the script, it was so full of holes it offended me to look at this thing. 'You gotta do this, you gotta do that, it's an obligatory moment,' and he'd listen with these big eyes, 'Let's do it, let's do it, write that down.' Then he called on us to come to work on it. We were writing at night, big chunks of that movie. We created the story line of the kidnapping of Melinda Dillon's little boy, Cary Guffey. He shot our script. Our names were not on it. We didn't care. In those days, there were no stakes. It was like you were being paid to sit in the sun and bullshit and then type it up. It was clear that Steven was really a talented director, and what I always liked best about working with him was that it made my own stuff better. He was full of ideas. They just poured off him. Even when they were lousy, they would provoke more ideas. Along with his ability, in those days, not to have a big ego about whose ideas they were. Kibitzing like this was sort of a game, and you expected the same kind of help on your stuff, and you got it." The two writers had done uncredited work on *Jaws* as well. Spielberg gave them a point each, explaining, "This is not just for this movie, it's for *Jaws* too."

The problems with *Jaws* had been so serious that Spielberg was worried that Columbia would never greenlight *CE3K*. It was an expensive film, and Columbia was still broke. Rob Cohen had set up *The Bingo Long Traveling All-Stars and Motor Kings* at Universal. The script had been written by Barwood and Robbins. Spielberg called Cohen, said, "Don't you like the way I direct?"

"What are you talking about, you're brilliant."

"How come you haven't offered me *Bingo Long?*"

" 'Cause I didn't think you'd be interested, it's a small picture."

"I love that script. I love Matt and Hal . . . "

"I'd be thrilled, are you kidding? Let's get together and talk about it."

Cohen says Spielberg told him, "I'm in a very difficult position. Begelman's giving me all this money to write this script, but I really want to do *Bingo Long*, so just call Sid, he's got options on me, and tell him to preempt me." Which is how Spielberg became attached to *Bingo Long* throughout its preproduction. But in that time, *Jaws* went from looking extremely iffy to looking like a hit, and the better *Jaws* looked, the less Spielberg was interested in *Bingo Long*, and the more he drifted back to what he really wanted to do, which was *Close Encounters of the Third Kind*. Continues Cohen, "He just wanted to be sure he had the next thing set up, and he knew that by pitting me against Julia Phillips, he would win either way, because either Julia would have a renewed sense of how important he was, and work harder to get *Close Encounters* made, or he would have another movie. He's a master at choreographing the elements of this business. He didn't get to be 'Steven Spielberg' just by being a good director."

Once *Jaws* opened, Spielberg knew what he had to do to get *Close Encounters*. "I marched in and shook those *Jaws* box-office receipts at them, and they gave in," he recalled. "I said I want $12 million to do this picture. They agreed."

Ten:
Citizen Cain
1976

• *How Paul Schrader crawled over the back of his brother to become the new Towne, who in turn fell out with Beatty, while* Days of Heaven *turned into months of hell for Schneider and Terry Malick.*

"Schrader is an original. I don't have much respect for screenwriters. Most of them couldn't carry my shoes. But I have respect for Paul."

— JOHN MILIUS

Right from the beginning, guns were an important prop for the growing legend of Paul Schrader. Of course it was Milius who led him on, if, indeed, he needed leading. "Milius and I were like fire and gasoline," says Schrader. Milius once took him to a sporting goods shop in Beverly Hills, in search of a pistol. The clerk showed him a .38 that felt good in his hand, cold and hard. He saw a girl over by the tennis racquets, sighted down the barrel at her head, and tracked her around the store as she moved, clicking the trigger a few times. "If there was ever a psycho you shouldn't sell a gun to, Paul was it," says Milius. "I told this story to Scorsese and he put it in *Taxi Driver.*"

Schrader kept a Smith & Wesson .38 on his bedside table, claiming someone was trying to break into his home, carried another in the glove compartment of his car, waved it around on appropriate occasions to make a point. One day Beverly Walker, his former girlfriend, came over with a script she had written, a Western about a female desperado, called *Pearl of the West.* According to her, Paul read it, reached for his weapon, waved it around, and said, "It needs more of this." Some years later, he was having a party, and Kiki Morris, his assistant, was tidying up the house. She put the gun in a drawer. He entered the bedroom, missed it, and told her, "Put it back. It's important for my image."

Schrader rarely fired his weapons; he was probably more dangerous to himself than to anyone else. Both he and his brother, Leonard, had a thing about suicide. Recalls director Penny Marshall, who knew Paul from those days, "He was always talking about it. From an anal-compulsive point of view. He was going to put a gun in his mouth and pull the trigger, but wrap a towel around his head so that he didn't make a mess."

Leonard, two years older, had a different attitude toward guns, perhaps because he took suicide more seriously. "I was afraid of them," he says, "for a very good reason: I was afraid of killing myself. I didn't want it to be easy. I would be sitting alone in some room at three o'clock in the morning with a loaded gun, thinking about blowing my brains out. It was not, 'I'm having a bad day, I want to kill myself'; no, the desire, the need, felt as real as a fucking table. I want to do this, and I never want to do this. I'm three seconds away from it, and I'm three million years away from it. I felt the fever of two things inside me fighting. I was breaking out in a sweat, my temperature was going up from the intensity of it. Sometimes I would just stare at the wall, trying to quiet the heat down, but sometimes the heat kept building, and that's when I was looking for the gun. Triggered by something physical, like I couldn't sleep. I found out that if I stuck the barrel in my mouth, like some infant's pacifier, I could fall asleep. It worked for two or three weeks, and all of a sudden, it didn't work. I'd been sucking on an empty gun. I knew if I loaded the sonofabitch, I was gonna sleep tonight."

Paul too slept with a loaded gun, "probably loaded," he says. "That's why I went into therapy."

It was hard to know what to make of the brothers' dark infatuation with death. It was strange, wildly anomalous in sun-baked Southern California, where the light is so bright it bleaches the shadows. For Milius, guns were shtick. For the Schraders, they were more, rooted in something gloomy and self-destructive in their childhood. The family of their father, though not Dutch Calvinists like their mother's, had its own peculiarities. Their father's brother committed suicide while his wife was pregnant with their eighth child, when Paul was six. Five years later, the eldest son committed suicide on the anniversary of his father's death. Five years after that, the second son committed suicide on the same day. Twenty years later, a third son showed up in Grand Rapids at their father's oil company, looking for a job because he was afraid *he* was going to kill himself on the same day. "This is what we grew up with," says Leonard. "We had Dutch Calvinism, which an expert told me is a permanent form of mild depression, just nudging us toward suicide, and then we had to keep this secret from everybody, that my dad's only relatives were blowing their brains out all the time."

•

LIKE SCORSESE, Paul Schrader was raised in a God-ridden enclave to one side of mainstream American secularism. Instead of the priests and gangsters of Little Italy, Schrader was breast-fed on the fire and brimstone of the fanatical Christian Reformed Church, a Dutch Calvinist breakaway sect, in Gerald Ford's hometown, Grand Rapids, Michigan, in the '50s. His parents regarded movies, TV, and rock 'n' roll as the work of the devil.

Schrader's family came from Friesland, in Holland. They traveled west around the time of the Civil War, until they found a place that seemed like home, the mucky shores of Lake Michigan, where they raised celery.

The cinema of the '70s was a cinema of younger brothers — Scorsese, Coppola, De Palma, Rafelson. Like these men, Paul had a complicated relationship with his older sibling, affectionate, but bitterly competitive in an undeclared way. Since — unlike the other sets of brothers — the Schraders would work together trying to get a foothold in Hollywood, the result was more dramatic.

Paul was a sickly child, and Leonard's mission in life, drummed into his head by his parents, was to take care of him, make sure he survived the vale of tears that was life on earth, particularly in Grand Rapids. "Leonard bore the brunt of my father's personality and in many ways he was crushed by it," says Paul. "But he helped me build up strength to confront my father. And I swore that when my time came to do battle with him, that I would not lose. And I didn't."

The Schraders' father was strict even by the standards of Dutch Calvinism. He would make the family — the boys dressed up in their Sunday best, starched white shirts, suffocating and stiff as boards — arrive at church an hour early so he could be sure to sit in the same spot in the same pew. "No matter what you did, you made too much noise and got the elbow in the ribs," recalls Leonard. "The third elbow meant you were gonna get whipped. I got whipped six, seven days a week. Just to be a normal human being for twenty-four hours, breathing, eating, going to the rest rooms, having a normal life, meant I was going to break twenty rules a day, and three of them were worth a beating. I took off my Sunday shirt, my father leaned me over the kitchen table, took the extension cord from his electric shaver, and he whipped my back with the plug so I'd get little pinpricks of blood, a nice little pattern of dots up and down my back. Like I'd been to the doctor for an allergy test."

Mother wasn't much better. In an effort to dramatize what hell was like for young Paul, she took his hand and jabbed him with a needle. When he cried out, she said, "Do you remember what it felt like the moment the needle hit your thumb? Well, that's what hell is like, all the time."

But she was an improvement on Dad. "What saved me was my mother was human," continues Leonard. "My father was like a machine. Always told me the number ahead of time, related to how bad my offense was. If he said he was going to beat me twenty times, he beat me twenty times. My mother whipped me with a broom handle. In the kitchen. Sometimes she'd break it right over my back. But if you made my mother laugh, she couldn't go on. I would save jokes for this occasion, not jokes that I thought were funny — some of them were the dumbest jokes I ever heard — but jokes that my mother's group of friends in the church basement thought were funny, that she hadn't heard yet. I'd always wait for the first blow, the one I could never stop. Then I'd tell a joke, straining to remember the punch line. Once she started to laugh, it was okay, always with that Freudian little cap, 'Don't tell your father, it's our secret,' the S&M beatings in the middle of the kitchen."

The brothers were not allowed to watch movies, of course, nor television. Paul didn't see his first movie until he was seventeen. One day, his mother caught him listening to a Pat Boone song and hurled the radio against the wall. The brothers chafed under the constraints. "I wanted to see one movie in my life, as an act of sin," recalls Leonard. "But I had no idea how to pick a movie. So I opened the paper, and I saw this ad, *Anatomy of a Murder*. It was about where I lived, a Michigan rape-murder trial. I was standing on the sidewalk in front of the theater, trying to bolster my courage. I'd been taught that Christ is your constant companion, so I was making jokes, going, 'Well, Christ, if you want to wait here on the curb, I should be back in about an hour and a half.' Finally, I bought the ticket, went in. I had also been taught that movie theaters, the buildings themselves, were dens of iniquity. I expected honey to be oozing down the walls. This one was like a Howard Johnson's. A man in a monkey suit, and a candy counter, so I thought, Why has this been forbidden? Where's the sin? I made a minimum commitment, sat down in the last seat, end, white knuckles, terrified. *Terrified*.

"Since puberty, I had had these hallucinations. I would see things and hear things that I knew weren't there. So all of a sudden the screen peeled back, and it was the Last Judgment Day. I saw the Lord God Jehovah and hosts of angels coming down, and I was gonna burn in hell forever, because I went to the fuckin' movies. I knew it was not real, yet I saw it, and I heard it. I ran out of the theater, two blocks, five blocks, till I calmed down, furious at myself. This is your first movie, and you're havin' these fuckin' visions, you freaked yourself right out of the theater. How you ever gonna get outta this town if this is how you're gonna be. I still had the stub in my pocket, so I went back, and watched the whole thing. That was my first movie!"

Paul planned to be a minister. But by the time he entered Calvin College, it was the '60s, and the rumblings of the antiwar movement were audible in Grand Rapids. Paul's parents were right: film was the snake in the Calvinist garden, the last temptation for someone like their itchy son. "I fell in love with movies because they were forbidden," he says. He was introduced to Pauline Kael at the West End Bar when he was taking film courses at Columbia in the summer of 1966, after his sophomore year. They talked film far into the night.

"The first time I met her, referring to some movie, a comedy, she said, 'The laughs are as sparse as pubic hairs on an old lady's cunt,'" he recalls. "I was shocked. I didn't know women talked like this." After he graduated in June of 1968, she helped him get a job reviewing films for the *L.A. Free Press*. Better yet, she got him into UCLA Film School. "Pauline plucked me out of nowhere," he says. "There was no way I could have gotten into UCLA without her. She was my only connection to a career. I was terrified that suddenly she would get hit by a car. What would I do?" Schrader lost his job at the Freep for panning *Easy Rider*.

After Beverly Walker left him, Schrader was devastated. He had abandoned his wife for Beverly, and now she had cut him loose. "I felt shit twice over," he recalls. His personal fortunes at a low ebb, he considered leaving L.A., but decided he would never forgive himself if he didn't try to write a script. The result was *Taxi Driver*, which he feverishly wrote in ten days (seven for the first draft, three for the rewrite), in the late spring of 1972, while he was staying on in Walker's apartment in Silverlake.

Schrader recalls, "These violent, self-destructive fantasies that one normally holds at bay started to prey upon me. I had this old Chevy Nova. I drove around at night drinking scotch and going into the peep shows — those damn 8mm loops where you threw a quarter in to keep the loop going. You passed the point where there's pleasure involved, and it just became a kind of abnegation. Then I started getting sick. I finally went to an emergency room in enormous pain. I had an ulcer. While I was in the hospital, I had this idea of the taxi driver, this anonymous angry person. It jumped out of my head like an animal. It was like, 'Oh, this is a fiction; it isn't really you. Put it in a picture where it belongs and get it out of your fucking life where it doesn't belong.' So I wrote that script and left L.A." He hit the road in his beat-up car on one of those suicidal, my-career-is-over-what-am-I-gonna-do-with-my-life trips around America.

WHILE PAUL WAS IN HOLLYWOOD, Leonard was in Japan. He had left the country in 1968 when he had gotten his induction notice. He ended up teaching English for four years at what he terms the Berkeley of Japan. As soon as he got there, radical students calling themselves the Red Army Faction armed with sticks and iron pipes dragged him out of his classroom and closed down his university. He had nothing to do, so he hung out in bars and got a taste of the Japanese underworld, the Japanese mob, called the *yakuza*. He came back in the early fall of 1972, when he turned twenty-eight, too old to be drafted. He had no idea where Paul was, and went back to Grand Rapids, where he stared at the wall of his parents' house for three weeks, lost, broke, and depressed.

One day, Paul called, told him to meet him in Winston-Salem, where he had been staying. Nixon was running for reelection against George McGovern, Jesse Helms was running for the Senate for the first time. Leonard borrowed a couple of bucks, bought a Greyhound ticket. "I traveled all night through these dogshit little towns in West Virginia, and all the while the idea for *The Yakuza* was getting clearer in my head," he recalls. "I got off at dawn, at this tiny bus station on the edge of town. And there was my brother playing pinball. I hadn't seen him in four, five years. I walked over. He didn't even look at me, said, 'I got another ball.' Finished his game, we got in this car, drove onto the freeway, which was empty, because it was so early. Two hotrod guys came flying along, cut us off. My brother hit the gas, we came up behind their car, touched them, then he floored it, we were pushing them over a hundred miles per hour down the freeway. I put my feet up on the dashboard, thinking, We're gonna die here, which was fine with me, I'd been looking at my parents' wall for three weeks. We came to an exit, my brother had had enough, let up on the gas, and that car took the exit, just went bam! My brother and I still hadn't spoken. He turned to me, said, 'That's how I feel, how do you feel?'

" 'About the same. 'Cept I got an idea.'

" 'Idea for what?'

" 'A novel.'

" 'Like what?' I told him. By the time we got to our friend's house, he had said to me, 'Novel, fine, first we write the screenplay. And I'm gonna call a guy right now, and get the money.' "

Leonard's idea, simply put, was Japanese gangsters. Paul made the call to his agent, Michael Hamilburg, said, "This is *The Godfather* meets Bruce Lee. It's gonna sell for sixty grand. You get a third of the money, I get a third, and Leonard gets a third."

Hamilburg gave them $5,000 on the spot. The brothers arrived in L.A. around Thanksgiving and rented a tiny apartment on Bicknell in Venice, a block from the beach, for $90 a month, which Hamilburg paid for. They took the bedroom doors off the hinges, stole some cinder blocks from a construction site, set up two desks, one in each bedroom, facing each other. The only other piece of furniture was a massive butcher block coffee table with wrought iron legs. It was scored with knife marks, made while Paul was writing *Taxi Driver*. They rented two electric typewriters, wrote three drafts in about eight weeks. They wrote around the clock, twenty, twenty-two hours a day, worked ten hours, slept one, very little food. The walls were so thin the German woman downstairs continually threatened to call the police until the brothers put blankets under the typewriters to deaden the clacking. Toward the end, around Christmas of '72, they were running out of money, even though they were spending less than a dollar a day, $7, $10 a week for food, stealing plastic envelopes of ketchup from restaurants, making tomato juice.

"We sat down, took a good look at the script, and said to each other, 'We gotta write it one more time,' " recalls Leonard. "We were just wiped out, needed to find the energy to write one more draft. For us, the only surefire source of that big a jolt was guilt. We talked about, 'How we gonna get' — you didn't wanna go out and rob somebody — 'the guilt?' My brother said to me, 'We'll go to Vegas, lose all our money, we'll feel so guilty, so pissed off, we'll come home and finish the script. Or, we'll get rich, and we won't care if we finish the script.' So we drove to Vegas. We each had forty bucks. We each played blackjack, we each won, I had about two hundred bucks, my brother had about three hundred bucks. He said, 'This is nuthin', I don't feel guilty enough.' I said, 'Neither do I. What're we gonna do?' We decided that we'd keep enough money to buy gas to get home, and take the rest of the money, which was almost $500, and put it on one number in roulette. We lost, started back to L.A. On the outskirts of Vegas, this car we'd been driving the crap out of broke down. It was the middle of the night, no gas stations open, and besides, we couldn't afford to get it fixed. So we locked it up, left it there, and hitchhiked into L.A.

"We rewrote the script in ten days, right over New Year's, and by January 5 it was finished, BAM, we got meetings, but we got no car. We had to hitchhike and walk to these meetings, and we had to hide that we got no car. 'Can we validate your parking?' 'No, we parked on the street,' " I said.

Calley and Wells brought them in for a forty-five-minute meeting. Paul was impressed. He recalls, "They turned off the phone. They were really interested in what we thought young people wanted to see. 'What kind of movies do you wanna make now?' There was nothing that was too outrageous, because everything was up for grabs." Afterward, as the brothers made their way off the lot, Paul said, "You saw those guys?"

"Yeah."

"In ten years, I could be sitting in that chair!"

Says Leonard, "That's where I realized the difference between my brother and me, the desire for power. If you're the older brother, you don't have to work for power, and getting it doesn't seem that hot a deal. All I wanted was, 'Thank you for the money, I want to make a good film.' My brother had a different agenda. Power was everything.

"There was an auction, sixteen bidders, it was the highest amount for original script ever sold at that point: $325,000. We got the money, and we went out to the desert and got the car. We didn't take no bus, we took a taxi."

When the dust settled, instead of an equal three-way split, *The Yakuza* money was split 40-40 between Paul and Hamilburg, with Leonard getting only 20 percent. "I became the older brother, and I was dictating the terms," says Paul. "I would break down the story, he would write the interim things, I would rewrite him. I used him as a sounding board." Most importantly, "I wanted to have that sole screenwriting credit, so I made him take shared story credit." Leonard looked the other way, pretended it hadn't happened.

Suddenly Paul had money. Milius accompanied him when he bought an Alfa Romeo. "The salesman took one look at him, and said, 'Ya know, with a new car, people have the most accidents in the first eight hours,' " recalls Milius. "Sure enough, Paul took the Sunset exit off the freeway too fast, went over the embankment, and totaled the car."

"When he sold his first script, *Yakuza*, his ego really went bananas, nuts," recalls Sandy Weintraub. "He was waving a gun around, and he seemed loaded a lot. He seemed crazy to me." In March, Paul used some of his money to buy a sprawling home in Brentwood on Carmelita, near the house in which Marilyn Monroe died. The living room was so big it accommodated four sofas. He bought two Wurlitzer juke boxes, which he put in the living room, and stocked with 45s from the '50s and '60s. Otherwise, the house was essentially bare, except for the table with the scarred butcher block top. He lived there with Leonard, who had an office in the back. Paul had an office in the front. Paul would write all night, Leonard during the day. De Palma would stay there when he was in L.A., and they used to gather at 6:00 A.M. to watch the Watergate hearings just starting in Washington. Every Tuesday, Paul and Leonard got letters from their mother, containing Sunday's sermons, three of them, one from each of the services they had attended. She knew they had strayed, wrote, "Father and I will miss you in heaven."

Somewhere Paul had gotten hold of a crown of thorns fashioned in brass. The thorns were so sharp that when he pressed it down on his head, they broke the skin, making a ring of pinpricks that trickled blood. It was a perfect accessory for the Schraders, a little memento mori of their youth. Paul kept the crown on the butcher block table alongside his .38. "Beer bottles would come and go, ashtrays come and go, but there would always be the crown of thorns — and the pistol," says Leonard. "Whenever strangers came over, it was empty, but when the strangers left, it was loaded. Pick your yin/yang opposites: sadism/masochism, homicide/suicide."

Paul was given an office at Warners. Despite his newly minted success, Paul was still very much the bad boy. You could dress him up, but you couldn't take him out, especially to a studio. At the entrance, "he would point his car right at the wooden gate to see if the guy would raise it in time," recalls Milius. "Often he wouldn't, and Paul would snap it right off."

Schrader had contempt for those who weren't making it, like Kit Carson, who in 1973 had a nervous breakdown, ended up selling his blood for pennies. Later, he recovered sufficiently to do a piece for *Esquire* on the New Hollywood. He interviewed Schrader at his office. "The first thing he said, when he sat down at the table, was, 'I thought you were dead.' It wasn't like, 'I knew you were having a hard time and I was trying to find you and help you,' it was like, 'I'm surprised that you're still alive.' People were getting a number put on their foreheads, a ranking. As soon as the ranking disappeared from your forehead, people just cut you right off. You were dangerous to have around, you might affect the number on their forehead. There was such a marketplace frenzy at that time, that people wanted to protect their position."

Schrader was turning out scripts like so many sausages. He wrote fast, ten, twelve pages a day, so that in ten days or so, he had a completed draft. He kept the .38 beside the typewriter. When he got stuck, he would nervously pull on the trigger: click, click, click. He was writing like a machine, and although he didn't know it then, he was writing himself out.

One of the scripts he wrote was *Déjà Vu*, later called *Obsession*, to be directed by De Palma. The two men had developed *Obsession* during the course of a long afternoon. It was a mixture of *Vertigo*, a film they both loved, and Ozu's *An Autumn Afternoon*, which Paul forced Brian to see. Says Paul, "Before video, it was a lot easier to knock things off because no one else had seen them." But they had a particularly disagreeable falling out, and Schrader threatened to take his name off it.

At Christmas, the Schraders' parents came out for a two-week visit, stayed at the house on Carmelita. Despite their conviction that movies were the devil's business, Calvinists have a great respect for money. "We didn't have to say a word, let the house talk for us," recalls Leonard. "There was my father, president of an oil company, came out to California where real estate was two, three times more than it was in Michigan, and his son's house was two, three times bigger than his. There were so many bedrooms my parents could have brought out everybody they knew, and they'd all have a room." When they left, Paul turned to Leonard, said, "I don't want the house anymore. I only bought it so that I could say to mom and dad, 'See, I'm not a failure.'" In the spring, Paul put it on the market.

Scorsese, meanwhile, had settled into a small, Spanish-style house off Mulholland, the wrong side of Beverly Glen, overlooking the Valley, west of the Brando and Nicholson homes. His doctor told him he had to live above the smog line. Sandy decorated it. She hired a muralist to paint an Arizona sunset that ran the length of the master bedroom. The windows were covered by orange, red, and yellow miniblinds that changed colors when they were opened or closed. The dining room walls were covered with paint dribbles. Marty and Sandy were broke; they bought a washer, but they couldn't afford a dryer, so Sandy took wet clothes and hung them on the line out back.

Marty and Sandy were not getting along. She was bored by Marty's total immersion in movies. She told him, "I don't give a fuck about the movies. I just want us to be together." They split up; they got back together. They argued, they fought, often in public.

Marty asked Sandy to accompany him to Cannes in the spring of 1974, with *Alice*. She didn't want to go. She knew she'd be left on her own while he hustled contacts and people fawned over Marty, telling him he was a genius. Finally, she said, "Okay, I'll go with you to Cannes on the condition that we find some time alone for the two of us. I'm sick of all these people coming at us all the time." He said, "Fine, I promise you I'll make some time." But when they got there, he could not seem to find a moment for her. One spectacularly sunny day, when they were planning to drive out of town to have a romantic lunch by the sea, he came to her, apologetic. Dustin Hoffman asked him to lunch, and he just couldn't turn him down. Sandy flipped out. They were in the lobby of the Carlton Hotel, the hub of the festival. The walls were hung with oversized movie posters, hundreds of people were milling about, looking to score. "That's it, I'm leaving," she screamed as heads swiveled. "I can't stand it anymore."

"Please, please forgive me," Marty implored her. "I'll do anything."

"You'll do anything? I want you down on your knees and beg me to stay." He fell to his knees in the middle of the Carlton lobby and begged her to forgive him.

Meanwhile, Schrader continued to write furiously. He desperately wanted to direct. "Somewhere in between how *Obsession* and *Yakuza* turned out I realized that if you were a critic or a novelist, you lived by your words," he says. "When you're a screenwriter, that didn't happen. You're half an artist. If you wanted to be in control of your own life, you had to be a filmmaker." He rewrote the *Taxi Driver* script, wanted it to be an American *Notes from the Underground*, an American *Pickpocket*. He read the diary of Arthur Bremer, the man who shot George Wallace. He discussed the project with Kael, who didn't think De Niro could carry a movie. One night, in a New York hotel, he picked up a girl in a bar. When he got her to his room, he realized that she was "1. a hooker, 2. underage, and 3. a junkie. At the end of the night, I sent Marty a note saying, 'Iris is in my room. We're having breakfast at nine. Will you please join us?' A lot of the character of Iris was rewritten from this girl who had the concentration span of about twenty seconds."

Schrader's shrink pointed out that his suicidal fantasies were all the same: they involved shooting himself in the head. Indeed, his head *was* filled with demons and bad thoughts, and many of them ended up in *Taxi Driver*. Schrader and De Niro discussed the meaning of the story. De Niro told Schrader that he always wanted to write a script about a lonely guy who walked around New York with a gun. He used to sit in the General Assembly of the United Nations, fantasizing about assassinating diplomats. Schrader said to De Niro, "You know what the gun is, don't you Bobby? It's your talent. At that time in your life you felt you were carrying that huge talent around and you didn't know what to do with it. You felt embarrassment. You knew that if you ever had a chance to take it out and shoot it, people would realize how important you were, and you would be acknowledged."

On the basis of his performance in *Mean Streets*, Bernardo Bertolucci offered De Niro *1900*, which was shot in Parma, Italy, while De Palma was in Florence, shooting *Obsession*. Then *Alice* came out, to excellent reviews, and De Niro won his Oscar for *Godfather II*. What with that, and Burstyn's for *Alice*, added to the one the Phillipses got the year before, the *Taxi Driver* package wasn't looking so bad. Julia lobbied Begelman, who had always detested Schrader's script, at every opportunity. She assured him that if Scorsese messed up, Spielberg, who had *Jaws* out by this time, and was prepping *Close Encounters*, would take over. She persuaded him she could bring in the picture for $1.5 million, and Begelman finally gave in. (Ultimately the budget rose to $1.9 million.) Scorsese got $65,000, Schrader $30,000. Says Michael Phillips, "What really made it happen was, after Bobby won his Oscar, he could have demanded several hundred thousand, which would have been enough to make Marty and everybody escalate their salaries, but he still agreed to honor his original deal and work for $35,000. He was a saint."

THE 1975 OSCAR for *Hearts and Minds* marked the high point of Bert Schneider's career. (He used to take the speech out at dinner and read it to people.) Shortly afterward, he led a trip to Cuba — the one that had been delayed by Artie Ross's death — that included Bergen, Coppola, and Terry Malick. Brackman had introduced Malick and Schneider, and in Cuba they began conversations that would lead to *Days of Heaven*, a story of three migrant workers who end up in the wheatfields of Texas.

Malick had already failed to get a bankable star for *Days of Heaven* — neither Dustin Hoffman nor Al Pacino would do it — and realized that with Schneider's name they could go ahead without one. Schneider agreed to produce, but as usual insisted that Malick hire his brother Harold to look after the nickels and dimes. They lined up a cast that included the young Richard Gere, playwright Sam Shepard, and Brooke Adams.

Diller had been wooing Bert, and the producer set up *Days of Heaven* at Paramount, where Sylbert then headed production. Diller was in the early days of his long tenure at the studio, and had nothing much in the way of hits to show for himself. He was not a warm and cozy person, and had earned a reputation for being smart but combative. He rarely lost his temper, but his sarcasm was withering, and he could lower the temperature in a room twenty degrees with a few well-chosen phrases. His note pads with his name at the top he apparently found too casual: when he dispatched a sheet to his minions, he put a slash through "Barry." He was particular about his clothes and cutting about the sartorial lapses of others. At the office, he wore conservative dark suits and thin Egyptian cotton shirts — pressed jeans on weekends. He took his own pillow with him when he traveled, in a Louis Vuitton carrying case. When he first came to the studio, he was in the habit of driving himself to the airport, abandoning the car in front of the American Airlines terminal, and leaving his secretary to deal with the consequences. Diller once barged into a meeting with outside vendors, was introduced around the room by a middle-level studio executive, became furious, and later told the malefactor, "Never introduce me to anyone I do not know."

Diller was unhappy with his production head. Sylbert's tastes ran to the literary, and Hollywood was fast moving in another direction, with Paramount at the head of the pack. Diller hired Michael Eisner, who had worked for him at ABC. Eisner was young and enthusiastic, the perpetual college kid. Recalls Sylbert, "When Eisner came in, the atmosphere at Paramount changed completely. They wanted to do what they had done for the network, manufacture product aimed at your knees." A production head has to be a cheerleader, and Sylbert was decidedly otherwise. A year and a half after Sylbert hired Simpson, Simpson had his job.

Days of Heaven was an anomaly, given Paramount's direction. But by this time Schneider was a legend, and there was no downside for the studio. He made very much the same kind of deal with Paramount that he had struck with Columbia seven years before. He guaranteed the budget, was personally responsible for overages. "Those were the kinda deals I liked to make," Bert has said, "because then I could have final cut, and not have to talk to nobody about why we're gonna use this person instead of that person."

Production began in the fall of 1976. Malick was a director, like De Palma, who was very much inside his own head. The actors and crew thought he was cold and distant, and he was having trouble getting decent performances. Two weeks into the picture, lookng at the dailies, it was clear it wasn't working, looked like bad *Playhouse 90*. Malick decided to toss the script, go Tolstoy instead of Dostoyevsky, wide instead of deep, shoot miles of film with the hope of solving the problems in the editing room.

The production proceeded at a snail's pace. The ancient harvesting machines were always breaking down, which meant that shooting often didn't start until late in the afternoon, allowing for only a few hours of daylight before it got too dark to continue, although the footage, suffused with the golden glow of sunset, looked great, despite the fact that DP Nestor Almendros was slowly going blind. He had one of his assistants take Polaroids of the scene, then examined them through very strong glasses and made his adjustments.

One day a couple of helicopters were scheduled to drop peanut shells that were supposed to look like locusts on film. But Malick decided to shoot period cars instead, keeping the choppers on hold at great expense, infuriating Harold, who was so angry he was virtually spitting blood.

Bert saw Terry blithely pissing away his money — for what? Just to make himself look a little better? — while Bert had to worry about losing his home. Malick ran $800,000 over, which caused a serious rift between the two men.

Then there was the editing, which took over two years—Malick was famously indecisive. Or just meticulous, depending on who's footing the bill. Says Jim Nelson, who worked on *Badlands*, "Terry wouldn't let go. He'd nitpick you to death." As more and more dialogue ended up on the floor, the plot became incomprehensible, and Malick struggled with various ways of holding it all together, finally seizing on a voice-over. Schneider showed a couple of reels to Richard Brooks, who was thinking of using Gere in *Looking for Mr. Goodbar*. *Days of Heaven* took so long to complete that "Brooks cast Gere, shot, edited, and released the picture while Malick was still editing. 'Cause Terry couldn't find the movie."

Some of the angry scenes between them were almost like interventions, with Bert presenting long, lawyerly briefs listing all Terry's broken promises, the deadlines he had violated, and so on. Terry would reply, "Well I didn't know this guy was going to fuck me, the guy who was doing the effects ran off, did nothing, there were a lot of mitigating circumstances." Bert, of course, didn't listen to any of this; from his point of view, Terry had betrayed him, plain and simple.

But Terry was similar to Lucas. He just dug in, frustrating Bert's attempts to gain control of the production. Unlike Harold, Terry could not endure a volcanic blow-up with someone and have lunch with him an hour later as if nothing had happened. He kept things inside. He absorbed Bert's assaults, and made a mental note to smack him over the head with a baseball bat in a dark alley sometime in the future. The elephant never forgets.

Terry's dilatory pace put Bert in the position of having to go to Diller, hat in hand, asking him to cover the overages. Bert had known Diller since the Screen Gems days, back when Diller was buying movies of the week for ABC, and this was something Bert did not want to do. He considered it groveling, and he resented Terry for putting him in that position. They cobbled together a demo reel, made their pitch—"We're giving you so much more than you expected, we're going to blow this up to 70mm," etc., etc.—and Paramount bought it. Bluhdorn, in particular, was knocked out, and as a result, he gave Malick a very sweet deal at the studio, carte blanche, essentially.

Going head to head with Malick had taken a lot out of Schneider, as well. Actor Bruce Dern, on his way back from Florida to L.A. after shooting *Black Sunday*, ran into him on a plane. Leaning back in his seat and speaking of himself in the third person, Bert said, "He's out, Derns, he's out, the Schneids, it's passed him by." Recalls Dern, "This was only 1976, and he just looked so tired."

Schneider had good reason to be tired. He dedicated his professional career to freeing himself from dependence on the studios, but without the studio system to sustain him, he had to invent the wheel every time he produced a movie. "I burned out on the movie business," he has said. "In order to have the kind of freedom to work comfortably, I would have had to continue to do what I was doing, which was to gamble my entire life on every movie. That got tiresome after a while. The second reason is that I really didn't have that much to say anymore. People make movies and people make movies. Some care, and some really care, have passion and commitment and so forth, and once that wanes — for me, if I'm not juiced up, I don't want to do it." Even the building on La Brea, once the hub of all that was hip and happening in Hollywood, had a dilapidated, down-at-the-heels air about it, the movie posters and blown-up stills of historic movement moments yellowing on the walls. By the second half of the decade, it seemed like a museum piece from another era: Head Shop, c. 1970. Schneider eventually sold it to Redd Foxx.

TAXI DRIVER was shot in the hot, humid streets of New York, in the summer of 1975, when *Jaws* was depopulating the beaches of America. De Niro borrowed Schrader's clothes for his characterization, lending credence to the suspicion that had the writer not been into masochism more than sadism, he could well have been Travis Bickle. Michael Chapman was the DP. Scorsese had liked his work in *The Last Detail*. The style was all Godard — and that of his cinematographer, Raoul Coutard, the poet of the pavements — down to a close-up of a glass of Alka-Seltzer, a homage to a notorious shot from *Two or Three Things I Know About Her*. "Godard was the great freeing influence for all of us," says Chapman. "He said, Look, you don't have to worry about this or that, you can do absolutely anything you want. There's a scene where De Niro drives the cab into the car barn on 57th, he gets out of the car and starts walking one way, the camera pans around the other way, and meets him when he gets to where he's going. The crew was scandalized by that. It was as if we were saying, 'Don't follow this guy, but look at the world he lives in.'"

Jodie Foster, then a mere twelve and a half, was cast as Iris, and Cybill Shepherd as Betsy. "We had been referring to that role as the Cybill Shepherd role," recalls Schrader. "Just as a kind of prototype." It never occurred to them they could actually hire her on their dirt-cheap budget. One day they got a call from Mengers. "At that time, after *Daisy Miller* and *At Long Last Love*, she was so cold she had icicles forming on her body," says the agent. She had even contemplated suicide. Continues Mengers, "Cybill had become a joke. She needed that role. She needed to work with a director with that cachet." Mengers said to Scorsese, "I hear you're looking for a Cybill Shepherd type. Why don't you hire Cybill?"

"We can't afford her."

"Well, she'll do it for what you can pay."

"Thirty-five thousand?"

"Yeah."

Marty and Paul were nonplussed. When they got her they weren't sure they wanted her, weren't sure she was a good enough actress. Paul said, "We always said we were looking for a Cybill Shepherd type. How much worse can she be than a Cybill Shepherd type?" Finally, they decided she would give the film some legitimacy. "But," said Schrader, "she was always a Cybill Shepherd 'type.'"

There was, however, a glitch. By that time, Cybill was such box office poison that Begelman had refused to let Bogdanovich cast her in his next picture, *Nickelodeon*. Peter and Sue went so far as to leak a story to the press to the effect that he and Cybill had separated in the hope that it would prompt Begelman to change his mind. But the studio head was obdurate, and warned Peter that if Peter didn't give in on Cybill, he wouldn't approve her for *Taxi Driver*. Peter was bitter; his two male leads, Burt Reynolds and Ryan O'Neal, wouldn't stand behind her. *Nickelodeon* was Peter's last picture with Ryan.

Meanwhile, on the *Taxi Driver* set, Shepherd was indeed treated as a Cybill Shepherd type, which is to say, badly, especially by De Niro. Bogdanovich says he hit on her, and was rejected. "He treated Jodie Foster like she was a queen," says one source. "He treated Cybill like a pile of dogshit. It was really hot. One of the grips or somebody gave her a little electric fan because she was in this really hot dress. De Niro would kind of like go — 'the princess' kind of a thing. It was horrendous to watch. The truth is, Bobby treated people badly if he decided they were not up to snuff."

Marty and Sandy stayed at the St. Regis, because that used to be Orson Welles's favorite hotel. "The pressure was enormous," she says. "I remember opening up the nightstand and finding vials [of coke] for the first time. When we started *Taxi Driver*, I felt like I was being sucked up by this energy, and kind of losing myself. So I said to him, 'I don't want to work on your next movie. I want to do some of my own stuff.' That was sort of the beginning of the end for us because he needed that devotion. His dilemma was that he wanted a woman who had her own mind and her own ideas and was independent and smart. But then he wanted her totally devoted to him. Everything was for the movie. If you weren't there for the movie, you couldn't be with him. I don't think that Marty would have a woman in his life unless it was absolutely necessary. The last thing he wanted to do was to have a real life. This was his life." He once summed up his relationship to women when he said, "They put up with us until they find out who we are, and then you have to get another one."

Sandy was spending a lot of time in L.A., while Marty was in New York. One day, a freelancer named Julia Cameron showed up at the hotel. She was attractive, petite, with reddish hair. Cameron was a political writer from Washington, D.C., and was doing a story for *Oui*. She interviewed Schrader, and hung around his suite after they were finished. He couldn't get rid of her, and told Michael Phillips about her, who said she had come on to him too. Schrader left for L.A., and when he returned to New York, Phillips said, "Guess what?" She had moved in on Marty, they had become an item.

Cameron says Scorsese gave her a script first thing. "I sat down and went, 'Your political speeches don't work, none of your campaign headquarters stuff works,' so I wrote that stuff all over again, 'and your cab driver stuff doesn't work,' so I wrote all the ambience of the cafeteria. I don't know if Paul knew where my scenes came from. He might have thought that Marty just wrote them." Cameron was not credited. She says, "Bogdanovich took Marty aside, and said, 'You know, if you give Julia writing credit, Pauline [Kael] will find great fault with your movies,' which is probably an accurate assessment. She was very possessive of the directors over whom she felt she had some sway, and the minute a woman appeared, she became very competitive. She had said things like, 'Oh my God, you look like a pornographic Angela Lansbury.' And she said to Marty, 'Whatever you do with this girl, don't marry her just for taxes.' There was a certain amount of mucking going on." (Bogdanovich says he has no recollection of any such conversation.)

Cameron was not popular with Marty's friends, to say the least. They felt she was trying to come between them and him, and they disliked her for it. Says Amy Jones, who was Scorsese's assistant, and would later become an editor and director, "Nobody liked her. She was kind of the aggressor in the relationship. There was a heat-seeking missile quality about her." According to Mardik Martin, Scorsese's longtime collaborator, who would find himself in competition with her rewriting *New York, New York*, she was "insanely jealous of anybody who came next to Marty, very possessive. Marty was easily fooled by women. He loved them, he more than loved them, he worshipped them. A lot of my conversations with him went, 'Jesus, what're you listening to her for? She's crazy.'" Says one source, who blamed her for getting Scorsese deeper into drugs, "She was a real nutcase, a real two-gram-a-day abuser." But, as Chapman puts it, "How do you push somebody who's jumping?" Says Cameron, "I was just madly in love."

Sandy didn't go quietly. She mangled the windshield wipers on Marty's Lotus. Scorsese and Cameron wed on December 30, 1975. Marty couldn't believe he was getting married in a place called Libertyville—her hometown, in Illinois. It was as far as he could get from Little Italy; it represented the ultimate assimilation to the American heartland, the ultimate in self-denial.

There is a famous scene in *Taxi Driver* where a gun dealer appears in Travis Bickle's apartment with a case of pistols. Recalls Sandy, "I told Marty that not only do I know a guy who could play the part but he could bring his own guns." Having worked for her father, Sandy had known "little Stevie" Prince since childhood. "He had been doing heroin on and off for years," she continues. "He had black circles under his eyes that went down to his elbows." Later, he became indispensable to Marty. "He was the guy with the gun," recalls Martin. "If something went wrong, hopefully he was sober enough to take care of it." Says Taplin, "He was like a bodyguard, the doorkeeper. Sometimes— like that Dirk Bogarde movie, *The Servant*—you had the feeling that he could appeal to Marty's paranoia in such a way that he could make Marty do things. In that sense he had quite a bit of power."

Even though Schrader suspected Scorsese of wishing to deviate from the text, Marty was determined to preserve the integrity of the concept. The studio "would have turned it into a love story" says Scorsese. "That's why I fought everybody and everything to get it made. I was ready to destroy the picture rather than have it compromised. I became obsessed with the film, and was quite unpleasant to be around when I was making it, because I had to fight. Every day was a battle to get what I wanted. . . . I came to realize the kind of film director I had become. . . . I was going to compromise? I might as well have made another genre film for Roger Corman."

SHAMPOO opened in early 1975. Begelman saw it for the first time at a screening room at Goldwyn. He was appalled by the notorious exchange in which B movie producer William Castle, who plays the fat cat sitting next to Julie Christie at a Republican fund-raiser, says, "I can get you anything you'd like, what would you like?" and she says, "Well, first of all," looking at Beatty, and diving under the table, "I'd like to suck his cock." He asked Beatty to remove it, and of course Beatty refused, it being the best line of the movie, in his opinion the very point of the movie. "It wasn't just a dirty moment where she says a dirty line," he says. "The subject of *Shampoo* is hypocrisy, the commingling of sexual hypocrisy and political hypocrisy. The reason Julie's line made for such an explosive moment was because it shredded that hypocrisy." Towne saw Beatty's character, George Roundy, as an innocent, a natural child, the only figure in the movie whose goal is pleasure, not money. He doesn't seduce anyone; he lets himself be used. He's the girl, the dumb blonde.

Shampoo turned out to be a huge success, pulling in about $24 million in rentals in its initial U.S. run. Despite the changes that were overtaking the country, the incipient move to the right, *Shampoo* was able to tap into the climate of disillusionment following Watergate. As Beatty puts it, "Vietnam polarized the town. *Shampoo*'s audience was the audience that didn't want to go to war, that used every means to end the war."

Begelman disliked *Shampoo* so much he was distressed when the raves started coming into his office from the East Coast reviewers over the teletype. Kael compared it to Renoir, Bergman, Ophuls. Beatty and Towne had been courting Kael, who some thought was sliding rapidly down the slippery slope from reviewing to advocacy to fraternization and favoritism. They concluded that she was susceptible to the blandishments of stars, especially star auteurs and glib writers who practiced on her vanity, dazzled her with their attention. Says Buck Henry, "Towne had Kael wrapped around his finger."

Kael was allergic to the sun, and when she came out to L.A., she was swathed in veils and wore white gloves. Towne and Julie Payne, his companion, took her out to dinner at Trader Vic's. She also had dinner with them and Beatty and Christie after the critics' screening of *Shampoo*. Indeed, Towne, rather than Beatty or Ashby, was the hero of her review. He has a cameo in the picture, and she flattered him by writing that he looked like Albrecht Dürer. He started dropping her name in a way that suggested to some people that he and Kael were intimates, that he had explained his views to her, that *Shampoo* was a version of *Smiles of a Summer Night*. When her review came out, it was sprinkled with references to Bergman's film. No one could prove it of course, but people were suspicious. "You think Kael recognized what was behind *Shampoo*?" continues Henry. "He told her."

Towne says he showed Kael the script for *Greystoke: The Legend of Tarzan, Lord of the Apes*, and years later, *Tequila Sunrise*. After *Tequila* came out, director James Toback says Kael complained, "Towne sent me the script, I told him what to do, gave him advice, he didn't listen to me, and fucked it up." Toback claims she asked him to send her scripts, but he refused. According to a Kael profile in *Time*, producer Ray Stark sent her the script for *Annie* and she spotted some flaws in plotting. Says Towne, "I just loved her because she was the one person in the last half of the twentieth century who raised criticism to the level of art. But if you got good reviews from her you were resented by the other reviewers. Vincent Canby always hated me because of her." Kael admits to reading *Greystoke* and *Tequila Sunrise*, but denies seeing any others. She says, "I didn't review things I'd been involved in in any way. I was never a great buddy of directors."

Shampoo helped everyone connected with it, but some people felt it did not help them enough. Ashby grumbled that he hadn't made as much on *Shampoo* — which nobody in the industry considered his picture — as he should have. However, it enabled him to add a silver Porsche and a Mercedes to his collection of cars, and a beautiful old pine and mahogany house in the Malibu Colony that had been built in 1925 for $350,000.

For Towne, *Shampoo* was the capstone of a phenomenal burst of creativity. He would be nominated for an Academy Award again, as he was for *The Last Detail* and *Chinatown*, his third in a row. Calley, who was close to Towne, brought him over to Warners as a "consultant," hiring Julie Payne to renovate Jack Warner's old bungalow, which the two men would share. It included a magnificent deco steam room and bath with black marble sinks and toilets, gold-plated fixtures, peach-colored glass. There was even some green space nearby described on the plans as "Hira's garden," eventually removed because it seemed embarrassingly rich even in these regal circumstances. (Somebody once complained to Frank Wells that Hira was leaving industrial-sized turds in the grass; Towne sent the offended party a large bag of fertilizer.) For a mere screenwriter, Towne had arrived.

But Towne felt he hadn't made as much from *Shampoo* as he should have. Towne had 5 percent of the gross from the point where the picture earned four times the cost of the negative, which was $16 million. (The movie cost $4 million.) He figured he was owed in the neighborhood of $1 million, but he hadn't seen anything near that. About a year after the picture was released, he met with Beatty at the Beverly Wilshire. According to Towne, Beatty explained for the first time that Begelman had forced him to accept a rolling gross deal, which meant less money all around. (Since Beatty produced *Shampoo*, Towne, like Ashby, Hawn, and Christie, was paid by his company.) "Beatty said, 'Begelman fucked us.'

" 'He fucked you, he didn't fuck me. My deal was with you, and you neglected to tell me that this deal was worth less than half of what I thought it was.'

" 'You know what they say about Hollywood. You don't get rich on your last picture, you get rich on your next picture.'

" 'That may have been true when I worked on *Bonnie and Clyde* for $8,000, but the future is now, as far as I'm concerned. I'm not gonna sue, and I'll still be your friend, but I'm never gonna work with you again. This is absolutely chickenshit.' " Still, Towne's deal was doubled twice, and his cut was bigger than Ashby's, Christie's, or Hawn's. His agent must have known what kind of deal he had, and for his account to be true, it must be assumed that his agent never told him and he never asked.

Despite the fact that Towne was making at least $500,000 a year throughout the second half of the '70s, he took sizable six-figure loans from Beatty, apparently with little intention of paying him back because he felt Beatty owed him for *Shampoo*. The co-screenwriting credit also rankled. Says David Geffen, "Bob always said that Warren extracted credit from him that he didn't deserve. I interceded on Bob's behalf with Warren, and it was one of the most embarrassing things that ever happened to me. I said, 'You know, Warren, I really think that you're out of line,' and he went crazy, said 'Who told you this?' And I said, 'Bob.' He said, 'I want him to tell you this in front of me.' So at a party that Goldie Hawn had, Warren was so furious that he grabbed me, and he grabbed Bob, and he said, 'Okay, he's telling me that you said all this shit, say it in front of me.' And with me standing there Bob said he didn't do it. And the reason he didn't have the guts was because it wasn't so. Warren called me up that night, and said, 'Don't ever do that again.' "

Says Beatty, "It was Towne that offered *me* the screen credit. I would have been happy to go to arbitration. The story had no political context with Robert, no Nixon, no nothing. All of that is 99 percent me, my work. We used to meet every fucking day and I'd have to tell him the goddamn story. It's absolutely not true that every line of dialogue is his. It's an outrageous lie. Both party sequences were written by me, none of those were in Towne's original draft at all. That's half of the movie." He adds, "This idea of his being upset about credit is insane. Half the fuckin' time the guy didn't show up on the set, he'd be at the doctor.

Towne's scripts were so lengthy and he was so reluctant to cut them himself that key creative decisions were left to the director, the producer, the star, or whoever was the strongman on the project. Says former wife Julie Payne, who admittedly dislikes him, "The great secret was, Roman could have easily asked for a credit on *Chinatown* and he would have gotten it. It wasn't just the ending. Roman simply took it over, structured the whole piece. But he couldn't be bothered. Directed it, got out of town."

Beatty and Towne had been friends since the '60s. They were as close as two men could be, but it is hard to maintain friendships in Hollywood where the stakes are so high, where there are vast disparities of money and power, where the lines between affection and business are blurred, and people never know whether their success is earned or accidental. Enough is never enough, and the poison of envy eats away at the fiber of friendships. Directors want to produce. Producers want to direct. Directors want to act. Writers, who are historically the lowest of the low, the monkeys with the typewriters, feel the sting most keenly. Says Payne, "Robert became very jealous of other people's work or success. It wasn't just Warren that Robert wanted to be. It was Francis, Jack."

SCORSESE WAS ALWAYS in the *Taxi Driver* cutting room, according to Julia Phillips, popping 'ludes and drinking Dom Perignon. Bogdanovich would drop by to make sure Marty was doing right by Cybill. He admired the movie, so unlike his own. At one point, he suggested a few trims, told Marty, "You're ten minutes away from a brilliant picture."

Relations between Schrader and Scorsese, never great, became increasingly tense. Schrader was competitive with Scorsese, envious of his success as a director. He accused Marty of betraying his vision. "Marty is not an easy person to work with," said Schrader. "When I first saw his cut, Marty and I had a talk about it; he ended up having an attack, screaming, accusing me of not knowing what the movie was about and of being against him. One of the reasons Marty's good is that he's headstrong and stubborn; he sees himself as an important entity, therefore he often takes criticism as a child takes a beating, wincing at every blow. If he gets enough of it, his health will go out. So arguing with him becomes a therapy session where you're reduced to pleading, screaming. . . . [But] you have to work with the best people, no matter how hard it is."

Talking about him in public angered Scorsese, but he would never confront Schrader directly. Rather, it was Cameron who told him, "Marty's upset about some things you said in print." Continues Schrader, "He was not very confrontational. Which I think is one of the reasons he gets so confrontational in the films, he's just letting all that out. All the stuff that he can't do in his day-to-day life."

They cut and recut the picture until they came up with a version that worked. But the Motion Picture Association of America (MPAA) threatened to give the film an X rating. Scorsese and Julia Phillips met with Begelman and Stanley Jaffe, who was Executive V.P. of worldwide production of Columbia at the time, who simply told them that if they didn't recut the film to an R, the studio would do it for them. Jaffe didn't like the shot in which De Niro watched an Alka-Seltzer fizz in his glass. Jaffe wasn't interested in homages to Godard, that film school shit, called it "an Alka-Seltzer commercial." Scorsese was furious. He thought, What's their problem? It was all in the script. He realized this was not going to be a meeting where people were going to be reasonable. It was a meeting where people were saying, in effect, "You do it or else." He realized he had to fight, although he had precious few weapons. He thought, The fight is going to have to go down in a very showy sort of way: "I'm an artist!" And the response to that, of course, is going to be, "So what!" They don't want to see you, they don't want to know you, they don't really want this movie, thank you very much. More than anything else, he was angry, reacted with the old Sicilian thing, "How *dare* you speak to me like that." But his face became like stone, revealed nothing.

Scorsese was shaken. He went home, summoned his friends, Milius, De Palma, Spielberg, to his house on Mulholland. "Can you come up here right away?"

"Why?" Spielberg asked.

"Well, it's an emergency." Spielberg jumped in his Mercedes and drove over from Laurel Canyon. "I had never seen Marty so upset," he recalls. "Verging on tears, but leaning toward rage. He shattered a glass Sparkletts bottle all over the kitchen floor. We were holding his arms, trying to calm him down, find out why he was so upset. He finally came out with the fact that Columbia had seen his movie, had hated the ending, and wanted him to take out all the violence, the entire shoot-out, to cut away from the splintering fingers and the blood spouting and puddling. They felt the film was bound for an X rating, and he was being forced to Disney-ize it. Eventually he began to tell us the story of an actor, Timothy Carey, when he was auditioning for Harry Cohn in the early

'50s. In the middle of his audition, he broke down and said, 'This is so humiliating standing up here and acting for you people who know nothing about actors,
nothing about my art,' and he pulled out a gun and fired at the executives,
full-load blanks, and then had trouble getting a job for years after that. That
was his fantasy. He pointed a finger at Stanley Jaffe, and said, 'He's the head of
the studio, he's the guy I'm angry at, so I'm gonna get a gun and shoot him.'
He wasn't serious about it, but he was relishing the rage, and he wanted us to
share his anger."

In an attempt to gather ammunition for the imminent blow-up with the
MPAA and the studio, Julia took the work print to New York to show to Kael
and a few other critics. Kael offered to write an open letter in her column to
Begelman if they needed it. Back on the lot, Julia let it slip that Kael loved the
movie. Begelman and Jaffe flipped out. Afraid they would seize the print,
Scorsese locked it in the trunk of his car and sneaked it off the lot.

Powerless as Marty thought he was, he did have a few cards he could use if
he had to. UA was wooing him. He and Michael Phillips had lunch with Eric
Pleskow one day at MGM. Pleskow offered to take *Taxi Driver*, sight unseen,
with an X. UA, which had released *Midnight Cowboy* and *Last Tango*, had
done very well with X-rated films. When Scorsese heard that, he thought,
These are the people I want to be with. But it wasn't up to him.

Scorsese agreed to cut a few frames that depicted blood spraying from the
severed digits. He also suggested desaturating the color in the sanguinary finale,
something he had wanted to try since he saw Huston do it in *Moby Dick*.
Appeased, the MPAA slapped an R rating on all the disputed footage. Marty
had the last laugh. He thought with the colors muted, the scene was even more
shocking.

Begelman hated *Taxi Driver* even more than he hated *Shampoo*. He couldn't
get past the grunge, the garbage, the people like pond scum, and of course
the blood-soaked denouement. He wanted to dump it in drive-ins in the
South.

DESPITE BACK-TO-BACK HITS, Friedkin hadn't changed much. After *The
Exorcist*, "we went around the world and he was given accolade after accolade,"
says Nairn-Smith. "Everyone he met told him he was a genius, but he already
thought he was a genius." Success had done little to dull the edge. He had a
photograph of Idi Amin on the wall of his office. Rolling in money, he decided
to buy a home. Nairn-Smith occupied herself with house hunting. She found
one in Bel Air on Udine Way, next door to Charles Bronson and Jill Ireland.
He bought it, she decorated it, shopped for furniture, selected wallpaper. "I'd have floral patterns," she says. "He would get George Grosz paintings, Francis Bacon stuff. He was very dark." Friedkin was embracing a way of

life he would come to regret. "When I started out, I lived in an apartment in New York, I rode the subways every day, I ate in lower-middle-class restaurants," he says. "When someone achieves a degree of success you tend to alter your lifestyle in a way that is not conducive to staying in touch with the zeitgeist. You ask a guy, 'Do you know how to play tennis?' He says, 'Yes,' you know it's the beginning of the end for him, that he's out of touch with the public, the vast majority of whom don't give a flying fuck about tennis."

Twice he decided they should get married, and twice he backed out, after her proper banking family in Tasmania had arranged the weddings. (One of the engagements was even announced in the gossip columns.) Her father died after the cancellation of the second ceremony. Nairn-Smith was in Tasmania for the funeral, when Friedkin invited her mother to accompany her back to L.A. to stay with them. But one night, toward the end of her visit, Jennifer's mother took him to task for canceling the weddings. According to Nairn-Smith, she said, " 'Why haven't you married my daughter, William? Is it because she isn't a Jewish girl?' William went insane. He had this terrible trait, he threw tantrums like a two-year-old. He foamed at the mouth, spittle flew out of it, he screamed at her, 'You're a racist!' My mother sat very upright, a houndstooth-suit, silver-caned kind of a lady, didn't flinch at all. I was quivering with terror. My mother calmly said, 'Well, William, I suggest we retire now and you think about what you've said.' William called to me, 'Come to bed with me. Come to bed with me.' I said, 'No, I'm going with my mother. Blood's thicker than water.' The next morning, he was on his best behavior. He sat there and blew bubbles in the milk, like a seven-year-old kid, like, 'Aren't I a good boy now.' My mother left the following day."

Meanwhile, Friedkin was beginning preproduction on *Sorcerer*, his quixotic attempt to remake *The Wages of Fear*. *Sorcerer* was supposed to be a little, $2.5 million in-between movie while he was waiting to launch his next big production, *The Devil's Triangle*, about the Bermuda triangle, except that instead of ships and planes sinking to the bottom, he had this notion that they would go up into space. But Spielberg beat him to it with *Close Encounters*.

Sorcerer revolves around the attempt of a small group of desperate men to drive a couple of trucks loaded with nitroglycerine across treacherous mountain terrain. "The feeling was," says *Sorcerer* screenwriter Walon Green, "we're really auteur filmmakers, we can do anything we want, we can go anywhere we want." Friedkin had always been competitive with Coppola. Coppola was going to the Philippines to shoot *Apocalypse Now*, Friedkin would go to South America to shoot *Sorcerer*, an ambitious, pricey foray into the heart of darkness. Friedkin was having a hard time lining up a cast. He gave the script to Steve McQueen. McQueen asked Friedkin, "This is the best script I've ever read. Can you make this movie in the U.S.?"

"Oh no, the location's real important, it's gotta be believable."

"I'm worried about my marriage to Ali. If I go outta the country for three months, I won't have a marriage when I come back. Can you write in something for her?"

"No, I can't write in a part for her. You told me it was the best script you ever read and there's no part for a woman in there."

"Would you consider making her associate producer so she can be with me?"

"No, I wouldn't consider that." After McQueen turned him down, Friedkin actually began shooting without a lead. Eventually, Roy Scheider, a veteran of *The French Connection* and hot from *Jaws*, took the role.

Friedkin had made his three-picture deal with Julie Stein, who had given him a $1 million signing bonus without consulting Wasserman. Now, as the budget started to climb, Wasserman wasn't happy. He pounded his desk and refused to back a $12 million picture in the jungle without stars. He closed Friedkin down. When the word got out, Bluhdorn called Friedkin, invited him to do the picture for Paramount in his backyard, the Dominican Republic. Eventually, the two studios co-produced.

Friedkin told Green he wanted "a sense of people in the Third World manipulated by these international companies that aren't even there." Bizarrely enough, a millionaire director like Friedkin was able to identify with the wretched of the earth by way of the studio boot he felt on his own neck, and in Bluhdorn he found a symbol too good to be true, at once his own personal oppressor and a capitalist buccaneer whose exploitation of the Third World through Gulf + Western he could actually document by using the conglomerate's client state as a location.

Sorcerer was shot in France, Israel, the Dominican Republic, and New Jersey. The budget skyrocketed to $22.5 million, making the *Jaws* overruns look like small change. Friedkin hated Israel. Recalls Nairn-Smith, "He said, 'I can't wait to get out of here, all these people are just so obnoxious. They're like my family.' " The trip was the end for the unhappy couple. "I said to William, 'You know, I think I'm pregnant again,' " she continues. He screamed, she recalls, "I don't have time for a baby, I don't want a baby. If you don't get rid of the baby, I'm getting rid of you." Continues Nairn-Smith, I said, 'That's not going to work this time.' He simply turned on his heels, saying, 'I'm going to a casting session.' The last time I saw him, he was blowing up a building. He had his Cartier wedding ring on his little finger and he waved to me and shouted across the town square, 'We'll work it out in New York.' "

Friedkin never had any intention of getting married. No one got married in the '70s, and commitments were day to day, "till the milk goes bad," as the saying went. Sex without strings was free and abundant. According to Friedkin, "All I ever thought about Jennifer was that she was a great-looking woman, but I never had any real attachment to her, nothing emotional, she was just a piece of ass. She sort of attached herself to me. I always thought she was *Fatal Attraction* personified. For about the last twenty years, Jennifer has been totally obsessed with me. Her home is like a shrine to me. She came to me one day in Israel, and said she was pregnant, and wanted me to marry her. I said, I'm not going to marry you."

Friedkin was focused on *Sorcerer*, not on Nairn-Smith. As a result of the unusual financing arrangements, he had not one, but two studios by the nether parts. Says Mark Johnson, who started the picture as a second AD trainee, "Billy had won an Oscar for *The French Connection*, and had directed what was then the third top grossing movie of all time, *The Exorcist*, so when he got down there, he was the Christ, and couldn't be touched." When he found out that Universal executives were seeing the dailies before he was, he had an extra who had been taught phonetic English peer into the camera and say, "More per diem Meester Waherman, more per diem, Meester Waherman," over and over for the length of a camera reel. Bluhdorn didn't fare any better. Friedkin couldn't help but notice that the Dominican Republic was a very poor country, dominated by Bluhdorn's holdings. "He virtually had President Balaguer and the whole government working for him," he recalls. So when Friedkin needed a photo for the office wall of the board of directors of the rapacious oil company that has a death grip on the fictional Latin American country where the action is set, he tore a photo out of Gulf + Western's annual report and used it. "To me, they looked like a bunch of thugs," says Friedkin. According to Green, "When Bluhdorn saw his picture, he had a shit hemorrhage."

Friedkin's behavior made a difficult situation nearly impossible. He invariably arrived at the remote jungle locations, discovered two or three things not to his liking, threw a fit, and only then, when everyone was thoroughly terrified, did he begin the day's shooting. He was a perfectionist, and when something wasn't right, there was hell to pay. He was said to have fired scores of people during the course of the production, including Dave Salven, his longtime line producer, and five production managers. Friedkin fired so many people that Johnson moved up to second AD. "If we had shot for another week or two, I could have become the producer," he jokes. "I was the only guy he couldn't fire, because I was the leading man," says Scheider. "I said to Billy, 'You gotta stop firing these people,' 'cause I'm getting tired of going to the airport and saying goodbye to them.' " Explains Bud Smith, Friedkin's editor, "At first it was like the old baseball thing, three strikes and you're out, three fuckups and you're gone. Then it got down to two, and then it got down to one. And sometimes it didn't matter if they made any fuckups at all, he fired them because he didn't want to look at them again. 'Get 'em out of my sight.' He fired the director of photography, Dick Bush, because Dick wanted to light the fucking jungle, and the whole camera crew left. He fired the head of the Teamsters, and all the Teamsters left. With all that rolling stock there must have been thirty, forty Teamsters there, so we had to bring in a whole new crew. And a new stunt crew." Friedkin assumed Salven's job himself, joining the flock of New Hollywood directors who tried to be their own producers. The results were disastrous.

On one occasion, Billy hired a local for a few pesos to drive the car carrying Scheider back into town, a scene that occurs at the end of the picture. He instructed the driver to stop for nothing and no one. The unhappy man ran over a pig, and continued on. Friedkin cut, screamed and ranted at the campesino, and fired him on the spot. "The pig was dying on the side of the road, screaming in pain," recalled Johnson. "Billy went over to it and started to cry. Every single person on the cast and crew had very snide comments about the fact that he shed a tear for this pig, and yet the location manager, who was a very sweet woman, had been fired and sent running from the set in tears. Yet this is how Billy chose to show his sympathy." He adds, "At that point, people were beginning to question whether or not he had a heart."

Friedkin and Nairn-Smith's baby was born in November 1976. Jennifer named him Cedric, after her father. What was left of the relationship quickly deteriorated into "he said, she said." Although she and Friedkin had lived together as man and wife for three years, she says he just abandoned her, refused to acknowledge the baby was his. According to Ellen Burstyn, who had an affair with him after *The Exorcist* (which he denies), he told her that he and Nairn-Smith "had broken up, gotten back together for one night, had sex, and she didn't use what she usually used. She got pregnant, and he felt it was on purpose, that she was doing it to keep him. He didn't want to have anything to do with it." Says Green, "She told him she was four months' pregnant, and he went crazy. He was hysterical, she was trying to put him to the wall. Within a few days she was the enemy. He didn't acknowledge the paternity until quite a ways in. I saw the baby, and it looked exactly like him. He said, 'I'm fighting this all the way to the end,' and I said, 'Billy, let me tell you something. If she walks into court with that kid you're gone.' " Friedkin says, "I had a blood test, initially, to make sure that it was mine, and the blood test came out that it was, and I never contested it. I never denied paternity, and I supported the child from the beginning."

Barry Diller and Sid Sheinberg had seen a cut of *Sorcerer* and knew they were in trouble, particularly since Friedkin was openly contemptuous of executives, particularly Sheinberg, who he thought was a moron. *Sorcerer* was filled with European actors like Francisco Rabal, Amidou, and Bruno Cremer. Sheinberg told him, "You know, a problem is, this picture, it seems like a foreign film because it's got all these foreign names in it."

"Well, I don't see where that's a problem. Let's just get these guys to change their names."

"Whaddya mean?"

"Well, like Francisco Rabal, could be Frank Roberts or something. And Amidou, he could be Joe Smith. And I'll change my name if you want, I don't care."

They asked for a meeting with the director, a lunch in the private dining room at Universal. Friedkin recalls, "At that time I thought I was invincible, and I thought that any notes that were gonna come from Sheinberg and Diller were not gonna be of any value." Friedkin asked Smith and Green to accompany him to the lunch, insisting that Green, who had been working on a house, wear bib overalls splattered with paint. He explained, "I want to show utter disrespect to these people." Billy himself was dressed liked a gas station attendant, in workman's coveralls. He told his pals, "These guys operate through intimidation. They talk and you listen, and they expect you to nod your head at what they say. I want you guys to remember one thing: no matter what they say, even if you like the suggestions you hear, do not nod your head. Don't look them in the eye, just stare at their ears. And if they say, 'Can such and such be done?' we're gonna say, 'Yeah sure, but we're gonna have to gear up again and get the whole company back and reshoot.' "

They went to lunch. Smith placed a Sony tape recorder on the tablecloth, as if he were going to record everything they said. (There was no tape, nor batteries.) The waiter came by, said, "Anyone want anything to drink? Iced tea, Coke, diet Pepsi?"

"Let me have some vodka," replied Friedkin.

"A glass?"

"No, a bottle of Smirnoff."

"Would you like some ice?"

"No." Friedkin didn't drink, and as he swigged vodka right out of the bottle, his complexion turned ruddy.

They had already shot for eleven months, cut and screened the film. It was too late in the day for major changes, but Diller and Sheinberg had a long list of tweaks. Among other things, they complained that the movie didn't make it clear how many miles the drivers had traveled with the nitro, and how many miles they still had to go. Maybe it would be a good idea to cut away to a shot of the odometer every so often. Friedkin knocked back some vodka, nodded his head, said, "If that's what you want, no problem. Okay, Bud, we have to call the actors, get the whole crew back. Let's see if we can get permission to do it in the DR. It shouldn't take more than a month to do it."

"Wait a minute, wait a minute," Diller remonstrated, waving his hand. "Why do we need the actors and why do we need the Dominican Republic? All I'm talking about is a shot of —"

"I don't shoot inserts."

Toward the end of the lunch, Sheinberg proudly showed him an ad line the studio had prepared. Friedkin simply pitched forward in his seat and fell on the floor. Sheinberg looked down at him and asked, "What happened to him?" Smith replied, "That ad line knocked him out!" Says Friedkin, "They thought I was fucking nuts and they simply withdrew."

A few days later, Sheinberg was in the publicity department, bending over some artwork. Billy came up behind him whistling a tune from the '40s, "Jumpin' with Symphony Sid," grabbed the air on either side of his waist, "doing one of these numbers," recalls Smith, who was watching, "fucking him in the ass."

When Tanen finally saw *Sorcerer* with Sheinberg, Wasserman, and the other top Universal executives, he was appalled, but also gratified in a perverse way, because his worst fears had been fulfilled. He said, "We're fucked. We went through all this, for *that?*"

Joe Hyams was at the screening. In front of the Universal brass, Friedkin turned to him, said, "Joe, you were with me the night that I got Clouzot to give me his permission to make this picture. What did I tell him? Do you remember?"

"You said you'd never make it as well as he did."

"I was right!"

TAXI DRIVER opened at the Cinema I in New York City on February 8, 1976, at noon. Schrader overslept on the morning of the premiere, got to the theater around 12:15. There was a line around the block comprised of Travis Bickle look-alikes: pale young men with buzz cuts in army surplus jackets. Schrader thought to himself, Oh fuck, something's gone wrong, they haven't let them in yet. Then he realized that this was the line for the next show. He ran into the theater as the credits were coming on, joined Marty, Michael, and Julia in the back. The word-of-mouth was so strong that as the words "Taxi Driver" came up, the audience started applauding. The three filmmakers hugged each other, danced in the lobby. "It was a moment of pure joy," says Schrader. "Not to speak of the vindication." There was another screening in L.A. at the Directors Guild. Julia bumped into Towne and Bert Schneider coming out of the screening, thought they didn't like the movie, but neither would say so. Five years later, after John Hinckley, apparently under the influence of *Taxi Driver*, shot Reagan, Julia again ran into Schneider. "See, it wasn't such a bad movie," she said, smiling. He replied, "If it was really great he would've killed him."

Taxi Driver flabbergasted everyone by becoming a commercial hit; it did $58,000 the first week in New York, and $12.5 million in rentals before it played out. It also got generally good reviews. Kael indeed loved it, and she also understood that for all of Scorsese's Cassavetes- and Godard-inflected street realism, he had a Catholic, Wellesian Expressionist streak that lent the streets of New York City the kind of trippy intensity that Coppola would shortly achieve for Vietnam in the Philippines.

It was *Taxi Driver*'s ambition to take *Bonnie and Clyde* one better, extending its inquiry into the phenomenon of celebrity. When the media treat Travis Bickle as a hero, it is meant as a criticism of the media. "Characters like Travis are justified by publicity," said Schrader. "If you're on the cover of *Newsweek*, like Lynette Fromme, then you're important. The reason *why* you're on that cover is unimportant." Ultimately, however, the critique got lost in the shuffle. "One of the reasons we wanted to make this movie was because of the message," recalls Weintraub. "Marty may not have said, 'I want to make political message movies,' but I certainly think he had a consciousness about it. He was around for the '60s. Woodstock did blow his mind. Marty hoped that by becoming that violent he would capture a big audience, but they were overwhelmed by the violence of the film, all that blood and gore. They missed that message. I was really disappointed."

And if Schrader thought he was contriving a commentary on the moral bankruptcy of the media, he was wrong. He was not glossing *Bonnie and Clyde*; he was turning it inside out. Although the movie brats were '60s people, they were half a decade younger than the Beatty-Nicholson-Hopper generation, and those years were crucial. Pace Weintraub, they were not into prescriptive, politically correct cinema. Schrader brought the war home, but drained it of the passion that animated the peace movement (as Scorsese was forced to desaturate the color of the blood), and inflected it instead with European alienation and American vigilantism. To paraphrase Schrader, if you put Penn and Antonioni in bed together, put a gun to their heads and told them to fuck while Bresson watched through the keyhole, you got *Taxi Driver*.

Although *Bonnie and Clyde* had been attacked for its ironic refusal to judge its characters, *Taxi Driver* made *Bonnie and Clyde* look positively moralistic, and rendered its implicit liberal — once radical — politic more evident in retrospect than it was when the film was released nine years earlier. By darkening and deglamorizing *Bonnie and Clyde*, by putting Bickle and Betsy into a sleazy, contemporary, urban environment and frustrating the love affair altogether, Scorsese and Schrader stripped the Depression-era outlaws of their aura of populist romance and turned their story into one of simple brutality redeemed only by Schrader's Calvinist fascination with the cleansing violence of the Manson figure.

Taxi Driver was a picture completely in keeping with the new centrist administration of Jimmy Carter, who turned his back on the left wing of his party, the McGovernites. As Beatty puts it, "What animated Hollywood in the '70s was politics. You can mark the end of that with the election of Carter. There's nothing that can destroy the Democratic party like a Democrat." The only part of *Bonnie and Clyde* that survived was the violence.

•

THE ACADEMY AWARDS for 1975 were held on March 29, 1976. *One Flew Over the Cuckoo's Nest*, which beat *Barry Lyndon, Dog Day Afternoon, Jaws,* and *Nashville*, was the first of an unprecedented run of three Oscars in a row for UA, after years of floundering. Verna Fields took Best Editing for *Jaws.* Louise Fletcher won Best Actress for her portrayal of Nurse Ratched in *Cuckoo's Nest.* She still bore the wound Altman had inflicted when he gave the role based on her parents to Lily Tomlin, a wound that was reopened when Tomlin was nominated for Best Supporting Actress for *Nashville.* "What drove me crazy was I could have done both," she says. "But the worst thing Bob did, at the Academy Awards, when I won — it was the Bicentennial — we all went out on stage and sang 'America the Beautiful,' and I thanked my parents in sign language. I looked down, and there in one of the front rows was Bob." His face distorted into a grimace, he was mimicking her signing movements, his hands dancing about as if they had a life of their own. He was making fun of Fletcher signing to her deaf parents. She tried to put the best face on it. "I can't believe that Bob meant it in that malicious way," she says. "I think he meant it as a kind of joke, but I thought it was incredibly ironic, with *Nashville*, and then what had happened that night, and then to have Bob put this tag on it."

In May, the *Taxi Driver* gang went to Cannes. It was a heady time for Schrader, who also had *Obsession* in competition. He sat on the terrace of the Carlton, late into the night, with Marty, Brian, Sergio Leone, and Rainer Werner Fassbinder, inhaling the scented air of the Riviera springtime, sipping scotch, talking to them like an equal. *Taxi Driver* won the Palme d'Or. Schrader had arrived.

Obsession was released in August, and did surprising box office. That, combined with the vast success of *Taxi Driver*, enabled Schrader to move from writing to directing, with *Blue Collar.*

Fueled by his big hit, Scorsese moved full speed ahead on *New York, New York*, which he was doing with UA. *New York, New York* would be a New Hollywood musical, a big budget homage to the musicals of the past with a film student's inflection, a sort of cross between Vincente Minnelli and John Cassavetes. It starred De Niro and Liza Minnelli.

But there was a price to pay. Perhaps it was the success, perhaps it was the drugs, but Scorsese was setting himself up for a fall. "One of the things I will always thank the French for was giving me that grand prize at Cannes for *Taxi Driver* that allowed me to reveal to myself what a total failure I could be," he says. "It was a few weeks after the night when *Taxi Driver* opened that I remember I started playing with drugs when I was doing *New York, New York.* For me it was just the beginning of going into an abyss for about two years and coming out of it just barely alive."

Eleven:
Star Bucks
1977

- *How George Lucas finished with* **Star Wars** *what* **Jaws** *started, Friedkin was bewitched by* **Sorcerer,** *and Spielberg had a close encounter with Amy Irving.*

"Star Wars *was the film that ate the heart and the soul of Hollywood. It created the big-budget comic book mentality."*

— PAUL SCHRADER

Martin Scorsese was mixing the sound for *New York, New York* at the old Samuel Goldwyn Studios during the day. Marcia Lucas had been one of the editors on the picture, and George was finishing *Star Wars* at night at the same facility. The word on the street was that *New York, New York,* with its lush sets, extravagant production numbers, and hip modern story, complete with the de rigueur unhappy ending, was a masterpiece. Marcia told George, "*New York, New York* is a film for grown-ups, yours is just a kids' movie, and nobody's going to take it seriously." George was depressed that *Star Wars* was going over budget and certain it wasn't going to make any money. It faced stiff competition that summer: a *Jaws* rip-off called *The Deep, A Bridge Too Far, Smokey and the Bandit,* and *Damnation Alley,* another sci-fi picture, were all slotted for Memorial Day. George called his friends, Willard Huyck and Gloria Katz, and complained, "They're all being released at once; my movie's going to be the fourth best."

George was so worried about *New York, New York,* he wanted the couple to sneak into a screening and report back. Jay Cocks got them an invitation. Huyck saw the movie, called up George, and said, "I just don't get it. I just don't understand why people think this is going to be such a successful movie. It's really boring." He wasn't sure George believed him, or just thought he was being loyal. Lucas continued to worry. Of course, worrying came naturally to him.

•

GEORGE LUCAS WAS BORN in Modesto, California, on May 14, 1944. He was raised in a rather conventional fashion, which he would later refer to wryly as his "Norman Rockwell upbringing." He grew up on the short side, five foot seven, and like most of the movie brats, he was an introverted kid who had great difficulty relating to others. He was frail, unathletic, and timid; although he didn't know it at the time, he had diabetes. He was frequently picked on by bullies, and had to rely on a younger sister to chase them away.

Compared to the tortures inflicted on the Schraders, the chilly Lutheranism and cultural impoverishment of small-town life in Modesto was nugatory, but of course, young George had nothing to compare it to, and felt it keenly. His father, George Sr., was a rock-ribbed Republican, a businessman who grew up during the Depression and ran an office supply store. He regarded young George, who never did particularly well in school, as a slacker who would probably come to no good. He once referred to his son disdainfully as a "scrawny little devil." He subscribed to the boot camp school of child-rearing, and every summer he shaved his son's hair off. He was in the habit of derogating Hollywood as Sin City, and wanted George to follow him into office supplies. Later he opposed George's decision to go to film school. Very much the disciplinarian, he ironically managed to instill a lifelong anti-authoritarian attitude in his repressed and angry son that would later express itself in his movies. It always seemed that his rupture with his father led him to seek paternal relationships elsewhere, like the one he formed with Coppola. At the same time, many of his father's values took root. George prized hard work and ambition, vowed to beat the adults at their own game, and early on identified money with power and freedom. This ambivalence was nicely expressed when, arguing with his father over going to film school, dad said, "You'll be back in a few years," and George shouted, "I'm never coming back," and then added, "I'm going to be a millionaire before I'm thirty."

Like Spielberg, Lucas was a child of television. "Movies had extremely little effect on me when I was growing up," he said. "Television had a much larger effect." It was during the two years he put in at Modesto Junior College that he started going to movies, making the trek to North Beach in San Francisco to watch local underground filmmakers such as Scott Bartlett, Bruce Conner, and Jordan Belson. He transferred to USC as a junior in 1964, moved over to film, and quickly realized he had found his vocation, plunging into it with a passion that was almost frightening in its intensity. He worked day and night, lived on candy bars. "What we had in common is we grew up in the '60s, protesting the Vietnam War," says Lucas. "We were gonna take over the world. The other thing was that we were passionate about movies. We never thought we were going to make money at it, or that it was a good way to become rich and famous. It was like an addiction. We were always scrambling to get our next fix, to get a little film in the camera and shoot something."

Lucas was such a star at USC that he scooped up the few training gigs available. He and a couple of other USC and UCLA students got a Columbia Pictures scholarship to shoot a short documentary on the making of *MacKenna's Gold*, which was being shot in Page, Arizona. It was a lumbering, elephantine studio Western, very much in the style of the bloated musicals of the '60s, and it was Lucas's introduction to the Old Hollywood. "We had never been around such opulence, zillions of dollars being spent every five minutes on this huge, unwieldly thing," he said. "It was mind-boggling to us because we had been making films for $300, and seeing this incredible waste — that was the worst of Hollywood." While the other students shot conventional "making-of" documentaries, Lucas shot an imagistic film about the beauty of the desert, with the production barely visible in the far distance. The experience confirmed his anti-studio attitude. He said, "L.A. is where they make deals, do business in the classic corporate way, which is screw everybody and do whatever you can to turn the biggest profit. . . . I don't want anything to do with them." He also got the fateful Warners scholarship that brought him to the set of *Finian's Rainbow*.

GRAFFITI convinced Lucas he was on the right track. "When I did *Graffiti*, I discovered that making a positive film is exhilarating," he said. "I thought, Maybe I should make a film like this for even younger kids. *Graffiti* was for sixteen-year-olds; this [*Star Wars*] is for ten- and twelve-year-olds, who have lost something even more significant than the teenager. I saw that kids today don't have any fantasy life the way we had — they don't have Westerns, they don't have pirate movies. . . . the real Errol Flynn, John Wayne kind of adventures. Disney had abdicated its reign over the children's market, and nothing had replaced it."

He had always wanted to do sci-fi, "a fantasy in the Buck Rogers, Flash Gordon tradition, a combination of *2001* and James Bond." He admired Kubrick's *2001*, but thought it was excessively opaque. *Star Wars* "was a conscious attempt at creating new myths, he continued. "I wanted to make a kids' film that would . . . introduce a kind of basic morality. Everybody's forgetting to tell the kids, 'Hey, this is right and this is wrong.' "

Lucas started writing the treatment for *Star Wars* in February 1972, about a month after the Northpoint screening of *Graffiti*. He was reading extensively through the literature of fairy tale and myth, discovering Joseph Campbell. He pored over Carlos Castaneda, recast Castaneda's hero, a Mexican shaman named Don Juan, as Obi-Wan Kenobi, and his "life force," into the Force. But as usual, he had trouble writing. More than a year later, by May of 1973, all he had to show was thirteen pages of virtual gobbledygook. The first sentence informed the reader that this was "the story of Mace Windu, a revered Jedi-bendu of Opuchi who was related to Usby C. J. Thape, padawaan learner of the famed Jedi."

Neither his lawyer, Tom Pollock, nor his agent, Jeff Berg, could make any sense of Lucas's treatment, but he *was* their client, and they gamely went out to try to sell it. They were still obliged to bring the project to Universal. "George didn't want it set up with Tanen," said Pollock. "We were pretty sure they would pass . . . because it was right in the middle of Ned's most angry period."

Meanwhile, three months before *Graffiti* released, Berg had smuggled a print to production head Alan Ladd, Jr., at Fox. Ladd saw it at 9:00 in the morning, and called Lucas that afternoon, saying he wanted to be in business with him. They had a meeting. Lucas pitched *Star Wars*, described the picture as a cross between Buck Rogers and Captain Blood, language Ladd could understand. He had none of Tanen's mishegoss; he was quiet, laid-back, and nonconfrontational, not unlike Lucas himself. He knew his place, and Lucas liked him for it. The two men reached an understanding.

According to Pollock, Universal had thirty days in which to respond. Right before the deadline, Tanen called Berg and said, "We're passing." Berg made a deal at Fox within a week after Tanen said no. Ladd paid Lucas $15,000 to develop a script, $50,000 to write, and another $100,000 to direct. Lucas's company, the Star Wars Corporation, would get 40 percent of the net. The budget was fixed at $3.5 million, which Lucas knew was wildly unrealistic, but he was afraid Fox would back off if Ladd realized what the true cost might be.

Graffiti opened on August 1, 1973. It broke house records, and earned a phenomenal $55.1 million in rentals. The picture's direct cost was $775,000, plus another $500,000 for prints, ads, and publicity, a staggering return on investment. "To this day, it's the most successful movie ever made," says Tanen. Lucas's cut came to about $7 million, around $4 million after taxes. This, after living on a combined income of $20,000 a year or less for longer than George and Marcia cared to remember. But for George, the glass was still half empty. So different from Francis, he made few changes in his lifestyle. Says Marcia, "He had this idea of being a flash in the pan, you hit it once and that's all you're ever going to have, there are no guarantees." But they did buy an old Victorian in San Anselmo and restored it. Marcia called it Parkhouse.

Like Spielberg, Lucas wanted to be taken seriously as an artist, be paid the kind of attention the critics lavished on Coppola and Scorsese. He told Friedkin that in *Graffiti*, he had made an American version of Fellini's *I Vitelloni*, and he wondered why none of the critics had picked up on it. Friedkin thought to himself, My God, he's filled up with himself. This guy really thinks that's what he's done?

Mean Streets opened six months later. "They're similar," observes Scorsese.

"One was about urban Italian-Americans and one was about small-town Americans. That's when I saw the handwriting on the wall. The movies I was going to make were going to be for specialized groups, while *Graffiti* and *Star Wars* would appeal to everyone."

Although Lucas had conceived the story and directed the picture, the press gave Coppola a lot of the credit. *Graffiti* was another example of his unfailing golden touch. Lucas distributed points to those he felt had made major contributions. Lucas and Coppola, who had promised points to DP Haskell Wexler and producer Gary Kurtz, fell to fighting over whose cut the points came out of. George wanted Francis to pay them out of his twenty-four points; Francis didn't see why he should. "George is just like an accountant when it comes to money," says Huyck. "The amount of money that George had to send to Francis upset him." Said Lucas, "Francis was questioning my honesty. It was one of the reasons we drifted apart." According to Dale Pollack, Lucas's biographer, George previously thought Coppola didn't know any better. After this quarrel, he felt Coppola was immoral. (Lucas says Pollack exaggerated the degree of animosity between himself and Coppola in the interest of a good story.)

Coppola in fact ended up paying Wexler and Kurtz, and his twenty-four points shrank to fourteen, netting him $3 million, although had he produced *Graffiti* himself, he could have made much more. "That movie could have brought me over $20 million," he said. "I lost the chance to earn enough money to set up my own studio. After that, I decided that I would finance all Zoetrope films myself." He always regretted his failure to finance *Graffiti*, for a long time blamed Ellie for it.

When *Graffiti* started cleaning up at the box office, Lucas had an opportunity to renegotiate his deal with Fox. Berg told him he could expect to get his salary raised to $500,000, and cash in his net points for gross. Lucas shrewdly decided to make his demands in another area. Wiser from his traumatic experiences with Warners and Universal, he wanted *Star Wars* produced by his own company so he could make sure that costs charged against the picture were genuine. Says Pollack, "He had been burned on control by studios. He really saw it first as a control issue rather than a money issue, because he was then and still is into control."

Lucas also insisted on the music rights and profits from sales of the soundtrack album, as well as the sequel rights. And last but not least, he wanted the merchandising rights. Until *Star Wars*, merchandising was a relatively trivial cash center. Lucas understood its importance. Just how much Lucas was motivated by money is a matter of debate. Someone who worked on *Raiders of the Lost Ark*, which Lucas produced, once volunteered that her favorite film of his was *THX*. He gave her a puzzled look and said, "But it didn't make any money!" As always, Coppola was the standard by which he measured himself. Recalls Milius, "George said to me, 'I'm going to make five times as much money as

Francis on these science fiction toys. And I won't have to make *The Godfather.*'
I thought, Where is this coming from?" Lucas had all the angles figured out.
He was under no illusions about the kind of picture he was making. "I've made
what I consider the most conventional kind of movie I can possibly make." He
added, "This is a Disney movie," he said. "All Disney movies make $16 million,
so this picture is going to make $16 million. It cost ten, so we're going to lose
money on the release, but I hope to make some of it back on the toys."

Recalls Huyck, "When George said, 'I'm gonna make my own movies,' it
wasn't, 'Fuck you, we're gonna make our movies,' because we kinda could
make our own movies in those days. What was upsetting him was the fact that
he felt he should be getting more of the movie. George looked at it like a
businessman, saying, 'Wait a minute. The studios borrowed money, took a 35
percent distribution fee off the top.' He said, 'This is crazy. Why don't we
borrow the money ourselves?' So some of the bravest and/or reckless acts were
not aesthetic, but financial."

From Fox's point of view, Lucas's demands were a joke. Everyone knew that
toys took eighteen months to design, manufacture, and distribute, and by that
time the movie would be history. It was axiomatic that you couldn't make
money on sequels, and the rights obviously didn't amount to much unless the
movie was a huge hit, which nobody expected.

MEANWHILE, Coppola approached Lucas about directing *Apocalypse Now.*
The period from *Godfather II* to *Apocalypse Now,* roughly a year and a half
from December 1974 to March 1976, marked the high tide of Coppola's power,
success, and fame. *Godfather II* had been all his, dispelling the doubts he and
others had harbored about its predecessor. A lot of people he respected thought
it was better than the first *Godfather.* Now that he had really come into his
own, his ego exploded. The overwhelming grosses of *Graffiti,* the double Oscar
nominations that greeted *Godfather II* and *The Conversation,* the *Godfather II*
sweep that followed, gilded his career — he was a triple threat as writer, producer, and director — with unparalleled triumph. He had done what every
young director dreamed of: achieved spectacular success in a mainstream
genre, managed to pursue personal filmmaking at the same time — and more,
combined the two in his risky *Godfather* sequel. It is fair to say that no other
figure, not even Welles at his most grandiose, or Spielberg at his height, enjoyed
the wild acclaim bestowed upon him. Not even the perfervid fantasies of the
polio-ridden child could equal the reality of his life. Coppola was still all of
thirty-five years old; the youth movement had come of age.

But the nonstop adulation was beginning to take its toll. "The success . . .
went to my head like a rush of perfume," Coppola recalled. "I thought I
couldn't do anything wrong." Francis wanted to get *Apocalypse* out for the

Bicentennial in 1976, but George had begun work on the *Star Wars* script, and demurred. Francis didn't think much of George's script, told him he was crazy to pursue it when he could do *Apocalypse* instead. George always regarded *Apocalypse* as his to direct whenever he decided he was ready. True, Coppola had folded it into his deal with Warners way back when, and Lucas had never objected, but he had presented Lucas with a fait accompli, never even discussed it with him, and Lucas believed he had a moral claim on the project.

"All Francis did was take a project I was working on, put it in a package deal, and suddenly he owned it," he says. After Zoetrope collapsed, Lucas took the script to the studios. When Begelman arrived at Columbia, the conversations went so far that Lucas's producer, Gary Kurtz, flew to the Philippines to scout locations. Lucas was all ready to begin, wanted to shoot it in 16mm for $2 or $3 million. "I couldn't get the same terms Francis had gotten at Warners, it was much less," continues Lucas. "But he was determined to hang on to the same number of points, his old number, so whatever Columbia took, I had to give up. My points were going to shrink way way down, and I wasn't going to do the film for free. He had a right to do it, it's in his nature, but at the same time I was annoyed about it." He was quoted as saying, "Whatever Francis does for you always winds up benefiting Francis the most. . . . He finds it incredible that people do things he doesn't wish them to do, since he's controlling it all and they're all here for *him*."

"I was always on Francis's side," says Milius. "George had nothing whatsoever to do with it, other than the fact that he was going to direct it. 'Just go do your Vietnam thing, John.' Francis gave George ample opportunity to make the movie. George never did. He was too good for it. Francis has a lot of terrible qualities; he is a supreme egotist, and he will take everything for himself. He is like what they said of Napoleon, he was great as a man can be without virtue. But if Francis hadn't done it, that movie never would have been made."

Once Coppola decided to do *Apocalypse* himself, he moved ahead quickly. He had absorbed the lesson of *Graffiti*, and he was determined to set it up without studio money. That way, he could control the production and retain a large slice of the profits. In spring of 1975, he sold off the foreign rights to European distributors for $7 million. But there was a string attached. He couldn't touch the money until he signed a couple of brand-name actors, the kind that would make his investors see dollar signs. Coppola thought it would be easy, just wave his Oscars in front of, say, Steve McQueen. But he was in for a surprise. He failed with McQueen, Pacino, Nicholson, and Redford, none of whom was eager to spend months in the jungle with Coppola, particularly since he was unwilling to offer them gross points. Pacino said, "I know what this is going to be like. You're gonna be up there in a helicopter telling me what to do, and I'm gonna be down there in a swamp for five months." Coppola failed with all of them. Ditto Brando. Furious, Francis threw his Oscars out the window, until all but one lay on the sidewalk, shattered. By this time, he had spent about $1 million of his own money on preproduction. He told his production designer, Dean Tavoularis, that if he couldn't get big stars, he'd cast unknowns, "young Al Pacinos. The war was fought by children. Redford and McQueen are too old."

The script, loosely based on Joseph Conrad's *Heart of Darkness*, told the story of a rogue Green Beret colonel named Kurtz, targeted for termination by the army, through the eyes of Willard, the officer sent to execute him. It was now six years old, and a lot had changed since Milius had written it in 1969. Although the U.S. had decimated Vietnam, it had lost the war. Coppola told everyone that the script was little more than a one-dimensional expression of Milius's neolithic jingoism: "The film continued through comic-strip episode and comic-strip episode until it came to a comic-strip resolution: Attila the Hun (i.e., Kurtz) with two bands of machine-gun bullets around him, taking the hero (Willard) by the hand, saying, 'Yes, yes, here! I have the power in my loins!'"

From the beginning, Francis had in mind a surrealistic treatment. "People used to ask me, 'What's this movie gonna be like?' And I would say, 'Like Ken Russell,' " he remarked. " 'The jungle will look psychedelic, fluorescent blues, yellows, and greens. . . . I mean the war is essentially a Los Angeles export, like acid rock. . . .' "

Coppola eventually settled on Harvey Keitel as Willard, and Robert Duvall as Colonel Kilgore. Desperate, he changed Brando's mind with an extremely rich deal: a million a week for three weeks and 11 percent of the gross. Other parts went to Sam Bottoms, Fred Forrest, Scott Glenn, and Dennis Hopper. With this cast on board, Francis turned around and sold U.S. rights to United Artists for $10 million. All told, he had about $17 million — a wildly inadequate sum, as it would turn out — but he had managed to retain control of the movie. UA optimistically announced a release date of April 7, 1977, Coppola's thirty-eighth birthday.

Francis called Roger Corman, who had shot several films in the Philippines. "I know you've been shooting your films in that area. What advice can you give me?"

"My advice, Francis, is, Don't go."

"It's too late to change. We've been in preproduction for weeks."

"You're going right into the rainy season — May through November. Nobody shoots there that time of year."

"It'll be a rainy picture."

On the eve of his departure, Coppola's mood was ebullient. Megalomania, never a stranger, came knocking once again. He startled a journalist by falling dramatically to his knees before the new pyramidal skyscraper that poked upward through the skyline of North Beach. It was the Transamerica headquarters at 600 Montgomery Street, home of UA's conglomerate parent. It dwarfed his own Sentinel Building across the street, a daily reminder of his humiliating dependence. "Someday I won't just own this," he bellowed, "but I'll own you too," gesturing at Transamerica's headquarters. As the *Apocalypse* budget climbed, it seemed that the tiny Sentinel Building threw an ever larger shadow on the glass facade of the Transamerica Tower behind it.

LUCAS WORKED on the *Star Wars* script for two and one half years, writing at the back of his house in San Anselmo in a room that he shared with a gaudy Wurlitzer juke box. A photograph of Sergei Eisenstein peered down at him from the wall behind his desk. The Emperor, corrupted by power, was based on Richard Nixon, although some of his friends suggested that it was only later, after the picture became a hit, that Lucas claimed this. He plundered Flash Gordon serials and other pulp sci-fi of the '30s for decor and costume. He wrote, revised, and revised some more. He puzzled over how to get the right "wholesome" tone, avoiding sex and violence, yet including "hip new stuff."

First there were too many characters, then too few. They combined, and then divided again. The plot was too simple, too complex. Princess Leia's role grew bigger, then smaller. Obi-Wan Kenobi and Darth Vader, initially one character, became two. The Force got a good side (Ashla) and a bad side (Bogan). Annikin Starkiller became Luke Skywalker. Kenobi began life as an elderly general, became an addled hermit, and then an elderly general again. A Kiber Crystal appeared, then disappeared.

Lucas, meanwhile, was afflicted by headaches, pains in the stomach and chest. He became compulsive about his writing materials, insisting on No. 2 pencils and blue and green lined paper. He took to slicing off bits of his hair with scissors, depositing them, along with crumpled sheets of paper, in the wastebasket. He could never remember how he had spelled the names of his characters, rendered Chewbacca differently every time he wrote it.

When Lucas finished a draft, he would show it to his friends: Coppola, Huyck and Katz, Robbins, and so on. No one was supportive. "They said, 'George, you should be making more of an artistic statement,'" Lucas recalled. "People said I should have made *Apocalypse Now* after *Graffiti*, and not *Star Wars*. They said I should be doing movies like *Taxi Driver*." He was depressed, convinced he was a failure. Marcia asked De Palma to talk to him. "George thinks he has no talent," she said. "He respects you. Tell him he does."

The third draft was finished on August 1, 1975, by which time Marcia had started work on *Taxi Driver*. Lucas wrote Coppola into his script as Han Solo, in a self-flattering version of their relationship. Solo outwitted the Empire (read, studios) and enjoyed skating along the edge of the precipice, but he gambled and lost heavily, never accumulating enough money to get any real power, and had a self-destructive streak a mile wide. And most important, he lost the girl to Luke, i.e., George. He was still anxious about the script, and begged Huyck and Katz to do a polish, swearing them to secrecy. "They're already nervous," he told them. "If they find out that I've gotten someone else to rewrite the script, they're gonna back out. I'll give you some points." He gave them two.

Meanwhile, Fox still hadn't given Lucas the green light. Finally, the time came when Ladd had to decide whether to shelve Lucas's movie, or let him begin. A few weeks before the Oscars, in March, he had put Lucas's one-paragraph synopsis in front of CEO Dennis Stanfill and the board of directors. He asked them to commit $8.5 million to a project in a despised genre, without names, without a presold book. Miraculously, the board agreed. Lucas had a go.

NEW YORK, NEW YORK went into production without a finished script. "They started shooting because Minnelli had a commitment to go to Vegas or something," recalls Mardik Martin, whom Scorsese called in to rewrite Earl Mac Raush's draft. Scorsese knew the script wasn't ready. He explains, "You get a big head. You think, 'Oh, I don't have to make up a script, I can work it out on the soundstage when I'm there.' Sure. A lot of guys work that way. Evidently, I couldn't." Adds Sandy Weintraub, "After *Mean Streets*, the critics called Marty 'The King of Improv.' And he decided that he *was* 'The King of Improv.' So on *Alice*, he was just gonna have everybody improv up a storm. That continued through *Taxi* and obviously the result you see is *New York, New York*, where it got out of control." Continues Martin, "It was a nightmare. I was writing up till the final frame. You don't make movies like that."

Scorsese says he used coke as a creative tool: "I didn't know how to get to these feelings. I kept pushing and shoving and twisting and turning myself in different ways, and I started taking drugs to explore, and got sidetracked a lot of the time. We put ourselves through a lot of pain." One day, he kept over 150 fully costumed extras waiting while he talked to his shrink from his trailer. He was sick a lot, and late to the set. Says Martin, "I blame all that on coke."

The movie was intensely personal, for both Scorsese and De Niro. Consciously or unconsciously, De Niro's jazz musician (Jimmy Doyle) — the artist as a young man — was very much Scorsese at that time, torn between the claims of his family and his art, intoxicated with his own talent, and honeycombed by self-hatred. Doyle rejects his baby just like Scorsese rejected his. The Minnelli character is a version of Julia Cameron, Sandy Weintraub, and other women Scorsese knew. Scorsese called it a $10 million "home movie." Cameron continued to irritate Marty's friends. Says Martin, "She conned her way into doing a lot of rewriting, then told everyone she wrote *New York, New York*, which is total bullshit. She was a really bad drunk, a Jekyll and Hyde. I had a brand-new, beautiful Cadillac Seville, and I used to pick her up when she was drunk, and take her home. She threw up in my car twice. Marty said, 'I'm sorry, I'm sorry.' "

Cameron was pregnant, but Scorsese, mimicking the De Niro character, was carrying on an open affair with Minnelli, who was married to Jack Haley, Jr., (whose father played the Tin Man in *The Wizard of Oz*), and herself having a liaison with Mikhail Baryshnikov. Running into her with Haley on the street one day, Marty is supposed to have berated her about Baryshnikov. "How could you!" he shouted, while Haley looked on. On another occasion, according to Andy Warhol's *Diary*, Minnelli appeared on Halston's doorstep pleading, "Give me every drug you've got," while Marty, ever dapper in his white suit, but shaking badly — apparently from the coke he'd taken — waited in the shadows. Halston gave her four 'ludes, a Valium, a vial of coke, and four joints. The couple went off into the night.

In the middle of the pregnancy, Marty realized it wasn't going to work out between him and Cameron, and when the baby was born, a girl named Domenica, he left her. Fueled by an I-am-a-genius ego and surrounded now by an adoring circle of friends, with *New York, New York* shaping up as an unprecedented triumph, Scorsese had begun to change. Says Chris Mankiewicz, who had been in Europe and hadn't seen Marty since he had known him in New York in the '60s, "By the time I came back, I was surprised to see how much more — I won't say arrogant, but self-assured and bordering on arrogance — he had become. He was already a superstar director, and it was clear that he didn't tolerate [criticism]." Adds Huyck, "De Palma, who I always thought of as Marty's best friend, thought that Marty was so egocentric that he just became very difficult to relate to. [At one point, Brian] hadn't seen him in years, and there was no interest in anything that Brian had gone through. It was all what Marty was doing. I never liked him personally, but compared to everybody else, I always felt that Marty was the artist."

WHILE LUCAS WAS FINISHING the last draft of the *Star Wars* script, post-production whiz Jim Nelson was putting together Industrial Light and Magic (ILM) from scratch in an old warehouse on Valjean in Van Nuys, next to the airport. "There was no ILM," recalls Nelson. "There were four walls, no rooms, even. We had to build rooms, buy equipment, make equipment, because the equipment that made that film didn't exist." Nelson hired John Dykstra, the special photographic effects supervisor who had worked for Doug Trumbull on *2001*. Dykstra's breakthrough was to create a computer-controlled camera that moved around the models in a pattern that could be replicated again and again, so that shots could be built up out of layers.

Lucas was afraid from the start that ILM would be a sinkhole of money, and relations between him and the effects wizards he had hired were tense. "Having been a clever filmmaker who did things on his own, George's idea was that ILM was going to be this little squad of techies," says Robbins. "They'd figure out how to make these shots in a garage for $1.98. I remember Dykstra saying, 'If it were up to George, we would have hung a black backing, and put the ships on broomsticks and waved them around. Like twelve-year-olds.' I think George actually did propose that. Dykstra, of course, knew they were going to have to hire a lot of people and buy a lot of equipment. George, who was very much his father's son in terms of business, felt he was being ripped off, that all the expenses and technical mumbojumbo were about creating an empire for John Dykstra, founding John Dykstra, Inc."

On several occasions the two men engaged in shouting matches. Says Marcia, "ILM was a mess. They spent a million dollars, and the fx shots they'd been able to composite were just completely unacceptable, like cardboard cutouts, the matte lines were showing." Remembers Nelson, "We were under a great deal of pressure, we had nothing to show anybody, and we kept spending all this money. We didn't have a shot for over a year." Three million dollars of Lucas's budget had been earmarked for ILM. By the end of the first year, they had spent $4 or $5 million, with few results. Lucas came down from the Bay Area once a week, on Tuesdays, expressed his disappointment, and went home. Continues Nelson, "I always had to be the bearer of bad news, which he never wanted to hear. You couldn't argue with him, he didn't want to hear no, he didn't want to hear, 'You're wrong, George.' "

That same fall of 1975, while Marcia was still editing *Taxi Driver*, Lucas went down to L.A. to begin casting. She was nervous. "I knew he was going to be looking at the most beautiful eighteen- and nineteen-year-old girls in Hollywood for Princess Leia, and I felt insecure." She said, "George, are you going to be a good boy when you're there?" He and Marcia had promised to tell each other if either one strayed, hoping that that unpleasant duty would deter them. "My first vow when I came to a film studio was never to date an actress," said Lucas. "You're just a funny kid, and someone like a Playmate of the Month is coming after you — life is just too short for that."

Despite the fact that *Star Wars* was about as far as you can get from a realistic drama, Lucas, like his peers, did not want to cast stars, despite Fox's pressure to do so. De Palma was casting *Carrie* at the same time, and also looking for new faces of similar ages, so the directors held readings for the two films together, working out of the Goldwyn Studios, seeing thirty to forty actors a day in a cattle call. De Palma was relaxed and garrulous. Lucas sat at his side in silence, obviously uncomfortable. George would make the opening speech, and Brian would make the closing speech. If the actor was somebody they were not interested in, Brian would start the closing speech before George had finished the opening speech.

Fred Roos, who was advising Lucas on casting, persuaded Lucas to use

Carrie Fisher instead of Amy Irving or Jodie Foster. Harrison Ford was cast as Han Solo, Mark Hamill as Luke. Lucas wanted young and callow, that is, Hamill and Fisher, as opposed to, say, Ford as Luke and Raquel Welch, or a Playboy bunny type to play the princess. He said, "You can make this picture for teenagers, late teenagers, early twenties, or you play it for kids, and that's what we're going for, eight- and nine-year-olds. This is a Disney movie." During production, he bound Fisher's breasts with gaffer's tape. "No breasts bouncing in space, there's no jiggling in the Empire," she observed, wryly.

De Palma ended up using Irving in *Carrie*. With her emerald eyes and high cheekbones, Irving made a striking impression. She was smart and ambitious, and had a crush on De Palma, who did not reciprocate. Instead he introduced her to Spielberg. Steven was still very awkward with women. Says Gottlieb, "By the time he was thirty-five, he was where normally a twenty-five-year-old would be, sexually." He felt he was unattractive to women, and the only way he could attract them was through power, which made him uncomfortable. Occasionally, when he would go to Show West, the annual exhibitors confab, they would fix him up with a model.

Marginally more hip than he had been, with his Prince Valiant haircut, aviator glasses, brown suede jacket, and Levi's, Spielberg had become quite the catch. Steven, Irving, and De Palma went to Nick's Fish Place on Sunset. "They hit it off right away," says De Palma. The daughter of actress Priscilla Pointer and actor-director Jules Irving, one of the founders of Lincoln Center Repertory Theater, she was considerably more worldly than Spielberg, whose horizons were limited to film, movie music, TV, and video games, which were just beginning to catch on. Irving took her career extremely seriously. She was humorless and driven. A few years later, De Palma cast her in the lead of *The Fury*, a Stephen King rip-off about a girl with telekinetic powers. Several members of the cast, including John Cassavetes, thought the picture was garbage, and made fun of Irving for treating it like Shakespeare, like it was a big career move. She worked on her character with a great earnestness. "You'd think she was playing Joan of Arc," Cassavetes joked to another actor.

Steven, who up to this point had not had a real relationship, fell hard. She was often cruel to him in public; he took what she dished out. His friends needled him for being "pussy-whipped," and few of them either liked or trusted her. Says producer Rob Cohen, "She was a lynx-eyed beauty, but I found her cold, and I didn't feel like they were a good match. He was so sweet in many ways, and such a gentle person, and she just had that air of actor's ruthlessness about her, like she was gonna get to be a star no matter what it took. Their relationship was very volatile." Like Brooke Hayward on *Easy Rider*, and Marcia Lucas on *Star Wars*, she derided Spielberg's pictures, saying, "I know he's an incredible moviemaker, but the kind of films he makes aren't necessarily the kind I want to be in," and complained that "our social life was going out to dinner with studio heads."

STAR WARS went into production at Elstree Studios outside London on March 25, 1976. Lucas chose to shoot in London to get away from the studio and to save money, but right away he ran into trouble. His relationship with the cast and crew was prickly, to say the least. He was a proud man who would not beg for what he wanted. "George does not ask people more than once," says Howard Kazanjian, who was producer of *More American Graffiti*. "If you say no to him, you don't get asked a second time." George never said thank you, and the people who worked for him thought he was cold and remote. Most of the time he had no contact with them at all, didn't know who they were. Recalls Huyck, "When George and Gary Kurtz, who was also not Mr. Warmth, got to England, they offended the English crew because they just don't know how to deal with people." Lucas, looking back on the production later, observed, "I realized why directors are such horrible people, because you want things to be right, and people will just not listen to you, and there is no time to be nice, to be delicate. I spent all my time yelling and screaming at people."

Once again, George was not terribly helpful to the actors. The dialogue was awful. As Harrison Ford famously told him, "George, you can type this shit, but you sure can't say it." Lucas's kit bag of moves contained only two instructions: "O.K., same thing, only better"; "Faster, more intense."

Huyck and Katz visited their friend on the set in London. Recalls Katz, "George would sit on the edge of his bed every morning — he had these terrible foot infections. We would sit with him; we didn't think he would even make it to the set. We walked him around, tried to convince him not to kill himself. He was so disappointed he couldn't get anything he wanted, the crew was making fun of him. The cameraman was surly, would say, 'Bring the dawg in, put light on the dawg,' talking about Chewbacca. George kept saying, 'I just can't take this,' and we kept saying, 'Come on, George, you can do it, you can get up, you can get to the set.' He was really in a very fragile state. The final insult was the English crew voted the last day of the movie whether they were going to do overtime. They voted no. He hasn't directed since."

The problems that afflicted the script wouldn't go away. When Luke, Han, and Princess Leia were trapped on the Deathstar, George complained, "I got fifty storm troopers shooting at three people from ten feet away, and nobody ever gets hurt. Who's gonna believe this?"

Spielberg offered to shoot second unit on *Star Wars*, figure out a way for the storm troopers to die in a spume of green vapor. "George wouldn't let me," he remembers. "He was always more competitive with me than I was with him.

He kept saying, 'I'm sure *Star Wars* is going to beat *Jaws* at some point, or if not *Star Wars*, something else.' I was admiring and jealous of his style, his proximity to audiences. But he did not want my fingerprints anywhere around *Star Wars*." Spielberg put down Lucas because Lucas never moved his camera, just plunked it down on sticks and shot what happened in front of it.

When he returned from London, Lucas was about as depressed, upset, and bitter as his friends had ever seen him. He called it a $10 million trailer, kept saying, "I only got 30 percent, 30 percent." Initially, the plan was that Marcia would not edit *Star Wars;* she would take some time off, get pregnant. But she never did get pregnant, and George, unhappy with his English editor, who was cutting to create a campy effect, asked Marcia to take over. She was working on the climactic battle scenes at the end, when Scorsese called, shortly after Christmas 1976. His editor on *New York, New York* had died. "I'm fucked," he said. "I really need you. Could you come down to L.A. and help me out?" Says Paul Hirsch, who was cutting *Star Wars* with her, "Marcia respected Marty above all other directors, and didn't believe in *Star Wars* terribly much. It was not her thing." So she went. "She abandoned George to work on this serious, artistic film," says Katz. "For George, the whole thing was that Marcia was going off to this den of iniquity," adds Huyck. "Marty was wild and he took a lot of drugs and he stayed up late at night, had lots of girlfriends. George was a family homebody. He couldn't believe the stories that Marcia told him. George would fume because Marcia was running with these people. She loved being with Marty."

One day, Lucas stopped by Scorsese's editing room. In a rerun of the dispute over the ending of *Alice,* he told Marty that he could gross an additional $10 million if De Niro and Minnelli walked off into the sunset a happy couple instead of going their separate ways. "When I heard him say that, I knew I was doomed, that I would not make it in this business, that I cannot make entertainment pictures, I cannot be a director of Hollywood films," recalls Scorsese. " 'Cause I knew I wasn't going to do it. I knew that what the two characters had gone through in that film, I had gone through in my own life, and I knew I wouldn't be able to face myself or them if Bob and Liza were to go off together."

TO HIS CREDIT, Spielberg resisted studio pressure to do a sequel to *Jaws.* Sequels were considered déclassé, and for all his commercial inclinations, he was too much a child of the '70s to sully his hands with an exclusively pecuniary enterprise. Of course, Universal went ahead without him, and *Jaws* 2 became the first example — quickly followed by the *Rockys* — of a practice that would fly in the face of all that the New Hollywood stood for.

Close Encounters began principal photography in May 1976, about a month after Lucas started *Star Wars.* Spielberg was nervous. "I didn't think it was going to do well," he recalls. "I didn't know if I was the only person interested in UFOs. I didn't know if anyone in America could identify with a man who gives up his entire family, including his children, perhaps never to return." He had managed to land François Truffaut for the role of the scientist. Truffaut liked Spielberg, but condescended to him; he couldn't resist pointing out that Steven's favorite French directors were Claude Lelouch, best known for smarmy romances, and Robert Enrico, who made a couple of commercial pictures with Lino Ventura. He was also amused by the idea that Spielberg had seen Philippe de Broca's *That Man from Rio* nine times. In a letter to a friend, he wrote, "I knew that what he was after was a grand cartoon strip and that I could put back in my suitcase the book by Stanislavsky that I had bought for the occasion." Once, during production, when Steven was arguing with Vilmos Zsigmond, the DP is reputed to have said, pointing to Truffaut, "Why don't you turn the film over to a real director!"

The script for Spielberg's next film, *1941*, was already under way, written by the two Bobs, Zemeckis and Gale. It was a broad comedy about an abortive Japanese attack on L.A. during World War II. Spielberg brought the script to Tanen, at Universal. According to Spielberg, Tanen hated it, ranted and raged, yelling, "I asked for a shootable movie, not the battle plan for Europe," and threw it against the wall with such violence that the binding broke and the pages flew all over his office. "He frightened me," says Spielberg, who took it to Columbia, which was eager to have it.

Before *Close Encounters* went into production, Spielberg bought a sprawling home on Alto Cedro, off Cherokee in Coldwater Canyon. John Belushi used to call it the House of Fear, because of its vast size and intimidating gates. Steven loved toys, and installed video arcade games like Space Invaders, Pong, and Tank. The Alto Cedro house was decorated like the Hyatt Regency, down to the $40 Italian architecture books casually lying open on coffee tables to what guests suspected were carefully selected illustrations color coordinated with the rugs. One wall was covered with macramé "art." None of this was Steven, but he didn't much care, didn't have a personal aesthetic, personal taste, outside of what he guessed was cool, or what rich people had.

Spielberg's mother opened a kosher dairy restaurant in Beverly Hills, but her son avoided it. He disliked his stepfather, who was an Orthodox Jew. Some of his more Jewish-identified friends regarded him as a self-hating Jew. Director John Landis used to call him "Shmuel," his Hebrew name, to annoy him.

As his success and power increased, Spielberg became inordinately concerned with his own personal safety. He made it a practice never to accept packages through the mail. Picking up a cue from Watergate, he bought himself a shredder. He was one of the first of the movie brats to install an elaborate security system, and he traveled out of Beverly Hills with reluctance, worried about driving and parking his Porsche in, say, West Hollywood.

Spielberg was still seeing Irving, but the relationship was rocky. She visited him on the set, but he was preoccupied with the movie and had no time for her. She cried, and he apologized, saying, "Don't you understand, I'm fucking my movie." According to Rob Cohen, "Feminism was really coming into its own, and a lot of women were caught between a new spirit of independence and a desire to re-create the old Hollywood dynamic between men and women, where women were commodities of beauty and sexuality. If you were dating an actress, it was just presumed that one of the reasons she was dating you was you had the Jag XKE, and the job, and she was pretty and looked good in a halter top.

"On the one hand, there was all this easy sexuality, and on the other, there were these new kinds of women, young agents, young producers, and some actresses, who were writing a new script for themselves. Male-female relationships were extremely contentious, 'What makes you decide where we go on Friday night, I have work also, I have to go to this screening,' and so on. There were some really wild rides, on again, off again, angry, loving, vindictive, up and down — and Steve and Amy's was one of them."

Irving was afraid her career was going to be eclipsed by Spielberg's, and it made her resentful and angry. His friends felt she used her considerable powers of seduction to humiliate and undermine him. She would say she had a headache, didn't want to see him, and then go out with someone else. She was alleged to have gone to bed with Woody Allen and Dustin Hoffman. Later, rumors of Irving's affair with Willie Nelson during the shooting of *Honeysuckle Rose* reached the press, although she always denied them.

According to a friend, Steven complained that Amy had slept with Dustin Hoffman while he was casting *Straight Time*. The friend told Steven to get rid of her.

"Why? She fucked Dustin Hoffman?"

"No, because she came home and she told you about it. She did it to tell you, to hurt you, to leverage you, for some reason, she's manipulating you."

"Oh, Amy, you know, she's insecure, she needs to be reassured that she's talented . . ." (Irving denies sleeping with Hoffman.)

His friends thought she worked him. Says Gottlieb, "I could tell from her behavior when he wasn't on the scene, the way she talked to Penny Marshall and Carrie Fisher, that she had a fairly cynical take on their relationship. Basically, it was professionally useful. And that it was going to be very expensive for him to get out of it, and if it took having a child to cement that relationship, so be it."

But the guys always felt defensive when a new woman appeared on the scene and changed the chemistry. "I liked Amy," says Marcia Lucas. "Terrific gal, just tons of vulnerabilities." The fact of the matter was, Irving just didn't fit in, coming, as she did, from a considerably more sophisticated and intellectual background than Spielberg and his circle. Although she was able to delude herself about *The Fury*, she couldn't help recognizing the limitations of the kinds of films they were making. At the time, she said, "I'm glad I didn't do *Star Wars* because it was a nothing part. I would not want to get famous because of that movie."

Steven fooled around as well. He thumbed through John Casablanca's books looking for Elite models to date, a resource he had learned of through De Palma. Sometimes he told friends he didn't want to date actresses, wanted to find a regular girl, a teacher. It was hard to say who had the upper hand, Steven or Amy. It was evident to his friends that her infidelities hurt him. He adored her, which made him vulnerable. At the same time, he was coming up fast, had the big house, the cars, and Irving was still a struggling actress. Adds Marcia Lucas, "Amy was like the houseguest." She couldn't use the leverage his infatuation gave her, because, continues Marcia, "I don't think she felt she was worthy of that love."

In any event, Amy moved in, and the couple began to entertain. One young director he invited to dinner recalls that there was a large assemblage hanging over the dining room table, comprised of a parchment sheet music to which were affixed real instruments — violins, horns, and so on — the kind of thing that might decorate the lobby of a bank. One guest politely asked, "Who made it?" Steven astounded everyone by replying, "I did," while Amy rolled her eyes.

IN MARCH 1977, George and Marcia took a moment out to watch the Oscars. They had a rooting interest in *Taxi Driver*, which was up for Best Picture, along with *All the President's Men*, *Bound for Glory*, *Network*, and *Rocky*. Jodie Foster had been nominated for Best Supporting Actress. A few days before, Scorsese had received a letter threatening his life if Jodie won. It read something like, "If little Jodie wins on March 29 for what you made her do in *Taxi Driver*, you will pay with your life. I am serious. I am not a sicko. I love little Jodie. I would never do anything to hurt her. Never, never, never." Several years later, after John Hinckley shot Reagan, a couple of Marty's friends became convinced that he had sent it. "Without thinking, [Steve Prince] called the FBI after that letter came in," says Jonathan Taplin. "They smuggled the stash out before they got there." The coke was hidden in a thousand-foot can of raw stock sitting on a shelf in an editing room in plain view. FBI agents disguised as guests descended on Scorsese at the awards ceremony. Marty had his own agent, a woman in a gown with a gun in her bag. "Imagine ducking into the bathroom [for a few toots] with the FBI all over you," chuckles Taplin. (At the same time, Scorsese was also receiving death threats from members of the Manson family, after he had been asked to play Manson in a made-for-TV movie, *Helter Skelter*.)

Bound for Glory, which hadn't done very well at the box office, had gotten five nominations, including one for Best Picture. Wexler won for Best Cinematography. The threat against Scorsese said he would be killed a minute after midnight. Foster lost (to Beatrice Straight for *Network*), and Scorsese walked off into the night to the *New York, New York* editing rooms at MGM.

Lucas felt he was ready to screen *Star Wars*. The special effects weren't finished, and George had cut in black and white dogfights from old World War II films, but you got the general idea. Alan Ladd flew up to his home in San Anselmo; it was the first time he would be seeing anything. De Palma, Spielberg, Huyck and Katz, Cocks, and Scorsese met at the Burbank airport. It was foggy, and the flight to San Francisco was delayed. When it finally took off, Scorsese wasn't on board. He was as nervous about *Star Wars* as Lucas was about *New York, New York*. He hated flying, but Huyck and Katz thought, Well, he's very competitive, he really didn't want to see it, didn't want to know about the film. As Scorsese puts it, "You'd have the anxiety — if it's better than yours, or even if it isn't better than yours, you think it is. And your friends will tell you it is. And you believe it. For years."

The screening ended, there was no applause, just an embarrassed silence. Without the effects, the picture look ridiculous. Marcia was upset, said, "It's the *At Long Last Love* of science fiction. It's awful!" and started to cry. Katz took her aside and warned her, "Shhh! Laddie's watching — Marcia, just look cheery." Lucas felt like he'd failed, that it wouldn't cross over to adults. He kept repeating, "Only kids — I've made a Walt Disney movie, a cross between *Willy Wonka and the Chocolate Factory* and *The Computer Wore Tennis Shoes*. It's gonna do maybe eight, ten million." Several people just left, and those that remained went to eat at a Chinese restaurant. George was quiet in the car, a little shell-shocked.

As he picked over his dumplings, George asked, "All right, whaddya guys really think?" Brian started in on him, was merciless, as George took notes. In the cut they had seen, the Force was called the Force of Others. Brian said, "What's this Farts of Others? And the crawl at the beginning looks like it was written on a driveway. It goes on forever. It's gibberish." De Palma paused, looking at George to gauge the effect of his words, before continuing. "The first act, where are we? Who are these fuzzy guys? Who are these guys dressed up like the Tin Man from Oz? What kind of a movie are you making here? You've left the audience out — you've vaporized the audience. They don't know what's going on." He attacked Lucas for making an obscure movie that only pretended to be accessible. Recalls Katz, "Brian wouldn't let up, he was out of control. He was like a crazed dog. Marcia was getting angry at Brian, and she never forgot." George needled Brian in return: "You should talk, none of your films have made a dime. At least I've made some profit." They tried to rewrite the crawl so it made sense. "You gotta drop the Jedi Bendu shit, nobody's gonna know what you're talking about," continued De Palma, relentless. Katz thought, This is hopeless. It's never going to make any sense. George was ashen, but he was taking it all in, writing it all down.

Spielberg dissented, said, "George, it's great. It's gonna make $100 million." In those days, almost nothing made $100 million. Katz thought, Steve is a moron. Lucas said, "I promise you, *Close Encounters* will make four to five times more than *Star Wars*." Spielberg replied, "No, no, George, this time *I've* made the esoteric science fiction movie, you've made the crossover one." They made a bet with each other on the relative box office of *Star Wars* and *Close Encounters*, wrote the figures down on matchbook covers and traded them.

That night, Ladd called Spielberg. "What do we have here?" he asked. "Is *Star Wars* going to be any good, is anybody ever going to come see this movie?"

"It's gonna be a huge hit. You're gonna be the happiest film studio executive in Hollywood."

"How huge is huge?"

"At least $35 million in rentals. Maybe more."

At the end, the ILM folks were working around the clock, seven days a week, three shifts. "I remember the day I made a loop of the first shot we finished for Laddie," recalls Nelson. "It was about two seconds long, it was nothing, a shot of a starship going by real quick, so quick you couldn't even tell what it was. All this money spent, here's this one shot going around and around. He just sat there laughing. My hair was like dark when I started that movie. I came out of it totally gray." But for Lucas, it was too little, too late. He did not come to the wrap party, angering a lot of people who had worked very hard.

Like the other Bay Area filmmakers, Lucas had always been interested in sound. Over Fox's objections, he insisted on using Dolby Stereo. Says Walter Murch, "*Star Wars* was the can opener that made people realize not only the effect of sound, but the effect that good sound had at the box office. Theaters that had never played stereo were forced to do it if they wanted *Star Wars*."

With the effects and sound finally finished, Lucas screened it again at the Northpoint, just like *Graffiti*. Marcia had taken a week off from *New York, New York* to help George. "Previews always mean recutting," Lucas said gloomily, obviously thinking about THX and *Graffiti*, and anticipating the worst. The suits were there, Ladd and his executives. Marcia had always said, "If the audience doesn't cheer when Han Solo comes in at the last second in the Millennium Falcon to help Luke when he's being chased by Darth Vader, the picture doesn't work." From the opening shot of the majestic Imperial Starship drifting over the heads of the audience across the black vastness of space studded with stars blinking like diamonds, the place was electric. "They made the jump to hyperspace, and you could see bodies flying around the room in excitement," recalls Hirsch. "When they get to that shot where the

Millennium Falcon appears at the last minute, not only did they cheer, they stood up in their seats and raised their arms like a home run in the ninth inning of the seventh game of the World Series. I looked over at Marcia, and she gave me a look like, I guess it works, ya know? So we came out, I said to George, 'So whaddya think?' He said, 'I guess we won't recut it after all.' " Still, the signs were mixed. Word got back that when the picture was screened for the ratings board, several people fell asleep.

George made plans to be out of town, in Hawaii with Marcia and the Huycks for the opening of *Star Wars*, the way he was when *Graffiti* premiered. He was still afraid the movie was going to be a huge embarrassment. His attitude was, "I've done everything I can do, it is what it is. I'm not going to read a review, I'm not going to talk to anyone from the studio." They were leaving on a Saturday. The Wednesday before, May 25, 1977, they were both still working at Goldwyn, Marcia on *New York, New York*, during the day, and George at night, on the monaural track. The only time they ever saw each other was when she was leaving and he was just arriving — for dinner. They were both so exhausted they had forgotten Wednesday night was the premiere of *Star Wars*, and went to the Hamburger Hamlet that happened to be directly across from the Chinese Theater on Hollywood Boulevard. They didn't notice anything going on, and it wasn't until they were seated that they looked out through the windows onto the street and saw a commotion in front of the theater. "There were people all over the place, like a thousand people, two lanes of the street were closed off, there were limos out in front, it was just amazing," recalls Lucas. But they still couldn't see the marquee. When they finally finished and emerged from the restaurant, they recognized the distinctive *Star Wars* logo. As soon as George got to work, Ladd was on the phone, said, "The film's a hit, the first screenings are great." Lucas replied, "Look, Laddie, science fiction movies, they always open big, but it doesn't really count until we get to the second or third week. So let's not get too excited about this." Then he and Marcia went to Maui.

By the time they got to the hotel, their box was stuffed with messages from Fox. They said, "Watch the six o'clock news." George and Marcia and Willard and Gloria crowded in front of the TV and saw Walter Cronkite report that the lines were around the block. Lucas couldn't believe it. They figured, We're rich, we're rich. The next day they went into town trying to spend some of their future earnings, but they were in Hawaii; the only thing they could buy was suntan lotion and shells. George said, "You know, these yogurt things are really going to take off, maybe I'll buy a yogurt franchise." He wanted to return to California to enjoy his success, but he couldn't, because he had made such a big point of saying, "I don't care what happens, I'm above all this crap." Coppola, who was looking for financing to finish *Apocalypse Now*, sent him a telegram that said, "Send Money. Francis." After a week or so, the Huycks left, and Spielberg arrived with Amy. George and Steven built sand castles on the beach, talked about an idea that would become *Raiders of the Lost Ark*. George would produce, and Steven, whom he had once looked down on because he worked inside the system, would direct. Spielberg hadn't changed. Had Lucas?

Soon after *Star Wars* opened, Cocks was at director Jeremy Kagan's house. Harrison Ford arrived, totally disheveled, his shirt half ripped off, looking like William Holden in *Picnic*. "Jesus, Harrison, what happened?" asked Cocks. "I went into Tower Records to buy an album, and these people jumped on me."

THE *SORCERER* TRAILER Bud Smith cut played in front of *Star Wars* at the Chinese Theater. Says Smith, "When our trailer faded to black, the curtains closed and opened again, and they kept opening and opening, and you started feeling this huge thing coming over your shoulder overwhelming you, and heard this noise, and you went right off into space. It made our film look like this little, amateurish piece of shit. I told Billy, 'We're fucking being blown off the screen. You gotta go see this.'"

Friedkin went with his new wife, French actress Jeanne Moreau. Afterward, he fell into conversation with the manager of the theater. Nodding his head toward the river of humanity cascading through the theater's doors, the man said, "This film's doing amazing business."

"Yeah, and my film's going in in a week," replied Billy nervously.

"Well, if it doesn't work, this one'll go back in again."

"Jesus!" Friedkin looked like he had been punched in the stomach. He turned to Moreau, said, "I dunno, little sweet robots and stuff, maybe we're on the wrong horse." A week later, *Sorcerer* did follow *Star Wars* into the Chinese. Dark and relentless, especially compared to Lucas's upbeat space opera, it played to an empty house, and was unceremoniously pulled to make room for the return of C3PO et al.

Sorcerer was a major disaster, grossing only a piddling $9 million worldwide. Friedkin was dumbstruck. He could not believe the public didn't like it. He could not believe the critics didn't like it. Says Smith, "He probably put more into *Sorcerer* than any other film he'd ever done—time, energy, labor, and thought." The picture is punctuated by some striking images, but it is self-consciously arty and pretentious, ironic in view of the way Friedkin had once put down film art in favor of commercialism, derided Coppola and Bogdanovich for their artistic aspirations.

Friedkin says now, "I probably shouldn't have done *Sorcerer*, 'cause it was written to be a star-driven vehicle, and there were no stars in it. I made a big mistake with McQueen. I didn't realize that the close-up is more important than the wide shot. A shot of Steve's face was worth more than any landscape I could have shot. That was great hubris on my part. But the mere fact that the studio didn't want me to make it kept me persevering and overlooking all of these things."

Fatally trapped between America and Europe, commerce and art, Friedkin had finally achieved the worst of both worlds, an American remake of a French classic that was too episodic, dark, and star-challenged for a late '70s American audience that was very different from the audience that flocked to *The French Connection*. Like many Hollywood directors of the '70s, he wanted to be Godard, Bergman, or Antonioni, but he was never able to find an idiom that melded American subjects with a European sensibility, the way Beatty and Penn had with *Bonnie and Clyde*, Bogdanovich with *The Last Picture Show*, or Rafelson with *Five Easy Pieces*.

Nairn-Smith had met Jules Stein and his wife, now in their eighties, through Friedkin, but they'd remained friends after the split. She would see them at the home of Mervyn and Kitty LeRoy. "The four of them would be sitting there talking about their plots at Forest Lawn," she recalls. Every time he'd see her Stein would say, "Your William cost me $20 million." And then he died. Adds Friedkin, "For a while I was regularly invited to Wasserman's house, but then, after *Sorcerer*, that stopped."

Friedkin took refuge on Jeanne Moreau's farm in the south of France. They had been married in February, in Paris. Burstyn read about it in a magazine. "I thought I was still going out with him," she recalls. "He didn't tell me. Let's say, he auditioned us both, and she got the part." The marriage made a certain amount of sense, at least from his side. If he couldn't wed Clouzot or Truffaut, Moreau, the star of so many Nouvelle Vague films, was the next best thing. After he took her out for the first time, he said, "God, I've wanted her ever since I saw *Les Amants* [*The Lovers*]." He liked older women, perhaps a residue of his attachment to his mother. In 1977, Friedkin was forty-three, Moreau fifty. He worked, she cooked. When they were together, he would pull her down into his lap, kiss her breasts, and say, "Jeen, Jeen," in his atrocious French accent.

NEW YORK, NEW YORK opened on June 21. It was a darker movie than UA wanted. They thought it was going to be some sort of breakthrough musical of the old MGM school. Marty refused to change a frame. He was stubborn, and convinced of his own vision. The picture didn't fare much better than *Sorcerer*. The plot was ragged and desultory, overwhelmed by the big, static production numbers. Even the critics, whom Scorsese had always been able to count on, deserted him. The lukewarm reception of *New York, New York* devastated him. He had gone from hit to hit. This was his first taste of failure, and he didn't like it. He says, "I was angry, especially about being treated as if I had gotten a comeuppance — for what? For making *Mean Streets? Alice* and *Taxi Driver?* It wasn't the criticism, it was a lack of respect, so what I did was to behave in such a way that you could be guaranteed no respect at all." Later he admitted, "I was just too drugged out to solve the structure." He was put on lithium in an effort to dampen his anger and control his violent outbursts. He took it for four months, but his drug of choice remained coke. It was as if he were lost in another world, Luke Skywalker stumbling about the ice planet Hoth in the opening scene of *The Empire Strikes Back,* lost in a blizzard of snow.

Not even De Niro could bring him back. He was still carrying around his well-thumbed copy of Jake La Motta's book, which he brought to Irwin Winkler. Winkler agreed to produce it, if they could get Marty to commit. But De Niro had a hard time getting his attention. Scorsese read a couple of chapters, gave the book to Mardik. He had no interest in boxing, never went to fights. Besides, La Motta wasn't much of a boxer. His singular talent lay in his ability to absorb punishment. Mardik read it, told Scorsese, "The trouble with *Raging Bull* is that the damn thing has been done a hundred times — a fighter who has trouble with his brother and his wife, and the mob is after him. I don't want to do another brother-fighter story because that was done in *Champion.* And *Rocky* is out, same company. Same producers! Plus, I think this book is full of shit. It's made-up stuff, looks like a PR job."

Scorsese, depressed, was more than willing to be discouraged. All the New Hollywood directors believed that being an auteur meant making personal movies. If they didn't generate their own material, they couldn't proceed until somehow they had made it their own. Through his affair with Cybill Shepherd, Bogdanovich experienced the vertigo of adolescence, which was the subject of *The Last Picture Show.* Francis Coppola *became* the Godfather. "I really didn't want to do *Raging Bull,*" Scorsese says. "I had to find the key for myself. And I wasn't interested in finding the key, because I'd tried something, *New York, New York,* and it was a failure."

WHEN EVERYTHING WAS IN, *Star Wars* cost only $9.5 million, with an additional couple of million for prints, ads, and publicity. It took in over $100 million in only three months. The novelization, released quietly by Bantam, reached number four on the paperback best-seller list, selling two million copies by August 25. In November, *Star Wars* bested *Jaws* to become the biggest money-maker of all time, racking up an astounding $193.5 million in rentals.

Star Wars made Lucas's friends rich, or at least some of them: Huyck and Katz had gotten two points. He gave out quarter points to Ford, Fisher, Hamill, and sound wizard Ben Burtt. The point trading had reached such a pitch that Lucas gave Milius points in *Star Wars* in exchange for points in *Big Wednesday,* which he was prepping. *Big Wednesday* was supposed to put Milius on the map. He was Mr. Surfer, and if anyone could capture that scene, it was presumably Milius. (Spielberg gave him a point on *CE3K* in exchange for one on *Big Wednesday*, as well.) Pollock, speaking as Lucas's lawyer, said, "Why are you doing this? You're going to feel like an idiot." George's response was, "Look, the studios are going to cheat us out of everything anyway, what's the difference, it'll give us all a rooting interest in each other's movies." (Later, after *Big Wednesday* flopped, Lucas asked for his points back.)

Ironically, Lucas was not pleased with ILM, and punished the effects crew by passing them over. Nelson did not get any points, nor did Dykstra, although some people got bonuses. Nelson and Dykstra were furious. Dykstra left to start his own company, taking much of the staff with him. Lucas moved the remaining six or so loyalists up north to Marin County.

When it was clear *Star Wars* was going to be a gigantic hit, Lucas came to Coppola, said, "Oh, I'm gonna have all this money, we can do all the dreams we always wanted to, and I want to do it with you."

"Well, George, you wait until you get the dough, and then see if you still feel that way." George took him to a few meetings. They talked about buying the Mann theaters, had a great deal on them, $25 million. They talked about buying Fox. "But now I was clearly in the subordinate position," says Coppola, "and then about six months later there was less of that talk, and then there was a period of falling out. I never understood what it was about."

Coppola wasn't the only one. The money changed everything. Says Milius, of Spielberg as well as Lucas, "These guys got too good for everyone. Everybody got very, very distant. George had his entourage around him. Could do no wrong. Everything was for George. And Steven you can't talk to. He's not a human being anymore."

Star Wars put Fox on the map. Suddenly, Ladd was a genius. He had seen something in Lucas's *Star Wars* script where no one else had. Like Calley, Tanen, and Evans, Ladd wanted to attract talented directors, and the *Star Wars* profits made it possible for Ladd to shelter Altman during the second half of the decade.

Buffalo Bill and the Indians had been a major disappointment for Altman. It had a hefty budget, a big star (Paul Newman), and an interesting cast, but still it flopped. Even Kael didn't like it. One problem may have been that when Altman did use stars — witness his treatment of Beatty in *McCabe* — he still couldn't curb his subversive instincts. He somehow neglected to introduce Newman until the second reel, and then withheld close-ups of the famous blue eyes and grin.

But Ladd admired him. Once, Altman and Tommy Thompson were driving to the airport when Altman said, "Let's stop at Twentieth. I had a dream last night, I want to sell it to Laddie. Keep the engine running, it'll only take a minute." Altman darted into Ladd's office, made a deal for 3 *Women*, and was back in the car in time to make the flight. "Ladd left me totally alone," he says. "When we finished 3 *Women*, I showed it to him and a bunch of guys in the studio. The lights came up and he said, 'Well, I don't know who you think you're going to sell this picture to, but good luck.'" Of course, the economics more or less made sense from the studio's point of view, because Altman worked nonunion and kept his budgets low. He made 3 *Women*, *A Wedding*, *H.E.A.L.T.H.*, *Quintet*, and *A Perfect Couple* for Fox, all for next to nothing. (*A Perfect Couple* cost only $1.5 million.) In Florida, when he was shooting *H.E.A.L.T.H.*, he was threatened with a Teamster picket. He proceeded to publish the cast and crew salaries in the local newspaper, showing the Teamster drivers at the top of the list.

But the same success that gave Ladd new power, qualified it as well. As Spielberg puts it, "If you're the executive, suddenly you realize that if you're going to go into business with George Lucas, you are no longer in the 20th Century-Fox business, you are in the George Lucas business, and George is going to call every shot. You lose the power to say 'No, I don't like this, I'd like you to change it.'"

In case Ladd didn't get it, Lucas quickly drove the point home with the stingingly punitive deal he demanded for the *Star Wars* sequel, *The Empire Strikes Back*. Having seized the baton from his mentor Coppola, Lucas's grand plan envisioned financial independence from the studios. He wanted to finance *Empire* himself, and insisted on 50, and then an unprecedented 77 percent of the gross after a specified threshold had been reached, ownership of the negative, and TV and merchandising rights. He enjoyed sticking it to the studio, explaining, "I got screwed in the beginning and now I'm able to do it to them."

Star Wars drove home the lessons of *Jaws*, that kids and young adults would come back again and again to a movie without stars. But unlike *Jaws*, it showed that a phenomenally successful movie could be made from original material. It woke up the studios to the potential of merchandising, showed that the sale of books, T-shirts, and action figures could be a significant profit center. *Star Wars*'s merchandising efforts, instead of merely promoting the movie, as had been the case in the past, took on a life of their own and sucked up well over $3 billion in licensing fees as of the re-release of the *Star Wars* trilogy in 1997, adding an incentive to replace complex characters with simple figures that could be turned into toys.

Beyond its impact on movie marketing and merchandising, *Star Wars* had a profound effect on the culture. It benefited from the retrenchment of the Carter years, the march to the center that followed the end of the Vietnam War. As Lucas was the first to notice, audiences were exhausted by the Sturm und Drang of the '60s, tired of being actors on a historical stage, exciting though that may have been for a while. As the pundits of the time put it, the activists of the '60s turned to cultivating their own gardens. In an omnibus review entitled "Fear of Movies," Kael echoed Lucas, but drew the opposite conclusions. She too noticed a reaction against the violence; people were tired of movies "that are all car crashes and killings and perversity," she wrote. "Discriminating moviegoers want the placidity of *nice* art — of movies tamed so that they are no more arousing than what used to be called polite theater. So we've been getting a new cultural puritanism — people go to the innocuous hoping for the charming, or they settle for imported sobriety, and the press is full of snide references to Coppola's huge film in progress. . . ." And there was no nicer art than *Star Wars*, which reestablished the family film.

Blockbusters have to offer something for everyone, and like *The Godfather*, like *The Exorcist*, like *Jaws*, *Star Wars* did so, sending mixed, often contradictory messages to both the left and the right, the boomers who had lived through Vietnam, and the next generation, the baby baby boomers for whom the war was only a fading memory. On the one hand, despite the famous fairy-tale crawl at the beginning of *Star Wars* — "the galaxy far away" — Lucas's picture was not so far from Vietnam as it appeared. Lucas was personally rather conservative — cautious, drug-resistant, and essentially apolitical — but his deep-seated anti-authoritarianism and his battles with the studios inevitably branded him a child of the counterculture, of Carlos Castaneda and Tom Hayden. If, as he insisted, the Emperor was Nixon, his trilogy could be taken as a distanced, but nevertheless transparent allegory of the tumultuous decade in which the director had come of age. The vast, powerful Empire could only be the United States (more specifically, Hollywood), and the raggedy band of rebels, with their improvised, patchwork, rubberband and chewing gum weapons, the Vietcong (or the New Hollywood movie brats). What was subtext in *Star Wars* became text in the Moon of Endor sequence in *Return of the Jedi*, where the furry little Ewoks deep in the forest carry on guerrilla warfare with sticks and stones against Imperial Walkers and whatnot — the power of the people triumphant against the man's technology, as the slogan went in the '60s.

On the other hand, this Luddite strain in the *Star Wars* story existed cheek by jowl with the cold, clean, high-tech look of the film itself. As Milius rightly put it, *Star Wars* "brought kids out of the residue of the counterculture and interested them in American technology again."

Moreover, whereas the most sophisticated directors of the '70s, like Altman, Penn, Scorsese, and Hopper, were deconstructing genre, Lucas, like Spielberg, was doing the reverse, gentrifying discredited genres of the past, in this case by yoking the dazzling special effects Kubrick pioneered in *2001* to the matinee serials of the '30s, thereby revitalizing them.

Lucas knew that genres and cinematic conventions depend on consensus, the web of shared assumptions that had been sundered in the '60s. He was re-creating and reaffirming these values, and *Star Wars*, with its Manichaean moral fundamentalism, its white hats and black hats, restored the luster to threadbare values like heroism and individualism. At the same time, after half a decade of character- or theme-driven movies, unhappy endings, fractured narratives riven by flashbacks and psychedelic dream sequences, Lucas reasserted the pleasures of straightforward, unironic storytelling, along with accessible two-dimensional characters whose adventures ended happily. As Ladd put it, Lucas "showed people it was all right to become totally involved in a movie again; to yell and scream and applaud and really roll with it." Lucas insisted that the actors deliver the improbable dialogue straight, without mugging or snickering. As he said, "It wasn't camp, it was not making fun of itself." Again, Milius summed it up: "What my generation has done is bring back a certain innocence. . . . It's easy to be cynical. It's hard to be corny."

But even the revitalization of narrative wasn't the point of *Star Wars*. True, the set pieces were strung like beads along an easy-to-see thread, but it was the beads, not the thread, that was the point. As Lucas puts it, "I'm an advocate of pure cinema. I'm not that interested in narrative. The dialogue doesn't have much meaning in any of my movies. I'm very much of a visual filmmaker, and very much of a filmmaker who is going for emotions over ideas."

Lucas and Spielberg were only six and seven years younger than Coppola, but they might as well have been on a galaxy far away. For one thing, Coppola was largely raised in New York, and if New York Gothamized Hollywood in the '70s, Lucas and Spielberg were in the vanguard of the counterattack by small-town and suburban values that were to reclaim Hollywood as their own. Moreover, Coppola was a child of the written word, drama and the novel. When he was helping Lucas write *THX*, he urged him to use Shakespearean themes, which he himself would employ to brilliant effect in the *Godfather*s, as he would turn to Joseph Conrad for *Apocalypse Now*. Lucas and Spielberg, on the other hand, had little use for literary tropes. "I love to tell the story graphically, not with people saying words," Lucas explains. "Words are great in the theater, but that's not movies."

Lucas's genius was to strip away the Marxist ideology of a master of editing like Eisenstein, or the critical irony of an avant-garde filmmaker like Bruce Conner, and wed their montage technique to American pulp. *Star Wars* pioneered the cinema of moments, of images, of sensory stimuli increasingly divorced from story, which is why it translates so well into video games. Indeed, the movie leapt ahead — through hyperspace, if you will — to the '80s and '90s, the era of non-narrative music videos, and VCRs, which allowed users to view film in a non-narrative way, surfing the action beats with fast-forward.

When all was said and done, Lucas and Spielberg returned the '70s audience, grown sophisticated on a diet of European and New Hollywood films, to the simplicities of the pre-'60s Golden Age of movies, the era Lucas had memorialized so well in *Graffiti*. They marched backward through the looking glass, producing pictures that were the mirror opposite of the New Hollywood films of their peers. They were, as Kael first pointed out, infantilizing the audience, reconstituting the spectator as child, then overwhelming him and her with sound and spectacle, obliterating irony, aesthetic self-consciousness, and critical reflection. So thoroughly did *Star Wars* redraw the landscape of popular cinema, so thoroughly did it make the future safe for itself that the trilogy could, in 1997, be re-released in two thousand theaters and gross $250 million. The simultaneous re-release of *The Godfather,* an immeasurably better picture, paled in comparison. We are the children of Lucas, not Coppola.

Simply put, the success of *Star Wars,* coupled with the failure of *New York, New York,* meant that the kind of movies Scorsese made were replaced by the kind of movies Lucas (and Spielberg) made. Says Scorsese, "*Star Wars* was in. Spielberg was in. We were finished." And Milius, "When I was at USC, people were flocking to *Blow-Up,* not going to the theaters to be jolted by a cheap amusement park ride. But [Lucas and Spielberg] showed there was twice as much money out there, and the studios couldn't resist that. No one had any idea you could get as rich as this, like ancient Rome. You can clearly blame them." And Friedkin, "*Star Wars* swept all the chips off the table. What happened with *Star Wars* was like when McDonald's got a foothold, the taste for good food just disappeared. Now we're in a period of devolution. Everything has gone backward toward a big sucking hole."

Naturally enough, Lucas rejects the idea that *Star Wars* ruined American movies, and puts a Reagan-era trickle-down spin on the situation, arguing, somewhat contradictorily, that movies are better than ever. "*Star Wars* didn't kill the film industry, or infantilize it," he says. "Popcorn pictures have always ruled. Why do people go see these popcorn pictures when they're not good? Why is the public so stupid? That's not my fault. I just understood what people liked to go see, and Steven has too, and we go for that." Blockbusters subsidize serious smaller films, much the way *Star Wars* allowed Ladd to make a home for Altman. "People forget that there's an ecology, a loop of symbiotic relationships that exists in the film business where you need movies that make a lot of money in order to finance the ones that don't make money," Lucas continues. "Of the billion and a half dollars that *Star Wars* made, half of it, $700 million of it, went to the theater owners. And what did the theater owners do with that? They built multiplexes. Once they had all these screens, they had to book them with something, which meant that the art films that were being shown in tiny places in the middle of nowhere, suddenly were playing in mainstream cinemas, and started making money. And once they started making money, you got Miramax and Fine Line, and the studios got interested, and so now you have this really thriving American art film industry that didn't exist twenty years ago. So in a way, I did destroy the Hollywood film industry, only I destroyed it by making films more intelligent, not by making films infantile."

Scorsese and Altman take a darker view. "They're not subsidizing everything else," says Scorsese. "They are it. That's all. The person who has something to say in a movie has got to make a picture for $50. They're smothering everything." And Altman, "Last summer trying to find a picture to see, I went to the two multiplexes in Beverly Hills. Every single screen was playing *Lost World*, *Con Air*, *My Best Friend's Wedding*, and *Face/Off*. There wasn't one picture that an intelligent person could say, 'Oh, I want to see this.' It's just become one big amusement park. It's the death of film."

Marcia Lucas concurs. "Right now, I'm just disgusted by the American film industry. There are so few good films, and part of me thinks *Star Wars* is partly responsible for the direction the industry has gone in, and I feel badly about that."

Twelve:
Coming Apart
1979

● *How Coppola returned from his heart of darkness with* **Apocalypse Now,** *nearly leaving his sanity behind, while Ashby came home and Beatty finally seduced Kael.*

"*Everyone was against me. I was doing something on a subject no one dared touch with my own money, and I was getting all this flak. I collapsed.*"

— FRANCIS COPPOLA

Francis Coppola was not altogether impressed by Lucas's space opera. He disliked the script, disliked the rough cut, said the gunplay was boring. His pal from the UCLA days, Dennis Jakob, coined the phrase "twerp cinema" for the movies of Lucas and Spielberg. During a car ride a few days after Francis and his friends saw *Star Wars*, someone scoffed, " 'The Force be with you,' what a crock." Francis was in the throes of *Apocalypse Now*, a film that seemed as far from Lucas's picture as you could get, a film about the Vietnam War, a subject that was still too sensitive for Hollywood to touch. Jakob turned to Francis and said, over and over, "Francis, it's all up to you now, you're the only one." It was as if Coppola, the last man standing, had inherited the historical obligation of the New Hollywood — to make cinematic art of the seminal event of their generation. Never one to shrug off the hand of history, Francis willingly embraced this destiny, for if not he, who? After all, he had shown the way; his entire career had been no more than a preamble to this project, combining, as it did, his talents as a showman, a producer, an artist. Still, it was a heavy burden. Francis struggled with it, faltered under it, and although he produced a masterpiece, albeit flawed, he was never the same.

●

ON MARCH 1, 1976, Coppola, accompanied by his family, finally left for the Philippines for what was expected to be a fourteen-week shoot. Dean Tavoularis had picked out locations all over the jungle island of Luzon, and the idea was that they would simply hop from location to location. This required the production to rely on air transportation, assumed that the Philippines had a modern, efficient airline system like that of the United States. But such was not the case, and the mountains were dangerous for helicopters. Moreover, the rivers were so treacherous that the boatmen who ferried around the location scouts wore T-shirts with numbers on the back to make it easier to identify them if they drowned. During the scout, one crew member told Coppola, "Don't come here, it's dangerous. Go to Australia, go to Thailand, go to Stockton! You're talking about building a $20 million set. This is November. On May 15, the first typhoon's gonna hit, and it's gonna rain until October 15. The water rises fifty feet. The sets are going to be washed out to sea." Coppola said, "What're you, a fuckin' weatherman?" He simply didn't want to hear it.

It was a hellish shoot, the difficulties compounded by Coppola's arrogance. The logistics were impossible, and he went through assistant directors like Kleenex. The first were Italians, hired for their ability to communicate with DP Vittorio Storaro's crew, but they fell behind immediately. Coppola fired them, and sent for David Lean's first AD on *The Bridge on the River Kwai*. In the meantime, he improvised. Jonathan Reynolds, a writer pal there maybe to write a "making of" book, had rarely, if ever, been on a set before. Francis made him first AD of this enormous production. When Lean's guy finally arrived, it turned out he was too old to do the job. (*Kwai* was made in 1957.) As actor Fred Forrest, who played Chef, put it, "In the movie, when Martin Sheen walks up to that guy in the trench and says, 'Who's the commanding officer here?' And the guy says, 'Ain't you?' — that was the essence of *Apocalypse Now*. We didn't know who was in charge, man."

The conditions were so bad that the cast and crew partied like it was their last day on earth. The Philippines had long been the home of the U.S. Seventh Fleet, headquartered at Subic Bay, so that hookers, drugs, and booze were easy to come by, almost as cheap as air. When actor Sam Bottoms arrived at the building that housed the production office in Manila, he noticed a massage parlor on the first floor. "You could go in there and get jerked off for five bucks," he recalls.

Coppola treated himself like a potentate, replicating America's intervention in the Third World in more ways than one. He enjoyed the finest of creature comforts: the best wine, Lalique crystal, stereo equipment, cooking utensils, and shoes. Not all of this was entirely his fault. He was convinced, with some reason, that *Apocalypse Now* was a major artistic event, and he surrounded himself with true believers whose job it was to serve Francis and his vision. Money was no object. If Francis made an offhand remark about champagne glasses from Tiffany, they were sure to arrive in the next shipment from San Francisco. No one wanted to incur Coppola's wrath. The practice on the set was, when in doubt, buy it!

On the eighth of April, one day after his thirty-seventh birthday, he had a party on the beach near the location. Three hundred Americans, Filipinos, and Vietnamese extras were invited to consume hundreds of pounds of hamburgers and hot dogs flown in from San Francisco. The cake was six by eight feet, decorated with mountains, a river, an ocean with waves of icing, palm trees, and so on. The shipping and duty alone for the food came to $8,000.

No sooner did Coppola finally sort out the AD situation than he decided to fire his lead actor, Harvey Keitel, just before Easter, and replace him with Martin Sheen. Sheen arrived at the Philippine location on April 24, to find chaos. All the Keitel footage had to be reshot.

Francis was rewriting the script as he went along. As he had often done in the past, he was finding the film as he was making it. This was all very well with the inexpensive *Rain People*, but courting disaster with a $20 million production in the jungle. Perhaps taking a cue from the laborers who were carving out a swimming pool at his temporary home in Manila with their bare hands, Coppola was digging a very deep hole for himself—aided by all the technology at his disposal. Storaro was a laid-back guy who went with the flow. Without the gravitational pull exercised by a strong personality like Willis, Francis just spun off into space.

KEITEL SEGUED into *Fingers* for Jim Toback, and then *Blue Collar*, for Paul Schrader. Schrader was still trying to figure out how to move from writing to directing. The studios were not lining up to give him a directing gig, and he felt burned out. Once again, it was his brother, Leonard, who came up with the idea, and he drew on their shared childhood in Grand Rapids. They grew up around Polish autoworkers whom Leonard had always wanted to write about. "I saw how to do this story, the same as *The Yakuza*, two guys, one black, one white, from different traditions, but both stuck in blue-collar autoworker jobs," recalls Leonard. But he couldn't come up with a plot. "Then one day I came across the Lordstown, Ohio, strike, the Chevy Vega plant," he continues. "All the autoworkers were under twenty-five, they were not interested in what the union had done for dad and grandpa. What it had done for them was nothing. They called their own strike, and the union told them they better get back to work. 'Yes, we hate management, but you know who we hate worse? Our union. It betrays us.' Never seen a movie about that before."

According to Leonard, Paul couldn't have cared less about autoworkers. It was more, "You mean I can get money for this?" There was no way Steve McQueen was going to work for him, but nobody had been able to find a script for Richard Pryor, who was very hot as a standup comic. The Schraders set to work. Leonard wrote and Paul polished. They had a hard time raising money, with two black leads and one white. Recalls Leonard, "All the investors said, 'You've made a mistake, there's supposed to be two white and one black, this is America.' We said, 'No, no . . .' It almost never got made for that reason."

Once again, Leonard got much less than Paul. They split the script fee, $100,000 or so, but Paul got approximately $200,000 for directing, so he ended up with $250,000 to Leonard's $50,000. And once again, the name of the game was sacrifice in the interest of Paul's directing career. This made perfect sense to Paul, who still had a hard time regarding Leonard as an equal. "I broke the structure down, and I described the scenes to him," Paul recalls. "I would say, 'Write this scene, he says this, she says this, blah, blah . . . in four or five pages and bring it back tomorrow.' In a word, I was using him as an employee." Once the shooting started, Paul didn't want Leonard on the set. The experience further alienated the two brothers.

Schrader had hired Harold Schneider to line-produce. Harold put a vial of white powder on Schrader's desk, saying, "Try this, it'll make you work better." Schrader, who would become a major cokehead a few years later, was shocked.

The set was a powder keg, with homicidal competition between Pryor and co-star Yaphet Kotto, the two of them arrayed against the other lead, Keitel, and all of them sparking with Paul. Coming from the writing end, this man who could barely communicate with his friends had no idea how to handle actors. "There's a kind of anger I have which tends to create a tense environment," he says. "My psychiatrist pointed this out to me years ago. He said, 'Just the way you speak creates tension. The way you withhold words. The way you spit words. You unrelax people."

To get them to commit, Paul had assured each actor he was the star of the movie. Once the shooting started, each one thought he was playing second fiddle to the others and concluded he had been lied to — not far from the truth. According to Schrader, "Richard was starting to coke up again. He was in this whole mode of, I'm gonna be the sidekick to Terry Malloy, you set me up to be the funny nigger, while Harvey's take on it was just the opposite: I'm gonna be Ed McMahon to his Johnny Carson. So they wouldn't talk to each other. Right after you said, 'Cut,' a fight would start." Continues Paul, "After about three weeks in, all of a sudden I started crying, and I just couldn't stop. Richard looked at me and said, 'You pussy — are you gonna be a man or not?'"

In the fall, his down-and-dirty *Blue Collar* was nearly finished. Says editorial assistant Janice Hampton, "I always thought Paul was trying to be Marty. He had the asthma, the 'ludes, the coke." With only the credits remaining to be shot, according to Toback, Schrader, drunk, confided to him at a party, 'Ya know, I could actually fuck my brother out of a credit on this, and I was thinking about it, but then I thought, If you fuck your brother, who won't you fuck.' He was like waiting to be patted on the back because he wasn't gonna fuck his brother." Universal effectively dumped the picture, but Paul got plenty of good reviews. And indeed, the picture was raw and powerful, one of the few unsparing and politically sophisticated portrayals of blue-collar life in America. Schrader was a director.

COPPOLA HAD ONCE TOLD LUCAS that the shock of sudden success "is no different from the shock of death, and when you come out of it, you're a different person." Recalls Nancy Tonery, the script supervisor who had been with Coppola since the first *Godfather*, "His personality had changed. Something happened to him either before or during the filming in the Philippines. He was no longer bound by any normal conventions. Francis would tread on anyone he could tread on. Anytime anybody had his belly full or annoyed Francis, he or she would be fired. There was a constant parade of people coming and going. Each time anybody left, the next person wouldn't come for any less than twice as much as his predecessor had been making."

Ellie was alarmed that her husband was identifying with the demonic Kurtz, rather than with the relatively benign Willard. Coppola always had a nasty temper, and nothing inhibited him from publicly humiliating those closest to him, cursing, yelling, tearing doors off hinges. Fred Roos had been the whipping boy on *Godfather II*, and with the pressure of *Apocalypse*, this kind of behavior got worse. One day Coppola threw a two-by-four at Gray Frederickson, one of the producers. Says *Godfather* producer Al Ruddy, who was a good friend of Frederickson's, "Francis didn't pay anyone anything. And he treated these guys — Gray and Fred Roos — like they were like fuckin' slaves. But, hey, if you buy into 'he's the emperor and he can do what the hell he wants,' then you gotta take it."

Muslim rebels were battling Ferdinand Marcos in the south, and the Philippine strongman was convinced that they were going to bomb Manila airport at night, when it was lit up, so he closed it down every day at sundown. Consequently, aircraft were not allowed to fly after dark. One evening, the sun had set, and Francis's pilot refused to take off in his Mitsubishi. Francis went ballistic. The pilot just shrugged, said, "It's your plane, you fly it." Francis took his brand-new, state-of-the-art miniature Nagra NSN tape recorder that he had purchased in Hong Kong, threw it to the ground and stomped on it with his heel. Then, regarding it mournfully, he said, "I'm sorry, I've killed my little Nagra."

Coppola was a raw wound, and the insecurities he harbored about himself as an artist, which he had papered over with the phenomenal success of the last few years, leaked out like the juice of a bruised mango. He worried that he

was a better adapter of other people's work than a creator of original material. He worried that he was making a pompous film on an important subject. One evening, after the day's shooting was over, he recalled a humiliating incident that occurred during the production of *The Godfather*. He was in the men's room, sitting on the toilet, when two members of the crew came through the door. They were talking about "how the film was a load of shit and the asshole director didn't know what he was doing." Coppola lifted up his feet so that they wouldn't recognize his shoes. Now he feared that everybody was thinking the same thing, *Apocalypse* was a load of shit and the director was an asshole. But it was too late to lift up his feet.

Morale was at a low ebb. Despite Coppola's determination to do it differently, he operated like any studio, lavishing money on himself and the talent, while nickel-and-diming everyone else. Storaro and the Italian camera crew were treated like royalty, had pasta flown in from Italy every week. On the other hand, Coppola stopped paying the rest of the crew their per diems, provoking a near mutiny. Things got so bad that when cast and crew scrambled onto a transport plane destined for Manila on their day off so they could bathe, make calls, and get milk products, a guy with a submachine gun prevented people from forcing their way on. "It was a state of siege," says Tonery. "It was like the people clinging to the landing struts of a helicopter trying to get out of Saigon."

Then, as if conditions were not bad enough already, at the beginning of the third week in May, as predicted, a typhoon slammed into the island like a fist. It rained and rained, an endless torrent of water drumming on buildings, eight days, nine days, ten days straight. The typhoon scored a direct hit on one of the locations, turning it into an island, burying the sets in mud, dumping a speed-boat on top of a helicopter pad. Small clusters of people were stranded every-where, without food, drinkable water, or toilet facilities. There was no electricity, and the beds were soaking wet because the roofs had blown off. Then the vodka ran out.

Coppola spent part of the typhoon with a porn actress he had met during *Godfather II*. They were at a hotel in Olongapo, when skylarking actors and stuntmen broke down the door of his room to throw him in the pool. He just had time to wrap himself in a sheet.

The storm forced the production to shut down. On June 8, Francis dismissed the cast, returned to San Francisco with ninety hours of rushes, and only eight minutes of usable, cut film. It was the end of Phase I. The production was six weeks behind schedule and $3 million over budget, hemorrhaging dollars. However, the break gave Coppola some breathing space to regroup and rethink the script.

Many on the production who were laid low with tropical diseases, exotic parasites of various stripes, took the opportunity to get medical treatment. There was no doctor on the set, and people had simply poured diluted Clorox and vodka on their cuts and sores. Bottoms had hookworm, which wrecked his liver. Fred Forrest had collapsed, his ears oozing blood. A Filipino construction worker died of rabies, and was buried in his *Apocalypse Now* T-shirt.

Coppola was scared and depressed. Land-rich and cash-poor, he found that his home phone in Napa had been turned off because he had failed to pay the bill. He picked up a $3 million loan from UA, but the company drove a hard bargain. If the film didn't exceed $40 million in rentals, he would be held personally liable for the overages. If *Apocalypse* just did good, but not great, business, if it did not become a blockbuster, he stood a reasonable chance of being wiped out.

BY THE SECOND HALF of the decade, America finally seemed ready to deal with Vietnam, at least on a movie screen. While Francis was foraging for money, Hal Ashby was going ahead with *Coming Home*, which starred Jane Fonda, Jon Voight, and Bruce Dern, and was shot by Haskell Wexler. It was also set up at UA by Jerome Hellman, who had produced *Midnight Cowboy*.

Hellman had loved *The Last Detail*, had written Ashby a fan letter. The two men met. Like Zaentz before him, Hellman had a hard time figuring out if they were on the same wavelength. But he liked Hal, and decided to take a chance. "We had a couple of tough times," the producer says. "Hal tended to view any comment, or a suggestion even, as criticism, an incursion into his domain. We were friends for years and years, and we worked together intimately, but I would only know if he was upset with me because he wouldn't want to see me, but as to what was bothering him, I'd never find out. Once I had to go into the steam room at his house, fully dressed, and confront him there in the nude, and demand to know why he was suddenly trying to have a screening without me. Of course, he denied it. 'Oh, nooo, Jerry, I don't know where — I wouldn't do that to you.' Of course, I knew it was true."

Ashby and Mimi Machu were still living together in Malibu. The relationship had turned stormy. During post-production on *Bound for Glory*, at the Appian Way house, she threw an ashtray at the screen of his Advent, denting it badly. "He found it very difficult to be loved," she says. "That really scared him, having someone too dependent on him, and as much as he loved the person, he would do things to drive them away. Hal was a very jealous man. He was jealous of all my past boyfriends, couldn't stand to hear anything about my son's father, [Sonny Bono]. It drove him crazy. We'd have big fights and then make up."

When *Coming Home* opened in early 1978, it was a surprise hit. Ashby had again worked his magic in the editing room. Says Wexler's son Jeff, who did the sound, "After we were done shooting Voight's speech to the high school at the end, I turned to Haskell and I said, 'We're in big trouble, it just doesn't work.' Hal had let Jon ramble on, and Jon did a lot of stuff that was really stupid, that would have been an embarrassment had it ended up in the movie. Pop said, 'Give it a chance. You know the way Hal is in the editing room.' Sure enough, he put together a great scene that probably won Jon the Oscar."

Ashby went on to direct yet another film, *Being There* — starring Peter Sellers in a script by Jerzy Kosinski — that opened to enthusiastic reviews. He started his own company, North Star, with a deal at Lorimar. Then the bottom fell out. Recalls Peter Bart, who was head of production at Lorimar, "After *Being There*, Hal got more and more isolated, stayed around the house too much. When I talked to him, I was obviously talking to somebody who was smoking dope all the time." He became increasingly eccentric. It got to the point where Hal would not allow anyone to see him eating.

Lookin' to Get Out, a film about four gamblers, starring Voight, was not a promising script, but Hal thought he had a charmed life. He had gone into production on *Coming Home* with only a handful of pages of shooting script, and the movie had become a success. (The script actually won an Oscar.) "One of the reasons he made *Lookin' to Get Out* with a lousy script, *Second-Hand Hearts* the same way, was he was very arrogant about what he could fix in the editing," says Haskell Wexler. "Rather than try and rewrite it, he would say, 'We'll shoot this, and I'll cut to the reaction of this guy, it'll be fine.'" Rumor had it that he prepared for the film on the six-hour drive from L.A. to Las Vegas. Adds Wexler, "There were a lot of bad vibes coming from that picture. Hal went crazy. We had this casino set, and we spent ten, twelve days with multiple cameras, shooting inserts — dice, cards. Hal wanted the second camera guy to pan to one card, and the guy missed. Hal got furious, fired him right there. I just felt Hal had lost it. Something flipped." Indeed, Ashby was getting still deeper into drugs, freebasing and smack. After a night of hard partying with Mick Jagger and company while he was shooting his Stones documentary, *Let's Spend the Night Together*, he OD'd and collapsed at Sun Devil Stadium in Phoenix. He had to be wheeled out on a gurney with an I.V. stuck in his arm.

Hal hired all his old girlfriends and put them on the editing payroll. It was his way of saying he was sorry, of taking care of them. None of them knew anything about editing, nor even showed up, outside of Machu. Still an insomniac, he'd arrive at the cutting room at 4:00 A.M. wearing his embroidered Levi's jacket, or maybe the towel he'd wrap around him like a skirt, attached at the front with Velcro. "When he showed up, you never knew what Hal had had, whether he had eaten mushrooms, whether he was on acid or coke," recalls Janice Hampton, an editor. "We would hear his Mercedes, and we would say, Here comes Captain Wacky to the bridge. He would walk in, barefoot, no 'Hello, how are you.' He'd sit down, look at film for two or three hours and never say a word. It was like watching an insane genius, back and forth, back and forth. He'd light up a joint, and if he knew you smoked dope and didn't smoke with him, he would pout, wouldn't talk to you. He watched the reflection in the screen of the KEM as everybody would take a hit. Once he knew you were high, he started in with the mind games, he'd really try to fuck you over. Sadistic. 'Okay, if I do this and I do that, how much have I taken out and how come we're still in sync.' But he could never stay in sync himself, he was too loaded. This is how our days went, like Chinese water torture." He would often lose his temper if he couldn't find something or someone didn't move fast enough, and heave the heavy splicer through the air in the direction of the offending party. Once, in a relaxed moment, he told a story on himself about how he'd decided to commit suicide by swimming out into the ocean, then went shopping for the right bathing suit. He couldn't find one he liked, so he never followed through on the suicide.

Still, Hampton liked him. A redhead, she first met him in the bedroom of his Malibu home where she had come, notebook clutched in her hand, all business, to discuss the editing. He was sitting shirtless and cross-legged in the middle of a king-sized bed with wisps of graying blond hair hanging down over his face like tassels of corn, resembling an Indian guru, surrounded by jars full of different kinds of marijuana, rolling joints from a silver bowl full of loose grass. "I think that everything I've learned of value I learned from Hal," she continues. "He had an eye like nobody I've ever seen in my life." He came on to her, of course, but she always kept her distance. "There was always that fine line with Hal," she says. "You had to keep him interested, but not really get involved with him, otherwise he got bored."

On *Lookin' to Get Out*, Ashby disappeared for two months after the production ended, leaving the editors unsupervised. When he returned, with a stoner's attention to detail, he spent weeks cutting seven-, eight-minute montages — a dozen versions — of Vegas nightclub acts set to the Police's "Message in a Bottle" that the editors knew would never be used. "I don't remember ever sitting down and looking at the entire movie," says Eva Gardos, one of Hal's cutters. It was nearly two years in the editing room.

Lorimar finally tried to seize the film, particularly humiliating for a fine editor like Ashby, and took legal action to prevent him from working elsewhere, one reason he lost *Tootsie*. Ashby carried the reels around in the trunk of his car for a month, but finally gave them up. It was something he would never have allowed in the past. Now, however, he just holed up in his beach house, wouldn't speak to anyone. Voight talked the studio into letting him cut his version, with Bob Jones. Recalls Jones, "I called him, said, 'Hal, we're screening this, I want you to see it,' and I couldn't get any response. 'Hal, it's being released,' no response."

Hal was bitter, blamed his lawyer, Jack Schwartzman — who was married to Coppola's sister, Talia Shire — for his financial troubles. "But Hal was so

zonked out of his mind," says Bart, "he didn't need any help self-destructing."
Adds Jeff Berg, who was his agent, "More often than not, you couldn't
reach him. You left a message, guy didn't call back. I had to drive out to
the beach and knock on his door. I said to myself, What is this about?
What Hal really meant was, 'Yes, you are my agent, you're my link to the
world of commerce, you are my facilitator, but you're not on my side.' *No
one* was on his side."

AT THE END OF JULY, Coppola, Ellie, and their daughter, Sophia, returned
to the Philippines for the beginning of Phase II. Nobody wanted to go back,
and many didn't. Sheen was particularly reluctant. "When Marty came home
after the typhoon, he was real scared," recalled Gary Morgan, a friend. "He
said, 'I don't know if I am going to live through this. Those fuckers are crazy.'
At the airport, he kept saying goodbye to everyone."

Until *Apocalypse*, Coppola had never done much in the way of drugs. "I
started smoking grass," he said. "The grass affected me a little bit: I was more
able to say how I felt. It was like Vietnam — it was there, and everybody was
doing it. I also started getting very paranoid."

Dennis Hopper had known Coppola since the late '60s, when Francis was
writing *Patton*. Hopper arrived, drunk and stoned, at the beginning of September. Throughout the late '70s, he had continued his downward slide, in and
out of rehab; nothing worked. At one point, he decided he was essentially an
alcoholic, and stopped drinking, while continuing with drugs. He would show
up at Alcoholics Anonymous meetings with half an ounce of coke in his pocket.
He was so out of it that sometimes he'd show up at Narcotics Anonymous
meetings by mistake, look around him at the waxy faces of the ex-junkies and
dramatically announce, "I'm an alcoholic."

Hopper would shortly appear in his usual regalia — cowboy hat and boots —
stoned, at his daughter Marin's graduation from the prim and proper Wooster
Academy, near Ridgefield, Connecticut, and, according to his ex-wife, Brooke
Hayward, "He tried to seduce her best friend, it was a nightmare. We're talking
about children who were sixteen, seventeen years old. Dennis always had that
thing about young girls."

After Marin graduated, she paid him one of her rare visits. (Her mother says
she always became catatonic when his name came up.) Her plane was late,
and Dennis had plenty of time to get loaded at the Albuquerque airport bar.
On the way to Taos, he stopped at a house by the side of the road to pick up
something, possibly a gun. It was already dark. Hopper's girlfriend tried to get
the car keys away from him, but he threw them into the bushes. When they
were out of the car, recalls Marin, "he fired shots over our heads with this gun
he had in the car. Amazingly, he found the keys and drove off, leaving us

there." Later, Brooke got a call while she was at a dinner party in Southampton. She remembers a friend saying, " 'You've got to get Marin out of here. Dennis has gone berserk again.' I thought, Oh, no, will it never end?" (Hopper denies this event took place.)

Hopper appeared in the Philippines with his companion, Caterine Milinaire, a photographer and the daughter of the Duchess of Bedford. Several people recall seeing a flaming mattress fly out of a window and hearing a shot during one wild night at the Pagsanjan Rapids Hotel where everyone was staying, although she denies he fired at her. Others saw her with a black eye the next day. "She definitely was hit across the face, had a nice shiner," says one former crew member. (Milinaire refuses to comment.)

The Kurtz compound was finally ready. It was strewn with corpses, many of which were real. Recalls Frederickson, "It turned out that the guy procuring the dead bodies who said he was getting them from a medical research lab, had actually been robbing graves."

When Brando arrived in early September, four months late, the cost of the production went from $100,000 a day to $150,000 a day. He insisted on sleeping on a houseboat, which had to be carried overland to a nearby lake. Coppola realized immediately that Brando had not read Conrad's *Heart of Darkness*, had done absolutely nothing to prepare himself for playing Kurtz. Francis disappeared into his trailer and never came out, as one person put it. "Everybody was waiting to shoot, hundreds of people, while Francis and Brando were play-acting, Brando playing Westmoreland, and Francis playing Ho Chi Minh," says a crew member. According to Hopper, Coppola spent days actually reading Brando Conrad's novel out loud. When it came to the last shot of the last day of Brando's scenes, Coppola turned the direction over to the AD and left in his helicopter. It was his way of saying "Fuck you" to Brando.

Meanwhile, with excruciating slowness, Coppola puzzled his way toward a denouement. Willard, embracing primitivism, finally kills Kurtz. But then what? He could not come up with an ending. The film had been freighted with so much Significance, so much Joseph Campbell, what with ritual sacrifices, magical beasts, and dying gods, that the rather conventional battle scene of the script seemed hardly adequate. "Letting the movie get more surrealistic, more heightened, I was painting myself in a corner and I had no way to get out," he explains. Coppola's moods continued to swing wildly between deliriums of self-intoxication and black depression.

Francis had been carrying on various affairs with the women on the set, complaining that he wanted to have more children, but Ellie refused. In addition to the porn actress, he had an affair with a nubile young starlet playing one of the Playboy bunnies, Linda Carpenter, who had been a Playmate of the Month in August 1976, under the name of Linda Beatty. (Coppola denies that he had affairs with the porn actress and Carpenter.) Then there was Melissa

Mathison, whom Francis had asked to do a rewrite on the script of *Black Stallion*, who occasionally visited the set.

Once, Mathison accompanied Francis and a few others when he screened footage for President Marcos and his wife, Imelda. "The palace was like a fortress, a den of evil," she recalls. "There was a huge dining room table, twenty feet long, that was covered with row after row of candy bars, a hundred Clark Bars, a hundred Three Musketeers — for us. Imelda came in from one side of this giant room, with all of her ladies-in-waiting dressed to the nines in Chanel, while we were wearing Vietnamese black pajamas. Then Marcos came in from the other side, with all of his men. They nodded politely at each other. Obviously they hadn't seen each other in about three years. Vittorio set up this little projector in the back, while Francis was making a speech and Imelda's ladies were giggling and eating candy bars. She was sitting in front of me, and every time a handsome actor appeared on the screen, she'd say, 'Is that Marlon Brando?' It was surreal."

Coppola didn't much bother to conceal his dalliances from Ellie, nor did he treat her with much consideration. Says one crew member, "She was quiet, hung in the background and seemed to take a lot of abuse. It was embarrassing." According to another source, he would watch dailies seated in the first row, flanked by his editor on one side and his female flavor-of-the-week on the other. Behind them were ten or fifteen chairs for Storaro and the camera crew, and others. Ellie would wander in late, sit on the floor in the back. One day, like others, Francis arrived at the set in his plane. He jumped out, followed by his pilot and a girlfriend. Then the crew unloaded whatever equipment they had brought. Then came Ellie. People joked that she must have ridden in the cargo bay. Like Sandy Weintraub, it was hard for her to live with a man who was constantly the center of attention, who was always being told he was a genius. She felt forced to counterbalance the flattery by withholding her approval — which he resented, because she was the person whose approval he craved most. "I never felt that my wife had any confidence in me," he complained. "I felt she was meddling and lining up with the people that I — My wife [is] like a regular person. So she has the same kind of doubts about me as the so-called they at large."

Mathison's wide-eyed adoration, on the other hand, dispelled his self-doubts, was an aphrodisiac. It was "like the girl who has a crush on her professor" he explained. "Her confidence in me made me feel confident. . . . Confidence is a very important thing. When everyone is saying, 'You're going to fail. . . .' That's why . . . [she] always made me feel like a million dollars, in terms of 'I was talented, and I could do it.' "

When one crew member asked Francis how he could treat Ellie so badly, he said, "Look, I have these three women in my life, each one is very different, and each one has a place. I'm not hurting anybody. This whole thing is riding on me, and all of this I'm doing is making me very happy, and everybody is benefiting from it. Eleanor and my family are happy because I'm happy." A lot of people who weren't so happy felt he was more interested in getting laid and smoking dope than shooting the great work of art they thought they were there to create.

Coppola shut down the production again in December 1976, for a Christmas break, the end of Phase II. Back in the U.S., he ran into Kael. She was full of advice, as usual, and warned him against using the "Ride of the Valkyries" for the soon-to-be celebrated sequence in which a fleet of American helicopters descend like black birds of prey on a cluster of thatched huts where school-children are at play, firing missiles and dropping mustard yellow smoke bombs, while Robert Duvall, playing Colonel Kilgore, announces, "I love the smell of napalm in the morning," and watches his men surf. Coppola recalls, "She was a real know-it-all. She said it had been used by Lina Wertmuller in *Seven Beauties*. I always felt that Kael turned on me because I didn't kiss her ass as much as I was supposed to."

He screened a rough assemblage in San Francisco and was ecstatic, as manic as he was depressed a few weeks before. Ellie was suspicious. "He was never, on any of his films, excited and up like he is now. He was always a real tortured-sufferer type," she wrote in her journal. "There is a kind of franticness. . . . If I say anything to the contrary, it is taken for negativity, disloyalty or jealousy. I think that Francis is truly a visionary, but part of me is filled with anxiety. I feel as though a certain discrimination is missing, that fine discrimina-tion that draws the line between what is visionary and what is madness. I am terrified."

ALMOST IMMEDIATELY after scoring big with *Shampoo*, Beatty plunged into a light comedy, *Heaven Can Wait*, with a script by Elaine May. Beatty set the picture up at Warners. But once again, as with *Shampoo*, there was trouble. The business people began to nickel-and-dime him, no water cooler in the production office, that sort of thing. There was trouble at the top. Ted Ashley felt, in his words, that "Warren, who was among the most finicky, obsessive people, might take a picture that we thought was commercially marginal, and bring it to the point where we'd lose a bunch of money." According to one source, Beatty wasn't coming up with a budget for the heaven scene. Wells asked, Beatty procrastinated. Wells asked again, Beatty procrastinated again. Wells and Beatty were both tough negotiators; they pushed each other's buttons. Finally, there was a meeting among Wells, Calley, and Beatty, shortly before they were scheduled to begin production. Wells asked him yet again for the numbers on the heaven scene. Beatty, irritated, said, "Do you want to make a budget, or do you want to make a movie?" As usual, Wells wanted to make a budget, and let him walk. Wells and Towne had gone to the same school, played water polo. Wells had been a goalie, and Towne quipped, "He's still a goalie. He won't let anybody score."

Warners would regret it. Beatty always had a backup. He had devoted his considerable charms to wooing Barry Diller, who prided himself on being a hardnose. But Diller was no match for Beatty, who used to refer to him, playfully, as "The Chairman." Says Simpson, "Barry had his pets and his favorites. He loved to play with Beatty and Redford, while a lot of other things fell through the cracks." In any event, Diller stepped in, and the very same day Wells said no, he said yes.

This time, Beatty decided to direct it himself, but since he was starring as well, he asked Buck Henry to co-direct it with him. The rest of the cast included Charles Grodin and Dyan Cannon. After Henry had been profiled as the "hottest writer in Hollywood" in the *New York Times Magazine* in 1970, his career had not gone well. He was clever and wickedly funny, a gregarious man who had to be at every gallery opening, every new theater piece, every party, and would take every acting job that came along. He had a hard time making himself sit down alone and write. Directing, even co-directing, a Beatty movie was a big break. But it was a mixed blessing. "Warren is a master manipulator," says Henry. "When I arrived at Paramount the first day, there was a sign on the front gate, 'Welcome to Paramount, the Home of Buck Henry.' Of course, a few days later, there was a sign that said, 'Welcome to Paramount, the Home of Charles Grodin.' "

Beatty and Henry began the search for the female lead. Beatty tested actresses, and tested more actresses. After every test, he would turn to Henry and say, wistfully, "She's no Julie." Recalls Henry, "I didn't realize this was a pretend search for a lead actress until late in, after hearing 'But she's no Julie' for the fiftieth time." Julie and Warren were long over, and she had no interest in acting in the picture. Nor were they on particularly good terms. Beatty had to send his cousin, David MacLeod, over to England to intercede for him. Eventually, she gave in. "I think he always knew it was going to be Julie," says Henry. "But they were so edgy, that he also knew — he's so weirdly smart about this kind of shit — that at the end of this movie, he wasn't going to be able to say, 'Julie, I want you to look me in the eyes in this scene,' without her getting irritated. He needed somebody who could take the place of the director, and say, 'Just stare at him while he's talking.' That was me."

Indeed, there is a scene in the movie in which Warren and Julie are walking through the rose gardens of a grand estate. He is wearing a stylish leather jacket, and she has a haircut she hated, the one she sneeringly called her "dolly girl" hairdo. In the film, romantic music is swelling up on the soundtrack, drowning out their conversation, wherein Christie was saying, in her clipped British accent, "I can't believe you're still making these fucking dumb movies when, I mean, there are people all over Europe making fabulous films, about real things, Fassbinder and so on, and you're still doing this shit," and then she'd smile at him as if she had honey on her tongue. Beatty just laughed, but there it was again, the old itch that needed to be scratched: Was he a serious filmmaker? His next film, *Reds*, would dispel any lingering doubts.

Beatty had always been afflicted with the disease of perfectionism, and as his power grew, he was increasingly able to indulge it. "Warren is the only director I've ever really had fights with," recalls Henry. "We used to fight a lot about dumb things, like he would say, 'It's midnight, let's do another two hours.'

" 'Fuck you, we've got to get up at six.'

" 'Well, we need to work on this.'

" 'No we don't. It's perfectly fine the way it is.' He liked to worry things to death, like, 'I don't like take thirty-two.' I think that tires out the actors. The last day, we shot well into the night, two or three in the morning. When we finished, the crew and the actors just walked off into the night, while Warren sat at a playback machine watching the takes, not saying goodbye, just letting everybody sort of dissolve."

IN LATE JANUARY 1977, Coppola returned to the Philippines for what he believed would be the final few weeks of shooting. Eleanor remained in San Francisco, furnishing him with the usual supply of air-conditioners, table linens, frozen steaks, wine, and kitchen utensils, and brooded over her husband's state of mind. Finally she sent him a telex that conveyed her fears. She told him that with his supply lines of food and equipment, he was creating his own Vietnam, creating "the very situation he went there to expose." She called him an "asshole," and copied Tavoularis, Storaro, and even the production manager. Francis was furious. At this moment, when his professional life hung in the balance, she had stabbed him in the back. Five days later, on March 5, 1977, Martin Sheen had a heart attack. Coppola knew that if the news reached L.A. or New York, he would be shut down. If Sheen could not return to work, it was all over, he would lose everything. He was appalled and frightened when he heard that crew members were calling home, saying that the actor had died.

Coppola's mood swings were getting more erratic. As he put it, "We were in the jungle, there were too many of us, we had access to too much money, too much equipment — and little by little we went insane." Francis was now living in Hidden Valley, a spectacular resort inside an inactive volcano, smoking lots of dope. Despite a change for the better in the weather — the oppressive heat had broken, and a dry, cool wind had come up — Francis was in a black humor. Melissa had just left. He was blaming himself for Sheen's heart attack. One evening in the middle of March, Coppola had flown in a chef from Japan to prepare an elaborate meal of Kobe beef. Suddenly he sank to his knees, weeping, then had a classic epileptic seizure, banging his head against the wall, thrashing about on the floor, foaming at the mouth. His pilot thrust a belt between his jaws to prevent him from biting his tongue. He had been about to rehearse Linda Carpenter in a scene in which she read tarot cards, and now, in his delirium, he was convinced that she was a witch, he the devil, the movie evil, and that the apocalypse of the title was actually at hand. He swore he had seen the white light, was going to die. His last request was that Lucas finish the picture. Two days later he appeared to be fine, flew in a print of one of his favorite movies, Lubitsch's *To Be or Not to Be*, to screen.

Eleanor, who was in San Francisco, flew to his side. According to Cyndi Wood, who played another Bunny and was also staying at Hidden Valley, Coppola asked her to tell his wife about his relationship with Carpenter. She did. Francis and Ellie discussed separation or divorce. "I was in, like, love triangles, beyond my thing, and I almost — and I was tired, and Marty had just had a heart attack, and it was my own money, and I didn't feel good about my relationship with my wife," Francis recalled. But he couldn't bring himself to make the break. "I didn't want to lose my children," he said. "A lot of men can do that. But I was just not the kind of person who could go and wipe out my family like that and do a second family. I will never do that. I just can't." He lay at Eleanor's feet, stroking her ankles, moaning, "I'll never do it again, I'll never do it again."

March 20, the one-year anniversary of the beginning of principal photography, came and went, unremarked. Sheen recovered surprisingly quickly, and was working again by mid-April. In early May, Coppola wrapped. He finally returned to San Francisco in the middle of June 1977, in a BAC 111 — a sizable plane about four times the size of a Gulfstream, seating eighty, that he had wangled from a South African manure millionaire, after a 238-day shoot (double that of *Jaws*), with 250 hours of footage, a few weeks after the premiere of *Star Wars*, which he missed. The budget, which had begun at $13 million, had reached nearly $30 million and was still climbing. Francis had lost nearly a hundred pounds. He owed $14 million in overruns. UA had sunk $25 million in the film and found it prudent to take out a $15 million insurance policy on his life. If he died, UA would walk away with a $1 million profit. He joked that he was worth more dead than alive.

Coppola still needed another $10 million for post-production, and was forced to put up the rest of his assets, including the Napa house, future profits from *The Black Stallion*, which was then in production under his aegis with Carroll Ballard directing.

Coppola intended to make a big push to finish the picture quickly. A crew of carpenters set to work building customized editing tables out of mahogany brought back from the Philippines, and laminated maple plywood. Francis divided the picture among several teams of editors, and beefed up the editorial staff. He promoted one of his former baby-sitters, and hired almost any warm body that walked through the door. Some of the veteran editors raised their eyebrows. "The cutting was turned over to Francis groupies," grumbles one. But he also gave work to aspiring filmmakers who would never have been able to break into the business in L.A. or New York because they were not members of the union. Says Jerry Ross, a sound editor, "I owe everything I have to his wonderful madness."

Yet Francis was so depressed the work ground to a halt. "We'd come to work every morning and for three months there was literally nothing to do," says Richard Candib, an editorial assistant. In the fall, a number of people were laid off, and Francis took off for Europe in his BAC 111. (Tavoularis was responsible for the deco design of the interiors, which reflected the decor of his office. He also designed the crew's uniforms.) Some people suspected Melissa was with him.

In October, Francis had told Eleanor that he was in love with another woman. "The emotion rose up from my feet like a tide," she wrote. "It hit me in the chest and knocked me backward." He said he loved both of them. "I have been comfortable believing the lies," she continued. "Just like Kay in the last scene of *The Godfather*. All of the evidence tells her that her husband has had people killed, and when she asks him, he says no, and she believed his words. All the evidence through the years, the little presents, notes, things I would find in Francis's pockets after a trip, the pin sent to him in the Philippines that he wore on his hat as a good luck charm. And when I would ask, I would hear, 'Ellie, she is a friend, she has been a big help to me—she is no threat to you.' I believed the words, I denied the evidence. I didn't want to see the truth." Ellie thought about Jackie Kennedy, how after the president was assassinated, she came into her own, was allowed to live her own life. "There is part of me that has been waiting for Francis to leave me, or die, so that I can get my life the way I want it." She finally let go. She went into the kitchen and threw bone china against the walls.

Coppola promised to break it off with Mathison, but continued to see her. She accompanied him to a special screening of *The Last Waltz* in L.A. that Scorsese arranged for him. She moved into a house on Wolfback Ridge Road high up on the Marin Headlands in Sausalito, with a sweeping view of the bay. Francis paid the rent. When Ellie was not around, which was often—she was busy decorating the Napa house—he would bring Melissa to screenings.

Francis's pal Dennis Jakob joined the editing team. Jakob was eccentric, to say the least. But the director regarded him as a genius. It is said that he worked with a skull in his lap, nervously rubbing his fingertips across the surface. Francis was having a dalliance with a pretty editorial apprentice whom Dennis apparently fancied. Telling Francis, "You can have her or Melissa, but not both," Jakob walked off with several reels of work print that contained the last third of *Apocalypse*. One day Francis received a baggie filled with ashes that Jakob claimed were burned film. When two assistant editors went to negotiate with Jakob, he said he would return the reels if Francis sent Mathison to sleep with him. Eventually he was convinced to return the film anyway. (Jakob could not be reached for comment.)

WHILE COPPOLA FIDDLED, other pictures stole his thunder. *Close Encounters*, which ended up costing a whopping $19.5 million, was released on November 16, 1977, and the same week, *Star Wars* supplanted *Jaws* as the top grossing picture of all time. Spielberg believed that if *Close Encounters* had beaten *Star Wars* to the screen, it would have done better. The reviews were gushy and adoring. Kael called Spielberg a "magician."

The politics of Spielberg's picture appeared to be not that different from that of the Watergate-inflected, *Jaws*: government conspires to keep an important truth from the people, and only an ordinary joe can get to the bottom of it. But somewhere along the road to *Close Encounters*, Spielberg must have understood the same thing Lucas understood after *THX*: audiences were tired of bad news. Although they loved being vicariously sliced and diced, dismembered by a mouthful of razor-sharp teeth, they loved to be uplifted even more, overwhelmed by a power that was benevolent, *The Exorcist* stood on its head. More money could be made by taking the high road and appealing to our better selves; awe was more commercial than fear.

And an even richer vein was our sentimental view of our better self as the inner child, the innocent youth we used to be. Dreyfuss's Neary is the first of Spielberg's childlike, regressed adults. Absorbed with his obsession, he plays with mashed potatoes, making of them a model of Devils Tower, where the mother ship comes to earth and reabsorbs him, returns him to the womb. "I really wanted to take a child's point of view," Spielberg said, "the uneducated innocence that allows a person to take this kind of quantum jump. Neary is no different than any of the kids."

At the same time, Neary is a version of Spielberg's father, Arnold, a man obsessed with his work who was never there for the family. Because as much as Spielberg and Lucas wanted to indulge their Peter Pan complexes, return the boomers to the sandbox, much as they backed kids against adults, Spielberg's movies in particular are colored by longing for the absent dad, a nostalgia for authority. His families are often fatherless; the plots are set in motion by the moral and emotional vacuum at the center of the home, and resolved by father surrogates. Both the *Star Wars* trilogy and the Indiana Jones trilogy end on a note of generational harmony, with the revelation that the repentant Darth

Vader is Luke's father, and the reconciliation of Indy with *his* father in *Indiana Jones and the Last Crusade*. Indy's final words are, "Yes, sir!" In *Close Encounters*, Neary-the-child, entering the mother ship in a trancelike daze, surrenders himself to the superior power of idealized grown-ups, grown-ups as they appear to children, in the same way that *Star Wars* ends with the famous parody of *Triumph of the Will*. The evil over-thirties of the Nixon era would become the avuncular adults of the Reagan era — Reagan himself in particular. Lucas and Spielberg finally succeeded in turning the counterculture upside down.

With two blockbusters in a row, *Close Encounters* confirmed Spielberg's place, along with Lucas's, in the pantheon of profit. The studio blew up his first check to poster size. The amount? Four and one half million dollars. At the Alto Cedro house, he had a vast pine desk in which was planted a state-of-the-art phone system, flush with the top. It was one of the first to feature a speed dialer, and Spielberg loved to show it off to friends. "Look, I just press this, I don't have to do anything," he said happily. The list of names next to the Lucite buttons included Begelman, Sheinberg, Calley, Diller, Ladd, Medavoy — every one the head of a studio. The road had forked. Speilberg had gone one way; his peers, for the most part, had gone another.

On November 16, 1977, Coppola flew to Washington for a shindig at the Carter White House with Spielberg and Lucas. Among them they represented three of the top grossing films of all time. Spielberg referred to them as the Billion Dollar Boys. He described to them the trip around the world he took after *Jaws*. India and Russia were the only countries he visited where people weren't wearing *Jaws* T-shirts. In Washington the directors stayed at the Watergate. A photographer from *Amercian Film* magazine took a picture of the three of them. It reminded Francis of another group shot, this one taken in 1974 when he posed with Bogdanovich and Freidkin. Peter and Billy had fallen by the wayside. Francis was the last man standing.

LIKE COPPOLA, by the end of the decade Beatty had gotten to the point where he could do anything he wanted. What he wanted to do was *Reds*, a sprawling epic about John Reed, the American radical journalist, the only American buried in the Kremlin, that would be shot in six countries over a considerable period of time. This was a project he had been noodling for nearly a decade, and after two comedies, and Christie's gibes ringing in his ears, it was time. *Reds* was deeply personal. "Warren sees himself as John Reed," ventured Jerzy Kosinski, who played Zinoviev, at the time. "In his movies so far, Warren has been as socially insignificant as John Reed before he began writing about the revolution. What could Warren possibly do . . . that would be revolutionary, truly qualitatively different from what Brando or Eastwood or Reynolds has done?" Kosinski was more than a little patronizing and wrong to dismiss *Bonnie and Clyde* and *Shampoo*, but he was correct to the extent that Beatty regarded *Reds* as the crowning work of his career.

Unlike Coppola, Beatty was not about to undertake a production of this magnitude without the backing of a studio. He was at the height of his power, and nothing symbolized it more than this project; only Beatty had the clout to launch a major motion picture that would dramatize the Russian Revolution from a not unsympathetic perspective — and get a studio to pay for it.

Still, it wasn't easy. *Reds* was an expensive pill for Paramount to swallow. It was no low-budget trifle, a *Days of Heaven*. Says Simpson, "Even Barry Diller passed on *Reds*. He said, 'We're not making a picture about communists. We're not glorifying them.' Warren said, 'You owe it to me to have a meeting with Charlie and yourself.' Now Charlie *really* loved Warren — he was such a star-fucker — and Charlie's the one who committed." But Bluhdorn was far from wild about the idea. Not only was it an expensive picture about a communist, Reed doesn't go off with the girl, and he dies at the end. Bluhdorn did every-thing in his power to dissuade Beatty from proceeding, even said, "Do me a favor, take the budget, $25 million. Go to Mexico. Keep twenty-four million for yourself. Spend the one million on a picture. Just don't make this one." As Evans puts it, "Warren could dictate what he wanted to make. It was his come shot after *Heaven Can Wait*."

The picture was rushed into production to meet the schedules of the huge, high-profile cast. It immediately became clear that the budget had been wildly underestimated. "I got very frustrated," said Diller. "My knee-jerk reaction was to get angry with Warren. At the worst stage, I refused to talk to him." He stopped taking Beatty's calls. Then, at Christmas 1979, he saw five hours of footage in London, realized he had been wrong, and apologized. From then on, Paramount was fully behind the picture.

In early 1979, the trades reported the astonishing news that Pauline Kael had made a production deal with Paramount. She took a five-month leave of absence from *The New Yorker*, moved out to L.A., and was set up in an office on the lot. Kael and Beatty had a history. Her review of *Bonnie and Clyde* had been key to both their careers, she had loved *Shampoo*, and over the years a relationship developed. But she had disliked *Heaven Can Wait*, deriding it as a "prefab" picture, "image-conscious celebrity moviemaking," and nastily de-scribed Beatty's character as "the elfin sweet Jesus," accused him of turning into a "baby-kissing politican." For his part, Beatty disparaged her and the Paulettes as "Ma Barker and her gang." But if Kael thought Beatty was "Jesus," he would shortly appear to her in an altogether different guise, and offer her the apple that might have ended her career.

Kael had given Toback's *Fingers* a rave, and when Beatty was trying to decide whether or not to produce Toback's next film, *Love and Money*, he flattered her by asking for advice. Recalls Beatty, "I thought he was off his trolley, and I was going away to do *Reds*. She said, 'Do *Love and Money*. Forget *Reds*. Why make a film on the communist party?' " He replied, "You tell Fellini how to make movies. If you think it's so easy, you ought to try it yourself." She replied, "Maybe I should." So he hired her to produce *Love and Money*. Says Beatty, "It was the stupidest thing I've ever done. I told her there was one condition: she would meet a lot of people in Hollywood who would appear dumb to her. And that if she decided to go back to reviewing, she could not write about them, because she would destroy them. And she agreed. She immediately became completely competitive with Toback, rewriting the script over and over. Finally she said, 'What should I do? Should I give him the money?' I said, 'Yes. You're the one who convinced me what a genius he is.' And she still hadn't given up on *Reds*. She even called Diane Keaton, called my fucking girlfriend to get her to persuade me not to do *Reds!*" Adds Toback, "After six weeks of working with her, I couldn't stand it. I said to Beatty, 'Either I'm going or she's going. I just cannot do this movie with her around.' I was polite in the press, making it seem as if it were a mutual decision, but it wasn't a mutual decision at all. I had her fired from *Love and Money*. I got rid of her."

No one could figure out exactly what all this was about, but the Warrenologists in Hollywood, who always looked for deeper motives, couldn't help seeing Beatty's move as the pièce de résistance of the campaign to finesse Kael. "Because of her power, executives used to be terrified of her," says Paul Schrader. "There was a feeling in the industry that Warren was the only one who could bring Pauline down. The ultimate smooth move was to flatter her to death, give her a little power, and put her in an office until she was gradually exposed as being one of us and therefore not dangerous. I really believe he brought her out there to humiliate her, maybe not consciously, but some part of him did. He gathered a lot of respect from the industry for that."

Adds Buck Henry, "We're talking about manipulation on a level unknown to man. This is so Machiavellian, even I can't quite believe it, except that it was Warren. He knew he was going to make *Reds*, and he knew that Kael was always incredibly patronizing about him, and he knew she adored Toback. I think he thought, I've got to find a way to get her to back off. If I put her together with Toback, and make her think she's part of a company, even if I dump her in a year, she can't come back and slam me."

If that was Beatty's intent, it almost worked. After she got fired from *Love and Money*, she sat in her office twiddling her thumbs until her contract ran out. She used to go over to director Richard Brooks's office, complain that she had been compromised and put out to pasture, and weep. She never knew what hit her. Beatty introduced her to Diller, who offered her a production deal that would enable her to work out of her home in Great Barrington, Massachusetts. "They were really wonderful to me," she says today, although she turned Diller down. "Don Simpson was head of production, and he would have had no interest in any projects of mine." However, when she finally got back to *The New Yorker,* she wrote the very article Beatty says she promised she wouldn't, a scathing and prescient analysis of the future of the movie business. Although she didn't mention Paramount by name, those in the know could read between the lines. And when *Reds* came out, she gave it a bad review.

APOCALYPSE WAS CUT and recut. Says one member of the team, "For months, Francis would just sit in the screening room at night, look at cuts of the film, get stoned, and trip on music." Says one editor, "We'd be working for months without feedback, and then we'd get an insane note from his office in the penthouse, 'Francis would like you to recut the scene to the Doors' "L.A. Woman." ' He was in another world." Adds another editor, "I'd ask Francis, 'Whaddya want me to do with this scene?' He would go into this exegesis of *The Golden Bough,* the father killing the son, and I'd be sitting there mesmerized by his wonderful eloquence, and then he'd leave, and I'd think, Yeah, but what am I supposed to do with this scene?" *Apocalypse* was to have been UA's big Christmas movie in 1977, after having been pushed back from April. But Christmas came and went without a Coppola movie in the company's stocking. A new date was set, April 7, 1978, Francis's thirty-ninth birthday.

Meanwhile, many of the people whom Coppola had inspired with his passion fell away. It was all too insane, the self-indulgence, the megalomania, the false hopes Francis held out to people, the drama between Francis and Ellie. "It was like walking on eggshells, seeing the personal side, and then trying to carry on a professional relationship," says Bottoms. "The key to that was to put on blinders. You just didn't see it." He adds, "One of his big dreams was that we'd all work together in harmony for the good of the project, like communists. That's why I was attracted to him in the first place. But like any utopia, the truth is there is one person who gained, and everyone else suffered. He was living like a king — the cigars, the limos, the mansions — and complaining he didn't have any money. When someone's abusing their power to the point where they become inhuman, lashing out at people, criticizing people who were working for nothing, where's the humility there? After *Apocalypse Now,* it was like, 'I only make commercial movies, I don't even write my own scripts anymore.' So because of that illness — not wanting to share — he never was really able to tap into the fledgling artists. I learned that I couldn't wait for someone like Francis to take me by the hand anymore, because guys like him can't even take care of themselves."

"Part of the dynamic of the place which I found difficult to be around, was an elitism, the sense that we're all really special," says Mathison. "Maybe they were, maybe they weren't. They were just making movies, and there isn't anything that special about that. I'm sure a lot of people who were part of the 'we,' felt like they suddenly became a 'you' or a 'them,' and that was hard to take."

UA acquiesced to a mid-August date—1979. There were different versions, with different endings. Coppola says Lucas came to him, asked to use his spectacular helicopter footage for *More American Graffiti*. Francis knew Lucas's picture would come out first, and at that juncture, he felt that the helicopter footage was all he had. He was on the brink of disaster and refused his friend's request.

Apocalypse was taking so long that UA was collapsing under him. In late January 1978, Arthur Krim and company shocked the industry by exiting—taking Medavoy with them—to form a new company, Orion. In a scramble for credibility, Transamerica reached deep into the company and came up with Andy Albeck, a lifer who had worked for Krim forever. Albeck was not part of the club, and would become the perfect scapegoat in the disaster that would soon be upon the company like an on-rushing locomotive. When the dust settled, production was headed by two kids with little experience, Steven Bach and David Field.

Bach and Field were hungry for product. In the summer of 1978, the buzz on the street was all about *The Deer Hunter*, scheduled for release in the fall. It had cost $15 million, twice the budget going in, and director Michael Cimino's cut was three hours and four minutes, over which he was involved in a brutal fight with Universal. In August, Cimino's agent, Stan Kamen, approached UA with a pay-or-play deal for the director's next movie, tentatively entitled *The Johnson County War*, with a modest $7.5 million price tag. UA executives screened *The Deer Hunter* in New York on Wednesday, August 16, at their headquarters, on Seventh Avenue. Wrote Bach in his book, *Final Cut*, "We didn't know what it meant to Cimino—politically or otherwise—but we knew what it felt like was, well . . . poetry."

About a month later, Bach met with Cimino and his producer, Joann Carelli, at the Polo Lounge in Beverly Hills. Cimino was short and stocky. His large head, set off by a dramatic mane of dark hair, sat atop his shoulders like a melon. He dressed casually in a black leather jacket and jeans. Carelli handed Bach a script she described as "a passion of his [Cimino's]." Bach read it, liked it. It struck him as another exercise in genre revisionism like *The Godfather*, or better, *The Missouri Breaks*, except that it dealt with large themes that had to do with cattlemen hiring mercenaries to slaughter immigrant homesteaders. His only reservation concerned the ending, in which all the major characters were killed.

By that time, word was out on *The Deer Hunter*, and other studios were beginning to swarm around Cimino. On September 25, Bach and Field called Kamen and gave Cimino the deal he asked for. *The Johnson County War*—eventually known as *Heaven's Gate*—was theirs.

•

EVANS HUNG ON in the shadow of Diller's whiz kids—Michael Eisner and
Don Simpson, with Simpson's assistant Jeffrey Katzenberg lurking in the wings
—a throwback to a bolder time. Still under the protection of Bluhdorn, he
could always go over Diller's head when he needed to, and he continued to
behave as if he were head of the studio. "Eisner was scared of him," says
Simpson. "Evans believed he was this living legend. He would come in with
his sunglasses and his black clothes, and Eisner freaked. He would buzz me.
He'd go, 'Don, Don! You gotta get in here!' I'd say, 'What's wrong?' He'd say,
'Evans is here.' Like I was the witch doctor that could deal with this maniac.
When I was first head of production, he had to work for me as a producer. He
would invite me over to his office, and he couldn't sit at his desk for more than
ten minutes without going to his bathroom and reemerging with a mountain
of white substance all over him. Later on, when I got to know him better I'd
say, 'Bob, you can't go out in public with a fuckin' ounce of blow on your
chest.' He'd sit there and basically try to bribe me, said if I helped him with his
project, he'd get me pussy. It drove me crazy, not that I was any paragon of
virtue, because he was so sleazy."

Evans wanted to do a picture based on the *Popeye* comic strip. The studio
was less than enthusiastic, but when Disney agreed to defray half the cost,
Eisner finally agreed. Evans got a tubful of turndowns, but finally talked Altman
into doing it. Evans had often expressed his preference for hiring a good
director after a flop, and Altman neatly fit the bill. He had a good thing going
with Ladd, who would have backed one of Altman's laundry stubs so long as
the director kept the budget down. But none of these films had prospered.
"Princess Grace was on the board of directors of Fox, and they had their annual
meeting at Monaco," the director recalls. "Princess Grace said, 'Why would
you allow Mr. Altman to make such a terrible film with such a great actor, Paul
Newman,' talking about *Quintet*. And Laddie said, 'Oh, why don't you go fuck
yourself,' or something like that. And got up and left, left the company." (Actually, it was more probable that Ladd was forced out by his rival, CEO Dennis
Stanfill, who took advantage of the unfavorable deal Ladd had negotiated with
Lucas for *The Empire Strikes Back* to embarrass him with the board.)

To say that Altman's name stirred little enthusiasm at Paramount is an
understatement. Says Simpson, "None of us really wanted to make *Popeye*, and
we hated Altman, who was a true fraud. I used to go into Altman's bathroom at
Lion's Gate at six o'clock at night and there would be an empty fifth of scotch
—that was from lunch till then, he was such an alcoholic. He was full of
gibberish and full of himself, a pompous, pretentious asshole. I guess Evans
wanted him, because Evans thought they could party together. So the fucking
director was beyond a fucking drunken disaster, and then we had Evans, who

didn't even know what a fucking setup was. The two of them together were a dangerous combination."

The studio had scheduled *Popeye* for Christmas 1980, to go up against *Heaven's Gate* and Scorsese's *Raging Bull*. The fall of 1979, from October to New Year's, was spent casting. Shelley Duvall, one of Altman's regulars, was the spitting image of Olive Oyl, but Eisner preferred Gilda Radner, who was hot from *Saturday Night Live*. Altman didn't want to make the picture without Duvall, so for him it was a deal-breaker. He showed a twelve-minute reel of Duvall's work to Bluhdorn and the other Paramount executives, who came over to Lion's Gate to see it. Recalls the director, "After the reel finished, Simpson stood up and said, 'Well, I wouldn't want to fuck her. And if I don't want to fuck her, she shouldn't be in the movie.' I was appalled. Simpson was a bad guy, a bum. That was the kind of guy who was taking over the studios. It's a big plus to our industry that he's not here anymore. [Simpson died suddenly in 1996.] I'm only sorry he didn't live longer and suffer more."

Popeye was shot in Malta. "There was a lot of cocaine and a lot of drugs going around," recalls Altman. "Everybody was shipping stuff in." In January 1980, Evans flew out to the location. Right away, Simpson got a call, at home, midnight. He was in bed.

A hoarse voice whispered, "Don, Don."

"Who *is* this?"

"It's Robert . . . Evans."

"Where are you?"

"I'm in Malta. I got a problem. I need your help."

"Bob, could we talk about it tomorrow?"

"No, we can't. They lost my bags."

What Simpson wanted to say was, "I'm president of production. I'm not in charge of bags," but instead he said, "Gee Bob, I'm sorry."

"You understand. . . . They lost my bags . . . and everything in them."

"Yeah?"

"Don. I had things in them. Don, a lot of things, because I was helping Altman out too. This is for the film."

"Holy shit!"

"You got to get on the phone and call Henry."

"Henry?"

"Kissinger. Get ahold of my secretary, Mary Ellen, and she'll give you his number in D.C." The next day, he got his luggage. But this was only the beginning of Evans's problems. In May, on the set of *Popeye*, Evans was informed he would be indicted on fifteen felony counts for a coke buy (about five ounces) that his brother Charlie had made weeks earlier. When the word got out, Polanski called Sylbert, said, "Deek, Deek, thirty-five pounds! What was he trying to do, make a line from New York to Paris?"

On July 31, 1980, while *Popeye* was still in post, Evans pleaded guilty to a misdemeanor charge of cocaine possession. Needless to say, Disney was not happy with all the bad publicity swirling around the producer. "*Popeye* was the first time the Walt Disney Company opened their arms to an outside partner, and I was arrested for cocaine!" continues Evans. "There was a headline every other day, 'Bob "Cocaine" Evans.' Can you imagine Walt Disney turning over in his grave, just thinking about opening his doors to do business with a Jew — and then this?"

Altman had his own troubles with Disney and supported Evans throughout his. "There's one scene when Popeye jumps into the water and he goes, 'Oh, shit!' An executive called me, just reamed me out, saying, 'No Disney film has ever had the word 'shit' in it, and no Disney film is going to have it as long as I am here.' "

It was on *Popeye* that Scottie Bushnell finally consolidated her power. "After Scottie came on the scene, you could never again have a meeting with Bob that wasn't shaded and jaded," says Tommy Thompson. "Anything anyone was trying to do, she would undermine. She'd be curled up on the sofa, somebody'd come in to talk about something, and when they'd leave, she'd nail 'em. 'Well, I wonder what that was all about.' 'Whaddya mean? He wants to take a vacation.' 'Sure he does.' Bob loved that, ate that up. He wouldn't get rid of her. Scottie was the personification of evil, a witch who just nourished his blackness, that terrible, terrible black hole that's in Bob that would come out when he drank." Joan Tewkesbury, who wrote *Nashville*, and was later fired by Altman, says, "She was a real pain in the ass. She was a facilitator for Bob, but she was not a facilitator for some of the rest of us, and a lot of us were let go. *McCabe*, *Thieves*, *Nashville*, were actively collaborative. Everybody had something to give. That atmosphere changed, and I hated to see it happen." Although many people laid Altman's post-*Nashville* decline to Bushnell's influence, Altman empowered Bushnell for his own reasons. It was not an accident, and may have been his version of the syndrome that afflicted other directors: if he was indeed a genius, as everyone said he was, collaboration was unnecessary.

Says Altman, "A lot of people hated Scottie. She had an abrasive manner. But she took a big load off my shoulders, and she was very good at casting, she was very good with wardrobe. I used her as a way to deal with things that I didn't want to deal with. But it went on too long. That relationship was starting to hurt the pictures, the talent, but I didn't know what to do with her."

When *Popeye* opened at the end of 1980, it didn't do as well as expected, and was widely regarded as a failure. Says Altman, "The picture got an odor because it wasn't *Superman*, and that's what they were looking for." This was Altman's last studio film. He was slated to do *Ragtime* for Dino De Laurentiis, but De Laurentiis, insisting he wanted Redford to star, kicked him off. Altman's world was turning to sand, sifting through his fingers. Says longtime collaborator Allan Nicholls, "Bob always had this studio pyromania, burning studios right and left, and finally, it became, Who do you go to?" (Years later, Altman wrote a song entitled "I'm Swimming Through the Ashes of the Bridges I've Burned.")

FRANCIS AND ELEANOR went to New York. They ate dinner at Elaine's, where they ran into a number of movie folk. Bernardo Bertolucci was at the next table, looking grim. Bob Fosse, haggard and ill, was at another, with one of his dancers. Eleanor thought, What is happening to all these directors?

In December, Coppola endured the indignity of seeing Cimino's Vietnam picture, now disrespectfully dubbed *Apocalypse First* by the waggish press, beat his own film to the screen. He attended a screening in New York, was elaborately courteous to Cimino, only to have the upstart make not-so-veiled digs at *Apocalypse* in his interviews. It would get worse. Although *Superman* dominated the Christmas 1978 box office (ironically, it was written by David Newman, the co-writer of *Bonnie and Clyde*, and co-starred Margot Kidder, the siren of Nicholas Beach), *The Deer Hunter* was greeted with the kind of ecstatic reviews Coppola coveted for his own movie, punctuated by some sharp and angry dissent from what remained of the New Left, for its distortion of the facts.

The Deer Hunter was nominated for nine Oscars, and on April 9, 1979, it won five, including Best Film and Best Director, beating *Coming Home*, *Heaven Can Wait*, *Midnight Express*, and *An Unmarried Woman*. Coppola, in a moment freighted with drama, handed Cimino his award, and John Wayne, in his last public appearance before his death, handed out the Oscar for Best Picture. The writers of *Coming Home* picked up awards for Best Original Screenplay, as did Jane Fonda, for Best Actress. Backstage, Fonda lit into Cimino for making a "racist, Pentagon version of the war." Vietnam Veterans Against the War picketed outside the Dorothy Chandler Pavilion. Coppola could do little but watch.

Rumors were rife that *Apocalypse* was unreleasable. *The Black Stallion* too was a year behind. UA tested *Black Stallion* in Seattle, at a screening attended by the filmmakers, Coppola, and David Field, UA's new head of West Coast production. It was not a great success. The movie was too long and there was no ending. Afterward, they all went out to eat. Field reached into the pocket of his jacket, pulled out a piece of paper, and said, "Francis, I have some notes on the picture." Director Carroll Ballard steeled himself for a fight, but before Field could finish another sentence, Francis raised his hand, said, "David, wait a second. You've got to understand that if this is the way Carroll wants this movie to go out, this is the way the movie's going to go out." Without another word, Field folded up the paper and stuffed it into his pocket. This was the way it was supposed to be, Coppola using his power to produce his friends' movies and shield them from the clumsy hand of the studios. Says director Bob Dalva, who was there, "Francis protected Carroll. He protected me when I directed *The Black Stallion Returns*. He protected Caleb Deschanel on *The Escape Artist*. He used his power, and he stood up for his friends."

But other things happened too that were not the way they were supposed to be. Coppola sent the BAC 111 to Paris to buy copper cookware for his kitchen. He became diverted by the prospect of buying UA, now limping along with its well-intentioned, but inexperienced production executives. He started making calls, trying to round up a group of filmmaker-investors. He called Beatty, who wasn't interested. Undeterred, Coppola went on and on about the new digital technology, about creating a digital studio. "You know, Warren," he said, "I'm telling you that when the cinema becomes electronic, actors can play more than one part. Sets can be made out of nothing." Beatty remained noncommittal. Coppola called again, and again. Every time his mood was different. He was up, he was down. Francis recalls, "The next thing I know I was in this speeding car — it wasn't an ambulance, but it felt like that — with my wife going to some doctor that Warren had told her about, and they're suddenly shoving lithium down my throat. Warren had told my wife, 'Your husband is in serious trouble. He could really be irreparably damaged.' Like, I'm the crazy guy that Warren isn't." Sometime later, Beatty ran into Ellie at a Hollywood function. She thanked him for saving her husband's life.

To those around him, it was evident that Coppola was in the grip of a full-blown, clinical case of manic depression. One day in 1979, near the end of post on *Apocalypse*, he virtually held a roomful of editors prisoner for several hours, haranguing them with a machine-gun fusillade of wild ideas. Word processors had just come out, and he described them as the key to a new way of making movies. He wanted to do a ten-hour film version of Goethe's *Elective Affinities*, in 3D, which people attributed to Melissa's influence. He began negotiating to buy Hollywood General Studios in L.A., and started to talk about taking over Hollywood, building an empire. When the mania ebbed, he became depressed and paranoid, convinced that everyone was out to get him.

Coppola took lithium for about four years. It calmed him down, but he didn't like it; it made him nauseous. He always said, "I don't want lead in my body. What do I need this for?" The doctors told him, "You'll be depressed." He replied, "Well, I'll be depressed." They said, "Just don't shoot yourself."

Francis turned forty on April 7, 1979. A week later, he threw a Coppola-sized party, where the guests, who included Lucas, De Niro, and Hopper, chanted, "We will rule Hollywood! We will rule Hollywood!" while cheerleaders chanted, "Francis has the power!"

Coppola began to complain that he couldn't satisfy Melissa, that she was insatiable. Eventually, it became clear to Coppola that he was not going to leave Ellie. "I have wept over the impossible question of dual loyalties," he said. "You feel loyal to your wife and your family, but you feel loyal to another person whom you have singled out for mutual confidence. . . . That's probably the most destructive thing I've ever been through. But also, as I look back, I don't think I was so much in love. . . . I think it was all about the project and needing that kind of muse to get myself together. . . . I realized you could change wives every ten years and be in the same situation. That it's better to just have one wife. That marriage is best in the long term." He took to introducing Ellie as "my first wife." He said he meant it as a compliment; everyone they knew was divorced and they were still married, but the implied threat was evident. Melissa, meanwhile, started seeing Harrison Ford.

Coppola took the "work-in-progress" to Cannes in May, winning the Palme d'Or for an unprecedented second time. He held a press conference in which he excoriated rapt journalists packed into the two-thousand-seat Grand Salle theater, blaming them for the picture's problems. At a dinner of some twenty or thirty people, including the editing crew, an attractive young woman flagrantly flirted with Francis, who did nothing to discourage her. Reaching the end of her rope, Ellie threw a glass of wine at her, initiating a wine-tossing melee.

When Milius first saw Apocalypse, he was so upset that Coppola had ruined his script that he reportedly put his fist through a door. Nor did Lucas like the picture, complaining he'd invested six years of his life in it, "only to see [my] original concept distorted by Coppola's fervid imagination." Apocalypse was not the smash that the first Godfather was, nor even Godfather II. The reviews were decidedly mixed. Critics were stunned by the hallucinatory first two thirds of the film, but the consensus was that the turgid and inconclusive last third did not work. Tavoularis's corpse-strewn, skull-ornamented Kurtz compound was arresting, as was the mysterioso image of Brando's ovoid, hairless head, but Coppola had indeed lost his way. The pressure he felt to live up to his (self-imposed) reputation simply deprived him of his voice. The picture was sensational in places, but it worked only intemittently. As Towne put it, "It was Apocalypse Now and Then."

Once again, like Star Wars, The Godfather, and Taxi Driver, Apocalypse revolved around the issue of parricide. The New Hollywood directors were created in the crucible of generational conflict, and the highly charged relationship between fathers and sons became their core theme. Like the other Vietnam films, Apocalypse was less an attempt to grapple with the war in any realistic way than an occasion to hold up a mirror to the home-front struggles it provoked. Brando, of course, was the ur-father of this generation, the actor whose performances and rebellious example inspired its best work, yet who now stood a colossus astride the road to greatness, an obstacle Coppola — who long enjoyed a complicated love-hate relationship with the actor — had to overcome. Kurtz, lurking in shadow, clad in black, at once model and caution, became his Darth Vader, another incarnation of Charlie Manson, the scourge figure who had gone native and now, unchallenged, ruled over his family. The compound was his Spahn ranch. From another angle, Kurtz was one more incarnation of Coppola himself, or at least the monster of self-indulgence he had become.

Violating the boundaries between life and art to make their material their own was a dangerous way for these filmmakers to work. It was successful for a while, enriching both the life and the art, but as the two became more extravagant and interchangeable, New Hollywood directors lost the detachment of artists, and their lives and art sank into quicksand, joined in a fatal embrace. It was no wonder Coppola could not figure out what to do with Kurtz. He existed at the intersection of too many issues that were deeply personal. To kill him would be to indict himself, commit suicide, metaphorically speaking. To let him live would be to capitulate to the dark side. Coppola's inability to resolve this dilemma prevented *Apocalypse* from becoming the masterpiece it might have been.

When all was said and done, *Apocalypse*, originally budgeted at $12 million, had cost well over $30 million, very likely over $40 million. It made a big splash when it finally landed but, as Bogdanovich puts it, the suits were not "thrilled about *Apocalypse*, let's face it, 'cause it cost a fortune. It made its money back, but that wasn't what they wanted." From this point forward, Coppola would be regarded in many quarters as damaged goods.

Still, he was pleased. He had become the poet of the imperfect. "Filmmaking is like winemaking," he says. "You got all these grapes, some of them are burnt, some of them are not quite ripe, some of them the sugar isn't right, and with the winemaker's sweat, you make great wine." He personally cleared $10 to $15 million from the picture, enough to take the next and fatal step on the road to disaster that had started with his modest establishment on Folsom Street in November 1969.

Coppola had moved to San Francisco in the first place to get away from the studios and the stultifying, movie-obsessed atmosphere of L.A. Ironically, he had internalized Hollywood, carried the studio system inside him—like Rosemary's baby. But it grew too large. The Bay Area wasn't enough. Nothing was ever enough. Always ambivalent, torn between being a filmmaker and a mogul, Coppola characteristically tried to do both, and resolved to carry the battle to the enemy. He expanded his operation to Hollywood.

- *How Scorsese redeemed the movie brats with* **Raging Bull,** *while a blanket of coke descended on Beverly Hills, Bogdanovich tumbled into tabloid hell, and* **Heaven's Gate** *buried the New Hollywood.*

"We poured all of ourselves into one movie, and if it didn't hit, our whole career went down with it. There are directors who, after certain titles, didn't have anything more left, any more fight."

— MARTIN SCORSESE

By the late '70s, there was a hard white snow falling on Hollywood. Coke was so widespread that people wore small gold spoons around their necks as jewelry. Drug connections became intimates, friends, and boyfriends. You went out to eat, you'd leave a line of coke on the table for the waitress as a tip. Scorsese, exhausted, in poor health, and fueled by a perpetual coke high, tried to do everything. He promiscuously took on several projects at once. Then, toward the end of *New York, New York*, producer Jonathan Taplin called. The Band was going to break up, and he asked Scorsese to shoot a documentary about the group's final concert on Thanksgiving Day 1976, which would become *The Last Waltz*. Without giving it a second thought, Scorsese agreed. "He never could resist Robbie Robertson and the Band," says Irwin Winkler, who produced *New York, New York*. In the frame of mind he was in, he figured he could cut the film at night while he edited the feature during the day. Adds Taplin, "Marty was just so wired he could show up at any hour of the day or night, go into the editing room, do a sequence, and go on to the next thing."

After Julia Cameron moved out in January 1977, Robertson left his family to move into Scorsese's Mulholland Drive house. He had delusions about becoming a movie star, and Marty was his ticket. "We were the odd couple — looking for trouble," says Robertson. Reflects Sandy Weintraub, "It was a shame that Marty wasn't gay. The best relationship he ever had was probably with Robbie."

The Mulholland house was barely furnished, and notable for a seventeenth-century wooden crucifix concealing a dagger that hung over Marty's bed. His friends puzzled over the symbolism. The house looked like a hotel for transients, filled with the groupies, visiting filmmakers, musicians, and druggies who made up Scorsese's circle. The regulars, Steve Prince, Mardik Martin, Jay Cocks, and assorted hangers-on, used to gather in Scorsese's projection room in the garage — which doubled as Robertson's bedroom — and watch four or five movies a night. "Marty's house was blacked out with blinds," says Robertson, "soundproofed, and he installed an air system so you could breathe without opening the windows. We only had two problems: the light and the birds."

"We were like vampires," recalls Martin. "It was like, 'Oh no, the sun is coming up.' We never got to sleep before seven, eight A.M., for six months." Marty had also put in an elaborate security system, which invariably malfunctioned, bringing unwelcome visits from rent-a-cops. Outside of watching movies and doing drugs, Marty's only relaxation was playing with his collection of toy soldiers.

Marty had been taking pills since he was three, so by this time it was second nature to him. He took drugs like aspirin. He was still going up and down in weight. Coke depresses the appetite, but after going without food for two or three days, there was a lot of binge eating, a lot of junk food, anything that was at hand. Moreover, he and his friends needed booze to come down, so they knocked back a couple bottles of wine or vodka just to get to sleep. According to Taplin, "They would call the editor of The Last Waltz, Yeu-Bun Yee, in the middle of the night with ideas. They were so stoked they thought everyone else was up all night too."

"At first you felt like you could make five films at once," Scorsese recalls. "And then you wound up spending four days in bed every week because you were exhausted and your body couldn't take it." He had been in and out of the hospital a number of times with asthma attacks. "The doctor would say, 'Take these pills. You're suffering from exhaustion,'" says Robertson. "But we had places to go, people to see." The rule was, live-fast-and-leave-a-good-looking-corpse. Scorsese was convinced he wouldn't see forty. "It was a matter of pushing the envelope, of being bad, seeing how much you can do," he continues. "Embracing a way of life to its limit. I did a lot of drugs because I wanted to do a lot, I wanted to push all the way to the very very end, and see if I could die. That was the key thing, to see what it would be like getting close to death." This kind of recklessness lent his work a high passion that hoisted it above the ordinary, but it was dangerous. "I've always felt that there's something self-destructive in directors," says Ned Tanen — himself no slouch in that department — contemplating the sorry spectacle of the New Hollywood directors careening pell-mell down the mountain, arriving in a heap at the bottom, careers shattered, marriages sundered, friendships broken, lives in ruins. "I once asked Howard Hawks, my former father-in-law, about it, and he said, 'The studio system worked because we couldn't be excessive, we couldn't just do what we wanted to do.' "

One day there was a party at Winkler's home. Scorsese, Martin, and Robertson came late, stoned out of their minds, hung out by themselves at the far end of the pool. Scorsese was dressed in the crisp white suit he favored above all others. All of a sudden John Cassavetes walked up, pulled Marty aside, started in on him for doing drugs. "Whatsamatter with you?" he growled. "Why are you doing this, ruining yourself? You're fucking up your talent. Shape up." Scorsese broke out into a sweat. Cassavetes was a notorious drunk himself, but no one could call him on what he said, because they knew it was true.

De Niro had not given up on *Raging Bull*. But he was still having a hard time getting Scorsese's attention. Marty's personal life was in such turmoil he couldn't concentrate on his work. Despite his success, Scorsese was still extremely fragile, emotionally speaking, a state of affairs that doubtless stemmed from the aggravations of his childhood: his diminutive stature, his frailty, his perception of himself as unattractive. His feelings were easily hurt; he was quick to feel slighted and slow to forgive. He nursed grudges for years. He built a wall around himself. "He was lost personally," says Martin. "Secure as he was on a film set, he was very insecure with himself as a man, dealing with people." Martin once invited him to a party. "I said to him, 'We'll have a lot of fun, girls, orgies . . .' He said, 'Nah . . . somebody will know who I am . . .' I said, 'You don't have to tell them who you are. Nobody cares.' He said, 'No, no, no, I can't deal with a woman who doesn't know who I am.' He had to be 'Martin Scorsese' for him to deal with a woman, but then he worried she would only like him because he was 'Martin Scorsese.' "

"I was making love to different women, but I didn't find that very interesting," Scorsese recalls. He was doing it more, enjoying it less. He got into a tempestuous relationship with an assistant, and one night he went to a party where he encountered her, Liza Minnelli, and Julia Cameron, all at the same time. She was the kind of woman who always had another man in her life, which drove Marty insane with jealousy. She threatened suicide every other day, which is to say, she was perfect for him. "Marty sort of likes a little bit of drama, and if it's not there, he creates it," says Martin. "It was a typical living-dangerously mentality. She brought out the worst in him." Scorsese could never stand to be alone. One night, he drove her out and then ran naked down Mulholland after her, screaming, "Come back, don't leave me."

Scorsese knew he was acting badly, driving people away from him, but he couldn't help it. He says, "I was always angry, throwing glasses, provoking people, really unpleasant to be around. I always found, no matter what anybody said, something to take offense at. I'd be the host, but at some point during the evening I'd flip out, just like when I'm shooting." He began to have paranoid hallucinations. He'd say, "I think somebody's watching me," or, "Somebody's trying to get in." Marty had a one-night stand with Yeu-Bun Yee's girlfriend, who looked like a model, and was afraid that he would come up in the middle of the night and kill him. One of Steve Prince's jobs was to protect him from real or imagined dangers.

Scorsese and Robertson took *The Last Waltz* to Cannes in the spring of 1978. Fueled by coke, Marty was doing back-to-back interviews, but even he eventually ran out of words. And coke. He joked, "No more coke, no more interviews." He couldn't score in Cannes, so a private plane was dispatched to Paris to bring back more coke.

"It hit me finally, when I was watching the end credits crawl of *The Last Waltz* at the Cinerama Dome, that I didn't enjoy it anymore," says Scorsese. "There was nothing left. I knew when I broke up the second marriage — I had a child, I knew I was not going to see the child for a while — but I always had a bottom line: the work, and felt good about having been able to say something in a movie, but this one day, it was like rock bottom. I thought, I've lost my voice."

Scorsese kept everyone at bay, just yessing them to death, but refusing to move forward on *Raging Bull*. He was emotionally and spiritually tapped out. "We were just circling the globe constantly, going from party to party, trying to find what it was that would inspire us again to do work," he recalls. "I knew what I wanted to say in *Mean Streets*, like I knew what I wanted to say in *Taxi Driver*. I even knew what I wanted to say in *New York, New York*. But I know I didn't know what the hell *Raging Bull* was about." He had done three straight pictures with De Niro. "After a while, you want to do movies just on your own, especially after the unhappy experience with *New York, New York*," he adds. "I just didn't want to play anymore."

Mardik was already on salary at Winkler's company, in which he was partnered with Robert Chartoff. Winkler told him to go ahead anyway, write a script. Mardik did a draft, which Scorsese couldn't even bring himself to read. One day, after Mardik pestered him for the hundredth time, the director asked, "Okay, whaddya got?"

"I got one good scene that you're gonna like. You have these gladiators, see, just like in Rome, two guys, fighting each other, and you got all these rich people, fur coats, tuxedos, sitting in the front row, and Bobby gets punched in the face, and his nose starts to squirt blood, and it splatters all over these rich people's clothes and furs."

"Whew, that's great, I love that. Lemme read the script." Scorsese read the script, told Mardik, "I wanna make it more personal." His grandfather, who used to live on Staten Island, owned a fine fig tree, and one day he said, "If the fig tree dies, I'm gonna die." And sure enough, the fig tree died, and he died. Recalls Mardik, "He wanted me to put that in the movie, a lot of crazy stuff that had nothing to do with Jake La Motta. I didn't want him to say no, so I catered to his whims and bullshit. It was driving me crazy. I said, 'Marty, I don't think this makes any sense, Bobby's gonna kill me.'" Indeed, De Niro hated it, said, "What's going on? This is not the picture we agreed upon."

Continues Mardik, "One day, Marty said to me, 'Whaddya think of Paul Schrader coming in for a polish.' Because Marty was not listening to me anymore, he was doing his Godfather bit. I said, 'Sure, why not.' Paul didn't even come to me. He sent somebody to get all my research, all my versions, three of them. I gave it to the guy, said, 'Good luck.'"

AFTER HIS TRAUMATIC EXPERIENCE on *Star Wars*, Lucas decided he'd had it with directing. Just as he had read the post-Vietnam cultural tea leaves and exploited what he sensed in *Graffiti* and *Star Wars*, so his move from directing to producing would prove to be equally prescient. He hired Irvin Kershner, who had taught at USC and been something of a mentor for George and his friends. Even so, *The Empire Strikes Back*, also shot in London, was another difficult production. Kershner was unhappy, Lucas was unhappy. Kershner was good with actors, used to edgy contemporary material, had been widely praised for a film called *Loving*. But he had never directed a special effects picture. He complained, to anyone who would listen, "It's amazing. I direct the actors, and then [the footage] goes to California and then I find out what the scene is about."

He was also known as a ditherer, a director who could turn a green light into a development deal, someone who would change his mind by the end of a long sentence, and he had a slow DP. One day, as the shooting spilled over the wrap date, it became evident that Kershner had exceeded the budget by a good $5 million, with six unanticipated weeks to go. Lucas, who was financing the picture himself, was apoplectic, and blamed his long-term friend and associate, producer Gary Kurtz. Eventually, *Empire* ran over by eight weeks and $10 million, with the budget finally coming in at $33 million, roughly three times the cost of *Star Wars*. Lucas never worked with Kurtz again.

The huge budget overruns nearly sank Lucas. Stretched to the breaking point, he was forced to take a bank loan, and worse, was humiliated by having to beg Fox to guarantee the loan. In exchange, Fox insisted on renegotiating the deal. Still, he came out with $430 million worth of tickets worldwide, recouping his $33 million in only three months — and finally achieved his dream: financial independence from the studios.

Less flexible and forgiving than his mentor, George disliked the Hollywood establishment even more than Francis did. In 1981, the man who had once called Hollywood "a foreign country," got into a tiff with the guilds because he had placed Kershner's director's credit at the end of the film instead of at the beginning, as DGA rules required. He also crossed swords with the Writers Guild. Both guilds fined him, and in response, Lucas resigned from the Motion Picture Academy and tore up his membership card to the Directors Guild. Around Memorial Day, he dramatically severed his last remaining ties to Hollywood. Lucasfilm closed its offices across the street from Universal, and moved north of San Francisco to San Rafael, where ILM was located. Says Lucas, "Once the corporations bought in, and once the agents, lawyers, and accountants took over, people who read the *Wall Street Journal* and cared less about the movies than the price of the stock, that's when that whole thing died."

Lucas was determined to build his own version of Zoetrope, a full-service state-of-the-art production facility where his friends could come and work on their films in an idyllic, Northern California setting far from the fleshpots of tinsel town — the agents and the drugs, the limos and the trendy restaurants. He bought four-thousand odd hilly acres of scrub off Lucas (no relation) Valley Road in Marin County and called it Skywalker Ranch. Skywalker included a library, a lake, a baseball diamond, stables, and a vineyard. No building was visible from any other building. The three-acre lake was stocked with trout.

Lucas imagined that Skywalker would be a cinematic think tank. There would be lectures, conferences, retreats, and all his friends would have offices there. Predictably, Skywalker was the flip side of Zoetrope, where the food was great but the toilets were always broken. It ran like clockwork, but was antiseptic and anonymous, with Big Brother vibes.

Marcia told him he was crazy. "By the time George could afford to have a film facility, he no longer wanted to direct," she says. "After *Star Wars*, he insisted, 'I'm never going to direct another establishment-type movie again.' I used to say, 'For someone who wants to be an experimental filmmaker, why are you spending this fortune on a facility to make Hollywood movies? We edited *THX* in our attic, we edited *American Graffiti* over Francis's garage, I just don't get it, George.' The Lucasfilm empire — the computer division, ILM, the licensing and lawyers — seemed to me to be this inverted triangle sitting on a pea, which was the *Star Wars* trilogy. But he wasn't going to make any more *Star Wars*, and the pea was going to dry up and crumble, and then he was going to be left with this huge facility with its enormous overhead. And why did he want to do that if he wasn't going to make movies? I still don't get it."

Coppola was at once envious and disappointed that he wasn't part of it. "I'm the only one of all his friends who never had a piece of *Star Wars*," he says. "Although I was the one whom he would talk to about it. I helped him, but clearly, once he went on, he went on. It was clear to me he just wanted his own show. I had brought him along with me everywhere I went, but he didn't bring me along with him."

•

SCHRADER TOOK TO COKE like mother's milk; he plunged into the drug scene with the enthusiasm of a lapsed fundamentalist. Like Scorsese, he believed coke helped him creatively. He had always been in the habit of writing while intoxicated, so the transition to drugs was easy. "I would write stoned and revise sober," he says. "When you're very, very stoned you have access to fantasies that are harder to get at when you're straight, particularly for somebody like me that didn't have access to that inner life. The prose gets sometimes a little excessive, and the syntax gets a little wacked. But it's basically what you want to say, and often, very, very alive. I would write a scene at three o'clock in the morning, and I would be all jacked up, so excited I would be singing and dancing around the room. Substance abuse was the key that opened that door. It would be hypocritical to look back and blame the key."

A gram cost about $100 in the late '70s, which included the packaging and the convenience of delivery. (It was cheaper on the street.) Schrader's dealer supplied grams in little envelopes fashioned from pages torn out of *Playboy* and *Penthouse*, with the grade (the highest was SG — Show Girl), marked on the front. Schrader was doing an ounce (twenty-eight grams) a week, a habit that cost him about $12,000 a month, or $144,000 a year. He bought a quarter of an ounce (seven grams) at a time, never more than nineteen grams, because in a bust, twenty grams could pull down a conviction for dealing, rather than mere possession.

Schrader was working hard and playing hard. He became very much a part of the gay party scene, which he had been flirting with since the *Taxi Driver* days in 1975. "This was a kind of heady period, where for the first time in American culture, gay choices about music, clothes, design were considered to be the future," says Rosenman. "This was the cutting edge, but it was so exciting and gorgeous and glamorous that everybody knew that it was leading toward an abyss. And that was attractive in and of itself. There was a mystic wildness about the partying, the music, the drugs, the clothes, the free sexuality — the interchange of partners, the constant fucking of boys, girls, it was so shocking and exhilarating. People like Schrader were attracted to it because they understood there was something religious in the intertwining of sex, death, and ecstasy."

Schrader's friends wondered how far Schrader went. Although it would be hard to imagine a less sympathetic audience than the gun-crazed Milius, Schrader used to lecture his friend on the importance of the gay aesthetic. "The arbiters of taste in our society are gay. Most of my friends are gay."

"Well, Paul, are you gay?"

"I can't do it, I can't even succeed here."

Says Milius, "Schrader was this character who had fallen from his Calvinist grace, and was really enjoying his time in hell, sampling every part of it. He loved perversion, but all sexuality in some way was a failure for him. One night, when he was making *Hardcore*, I noticed his wrists were marked. He explained, 'I went to Mistress Vicky and she hung me up and cuffed me. I could only take it for three minutes.' Like, he wasn't a true pervert. He couldn't take it for a half an hour like a real-man pervert. The same thing with being gay, he failed at that too, couldn't get it up for boys."

But Schrader's sexual preferences were less interesting than his cultural ones. For a while, at any rate, he was able to anticipate the sudden and not so sudden changes in the cultural weather, and when he joked to Milius that he'd exchanged "violence for design," he was expressing more than a personal inclination. As Kael noted, there was a rising revulsion against violence in movies. Schrader's carefully nurtured reputation as a wild man had run its course and was now a liability. Whereas *Time*'s cover story on *Bonnie and Clyde* in December 1967 lauded shockers like *Point Blank*, in October 1980, Schrader was featured on the cover of *Saturday Review* with Scorsese, De Palma, and Walter Hill under the cover line, "The Brutalists: Making Movies Mean and Ugly." He recalls, "I started getting labeled as a filmmaker who was only into violence. I winced at that, realized I really had to change my image." It was part of the backlash against the New Hollywood — and Schrader sensed that what worked for *Taxi Driver* would work no longer.

THE MOVIE *1941* went into production in October 1978. It was a quixotic venture from the start. Spielberg's friends wondered, "Why is Steven doing comedy. Where has Steven been funny?" But *Animal House* had been a huge hit, *Saturday Night Live* was all the rage and, funny or not, Spielberg felt he had to join the party. He cast John Belushi and Dan Aykroyd, among others; Milius produced, and did some work on the script. He didn't much like working with his friend. He says, "Steve just wouldn't listen. He would never say, 'Well you're wrong, come up with something better,' like Francis would do. Instead, he'd go talk to his other team of writers that you didn't know existed."

It was Spielberg's only foray into genre deconstruction, à la Altman et al., and it quickly became clear even to him that he wasn't good at it. The director had snatched victory from the jaws of a shark once before, but this time it was different. The budget was out of control. Spielberg was suffering from auteur's disease. He was using a Louma crane — an extremely costly piece of equipment — to shoot inserts, an elephant stepping on a pea. When the picture wrapped on May 16, 1979, Spielberg had been shooting for 178 days, nearly a month longer than *Jaws*, and eventually the budget peaked at $31.5 million (some placed it at $40 million), giving *Apocalypse Now* a run for its money. Before the movie came out, *Saturday Night Live* writer Michael O'Donoghue had distributed buttons that read, "John Belushi: 1952–1941."

Later, Spielberg explained, with a degree of candor unusual for Hollywood,

"We would have been better off with $10 million less, because we went from one plot to seven subplots. But at the time, I wanted it — the bigness, the power, hundreds of people at my beck and call, millions of dollars at my disposal, and everybody saying, Yes, yes, yes." Now, he elaborates, "Power can go right to the head. I felt immortal after a critical hit and two box office hits, one being the biggest hit in history up to that moment. But 1941 was not a screw-you film, I can do anything I want, watch me fail upward. I was very indulgent on 1941, simply because I was insecure with the material. It wasn't making me laugh, or any of us laugh, either in dailies or on the set. So I shot that movie every way I knew how, to try to save it from what I thought it actually became, which is a demolition derby."

Spielberg was so certain 1941 was going to be a disaster that on the night of the December 14, 1979, premiere, he fled the country, decamped with Amy to Japan, where they planned, finally, to get married. They had been engaged for months, sent out Christmas cards signed, "the Spielbergs." Amy told friends, "I'll be pregnant by April." They never did get married there; by the time the plane landed in Tokyo, the two had called it off. Explains Irving, "I fell in love with Willie Nelson." So low was Amy's standing among Spielberg's friends that they speculated she left him because the picture flopped. Says one friend, "He was so relieved that they broke up, because he wanted to marry her, and he just saw it as a narrow escape from years of alimony, because the marriage would not have lasted."

Spielberg was right — about Amy, about 1941. The reviews were awful, and the picture went down with a resounding thud. In the press, Steven ungallantly blamed the writers, Zemeckis and Gale, who "caught me at a weak moment," he said. Amy moved to Santa Fe. It was a low point in Spielberg's life and career, perhaps the lowest. 1941 popped the wunderkind balloon, and now, after advertising his marriage plans to everyone he knew, the squeaky-clean director had just managed to prove that his personal life was as out of control as his budgets. It took him a long time to recover. "It's a lot easier to commit to a movie than a personal relationship," he said, adding, "Life has finally caught up with me. I've spent so many years hiding from pain and fear behind a camera. . . . [But] I didn't escape suffering. I only delayed it."

DURING THE LAST WEEK of Hardcore, when De Niro paid a visit to the set, Schrader knew something was up. The actor was not the sort to casually drop by. He told Schrader that UA wouldn't make Raging Bull with Mardik's script; he asked Schrader to rewrite it. He also told him he was fed up with Scorsese's indifference to the project. By that time, Schrader had firmly established himself as a director, and he was not eager to work on other people's scripts. At a dinner with Bob and Marty at Musso and Frank's Grill in the summer of 1978, he agreed to do a polish, but he made sure they knew he was doing them a favor. This did not sit well with Marty.

After reading Mardik's drafts, Schrader concluded that more was needed than just a fix. He knew he had to go back to the sources, do his own research. It was then that he discovered Jake's brother, Joey. Recalls Schrader, "They were both boxers. Joey was younger, better looking, and a real smooth talker. It occurred to Joey that he could do better at managing his brother. He wouldn't have to get beat up, he'd still get the girls, and he would get the money. And having a brother myself, it was very easy for me to tap into that tension. I realized there was a movie there." *Raging Bull*, among other things, became a version of Schrader's relationship with Leonard.

Meanwhile, the movie was coming together for De Niro. One day, at Scorsese's suite in the Sherry, La Motta just got up and banged his head against the wall. Recalls Scorsese, "De Niro saw this movement and suddenly he got the whole character from him, the whole movie. We knew we wanted to make a movie that would reach a man at the point of making that gesture with the line, 'I'm not an animal.' "

Schrader wrote at Nickodell's, a bar on Melrose next to Paramount that, in Simpson's words, "was a great place to get fucked up, because it was dark and cavernous." He remembers Schrader retiring to the bathroom for some moments, then emerging to take a seat at the bar, where he feverishly scribbled on a napkin. It was a scene in which La Motta, in jail and at the nadir of his fortunes, tries to masturbate. But he can't get off, because his mind is flooded with guilt, memories of how terrible he's been to the various women in his life. This was Schrader at his best, going places nobody else would go, raw and fearless.

But material of this kind was way too rich for UA. Winkler met with the executives at Eric Pleskow's apartment on Ocean Avenue in Santa Monica, near the beach. "We'd just done a boxing movie, *Rocky*," recalls Medavoy, "and this was a real downer." According to Winkler, the company wanted no part of *Raging Bull*. Still, the producer had a trump. "We were in a unique position, 'cause we owned the rights to *Rocky*," he says. UA had released *Rocky* in 1976. It was one of the coming crop of post–New Hollywood feel-good films, a throwback to the '50s, and a peek at the '80s, a racist, Great White Hope slap at Muhammad Ali — on whom the character of Rocky's opponent was all too obviously based — and everything he stood for, the generation of uppity black folk and the antiwar, "nigger-loving" white kids who admired him. *Rocky* was a huge success, taking in about $110 million before it played out, making it the fifth highest grossing picture of all time. So all Winkler had to say was, "Want to make *Raging Bull*? No? Want to make *Rocky II*? Yes? Okay, let's make a deal."

Even the writer of *Taxi Driver* found the characters repellent. Schrader told

Marty, "We have to give Jake a depth, a stature he does not possess, otherwise he's not worth making a movie about." He says Scorsese didn't get it. For Scorsese, Jake's Neanderthal sensibility was the whole point. "Bob and I sort of pushed each other in terms of how unpleasant a character could be, and still people cared for him," he says. "Because there's something in Bob as an actor, something about his face, that people see the humanity."

Scorsese, De Niro, and Winkler met with Schrader at the Sherry to discuss the script. It was a tense meeting. Marty thought Schrader's new draft was a breakthrough. He too responded to the sibling aspects of the script. Still, both he and De Niro had reservations. Recalls Schrader, "De Niro was balking at a lot of the heavier stuff, the raw, controversial stuff, the cock and the ice and all that, 'Why do we have to do these things?' Marty wasn't going to take on Bob, because he had to work with him, so he was letting me fight those fights. It was a bold, original kind of scene. But looking at it from De Niro's point of view, it was pretty hard to make it work, sitting there with your dick in your hand." To Marty and Bob, Schrader's attitude was, Here's your script, I don't need this, I want to get back to my own projects. At one point, Paul threw the script across the room, yelling, "If you want a secretary to take dictation, hire one. But I'm here to try to write a real story about someone that people care about," and stormed out. Says Scorsese, "I'll do anything and say anything to get what I want on the screen. Throw something at me, curse at me, do what you want to do as long as I get what I want. I sit there and smile and take it and run, which is what I did. He broke the icejam and gave us something special. But I certainly couldn't embrace the person afterward. Not after years of slights and insults, it was just too much."

But Scorsese's world came crashing down around his ears right after Labor Day 1978. He had been living with Isabella Rossellini since early summer. He, Rossellini, De Niro, and Martin, went to the Telluride Film Festival. "We didn't have any coke, somebody gave us some garbage, it made us sick," recalls Mardik. That weekend, Scorsese started coughing up blood, and blacked out for the first time in his life. From Telluride, he went to New York, where he collapsed. "He was bleeding from his mouth, bleeding from his nose, bleeding from his eyes, ass. He was very near death," Martin adds. Rossellini had to go to Italy for work, and when she left, after that weekend, she thought she was never going to see him alive again.

Steve Prince took Scorsese to New York Hospital. A doctor came running down to the ER carrying a sample of his blood, yelling, "Is this your blood?"

"Yeah," Scorsese replied, blankly.

"Do you realize you have no platelets?"

"I don't know what that means."

"It means you're bleeding internally everywhere."

"I want to get back to work."

"You can't go anywhere, you may get a brain hemorrhage any second."

Scorsese's condition appeared to be a result of the interaction among his asthma medication, other prescription drugs, and the bad coke he had taken over the weekend. He was down to 109 pounds. The doctor stopped all the drugs and pumped him full of cortisone. He was put in a palatial room previously occupied by the Shah of Iran, but he couldn't sleep, and the first three nights he stayed up watching movies, among them, *Dr. Jekyll and Mr. Hyde*, appropriately enough. Eventually, the cortisone worked, and his platelet count started to rise, stopping the bleeding.

"Finally," says Robertson, "Marty got a doctor who conveyed the message that either he changed his life or he was going to die. We knew we had to change trains. Our lives were way too rich. The cholesterol level was unimaginable. I went back to my family, hoping they would overlook my fool heart."

De Niro came into Scorsese's room, said, "What's the matter with you, Marty? Don't you wanna live to see if your daughter is gonna grow up and get married? Are you gonna be one of those flash-in-the-pan directors who does a couple of good movies and it's over for them?" He changed the subject to *Raging Bull*, said, "You know, we can make this picture. We can really do a great job. Are we doing it or not?" Scorsese replied, "Yes." He had finally found the hook: the self-destructiveness, the wanton damage to the people around him, just for its own sake. He thought: I am Jake.

AFTER HIS STRING of high-profile reverses, Peter Bogdanovich's ill-wishers whispered that he was washed up, could no longer get a studio deal. Cybill Shepherd had left him to marry a former bartender and parts manager for a Memphis-based Mercedes-Benz dealership, three years her junior. Bogdanovich derisively referred to him as "that garage mechanic." He was depressed and at loose ends.

Bogdanovich had become a frequent visitor at the Playboy Mansion, where he met Dorothy Stratten, in October 1978. She was a former Dairy Queen waitress from a cowtown in Canada, eighteen years old, and unhappily married to Paul Snider, twenty-nine, a sleazy hustler who was managing her career. Snider had sent her nude pictures to *Playboy*, where she had been featured as Miss August 1979, going on to become Playmate of the Year in 1980. Stratten was from the same mold as Shepherd, a stunning blonde, statuesque (five foot eleven), with great bone structure, full breasts, and was, of course, an aspiring actress. Dorothy was a pothead, spent her days stoned playing checkers and roller skating. She was almost comically nearsighted, but refused to wear glasses because they spoiled her looks. When she walked down Sunset to Mirabelle's, a restaurant, perched on platform heels and wearing indecently brief terrycloth shorts with a tiny top, head high in the air, she invariably caused rear-enders — to which she was entirely oblivious because she was nearly blind.

Bogdanovich took one look at Stratten and thought, This is the most beautiful girl I've ever seen in my life. He told her he was casting a picture, which he wasn't, and gave her his number. She never called. Exactly one year later, in October 1979, he ran into her again, and they started seeing each other. He told her he had made a star of Shepherd, he would do it again with her. She cried on his shoulder, complained about Snider. He clucked sympathetically. It was the old body-of-a-woman, mind-of-a-girl thing. Not yet twenty, she always had a man in her life to tell her what to do. Peter was more than happy to fill the bill. "She was not in love with Peter," says someone who knew them both. "Every time she talked to me about Peter, it was, 'Peter is okay.' It was not like when I talked to Peter, 'Oh, we love each other.' She was along for the ride." But, according to actress Colleen Camp, who was a friend, "She was totally smitten with Peter."

Several of Dorothy's friends warned the couple that Snider was unstable. Dorothy always dismissed the idea, saying, "Oh, he'd never do anything. He's very gentle." Peter said, "I guess I should pay him some money."

Peter wrote Dorothy into *They All Laughed*, an $8.6 million romantic comedy with Audrey Hepburn, Ben Gazzara, and John Ritter. It was produced by a wannabe Hollywood company, Time-Life Films. Peter kissed her for the first time in mid-January of the new year, as they walked on the beach in Santa Monica. In the spring, she wrote Snider a letter informing him she wanted a separation.

They All Laughed started up in New York. At that point in his career Peter, who always fancied himself an actor, was better at playing the director than actually directing, so much so that when Buck Henry was walking down Fifth Avenue past the Plaza and stumbled across the production, he saw a guy in a big Stetson and cowboy boots behind the camera, and said to his girlfriend, "Look, somebody's making a movie about making a movie."

Snider was desperately trying to reach Dorothy, who had put a "Do Not Disturb" on her phone at the Wyndham Hotel. People warned her that it would drive Snider crazy if he did not have access to his wife. She paid no attention. After the picture wrapped in July, Stratten moved into Peter's house. Snider, meanwhile, was starting to behave erratically. He bought a shotgun and shot pigeons in his backyard. One afternoon, he called Platt's home, shouting, hoarsely, "Where's Peter Bogdanovich, where's Peter Bogdanovich?" Platt thought it was an out-of-work actor.

Snider had convinced Stratten she still owed him for making her a centerfold, and she was giving him money. On the morning of August 14, she left Peter's house without telling anyone where she was going. She was on her way to Snider's home, apparently to make another payment. When she had not returned by noon, Peter began to worry. Trying to calm him down, his daughter Antonia said — ironically, as it turned out — "At least she's not dead."

Probably loaded on booze and 'ludes, Snider blew Stratten's head off with the shotgun, and then placed her prostrate on an exercise bench (later referred to in the press as a "bondage machine") and had sex with her corpse. Her butt was slightly elevated by the bench, on which there were semen stains; there were two bloody handprints on her bottom. One of her fingers, apparently blown off when she raised her hands to protect herself, was stuck to the wall, along with a fair amount of blood. She was twenty. Snider then shot himself in the head. When the police discovered the body, one of his eyes had been moved to the center of his forehead by the force of the blast, so that he looked like a Cyclops.

Bogdanovich was told about the murder-suicide by Hugh Hefner, who phoned him around midnight. "I dropped the phone, fell down, tried to scratch through the linoleum," he recalls. "It was the way people reacted to heavy bombing during the war. They tried to dig through the ground. I wanted to get away from it, that's what that crawling thing was about, but then it hit me, that no matter where I went, the problem was that I'd be there. Nobody would let me out of the house, which was just as well. I would've driven off a cliff or something. They gave me a whole shitload of Valium, and took me upstairs and put me to sleep."

LIKE ARTHUR KRIM AND COMPANY, the new production heads at UA, Steven Bach and David Field, found the *Raging Bull* script scabrous and depressing, thought it made *Rocky* look like a dust-up between two sissies in the sandbox. One of Winkler's jobs was to keep bad news away from his volatile director. Scorsese had no idea the project was in jeopardy. He recalls, "I thought I could get any picture made, particularly with De Niro. He was a big star. I was naive about that."

Winkler finally called Marty, said, "We better have a meeting with the UA guys. Just say hello and talk about the script."

"What do they want to know? What do we have to talk about?"

"Just say hello. It's a hello meeting. It's just something so they feel part of it." At the end of November 1978, just after Thanksgiving, Bach and Field accompanied Winkler to Scorsese's co-op in the Galleria on East 57th Street in New York. De Niro was there as well. Winkler wasn't worried. He still had the *Rocky* trump. But Scorsese startled them by announcing he wanted to do the film in black and white. He wanted *Raging Bull* to have a tabloid look, like Weegee. Bach and Field demurred, eventually gave in, but came up with a series of objections to the script.

"This picture is written as an X, and I don't think we can afford that," said Bach.

"What makes you so sure it's an X?"

"When I read in a script 'close-up on Jake La Motta's erection as he pours ice water over it prior to the fight,' then I think we're in the land of X . . ."

"Look," interrupted Field, "it isn't about the language or the things the writers wrote that you probably won't shoot anyway. It's the whole script. It's this *man*," Field said, quietly. "I don't know who wants to see a movie that begins with a man so angry, so . . . choked with rage, that because his pregnant wife burns the steak, he slugs her to the kitchen floor and then kicks her in the abdomen until she aborts."

"We'll find a writer who can lick it," said Winkler, blandly.

"It's not finally about the writer," said Field. "Can any writer make him more than what he seems to be in the scripts we've seen?"

"Which is what?" asked Marty, brows knitted.

Field regarded him with a faint smile. "A cockroach."

A suffocating silence fell over the room like a blanket. De Niro, in jeans and bare feet, slumped in an easy chair, had said nothing. He roused himself, and said, quietly but distinctly, "He is not a cockroach. . . . He is *not* a cockroach."

Bob and Marty took off for St. Martin, and completely reworked the script. Scorsese didn't like islands, his asthma was killing him. He was taking Tedral to clear his lungs, but it sent him into bouts of trembling. De Niro nursed him, made him coffee in the mornings. They knew this was it; either they came back with a usable screenplay, or the project was history. But right away they found the zone. Once again, Scorsese dipped into himself. He recalls, "The key thing was the writing of the scene where Jake is fixing the television, and he accuses his brother of sleeping with his wife. What I took from myself was the tenacity of a man who is so paranoid and so self-destructive that even though he knows nothing, he will conduct an investigation of the person closest to him as if he knows exactly what happened, and he will not accept no for an answer, which means he sets up everything to destroy himself."

Weeks later, UA approved it. Bach and Field had other things on their mind besides *Raging Bull*. They were preoccupied with gearing up for *Heaven's Gate*.

PUFFED UP BY his Oscars, stubborn and so megalomaniacal he made Coppola look like Mary Poppins, Cimino had won all the preproduction skirmishes, including a cast of sub-marquee names that included Kris Kristofferson, Isabelle Huppert, Christopher Walken, and John Hurt, and most important, the contractual right to go over budget, if necessary, to make the Christmas 1979 release date UA wanted. After many delays, he began production on April 16, 1979, in Kalispell, Montana, on a budget of $10 million.

Cimino's perfectionism knew no bounds, and it soon became clear that he was shooting at an exceedingly slow pace. While the budget visualized two script pages a day of a 133-page script, the actual rate was closer to five eighths of a page. After the first twelve days, he was ten days and fifteen pages behind. He started losing ground at the rate of one day for every day shot. He was building, tearing down, and rebuilding sets, as well as piling on extras by the

cartload. Cimino was shooting ten, twenty, thirty takes of every shot and print-
ing almost every one, ten thousand feet of film a day (two hours plus of film),
which cost $200,000 per day or about $1 million a week. By June 1, a month
and a half into the shoot, Cimino had reached the $10 million mark, equal to
the original budget. But there were still 107⅜ pages to go. Albeck projected
that if Cimino continued at that pace, the film would cost the company,
excluding prints and ads, in the neighborhood of $43.4 million. When Field
visited the set, Cimino refused to speak with him. Bach and Field were virtually
helpless. As Tanen put it, "It had become more risky to say, 'We're stopping the
picture, you're off the film.' The Directors Guild came in with these rules that
you could only fire for cause, and in the end, you just couldn't put somebody
off a movie. So the attitude became, just get to the end of the tunnel."

Bach and Field visited the set on another occasion, with the intention of
reading Cimino the riot act. But when he showed them his rough assemblage,
they were stunned by its beauty — and won over. "It looks like David Lean
decided to make a Western," Bach later told Albeck, breathlessly. Instead of
disciplining their intractable director, they congratulated him and went home.
According to UA executive Chris Mankiewicz, who had resigned in anger just
before the elevation of Bach and Field, "They were so attached to becoming
somebody by making a 'Michael Cimino movie,' that they just let him roll over
them in the most shameful manner."

By the time he wrapped, on October 2, four and a half months after he
started, Cimino had shot 1.5 million feet of film (about 220 hours' worth), and
printed 1.3 million feet. The press smelled blood, and was all over the story.
UA was already saddled with *Apocalypse Never*. Now *Time* magazine called
Heaven's Gate Apocalypse Next.

SCORSESE WENT INTO *Raging Bull* twisted into a knot of bitterness, defi-
ance, and self-doubt. He was overwhelmed by a sense of fatality, a certainty
that this was his last movie. "I was dead serious about it," he says. "I was
throwing it back at them, like, This is what I think I can do, and I don't know
if I have any more in me." He was lucky he never had the huge hits, *The
Godfather*, *Star Wars*. He had nothing to protect. "After *New York, New York*, I
thought, I'll never have the audience of Spielberg, not even of Francis. My
audience is the guys I grew up around, wiseguys, guys from Queens, truck
drivers, guys loading furniture. If they think it's good, I'm fine. Maybe I'm
crazy. But rather than compromise the story and make ten other pictures
afterward, I'd rather leave it alone and not make any more movies after this. So
what the hell!" The conviction that he had cut himself loose from conventional
Hollywood filmmaking, that he had nothing to lose and nowhere else to go,
freed him to do the best work of his career.

Raging Bull commenced principal photography in April of 1979, the same month *Heaven's Gate* went into production. Scorsese was edgy and irritable as ever, prone to sudden outbursts of anger. He got frustrated waiting for the DP, Michael Chapman, to set up shots. He would go into his trailer, put on the Clash at top volume, and sit there, revved up by the music, pacing back and forth, counting the seconds. After forty-five minutes, he'd come storming out, yelling, "It's more than one side of the Clash, Michael. What are you doing?" Then he picked up a folding chair and heaved it against the side of the trailer, making big dents and chipping the paint. The beefy Teamster driver tried to stop him, shouting, "Hey, you can't do that." Scorsese's tiny mother, Catharine, sprang to his defense. "Leave him alone," she snapped. "He's waiting, he's upset."

They took a break while De Niro ate his way through Tuscany and Rome for two months to gain the fifty pounds he needed to impersonate La Motta in his decline. "He stuffed himself with ice cream and spaghetti every night until he looked like a pig," recalls Martin. Scorsese and Rossellini got married in Rome on September 30. Sandy Weintraub joked that he was sleeping his way through the daughters of his favorite directors. The couple went to Japan where she had two weeks of work. Scorsese had such a severe anxiety attack on the bullet train from Kyoto to Tokyo that he couldn't catch his breath and was convinced he was having a coronary. They took him from the train to the hospital in Tokyo in an ambulance. A doctor asked him to breathe into a paper bag. The next day, he was fine. But it was in a disturbed frame of mind that he returned to shoot the last two weeks of the picture. When it was finished, DP Chapman went to work for Robert Towne.

"A LOT of what made me hesitate to direct was my health," says Towne. "Depending on how you put it, I was either neurasthenic or genuinely ill for a number of years, and I didn't feel I had the ability to sustain the fifty, sixty, seventy, eighty days on the film."

Beatty had asked Towne to polish the script for *Heaven Can Wait*, but Towne wouldn't do more than one scene, busy as he was with his life's great work, *Greystoke*. *Greystoke* was shaping up as a $30 million film, and Beatty warned Towne that Warners would never entrust a project of that magnitude to a first-time director, no matter how much Calley liked him, particularly because a major portion of it was to be shot in Africa. And then there were the usual Towne danger signs. He never finished the script, which ran 240 pages without the last act.

Greystoke was the story of a feral child raised by an ape, Kala. The child is physically inferior to his playmates, the young apes, and has to live by his wits. Like every Hollywood movie, on some level it was about the business. After all, he was a defenseless screenwriter, at a disadvantage against the ferocious

carnivores around him, condemned to live on scraps from the tables of friends
— Beatty, Nicholson, Evans, and Calley — who were way more powerful than
he. Indeed, for him, Hollywood was the planet of the apes. As he grew older
and more wily in the ways of the town, tainted himself, in fact, he increasingly
sentimentalized innocence, became mesmerized by the theme of innocence
and experience, purity and corruption, which was, after all, the preoccupation
of *The Last Detail, Chinatown,* and *Shampoo.*

Preproduction on *Greystoke* was proceeding at full speed, including a trip to
Africa to scout locations. Meanwhile, Towne and Julie Payne got married in
November 1977. In the fall of the following year she gave birth to a girl. Robert
oddly named her Katherine — oddly, because it appeared she was named after
Katherine Cross Mulwray, the incestuous issue of Evelyn Mulwray and her
father, Noah, in *Chinatown.* They called her Skip.

Anthea Sylbert had just become a production executive at Warners. She was
assigned *Greystoke* as her first project. She lived on the Old Malibu Road, near
the Townes, who had finally left Benedict Canyon and moved to the Colony.
Every Sunday Anthea drove down to Robert's house. They walked on the beach
together. She always asked the same question: "So whaddya think, Towne, how
much longer before the third act will be finished?" Likewise, his answer was
always the same: "Another two or three weeks." Towne had spoken the story to
her, talked her an outline so detailed she could almost write it herself. She
loved it, was moved to tears every time she heard it. But he could never put it
down on paper.

Every Monday morning Anthea had a staff meeting at the studio. The discussion would turn to *Greystoke,* and she would say, "Towne says, another two or
three weeks." Wells's face turned dark red, because he knew in his future lay
another renegotiation with the Edgar Rice Burroughs estate, which controlled
the rights to Tarzan. Then, one day, during their walk, Anthea saw several
muscular women doing push-ups on the beach in front of Robert's house. She
asked, "Who are those women, Towne?"

"Aren't they great?"

"I don't know if they're great or not, but who are they?"

"They're all going to be trying out for the Olympics."

"Oh — but what are they doing around here? Do they have anything to do
with the fact that you're not — that you've got this block?"

"Actually, I have this story roaming around in my head."

"Oh, really."

"It's got everything, heterosexuality, homosexuality, great bodies. I'll write it
for Jack. I want to call it *Personal Best.*"

Sylbert felt her jaw clench, but the next day, she gamely went to her staff
meeting, said, "Listen, Towne has this other story that's got heterosexuality,
homosexuality, great bodies . . ." Wells rose from his seat. She thought he was

going to leap across the room and kill her. She said, "I know, I know, don't get excited, because — Let's look at it this way. From the practical side, isn't it better to have Towne do a movie that's controlled, right here, with adults, rather than off in Africa with babies, and live chimps, and mechanical chimps. It seems to me that not only does this make creative sense, but it probably makes business sense." She talked everyone into being happy about the fact that instead of getting *Greystoke*, they were getting *Personal Best*.

The story for *Personal Best* was loosely based on a scandal about a coach who had sex with one of his female athletes. It may seem a leap from a movie about apes to one about athletes, but it was still another story about innocence despoiled, primitive grace, pre- or subverbal natural man, or in this case, woman.

As Payne nursed Skip, the Malibu house was invaded by Amazons. On a typical day, there were three or four topless women, none of whom was under five foot eleven, slicked down and lying on towels on the beach. "I've never seen such emotionally retarded crippled people as these women," says Payne. "They were all javelin throwers, shot-putters, the crème de la crème. There was sand all over the place, piles of dirty socks. Robert was always so fastidious, I couldn't believe it. The socks alone were enough to kill off everyone. 'I'd've rather had apes around the house." She adds, "He abandoned everything for *Personal Best*, and went off on this wild journey that never ended."

Towne drove to his bungalow on the Warners lot in a red Mercedes, wearing the same outfit every day: a $175 Hawaiian shirt, jeans, and Birkenstocks, his graying, Old Testament locks flying in all directions, walking around the office with only a pink towel wrapped around his waist. He finished the script, in record time for him, racing a threatened actors strike. He couldn't postpone the film because his Olympic hopefuls had to leave for the Moscow games. Nicholson had turned it down, and Towne cast Scott Glenn instead. He cast Mariel Hemingway as one of the lead actresses, Patrice Donnelly, an athlete, as the other.

Even in preproduction, Towne struck several people as someone out of his depth. "He was overwhelmed by directing and producing and the writing, dealing with a lot of people, needing to make decisions minute after minute," says Patty James, his assistant. Adds Michael Chapman, the DP for the bulk of the shooting, "He couldn't make a decision, and that drives you crazy." Towne complained that people needing answers followed him into the men's room, talking through the door of the stall where he took refuge on the john. And, continues James, "If he really couldn't handle it, then he would be on the phone to Warren."

Personal Best started production in early summer of 1979. A few weeks later, when the actors strike hit, the film was already behind schedule. Towne had begun an affair with Patrice Donnelly. Now he realized that with the production suspended, and the cast and crew returning to L.A., Julie would probably find out. She was recovering from a hysterectomy. Just as she was beginning to feel like her old self, Towne confessed his affair with Donnelly. With tears streaming down his cheeks, he said, "I've made a mess, I'm sorry, I didn't mean to do it." He swore it was just a location fling, but Payne was determined to get a divorce. Trying to change her mind he said, according to her, "You're middle-aged, no one will want you. You'll be in the street, and Skip will hate you forever, I'll make sure of that."

Towne ran into David Geffen at Michael Eisner and Neil Diamond's annual Labor Day party on the beach. Geffen was setting himself up as an independent after leaving Warners and selling his music company to MCA. The director asked Geffen to help him. Geffen went to the same psychiatrist as Towne and Beatty. Dr. Martin Grotjahn advised him not to get involved because Towne was "crazy." But Grotjahn said a lot of people were crazy, including Geffen, and Towne was an old friend. So Geffen agreed to bridge the cost of starting it up again — with his own money — until his pal Diller at Paramount took it off his hands.

Both Towne and Geffen would regret it. According to one version of the story, the trouble began when Geffen tried to get options on two future Towne scripts in exchange for using his money to restart the picture, the theory being that he was at personal risk for the money. But Diller called, ostensibly told Towne, "Let me be very clear about this, David Geffen is not risking a dime, I have your picture." It was said that Towne never knew about Diller's involvement, and came to believe Geffen was trying to trick him. Says Geffen, "It's an absolute lie. Made up stuff. As part of the agreement for my putting up the money on an interim basis — just through the strike — I got an option on his next picture, *Tequila Sunrise*. The deal was very clear. Everything was known to him."

In any event, *Personal Best* resumed shooting. It was a cokey set. A costume designer referred to him as "ol' write a line, snort a line Robert Towne." Says Bud Smith, who cut the picture, "If you were close to Robert, there was just an abundance of incredible cocaine. Patrice and Robert would be in the hallways at four in the morning, arguing, crying. The next day she'd look like dogshit. He wasn't paying as much attention to what he was shooting because he was chasing the girls. He was basically a playboy, he loved women, he loved drink, and he loved drugs. That to him would be a full life."

When Towne moved from one suite of rooms to another in the Westwood Marquis, Patty James was in charge of the move. "In one of the dresser drawers was a plastic bag of what obviously was cocaine," she says. "It was stuffed under his cashmere sweaters. I put it in the same place in the new suite. Then I left for the day. When he realized I must have found the cocaine, he sent half the staff running after me in the parking lot, saying, 'Miss James, you cannot leave.

Mr. Towne must see you.' I thought, What the hell is going on? I went upstairs, and I said, 'You know what? Your goddamn fucking cocaine is exactly where you left it in the other suite,' and I turned around and walked out. That was the first time I had actually seen any cocaine."

Meanwhile, Geffen was not impressed with the film he was seeing. "A lot of terrible stuff was going on," he says. "For instance, Robert had this scene where Donnelly and Hemingway were arm wrestling, and he made them shoot it from the waist down naked. There was not a reason in the world for that." Says Smith, "Bob would go from the set to his office where he had a steam room, and he and the girls would sit in the steam room snorting coke all day long, while the crew was sitting on the set waiting for him. He probably spent less time in the cutting room than he did with his dog." (Towne denies he used coke.)

"I remember Geffen storming around the stage," recalls Chapman. "We only heard Robert's side of it. Geffen was this devil incarnate, this awful man who was going to stand between us and art. But as things went from loonier to loonier, we began to think perhaps he had a point."

"It went wildly over budget," Geffen continues. "Towne behaved despicably during every aspect of this. I called up the security department at Warners, and I arranged to have everything surrounded by guards the next morning so he couldn't make off with the negative. I had the trailer where he was editing padlocked, the sound and the negative taken care of, and threw him off the lot." But unbeknownst to Geffen, the print was out for duping. When it came back, Towne asked Bud Smith to hide it in Friedkin's office, and then get out of town so nobody could question him as to the whereabouts of the print. Smith left for Colorado. Towne filed a $110 million suit against Geffen and Warners.

Now living at the Westwood Marquis, Towne was chronically short of cash. Beatty lent him $100,000 in 1980, the first of a series of five- and six-figure loans. He borrowed six-figure amounts from his agents. He borrowed $250,000 from Warners. He and Payne became embroiled in a brutal custody battle over Skip. They traded charges of child and substance abuse. "Robert had become extremely violent," recalls Payne. "He came walking in the door one day and said, I want to see you alone. He shut the door. I was sitting in a chair, and he knocked me across the room, five feet, with his fist in my eye. The damage from the blow was so horrifying—I heard the orbital bone break—that it smashed the septum and ripped the muscles off my cheekbone, so that one half of my face was being held up by the skin only." (Towne denies this.)

After Donnelly dumped him for a grip, Towne took up with Mariel Hemingway. Subsequently, Hemingway won the Dorothy Stratten role in *Star 80*, Bob Fosse's biography of the slain *Playboy* centerfold, and had to have her breasts enlarged. In their kitchen, on the bulletin board, mounted on a piece of paper, were two corn kernels, one regular and one popped. The caption under them read, "Before and after."

By the time *Personal Best* was finished, after two years of struggle, the small, $7 million picture that was supposed to be an out-of-town tryout for *Greystoke* had ballooned to $16 million. Eventually, Geffen and Towne settled, Warners took *Personal Best* off Geffen's hands, and Towne gave the studio *Greystoke* in exchange for finishing money for *Personal Best*. For his part, Towne felt Geffen tried to manipulate him into relinquishing the script. Asked about Geffen, he cites a scene from *Giant*, where Jett Rink (James Dean), who has just struck oil, confronts Bick Benedict (Rock Hudson), twice his size. In Towne's words, Jett says, " 'I'm a rich'n, Bick,' and makes suggestive comments to Elizabeth Taylor, playing Bick's wife. Bick hits him, and his men pull him off. While they're restraining him, Jett Rink punches him in the stomach, hops in his truck, and drives off. As he does, one of Bick's pals observes, 'You shoulda shot that fella a long time ago, Bick. Now he's too rich to kill.' "

When *Greystoke* was eventually produced with Hugh Hudson directing, the co-screenplay credit read "P. H. Vazak," Towne's dog. Hira was nominated for an Oscar. *Personal Best* opened in 1982 and immediately disappeared.

BLUHDORN, who had loved *Days of Heaven*, told Diller to make a deal with Bert Schneider. Bert turned around and hired Steve Blauner. It was ironic that Schneider, the same person who had kicked off the New Hollywood at the beginning of the decade, was now in business at the decade's end with the TV regime at Paramount that helped to put the New Hollywood in its grave.

Schneider had a book called *Obsession*, which Godard had earlier made into *Pierrot le Fou*. It was about the relationship between an older man and a teenage girl, a subject of more than routine interest to Bert. Monte Hellman was set to direct. Charlie Eastman, another ghost from the early '70s, was doing a rewrite. Eisner had green-lighted the film. At the eleventh hour, just as they were about to start casting and location scouting, the green light turned red: "Diller said no to Eisner, but Eisner had already said yes to Schneider," says a source. Eisner called Schneider, said, "You gotta do me a favor, you gotta meet with Barry."

"Barry is not my problem, he's your problem," Schneider replied. As Hellman remembers it, Bert refused to go to Barry's office, and Barry refused to come to his. "Bert was competitive with Barry, Barry with Bert, each not wanting to give up his pride," he says. Instead, Schneider sent Blauner, who always did Bert's dirty work. Blauner walked into Diller's office, remonstrated, said, "How could you do this? Come in now, after a year's work, say, 'Who cares about an older man with a younger woman?' So fine, we'll make it an older man with a younger boy! *Now* do you understand it?" Needless to say, after an exchange like this, the picture was never made, and the improbable deal fell apart.

After his unhappy experience with Paramount, Bert was again on his own. He decided to produce a script written by his former assistant, Michie Gleason, now living with Terry Malick, who had divorced his wife. The subject was close to his heart, gun-running to Third World revolutionaries. Gleason considered herself extremely lucky to have hooked up with Bert. Despite his reverses, he still had the reputation for being one of the few truly serious producers in town, one who would back a first-time director, a woman to boot—this at a time when there were virtually no woman directors save for Joan Micklin Silver and Claudia Weill—and beyond that, he shared her politics. The film was called *Broken English*, and Bert set it up at Lorimar. But then she ran up against the realities of Hollywood—and Schneider.

First came the casting. She had her ideas, and he had his, namely his new wife, Greta Ronningen, whom he had unsuccessfully put up for *Days of Heaven*. "I wanted experienced actors, the best I could get, which I thought I could get because of who he was," says Gleason. "But he wanted a movie where his wife would be a star, and he would be in charge. The compromise was she got the secondary role instead of the lead role. But I had to write that part for her, because she had never done anything before." Then Bert, according to Gleason, surprised her again, insisting on a lesbian scene, despite the fact that neither of the two female characters was written as a lesbian. "Those guys, that was their social life, sex, drugs, rock 'n' roll, sex with two girls," says Gleason. She said, "Yeah, yeah, yeah," hoping he would forget about it.

The production was based in Paris. Gleason and Schneider conducted a movable battle over sexual politics in three-star restaurants all over Paris. Bert was a person who would go from a whisper to a scream in a nanosecond. He would yell, "Fine, you're dealing with a man, fine, I have balls, I have a cock!" and clear the restaurant.

When the picture was finished, they screened it for Merv Adelson at Lorimar. Gleason recalls, "He said, 'What I wanted was an X-rated movie that we would show in European art theaters.' I was stunned. All of a sudden, a light bulb went on in my head and I thought, Oh, maybe that's why I had so much pressure." In other words, she came to believe that Bert might have misrepresented her picture as a soft-core art film—hence the lesbian scenes—to Lorimar in order to make the deal, confident that he could nudge Gleason in that direction.

In any event, Lorimar refused to accept the picture, and Schneider sued and won, but the picture never was released. It turned out to be the last picture Bert would ever make, a sorry conclusion to his career as a producer.

•

RAGING BULL was in post-production throughout the spring, summer, and fall of 1980. The sound mix alone took six months. According to Winkler, while Scorsese was editing, UA was quietly trying to sell the picture, but none of the studios would touch it.

If Scorsese was in fragile emotional and physical shape when he started *Raging Bull*, he was a mess when he finished it. He says, "I didn't achieve any of the peace that Jake had with himself in the movie where he could sit down and look at himself in the mirror calmly and recite those lines. I just didn't."

Scorsese showed the picture to Albeck, Bach, and a few other people in the middle of July at the MGM screening room on 55th Street and Sixth Avenue. As Bach described it, "The lights came up slowly in a room full of silence, as if the viewers had lost all power of speech. Nor was there the customary applause. Martin Scorsese leaned against the back wall of the screening room as if cowering from the silence. Then Andy Albeck rose from his seat, marched briskly to him, shook his hand just once, and said quietly, 'Mr. Scorsese, you are an Artist.' " Scorsese asked a young woman after the screening what she had thought. She burst into tears and ran down the hall. The director knew he was not making a "likable" movie. He says, "The poster with the picture of Bob's face all beaten and battered — I mean, if you're a girl, nineteen years old, I don't know if you'd say, 'Let's go see this one.' " But he didn't realize just how unlikable it was, just as he never seemed to understand how disturbing the ending of *Taxi Driver* was.

Raging Bull opened on November 14, 1980, at the Sutton Theater in New York. Jack Kroll called it "the best movie of the year" in *Newsweek*, and Vincent Canby gave it a rave in the *New York Times*. But it was Kathleen Carroll in the New York *Daily News* who struck the prevailing note when she called Jake "one of the most repugnant characters in the history of the movies," and went on to criticize Scorsese because the movie "totally ignores [La Motta's] reform school background, offering no explanation as to his anti-social behavior." Worse, UA was too preoccupied with *Heaven's Gate* to give it a proper promotional campaign. Scorsese's movie bombed.

Although *Raging Bull* was later selected in a *Premiere* magazine poll as the best movie of the '80s, it was very much a movie of the '70s, very much a beached whale on the shores of the new decade. It was an actor's movie, a film that valued character over plot, that indeed contained no one to "root for." With its unromantic, black and white, in-your-face tabloid look, its ferocious violence, and its pond scum characters layered with ghostly images of Italian Renaissance pietas and echoes of *verismo* operas such as *Cavalleria Rusticana* and *Pagliacci*, it was at the furthest remove from the smarmy, feel-good pap of the coming cultural counterrevolution. Scorsese had refused to get with the program, had made an anti-*Rocky*, thumbed his nose at *Star Wars*, and he would pay for it.

A scant four days later, on a cold, raw Tuesday, November 18, Cimino's three-hour-and-thirty-four-minute cut of *Heaven's Gate* opened at the Cinema I and Cinema II on Third Avenue. Arthur Krim was in the audience to witness the debacle, the immolation of the company he had built. The party afterward was at the Four Seasons. Almost no one showed up, a premonition of the reviews—which were devastating. In the *Times*, Canby wrote, "*Heaven's Gate* fails so completely, you might suspect Mr. Cimino sold his soul to the Devil to obtain the success of *The Deer Hunter*, and the Devil has just come around to collect." He went on to call it an "unqualified disaster." In an unprecedented move, UA withdrew the picture to cut it down to a reasonable length—this time at Cimino's request—and canceled the L.A. premiere, which was to have been held two days later. A version was released on April 24, 1981, at the Chinese Theater on Hollywood Boulevard to barely better reviews than the first version received. When the costs were all in, including prints and ads, *Heaven's Gate* wound up at $44 million. Re-released in a two-and-a-half-hour version, it grossed only $1.3 million in 830 theaters, or an average of $500 a night for each theater, a pathetic sum.

The chorus of outrage was quickly transformed into an attack on the studio that made the film, and then the system that made it possible. Although Albeck bore the brunt of the blame (he took early retirement), *Heaven's Gate* was an accident waiting to happen. The film that caused the crisis could have been *Sorcerer* or *Apocalypse Now* or *1941* or even *Reds*. So far as the ambition and budget were concerned, Cimino didn't do anything Friedkin, Coppola, Spielberg, and Beatty hadn't done. *Heaven's Gate* was as much a product of the '70s as *Raging Bull*, the result of the empowerment, nay, deification of the director, on the one hand, and the consequent, or congruent, demonization of the producer, on the other. When Calley swept the producers out of Warners a decade earlier, little could he have anticipated the result. As producer Jerry Hellman puts it, "Yes, the director is in creative respects the most important part of the team. But directors are not producers, by and large, and if you look at the cost overruns and films out of control, and huge, terrible movies being made by guys with two credits like Cimino, you begin to see how they built a disaster in there. It was a case of the baby getting thrown out with the bathwater."

The system of social Darwinism that is Hollywood took care of the problem in short order. UA, stripped of credibility, was devoured. Transamerica sold it to MGM's Kirk Kerkorian for $350 million. MGM itself was no more than a plaything for the buccaneering Kerkorian, and despite a momentary respite in the hands of Yablans in the early '80s, it was all over for both companies for the foreseeable future. UA became the symbol of a discredited, directorcentric system, and in its ruins, Paramount, the studio that boldly changed the rules of the game, flourished.

•

To MANY, it seemed that *Heaven's Gate* had rung down the curtain on the New Hollywood. Indeed, Altman had a project in preproduction at UA that was knocked out by *Heaven's Gate*. It was called *Lone Star*, and was to feature Sigourney Weaver and Powers Boothe. The locations had already been selected. For him, it was the last straw. He sold Lion's Gate, and announced that he would no longer make feature films. At the beginning of the '70s he said, "Suddenly there was a moment when it seemed as if the pictures you wanted to make, they wanted to make." Now he complained, "The pictures that they have to make to keep their machine running are not the kind of pictures I want to make. And the pictures I want to make they don't want to make because they don't know how to distribute them." It had come full circle.

The perception was that one director run amok had done in a studio and transformed the climate in which films were made. Says Scorsese, *"Heaven's Gate* undercut all of us. I knew at the time it was the end of something, that something had died." And Coppola, "There was a kind of coupe d'etat that happened after *Heaven's Gate*, started by Paramount. It was a time when the studios were outraged that the cost of movies was going up so rapidly, that directors were making such incredible amounts of money, and had all the control. So they took the control back."

Scorsese and Coppola were right. There was a counterrevolution at the beginning of the '80s, but *Heaven's Gate* was merely an excuse, a shorthand way of designating changes that had been in the works since *The Godfather* had transformed the way the studios did business eight years earlier.

The new Paramount regime of Diller, Eisner, and Simpson — with assistant Jeffrey Katzenberg studying their every move — embarked on a course that would eventually transform Hollywood filmmaking. Diller and Eisner, former network executives, had a TV mind-set that burned through feature production like a laser, focusing everything on one idea, one image so that the films could be shoehorned into promotional spots. "I went to see Brandon Tartikoff, when he was head of Paramount," recalls John Boorman. "I was pitching a film, and he said, 'Tell me what the thirty-second TV commercial is.' I said, 'I don't think I could express it in — .' He said, 'Then I can't make the picture. How am I going to sell it?' " As Milius puts it, "The stuff that brought it all to an end came from within. Diller, Eisner, and Katzenberg — they ruined the movies."

Increasingly films resembled comic books, were even based on comic books, like the *Superman* and *Batman* films to follow. This phenomenon was later dubbed "high concept," and has been variously defined, but the most scandalous explication of the term has always been attributed to Spielberg: "If a person can tell me the idea in twenty-five words or less, it's going to make a pretty good movie. I like ideas, especially movie ideas, that you can hold in your hand." As the studios became stronger, the power shifted from the director back to the executives, who were beginning to emerge from the shadow of auteurs to become celebrities in their own right. Whereas a key piece by Kit Carson in *Esquire* in the early '70s focused on directors, a similarly influential piece by Tony Schwartz that appeared in *New York* in the early '80s focused on the front office at Paramount.

Simpson led the way. "Don redesigned the way studios related to the material they produced," says Craig Baumgarten, who was also an executive at Paramount at the time. "The '80s would become a period in which studios took charge of their movies. It wasn't like, Gee, we like it, or we don't like it, or why don't you try this or why don't you try that? We began to issue blueprints. We came up with our own ideas." Recalls producer Rob Cohen, "Don would dictate easily, twenty- to thirty-page memos, single-spaced, that would go through the script from the beginning to the end, every scene."

As a delayed result of the conglomeratization of the late '60s, and the blockbuster money that flooded Hollywood, the new crop of executives were businessmen first, movie people second. As bright as Diller, Eisner, and Katzenberg were, they could easily have made themselves at home in any large corporation. "Diller would always make remarks like, 'Oh, I hate the movie business, it's disgusting,' " says Yablans, who admittedly detested him. But Simpson adds, Diller "never really cared much about movies, which is probably the reason he's now working for HSN selling dresses." And as for Katzenberg, he continues, "Jeffrey's not creative at all. He is a businessman. He's about commerce, and product, and shelf life, and crap like that."

The net effect was that the studios began to resemble other large corporations. They became bloated bureaucracies, with a proliferation of so-called creative executives. The days when production at Paramount was run by two men, Evans and Bart, were long gone. The comeback of the studios would be accompanied by the reemergence of the producers through whose hearts Calley had driven a stake in the early '70s. They would crack the coffin lids, shrug off their shrouds, and rise again — not creative producers like Tony Bill, Julia and Michael Phillips, or Jerry Hellman, but a new breed of hustler who just smelled money, megaproducers like Jon Peters, Mario Kassar, and Andy Vajna. As Bogdanovich puts it, "The cinema of the director went into eclipse at the end of the '70s. There was a general movement away from the auteurism toward producer-oriented movies."

By the end of the decade, costs were skyrocketing, not only production costs, but the cost of expensive TV promotion and wide breaks into thousands of theaters. The average cost of making and selling a movie at the beginning of the '70s was $8 million. Up to 1975, no picture cost more than $15 million. By 1980, an ominously large number of pictures — not only *Heaven's Gate*, but

Meteor, The Black Hole, Popeye ($20 million each); The Empire Strikes Back ($23 million); King Kong ($20 million); A Bridge Too Far ($20 million); The Wiz ($24 million); Moonraker ($30 million); Superman ($55 million); 1941, The Blues Brothers ($30 million); Flash Gordon ($40 million); Star Trek — The Movie ($45 million); Raise the Titanic! ($36 million), Reds ($33.5 million) — had shot up into the $20 to $30 million and above range.

With above the line and marketing costs skyrocketing, interest rates — spiking near 20 percent, and tax shelters eliminated, many of the smaller companies that contributed to the vitality of the '70s were forced out of the business. The majors consolidated their control of the market. Studios were increasingly reluctant to take risks on projects that did not seem to guarantee an enormous return on their investment. Distribution steamrolled production. The failure of the talent-run companies was used to prove the point. "We all remember the Directors Company," says Tanen. "We all do remember First Artists. Do you really want to discuss American Zoetrope? . . . If you put four directors in charge of choosing what films are to be made in the course of a year, they'll end up shooting each other. . . ."

Meanwhile, dazzled with the prospect of big-buck profits, new independents like Kassar and Vajna's Carolco, anxious to gain credibility with the exhibitors, struggled to attract talent. Abetted by agents and the other megaproducers, they bid star salaries upward, injecting high-octane dollars into an already over-heated star system, fueling an unprecedented escalation of salaries that put the most extravagant directors of the '70s to shame. Simpson and Bruckheimer sired Tom Cruise and Eddie Murphy, Kassar and Vajna fattened Arnold Schwarzenegger and Sylvester Stallone. Reynolds got $5 million for The Cannonball Run.

It was becoming a first-weekend business. Recalls producer Art Linson, then a novice, "I had a film, American Hot Wax, I went to the National Theater in L.A. on Friday night, I was in the lobby, Simpson was there, Katzenberg was there, and Katzenberg said, 'It's over.' I mean, it was opening night. I went, 'What do you mean it's over?' 'The picture, it's a flop.' I said, 'God, it's only Friday night at six o'clock, maybe it'll build, it's a good movie, let's advertise tomorrow, how do you know this?' 'We know it. We got the numbers back from New York. It's over.' "

So much was riding on every picture, even the superstar directors came to be terrified of failure. Directors were no longer given a second chance. "Realizing his life is going to be affected with one throw of the dice the director starts protecting himself by trying to make it beautiful, spectacular, and one of a kind — almost without regard for what were the original priorities of the piece," said Coppola. Even Spielberg agreed: "It used to be you only had to debut once, and then you had a career. Now, every single movie that I make, I'm debuting again, everybody's judging me like it's my first film." Concludes Friedkin, "In the '70s, if you had a flop, the attitude was, 'That's too bad, but it was a good picture.' Then it became, if you made a film that was not a hit, they put you under indictment. You were a fuckin' criminal."

With movies so expensive, the studios less intrepid than Paramount assumed a defensive stance. As Tanen put it in 1983, "It's really about hedges — what is our *exposure* on this movie? How much can we lose?" The studios also tried to minimize risk by conducting the kind of product research employed by manufacturers of consumer goods. Scorsese was never forced to test-screen a picture until *GoodFellas*, in 1990. Says Bart, "Testing changed the nature of the dialogue within the studio. The questions we asked — like, 'Does it work?' 'Is it a good movie?' — started to sound stupid and old-fashioned. Instead, they were asking, 'What sort of demos are we going to get?' 'Are the kids going to like it?' 'Does it skew toward women?' "

As producer Michael Phillips puts it, "In the '70s, the U.S. domestic market accounted for 85 percent of the business. If an executive had a hunch, he would take a shot. It was a seat-of-the-pants business. There was no more than two, three million dollars on the line, and virtually nothing in releasing costs, because it was a pay-as-you-go process. You opened in one or two theaters in each of the major cities, saw how it went. Nurse it along. When the economics started to drive film distribution in the direction of thousand- to two-thousand-print releases and big national buys of media and launch costs of ten, thirteen million dollars, the stakes were so high that each decision was fraught with sheer terror. Instead of a seat-of-the-pants process, people were grasping for a rational framework to make decisions, and the only rational process available was precedent and analogy. So the mentality of the sequel or the look-alike emerged in the '80s. '*Jaws* in Outer Space.' Movies were designed to be sequelized."

Eventually, Simpson was eased out of Paramount and became a producer. Although he was, so far as anyone could tell, aggressively hetero, he took gay culture, with its conflation of fashion, movies, disco, and advertising — images and sound — and used it as a bridge between the "naive" high-concept pictures of Spielberg and Lucas in the '70s, and highly designed, highly self-conscious high-concept pictures like *Flashdance*, the *Beverly Hills Cop* films, and *Top Gun* of the '80s. (Recall the discussion of the gay subtext of that movie by Quentin Tarantino in *Sleep with Me*.) It was no accident that high concept was born and raised at Paramount, which some people considered the gayest studio in Hollywood. Simpson was to gay culture what Elvis Presley was to rhythm and blues, ripping it off and repackaging it for a straight audience. The blockbusters Simpson made with Bruckheimer were star vehicles comprised of little more than a series of movie moments set to a pounding score. If, as Susan Sontag observed, the essential movie experience lay in the desire "to be kidnapped by the movie . . . overwhelmed by the physical presence of the image," the

Simpson-Bruckheimer movies — *Top Gun*, *Days of Thunder* — upped the ante. They took the audience by force. It was little better than rape.

The Don-and-Jerry pictures were perfect for the Reagan '80s. As Towne puts it, "So much of the '70s was about revealing the disparity between what the country said it was, and what the filmmakers perceived it to be, and they had an audience that was interested in that. When the '80s came along, we entered a world of steroided-out superheroes, starting with Superman. Sly, Arnold, even Bruce Willis would re-fight the Vietnam war, and win. A country that in LBJ's words had truly become a helpless giant, needed a fantasy where it was not impotent, where it was as strong as Arnold, as invulnerable as Robocop."

THE COMMERCIAL FAILURE of *Raging Bull*, on top of *New York, New York*, was a crushing blow for Scorsese. "Marty wanted the kind of success that Lucas and Coppola had," says Sandy Weintraub. "He was afraid he would always be the critics' darling, but the American public never would love him." He was terrified that he wouldn't be allowed to continue making movies if he didn't make money. She adds, "There was nothing in his life besides movies. What would he do?"

Later, when *Ordinary People* beat out *Raging Bull* for the Oscar, Scorsese was bitter. He always thought he could work within the system and maintain his vision, and for a while, he had. "When I lost for *Raging Bull*, that's when I realized what my place in the system would be, if I did survive at all — on the outside looking in."

After *Raging Bull* landed with a resounding thud, Scorsese directed *The King of Comedy*, which he did as a favor to De Niro. He regretted it: "We had explored everything that we could with each other on *Raging Bull*. I should not have done *The King of Comedy*, I should have waited for something that came from me." It turned into another troubled production. He says, "I found that I had to convince myself every day to be a pro and go into work, and I disappointed myself, like very often I was late in the morning and that sort of thing, and the picture went over budget."

During the editing, Scorsese hit a stone wall. "It was partly because I shot so much footage, almost a million feet of film I had to sit through. There were twenty, twenty-five takes of one shot, forty variations on a line. For the first two months, I just couldn't do it. At the same time, from November '81 to March '82, my marriage with Isabella was breaking up." When Scorsese met her, she was a TV journalist. He had not been pleased when she decided to become an actress, and when she divorced him in 1983, she complained to *Time*, "he wanted me to spend life between the cookstove and the kids."

"That left me flat, and crazed," continues Scorsese. "I sought out a doctor, and that started very intense therapy, five days a week, and phone calls on weekends, all through '82 and '83, '84, into '85. I got myself into such a state of anxiety that I just completely crashed. I'd come downstairs from the editing room, and I'd see a message from somebody about some problem and I'd say, 'I can't work today. It's impossible.' My friends said, 'Marty, the negative is sitting there. The studio is going crazy. They're paying *interest!* You've got to finish the film.' Finally, I began to understand a lesson I learned when I went to NYU. It was up to me. Nobody cared, ultimately, even your closest friends. You're gonna act crazy? You're gonna get into a situation where you can't work? Nobody gives a damn. And you wind up alone. You face yourself anyway. It's Jake La Motta looking in the mirror at the end of *Raging Bull.*"

The King of Comedy was plagued by negative word on the street, and when it was finally released, it bombed. Despite his disappointment, Scorsese plunged ahead with *The Last Temptation of Christ*, a labor of love he had been gestating since Barbara Hershey first gave him the Nikos Kazantzakis novel in 1971, on the set of *Boxcar Bertha.* While he was trying to set it up, he found himself the object of ridicule on the Hollywood–New York party axis. "Big people in the business were turning around saying, 'Yeah, I know the pictures you make,' " he recalls. "One guy introduced me to someone who was the head of some company. He says, 'This guy's gonna make *Last Temptation.*' The guy looked at me and laughed in my face. Walked away. 'Yeah, right. Call me next week.' I mean, I'd come through all those years to get that? It was like a kick in the heart."

Although Scorsese (and Coppola) blamed *Heaven's Gate*, in many respects, the movie brats did themselves in. Says Bart, "At the beginning of the decade, you have a group of people who really wanted to be on budget and on schedule. They were earnest young people who couldn't believe that they were being allowed to work within this system, and that the studios would be able to accommodate them. By the end of the decade, they became the big exploiters of the system."

It all came home to Scorsese when he had a meeting with Fox about *King of Comedy.* "They explained that it didn't pay for them to support *King of Comedy* any further at the box office, so after a month, they were going to pull it," he recalls. "Basically, it was, Screw you, forget the picture. The same thing happened that year at Fox with Robert Altman's *H.E.A.L.T.H.* They didn't even release the film, and Altman didn't do another studio picture for, like, ten years. I realized at that point nobody cared, and that was when I really understood that the '70s were over for me, that the directors, the ones with the personal voices, had lost. The studios got the power back. Today you look at an ad you don't even know who directed a picture."

Last Temptation was set up at Paramount, only to have the studio pull the plug well into preproduction when it realized the flak it would have to take from the religious right if it proceeded. Scorsese had not had a hit in nearly a decade, since *Taxi Driver* in 1976. After the successive failures of *New York, New York, Raging Bull,* and *The King of Comedy,* it was a crushing blow. "I had to make up my mind whether I really wanted to continue making films." he says. "There was such negativity that you might as well stop. So what do you do? Stay down dead? No. I realized then, you can't let the system crush your spirit. I really did want to continue making pictures. I'm a director, I'll make a low-budget picture, *After Hours.* I'm going to try to be a pro and start all over again." He did, and he survived.

Fourteen:
"We Blew It"
1980s

- *How Coppola finally bankrupted Zoetrope, while* **The Two Jakes** *broke up the old gang, Lucas's empire struck back, Spielberg's life became a soap, Friedkin glimpsed a better world, and Ashby took leave of this one.*

"Now, here we are, twenty years after Heaven's Gate. Directors don't have much power anymore, the executives make unheard of amounts of money, and budgets are more out of control than they ever were. And there hasn't been a classic in ten years."

— FRANCIS COPPOLA

What a long, strange trip it was. At the end of *Easy Rider*, when Wyatt tells Billy, "We blew it," he would be proved correct, although it would take over a decade to see it. Dennis Hopper and Peter Fonda had created an anthem for a generation, but they had also imagined its apocalyptic destruction, which many of the decade's directors did their best to emulate. Like Billy and Wyatt, they blew it. Says Bogdanovich, "I felt that by the mid-'70s, I'd blown it, Friedkin had blown it, Altman went into eclipse, one flop after another, Francis went crazy, even *Raging Bull* didn't do any business. Everybody kind of blew it in varying shapes and sizes." All but the most tenacious and disciplined directors of the '70s who had managed to walk the tightrope between art and commerce, fell to their deaths in the '80s.

Whereas Hollywood directors of earlier eras worked into their sixties and seventies, sometimes longer, as did such great foreign directors as Buñuel,

Kurosawa, Fellini, and Bergman, the American directors of the '70s, with few exceptions, burned out like Roman candles after an all-too-brief flash of brilliance, cut off in mid-career. Friedkin, Bogdanovich, Ashby, Schrader, Rafelson, and Penn, all went down. Only Scorsese, and to a lesser extent Altman, came back. Polanski fled the country in 1977 after he was convicted of rape. Milius never recovered from *Big Wednesday*. Malick left the business, simply disappeared for twenty years. Hopper's career also ended for some twenty years after *The Last Movie*. Although Beatty, De Palma, Lucas, and Spielberg hit their peak as the decade ended, of that group, only Spielberg cruised through the next decade, going from blockbuster to blockbuster.

Most of the other figures of the '70s suffered as well. "None of us were prepared for the '80s," says Margot Kidder. "Our heads were still in the '70s, and we were at sea in a business run by young agents with blow-dried hairdos." Bert Schneider never again equaled the high times of BBS. Nicholson struggled through a dry spell that lasted almost half a decade. Pacino and De Niro suffered through the '80s, while the careers of Voight, Caan, O'Neal, Reynolds, Gould, Segal, Cannon, Burstyn, Christie, and Clayburgh all collapsed. Towne never even approximated the run of scripts he wrote in the early '70s, and flopped badly as a director. Carole and Charles Eastman disappeared. Buck Henry only sporadically fulfilled his early promise, as did such other writers as Jeremy Larner, Rudy Wurlitzer, W. D. Richter, David Ward, Leonard Schrader, Mardik Martin, William Goldman, Alvin Sargent, and Frank Pierson. Mengers burned out, Begelman's career was ruined by a check forging scandal, and terminated by suicide in 1995. Simpson died prematurely, a victim of a life of drug abuse. Of the major '70s executives, Tanen survived for a few years in the '80s before he hit the skids; Evans destroyed himself in a self-inflicted auto-da-fé of legendary proportions, returning in the '90s as a grim parody of his former self, a wax figure from Madame Tussaud attached to a couple of pictures that were doomed from the start. Only Calley showed any real sense. He sat out the decade, resurfaced in 1993, and now heads Sony Entertainment.

For those few who did survive, the cost was high. "The trick, for me personally, has been to divest my life of complications," says Scorsese. "Your friends become less and less important. I adore Francis and Steven, but we don't see each other that often. I don't expect much from people anymore, and I don't want them to expect much from me. I just want to be left alone."

By the mid-'80s, at a meeting of the New York Society of Film Critics, Kael leaned over to Richard Schickel and whispered, sadly, "It isn't any fun anymore."

"Why do you say that?"

"Remember how it was in the '60s and '70s, when movies were hot, when *we* were hot? Movies seemed to matter."

•

IF MOST of the New Hollywood directors crashed and burned in the '80s, few were obliging enough to do it neatly, at the turn of the decade. Each did it in his own time, in his own way. And each fashioned the climax of his story with the degree of finesse accorded him by his gift.

IT WOULD TAKE a couple of years for the topography of the post–New Hollywood landscape to emerge from the blizzard of coke. Meanwhile, the director's cinema entered its decadent phase, lingering into the first half of the '80s — it still exists in a debased form even today — in the guise of several megabuck projects — Beatty's *Reds*, Coppola's *One from the Heart*, Evans and Coppola's *The Cotton Club*, and the abortive Nicholson-Towne-Evans sequel to *Chinatown*, *The Two Jakes*. These pictures were the New Hollywood's version of the Old Hollywood's big budget musicals of the late '60s, and of them, only *Reds* was a commercial and critical success (it won Beatty an Oscar for Best Director).

Schrader's *Paint Your Wagon* was an ambitious horror movie called *Cat People* that he made for Tanen at Universal. As the '70s ended, Schrader was riding high — on the back of *American Gigolo*. He was taking truckloads of powder and pills. "When you could get away with doing half a gram on a weekend, it was great fun," he recalls. "But when I moved up to a gram a day, then it wasn't fun anymore. After writing all night, and finding the next morning I only had a page and a half, I realized I wasn't producing. I was having motor problems. It got to the point where I couldn't hit the keys. I got paranoid, I couldn't focus. The whole balance of life shifted from day to night, the quality of the people in my life was getting scuzzier and scuzzier, darker and darker, until I was dealing with drug dealers and pimps and guns, and it got really ugly. In your forties, you really have to want to be a drug user, because it's so hard to keep the hours."

Tanen thought that in *Cat People* he would get a classy exploitation film starring Nastassja Kinski, while Schrader was happy to finally get a big studio movie with lots of special effects. But he gave Tanen more than he bargained for, a lyrical ode to sensuality, incest, and death, which only Schrader could have imagined would change his image. "Everybody on the film was doing drugs except Nastassja," he continues. "The drugs were really fucking me up. One day, I had been doing some coke in my trailer, I didn't want to come out. My AD came in to get me. He started doing drugs. The second AD came in to try and get us both out. Then the three of us were there, doing coke. All the PAs were standing around the trailer, because they didn't have anybody left. Somebody said, 'How are we gonna get anybody to direct this movie?'"

Then there was Schrader's intense affair with his leading lady. Coming off Roman Polanski's *Tess*, Kinski was being touted as the next Ingrid Bergman. Flat-chested and boyish-looking, she had a sensual face with full lips, perfect for Schrader in his neo-gay phase. He proposed marriage, even though he had just proposed to his long-term (seven years) housemate, Michelle Rappaport, telling her he wanted children. In fact, "I had two marriage and honeymoon plans," he recalls. "I had agreed to marry Nastassja, I had agreed to marry Michelle, and I said to my secretary, 'Kook, I can't handle this anymore. Whichever one says yes, that's what I'll do.'"

Not only had he agreed to marry two women, but he had two psychiatrists as well. Recalls Bud Smith, whom the director hired because he loved *Sorcerer*, "He would call one shrink, talk to him about whatever the problem was, then he would call the other one to find out if the first one was lying to him."

Toward the end of production, Kinski broke off the relationship. Schrader was devastated, furious. They ceased speaking to each other, and on one occasion, he directed her by proxy from his limousine. Says Milius, "When the movie was over, she disappeared. He pursued her to Paris and finally cornered her with some young stud. She said, 'Paul, I always fuck my directors. And with you it was difficult.'"

One day, during post-production, Kinski showed up at the Black Tower visibly agitated. Tanen's assistant announced, "Nastassja Kinski is insisting on seeing you. She's crying." Kinski entered, indeed weeping copiously.

"Please sit down," said Tanen, gesturing to a chair. "What's wrong?"

"He shoot me here."

"What?"

"He shoot me *here*."

"Somebody shot at you?"

"No, no, no—he shoot me *here*!"

"Okay, let's start from the beginning. Who shot you?"

"Paul."

"Paul took a shot at you?"

"No, he shoot me *here*!" Kinski was jabbing her finger downward. Tanen cast his eyes down toward the Oriental rug. "No, not there, *here*!" He raised his eyes to her crotch. A light slowly dawned in his eyes.

"He promise he never put it in movie."

"You're saying that he took some shots of your . . . genitalia area . . . ?"

"Yes!"

"Why did you let him do that?"

"Because he was my boyfriend and I believed him, but now he tells me he's going to put this in the movie." She began to hiccup hysterically.

Tanen rolled his eyes, picked up the phone, called Schrader. "Listen, you fucking idiot, this girl is running around telling everybody you shot her crotch and you're going to put beaver shots in the middle of this movie, what the fuck are you doing?"

"Oh man, she fucked me over and I'm going to fuck her, nobody's going to treat me this way . . ."

"Jesus Christ, you asshole, don't put any beaver shots in this movie! You'll get an X rating."

Tanen recalls, "At one of the previews, we were sitting in the theater and he was popping pills and drinking vodka out of the bottle. He was so fucking gone you could have pickled him and he wouldn't have known the difference. I said, 'Listen, Paul, if I have to sit through this piece of shit, you have to sit through it too, you're the one who made it!' "

The picture fared poorly at the box office. Schrader's image problem, if anything, was made worse by his behavior on the set, and he couldn't get work. "Jerry Hellman asked me to write *Mosquito Coast*," he says. "We sort of made a deal. My agent said he wanted to meet me. I said, 'What's this meeting about? We've met.' And he said, 'Jerry's upset; the studio is telling him not to make this deal because of your drug problem.' That was the first time I really realized that straight Hollywood was not the Hollywood that I was living in. And all of these eyes were trained on my sort of socio subgroup with reprobation. Then I wanted to do this film *Born in the U.S.A.* that Paramount had developed. Eisner wanted it to be more upbeat than it was. I refused. And I suspect that my reputation as a junkie wasn't helping." Like *Nickelodeon* for Bogdanovich, *Popeye* for Altman, *Cat People* was Schrader's last studio picture for many years.

It was then that his gun thing finally played itself out. He was in his Jacuzzi with a friend. "I was trying to get him to play Russian roulette," says Schrader, who aimed the weapon at his own head, squeezed the trigger once, handed it to his pal, who refused to play, and left. "I started getting into a suicidal funk," he continues. "At which point I called another friend. He called my shrink, and my shrink came over. He told me that if I didn't give him the gun, he was going to have me committed. So I gave it to him."

Schrader was shaken. He had been in the Black Tower going over the ad campaign for *Cat People* on March 5, 1982, when Universal executive Sean Daniel walked in, announced that John Belushi had been found dead in Bungalow 3 at the Château Marmont from a drug overdose. It was another one of those watershed moments. "The game was up," says Schrader. "Some people quit right away, but the feeling was, the rules have changed. My life was completely fucked up by women and drugs and my career had gone dead. The Russian roulette was the event that made it clear to me it was time to leave L.A., go to New York, and start over. So I did."

AT LORIMAR, Peter Bart was putting into practice his old boss's adage, Get 'em when they're down, and not only financed Schneider and Bogdanovich, but Friedkin as well. But after *Cruising* tanked, his third flop in a row, Friedkin too had trouble getting work. On March 6, 1981, he was driving on the San Diego Freeway to his office in Bungalow 50 on the Warners lot when, he recalls, "Suddenly this pain cut across my ribs from arm to arm. It was like an elephant standing on my chest. I couldn't move, I couldn't breathe. I thought, This must be a muscle spasm." He pulled over, tried to get the car door open, but he couldn't. Arranging his hands into the most comfortable position he could manage, on the bottom of the steering wheel, he pulled back onto the 405, crept slowly to the Burbank exit, and managed to reach the paramedics' station at the main gate of the studio, where he passed out. They put a nitroglycerin capsule under his tongue, stuck an IV into his arm, pounded on his chest with their fists. Friedkin recalls, "I heard the paramedic say, 'I'm not getting anything.' Those were the last words I heard. And then I was gone. I remember passing through a dark space as though I was on an escalator, right out of *All That Jazz*, and I was moving toward a light and thinking to myself, I'm dying, I'm fucking dying, and I've accomplished nothing with my life. It's fucking worthless and now it's over!"

Friedkin was pretty far gone, well on his way to the place to which his many enemies would have happily consigned him. The joke was, he couldn't find anyone who would call 911. "The next thing I knew I woke up and I was in the St. Joseph Medical Center in the emergency ward and the pain was back strong. I was looking into these white lights right above me. There was an oxygen mask on my face and I couldn't breathe and I thought, I'm in hell." Later, he liked to tell friends he'd been clinically dead for twelve seconds. It turned out he had a genetic defect in the circumflex artery. He didn't need surgery, and after several months of rehabilitation, he was all better. When he recovered, he didn't dedicate himself to medical missionary work in Africa; he merely continued to make bad movies. However, according to Bud Smith, he said, " 'I know I'm a total asshole, a prick, but I'm on a five year plan to become a really nice guy.' Five years later, he was still firing everyone right and left, hated them, hated the movie." Later he said, "I would like to tell you that the heart attack made me a better person, but I don't think so."

Professionally speaking, Friedkin might just as well have ended it all when he had his coronary. His career was essentially over. The new celebrity executives were slow to forgive directors who had treated them badly. The '80s were payback time. Says Coppola, "The way it works is, the grandpas, the *alter cockers*, sit around and say, 'That's a good kid, that's not a good kid.' A good kid is someone who's respectful of the establishment, who doesn't bite the hand that feeds him. Steven Spielberg, who always thanks Sid Sheinberg, who always thanks Universal, who never used his money or power to compete with them, is a good kid." Coppola was not a good kid. Neither were Altman, Rafelson, and Friedkin, especially not Friedkin. "They hated Billy," says writer Walon Green. "Hated him. They were thrilled when he started bombing." Muses

Friedkin, "I burned a lot of bridges. I treated Diller and Sheinberg and Eisner with contempt. The more powerful they got, the easier it was for them to remember the way I had carried on with them. Those people I snubbed on the elevator going up, were the ones I met going down. There was a lot of resistance to my doing films at some of these studios."

But it wasn't just a question of settling old scores. The new megaproducers didn't want to use New Hollywood veterans like Friedkin because these directors were too powerful, independent, and costly. Simpson and Joel Silver preferred novices they could hire for a song and push around, like the young Adrian Lyne or Tony Scott. The producers were the auteurs — of crash-and-burn action pictures — but their medium was not so much film as money.

The kind of reckless passion that Scorsese brought to *Raging Bull* is the privilege of the young, and as the New Hollywood directors got older, as they had more to protect and more to lose, as they grew familiar with failure, the passions of their youth were replaced by lassitude and cynicism. "When I first came out here, in the late '60s, I met guys like Richard Brooks and Billy Wilder who were still active," says Friedkin. "The two of them would invariably talk about what shit was being produced then. I thought, These guys who made films that I thought were astounding, are totally out of it today. How can this happen? The truth is, in America, film is a young man's game. When I made *French Connection* and *The Exorcist* there was no doubt in my mind that those pictures would be popular. Because they were exactly what I wanted to see and what I wanted to see was what most people wanted to see. Now, to be very honest about it, I'm really not sure of what people want to see. I feel like Wilder and Brooks, like an old nag. And, like them in the early '70s, I think that most of the films being made in this country today are garbage, just garbage."

Friedkin lost the ability to distinguish between a good film and a bad one. "I never set out to make a bad film," he says. "I thought in each case they were going to be as good or better than anything I had done. I went through this long period of wondering why I wasn't being received in the same way. Now I've reached the point where I know why. These films just weren't any fucking good. They have no soul, no heart, they don't even have any technical expertise. It's as though someone reached up inside of an animal and pulled the guts out. The thing that drove me and still keeps me going is *Citizen Kane*. I hope to one day make a film to rank with that. I haven't yet."

The ugly truth is that some directors never had much to say in the first place. Their own self-estimation to the contrary, most of them were not auteurs, not in the sense that Woody Allen is an auteur. Few directed movies from their own scripts; they were hostage to the material they were given. Says Coppola, "Even the great directors are not all great screenwriters. Scorsese is not the kind of guy who's going to sit in a room alone and just write about something. He needs that perfect book." Or, as Frank Yablans put it, "The directors still had to make movies whether the studios were developing good material or not. If out of desperation they finally said, 'I gotta make it work,' you're gonna get lousy pictures."

Defeated by failure, exhausted, crazy, some of the great directors of the '70s reached for the mainstream like a life preserver, only to drown in mediocrity. They became directors for hire. As Spielberg, of all people, puts it, "Francis has only floundered when he determined to succeed commercially. I've been unimpressed with films like *Dracula* and *Jack,* because those films don't feel like Francis Coppola movies. They feel like any number of directors could have done the same job. I expect Francis to take risks."

Like the others, Friedkin was a victim of the too-much-too-soon disease. "Arrogance and pussy were the double-pronged temptress for guys in our position," he says. "We all thought that where we were was the center of the universe and that everything revolved around our problems, our needs, our ambitions. I would never have stated it this baldly, but I really thought that directing films was the most important job in the world. We were endowed with some kind of magic." Adds Bogdanovich, "We didn't know how to deal with success, which is a much more difficult thing to deal with than failure. By the time the Old Hollywood veterans gained some power, they'd made a lot of pictures. John Ford's first big success was *Iron Horse* in 1924, and he'd been directing since 1917, movie after movie after movie. We didn't have the experience to do some of the things we thought we could do, in my case, a musical. It was lunatic." Mardik Martin sums it up: "The auteur theory killed all these people. One or two films, the magazines told them they were geniuses, that they could do anything. They went completely bananas. They thought they were God."

PETER BOGDANOVICH TURNED FORTY in 1979. Just as *They All Laughed* was to be released, Time, Inc., shut down its movie division. Fox, which was set to distribute, lost its enthusiasm after three test screenings had gone badly. Bogdanovich decided to do it himself, invested $5 million of his own money. *They All Laughed* was released in 1981, and grossed under $1 million. "I fell apart then, a delayed reaction to Dorothy's death," he says. "I went insane. I blew five million bucks distributing the movie, which was everything I had, including the house, cash, and everything—gone."

Bogdanovich had always behaved as if his life were a movie in which inconvenient scenes could be reshot or recut. He used his life as material for his movies, employed actors like Ryan O'Neal and John Ritter as ill-disguised surrogates for himself. This was by no means a vanity unique to Bogdanovich. Coppola, Spielberg, Schneider, Schrader — many tried to live their movies, or make their lives into movies, but none managed to fuse reality and fantasy to such a painful degree as Bogdanovich, and none was so rudely reminded of the discrepancy. "About a year or so after Dorothy's death," he recalls, "I was in Beverly Hills, and Billy Wilder walked up to me, and he started to talk about what had happened to me. I didn't know what he meant at first, but then I understood he was talking about my life as a script!" It came home to Peter, as he put it, "When Dorothy got murdered, it changed everything. It wasn't a movie. It was life. We all make movies about murder— but we don't really know what it means. We just think we do. But when something *happens*, and it's real, and there's no way to change it, no way to rewrite it, no way to recut it or reshoot it, you suddenly say, 'What *is* the point of making pictures? What is the point of doing anything? Because *this* is *real*.' " Bogdanovich could no longer work. "The day Dorothy was killed, I just didn't care about my career anymore; it was like a bomb went off, and I was left standing, but I wasn't the same person. That took away a decade."

Still, he courted and married Dorothy's (much) younger sister, L.B. "My excuse is my mother was twenty when she had me," he says. "And so the first woman I loved was twenty, so I guess it's this idée fixe of some sort." He was angered when *People* magazine claimed he was remaking her in Dorothy's image, paying for dental work that made her look more like her older sister. He threatened to sue. Bogdanovich was again living a movie, this time a picture by one of his mentors, Alfred Hitchcock: *Vertigo*. During the rest of the '80s, he was largely persona non grata at the studios, his career in ruins. He declared bankruptcy.

Peter had always aspired to be Orson Welles, and early in his career the critics flattered him by speaking of the two men in the same breath. Peter supported Welles in his time of troubles. When Welles was broke, he stayed with Bogdanovich. When Bogdanovich declared bankruptcy for a second time in 1997, and lost his home, he stayed in his friend Henry Jaglom's apartment in New York. He *had* become Welles, but not in the way he imagined. Irwin Winkler once ran into him at a party, where he said, "Remember me? I used to be Peter Bogdanovich."

COPPOLA HAD a clearer idea of the opportunity the '70s presented for revolutionary change than anyone else. He always claimed he was a visionary, and he was right. Coming off *Apocalypse Now*, and *The Black Stallion*, which he produced and which had been an unexpected hit in the fall of 1979, and frustrated in his attempts to acquire UA, Coppola, as was his wont, marched full speed ahead over the precipice. He bought Hollywood General Studios, a ten-and-one-half-acre lot on the corner of Santa Monica and Las Palmas, on March 25, 1980, for a song, $6.7 million. He asked Spielberg for help, a $1 million loan. Spielberg refused, saying, "I don't do that kind of thing." Lucas refused as well. He was still struggling with the financial burden of *The Empire Strikes Back*, and told Francis he didn't have the money to lend him. Coppola was incensed and vowed he would never ask Lucas for money again. "It's like your brother wouldn't help you out," said Mona Skager, then Coppola's producer. Added Francis, "Some people have that kind of generosity in their nature, it's easy for them. For other people, it's just not. I don't think George is wired that way." Responded Lucas, tartly, "Francis helped me and gave me a chance, but at the same time he made a lot of money off me. Francis has a tendency to see the parade marching down the street and to run in front of it with a flag and become the leader." He attacked his mentor for moving south, commenting, "I thought Francis was betraying all of us in San Francisco who had been struggling to make this community a viable film alternative."

The new Zoetrope would not only enjoy total independence from the studios, controlling its own pictures from inception through release, Coppola would show the studios how it was done. Using the latest video technology supplied by Sony, he would transform the production process so it would be as smooth and streamlined as the high-tech aluminum Air Stream — dubbed the Silverfish — he now called his office. With actors reading the script into a Betacam, standing in front of Polaroids of the storyboards, with songs and the occasional effects laid in, Coppola would "previsualize" his pictures, edit before a single frame of film was shot, thereby reducing costs, making movies faster, with less muss and fuss than the studios with their old, cumbersome methods of production. At least, that was the theory. In *Newsweek*, Coppola announced, sounding much like Dennis Hopper a decade earlier, "It's going to be the survival of the fittest, and the long-established studios will be brought down. . . ."

Coppola saw Zoetrope as a petri dish of creative talent, a repertory company, a sanctuary that would shelter talent cast off by the studios: Hollywood veterans, rich in experience; European auteurs the studios regarded as uncommercial; a new generation of kids, too independent and crazy to work within the system; and veterans of the other crafts — writers, DPs, sound designers — who wanted to break into directing. He gave an office to British director Michael Powell (*Peeping Tom*), whom Scorsese had rescued from oblivion. Courtesy of Tom Luddy, directors like Godard, Wim Wenders, Werner Herzog, and other great Europeans prowled the lot. He signed such actors as Fred Forrest and Teri Garr to long-term contracts, like the old studios.

"I was excited when it seemed that Zoetrope could set up right there in Hollywood," recalls Matthew Robbins. "It was like, We'll show them there's another way of making films, a collaborative way. There's such a thing as a community of filmmakers. It was like a Trojan horse, looked like a studio, but it was just us guys."

The first of Zoetrope's slate of films was scheduled to be released in 1982. Coppola himself would direct *One from the Heart* — insiders would eventually call it *One Through the Heart* — herald of a new, non-narrative American cinema. But there was one flaw: Francis's megalomania. Intended as a small, delicate porcelain figure of a film to be shot entirely on a soundstage, at the furthest remove from the excesses of *Apocalypse, One from the Heart* went way out of control, burying the dreams for a new cinema under its leviathan budget. Coppola locked himself away in the Silverfish and conveyed his instructions to the actors over a loudspeaker. Says former Zoetropian Bob Dalva, "Francis's voice was asking Teri Garr to do this emotional thing, and she was looking up at the ceiling talking back to him. Everybody on the stage stopped what they were doing and listened to this conversation. It was bizarre." This was a director who loved actors, who inspired them to great work. Something was seriously awry.

"Francis never wanted to hear 'No,' " says Skager. But by the early '80s, his aversion to the "n" word was considerably more extreme, and he had gathered around him a new group of people to run the studio, none of whom would speak the taboo syllable. Continues Dalva, "Francis was a man who could talk you into anything. 'Walk off the bridge!' 'Okay, that's a great idea, I'm gonna do it.' The new guys never caught themselves, and they all went off the bridge." And Skager, "*One from the Heart* started at $12 million, and the way it was going, I said, I don't think it's twelve, I think it's twenty-two. He really got upset. He took it as a betrayal." In fact, the budget rose to $23 million almost before the shooting had begun. Ultimately, the picture cost $27 million, making a mockery of Coppola's claim that the new video technology would reduce costs.

After a disastrous exhibitors' screening on August 18, 1981, and then a similarly catastrophic preview at Radio City Music Hall in New York in January 1982, *One from the Heart* was deemed so uncommercial Coppola had a hard time even getting a distributor for his flagship film. He finally reached an agreement with Columbia, and the picture opened on Valentine's Day of that year. It closed seven weeks later at the end of April, buried in an avalanche of viciously negative reviews. *One from the Heart* made less than $2.5 million. It was Coppola's first flop in a decade and a half, but it was a resounding and embarrassing one. "*One from the Heart* sank a lot of people's hopes and dreams," says Robbins. "It was really a bitter moment. Because he could have done it, but there was some gambler beast within him, and he was seized with an irresistible urge to bet everything, and he lost. It was unforgivable."

Francis was mortgaged to the eyeballs. He had made Robert Spiotta, devoid of any obvious qualifications save for an old friendship going back to their college days, head of his studio. "Spiotta was in way over his head," he says. "Originally, I didn't have any of the liability of *One from the Heart*. The Chase Manhattan Bank would come to my house every night, asking me to take personal responsibility, and I kept saying no, so they kept pressuring Spiotta.

One night he knocked on the door, I was in bed, he told me they had worked it out, and I just had to sign this document and we could go on. Stupidly, I signed it, and that was the signature that caused me to take the responsibility from the bank onto me."

Still, Coppola gambled, as he had when he indebted himself to UA to finish *Apocalypse*, that none of his backers could live with the stigma of being the one to pull the plug. But he hadn't counted on Jack Singer, a Canadian real estate mogul who had lent him several million dollars, secured by Coppola's real estate. Singer called in the loan and ruined Coppola.

"George couldn't understand how Francis got away with it for years and years," says Huyck. "He would say, 'I don't get it. When I go to a bank and I borrow money to make a movie, I have to pay it back.' After the banks finally closed Francis down, he said, 'See, it caught up with him.' " But he offered to buy the Sentinel Building and Francis's Napa home and hold them like an interest-free loan until Coppola was able to buy them back. Ultimately, Francis didn't need to do that, but he was grateful.

"Every Friday I would have to notarize some more documents to sign over more property" recalls Skager. "He lost the block in Mill Valley, the apartment house, the Hancock Park house in L.A., the Broadway house, the Little Fox Theater. The only things that survived were the Sentinel Tower and the vineyard in Napa." His dream — to provide the directors' cinema of the '70s with an independent base for production and distribution, lay in ruins.

Coppola filed for bankruptcy, and on April 20, 1982, he announced that the studio would be offered to the highest bidder. Said Coppola at the time, "With the collapse of my studio, everything fell into a black hole. I have no present at all. I live like a flea, in between two blocks of granite. There's no space. It's horrible."

Francis was in New York for Scorsese's fortieth birthday in November. Marty was in a funk, still reeling from the *King of Comedy* disaster, and his failing marriage to Isabella Rossellini. After a late dinner at Odeon, a hip restaurant in New York's downtown TriBeCa district, he was pacing his loft, complaining that his business manager had confiscated his credit cards. "I'm broke, I'm broke, I don't have a cent," he said over and over. Francis responded, "Marty, would you calm down? You're broke, I owe $50 million!"

Part of Coppola feels that he was the victim of a conspiracy. "*Apocalypse Now* was totally financed outside of the establishment," he says. "People felt that if directors started to realize that all they needed to do was that, there would be no place for the traditional hierarchy of agents and studios. Zoetrope was considered a threat. With my interest in technology, my studio was a dangerous precedent. And someone who (a) made the kind of megalomaniac kind of comments that I did, and (b) actually was doing it, I think you have to brand a person like that a little bit of a nut."

Coppola never again made a picture comparable to the masterpieces of the

'70s. He once said that the man who made the *Godfathers* died in the jungle, and perhaps he was right. Maybe it was the lithium that lobotomized his work. Says producer Al Ruddy, who watched his career from a distance after they fell out over *The Godfather*, "Before *The Godfather*, he was a nobody. After, he was one of the most important directors in the world. Nobody is prepared for a trip that heavy. He got very caught up in being the kind of man that Charlie Bluhdorn was. He lost some of his focus, was another example of a director destroyed by living the movie."

BY 1983, Spielberg and Irving were back together, but Steven had still not decided whether to marry her. Around the time of the celebrated Lee Marvin palimony case, all the business managers in Hollywood became nervous about their clients. According to a source, Sandy Breslauer, Spielberg's business agent, called him up, and said something like, "Steve, if you're going to be living with Amy and you're not going to get married, you have got to come up with this prenuptial agreement that we will write up, and you've got to get Amy to sign it. Because the consequences if you don't are extreme." But Spielberg was afraid of Irving's reaction, and he put it off. Breslauer kept pestering him. One night, as they were going out, the phone rang. It was the business manager. He said, "Steve, did you talk to Amy about the living together?" He said, "No, but I'm going to do it right now." So he knocked on the door of the bedroom, said, "Amy!"

"What?"

"That was the Breslauer office, and they—I gotta talk to you about . . . there's this thing they want us to sign."

"What are you talking about?"

"It's like this prenuptial thing, and you gotta—"

"Steve, are we going to get married?"

"Whaddya mean?"

"You said, prenuptial!"

"No, no, no, I don't mean prenuptial, I mean this living together deal." She slammed the bedroom door in his face.

Irving got pregnant in 1984, on her thirty-first birthday, September 10. One night, Spielberg was over to De Palma's for dinner in New York with a group of friends. As usual, he was complaining about Amy, saying, "I don't know if I want to get married, but she's pregnant, what am I going to do?" Brian said, sweetly, "Maybe we ought to have anybody who hasn't slept with Amy stand up."

Steve and Amy finally married on November 27, 1985, five months after the birth of their son, Max. De Palma was the godfather. Said Robbins: "When Steven decided to marry her, I was very worried. It was no fun to go over there, because there was an electric tension in the air. It was competitive as to whose dining table this is, whose career we're going to talk about, or whether he even approved of what she was interested in — her friends and her actor life. He really was uncomfortable. The child in Spielberg believed so thoroughly in the possibility of perfect marriage, the institutions of marriage, the Norman Rockwell turkey on the table, everyone's head bowed in prayer — all this stuff. And Amy was sort of a glittering prize, smart as hell, gifted, and beautiful, but definitely edgy and provocative and competitive. She would not provide him any ease. There was nothing to go home to that was cozy."

Marriage and parenthood did nothing for the relationship. The baby took her out of the career loop, and she was no longer an ingenue. "I had a baby and lost my place on line," she said. In 1986, Irving complained publicly, "I started my career as the daughter of Jules Irving. I don't want to finish it as the wife of Spielberg or the mother of Max." She groused that marriage to Spielberg made her feel like a politician's wife.

Eventually, Spielberg divorced Irving, who is said to have gotten the largest settlement in history — in the neighborhood of $100 million. He married Kate Capshaw, with whom he had had an affair during the filming of *Indiana Jones and the Temple of Doom.* Says Gloria Katz, "Kate outmanipulated the most manipulative woman who ever lived."

As Spielberg became even more wealthy and powerful, many of the friendships forged in the '70s fell away. "It started out that everybody worked together, helped everyone else," says Milius. "But as soon as they got money, everyone turned on each other. Suddenly you were hot, you were special. You could now move into that house in Bel Air. You could have your own offices, editing rooms, all these appurtenances of power that in the studio system only came to people after twenty years of making films. Steven and George had tremendous power, and they never asked me to do anything for them."

Robbins had done uncredited work on *Jaws* and *Close Encounters,* and Spielberg had rewarded him with a point on the latter. His own film, which he had written and directed, *Dragonslayer,* flopped in 1981. Spielberg was in the midst of preproduction on *E.T.,* but invited him down from the Bay Area to stay at his Malibu beach house while he recovered his spirits. To divert himself, he read Melissa Mathison's script for *E.T.* He recalls, "I said, 'What is this doing in here? Why don't you do this, why don't you do that?'" Spielberg reacted very much like he always reacted in these situations. He said, continues Robbins, "'That's great, that's great. I gotta write it down.' I said, 'I'll do it, give me a typewriter.' The script was 143 pages long. I cut over twenty-five pages for him, took out a key character, a neighbor kid who figured out what was going on with E.T. I got this idea they should tarp in the house, just bag it, like when your house is being fumigated. I lost myself in this rewrite, and I felt really proud of myself at the end of it. By that time, I'd been around enough to feel that this was not a joke, but was getting serious. I had to leave for the airport at the end of my ten days. I poked my head into Steve's office, said, 'Well, gotta go!' He looked up and said, 'Okay, uh, thanks, Matt!' I went home. No point, no nuthin'. For me, that was the end of those great days where you could fool around like that, where you were working on everyone else's movies as much as you were working on your own, like being at film school, swapping points back and forth, like it was Monopoly money. It's really a shame. I guess I miss that more than anything."

Money was the solvent that dissolved the tissue of the '70s like acid on flesh. Years later, at Robin Williams's fortieth birthday party in Napa, Steven and Kate were hanging around with John Travolta, Kirstie Alley, and a few others. Travolta is licensed for multi-engine jets. Somebody asked, "So John, you flew your own plane up here? What kind?"

"A Learjet."

Steven broke in, "Oh yeah, a Learjet. Do you have the kind where you can just walk into it, or do you have to duck your head?"

"You have to duck your head," replied Travolta.

Steven turned to Kate and said, "We don't have to duck our heads on ours, do we?" It wasn't meant as Learjet one-upmanship, but that's what it was. The kid from Laurel Canyon with an orange Trans-Am had come a long way.

LUCAS WAS FINISHING his trilogy, and he turned the job of supervising the ranch to Marcia. But she had no interest in what she derisively called "decorating." Unbeknownst to their friends, George and Marcia's marriage was in trouble. "For me, the bottom line was just that he was all work and no play," says Marcia. "I felt that we paid our dues, fought our battles, worked eight days a week, twenty-five hours a day. I wanted to stop and smell the flowers. I wanted joy in my life. And George just didn't. He was very emotionally blocked, incapable of sharing feelings. He wanted to stay on that workaholic track. The empire builder, the dynamo. And I couldn't see myself living that way for the rest of my life.

"I felt we were partners, partners in the ranch, partners in our home, and we did these films together. I wasn't a fifty percent partner, but I felt I had something to bring to the table. I was the more emotional person who came from the heart, and George was the more intellectual and visual, and I thought I provided a nice balance. But George would never acknowledge that to me. I think he resented my criticisms, felt that all I ever did was put him down. In his mind, I always stayed the stupid Valley girl. He never felt I had any talent, he never felt I was very smart, he never gave me much credit. When we were finishing *Jedi*, George told me he thought I was a pretty good editor. In the sixteen years of our being together I think that was the only time he ever complimented me."

Marcia suggested that they see a therapist, but Lucas had that small-town animus against psychotherapy, probably absorbed from his father, and he discouraged her. "His general feeling was that shrinks are fucked-up people or they wouldn't have been shrinks in the first place," she says. Marcia began to withdraw from the marriage, suggested a trial separation. George rejected that; for him, it was all or nothing. He implored her to wait until *Jedi* was released. She did, and then got involved with Tom Rodriguez, an artist who created the dramatic stained glass dome over the Skywalker library.

Lucas was crushed. Divorce was the daily coin of Hollywood, not Marin County. "It violated all of the small-town traditions and virtues, all his certainties about himself," says Robbins. For all his inability to express it, he was very much in love with her. "I know he wanted me to stay, but it was just too little too late," she says. Their friends were shocked, although some saw it coming. Says Ronda Gomez, who, with her husband, Howard Zieff, used to spend a lot of time with the Lucases, "He just didn't want to have fun. Marcia wanted to go to Europe and see things. George wanted to stay in the hotel room and have his TV dinners." From a lower-middle-class background, Marcia had always lived modestly, and she was uncomfortable with Lucas's new Hearst-like Xanadu. Says Murch, "I think what Marcia saw was that his success was winding him tighter and tighter into a workaholic control-driven person, and she thought that this was destructive, which it probably is in the long run."

Marcia took a reported $50 million in settlement money with her. "He was very bitter and vindictive about the divorce," she says of her ex-husband. "Francis and Ellie used to have an Easter party out in Napa, and the first couple of years after the divorce, I used to get to see everyone, the Barwoods, the Robbinses, and then I stopped being invited. Years later I ran into Ellie down in L.A., and she said, 'I always wanted to call you to explain that when Francis and George were working on *Tucker*, George asked him not to invite you, because he was very uncomfortable around you.' That really hurt. It's not enough that I'm erased from his life, he wants to blackball me too, with people who were my friends. It's like I never existed."

"When he got divorced, George came to me and wanted to be my friend," recalls Francis. "He apologized."

The '80s were not kind to Lucas. He threw a party, and nobody came. Locating an expensive, state-of-the-art post-production facility so far from L.A. just didn't make sense, and until the recent spate of effects-heavy movies finally made Industrial Light and Magic a profit center, it was always a struggle to make ends meet.

Worse, he didn't seem to enjoy running it. Instead, he discovered that what he actually bought with all that money was a huge burden. Shouldering the responsibility for the hundreds of people on his payroll was oppressive, and he resented them, was cold and distant. He sabotaged his own business, hiring and firing executives, starting up in L.A., closing down, moving north, moving south. The Indiana Jones movies, which Lucas produced, were phenomenally successful, but Spielberg seemed to get all the credit. When his few attempts at filmmaking, most notoriously, *Howard the Duck*, and then the ridiculous *Willow* failed, he became increasingly bitter. In 1987, Aljean Harmetz, writing in the *New York Times*, called him "almost a total recluse." Says Milius, "Francis really tried to do things with his power. He made movies with Wim Wenders, produced *The Black Stallion*, produced George Lucas. George built Lucasland up there, his own private little duchy—which was producing what? A bunch of pap."

Coppola had always complained that the success of *The Godfather* derailed his career. Says Lucas, "The same thing happened to me." Like Coppola, his aspirations were inflected by the market. Says Marcia, "George would have remained an experimental filmmaker if it had not been for *Graffiti* leading to *Star Wars*." He always vowed he would never return to *Star Wars*.

The great irony is that Lucas is the only New Hollywood director who succeeded in establishing his financial independence from Hollywood, the only one who is in the position to do whatever he wants, and yet he is imprisoned by the very Hollywood films—the *Star Wars* trilogy—whose success gave him that independence in the first place.

Lucas used to regard his career as a failure. He had a fantasy that when he died, God would look down on him and say, "You've had your chance, and you blew it. Get out." Now he's reconciled to spending the rest of his life churning out *Star Wars* prequels, tending the pea at the bottom of the inverted Lucasfilm pyramid, as Marcia puts it.

When Darth Vader begs Luke to serve the Empire and join the Dark Side at the end of *The Empire Strikes Back*, saying, "It's your destiny," Luke defies him, taking a risky plunge into nowhere. But real life is different. When Lucas's self-created empire begged the producer-director to serve it, he gave in. "It took a long time for me to adjust to *Star Wars*," he says, bemusedly. "I finally did, and I'm going back to it. *Star Wars* is my destiny."

ON DECEMBER 12, 1981, Evans announced, with the fanfare he was so good at orchestrating, a new project called *The Cotton Club*. He described it as "*The Godfather* with music," or, more pungently, a movie with "gangsters, music, pussy." Evans intended to direct himself. But after months of struggling, the script was in disarray, and he found himself strapped for money. He called Coppola. His voice shaking, he said, "I really need your help, my child is in trouble." Francis thought he was talking about his boy, Josh, so he said, "Yes, Bob, yes, I'll do anything I can. What happened?" Evans explained he was talking about his movie. One thing led to another, and Coppola, against his better judgment, became the director. He was still living in the shadow of bankruptcy; as Sylbert puts it, "the IRS was in his wife's jewelry drawer." Recalls Francis, "I didn't want to do *The Cotton Club*, it was a nightmare, it was already $25 million over budget, there was no script, I had Richard Gere in a gangster movie who didn't want to play a gangster, and I had to start in a month."

Evans knew he was going to need more money, and he fell in with Laynie Jacobs, an attractive, thirtyish blonde and a mid-level coke dealer, who introduced Evans to Roy Radin, an overweight, sleazy promoter from New York. But Jacobs and Radin fell out over Jacobs's standing in the project, and Radin disappeared on his way to meet her for dinner at La Scala. A few weeks later, the missing person's case turned into a murder when his body was found in a canyon north of L.A. Evans fell under suspicion. LAPD homicide investigators interviewed Evans for four hours, and emerged from his office with autographed copies of the *Chinatown* script clutched in their hands.

Meanwhile, Coppola hired novelist William Kennedy for a ten-day polish. Every once in a while, Coppola's mania would peep out from under the blanket of lithium. Driving around New York one day, he passed the Chrysler Building and told Sylbert, "Gee, I'd like to have an office in there. I'm going to buy that building." On another occasion, at a screening of a recently restored print of Abel Gance's 1927 masterpiece, *Napoleon*, which Francis was releasing under the Zoetrope imprimatur, at the moment when the single image becomes three, filling the wide screen with a breathtaking, panoramic vista, Francis turned to the person next to him and exclaimed, "I want to be him."

"Who, Gance?" she replied.

"No, Napoleon!"

The *Cotton Club* shoot, which started on August 28, 1983, was a disaster, lasting twenty-two months. Payrolls were missed. Kennedy's ten-day polish lasted eighty-seven days, the length of the production, at $12,500 a week. He wrote twenty-eight drafts. The budget more than doubled, from $20 to $48 million.

Evans *was* replaying *The Godfather*. But this time there was no happy ending. Coppola banned Evans from the set. "I wanted to pick him up and throw him, the fat fuck, outta the fuckin' window," says Evans.

From Coppola's point of view, the situation looked considerably different. In exchange for agreeing to direct, he says, Evans was supposed to relinquish creative control. But, he claims, as soon as Evans raised the rest of the money on the basis of his name, Evans tried to interfere. *The Cotton Club* opened on December 8, 1984, in New York, and disappeared shortly thereafter.

For Coppola, worse was yet to happen. Two years later, in 1986, during the production of *Gardens of Stone*, a story about the relationship between an old soldier and a surrogate son who will die in Vietnam, Coppola's twenty-two-year-old son, Gio, was killed in a boating accident.

Like Friedkin, Coppola eventually became a director for hire, even stooping to direct a John Grisham movie, *The Rainmaker*. He, too, feels he never really became an auteur. "Woody Allen sits down, writes the script, goes out and makes the movie, one after another. *He* would never do a Grisham book. His career is the one that I most respect. I always wished that I could have done that."

In the '90s, Coppola went into the wine business in a big way, and turned his vineyard into a tourist attraction. He sits outside at a long wooden table, the padrone, greeting tourists, autographing the labels of wine bottles, and having his picture taken with pretty young things from the Midwest sitting on his knee. There is a sadness about him, the sadness of a man who had greatness in him, but only intermittently achieved it.

BY 1984, when the Schrader brothers made *Mishima*, a study of the right-wing Japanese writer who committed hara-kiri in a sensational act of political theater, death was in the air. Paul's group was being decimated by drugs, which cast a lengthening shadow over the Hollywood community. His friends were getting sick as well, cancer here, pneumonia there. Howard Rosenman had gone to medical school, still followed the journals. "I started warning people. I kept saying, 'Something terrible is going to happen to us.' I told Paul about it, and he thought I was paranoid, said I should see a psychiatrist. But I was right. AIDS killed everything, shattered it into a thousand billion fragments." (Adds Schrader, "Howard claims that he's only still alive because he had hemorrhoids.")

Mishima, despite the drama of the story, was a cold, stylized script that attracted little interest. Paul persuaded Coppola to produce it, and he in turn asked Lucas to finance it. Lucas surprised everybody by instantly agreeing. If he wasn't going to make these kinds of movies himself, he was apparently willing to support others who were. "If you compare people like Francis and George to Spielberg, there's a world of difference," says Schrader, who had never forgiven Spielberg for *Close Encounters*. "Francis and George were always willing to risk their fortune and their fame for other people. Spielberg is a very conservative man. He probably still has the first dollar he ever made — screwed to the wall."

But during the course of the production, the festering, if subterranean, resentments between Paul and Leonard surfaced. Admits Paul, "I had always treated Leonard badly. Taking sole screenwriting credit on *The Yakuza* wasn't very nice. Treating him as an employee wasn't very nice. Throughout all that, he had one thing that I didn't have, which was Japan. And then came *Mishima*, and I stole Japan from him. To do *Mishima* was his idea. He had all the connections. But once I got there, I took the big suite in the hotel because I was the director, and he had the small room. I was having all the meetings, and my friend Alan Poul, who was fluent in Japanese, was my first lieutenant, and Chieko, Leonard's wife, was the interpreter for the actors. Leonard was out of the loop. Rarely did he ever come to the set. Looking back, I was too busy trying to make this goddamn movie to really care that he was obviously just sitting there stewing."

But Leonard had been having success on his own. He wrote the script for *Kiss of the Spider Woman* (1985), which won him an Oscar nomination, became an art house hit, and went to the Cannes Film Festival the same year as *Mishima*. "I wanted Chieko to come to Cannes very badly, because we had an image problem," continues Paul. "I wanted a Japanese presence so that the press would think this was more indigenous. But Leonard didn't want to come, because he didn't want to be the girlfriend staying in the background. And if he wouldn't come, she wouldn't come. But I got on the phone with her, said, 'If Len wants to be self-destructive and throw a snit, that's fine, but you have to come.' So she came, adding insult to injury. I can only imagine how much that hurt. We haven't spoken since *Mishima*. That was the end."

After *Mishima*, Schrader was rarely heard from again, and he never approached, either as a writer or a director, his films of the '70s. Says Rosenman, "Stephen Sondheim says that all art is born out of anger, and in Schrader's case I think it was true. But the demons, the beasts that drove him were quieted." Perhaps it is as Kael says, "He's smarter than he's talented." Ironically, his best film as a director was his first, *Blue Collar*, which he more or less disavowed. Says Leonard, "My brother finds *Blue Collar* embarrassing. One reason is, he hadn't yet developed his polished-jewel *Cat People* style. The other is, he didn't write it." Meaning, of course, that Leonard wrote it.

BY THE EARLY '80S, Dennis Hopper had reached rock bottom. He would consume half a gallon of rum, twenty-eight beers, and three grams of coke — a day. His drink of choice had been rum and Coke, but he decided that rum and cranberry juice would be better for his liver, and made the switch. Despite his drinking and drugging, he felt he was able to function tolerably well. He pitied those who would fall apart after a couple of drinks or a line of coke. They were the ones who should join the twelve-steppers; he was fine.

But Hopper was getting still more paranoid, if possible, and was convinced the Mafia had put out a contract on him. He decided to bring things to a head by pulling a stunt called the Russian Suicide Death Chair, at an art happening at the Big-H Speedway outside Houston. He lay down in a coffin made out of paper and surrounded himself with sticks of dynamite. It was the trick he'd seen done when he was a boy that he'd wanted to use for the beginning of *Easy Rider*. Hopper figured he'd either be killed by the dynamite or the Mafia, which would hear about it and then would find him. His friends flew in from all over to see if he would finally manage to do himself in.

Still convinced the mob was on his trail, he pulled a "geographic," ending up in L.A. shooting coke and heroin, and then on to Mexico, where he had an acting gig. Suffering from DTs and hallucinations, he stripped off his clothes and disappeared into the jungle. After he punched a Mexican detective, the film company put him on a flight back to the States. As he was boarding, however, he became convinced that two of his former directors, Coppola and Wim Wenders, were filming him from the plane. Somehow he crawled out on the wing while the plane was still on the ground, and when he eventually debarked in L.A., he ended up in a hospital in Century City, then a celebrity drug program called Studio 8, then a state hospital. As he puts it, "I checked myself in, but I couldn't check myself out. The state was gonna keep me for two and a half years. They decided that I could not be allowed outside." Bob Rafelson located him through his agent, visited him on Father's Day, got him out, and took him over to Bert Schneider's. Bert put him up until he got straight, even found a counselor for him. "I was taking these antipsychotic drugs that were making me shuffle, and she said, 'What are those things?' I said, 'Those are my pills, I gotta take my pills, 'cause I'm a psychotic.' She said, 'Gimme those fuckin' things,' and she took 'em, and she flushed 'em down the toilet. She said, 'Fuck off, you're just a fuckin' alcoholic.'

"When I was younger, I could never imagine a life without alcohol," he continues. "My idea of retiring, of heaven, was to have a rocking chair with a bunch of scotch and some cocaine, some marijuana, and a lot of cigarettes. Drugs opened up some doors for you, but they closed rapidly, and pretty soon you were working for the drug, basing your whole life around where you could get it, who you could trust, and how you could avoid getting busted. The people you hurt worst are the people that love you, because those are the only ones who hang around. It's a terrible thing."

ROBERT TOWNE STUMBLED along after *Personal Best*, involving Beatty and Penn in a script called *Mermaid*, but he took so long writing it that it was knocked out of the box by *Splash*. He also did some script doctoring, rewriting an Oliver Stone script called *8 Million Ways to Die* for Ashby. But the director changed some details while he was staging a scene and, according to the producer, Steve Roth, "Robert went ballistic. Psychotic. He thought he was the greatest thing since sliced bread. He was this raging egomaniac with a whole group of sycophants around him. He was envious of Hal being a big director, and he thought he did him this big favor in rewriting the movie. It was the ugliest fight I ever saw in my life. Hal was down on his luck at that point. All kinds of accusations about drug abuse had been leveled at him. Towne was vicious. Said he was over-the-hill and gone. A cripple. 'I'm not gonna be fucked by this guy one more fucking time.' What was sad was these guys genuinely liked each other. They took an entire relationship and threw it away. I don't think they ever spoke again."

Bob Evans had promised Nicholson a dinner if he won an Oscar for his comeback film, *Terms of Endearment*. In the warm afterglow of the dessert — crème brûlée with grapes — Evans tearily toasted Jack, announced that Towne was almost finished with *The Two Jakes*, the second of what the writer conceived of as a trilogy. Whereas *Chinatown*, set in the '30s, dealt with water and the oligopoly of old wealth, *The Two Jakes* would be set in the postwar era, 1947, where oil and real estate, which is to say, WASPs and Jews, struggled for dominion over L.A. Jake Gittes searches for Katharine Mulwray (Evelyn's daughter by her father), to find that she is married to the second Jake, a character loosely based on Towne's father, Lou. (The sequel was jokingly referred to as *The Iron Jew*.) Lubricated by generous amounts of booze and blow, the three friends decided that Evans, who had not acted in twenty-six years, would play the second Jake. It made a certain amount of sense. "Evans was that person, was the other Jake," says a source. "A real sleazeball." Besides, Jack would be there to help him.

The other twist was that Towne would direct. Towne was in a bad way. *Personal Best* had been a commercial failure and had left a trail of lawsuits in its wake. And he had lost the two things he most cared for in life: *Greystoke* went to Warners and Hira died in his arms in 1982, sending him into seclusion. Geffen warned Nicholson against Towne, but the actor wouldn't listen. Jack called Diller from Evans's screening room, proposed they do it for scale, cap the budget at $12 or $13 million, and the three men, all producers who would organize their own company, Ten Productions (named for Towne, Evans, and Nicholson), would split the take with Paramount, after the picture hit $18 million. It looked like a win-win proposition, in which everyone shared the risk — and the profits, which were certain to be huge.

But before they began production, Bluhdorn died suddenly on February 19, 1983. Martin Davis, a former PR man, won a vicious power struggle and succeeded his boss. He quarreled with Diller, who had supported him, over his bonuses. Diller abruptly resigned to go to Fox, and then Davis told the *Wall Street Journal* he was firing Eisner and Katzenberg while the two men were in the air on a commercial flight (the company jet having been refused them) on their way to renegotiate their contracts with him in New York. Eisner went to Disney, and took Katzenberg with him. Like a '50s sci-fi movie, the diaspora of the Paramount pods had serious consequences for the rest of Hollywood. The high-concept formula they had evolved and so assiduously practiced, along with hands-on supervision by creative executives, infected the studios like an emergent virus, and the effects are still being felt today.

Bluhdorn was buried a Christian. Says Evans, "There are more crosses around his crypt than there are around the Popes'."

Frank Mancuso, head of marketing, replaced Diller, and Tanen, who had left Universal, replaced Eisner. The executives were eager to hit the ground running, and embraced *The Two Jakes* as the kind of project they needed to put the all too successful Diller era behind them. *The Two Jakes* was scheduled for Christmas 1986. But Evans was having trouble getting the script out of Towne, who was getting engaged to Luisa Selveggio, formerly the hostess and wife of the owner of an Italian restaurant on Olympic. Evans promised to throw a wedding party at Woodland for the happy couple if Towne finished by the time of the ceremony, October 17, 1984. Towne made the deadline, and Evans was as good as his word, hosted 150-odd guests, although he complained about the cost for years after.

Evans and Towne were never ones to live within their incomes, and both were chronically broke. Evans had been paying a lot of the preproduction costs out of his own pocket. The writer's living expenses were running about $50,000 a month, and he needed cash to furnish his new home. Once again, Evans assembled the old gang. Sylbert came on to design. Caleb Deschanel, who shot part of *Personal Best*, was the DP. Nicholson insisted that Harold Schneider line-produce. *The Two Jakes* was set to begin principal photography on Monday, May 5, 1985.

If the notion that Towne could direct was questionable, the idea that Evans could act was ludicrous. Evans promised Towne three weeks of rehearsal. In *Personal Best*, Towne had extracted a passable performance from Patrice Donnelly, a nonactor, and was confident he could do the same for Evans. But Evans left for Tahiti to have Alain Delon's plastic surgeon work on his face. He wanted an exotic look, and brought along Polaroids of cats. He returned looking like "a Jewish Chinaman," as one source put it, and in his screen tests he was wooden and stiff. He was protective of his "image," refused to let his hair be cut for a '40s look—he reminded one person of a Las Vegas croupier—and worse, when his hair was cut, the sutures in his scalp became visible. During rehearsals, Kelly McGillis, who had a role, was openly giggling at Evans's lame attempts at acting. As the first day of principal photography approached, reality began to sink in, and Towne had second thoughts. "Evans had always said to me that he was the worst actor he ever knew, but it was really painful to watch," recalls Sylbert. "He had all the mannerisms of Faye Dunaway. He was a disaster. And there was no way we were going to get through a movie with Towne, who couldn't help him." Using Evans might easily make the picture days, even weeks, late. The overages were supposed to come out of Towne's cut of the profits, and he had just been through that on *Personal Best*. It finally dawned on the director that the amusing decision to cast Evans might cost him a fortune.

Towne went to Nicholson, said, "Jack, I don't think I can make it work with Bob."

"Oh, man, you don't think you can get him through it?"

"I don't think I can get him to it."

"He's gonna go crazy. Just let him do it, and if it doesn't work out in a few weeks, shitcan him."

"I'm on the hook for completion. Three weeks, I'll be broke forever."

According to Evans, Towne had told Nicholson that Evans was backing out because he didn't want to play a Jew. That night, Towne was supposed to join Sylbert at Deschanel's for an eight o'clock dinner of barbecued salmon. He finally showed up at 10:00, while everyone was cleaning the bones, looking exhausted. He announced, "I've fired Bob Evans." Recalls Sylbert, "Evans went crazy. He went *crazy*. The calls, the screaming, the threats. He wanted to *kill* Bob Towne. Jack wanted to beat the shit out of him [Towne] for doing what he did that night."

On Saturday Towne broke the news to Paramount. Mancuso and Tanen were aghast, rushed over to Evans's house for a meeting. Towne was there, represented by his lawyer, Bert Fields. They went 'round and 'round. Towne insisted that Evans was out. Nicholson, who had not in fact agreed to replace Evans, vehemently insisted he was in. In the middle of the meeting, the phone rang. Tanen's ex-wife, Max, had committed suicide. Their two daughters had found the body. Tanen left. Finally, Nicholson stood up. "Listen, Beener," he announced, using his nickname for Towne, "With Evans, I take nothin'. Without him, I want my six mil against 15 percent of the gross. Is that clear?" Then he offered to buy the script from Towne for $2 million. Towne refused.

Monday morning, they went up to the Pacific Palisades for the first day of shooting. The location was the Bel Air Bay Club, a sprawling structure built in 1928 up on the hills of the Pacific Palisades. It was a virgin location, never before used for a film, and it would not be, at least that day. Nothing was shot. Tanen desperately wanted to hold it together. For a moment, it looked like a compromise had been reached: all three principals, not just Towne, would guarantee the overruns. Towne and Evans agreed, but Nicholson balked, realizing he was the only one of the three with money and would be left holding the bag. Finally, Mancuso called Towne, told him he was pulling the plug.

Hollywood, inured to every kind of scandal and catastrophe, had never seen anything quite like this highly public meltdown. Rumor, paranoia, and wild speculation swirled around the unlucky principals. Everyone agreed that Evans would have been a disaster. But it was Towne's handling of the situation that left people wondering. Evans wasn't needed for a month to six weeks. The consensus was that Towne should have started shooting, and then let Evans go. With several weeks' film in the can, the studio would have been helpless.

Said Harold Schneider, "I think Towne didn't want to do the film because he didn't think he could direct. I think he was chickening out, and Evans was the excuse, the fall guy. Towne got lockjaw, his brains fried. . . . He was in a fetal position under the couch screaming, 'I can't go on. They're out there, and they're gonna kill me.' " Says Kael, "Towne has really blown his gift. It's tragic. He's got everything going for him except common sense." People whispered that Nicholson let it fall apart because he wanted to direct the film himself, which he did, several years later.

The Two Jakes was like the proverbial string that, once pulled, unraveled the skein of friendships, woven in the '60s and '70s, that these men held dear. Both Evans and Towne (not to mention Rafelson, Mike Nichols, and Ashby), were dependent on Nicholson's loyalty and resurgent box-office clout to free them from their respective albatrosses: *The Cotton Club* and *Personal Best*. Towne's friendship with Nicholson snapped. He says now, "Jack was one of the most important people in my life. We grew up together. He taught me how to write by watching him act. I swore he would become a movie star, and I would write for him, and one day that happened. He was the closest friend I had. I haven't spoken to Jack for ten years."

The Two Jakes fiasco sent Evans hurtling into the abyss. Although he avoided indictment in the Radin affair (he has always denied any wrongdoing), Evans had become an endless embarrassment to the studio. Evans was abandoned by his pals. Says Bart, "Bob was a Gatsby-like person. He only wanted to know important people. He didn't have friends, didn't have buddies." Evans too sank into depression. All day, he lay on his bed in a fetal position, refusing to go out of the house. On May 19, 1989, he checked himself into a depression clinic at the Scripps Memorial Hospital, just north of San Diego, afraid he would commit suicide. He was put in a barred room, shot full of sedatives. He realized right away he had made a mistake — the doctors were contemplating electroshock therapy — and when he wanted to leave, they wouldn't let him out. Three days later, he escaped. Evans eventually did get a second chance at Paramount, but he failed to make much of it.

When *The Two Jakes* was finally made in 1989, it ended Nicholson's twenty-five-year-old friendship with Bert Schneider. After *Broken English*, Schneider stopped trying. His world was falling apart. Not only had he seen his dreams of revolution come to nothing, but many of the people closest to him, first his brother Stanley, then Artie Ross, died. Abbie Hoffman committed suicide in 1989, and Huey Newton was ignominiously gunned down in a drug-related killing on a dark street in Oakland the same year. "When Huey went, I think a good piece of Bert went at the same time," says Rafelson. "Dying like a gangster with a bullet in the brain, it was a bad way for Bert to see his pal go."

There was no place for people like Bert in the Reagan-Bush '80s. In the early '70s, BBS thought it was riding the wave of the future, but a decade later, reality had set in. "Despite *Easy Rider's* gigantic success, I always thought of us as — for want of a better term — minority communicators," Schneider has said. "We were in touch with a very small segment of the population and had to make inexpensive movies, because that was how we could survive. Our movies didn't have to reach a lot of people." In 1979, the MPAA reported that 90 percent of ticket buyers were between the ages of twelve and thirty-nine. But this was no longer a counterculture audience. It was a *Porky's* audience. Despite his flaws, Schneider's authority was such that for those who knew him, his self-imposed exile even now stands as a rebuke to the Me Generation that followed him.

One night, Nicholson was bemoaning the fact that he was never going to be taken seriously as a director. Bert suggested he revive *The Two Jakes* and direct it himself. He offered to executive-produce, watch Jack's back with Paramount. Harold Schneider would manage the production. But Paramount, already burned once, drove a hard bargain, said it didn't need an executive producer. Schneider expected Nicholson to pay him out of his cut. Says Blauner, "Bert was pissed that Jack wouldn't eat this. Bert made Jack. Jack would still be doing bike movies if it wasn't for BBS."

"The money was not the point," says Harry Gittes, who heard the story from Harold. "The point was, Bert wasn't treated with the respect he felt he deserved. The point was, 'You — Jack — made a fuckin' blood bond with me, and you broke it, and you're dead.' That's how Bert plays. 'And you're gonna let my brother, my kid brother, the Doberman, give me this news? It's humiliating. How could you do this to me?' And he was probably right, because Harold didn't exactly wear a velvet glove."

The rift was compounded when Bert wanted Jack to do a cameo in a sequel to *Easy Rider*, written by Michael O'Donoghue. According to Blauner, Jack had once told Bert, "Whenever you want me for a movie, just tell me where to show up, I'm there." Jack liked the script, and agreed to do it. At $1 million for three days' work and a chunk of the gross from breakeven, it wasn't much of a favor. Hopper and Fonda and key crew were all set to go. Bert sent Blauner to close the deal. But Jack wouldn't commit. Blauner said, "Let's cut the bullshit. Bert needs this!" Still Jack wouldn't respond. Furious, Blauner jumped in his car and started down the driveway. Jack ran after him. "What's the big hurry, Blautown? In and out?" Blauner barked, "What's there to talk about?" and drove off. He says, "Jack didn't stand up for Bert, like he doesn't stand up for anyone. Jack has still got a lot of Jersey in him, all of Jersey in him."

Whatever was going on in Nicholson's mind, it was plain he didn't want to be pressured. Bert might have been able to get away with that twenty-five years ago, when he was on top of the world and Nicholson was a struggling young actor, but not now, and Jack just ignored him. Continues Gittes, "Jack is the king, and we bring to the king. Bert was one of the last guys that sort of held over him, 'I'm Bert and you're Jack. I'm the Godfather, and you're the soldier. You're close to the Godfather, you may be the star soldier, but you're still a soldier."

Hopper was the go-between for Bert and Jack, but he and Bert also had a falling out, and Bert cut him off. "I love Bert," says Hopper. "I'll always remember what Bert and Bob did for me, but they're mean-spirited. They're just lucky that I passed through their lives." Bert and Jack still go to Lakers games, but when they see each other, they don't speak.

Nor was Bert speaking to Harold when Harold died suddenly of a heart attack in the fall of 1994. Bert lost his mother the same year, and then his new, twenty-year-old French wife either committed suicide or OD'd.

Lightning struck often around Bert, hitting people on all sides of him, but sparing the great trunk itself. Brothers, wife, parents, friends. Bert, who regarded himself as above history, was finally left behind by it. His strengths, his specialness, became his downfall, and he ended up a veritable recluse, very much the Howard Hughes figure, everyone around him disillusioned or dead. As Buck Henry puts it, "When the marriages began to fall apart, and people began to die of drug overdoses, and talent began to wither too soon, nobody knew where to go or what to do about it. Some just hid out."

A few years later, after a picture called *Man Trouble* on which Rafelson and Nicholson seriously feuded, the director bought a house up on Mulholland, adjoining Jack's. Bob and Bert used to stand on the property line talking about the old days. They hollered, "Fuck you, Jack," into the canyon, waiting for the echo, bouncing from ridge to ridge, to come back to them. They took out their dicks, something they had always been good at, and peed over the property line onto Jack's land.

THE DIRECTORS of this decade were not unusual in their self-absorption, ruthlessness, or cruelty. Such behavior goes with the territory. "Directors, in order to stay in the game, are among the worst people we've got," observes producer Don Devlin, best known as the man who asked Lew Wasserman if he kept two sets of books. "You have to be absolutely ruthless. Many of them are sociopaths."

Could another group of directors have done it differently, broken the back of studio power, created little islands of self-sufficiency that would have supported them in the work they wanted to do? Could a hundred flowers ever have bloomed? Probably not. The strength of the economic forces arrayed against them was too great. "We had the naive notion that it was the equipment which would give us the means of production," said Coppola. "Of course, we learned much later that it wasn't the equipment, it was the money." Because the fact of the matter is that although individual revolutionaries succeeded, the revolution failed. The New Hollywood directors were like free-range chickens; they were let out of the coop to run around the barnyard and imagined they were free. But when they ceased laying those eggs, they were slaughtered.

As Coppola later recognized, the market selected and shaped these directors, snuffing out the careers of those whose films were not commercial, and boosting and molding the careers of those that were. Consider what might have been had Coppola dug in his heels, refused to direct *The Godfather*, made personal films instead. What if Spielberg had turned down *Jaws*, and had followed the path of *Sugarland Express*, made *Bingo Long*. Or if Lucas had followed *THX* with another dark, idiosyncratic picture. But of course, none of these "what ifs" was very likely. The rewards were too great for these filmmakers to walk away from them.

Still, just when the future seems darkest, when a picture like the ridiculous *Titanic* has apparently legitimized the studios' free-spending habits, a new generation of filmmakers, some inspired by the pictures of the '70s, sometimes even mentored by '70s directors, emerges at the bottom to inject new vitality into the system — the Oliver Stones and Coen brothers of the '80s, the Quentin Tarantinos and Atom Egoyans of the '90s. And there is always the hope that one of the great directors of the '70s — an Altman, a Schrader, a Friedkin — will find the resources to make the masterpiece that has so far eluded him.

Still, without a counterculture to nourish them, without a vigorous set of oppositional values, the independents are independent in name only, always at risk of being gobbled up and corrupted by the studios. It would be wonderful if Lucas's fantasy of multiplexes all over America playing independent features were a fact. But he has probably not been to a mall lately, where the reality is that six screens of the local multiplex will be showing *The Lost World* or a *Lost World* equivalent. Unfortunately, this story may not have a happy ending, and the last word could likely be that of Altman, who says, "You get tired painting your pictures and going down to the street corner and selling them for a dollar. You get the occasional *Fargo*, but you've still got to make them for nothing, and you get nothing back. It's disastrous for the film industry, disastrous for film art. I have no optimism whatsoever."

BY THE LATE '80s, Ashby had cleaned up, kicked the drugs, was very much in a rehab mode. "You know," he told producer Lester Persky, "I've lost eight years out of my life." He'd had a rough half decade, two pictures in a row taken away from him during the editing, *Lookin' to Get Out* and *The Slugger's Wife*, written by Neil Simon and produced by Ray Stark. The story went that Ashby had showed them a 20-minute rough cut of the beginning of the picture that had almost no dialogue, none of Simon's precious script, and that was that, they seized the film. Then came *8 Million Ways to Die*, the picture on which he feuded with Towne. Recalls Chuck Mulvehill, "We finished shooting the picture, a five-ton truck pulled up with a couple of palookas, they came up to the editing room, and they took the film away from him — the best editor in

Hollywood—for the third time in a row. Hal fought it through the Guild, and in the end, he settled. They gave him some money, and he just said, 'Ah, fuck it,' and he left. He would never have done that in the '70s—it would have been a fight to the death. The magic was gone." Hal told friends, "I just give up. I can't fight it, they're scumbags." Adds Bruce Dern, who lived down the beach from Ashby and had stayed in touch after *Coming Home*, "Hal said, 'I can understand anything except not letting me edit something, particularly something I shot.' I think he gave up then, and just let himself go. What happened to him, both what he did to himself, and they did to him, is as repulsive to me as anything I've seen in my forty years in the industry."

After years of reclusiveness, Hal started to appear at Hollywood parties wearing a double-breasted blue blazer, as if to send a message to the agents and producers in attendance: "I am no longer a drug addict, I am reliable, trust me." He was talking hopefully about starting over, making a "Hal Ashby" movie, had several projects at various stages of development. Then, one night, Hal was at Beatty's. He started to complain about an insect bite on his leg. "I got this on the other leg too, and it's bothering me," he said, showing what looked like a discolored bruise to Beatty, who replied, "I don't like the way that looks. It looks to me like phlebitis."

"What the hell is phlebitis?"

"You know, what Nixon had, a traveling clot, through the bloodstream. Let me send you to a doctor."

Ashby hated doctors, and shrugged off Beatty's concern. A few days later, he called Jerry Hellman, wanted to know if the script meeting they had scheduled could be moved from Hellman's house to his house. He didn't feel well. Recalls Hellman, "I got there, and one of his legs was propped up. It was black-and-blue and swollen, and looked fuckin' awful." Hellman asked, "What in the world is that?"

"Well, I don't know. It's funny, isn't it? Looks terrible."

"Yeah, it does look terrible. What does the doctor say about it?"

"Oh, I haven't been to the doctor. . . . It's the oddest thing, the damn thing keeps moving around."

"Whaddya mean it keeps moving around?"

"One day last week it was in my arm, my leg was fine, but my whole arm was swollen up."

Meanwhile, Beatty called some people he knew at Johns Hopkins, where his father had been treated before he died: "Is there such a thing as phlebitis in both legs?"

He was told, "There is a migratory phlebitis, which comes as a result of pancreatic cancer."

Recalls Beatty, "That scared the hell out of me. We had some CAT scans and pancreatic scans done at Hopkins, and of course he did have malignancies. I said, 'I think you should have the surgery,' but I couldn't talk him into it, and he came back to L.A. It was about five or six weeks — I felt they were crucial weeks — before me and Jack and Haskell finally talked him into going back and having the surgery." Dustin Hoffman flew back to Baltimore with him.

At Hopkins, they took out part of the liver and the pancreas, trying to get the tumors, gave him chemo, but the procedures were unsuccessful, and it was clear to everyone but Hal that he was dying. He resented the procedures, hated the hospital. All he knew was that he was in tremendous pain, so much pain that no amount of morphine seemed to dull the edge. He was losing his eyesight; the weak autumn sun hurt his eyes when they wheeled him onto the hospital grounds for some air. One day he just walked out of the hospital with an IV drip in him, checked into a hotel. He called Jeff Berg, told him the operation was the final humiliation of his life, and begged him to get him out of there. Berg called Warners co-head Bob Daly, got the company jet to fly him home.

Ashby was furious that he had allowed Beatty to talk him into the surgery. He refused to let him visit, and Beatty rarely saw him again. Hal's friends set up a kind of hospice in his house in the Colony. He had a big TV set, a couple of VCRs, and he was hooked up to a satellite. Hal's girlfriend, a New Ager, Griff, gave him herbs and natural remedies, didn't want to medicate him for his pain, but was finally convinced to do so by his friends, whom she angered by playing the gatekeeper, controlling who got to see him. Jerry Hellman came every night, sat by his bedside. Haskell Wexler, Bob Jones, Bruce Dern, Bob Downey came and held his hand.

Almost to the end, Hal was in denial. "The truth is, I've never seen anyone so frightened," recalls Hellman. "It was terrible to watch. Hal couldn't deal with reality. I don't think he ever recognized what was really wrong and accepted his death."

Chuck Mulvehill and Ashby had been estranged for years, and Mulvehill didn't want to see him, he was still too angry. Jones had to persuade him to visit. He and his wife, Shari, finally came over. They were shocked. Hal had become an old man. He looked bloated, was obviously in a lot of pain. "He saw Shari, and burst into tears, because they hadn't seen each other for about ten years," recalls Mulvehill. "We were trying to make light of the situation. Somebody made a joke, and we all laughed, and then Hal turned on everybody, I mean, it was vicious, like, whoops, talk about quieting the room. Everybody was on eggshells. I'd had a fantasy that he and I could sit down and be honest with one another, just bring it to a closure. It wasn't going to happen. I walked away one day thinking, It's too painful to watch."

But Hal knew more than his friends thought. One evening in the late fall after leaving the office, Berg drove up the coast into the setting sun to see him. It was hot; the Santa Ana winds were whipping through the canyons and rattling the shutters against Hal's house. Ashby told Berg, "Well, they're here."

"Who's here?"

"Them. Can't you hear them?"

"No, Hal, who is them and what am I not hearing?"

"The people who are taking me away." Berg thought, He's having a premonition of his death. The clattering of the shutters represents a knock on the door, saying, We're ready, are you?

A few days later, Jones went over to visit him. He sat at Hal's bedside watching him sleep, his skin pallid and dry as parchment, nearly translucent, his wispy beard matted and damp, his eyes buried in their sockets. Hal regained consciousness, said, "Bob, they're calling me from across the river. Don't let 'em get me. I don't want to die."

Hal Ashby did die just after Christmas, on a raw, rainy Tuesday, December 27, 1988, at the age of fifty-nine. The papers said it was liver and colon cancer, but it could just as well have been a broken heart.

There was a memorial service at the new DGA building on Sunset on Friday the 30th. Despite the fact that Hal had a lot of friends, the hall was only half full, because everyone was in Aspen or elsewhere for the holidays. The people who came sat alone, or in small clusters separated by rows of empty seats. They came because they cared about him, or they'd worked with him. Jeff Bridges presided over the procession of speakers, one from every film, and then some. He stood next to a jumbo-sized blow-up of Hal's face, smiling benignly down at the mourners. A L.A. street sign purloined by Sean Penn from an intersection on Overland that read "ASHBY" in white letters on a blue background, leaned against the base of the podium. Beatty spoke, Hellman, and Dern. So did Shirley MacLaine, Andy Garcia, and Bud Cort. Haskell Wexler was away on location, so was Nicholson, who sent a telegram. It was clear that they loved Hal, who despite the success of his films was more admired by the Hollywood community than by the reviewers. Kael never liked him much, put off perhaps by his politics and his deceptively relaxed mise-en-scène. But actors killed to work with him, even in the years of his decline. It was a wake as much for Hal as for themselves, for their dreams, for the best years of their lives.

Ashby had a thing about the ocean. He had made his way from the Wasatch mountains of Utah to the Coast, and then from Laurel Canyon down to the beach, which he dearly loved. He joked about ending it all by drowning himself, and there is a celebrated scene in *Coming Home* where Dern does just that, strips off his clothes and walks into the ocean. There is an equally celebrated scene in *Being There* — the last film clip shown at the memorial — in which Peter Sellers, impeccably dressed like an English gentleman, strolls casually across the surface of a pond. Hal had gone under, but his friends preferred to remember him as he portrayed himself, walking on water.

Beau Bridges, who had appeared in Ashby's first film, *The Landlord*, summed it all up. Ashby didn't like formal social occasions, Bridges recalled, and had he been there, like Tom Sawyer a witness to his own funeral, he would have been found sitting in the last row, mocking the gravity of the tributes. "And when the lights came up after the show," said Bridges, "and you looked around for him, he'd be gone. Hal always left early."

After the lights in fact came up, people filed out and got into their cars, no refreshments, no coffee, just drove off. In the weeks that followed, Griff occasionally invited small groups of Hal's friends over to the Colony house for a sort of service, to bring Hal's spirit back. Bob Jones was there once, on the deck, at night: "Griff saw a meteor streak across the sky, and she said, 'That's Hal.' I never heard from her again."

Cast of Characters

Julie Christie: actress, *McCabe & Mrs. Miller, Shampoo, Heaven Can Wait*; relationship with Warren Beatty.

Michael Cimino: director, *The Deer Hunter, Heaven's Gate.*

Rob Cohen: executive VP of motion picture division, Motown; later, producer and director.

Eleanor Coppola: married to Francis Coppola.

Francis Coppola: director, the *Godfathers, The Conversation, Apocalypse Now, The Cotton Club.*

Roger Corman: producer, *Targets, Boxcar Bertha*; director, *The Wild Angels.*

Bosley Crowther: movie reviewer, the *New York Times.*

Sean Daniel: production executive, Universal, under Ned Tanen, *Animal House.*

Robert Dalva: director, *The Black Stallion Returns*; associated with Zoetrope.

Peter Davis: director, *Hearts and Minds.*

Robert De Niro: actor, *Mean Streets; The Godfather, Part II; Taxi Driver; New York, New York; Raging Bull.*

Brian De Palma: director, *Obsession, Carrie, The Fury.*

Bruce Dern: actor, *The King of Marvin Gardens, Coming Home.*

Caleb Deschanel: cinematographer, *The Black Stallion, Being There.*

Barry Diller: CEO, Paramount.

Marion Dougherty: casting director.

Faye Dunaway: actress, *Bonnie and Clyde, Chinatown.*

Carole Eastman, aka Adrien Joyce: screenwriter, *Five Easy Pieces, The Fortune.*

Michael Eisner: president, COO, Paramount.

Robert Evans: executive VP of worldwide production, Paramount; producer, *Chinatown, Marathon Man, Popeye, The Cotton Club.*

David Field: president of West Coast production, United Artists.

Freddie Fields: head, CMA; founded First Artists; producer, *Looking for Mr. Goodbar, American Gigolo.*

Verna Fields: editor, *What's Up, Doc?, Paper Moon, American Graffiti, Jaws.*

Louise Fletcher: actress, *Thieves Like Us, One Flew Over the Cuckoo's Nest.*

Peter Fonda: actor-writer-producer, *Easy Rider.*

Gray Frederickson: associate producer, *The Godfather*; co-producer, *The Godfather, Part II, Apocalypse Now.*

William Friedkin: director, *The French Connection, The Exorcist, Sorcerer.*

David Geffen: executive, Warners; producer.

Michie Gleason: assistant to Bert Schneider, *Days of Heaven*; director, *Broken English*; relationship with Terrence Malick.

Harry Gittes: co-producer, *Drive, He Said.*

Ronda Gomez: executive under Peter Bart, Paramount.

Carl Gottlieb: writer, *Jaws, Jaws 2.*

Walon Green: writer, *Sorcerer.*

Charles Greenlaw: executive VP of worldwide management, Warners.

Dr. Martin Grotjahn: psychoanalyst for Warren Beatty, Robert Towne, and David Geffen.

Peter Guber: executive, Columbia.

Kitty Hawks: relationship with William Friedkin; daughter of Howard Hawks.

Bill Hayward: associate producer, *Easy Rider*; partner of Peter Fonda; brother of Brooke Hayward.

Brooke Hayward: married to Dennis Hopper; sister of Bill Hayward.

Patricia James: assistant to Robert Towne.

Gary Kurtz: producer, *American Graffiti, Star Wars, The Empire Strikes Back.*

Jerome Hellman: producer, *Midnight Cowboy, Coming Home.*

Buck Henry: writer, *The Graduate, Catch-22;* co-writer, *What's Up, Doc?;* co-director, *Heaven Can Wait.*

Paul Hirsch: editor, *Carrie, Star Wars, The Empire Strikes Back.*

Dennis Hopper: actor-director-writer, *Easy Rider, The Last Movie;* actor, *Tracks, Apocalypse Now;* married to Brooke Hayward, Michelle Phillips.

Willard Huyck: writer, *American Graffiti, Star Wars* (uncredited); married to Gloria Katz.

Joe Hyams: marketing executive, Warners.

Amy Irving: actress, *Carrie, The Fury;* married to Steven Spielberg.

Leo Jaffe: president, Columbia; father of Stanley Jaffe.

Stanley Jaffe: president, Paramount; executive VP of worldwide production, Columbia.

Henry Jaglom: director, *A Safe Place, Tracks.*

Dennis Jakob: creative consultant, *Apocalypse Now.*

Robert Jones: editor, *The Last Detail;* co-writer, *Coming Home.*

Pauline Kael: movie reviewer, *The New Yorker.*

Gloria Katz: writer, *American Graffiti, Star Wars* (uncredited); married to Willard Huyck.

Margot Kidder: actress, *Sisters, Superman;* housemate of Jennifer Salt.

Sidney Korshak: attorney for Charles Bluhdorn, Robert Evans.

Arthur Krim: CEO, United Artists.

Alan Ladd, Jr.: president, 20th Century-Fox.

Jeremy Larner: writer, *Drive, He Said, The Candidate.*

Richard Lederer: VP of production, VP of advertising/publicity, Warners.

Paul Lewis: unit production manager, *Easy Rider, What's Up, Doc?*

George Litto: agent for Robert Altman; producer for Altman and Brian De Palma.

Evan Lottman: editor, *The Exorcist, Apocalypse Now* (uncredited).

George Lucas: director, *THX: 1138, American Graffiti, Star Wars;* producer, *The Empire Strikes Back;* married to Marcia Lucas.

Marcia Lucas: editor, *American Graffiti; Alice Doesn't Live Here Anymore; Taxi Driver; New York, New York; Star Wars.*

Mimi Machu: relationships with Jack Nicholson and Hal Ashby.

Terrence Malick: director, *Badlands, Days of Heaven.*

Chris Mankiewicz: executive at Columbia, United Artists.

Mardik Martin: co-writer, *Mean Streets, New York, New York, Raging Bull.*

Melissa Mathison: co-writer, *The Black Stallion;* writer, *E.T.: The Extra-Terrestrial.*

Jim McBride: director, *David Holzman's Diary.*

Mike Medavoy: agent, IFA; head of West Coast production, United Artists.

Sue Mengers: agent, CMA; clients included Peter Bogdanovich, Barbra Streisand.

John Milius: writer, *Apocalypse Now;* director, *The Wind and the Lion.*

Susanna Moore: assistant to Warren Beatty; married to Richard Sylbert.

Charles Mulvehill: associate producer for Hal Ashby.

Walter Murch: sound designer-editor, *The Conversation, The Godfather, Part II, Apocalypse Now.*

Jennifer Nairn-Smith: dancer-actress, relationship with William Friedkin.

James Nelson: post-production sound for BBS, *The Exorcist.*

David Newman: co-writer, *Bonnie and Clyde, What's Up, Doc?, Superman.*

Huey Newton: leader, Black Panther party; friend of Bert Schneider.

Mike Nichols: director, *The Graduate, Catch-22, Carnal Knowledge, The Fortune.*

Jack Nicholson: actor, *Easy Rider, Five Easy Pieces, The King of Marvin Gardens, The Last Detail, Chinatown;* director, *Drive, He Said;* relationships with Mimi Machu and Michelle Phillips.

Julie Payne: married to Robert Towne.

Arthur Penn: director, *The Left-Handed Gun, Mickey One, Bonnie and Clyde, Night Moves, The Missouri Breaks.*

Lester Persky: producer, *Shampoo.*

Julia and Michael Phillips: producers, *The Sting, Taxi Driver, Close Encounters of the Third Kind;* married; partners of Tony Bill.

Michelle Phillips: singer, the Mamas and the Papas; married to Dennis Hopper; relationships with Jack Nicholson and Warren Beatty.

David Picker: head of production, United Artists.

Polly Platt: production designer, *The Last Picture Show, What's Up, Doc?, Paper Moon;* married to Peter Bogdanovich.

Roman Polanski: director, *Rosemary's Baby, Chinatown.*

Tom Pollock: attorney for George Lucas.

Ed Pressman: producer, *Sisters;* executive producer, *Badlands.*

Steve Prince: cameo in *Taxi Driver,* subject of Martin Scorsese's documentary, *American Boy.*

John Ptak: agent, IFA; clients included Paul Schrader.

Bob Rafelson: director, *Head, Five Easy Pieces, The King of Marvin Gardens, Stay Hungry;* partner, BBS; married to Toby Rafelson.

Toby Rafelson: production designer, *Five Easy Pieces, The King of Marvin Gardens, Alice Doesn't Live Here Anymore, Stay Hungry.*

Kathryn Reed: married to Robert Altman.

Matthew Robbins: writer, *The Sugarland Express.*

Robbie Robertson: musician, the Band; housemate of Martin Scorsese.

Fred Roos: casting, the *Godfathers, American Graffiti, Apocalypse Now;* co-producer, *The Godfather, Part II, Apocalypse Now.*

Howard Rosenman: producer, *Sparkle, The Main Event, Resurrection.*

Artie Ross: friend of Bert Schneider.

Albert S. Ruddy: producer, *The Godfather.*

Jennifer Salt: actress, *Midnight Cowboy, Sisters;* daughter of writer Waldo Salt; housemate of Margot Kidder.

Geoffrey Sanford: production executive, Warners.

Abe Schneider: CEO, Columbia; father of Bert, Harold, and Stanley.

Bert Schneider: partner, BBS; producer, *Days of Heaven, Broken English.*

Harold Schneider: associate producer, *Five Easy Pieces, The Last Picture Show;* producer, *Days of Heaven.*

Judy Schneider: married to Bert Schneider.

Stanley Schneider: president, Columbia.

Leonard Schrader: co-writer, *The Yakuza, Blue Collar, Mishima;* writer, *Kiss of the Spider Woman;* brother of Paul.

Paul Schrader: writer, *Taxi Driver, Obsession;* co-writer, *The Yakuza, Raging Bull, Mishima;* director, *Blue Collar, American Gigolo, Cat People, Mishima;* brother of Leonard.

Martin Scorsese: director, *Mean Streets, Alice Doesn't Live Here Anymore, Taxi Driver, New York, New York, The Last Waltz, Raging Bull.*

Cybill Shepherd: actress, *The Last Picture Show, Daisy Miller, At Long Last Love, Taxi Driver.*

Sidney Sheinberg: president and COO of MCA.

Don Simpson: president of worldwide production, Paramount.

Mona Skager: assistant and producer for Francis Coppola.

Bud Smith: editor, *The Exorcist, Sorcerer, Personal Best.*

Steven Spielberg: director, *The Sugarland Express, Jaws, Close Encounters of the Third Kind, 1941.*

Jules Stein: founded MCA with Lew Wasserman.

Anthea Sylbert: costume designer, *Chinatown, Shampoo;* VP of special projects, Warners.

Richard Sylbert: production designer, *The Graduate, Rosemary's Baby, Chinatown, Shampoo, The Fortune, Reds;* head of production, Paramount.

Ned Tanen: head of motion pictures, Universal.

Jonathan Taplin: producer, *Mean Streets.*

Joan Tewkesbury: script supervisor, *McCabe & Mrs. Miller;* screenwriter, *Nashville.*

Tommy Thompson: first assistant director, associate producer for Robert Altman.

James Toback: director, *Fingers, Love and Money.*

Robert Towne: writer, *The Last Detail, Chinatown, Shampoo, Greystoke;* director, *Personal Best;* married to Julie Payne.

Lew Wasserman: founded MCA with Jules Stein.

Fred Weintraub: VP of creative services, Warners.

Sandra Weintraub: associate producer, *Alice Doesn't Live Here Anymore;* relationship with Scorsese; daughter of Fred.

Frank Wells: president, Warners.

Haskell Wexler: director of photography, *American Graffiti, One Flew Over the Cuckoo's Nest, Bound for Glory, Coming Home.*

Gordon Willis: director of photography, the *Godfathers.*

Irwin Winkler: producer, *New York, New York, Rocky, Raging Bull.*

Frank Yablans: president, Paramount.

Richard Zanuck: producer, *The Sting, Jaws;* partner of David Brown.

Selected Filmography of Directors (1967–1982)

Robert Altman
That Cold Day in the Park (1969)
M*A*S*H (1970)
Brewster McCloud (1970)
McCabe & Mrs. Miller (1971)
Thieves Like Us (1974)
Nashville (1975)
Buffalo Bill and the Indians (1976)
Popeye (1980)

Hal Ashby
Harold and Maude (1972)
The Last Detail (1973)
Shampoo (1975)
Bound for Glory (1976)
Coming Home (1978)
Being There (1979)
Lookin' to Get Out (1982)

Warren Beatty
Heaven Can Wait (with Buck Henry) (1978)
Reds (1981)

Peter Bogdanovich
Targets (1968)
The Last Picture Show (1971)
What's Up, Doc? (1972)
Paper Moon (1973)
Daisy Miller (1974)
At Long Last Love (1975)
Nickelodeon (1976)

Michael Cimino
Heaven's Gate (1980)

Francis Ford Coppola
You're a Big Boy Now (1966)
Finian's Rainbow (1968)
The Rain People (1969)
The Godfather (1972)
The Conversation (1974)
The Godfather, Part II (1974)
Apocalypse Now (1979)
One from the Heart (1982)

William Friedkin
The French Connection (1971)
The Exorcist (1973)
Sorcerer (1977)

Dennis Hopper
Easy Rider (1969)
The Last Movie (1971)

George Lucas
THX: 1138 (1971)
American Graffiti (1973)
Star Wars (1977)

Terry Malick
Badlands (1973)
Days of Heaven (1978)

Bob Rafelson
Head (1968)
Five Easy Pieces (1970)
The King of Marvin Gardens (1972)
Stay Hungry (1976)

Paul Schrader
Blue Collar (1978)
Hardcore (1979)
American Gigolo (1980)
Cat People (1982)

Martin Scorsese
Boxcar Bertha (1972)
Mean Streets (1973)

Alice Doesn't Live Here Anymore (1974)
Taxi Driver (1976)
New York, New York (1977)
The Last Waltz (1978)
Raging Bull (1980)

Steven Spielberg
Duel (1971)
The Sugarland Express (1974)
Jaws (1975)
Close Encounters of the Third Kind (1977)
1941 (1979)

Robert Towne
Personal Best (1982)

Notes

A Note on the Research

This book is based on hundreds of interviews with the people who lived through the late '60s and '70s in Hollywood conducted over a period of five years. I have also availed myself of the voluminous body of secondary material that exists on this period, but I have endeavored to reinterview the sources cited whenever appropriate. Where my account differs from the recollections of one of the principals, I have indicated it, although often I had to choose between several conflicting accounts. Conversations are based on interviews with at least one of the participants. When thoughts are attributed to a principal, they are also derived from interviews.

AI = Author's interview.

Introduction: Knockin' on Heaven's Door

PAGE
13 *Epigraph:* Martin Scorsese, AI, 7/13/91.
13 *"I jumped out of bed":* Scorsese, AI, 5/23/94.
14 *"It was like the ground":* Peter Guber, AI, 11/10/92.
14 *"The '70s was the first time":* Steven Spielberg, AI, 12/9/96.
16 *"Reading Sarris":* Robert Benton, AI, 4/26/94.
16 *"We were just guys":* Scorsese, AI, 7/18/97.
16 *"the last great time":* Peter Bart, AI, 3/17/94.
17 *"It was at this specific moment":* Susan Sontag, "The Decay of Cinema," *New York Times Magazine,* 2/25/96, p. 61.
18 *"If you were these guys":* Ned Tanen, AI, 1/22/93.
18 *"Please, sir":* Irwin Winkler, AI, 3/17/92.
19 *"Directors weren't even":* John Calley, AI, 5/15/93.
20 *"The first day":* Walter Murch, AI, 11/18/93.
20 *"It was not like":* Spielberg, AI, 12/9/96.
20 *"The movie industry was":* Bart, AI, 4/17/92.
21 *"You saw Battle of Algiers":* Sean Daniel, AI, 11/13/93.
21 *"When the movie factories":* Scorsese, AI, 5/23/94.
22 *" 'No, no, no' ":* Paul Williams, AI, 7/23/93.
22 *"There was a complete":* John Boorman, AI, 2/22/95.
22 *"Because of the catastrophic":* Paul Schrader, AI, 12/3/91.
22 *"If you were young":* Guber, AI, 11/10/92.
22 *"This group of people":* Leonard Schrader, AI, 11/8/94.

Chapter 1: Before the Revolution

PAGE
23 *Epigraph:* Arthur Penn, AI, 1/12/93.
23 *"He always hated me":* Warren Beatty, AI, n.d.

24   *"Colonel!"*: Joe Hyams, AI, 4/9/92.
25   *"I wanted to do a comedy"*: Beatty, AI, 11/2/91.
25   *"Charlie taught Warren"*: Richard Sylbert, AI, 8/25/92.
25   *"Charlie would not be denied"*: Richard Sylbert, AI, 4/7/93, 5/26/93.
25   *"I want forty"*: Beatty, AI, n.d.
26   *"Warren said"*: Richard Sylbert, AI, 5/12/93.
26   *"I finally walked out"*: Beatty, AI, 11/2/91.
26   *"Warren went back"*: Richard Sylbert, AI, 8/25/92.
26   *"Woody was very unhappy"*: Beatty, AI, 11/2/91.
26   *"All the time" and following*: Benton, AI, 12/9/92.
27   *"Everyone knew somebody"*: Benton, AI, 4/26/92.
27   *"Being an outlaw"*: David Newman, AI, 7/30/92.
27   *"The French New Wave" and following*: Benton, AI, 12/9/92.
28   *"He was walking around"*: Robert Towne, AI, 3/3/94.
28   *"Some of these clowns"*: Letter from Beatty to Benton and Newman, 3/14/66.
28   *"Penn was a court"*: Towne, AI, 3/3/94.
28   *"I don't know"*: Benton, AI, 12/9/92.
29   *"I finished shooting"*: Penn, AI, 1/12/93.
29   *"Beatty and I"*: Bernard Weintraub, "Director Arthur Penn Takes on General Custer," *New York Times Magazine*, 12/21/69, p. 46.
29   *"Look, just give me"*: Beatty, AI, 6/11/94.
30   *"Warren said, 'He's' "*: Newman, AI, 2/15/94.
30   *"Who wants to see"*: Patrick Goldstein, "Blasts from the Past," *Los Angeles Times Calendar*, 8/24–25/97.
31   *"He had this ability"*: Gerald Ayres, AI, 6/14/94.
31   *"Bob was a very talented"*: David Geffen, AI, 4/18/96.
31   *"He set up a meeting" and following*: Towne, AI, 3/3/94.
32   *"We were trying"*: Benton, AI, 12/9/92.
32   *"You're making a mistake"*: Newman, AI, 7/30/92.
32   *"None of us felt"*: Towne, AI, 3/3/94.
33   *"When I was a kid"*: Towne, AI, 11/6/97.
33   *"It was like ordering"*: Marion Dougherty, AI, 4/11/94.
33   *"Most of the casting people"*: Nessa Hyams, AI, 4/1/94.
34   *"Warren and Arthur"*: Estelle Parsons, AI, n.d.
34   *"I was this sort of buffer"*: Towne, AI, 3/3/94.
35   *"It used to be" and following*: Penn, AI, 1/12/93.
35   *"I'll tell ya something" and following*: Penn, AI, 1/12/93; Beatty, AI, 6/11/94.
35   *"He kept running"*: Goldstein, "Blasts from the Past"; Beatty, AI, 10/31/97.
36   *"Ninety percent of them"*: John Ptak, AI, 1/30/92.
36   *"Francis was our idol"*: Margot Kidder, AI, 4/17/93.
36   *"It wasn't considered"*: Willard Huyck, AI, 6/16/94.
36   *"We had all gone"*: Murch, AI, 11/18/93.
36   *"Musical comedy"*: Michael Sragow, "Godfatherhood," *New Yorker*, 3/24/97, p. 46.
37   *"It was really hard"*: Marcia Lucas, AI, 3/3/97.
37   *"Because of his personality"*: Murch, AI, 11/18/93.
37   *"What do you mean"*: Dale Pollock, *Skywalking: The Life and Films of George Lucas*, New York, 1983, p. 74.
37   *"Francis had this closet"*: Milius, AI, 1/31/92.
38   *"September, in those days" and following*: Dick Lederer, AI, 6/23/92.
38   *"In those days"*: Beatty, AI, 6/11/94.

39 *"You guys are all crazy"*: Lederer, AI, 6/23/92.
39 *"I remembered"*: Joe Hyams, AI, 4/9/92.
39 *"What a reaction"*: Lederer, AI, 6/23/92.
39 *"a cheap piece"*: Mason Wiley and Damien Bona, *Inside Oscar*, New York, 1986, p. 403.
39 *"I was scared to death"*: Lederer, AI, 6/23/92.
39 *"Look, it's just another"*: Benton, AI, 12/9/92.
40 "Bonnie and Clyde is": Pauline Kael, *New Yorker*, 10/26/67.
40 *"The Pauline Kael review"*: Newman, AI, 7/30/92.
41 *"Without her"*: Towne, AI, 11/6/97.
41 *"he came on"*: Kael, AI, 8/5/95.
41 *"He was always saying"*: Lederer, AI, 6/23/92.
41 *"Let me pay you" and following*: Beatty, AI, 6/11/94.
41 *"I really think"*: Lederer, 6/23/92.
42 *"I'd always wanted"*: Peter Fonda, AI, 3/17/97.
42 *"I was a little"*: Lawrence Linderman, *Playboy*, 9/70.
42 *"Everyone knew that Kael"*: Buck Henry, AI, 12/7/94.
42 *"Peter, did they say"*: Dennis Hopper, AI, 7/15/97.
43 *"Heads are going"*: Brooke Hayward, AI, 4/24/97.
43 *"I was desperate"*: Mark Goodman, "Rebel Without a Pause," *New Times*, 10/2/78, p. 58.
43 *"the son of General Pershing"*: Bill Hayward, AI, 11/15/92.
43 *"He was an incredibly" and following*: Brooke Hayward, AI, 4/24/97.
44 *"rips off"*: Fonda, AI, 3/17/97.
44 *"He was completely crazy" and following*: Brooke Hayward, AI, 4/24/97.
44 *"It was hard"*: Hopper, AI, 7/15/97.
45 *"Nobody took"*: Brooke Hayward, AI, 4/24/97.
45 *"The day I started"*: Tom Burke, "Dennis Hopper saves the Movies," *Esquire*, 9/70, p. 170.
45 *"My wife"*: Fonda, AI, 3/17/97.
45 *"The audience will never"*: Fonda, AI, 3/17/97.
45 *"The New Cinema"*: Time, December 8, 1967, p. 66.
46 *"We have to rethink this." and following*: Beatty, AI, 6/11/94.
46 *"Julie was the most beautiful"*: Beatty, AI, 6/18/97.
47 *"If ever a movie star"*: Towne, AI, 11/6/97.
47 "You get slapped": Confidential source.
48 *"We were so fucking"*: Newman, AI, 7/30/92.
48 *"We're all disappointed"*: Michael Pearse, "Faye Dunaway: The Loves of a Passionate Woman," *Modern Screen*, 8/68.
48 *"There were people"*: Benton, AI, 12/9/92.
48 *"We didn't know"*: Penn, Jack Mathews, "Rebellious Times," *Los Angeles Times Calendar*, 1/24/86.
48 *"The Freudian nature"*: Curtis Hanson, "Warren Beatty as Producer," *Cinema*, Vol. 3, No. 5.
48 *"Andy Warhol was giving"*: Newman, AI, 7/30/92.
49 *"There's one last thing"*: Susanna Moore, AI, 5/5/93.
49 *"You couldn't get"*: Richard Sylbert, AI, 5/26/93.
50 *"Sharon was the sweetest" and following*: Sharmagne Leland-St. John, AI, 6/19/94.
50 *"They were crazy"*: Fiona Lewis, AI, 1/28/96.
50 *"I don't know"*: Dialogue in Film, Robert Towne, *American Film*, 12/75, p. 38.

50 *"I couldn't have"*: Jeremy Larner, AI, n.d.
50 *"Bob would love"*: Ayres, AI, 6/14/94.
51 *"Towne could talk"*: Robert Evans, AI, 2/27/94.
51 *"Robert had written"*: Beatty, AI, 6/11/94.
51 *"He would not"*: Towne, AI, 11/6/97.
51 *"Look, I don't wanna"*: Beatty, AI, 6/28/94.

Chapter 2: "Who Made Us Right?"

52 *Epigraph*: Hopper, unpublished interview by Robert Scheer.
52 *"The problem in moviemaking"*: Based on Bob Rafelson, AI, 11/10/93; Rex Reed, "Bob Rafelson: Director of the year?", *New York Sunday News*, 12/6/70, p. 26.
53 *"the house of" and following*: Toby Rafelson, AI, 6/12/94.
54 *"I don't want to see"*: Bob Rafelson, AI, 11/10/93.
55 *"it was all like"*: Confidential source.
55 *"He was the All-Star"*: Henry Jaglom, AI, 7/23/93.
55 *"Steve was Harold"*: Bruce Dern, AI, 6/17/95.
55 *"I kept turning"*: Steve Blauner, AI, 6/7/94.
56 *"I wasn't going"*: Judy Schneider, AI, 12/15/97.
56 *"I was into"*: Bo Burlingham, "Politics Under the Palms," *Esquire*, 2/77.
56 *"Bert and Judy went out"*: Toby Rafelson, AI, 6/12/94.
56 *"Within three or four"*: Henry, AI, 12/7/94.
57 *"I want to make"*: Blauner, AI, 2/28/94.
57 *"This is lame"*: William Friedkin, AI, 4/19/96.
57 *"I want to use"*: Donna Greenberg, AI, 2/3/95.
58 *"He was always pawing"*: Julie Payne, AI, 2/6/95.
58 *"They were princes"*: Paula Strachan, AI, 12/10/97.
58 *"Bob was a role model"*: Confidential source.
58 *"These were people"*: Toby Rafelson, AI, 6/12/94.
58 *"Never bring a woman"*: Patrick McGilligan, *Jack's Life: A Biography of Jack Nicholson*, New York, 1994, p. 181.
58 *"Bert would fuck"*: Confidential source.
59 *"One beautiful, sunny Sunday"*: Greenberg, AI, 2/3/95.
60 *"I think that repudiating"*: Toby Rafelson, AI, 6/12/94.
61 *"A lot of that stuff"*: Henry, AI, 12/7/94.
61 *"I wish they'd come"*: Confidential source.
61 *"You know Dennis"*: Rex Reed, "The Man Who Walked Off With *Easy Rider*," *New York Times*, 3/1/70.
61 *"This guy is fucking"*: Bob Rafelson, AI, 11/10/93.
61 *"How's your bike"*: Fonda, AI, 3/17/97.
61 *"Get the fuck"*: Bob Rafelson, AI, 11/10/93.
62 *"What makes us right?"*: Blauner, AI, 2/28/94.
62 *"All right, man"*: Bill Hayward, AI, 11/15/92.
62 *"You're making a big"*: Hopper, AI, 7/15/97.
63 *"There was disagreement"*: Peter Pilafian, AI, 4/22/93.
63 *"He went right off"*: Bill Hayward, AI, 11/15/92.
63 *"Every one of them"*: Hopper, AI, 7/15/97.
63 *"I was really"*: Hopper, AI, 7/15/97.
63 *"he just started"*: Baird Bryant, AI, 4/21/93.
63 *"This is my fucking"*: Fonda, AI, 3/17/97.

63 *"Jimmy wouldn't"*: Barry Feinstein, AI, 6/23/93.

63 *"Everybody was looking"*: Fonda, AI, 3/17/97.

63 *"On the final day"*: Bryant, AI, 4/21/93.

64 *"Here's what I want"*: Fonda, AI, 4/24/97.

64 *"It may not sound like"*: Bill Hayward, AI, 11/15/92.

64 *"I don't trust you"*: Hopper, AI, 7/15/97.

64 Account of fight: AIs, Hopper, Feinstein, and Karen Black.

64 *"We're finished"*: Brooke Hayward, AI, 4/24/97.

65 *"It was just"*: Bill Hayward, AI, 11/15/92.

65 *"It was just dreadful"*: Brooke Hayward, AI, 4/24/97.

65 *"He was now drinking"*: Brooke Hayward, AI, 4/24/97.

65 *"I want to tell you"*: Hopper, 7/15/97.

65 *"This is not"*: Fonda, AI, 3/17/97.

66 *"Don't you get near"* and following: Brooke Hayward, AI, 4/24/97.

66 *"They stopped me"*: Burke, "Dennis Hopper Saves," p. 172.

66 *"I called my lawyer"*: Brooke Hayward, AI, 4/24/97.

67 *"As long as I am"*: Ayres, AI, 6/14/94.

67 *"a creative bone"*: Nancy Griffin and Kim Masters, *Hit and Run*, New York, 1996, p. 73.

67 *"There was Dennis"*: Ayres, AI, 6/14/94.

67 *"How's the script"* and following: Hopper, AI, 7/15/97.

67 *"Aw, take it easy"* and following: Rip Torn, AI, 7/15/97.

68 *"Bert was a little nervous"*: Bob Rafelson, AI, 11/10/93.

68 *"You don't have"*: Hopper, AI, 7/15/97.

68 *"Terry never wrote"*: Hopper, AI, 7/15/97.

68 *"There was a"*: Neal Weaver, "I Have the Blood of Kings in My Veins." *After Dark*, 10/69.

68 *"Dennis Hopper didn't"*: Alix Sharkey, "Born to Be Wild," *Dazed and Confused*, 11/95.

68 *"In my mind"*: Terry Southern, AI, 8/94.

69 *"Neither of them"*: Patrick McGilligan, ed., *Backstory 3: Screenwriters of the 60's*, Berkeley, 1997.

69 *"It was supposed"* and following: Southern, AI, 8/94.

69 *"You have a director"*: Torn, AI, 12/16/97.

69 *"We're supposed"* and following: Hopper, AI, 7/15/97.

69 *"I was never"*: Fonda, AI, 3/17/97.

69 *"cinema verité"*: Elizabeth Campbell, "Easy Rider," *Rolling Stone*, 9/6/69, p. 19

69 *"I can't stand"*: Goodman, "Rebel Without a Pause."

70 *"It was Bruce Conner's"*: Fonda, AI, 3/17/97.

70 *"If we hate it"*: Bill Hayward, AI, 11/15/92.

71 *"Every day there was"*: Bob Rafelson, AI, 11/10/93.

71 *"Dennis, there is"*: Bill Hayward, AI, 11/15/92.

71 *"What we have here"*: Fonda, AI, 3/17/97.

71 *"Where's the picture?"*: Bill Hayward, AI, 11/15/92.

71 *"I wasn't going to"*: Fonda, AI, 4/24/97.

71 *"The film's too long"*: Hopper, AI, 7/15/97.

71 *"Dennis could go dick"*: Bill Hayward, AI, 11/15/92.

71 *"Bert was the heroic"*: Brooke Hayward, AI, 4/24/97.

71 *"I was just horrified"*: Bill Hayward, AI, 11/15/92.

72 *"Do you see"*: Bill Hayward, AI, 11/15/92.

72   *"You ruined my film.":* Hopper, AI, 7/15/97.
72   *"Hopper wants" and following:* Fonda, AI, 3/17/97.
72   *"I sabotaged that":* Hopper, AI, 7/15/97.
72   *"the little asshole" and following:* Bill Hayward, AI, 11/15/92.
73   *"He was sitting there" and following:* Blauner, AI, 2/28/94.
73   *"Wait'll you see" and following:* Bruce Dern, AI, 6/15/95.
73   *"The management":* Blauner, AI, 2/28/94.
74   *According to Bill Hayward:* The figure usually quoted is $360,000, which was the budget going in. Hayward says the picture went way over in post-production.
74   *"We made all":* CNN, *Showbiz Today,* 5:35 P.M., ET, 10/20/93, Transcript No. 399-2, by Sherri Sylvester.
74   *"Hollywood's hottest" and following:* Brad Darrach, "Dennis Hopper in the Andes," *Life,* 6/19/70.
74   *"The cocaine problem":* Hopper, AI, 7/15/97; Scheer, unpublished interview.
74   *"When we were making":* L. M. "Kit" Carson, *Evergreen Review.*
75   *"Nobody knew who wrote it":* Henry, AI, 12/7/94.
75   *"I want to make movies":* Darrach, "Dennis Hopper in the Andes"; Guy Flatley, "Henry Fonda Takes Aim at Dennis Hopper," *New York Times.*
75   *"The studio system":* Pollock, *Skywalking,* p. 246.
75   *"Everything seemed different":* Guber, AI, 11/10/92.
75   *"BBS fired a cannon":* Paul Schrader, AI, 12/3/91.
76   *"Normally, net means":* Blauner, 2/28/94.
76   *"Bert brought Columbia":* Brackman, AI, 4/30/93.
77   *"Orson [Welles] always said":* Jaglom, AI, 7/23/93.
77   *"The truth is":* Jim McBride, AI, 6/3/94.
77   *"I recall a time":* Joan Didion, "The White Album," *The White Album,* New York, 1979, p. 42.
78   *"On August 9":* Ibid.
78   *"I went up to look":* Beatty, AI, 3/16/95.
78   *"Roman was sitting":* Richard Sylbert, AI, 8/25/92.
78   *"He suspected a lot":* Richard Sylbert, AI, 6/7/94.
78   *"Roman was a brilliant":* Bart, AI, 4/17/92.
79   *"If half the people" and following:* Henry, AI, 12/7/94.
79   *"I walked up":* Hopper, AI, 7/15/97.
79   *"It was the end":* Richard Sylbert, AI, 8/25/92.

Chapter 3: Exile on Main Street
PAGE
81   *Epigraph:* Robert Altman, AI, 5/3/96.
81   *"Let's find a picture" and following:* Beatty, AI, 6/28/94.
82   *"Ted is ruthless":* Karl Fleming, *New York,* 6/24/74.
82   *"the pussy freak":* Don Simpson, AI, 12/24/92.
82   *"I just got":* Calley, AI, 5/15/93.
84   *"He knew where":* Henry, AI, 12/7/94.
84   *"You went to Universal":* Nessa Hyams, AI, 4/1/94.
84   *"It was sort of":* Jeff Sanford, AI, 3/13/92.
84   *"If McQueen" and following:* Calley, AI, 3/4/93.
85   *"Calley is a genius":* Confidential source.
85   *"Nobody supported me":* Fred Weintraub, AI, 12/19/97.
85   *"Wait a minute":* Calley, AI, 3/4/93.

86 *"It was so traumatic" and following*: Boorman, AI, 2/22/95.
86 *"Altman had this idea"*: Patrick McGilligan, *Robert Altman: Jumping off the Cliff*, New York, 1989, p. 93.
87 *"He was like"*: Tommy Thompson, AI, 10/18/95.
87 *"How are your morals?"*: Kathryn Reed, AI, 7/12/97.
88 *"All right, put me"*: McGilligan, *Robert Altman*, p. 175.
88 *"I couldn't fathom" and following*: George Litto, AI, 10/17/94.
89 *"Bob had a black side"*: Thompson, AI, 10/18/95.
89 *"I'll give you one of these"*: Confidential source.
90 *"Shape up"*: Francis Coppola, AI, 7/31/97.
90 *"To have had the guts to have plunked"*: Murch, AI, 11/18/93.
90 *"Francis could sell"*: Audie Bock, "Zoetrope and *Apocalypse Now*", *American Film* 9/79; Pollock, *Skywalking*, p. 79.
91 *"Francis saw Zoetrope"*: Pollock, *Skywalking*, p. 77; *Rolling Stone*, 11/5–12/10/87.
91 *"Francis was going"*: Sragow, "Godfatherhood," p. 44.
91 *"I think Francis"*: Marcia Lucas, AI, 3/3/97.
92 *"I betcha"*: Murch, AI, 11/18/93.
92 *"George was not"*: Marcia Lucas, AI, 3/3/97.
92 *"My life is"*: Pollock, *Skywalking*, p. 78.
92 *"seventy-year-old kid,"* Pollock, *Skywalking*, p. 78.
92 *"All directors have"*: Ibid.
92 *"George was like"*: Coppola, AI, 7/31/97.
93 *"Francis had this"*: Barry Beckerman, AI, 6/22/92.
93 *"Frankly, it was puerile"*: Confidential source.
93 *"The feeling from"*: Pollock, *Skywalking*, p. 100.
93 *"This is written" and following*: Litto, AI, 10/17/94.
95 *"It was more exciting"*: Altman, AI, 5/3/96.
95 *"I love his work" and following*: Gottlieb, AI, 6/13/97.
95 *"Another week"*: Litto, AI, 10/17/94.
96 *"Get away from"*: Altman, AI, 5/3/96.
96 *"It was the first time" and following*: Litto, AI, 10/17/94.
96 *"Darryl Zanuck had these"*: Altman, AI, 5/3/96.
97 *"The best American war comedy"*: Kael, *New Yorker*, 1/24/70.
97 *"they were very thick"*: Thompson, AI, 10/18/95.
97 *"Bob would cultivate"*: Joan Tewkesbury, AI, 10/13/95.
97 *"the first American movie"*: Mason Wiley and Damien Bona, *Inside Oscar*, New York, 1993.
97 *"Bob was never one" and following*: Litto, AI, 10/17/94.
98 *"work hard"*: Pollock, *Skywalking*, p. 90.
98 *"You've got to understand" and following*: Confidential source.
98 *"this is either" and following*: Murch, AI, 11/18/93.
99 *"You guys, wait"*: Matthew Robbins, AI, 5/2/97.
99 *"We weren't in"*: Ted Ashley, AI, 12/11/97.
99 *"Wells could never"*: Confidential source.
99 *"Listen, if you hook" and following*: Murch, AI, 11/18/93.
100 *"I like to become"*: Marcia Lucas, AI, 3/3/97.
100 *"Coppola was developing"*: Sanford, AI, 3/13/92.
100 *"Okay, we have a deal"*: Confidential source.
100 *"I'm not the oldest"*: Steve Kesten, AI, 4/6/97.
101 *"Calley and Ashley"*: Sanford, AI, 3/13/92.

101   *"They saw THX"*: George Lucas, AI, 5/2/97.

101   *"Wells was calling"*: Confidential source.

101   *"They had turned down"*: Coppola, AI, 7/31/97.

101   *"Francis was a gonif."*: Wexler, AI, 8/18/95.

101   *"This invitation cost" and following*: Pollock, *Skywalking*, p. 100.

102   *"You've run up"*: Coppola, AI, 7/31/97.

102   *"I needed to go"*: George Lucas, AI, 5/2/97.

102   *"I had always"*: Coppola, AI, 7/31/97.

102   *"If the director"*: Towne, *Time*, 7/3/78.

103   *"We had a director" and following*: Beatty, AI, 6/28/94.

103   *"It was one of"*: Altman, Walker Art Center Lecture, 4/25/92.

103   *"shared a sort"*: Beatty, AI, 6/28/94.

103   *"Bob didn't want" and following*: Thompson, AI, 10/18/95.

103   *"Bob had a talent"*: Beatty, AI, 6/28/94.

104   *"One of the big problems"*: Altman, AI, 5/3/96.

104   *"It was considered"*: Beatty, AI, 6/28/94.

104   *"nit-picking, the way"*: David Johnson, "Robert Altman," *Show*, 10/72, p. 49, quoted in
      Gerard Plecki, *Robert Altman*, Boston, 1985, p. 39.

104   *"Warren wouldn't start"*: Altman, AI, 5/3/96.

105   *"We shot it once"*: Thompson, AI, 10/18/95.

105   *"It was like"*: Jim Margellos, AI, 6/28/97.

105   *"The path to success"*: Tewkesbury, AI, 10/13/95.

105   *"A lot of times"*: Beatty, AI, 6/28/94.

105   *"Warren was buried"*: Margellos, AI, 6/28/97.

106   *"Towne's script didn't have"*: Beatty, AI, 6/28/94.

106   *"Hira was so big"*: Ayres, AI, 6/14/94.

106   *"I'm gonna make" and following*: Beatty, AI, 3/6/95.

106   *"Don't tell anybody"*: Confidential source.

106   *"Bob claims to have"*: Evans, AI, 6/11/94.

107   *"Towne was tremendously"*: Larner, AI, 3/9/95.

107   *"Towne treated Jack"*: Evans, AI, 2/27/94.

107   *"Towne was like this shadow"*: Henry, AI, 12/7/94.

107   *"I always felt"*: Towne, AI, 11/6/97.

107   *"I couldn't hear"*: Beatty, AI, 6/28/94.

108   *"The principals thought"*: Thompson, AI, 10/18/95.

108   *"Warren was infuriated"*: Bruce Williamson, *Playboy* interview, 8/76.

108   *"Sam Peckinpah is a prick"*: Margellos, AI, 6/28/97.

108   *"He stormed off"*: McGilligan, *Robert Altman*, p. 344.

108   *"You think we"*: Ashley, AI, 12/11/97.

108   *"Things had progressed"*: Beatty, AI, 6/28/94.

108   *"I can hear it" and following*: Altman, AI, 5/3/96.

109   *"a beautiful pipe dream"*: Kael, *New Yorker*, 7/3/71.

109   *"It still hasn't grossed" and following*: Altman, AI, 5/3/96.

109   *"It prevented it"*: AI, Beatty, 6/28/94.

Chapter 4: The Moviegoer
PAGE

110   *Epigraph*: Ellen Burstyn, AI, 4/10/96.

110   *"I just saw" and following*: Confidential source.

110   *"We really loved" and following*: Bogdanovich, AI, 11/16/93.

112   *"I've seen every American film"*: Benton, AI, 4/26/92.
112   *"One of the first"and following*: Bogdanovich, AI, 11/16/93.
113   *"You're a woman"*: Maureen McAndrew, "Polly Platt Sets the Style," *Cinema*, No. 35, 1976, p. 34.
113   *"Peter's father" and following*: Polly Platt, AI, 7/23/93.
114   *"Polly could be very"*: Bogdanovich, AI, 8/1/97.
114   *"I watched Hawks" and following*: Bogdanovich, AI, 11/16/93.
115   *"If you really want"*: Platt, AI, 7/23/93.
115   *"I went from"*: Bogdanovich, "Dialogue on Film," *American Film*, 1978.
115   *"Do you want"*: Bogdanovich, AI, 11/16/93.
115   *"You know how Hitchcock shoots"*: Roger Corman (with Jim Jerome), *How I Made a Hundred Movies in Hollywood and Never Lost a Dime*, New York, 1990, p. 142.
116   *"The ending of* Targets"*: Bogdanovich, AI, 11/16/93.
116   *"He's the locomotive"*: Platt, AI, 7/23/93.
116   *"Polly was a very strong"*: Paul Lewis, AI, 11/14/95.
116   *"If I was in charge" and following*: Platt, AI, 7/23/93.
116   *"I thought I was"*: Bob Rafelson, AI, 11/10/93.
117   *"They were close"*: Jim Nelson, AI, 11/11/94.
117   *"All we had was" and following*: Harry Gittes, AI, 12/12/94.
118   *"What was secretly"*: Larner, AI, 3/9/95.
118   *"Get out from under"*: Hopper, AI, 7/15/97.
118   *"She wouldn't step"*: Henry, AI, 12/7/94.
119   *"No film"*: John Russell Taylor, "Staying Vulnerable," *Sight and Sound*, fall 1976.
119   *"If he wrote ten words"*: Walon Green, AI, 12/3/96.
119   *"She felt she"*: Richard Wechsler, AI, 4/18/93.
119   *"If he could rewrite"*: Henry, AI, 12/7/94.
119   *"You know Bob"*: Confidential source.
119   *"a lot of the ideas" and following*: Toby Rafelson, AI, 6/22/94.
119   *"He'd say, 'Do you think' "*: Wechsler, AI, 4/18/93.
120   *"I think it's the best"*: Bob Rafelson, AI, 11/10/93.
120   *"There were all these" and following*: Platt, AI, 8/3/93.
121   *"Don't forget"*: Bogdanovich, AI, 3/2/94.
121   *"I've never had to say"*: Bogdanovich, AI, 11/16/93.
121   *"She had funny"*: Platt, AI, 8/10/93.
122   *"There was something"*: "Cybill and Peter—Who Needs Marriage?," *People*, 5/13/74.
122   *"You've got" and following*: Dougherty, AI, 4/11/94.
122   *"I knew"*: Platt, AI, 8/10/93.
122   *"Polly accused me"*: Bogdanovich, AI, 3/2/94.
123   *"We're going to bury"*: Platt, AI, 6/29/94.
123   *"Where's that pinko"*: Hopper, AI, 7/15/97.
123   *"Huey was beautiful"*: Brackman, AI, 4/30/93.
124   *"How can I put it?"*: Confidential source.
124   *"He just had"*: Wechsler, AI, 4/18/93.
124   *"a stunt man"*: Darrach, "Dennis Hopper in the Andes."
124   *"I can't find anybody" and following*: Blauner, AI, 2/28/94.
124   *"When we got involved"*: Confidential source.
124   *"If Hopper hadn't"*: Guber, AI, 11/10/92.
125   *"It was a miserable"*: Tony Bill, AI, 6/20/94.
125   *"It was frightening"*: Ned Tanen, AI, 1/22/93.
125   *"Wasserman said 'We've' "*: Danny Selznick, AI, 7/12/93.

125 *"He was clinically"*: Simpson, AI, 7/21/93.

125 *"Like Sid, he was"*: Spielberg, AI, 12/9/96.

125 *"For $5 million"*: Selznick, AI, 7/12/93.

125 *"When the companies"*: Tanen, AI, 1/22/93.

126 *"Are you sure"*: Tanen, AI, 1/22/93.

126 *"I just was laughing"*: Bob Rafelson, AI, 11/10/93.

126 *He sent a package*: Burke, "Dennis Hopper Saves," p. 170.

127 *"We felt we had"*: Blauner, AI, 3/1/94.

127 *"I can't understand"*: Bob Rafelson, AI, 11/10/93.

127 *"Peter was the only"*: Nelson, AI, 11/11/94.

127 *"I'm not sure" and following*: Bogdanovich, AI, 8/1/97.

128 *"I don't know" and following*: Platt, AI, 8/10/93.

128 *"Go home to what?"*: Rachel Abramowitz, "She's Done Everything," *Premiere*, 11/93, p. 94.

128 *"I'm going to kill"*: Platt, AI, 8/10/93.

128 *"They were like"*: Benton, AI, 4/26/92.

128 *"I felt terribly guilty."*: Bogdanovich, AI, 8/1/97.

129 *"My wife really likes"*: Confidential source.

129 *"Anyone who can have me"*: Jaglom, AI, 10/5/93.

131 *"You could go very" and following*: Brackman, AI, 4/30/93.

132 *"Don't worry, honey," and following*: Paul Rosenfield, "The Club Rules," *New York*, 1992, p. 129.

132 *"I'm so driven"*: Ibid.

132 *"You want to direct?"* Michael Black, AI, 1/31/92.

133 *"I sort of would"*: Bogdanovich, AI, 3/2/94.

133 *"she just won't"*: Tom Nolan, "You Can Bring Dennis Hopper to Hollywood but You Can't Take the Dodge City Out of Kansas," *Show*, 7/23/70, p. 23.

133 *"Dennis falls in love"*: Ibid.

133 *"Six Days' War"*: John Phillips, with Jim Jerome, *Papa John*, New York, 1986, p. 248.

133 *"one shot"*: Hopper, AI, 7/15/97.

133 *"I love you"*: Goodman, "Rebel Without a Pause," p. 58.

133 *"Dennis would run it"*: Tanen, AI, 1/22/93.

133 *"Dennis never showed up"*: Bob Rafelson, AI, 11/10/93.

134 *"Nobody influenced me."*: Hopper, AI, 7/15/97.

134 *"The editors would" and following*: Tanen, AI, 1/22/93.

134 *"They sure named"*: Lewis, AI, 11/14/95.

134 *"We had a thing" and following*: Tanen, AI, 1/22/93.

135 *"I won the Venice"*: Chris Hodenfield, "Citizen Hopper," *Film Comment*, 12/86, p. 70.

136 *"All the American audience's"*: John Russell Taylor, "Profession: Actor," *Sight and Sound*, Summer 1974, p. 150.

136 *"I was there before"*: Hopper, AI, 7/15/97.

136 *"There was no way"*: Rudy Wurlitzer, AI, 5/7/93.

137 *"The freedom that we"*: Lewis, AI, 11/14/95.

137 *"The Easy Rider period"*: Oliver Stone, AI, n.d.

137 *"I saw coming events"*: Selznick, AI, 7/12/93.

137 *"We had seen"*: Newman, AI, 2/15/94.

138 *"We were pay-or-play" and following*: Calley, AI, 3/4/93.

138 *"Using New York actors"*: Nessa Hyams, AI, 4/1/94.

138 *"He kept him"*: Altman, AI, 5/3/96.

138   *"I can pretty much"*: Bruce Williamson, *Playboy* interview, 8/76.
138   *"I slipped another"*: Confidential source.
138   *"Are you sitting"*: Bogdanovich, AI, 3/2/94.
139   *"the last person"*: Scorsese, AI, 5/23/94.
139   *"Are you satisfied"*: Sue Mengers, AI, 2/21/95.
139   *"I grew up in Manhattan"*: Bogdanovich, AI, 3/2/94.

Chapter 5: The Man Who Would Be King
PAGE
141   *Epigraph:* Milius, AI, 1/31/92.
141   *"the most exciting"*: AIs with Bogdanovich, Platt, Friedkin, Coppola, Burstyn.
142   *"I owe eleven Gs"*: Evans, AI, 2/27/94.
142   *"idolized gangsters"*: Bart, AI, n.d.
142   *"There was no great"*: Al Ruddy, AI, 8/26/92.
142   *"That's your esoteric"*: Robert Evans, *The Kid Stays in the Picture*, New York, 1994, p. 220.
143   *"Francis, you're just a kid"*: Bart, AI, 3/11/97.
143   *"He can't get a cartoon"*: Evans, *The Kid Stays*, p. 220.
143   *"Should I do this?" and following:* George Lucas, AI, 5/2/97.
143   *"Look, this kid"*: Bart, AI, 4/17/92.
144   *"Vile ve've been"*: Gordon Weaver, AI, 9/18/96.
144   *"these little white"*: Confidential source.
144   *"He was a thug"*: Bart, AI, 10/23/95.
144   *"Charlie had these black" and following:* Simpson, AI, 7/21/93.
145   *"Brooklyn Street Corner"*: Andrew Tobias, "The Apprenticeship of Frank Yablans," *New York*, 9/23/74.
145   *"Frank had the biggest"*: Friedkin, AI, 4/19/96.
145   *"a bully, crass, corny"*: Ruddy, AI, 8/26/92.
145   *"Nice tits today"*: Friedkin, AI, 4/19/96.
145   *"We were in London"*: Bart, AI, 10/23/95.
145   *"Charlie was" and following:* Frank Yablans, AI, 6/3/96.
146   *"He's gorgeous."*: Howard Koch, Sr., AI, 10/16/95.
146   *" 'The Paramount caca' "*: Evans, *The Kid Stays*, p. 107.
146   *"What a joke"*: Blauner, AI, 2/28/94.
146   *"Bob wasn't egocentric"*: Ruddy, AI, 8/26/92.
147   *Evans provided paragraphs:* Bart, interviewed by Terri Minsky, 5/89.
147   *"At Bob's house"*: Confidential source.
147   *"Ali was one of"*: Bart, AI, 4/17/92.
147   *"You have no idea"*: Friedkin, AI, 4/19/96.
147   *"You were dealing"*: Henry, AI, 12/7/94.
148   *"Everybody was looking"*: Bart, AI, 4/17/92.
148   *" 'Augie's the bright one' "*: David Breskin, *Inner Views*, Boston, 1992, p. 44.
148   *"a frustrated man"*: Michael Goodwin and Naomi Wise, *On the Edge: The Life and Times of Francis Coppola*, New York, 1989, p. 18.
148   *"All of us" and following:* Talia Shire, AI, 5/11/95.
149   *"I used to go"*: Breskin, *Inner Views*, p. 44.
149   *"All the kids" and following:* Coppola, AI, 6/27/96.
149   *"I was called"*: Dale Baker, *The Movie People*, New York, 1973, p. 67.
150   *"The way to come"*: Michael Pye and Lynda Myles, *The Movie Brats: How the Film Generation Took Over Hollywood*, New York, 1979, p. 83.
150   *"You have to set"*: Baker, *The Movie People*, p. 64.

150 *"is one of those"*: Goodwin and Wise, *On the Edge*, p. 70.

150 *"Francis was always"*: Friedkin, AI, 4/19/96.

151 *"I had a really hard time"*: Scorsese, AI, 5/23/94.

151 *"I never really got much"*: Scorsese, AI, 8/1/91.

151 *"What he was taking"*: Simpson, AI, 12/24/92.

151 *"We were all sitting"*: Jennifer Salt, AI, 3/14/92.

152 *"We were fighting"*: Scorsese, AI, 5/23/94.

152 *"Brian De Palma was"*: Calley, AI, 3/4/93.

152 *"I always felt"*: Brian De Palma, AI, 11/9/93.

152 *"I was not looking" and following*: Coppola, AI, 3/3/97.

153 *"He recorded my"*: David Rensin, *Playboy* interview, 4/91.

154 *"I knew it was" and following*: Coppola, AI, 3/3/97.

154 *"Early on, Francis said"*: Fred Roos, AI, 5/8/95.

154 *"Evans made Francis's life"*: Bart, interviewed by Terri Minsky, 5/89.

154 *"There weren't a lot"*: Gordon Willis, AI, 4/3/97.

154 *"We talked about"*: Coppola, AI, 3/3/97; Peter Biskind, "Making Crime Pay," *Premiere*, 8/97.

155 *"Screens were so blitzed"*: Sragow, "Godfatherhood," p. 49.

155 *"I'd always hear"*: Willis, AI, 4/3/97.

155 *"Francis's credentials"*: Kesten, AI, 4/6/97.

155 *"It had gone terribly"*: Coppola, AI, 3/3/97.

155 *"When that dark stuff"*: Willis, AI, 4/3/97.

155 *"They were black"*: Shire, AI, 5/11/95.

155 *"What's on the screen?"*: Bart, AI, 4/17/92.

155 *"They hated Brando"*: Coppola, AI, 3/3/97.

155 *"Is this movie"*: Bart, AI, 4/17/92.

155 *"The scene when" and following*: Gray Frederickson, AI, 5/23/90, 5/10/95.

156 *"That was not the way"*: Frederickson, AI, 5/10/95.

156 *"If you don't finish"*: Kesten, AI, 4/6/97.

156 *"It was hard for Francis"*: Willis, AI, 4/3/97.

156 *"I like to lay out"*: Sragow, "Godfatherland," p. 49; Willis, AI, 4/3/97.

156 *"hates and misuses actors"*: Susan Braudy, "Francis Ford Coppola: A Profile," *Atlantic Monthly*, 8/76, p. 71.

157 *"Francis just sat down"*: David Rensin, *Playboy* interview, 4/91.

157 *"Okay, but I'll have"*: Fred Gallo, AI, 3/5/97.

157 *"Why won't they"*: Confidential source.

157 *"When I was in New York"*: Ruddy, AI, 8/26/92.

157 *"He had a guy"*: Bart, interviewed by Terri Minsky, 5/89.

158 *"Do you want"*: Towne, AI, 11/6/97.

158 *"The picture stinks" and following*: Evans, *The Kid Stays*, p. 227ff.

158 *"The deal was"*: Coppola, AI, 3/3/97.

158 *"Evans felt"*: Calley, AI, 3/4/93.

159 *"Evans behaved very badly."*: Yablans, AI, 6/3/96.

159 *"Well, I guess" and following*: Coppola, AI, 3/3/97.

159 *"I had a great"*: Robin French, AI, 6/24/94.

160 *"Evans pushed them"*: Yablans, AI, 6/3/96.

160 *"It was just bad"*: Roman Polanski, AI, 3/14/94.

160 *"I went through a picture"*: Bart, interviewed by Terri Minsky, 5/89.

161 *"I was star fucking"*: Evans, AI, 2/27/94.

161 *"I don't want to hear"*: Bart, AI, n.d.

161 *"Lou wanted him"*: Payne, AI, 1/19/95.
161 *"What kind of script"*: Evans, AI, 2/27/94.
161 *"We said the script"*: Polanski, AI, 3/14/94.
162 *"This was the best"*: Evans, AI, 2/27/94.
162 *"It was the start"*: Ruddy, AI, 8/26/92.
163 *"When the picture had done"*: Coppola, AI, 3/3/97.
163 *"the best gangster"*: Kael, *New Yorker*, 10/8/73.
164 *"In the seventies"*: Sragow, "Godfatherland," p. 52.
165 *"Congratulations, Billy"*: Bogdanovich, AI, 11/16/93.
165 *"The goddamn dog"*: Polanski, AI, 3/14/94; Biskind, "The Long Road to *Chinatown*,"
     Premiere, 6/94.
165 *"We fought, every day"*: Towne, AI, 3/3/94.
166 *"Maybe it's enough"*: Richard Sylbert, AI, n.d.
166 *"I went to art"*: Towne, AI, 3/3/94.
166 *"I thought it was"*: Polanski, AI, 3/14/94.
166 *"Roman's argument was"*: Towne, AI, 3/3/94.
166 *"For a long time" and following*: Breskin, *Inner Views*.
166 *"In some ways" and following*: Sragow, "Godfatherland," p. 45.
167 *"I think I was just"*: Coppola, AI, 6/27/96.
168 *"My motive has been"*: Axel Madsen, "The New Hollywood," *New York*, 1975,
     p. 116.
168 *"When You're Rich"*: Robert Hillmann, AI, n.d.

Chapter 6: Like a Rolling Stone

PAGE
169 *Epigraph*: Bart, AI, 4/17/92.
169 *"Where's Hal?" and following*: Charles Mulvehill, AI, 8/22/94.
169 *"Hal sometimes had"*: Ayres, AI, 6/14/94.
169 *"Hal's in jail" and following*: Mulvehill, AI, 8/22/94.
170 *"I'm goin' to"*: Aljean Harmetz, "Gambling on a Film About the Great Depression,"
     New York Times, 12/15/76.
172 *"I saw what a force"*: Wexler, AI, 8/18/95.
172 *"I'd been working"*: Harmetz, "Gambling on a Film."
172 *"There was nothin' " and following*: Mulvehill, AI, 8/22/94.
173 *"To me, Harold and Maude"*: Bart, AI, 4/17/92.
173 *"We felt"*: Mulvehill, AI, 8/22/94.
174 *"They'd usually end up"*: Wexler, AI, 8/18/95.
174 *"There was this"*: Bart, AI, 10/23/95.
174 *"When one's gone"*: Robert Downey, Sr., AI, 1/11/98.
174 *"You couldn't drag"*: Mulvehill, AI, 8/22/94.
174 *"I didn't want"*: John Brady, *The Craft of the Screenwriter*, New York, 1981, p. 421.
174 *"I thought this was"*: Ayres, AI, 6/14/94.
175 *"Oh yeah, white sailor"*: Mulvehill, AI, 8/22/94.
175 *"The first seven"*: Guber, AI, 11/10/92.
175 *"Now that movies"*: Towne, 11/6/97.
175 *"I can get Burt"*: Ayres, AI, 6/14/94.
175 *"They were afraid"*: Guber, AI, 12/1/92.
176 *"Bob certainly saw himself"*: Brackman, AI, 4/30/93.
176 *"take away the audience's"*: Bob Rafelson, AI, 10/29/96.
176 *"She was luminous"*: Burstyn, AI, 5/2/96.

176   *"It was open adoration"*: Dern, AI, 6/17/95.

176   *"Nobody wanted him" and following*: Brackman, AI, 4/30/93.

176   *"Bob was a very cerebral"*: Burstyn, AI, 5/2/96.

177   *"On Marvin Gardens"*: Brackman, AI, 8/31/95.

177   *"I was watching"*: Dern, AI, 6/17/95.

177   *"At one point Bert"*: Bob Rafelson, AI, 10/29/96.

177   *"That was a major"*: Stephen Farber, "The Man Who Brought Us Greetings from the Vietcong," *New York Times*, 5/4/75.

178   *"What do you mean" and following*: Candice Bergen, *Knock Wood*, p. 254.

178   *"Most movie companies"*: Harmetz, "Gambling on a Film."

178   *"A lot of times" and following*: Mulvehill, AI, 8/23/94.

179   *"I can get behind"*: Towne, AI, 11/6/97.

179   *"I'd heard what a" and following*: Bob Jones, AI, 10/5/94.

179   *"He would come" and following*: Mulvehill, AI, 8/25/94.

180   *"We're coming up"*: Jones, AI, 10/5/94.

180   *"Bob Towne has always been" and following*: Ayres, AI, 6/14/94.

181   *"Let's go over"*: Lederer, 6/23/92.

181   *"Jack was always wild"*: Gittes, AI, 12/12/94.

181   *"Cocaine is 'in' "*: Richard Warren Lewis, *Playboy* interview, 4/72.

181   *"In your brain"*: Richard Sylbert, AI, 8/25/92.

181   *"What started as"*: Evans, *The Kid Stays*, p. 269.

182   *"The studio was falling"*: Richard Sylbert, AI, 8/25/92.

182   *"I felt that he"*: Bart, interviewed by Terri Minsky, 5/89.

182   *"If it bombs"*: William Murray, *Playboy* interview, 7/75.

182   *"I got the guy" and following*: Coppola, AI, 3/3/97.

183   *"Look, who was the star" and following*: Bart, AI, n.d.

183   *"Warners hurt me"*: Coppola, AI, 12/5/97.

184   *"Get home immediately." and following*: Bergen, *Knock Wood*, p. 263.

184   *"I knew Begelman" and following*: Blauner, AI, 3/1/94.

185   *"Bert's way of dealing" and following*: Bob Rafelson, AI, 11/10/93.

185   *"All these people"*: Henry, AI, 12/7/94.

185   *"Olinka would get up"*: Mengers, AI, 2/21/95.

186   *"Huey was pretty coked" and following*: Brackman, AI, 4/30/93.

186   *"I've always thought"*: Henry, AI, 12/7/94.

186   *"Bert really put"*: Toby Rafelson, AI, 6/12/94.

186   *The bereaved guests*: Richard Rutkowski, AI, 11/10/94.

186   *"I'm not going"*: Bob Rafelson, AI, 11/10/93.

187   *"Nobody ever recovers"*: Henry, AI, 12/7/94.

187   *"None of the women"*: Toby Rafelson, AI, 6/12/94.

188   *"That was the beginning"*: Richard Sylbert, AI, n.d.

188   *"Roman is Napoleon"*: Evans, AI, 2/27/94.

188   *"He'd say, 'In Poland' "*: Koch, Jr., AI, 3/15/94.

188   *"Jack was always amused."*: Anthea Sylbert, AI, 3/10/94.

189   *Dunaway was in the habit*: Anthea Sylbert, AI, 3/10/94; Koch, AI, 3/15/94.

189   *When she did use the john and following*: Koch, AI, 3/15/94.

189   *"Every time I shouted" and following*: Polanski, AI, 3/14/94.

189   *"There was a scene"*: John Alonzo, AI, 3/30/94; Koch, AI, 3/15/94.

189   *"He was so courageous"*: Richard Sylbert, AI, 6/12/94.

190   *"Did Warren really"*: Confidential source.

190   *"Robert's failure to deliver"*: Beatty, AI, 3/16/95.

190 *"She thinks"*: Towne, AI, 11/6/97.
190 *"It was very hard-hitting"*: Lester Persky, AI, 2/26/95.
190 *"Look, Bob, I'm"*: Evans, AI, 2/27/94.
191 *"People thought Columbia" and following*: Beatty, AI, 6/28/94.
192 *"He was devastated"*: Toby Rafelson, AI, 6/12/94.
192 *"Basically it would" and following*: Mulvehill, AI, 8/23/94.
193 *"Warren was a giant"*: Hellman, AI, 6/20/94.
193 *"Hal admired the way"*: Mulvehill, AI, 8/23/94.
193 *"Both Warren and Jack"*: Towne, AI, 11/6/97.
193 *"Hal hated authority"*: Mulvehill, AI, 8/23/94.
193 *"It was tough"*: Jones, AI, 10/5/94.
193 *"I visited the set"*: Wexler, AI, 8/18/95.
193 *"Hal walked up"*: Richard Sylbert, AI, 5/12/93.
194 *"It was a collaborative"*: Anthea Sylbert, AI, 7/22/93.
194 *"There were three of us"*: Towne, AI, 11/6/97.
194 *"If the director"*: Hank Moonjean, AI, 4/19/96.
194 *"You're being completely"and following*: Don Devlin, AI, 11/22/94.
195 *"He kept cutting"*: Platt, AI, 6/29/94.
195 *"Jack always has"*: Gittes, AI, 12/12/94.
195 *"didn't know whose"*: Richard Sylbert, AI, 8/25/92.
195 *"He loved that sense"*: Mimi Machu Mireille, AI, 2/4/95.
195 *"It'll be just like" and following*: Mulvehill, AI, 8/23/94.
196 *"Hal's lungs were"*: Mireille, AI, 2/4/95.
196 *"Hal was snorting"*: Wexler, AI, 8/18/95.

Chapter 7: Sympathy for the Devil
PAGE
197 *"There is a darkness"*: Friedkin, AI, 4/19/96.
197 *On December 8*: Porter Bibb, "Altamont: The Sixties On Stage," *The Variety History of Show Business*, New York, 1993, pp. 133–38.
198 *"I'm not going"*: William Peter Blatty, AI, 11/9/94.
198 *"If you don't"*: Bogdanovich, AI, 3/2/94.
198 *"the worst piece"*: William Friedkin, Seminar, *Dialogue in Film*, AFI Vols. 3 and 4, February/March 1974, p. 5.
198 *"Billy was a tough critter."*: Confidential source.
198 *"Someone who could"*: Blatty, AI, 11/9/94.
198 *"A good part"*: Friedkin, AI, 4/19/96.
198 *"It was all very well"*: Blatty, AI, 11/9/94.
199 *"I just want you"*: William Friedkin, Seminar, p. 6.
199 *"My grief could"*: Nat Segaloff, *Hurricane Billy*, New York, 1990, p. 137.
199 *"There was a certain" and following*: Blatty, AI, 11/9/94.
199 *"Did you read"*: Thomas D. Clagett, *William Friedkin: Films of Aberration, Obsession and Reality*, Jefferson, North Carolina, 1990, p. 111.
200 *"He never threw"*: Evan Lottman, AI, 10/24/96.
200 *"Charlie Greenlaw's on"*: Burstyn, AI, 4/10/96.
200 *"A lot of the guys"*: Friedkin, AI, 4/19/96.
200 *"It was a fucking"*: Segaloff, *Hurricane Billy*, p. 22.
200 *"My mother was"*: Friedkin, AI, 4/19/96.
201 *"He had Welles posters" and following*: Bill Butler, AI, 10/12/95.
201 *"I remember the day"*: Friedkin, AI, 4/19/96.

202 "*Mr. Friedkin, you're not*": William Friedkin Seminar, p. 3.

202 "*I don't give*": Clagett, *William Friedkin*, p. 28.

202 "*How'd'ya like the tie*": Segaloff, *Hurricane Billy*, p. 52.

202 "*the plotted film*": *Variety*, quoted in Segaloff, *Hurricane Billy*, p. 63.

202 "*aggressiveness and rank-pulling*": Ralph Rosenblum, *When the Shooting Stops, the Cutting Begins*, New York, 1979, p. 232.

203 "*I've got something*": Friedkin, AI, 4/19/96; Segaloff, *Hurricane Billy*, p. 99.

203 "*They really stayed*": Friedkin, AI, 4/19/96.

204 "*American films*": Segaloff, *Hurricane Billy*, p. 101.

204 "*I got an extra*" and following: Chris Chase, "Everyone's Reading It, Billy's Filming It," *New York Times*, 8/27/72.

204 "*Billy had a kind of*": Moore, AI, 5/5/93.

204 "*a lot of girls*" and following: Friedkin, AI, 4/19/96.

205 "*I came back*": Segaloff, *Hurricane Billy*, p. 113.

205 "*In those days*": Friedkin, AI, 4/19/96.

205 "*My career has ruined*": Gordon Gould and Bob Ellison, "A Devil of a Director," *Chicago Tribune Magazine*, 12/23/73.

205 "*I'm a millionaire*": Butler, AI, 10/12/95.

206 "*The next day was*": Friedkin, AI, 4/19/96.

206 "*I have no image*": Chase, "Everyone's Reading It."

206 "*I'm making commercial*": Gould and Ellison, "A Devil of a Director."

206 "*We'd get a bunch*": Bogdanovich, AI, 3/2/94.

206 "*Friedkin, vat's dat shit*": Friedkin, AI, 4/19/96.

207 "*Part of my desire*": Goodwin and Wise, *On the Edge*, p. 150.

207 "*You von't belief*": Yablans, AI, 6/3/96.

207 "*Frank, you're really*": Friedkin, AI, 4/19/96.

208 "*Coppola was playing*" and following: Yablans, AI, 6/3/96.

208 "*He was still*": Friedkin, AI, 4/19/96.

208 "*It was no secret*": Marcia Lucas, AI, 3/3/97.

208 "*I loved Francis*": Friedkin, AI, 4/19/96.

209 "*The first time*": Confidential source.

209 "*I don't judge myself*": Aljean Harmetz, "Peter Still Looks Forward to His *Citizen Kane*," *New York Times*, 11/71.

209 "*Cybill started out*": Rex Reed, "Peter and Cybill in the Chaos of Rome," *New York Daily News*, 9/23/73.

209 "*Will you stop*": Bogdanovich, AI, 8/1/97.

210 "*I don't drive*": Rosemary Edelman, "At Long Last . . . Love," *Los Angeles*, p. 88.

210 "*Naw, it's kindofa*" and following: Bogdanovich, AI, 3/2/94.

210 "*Frank, it's Peter*": Yablans, AI, 6/3/96.

211 "*Well, I'll do it if*": Platt, AI, 8/10/93.

211 "*The Conversation*": Friedkin, AI, 4/19/96.

211 "*Francis said it was*": Bogdanovich, AI, 3/2/94.

211 "*They've gone through*": Pye and Myles, *The Movie Brats*, p. 97.

211 "*I thought it was like*": Friedkin, AI, 4/19/96.

212 "*Once they took*": Yablans, AI, 6/3/96.

212 "*Francis always said*": Bogdanovich, AI, 3/2/94.

212 "*She's so right for it*": Donald Lyons, Jude Jade and Candy Darling, "Peter Bogdanovich on *Paper Moon*," *Interview*, I, 7/73.

212 "*The next thing I knew*": Friedkin, AI, 4/19/96.

212 "*I'll give you a job*": Platt, AI, 8/10/93.

212 "*I don't think*": Lewis, AI, 11/14/95.

213   *"a no-talent dame"*: Hillary Johnson, "Cybill Shepherd: Breaking the Ice," vol. 484, 1986.
213   *"After Daisy"*: Ibid.
213   *"When someone yells"*: Margie Rochlin, "Peter Bogdanovich," 3/85, p. 136.
213   *"I begged him"*: Mengers, AI, 2/21/95.
213   *"Billy said he wanted out"*: Bogdanovich, AI, 3/2/94.
213   *"I could see what"*: Friedkin, AI, 4/19/96.
213   *"They all wanted"*: Bob Rafelson, AI, 11/10/93.
213   *"He was not in good shape"*: Platt, AI, 11/11/93.
214   *"there was a lot"*: Chris Mankiewicz, AI, 6/21/94.
214   *"I won't do this"*: Altman, AI, 5/3/96.
214   *"Yeah, but we're all here" and following*: Tewkesbury, AI, 10/13/95.
214   *"Bob always did that"*: Litto, AI, 11/16/94.
215   *"There was this wonderful"*: Louise Fletcher, AI, 6/22/94.
215   *"He'd always position" and following*: Thompson, AI, 10/18/95.
215   *"He hated it" and following*: Altman, AI, 5/3/96.
216   *"Nashville was in development" and following*: Fletcher, AI, 6/22/94.
216   *"I hated the way"*: Platt, AI, 11/11/93.
216   *"I didn't know" and following*: Blatty, AI, 11/9/94.
217   *"He's the only guy"*: Confidential source.
218   *"I'd rather work with"*: Clagett, *William Friedkin*, p. 74.
218   *"Bill, you're doing it"*: William O'Malley, AI, 12/4/97.
218   *"He liked to"*: Burstyn, AI, 4/10/96.
219   *"I grew up in the '50s"*: Jennifer Nairn-Smith, AI, 9/29/94.
219   *"Jennifer was stunningly"*: Blatty, AI, 11/9/94.
219   *"Bill Blatty wants" and following*: Nairn-Smith, AI, 9/29/94.
220   *"Billy was really bad"*: Joe Hyams, AI, 4/9/92.
220   *"The movie was running"*: Lederer, 6/23/92.
221   *"I'm sure they were"*: Friedkin, AI, 4/19/96.
221   *"They had the tiger"*: Blatty, AI, 11/9/94.
221   *"There was a lot"*: Calley, AI, 3/4/93.
221   *"It was all about"*: Lottman, AI, 10/24/96.
221   *"Sounds like fuckin' "*: Bud Smith, AI, 12/13/96.
222   *"If I can't dance"*: Nairn-Smith, AI, 9/29/94.
222   *"She was a wonderful"*: Nelson, AI, 11/11/94.
222   *"What in the fuck"*: Smith, AI, 12/13/96.
222   *"If The Exorcist had"*: Friedkin, AI, 4/19/96.
223   *"There was a shot"*: Burstyn, AI, 4/10/96.
223   *"rather take a bath"*: David Batholomew, "The Exorcist: The Book, the Movie, the Phenomenon," *Cinefantastique*, Winter 1974, Vol. 3, No. 4, p. 13.
223   *"If it's a film"*: Kael, *New Yorker*, 1/7/74.
223   *"They didn't see"*: Friedkin, AI, 4/19/96.
224   *"Kid, the fun"*: Beckerman, AI, 6/22/92.
224   *"How could you keep"*: Joe Hyams, AI, 4/9/92.

Chapter 8: The Gospel According to St. Martin
PAGE
225   *Epigraph*: Scorsese, AI, 7/13/91.
225   *"Warners is bidding" and following*: Jonathan Taplin, AI, 7/30/91; Scorsese, AI, 5/23/94.
226   *"I really felt"*: Bart, AI, 5/27/92.

226 *"We had"*: Taplin, AI, 7/30/91.

227 *"I lived in a Sicilian"*: Scorsese, AI, 5/23/94, 5/7/96.

227 *"When you go to the movies"*: Scorsese, AI, 5/23/94.

227 *"Marty is basically"*: Mardik Martin, AI, 10/14/95.

227 *"As somebody coming"* and following: Scorsese, AI, 5/23/94.

228 *"He was on a whole"*: McBride, AI, 6/3/94.

228 *"Every morning at NYU"*: Corman, *How I Made*, p. 85.

228 *"What Godard was"* and following: Scorsese, AI, 5/23/94.

229 *"Our wives hated us"*: Martin, AI, 7/31/91; Peter Biskind, "Slouching Toward Holly-
      wood," *Premiere*, 11/91.

229 *"We were used"*: Scorsese, AI, 5/23/94.

229 *"It was all"*: David Ehrenstein, *The Scorsese Picture: The Art and Life of Martin
      Scorsese*, New York, 1992, p. 160.

229 *"This movie is as good"*: Jay Cocks, AI, 3/7/96.

230 *"Before they split up"*: Martin, AI, 10/14/95.

230 *"three big-titted daughters"*: Simpson, AI, 12/24/92.

230 *"I thought Marty"* and following: Sandy Weintraub, AI, 2/3/92.

231 *"It was so tacky"*: Salt, AI, 3/14/92.

231 *"Our attitude about drugs"*: Kidder, AI, 4/17/93.

232 *"I was always thinking"*: Salt, AI, 3/14/92.

232 *"The reality was"*: Kidder, AI, 4/17/93.

232 *"The goal of all"*: Carson, AI, 1/30/92.

232 *"We were the generation"* and following: Salt, AI, 3/14/92.

233 *"C'mon, let's go in"*: Spielberg, AI, 12/9/96.

233 *"Marty seemed"*: Kidder, AI, 4/17/93.

233 *"The period from"*: Scorsese, AI, 8/1/91.

233 *"People today complain"* and following: Paul Schrader, AI, 12/3/91.

234 *"He failed production"*: Katz, AI, 6/28/94.

234 *"What I couldn't stand"* and following: Walker, AI, 2/26/94.

234 *"I used to say"*: Leonard Schrader, AI, 11/8/94.

235 *"Paul was calling"*: Walker, AI, 2/26/94.

235 *"George thought not only"*: Robbins, AI, 5/2/97.

235 *"Don't be so weird"*: George Lucas, AI, 5/2/97.

235 *"After THX went down"*: Marcia Lucas, AI, 3/3/97.

235 *"Before American Graffiti"*: David Sheff, "George Lucas," *Rolling Stone*, 11/5–
      12/10/87; Paul Scanlon, "The Force Behind George Lucas," *Rolling Stone*, 8/25/77.

236 *"Yeah, sure, great."*: George Lucas, AI, 5/2/97.

236 *"Francis got the"*: Huyck, AI, 6/16/94.

237 *"George was given"*: Coppola, AI, 7/31/97.

237 *"George had no"*: Katz, AI, 6/16/94.

238 *"I was an opportunist"*: Scorsese, AI, 5/23/94.

238 *"No one succeeds"*: Paul Schrader, AI, 12/11/97.

238 *"He needed a lot"*: Sandy Weintraub, AI, 7/30/91.

238 *"Marty had a kind"*: Taplin, AI, 7/30/91.

238 *"She was very"*: Taplin, AI, 3/16/92.

239 *"He got angry"* and following: Sandy Weintraub, AI, 7/30/91.

239 *"Roger I swear"*: Simpson, AI, 4/8/92.

239 *"Nice work, but"*: Ehrenstein, *The Scorsese Picture*, p. 41.

240 *"This odd little"*: Kidder, AI, 4/17/93.

240 *"I'm basically depressive"*: Paul Schrader, AI, 12/3/91.

240 *"Paul was never"*: Rosenman, AI, 1/28/92.
240 *"It was impossible"*: Katz, AI, 6/16/94.
240 *"Schrader was attracted"*: Rosenman, AI, 1/28/92.
240 *"Schrader was in love"*: Carson, AI, 1/30/92.
240 *"Kiss me!" and following*: Kidder, AI, 4/17/93.
241 *"Paul was a very"*: Sandy Weintraub, AI, 2/3/92.
241 *"I didn't see what"*: Paul Schrader, AI, 12/6/95.
242 *"Communicating with Bob"*: Sandy Weintraub, AI, 7/30/91.
242 *"In order to get" and following*: Scorsese, AI, 5/23/94.
243 *"What Marty and Bob"*: Sandy Weintraub, AI, 7/30/91.
243 *"There was always" and following*: Scorsese, AI, 7/18/97.
243 *"Brian never believed"*: Litto, AI, 10/17/94.
243 *"Brian was more"*: Scorsese, AI, 7/18/97.
243 *"Ned wouldn't sit"*: Pollock, *Skywalking*, p. 118.
243 *"The movie started"*: Marcia Lucas, AI, 3/3/97.
243 *"This is in no"*: AIs with Coppola, 7/31/97; George Lucas, 5/2/97; Marcia Lucas, 3/3/97; Murch, 11/18/93; Robbins, 5/2/97; Tanen, 1/22/93; Paul Hirsch, 11/15/93.
244 *"Francis, who would"*: Tanen, AI, 1/22/93.
244 *"I don't know"*: Huyck and Katz, AI, 6/16/94.
244 *"Francis really stood"*: George Lucas, AI, 5/2/97.
244 *"I read the whole thing"*: De Palma, AI, 11/9/93.
245 *"It was like"*: John Landis, AI, 4/25/96.
245 *"Julia had a real eye"*: Salt, AI, 3/14/92.
245 *"In those days"*: Kidder, AI, 4/17/93.
245 *"Julia 'Yes, I am' "*: Simpson, AI, 6/9/92.
246 *"It's not true"*: Peter Biskind, "Good Night, Dark Prince," *Premiere*, 4/96.
246 *"The partnership foundered"*: Tony Bill, AI, 6/20/94.
246 *"Paul was never"*: Scorsese, AI, 5/8/96.
246 *"I was blind" and following*: Paul Schrader, AI, 12/19/91.
246 *"That's when Francis"*: Scorsese, AI, 8/1/91.
246 *"I don't think Francis"*: Sandy Weintraub, AI, 2/3/92.
247 *"Francis woke us up"*: Scorsese, AI, 8/1/91.
247 *"Marty, Bobby, and I" and following*: Taplin, AI, 3/16/92.
248 *"Ed was totally"*: Salt, AI, 3/1/94.
249 *"I'll put"*: Confidential source.
249 *"We're way over"*: Confidential source.
249 *"If you were a fucking man"*: Lou Stroller, AI, 10/24/96.
249 *"I would never"*: Jill Jakes, AI, 1/8/98.
249 *"They didn't listen"*: Confidential source.
250 *"Do it, because"*: Mary Pat Kelly, *Martin Scorsese: A Journey*, New York, 1991, p. 79.
250 *"Martin Scorsese's Mean Streets"*: Kael, *New Yorker*, 10/8/73; *New Yorker*, 3/18/74.
250 *"She'd never written"*: Taplin, AI, 3/16/92.
251 *"lets Bobby go over"*: Andy Dougan, *Untouchable: A Biography of Robert De Niro*, New York, 1996, p. 123.
251 *"I was raised"*: Kelly, *Martin Scorsese*, p. 31.
251 *"It's pretty tough"*: Scorsese, AI, 5/23/94.
251 *"He started an argument"*: Martin, AI, 10/14/95.
251 *"He's a different"*: Scorsese, AI, 5/23/94.
251 *"We thought the"*: Kelly, *Martin Scorsese*, p.79.
251 *"At Warners, we were"*: Taplin, AI, 7/30/91.

252   *"coyly botched film"*: "Cybill and Peter — Who Needs Marriage?" *People*, 5/13/74.
252   *"In every one" and following*: Burstyn, AI, 4/10/96.
252   *"I don't know"*: Sandy Weintraub, AI, 7/30/91.
253   *"Great, who'd you get" and following*: Burstyn, AI, 4/10/96.
253   *"We knew her"*: Weintraub, AI, 2/3/92.
253   *"Marty called"*: Marcia Lucas, AI, 3/3/97.
253   *"I know I stepped"*: Burstyn, AI, 4/10/96.
254   *"Warners was concerned"*: Scorsese, AI, 5/23/94.
254   *"He had a tremendous"*: Sandy Weintraub, AI, 2/3/92.
254   *"Marty wanted the people" and following*: Burstyn, AI, 4/10/96.
254   *"All I could think of"*: Ehrenstein, *The Scorsese Picture*, p. 116.

Chapter 9: The Revenge of the Nerd

PAGE
255   *Epigraph*: Bogdanovich, AI, 10/19/95.
255   *"They're overdoing it." and following*: Nancy Griffin, "In the Grip of *Jaws*," *Premiere*, 10/95, p. 90.
256   *"wimpy years"*: Michiko Kakutani, *New York Times*, 5/30/82.
256   *"I was a loner"*: Leo Janos, "Steven Spielberg: L'Enfant Directeur," *Cosmopolitan*, 6/80, p. 238.
256   *"I had friends"*: Lynn Hirschberg, "Will Hollywood's Mr. Perfect Ever Grow Up?" *Rolling Stone*, 7/19–8/2/84.
257   *"You should be"*: Ibid.
257   *"I didn't work"*: Spielberg, AI, 12/9/96.
257   *"Everybody was up"*: Carson, AI, 1/30/92.
257   *"He's a kid"*: Joseph McBride, *Steven Spielberg: A Biography*, New York, 1997, p. 187.
258   *"When I first heard" and following*: Robbins, AI, 5/2/97. Robbins is referring to a *Name of the Game* episode called "LA: 2017."
258   *"I saw in Francis's eyes" and following*: Spielberg, AI, 12/9/96.
258   *"the media were saying"*: Simpson, AI, 4/8/92.
259   *"We were out"*: Huyck, AI, 6/28/94.
260   *"Steven loved movies"*: Kidder, AI, 4/17/93.
260   *"He didn't want to be"*: Carson, AI, 1/30/92.
260   *"Steven was the one"*: John Baxter, *Steven Spielberg*, New York, 1996, p. 201.
260   *"That was why"*: Kidder, AI, 4/17/93.
260   *"I never took"*: McBride, *Steven Spielberg*, p. 127.
260   *"They had thousands"*: Huyck, AI, 6/28/94.
260   *"Every month he read"*: Milius, AI, 1/31/92.
260   *"Basically, I was"*: Kidder, AI, 4/17/93.
260   *"I'd like to get"*: Gottlieb, AI, 6/13/97.
261   *"Steven briefly brought"*: Kidder, AI, 4/17/93.
261   *"fresh crop of"*: Goodwin and Wise, *On the Edge*, p. 169.
261   *"She's the greatest" and following*: Frederickson, AI, 5/10/95.
262   *"There's a horizon" and following*: Leonard Schrader, AI, 11/17/94.
262   *"I want these people" and following*: Paul Schrader, AI, 12/6/95.
263   *"Steven didn't like"*: Robbins, AI, 5/2/97.
263   *"one of the most"*: McBride, *Steven Spielberg*, p. 266.
263   *"[I] swiped a copy"*: Judy Klemesrud, "Can He Make the 'Jaws' of Outer Space?" *New York Times*, 5/15/77.
263   *"I didn't know who"*: Spielberg, AI, 2/9/96.

263   *"There are two" and following*: Griffin, notes for "In the Grip of Jaws."
263   *"I was hell bent"*: Spielberg, AI, 12/9/96.
264   *"that rarity among"*: Kael, *New Yorker*, 3/18/74.
264   *"Steven was sitting"*: John Byrum, AI, 4/5/94.
265   *"My goal was"*: Baxter, *Steven Spielberg*, p. 125.
265   *"I wanted somewhat"*: Spielberg, AI, 12/9/96.
265   *"Then I saw"*: Griffin, "In the Grip of Jaws."
265   *"that it was just"*: Spielberg, AI, 12/9/96.
265   *"like a wake"*: McBride, *Steven Spielberg*, p. 400.
266   *"Jaws was not"*: "Summer of the Shark," *Time*, 6/23/75, p. 44.
266   *"turkey of the year"*: Ibid.
266   *"I knew what"*: McBride, *Steven Spielberg*, p. 238.
266   *"Because we had"*: Roy Scheider, AI, 9/16/97.
266   *"He would jump"*: McBride, *Steven Spielberg*, p. 244.
266   *"Steven, where is"*: Griffin, "In the Grip of Jaws."
267   *"Everywhere we went"*: Baxter, *Steven Spielberg*, p. 136.
267   *"You know, this"*: Griffin, "In the Grip of Jaws."
267   *"The week before"*: Gottlieb, AI, 6/13/97.
267   *"It was a shonda"*: Spielberg, AI, 12/9/96.
267   *"That night, I had"*: Griffin, notes for "In the Grip of Jaws."
268   *"Towne hated it"*: Evans, AI, 2/27/94.
268   *"Towne has this"*: Beatty, 3/16/95.
268   *"This is a great"*: Towne, AI, 3/3/94.
268   *"The first person"*: Evans, AI, 2/27/94.
269   *"It is indescribable"*: Bart, AI, 10/23/95.
269   *"If you're on"*: Evans, AI, 3/11/97.
269   *"They totally resented"*: Yablans, AI, 6/3/96.
269   *"How could they?"*: Confidential source.
269   *"Legally you're right" and following*: Evans, AI, 3/11/97.
269   *"He tried to"*: Ruddy, AI, 3/12/97.
269   *"I gotta tell"*: Yablans, AI, 6/3/96.
270   *"I'm asexual"*: Confidential source.
270   *"I knew it would" and following*: Yablans, AI, 6/3/96.
270   *"an orgy for"*: Kael, *New Yorker*, 3/3/75.
270   *"Because we didn't"*: Bruce Williamson, *Playboy* interview, 8/76.
271   *"When he walked" and following*: Blauner, AI, 3/1/94.
272   *"Uh, Bert, we have"*: Charlie Goldstein, AI, 11/22/94.
272   *"a Cuban exile"*: Bo Burlingham, "Politics Under the Palms," *Esquire*, 2/77.
272   *"I did everything" and following*: Blauner, AI, 3/1/94.
272   *"Artie's take on"*: Dorien Ross, AI, 11/3/93.
272   *Finally, Bert called*: Goldstein, AI, 11/22/94.
273   *"It wasn't out"*: Toby Rafelson, AI, 9/8/97.
273   *"In both Bob's"*: Burstyn, AI, 4/10/96.
273   *On January 17*: *Los Angeles Times*, 1/19/75.
274   *"At first, Francis"*: Richard Sylbert, AI, 8/25/92.
274   *"When Francis walked"*: Evans, AI, 3/11/97.
274   *"It was in my deal"*: Coppola, AI, 7/31/97.
274   *"If you don't"*: Andrew Tobias, "The Apprenticeship of Frank Yablans."
275   *"greetings of friendship" and following*: Wiley and Bona, *Inside Oscar*, p. 504.
275   *"Imagine, in 1975"*: William Murray, *Playboy* interview.

275   *"This movie was"*: Bogdanovich, AI, 6/29/94.

275   *"The audience was silent"*: Mengers, AI, 2/21/95.

275   *"It was just"*: Bogdanovich, AI, 10/19/95.

275   *"It was the most"*: Ronda Gomez, AI, 6/22/94.

276   *"People loathed Peter"*: Newman, AI, 2/15/94.

276   *"She wanted to"*: Bogdanovich, AI, 8/1/97.

276   *"It was treated"*: Margie Rochlin, "Peter Bogdanovich," *Interview*, 3/85, p. 134.

276   *"the debacle."*: Hal Rubinstein, "Cybill Shepherd," *Interview*, 11/86.

276   *"Because whenever there"*: Mengers, AI, 2/21/95.

276   *"Then the ushers"*: Platt, AI, 6/29/94.

276   *"There would be" and following*: Cohen, AI, 5/12/95.

277   *"The effects didn't work"*: Spielberg, AI, 1/15/97.

277   *"That decision was"*: Gottlieb, AI, 6/13/97.

277   *"It was definitely"*: Michael Chapman, AI, 3/28/97.

277   *"That's when I knew"*: Griffin, "In the Grip of *Jaws*."

278   *"My secretary handed me"*: Ibid.

278   *"My influences"*: Spielberg, AI, 12/9/96.

278   *"has no knowledge"*: McBride, *Steven Spielberg*, p. 396; Baxter, *Steven Spielberg*, p. 31.

279   *"The summer of '75"*: Griffin, notes for "In the Grip of *Jaws*."

279   *"I was giving"*: Judy Schneider AI, 12/15/97.

280   *"People had been warning"*: Brackman, AI, 4/30/93.

280   *"I knocked on"*: Blauner, AI, 3/1/94.

280   *"It may have been"*: Brackman, AI, 4/30/93.

280   *"There was such"*: Salt, AI, 3/1/94.

281   *"During my era"*: Yablans, AI, 6/3/96.

281   *"There's no audience"*: Kael, "On the Future of Movies," *New Yorker*, 8/5/74.

282   *"I can't believe it."*: Wiley and Bona, *Inside Oscar*, p. 515.

282   *"In the early '70's"*: Leonard Schrader, AI, 11/17/94.

283   *"The number of times"*: Confidential source.

283   *"I got a lot of credit"*: McBride, *Steven Spielberg*, p. 417.

283   *"Steven started to resent"*: Julia Phillips, *You'll Never Eat Lunch in This Town Again*, New York, 1991, p. 203.

283   *"Spielberg didn't write it." and following*: Gottlieb, AI, 6/13/97.

283   *"made me pressure"*: Phillips, *You'll Never Eat Lunch*, p. 203.

283   *"Steve felt he"*: Paul Schrader, AI, 12/19/91.

283   *"seemed to resent"*: McBride, *Steven Spielberg*, p. 418.

284   *"It surprises me"*: Baxter, *Steven Spielberg*, p. 155.

284   *"Steven started cutting"*: Robbins, AI, 5/2/97.

284   *"Don't you like"*: Cohen, AI, 5/12/95.

285   *"I marched in"*: Leo Janos, "Steven Spielberg: L'Enfant Directeur."

Chapter 10: Citizen Cain

PAGE

286   *Epigraph*: John Milius, AI, 1/9/92.

286   *"Milius and I"*: Paul Schrader, AI, 12/19/91; Biskind, "What a Long, Strange Trip It's Been," *Premiere*, 4/92.

286   *"If there was ever"*: Milius, AI, 1/9/92.

286   *"It needs more of this."*: Walker, AI, 2/26/94.

286   *"Put it back."*: Kiki Morris, AI, n.d.

287   *"He was always"*: Penny Marshall, AI, 2/9/92.

287   *"I was afraid of them" and following*: Leonard Schrader, AI, 11/8/94.

287   *"probably loaded"*: Paul Schrader, AI, 12/6/95.

287   *"this is what"*: Leonard Schrader, AI, 11/8/94.

288   *"Leonard bore the brunt"*: Paul Schrader, AI, 12/19/91.

288   *"No matter what"*: Leonard Schrader, AI, 11/17/94.

288   *"Do you remember"*: Laura De Coppet, "To Hell with Paul Schrader," *Interview*, 3/92, p. 53.

288   *"What saved me" and following*: Leonard Schrader, AI, 11/8/94.

289   *"I fell in love" and following*: Paul Schrader, AI, 12/3/91.

290   *"I felt shit" and following*: Paul Schrader, AI, 12/3/91; Diane Jacobs, "Mr. Taxi Driver," *Gallery*, 8/76, p. 89.

291   *"I traveled all night" and following*: Leonard Schrader, AI, 11/8/94.

292   *"They turned off"*: Paul Schrader, AI, 12/3/91.

292   *"That's where I"*: Leonard Schrader, AI, 11/8/94.

292   *"I became the older brother"*: Paul Schrader, AI, 12/13/95.

293   *"The salesman took"*: Milius, 1/9/92.

293   *"When he sold"*: Weintraub, AI, 2/3/92.

293   *"Father and I"*: Confidential source.

293   *"Beer bottles would"*: Leonard Schrader, AI, 11/8/94.

293   *"he would point"*: Milius, AI, 1/9/92.

293   *"The first thing"*: Carson, AI, 1/30/92.

294   *"Before video"*: Paul Schrader, AI, 12/19/91.

294   *"We didn't have"*: Leonard Schrader, AI, 11/17/94.

294   *"I don't give a fuck" and following*: Sandy Weintraub, AI, 2/3/92.

295   *"Somewhere in between*: Paul Schrader, AI, 12/19/91.

295   *"1. a hooker"*: Charles Michener, "Taxi Driver," *Film Comment*, 3–4/76, p. 11.

295   *"You know what the gun"*: Michener, "Taxi Driver," p. 19.

296   *"What really made"*: Michael Phillips, AI, 3/14/92.

297   *"Never introduce me"*: AI, Weaver, 10/8/96.

297   *"Those were the kinda"*: Confidential source.

298   *"Terry wouldn't let go"*: Nelson, 11/11/94.

298   *"That'll tell you"*: Bert Schneider, AI, 2/14/95.

298   *"Well I didn't know"*: Confidential source.

298   *"He's out, Derns"*: Dern, AI, 6/17/95.

298   *"I burned out"*: Confidential source.

299   *"Godard was the great"*: Chapman, AI, 3/28/97.

299   *"We had been referring"*: Paul Schrader, AI, 12/19/91.

299   *"At that time"*: Mengers, AI, 2/21/95.

300   *"We always said"*: Paul Schrader, AI, 12/19/91.

300   *"He treated Jodie"*: Confidential source.

300   *"The pressure was" and following*: Weintraub, AI, 7/30/91.

300   *"they put up"*: Confidential source.

301   *"I sat down" and following*: Julia Cameron, AI, 12/2/97.

301   *"Nobody liked her."*: Amy Jones, AI, 6/30/97.

301   *"insanely jealous"*: Martin, AI, 10/14/95.

301   *"She was a real"*: Confidential source.

301   *"How do you push"*: Chapman, AI, 3/28/97.

301   *"I was just"*: Cameron, AI, 12/2/97.

301   *"I told Marty"*: Sandy Weintraub, AI, 7/30/91.

302   *"He was the guy"*: Martin, AI, 10/14/95.

302   *"He was like"*: Taplin, AI, 7/30/91.

302   *"would have turned"*: Ehrenstein, *The Scorsese Picture*, p. 115.

302   *"It wasn't just"*: Beatty, AI, 6/28/94.

302   *"Vietnam polarized"*: Beatty, AI, 6/28/94.

303   *"Towne had Kael"*: Henry, AI, 12/7/94.

303   *"Towne sent me"*: James Toback, AI, n.d.

303   *"I just loved"*: Towne, AI, 11/6/97.

303   *"I didn't review"*: Pauline Kael, AI, 8/5/95.

304   *"Beatty said"*: Towne, AI, 11/6/97.

304   *"Bob always said"*: Geffen, AI, 4/18/96; Corrie Brown, "No Love Affair," *Premiere*, 2/95.

305   *"It was Towne" and following*: Beatty, AI, 3/6/95.

305   *"The great secret" and following*: Payne, AI, 1/19/95.

305   *"You're ten minutes"*: Confidential source.

305   *"Marty is not"*: Michener, "Taxi Driver," p. 13.

306   *"Marty's upset about" and following*: Paul Schrader, AI, 12/6/95.

306   *"I'm an artist"*: Ehrenstein, *The Scorsese Picture*, p. 116.

306   *"Can you come up here?"*: Spielberg, AI, 12/9/96.

307   *"we went around" and following*: Nairn-Smith, AI, 9/29/94.

308   *"When I started"*: Friedkin, AI, 4/19/96.

308   *" 'Why haven't you' " and following*: Nairn-Smith, AI, 9/29/94.

308   *"The feeling was"*: Green, AI, 12/3/96.

308   *"This is the best"*: Friedkin, AI, 4/19/96.

309   *"a sense of people"*: Clagett, *William Friedkin*, p. 140.

309   *"He said, 'I can't' "*: Nairn-Smith, AI, 9/29/94.

309   *"All I ever thought"*: Friedkin, AI, 4/19/96.

310   *"Billy had won"*: Mark Johnson, AI, 12/17/94.

310   *"More per diem" and following*: Friedkin, AI, 4/19/96.

310   *"When Bluhdorn saw"*: Segaloff, *Hurricane Billy*, p. 164.

310   *"If we had shot"*: Mark Johnson, AI, 12/17/94.

310   *"I was the only"*: Scheider, AI, 9/16/97.

310   *"At first it was"*: Smith, AI, 12/13/96.

311   *"The pig was dying"*: Segaloff, *Hurricane Billy*, p. 163.

311   *"had broken up"*: Burstyn, AI, 4/10/96.

311   *"She told him"*: Green, AI, 12/3/96.

311   *"I had a blood test"*: Friedkin, AI, 4/19/96.

311   *"You know"*: Green, AI, 12/3/96.

312   *"At that time"*: Friedkin, AI, 4/19/96.

312   *"I want to show"*: Friedkin, AI, 4/19/96.

312   *"These guys operate" and following*: Friedkin, AI, 4/19/96; Smith, AI, 12/13/96; Green, AI, 12/3/96.

313   *"doing one of these"*: Smith, AI, 12/3/96.

313   *"Joe, you were"*: Joe Hyams, AI, 4/9/92.

313   *"It was a moment"*: Paul Schrader, AI, 12/6/95.

313   *"we're fucked"*: Sean Daniel, AI, 11/13/93.

313   *"See, it wasn't"*: Phillips, *You'll Never Eat Lunch*, p. 253.

314   *"Characters like Travis"*: Jacobs, "Mr. Taxi Driver," p. 90.

314   *"One of the reasons"*: Sandy Weintraub, AI, 2/3/92.

314   *"What animated Hollywood"*: Beatty, AI, 1/7/98.

315   *"What drove me"*: Fletcher, AI, 6/22/94.
315   *"One of the things"*: Scorsese, AI, 2/91.

Chapter 11: Star Bucks

PAGE
316   *Epigraph*: Paul Schrader, AI, 12/3/91.
316   *"New York, New York" and following*: Katz, AI, 6/16/94.
316   *"I just don't"*: Huyck, AI, 6/16/94.
317   *"Norman Rockwell"*: Pollock, *Skywalking*, p. 39.
317   *"scrawny little devil"*: Gerald Clarke, "I Got to Get My Life Back Again," *Time*, 5/23/83, p. 68.
317   *"What we had"*: George Lucas, AI, 5/2/97.
317   *"You'll be back"*: Pollock, *Skywalking*, p. 38.
317   *"Movies had extremely"*: "Young Directors, New Films," *AFI Report*, 1974, p. 45.
318   *"We had never"*: Pollock, *Skywalking*, p. 70.
318   *"L.A. is where"*: David Thomson, *Overexposures*, New York, 1981, p. 40.
318   *"When I did Graffiti"*: Sheff, "George Lucas"; Scanlon, "The Force Behind George Lucas."
318   *"a fantasy"*: "Young Directors, New Films," p. 46.
318   *"was a conscious"*: Sheff, "George Lucas."
319   *"George didn't want"*: Pollock, *Skywalking*, p. 136.
319   *"To this day"*: Tanen, AI, 1/22/93.
319   *"He had this"*: Marcia Lucas, AI, 3/3/97.
319   *"They're similar"*: Scorsese, AI, 5/8/96.
320   *"George is just"*: Huyck, AI, 6/16/94.
320   *"Francis was questioning"*: Pollock, *Skywalking*, p. 128.
320   *"That movie could"*: Lillian Ross, "Some Figures on a Fantasy," *New Yorker*, 11/8/82, p. 63.
320   *"He had been burned"*: Pollock, AI, 1/21/93.
320   *"But it didn't"*: Confidential source.
320   *"George said to me"*: Milius, AI, 1/9/92.
321   *"I've made"*: Scanlon, "The Force Behind George Lucas."
321   *"When George said"*: Huyck, AI, 6/16/94.
322   *"All Francis did" and following*: George Lucas, AI, 5/2/97.
322   *"Whatever Francis does"*: Braudy, "Francis Ford Coppola: A Profile," p. 67.
322   *"I was always"*: Milius, AI, 1/9/92.
322   *"I know what"*: Confidential source.
323   *"young Al Pacinos"*: Braudy, "Francis Ford Coppola," p. 68.
323   *"The film continued"*: Greil Marcus, "Journey Up the River," *Rolling Stone*, 11/1/79, p. 52.
323   *"People used to"*: Ibid.
323   *"The jungle will"*: Braudy, "Francis Ford Coppola," p. 68
323   *"I know you've"*: Corman, *How I Made*, p. 40.
324   *"Someday I won't"*: Braudy, "Francis Ford Coppola," p. 66.
324   *"They said, 'George' "*: John Seabrook, "Why Is the Force Still with Us?," *New Yorker*, 1/6/97, p. 50.
324   *"George thinks"*: Nancy Allen, AI, 11/14/94.
325   *"They're already nervous"*: Huyck, AI, 6/16/94.
325   *"They started shooting"*: Martin, AI, 10/14/95.
325   *"You get a big"*: Scorsese, AI, 8/1/91.

325   *"After Mean Streets"*: Sandy Weintraub, AI, 2/3/92.

325   *"I didn't know"*: Scorsese, AI, 5/7/96.

325   *"I blame all that" and following*: Martin, AI, 10/14/95.

326   *"How could you!" and following*: Pat Hackett, *The Andy Warhol Diaries*, New York, 1989, p. 92.

326   *"By the time"*: Chris Mankiewicz, AI, 6/21/94.

326   *"De Palma, who I"*: Huyck, AI, 6/28/94.

326   *"There was no"*: Nelson, AI, 11/11/94.

327   *"Having been"*: Robbins, AI, 5/2/97.

327   *"ILM was a mess."*: Marcia Lucas, AI, 3/3/97.

327   *"We were under"*: Nelson, AI, 11/11/94.

327   *"I knew he was" and following*: Pollock, *Skywalking*, p. 150.

328   *"You can make"*: Ibid.

328   *"No breasts bouncing"*: Ibid., p. 165.

328   *"By the time" and following*: Gottlieb, AI, 6/13/97.

328   *"They hit it off"*: De Palma, AI, 11/9/93.

328   *"You'd think she"*: De Palma, AI, 11/9/93.

328   *"She was a"*: Cohen, AI, 5/12/95.

328   *"I know he's" and following*: McBride, *Steven Spielberg*, p. 295.

329   *"George does not"*: Howard Kazanjian, AI, 6/29/94.

329   *"When George and"*: Huyck, AI, 6/16/94.

329   *"I realized why"*: Scanlon, "The Force Behind George Lucas."

329   *"George, you can"*: Pollock, *Skywalking*, p. 64.

329   *"O.K., same thing"*: Seabrook, "Why is the Force Still with Us?" pp. 46, 48.

329   *"George would sit"*: Katz, AI, 6/16/94.

329   *"I got fifty"*: Marcia Lucas, AI, 3/3/97.

329   *"George wouldn't let me"*: Spielberg, AI, 12/9/96.

330   *"I only got 30 percent"*: Marcia Lucas, AI, 3/3/97.

330   *"Marcia respected Marty"*: Hirsch, AI, 11/15/93.

330   *"She abandoned George"*: Katz, AI, 6/16/94.

330   *"For George, the whole"*: Huyck, AI, 6/16/94.

330   *"When I heard him"*: Scorsese, AI, 5/7/96.

330   *"I didn't think"*: Spielberg, AI, 12/9/96.

331   *"I knew that"*: McBride, *Steven Spielberg*, p. 276.

331   *"Why don't you turn"*: Jim Bloom, AI, 3/3/97.

331   *"I asked for"*: Spielberg, AI, 12/9/96.

332   *"Don't you understand"*: McBride, *Steven Spielberg*, p. 296.

332   *"Feminism was really"*: Cohen, AI, 5/12/95.

332   *"I could tell"*: Gottlieb, AI, 6/13/97.

333   *"I liked Amy"*: Marcia Lucas, AI, 4/30/97.

333   *"I'm glad I didn't do Star Wars"*: Richard Licata, *New York Daily News*, 3/19/78.

333   *"Amy was like"*: Marcia Lucas, AI, 3/3/97.

333   *"Who made it?"*: Confidential source.

333   *"If little Jodie"*: Bert Lovitt, AI, 7/7–9/97.

333   *"Without thinking" and following*: Taplin, AI, 7/30/91.

334   *"You'd have the anxiety"*: Scorsese, AI, 7/18/97.

334   *"It's the At" and following*: AIs with Katz and Huyck, 6/16/94; George Lucas, 5/2/97; Marcia Lucas, 3/3/97; Spielberg, 12/9/96; Robbins, 5/2/97; Allen, 11/14/94; Cocks, 3/7/96.

335   *"I remember the day"*: Nelson, AI, 11/11/94.

335   "Star Wars *was the can opener*": Murch, AI, 4/20/97.
335   *"Previews always mean" and following*: Hirsch, AI, 11/15/93.
336   *"I've done everything"*: Huyck and Katz, AI, 6/28/94.
336   *"There were people" and following*: George Lucas, AI, 5/2/97.
336   *"You know, these"*: Huyck and Katz, AI, 6/16/94.
337   *"Send money."*: Baxter, *Steven Spielberg*, p. 2.
337   *"Jesus, Harrison"*: Cocks, AI, 3/7/96.
337   *"When our trailer"*: Smith, AI, 12/13/96.
337   *"This film's doing"*: Green, AI, 12/3/96.
337   *"He probably put"*: Smith, AI, 12/13/96.
338   *"I probably shouldn't"*: Friedkin, AI, 4/19/96.
338   *"The four of them"*: Nairn-Smith, AI, 9/29/94.
338   *"For a while"*: Friedkin, AI, 4/19/96.
338   *"I thought I was"*: Burstyn, AI, 4/10/96.
338   *"God, I've wanted"*: Friedkin, AI, 4/19/96.
339   *"I was angry"*: Scorsese, AI, 7/13/91.
339   *"I was just too" and following*: Scorsese, AI, 7/18/97.
339   *"The trouble with"*: Martin, AI, 10/14/95.
339   *"I really didn't want"*: Scorsese, AI, 8/1/91.
340   *"Why are you"*: Pollock, AI, 1/21/93.
340   *"Oh, I'm gonna" and following*: Coppola, AI, 7/31/97.
340   *"These guys got"*: Milius, AI, 1/31/92 and 3/16/92.
341   *"Let's stop"*: Thompson, AI, 10/18/95.
341   *"Ladd left me"*: Altman, AI, 5/3/96.
341   *"If you're the executive"*: Spielberg, AI, 12/9/96.
341   *"I got screwed"*: Pollock, *Skywalking*, p. 247.
342   *"that are all"*: Kael, "Fear of Movies," *New Yorker*, 9/25/87.
342   *"It was a vanishing"*: Kirk Honeycutt, *Newsday*, 12/8/91.
342   *"Blockbusters have to*: Peter Biskind, "The Last Crusade," in *Seeing Through Movies*, Mark Crispin Miller, ed., New York, 1990.
342   *"brought kids out"*: Kirk Honeycutt, "Milius the Barbarian," *American Film*, 5/82.
343   *"showed people it"*: Pollock, *Skywalking*, p. 186.
343   *"It wasn't camp"*: Scanlon, "The Force Behind George Lucas."
343   *"What my generation"*: Robert Lindsey, "The New New Wave of Film Makers," *New York Times*, 5/28/78.
343   *"I'm an advocate" and following*: George Lucas, AI, 5/2/97.
344   "Star Wars *was in."*: Scorsese, 5/7/96.
344   *"When I was at USC"*: Milius, AI, 1/9/92.
344   "Star Wars *swept"*: Friedkin, AI, 4/19/96.
344   "Star Wars *didn't" and following*: George Lucas, AI, 5/2/97.
345   *"They're not subsidizing"*: Scorsese, AI, 7/18/97.
345   *"Last summer trying"*: Altman, AI, 6/30/97.
345   *"Right now, I'm just"*: Marcia Lucas, AI, 3/3/97.

Chapter 12: Coming Apart
PAGE
346   *Epigraph*: Coppola, AI, 7/31/97.
346   " *'The Force be' " and following*: Confidential source.
347   *"Don't come here"*: Confidential source.
347   *"In the movie"*: Fred Forrest, AI, 11/23/97.

347 *"You could go in there"*: Sam Bottoms, AI, 4/20/96.

348 *"I saw how" and following*: Leonard Schrader, AI, 11/17/94.

349 *"I broke the structure"*: Paul Schrader, AI, 12/13/95.

349 *"Try this" and following*: Paul Schrader, AI, 12/19/91.

349 *"Richard was starting"*: Paul Schrader, AI, 12/11/97.

349 *"After about three"*: Paul Schrader, AI, n.d.

349 *"I always thought Paul"*: Janice Hampton, AI, 6/16/97.

349 *"Ya know, I could"*: Toback, AI, 12/12/94.

350 *"is no different"*: Pollock, *Skywalking*, p. 193.

350 *"His personality had changed."*: Nancy Tonery, AI, 4/9/97.

350 *"Francis didn't pay"*: Ruddy, AI, 3/12/97.

350 *"It's your plane"*: Skager, AI, 3/4/97.

351 *"how the film was"*: Eleanor Coppola, *Notes on the Making of Apocalypse Now*, New York, 1991, p. 63.

351 *"It was a state of seige"*: Tonery, AI, 4/9/97.

352 *"We had a couple"*: Hellman, AI, 6/20/94.

352 *"He found it"*: Mireille, AI, 2/4/95.

353 *"After Being There"*: Bart, AI, 10/23/95.

353 *"One of the reasons"*: Wexler, AI, 8/18/95.

353 *"When he showed up" and following*: Hampton, AI, 6/16/97.

354 *"I don't remember"*: Eva Gardos, AI, 12/6/97.

354 *"I called him"*: Jones, AI, 10/5/94.

354 *"But Hal was so zonked"*: Bart, AI, 10/23/95.

355 *"More often than not"*: Berg, AI, 10/20/95.

355 *"When Marty came home"*: Jean Vallely, "Martin Sheen: Heart of Darkness, Heart of Gold," *Rolling Stone*, 11/1/79, p. 48.

355 *"I started smoking"*: Breskin, *Inner Views*, p. 47.

355 *"tried to seduce" and following*: Brooke Hayward, AI, 4/24/97.

355 *"He fired shots"*: Maria Hopper, AI, 1/4/98.

356 *"You've got to get"*: Brooke Hayward, AI, 4/24/97.

356 *"She definitely"*: Confidential source.

356 *"It turned out"*: Frederickson, AI, 5/10/95.

356 *"Everybody was waiting"*: Confidential source.

356 *"Letting the movie"*: Coppola, AI, 7/31/97.

357 *"The palace was"*: Mathison, AI, 12/17/97.

357 *"She was quiet"*: Confidential source.

357 *"I never felt"*: Breskin, *Inner Views*, pp. 46–47.

357 *"like the girl who"*: ibid., p. 48.

357 *"Look, I have these"*: Confidential source.

358 *"She was a real"*: Coppola, AI, 7/31/97.

358 *"He was never"*: Eleanor Coppola, *Notes on the Making*, pp. 173, 176.

358 *"Warren, who was among"*: Ashley, AI, 12/11/97.

358 *"Do you want"*: Confidential source.

359 *"Barry had his pets"*: Simpson, AI, 7/21/93.

359 *"Warren is a master" and following*: Henry, AI, 12/7/94.

360 *"the very situation"*: Eleanor Coppola, *Notes on the Making*, p. 177.

360 *"We were in the jungle"*: *Heart of Darkness* documentary.

361 *"I was in, like"*: Breskin, *Inner Views*, p. 46.

362 *"The cutting was"*: Confidential source.

362 *"we'd come to work"*: Richard Candib, AI, 10/2/97.

362 *"I owe everything"*: Jerry Ross, AI, 10/6/97.

362 *"The emotion rose"*: Eleanor Coppola, *Notes on the Making*, pp. 211–12, 229–30.

363 *"You can have"*: Tim Holland, AI, 11/3/97.

363 *"I really wanted"*: Hodenfield, "The Sky Is Full of Questions," *Rolling Stone*, 1/26/78.

364 *"Look, I just"*: Cohen, AI, 5/12/95.

364 *"Warren sees himself"*: Aaron Lathem, "Warren Beatty Seriously," *Rolling Stone*, 4/1/82.

365 *"Even Barry [Diller]"*: Simpson, AI, 7/21/93.

365 *"Warren could dictate"*: Evans, AI, 6/11/94.

365 *"image-conscious" and following*: Kael, "Fear of Movies," 9/25/78.

365 *"Ma Barker"*: James Wolcott, *Vanity Fair*, 4/97.

365 *"I thought he was" and following*: Beatty, AI, n.d.

366 *"After six weeks"*: Toback, AI, n.d.

366 *"Because of her power"*: Paul Schrader, AI, 12/3/91.

366 *"We're talking about"*: Henry, AI, 12/7/94.

366 *"they were really"*: Kael, AI, 8/5/95.

367 *"For months"*: Confidential source.

367 *"I'd ask Francis"*: Confidential source.

367 *"It was like"*: Bottoms, AI, 4/20/96.

367 *"Part of the"*: Mathison, AI, 12/7/97.

368 *"We didn't know"*: Steven Bach, *Final Cut*, New York, 1985, p. 101.

369 *"Eisner was scared"*: Simpson, AI, 6/3/92, 6/14/92.

369 *"Princess Grace"*: Altman, AI, 5/3/96.

369 *"None of us"*: Simpson, AI, 6/14/92.

370 *"After the reel" and following*: Altman, AI, 5/3/96.

370 *"Don, Don."* Simpson, AI, 6/14/92.

370 *"Deek, Deek"*: Terri Minsky interview, n.d.

371 *"There's one scene"*: Altman, AI, 5/3/96.

371 *"After Scottie came"*: Thompson, AI, 10/18/95.

371 *"She was a real"*: Tewkesbury, AI, 10/13/95.

371 *"A lot of people" and following*: Altman, AI, 5/3/96.

372 *"Bob always had"*: Allan Nicholls, AI, 5/1/96.

372 *"racist, Pentagon"*: Bach, *Final Cut*, p. 211.

372 *"Francis, I have" and following*: Robert Dalva, AI, 3/10/97.

373 *"You know, Warren" and following*: Coppola, AI, 6/27/96.

373 *"I don't want lead"*: Skager, AI, 3/4/97.

373 *"You'll be depressed"*: Breskin, *Inner Views*, p. 45.

373 *"We will rule"*: Baxter, *Steven Spielberg*, p. 191.

373 *"I have wept"*: Breskin, *Inner Views*, p. 48.

374 *"only to see"*: Goodwin and Wise, *On the Edge*, p. 270.

374 *"It was"*: Towne, AI, 11/6/97.

375 *"thrilled about"*: Bogdanovich, AI, 10/19/95.

375 *"Filmmaking is like"*: Coppola, AI, 9/14/90.

Chapter 13: The Eve of Destruction

PAGE

376 *Epigraph*: Martin Scorsese, AI, 5/8/96.

376 *"He never could"*: Winkler, AI, 3/17/92.

376 *"Marty was just"*: Taplin, AI, 3/16/92.

376 *"We were the odd"*: Robbie Robertson, AI, n.d.

376   *"It was a shame"*: Sandy Weintraub, AI, 2/3/92.
377   *"Marty's house was"*: Robertson, AI, n.d.
377   *"We were like"*: Martin, AI, 10/14/95.
377   *"They would call"*: Taplin, AI, 3/16/92.
377   *"At first you felt"*: Scorsese, AI, 2/91.
377   *"The doctor would"*: Robertson, AI, n.d.
377   *"It was a matter"*: Scorsese, AI, 5/7/96.
377   *"I've always felt"*: Tanen, AI, 1/22/93.
378   *"Whatsamatter with you?" and following*: Martin, AI, 10/14/95.
378   *"I was making love"*: Scorsese, AI, 5/7/96.
378   *"Marty sort of likes"*: Martin, AI, 10/14/95.
378   *"I was always"*: Scorsese, AI, 5/7/96.
379   *"No more coke"*: Martin, AI, 10/14/95.
379   *"It hit me finally" and following*: Scorsese, AI, 5/7/96.
379   *"Okay, whaddya got?" and following*: Martin, AI, 10/14/95.
380   *"What's going on?"*: Kelly, *Martin Scorsese*, p. 123.
380   *"One day, Marty"*: Martin, AI, 10/14/95.
381   *"Once the corporations"*: George Lucas, AI, 5/2/97.
381   *"By the time George"*: Marcia Lucas, AI, 3/3/97.
381   *"I'm the only one"*: Coppola, AI, 7/31/97.
382   *"I would write stoned"*: Paul Schrader, AI, 12/19/91.
382   *"This was a kind"*: Rosenman, AI, 1/28/92.
382   *"The arbiters of taste" and following*: Milius, AI, 1/31/92.
383   *"I started getting labeled"*: Paul Schrader, AI, 12/13/95.
383   *"Steve just wouldn't"*: Milius, AI, 3/16/92.
384   *"We would have been"*: McBride, *Steven Spielberg*, p. 306.
384   *"Power can go right"*: Spielberg, AI, 12/9/96.
384   *"I'll be pregnant"*: McBride, *Steven Spielberg*, p. 525.
384   *"I fell in love"*: Amy Irving, AI, 1/22/98.
384   *"He was so relieved"*: Robbins, AI, 5/9/97.
384   *"It's a lot easier"*: Hirschberg, "Will Hollywood's Mr. Perfect Ever Grow Up?" p. 38.
384   *"Life has finally"*: Janos, "Steven Spielberg."
385   *"They were both"*: Paul Schrader, AI, 12/13/95.
385   *"De Niro saw this"*: Scorsese, AI, 5/8/96.
385   *"was a great place"*: Simpson, AI, 12/19/91.
385   *"We'd just done"*: Mike Medavoy, AI, 5/9/95.
385   *"We were in a" and following*: Winkler, AI, 3/17/92.
386   *"We have to give"*: Paul Schrader, AI, 12/13/95.
386   *"Bob and I sort of"*: Scorsese, AI, 5/7/96.
386   *"De Niro was balking" and following*: Paul Schrader, AI, 12/13/95.
386   *"I'll do anything"*: Scorsese, AI, 5/8/96.
386   *"We didn't have" and following*: Martin, AI, 10/14/95.
386   *"Is this your blood?"*: Scorsese, AI, 5/8/96.
387   *"Finally, Marty got a doctor"*: Robertson, AI, n.d.
387   *"What's the matter"*: Martin, AI, 10/14/95.
387   *"that garage mechanic"*: Hillary Johnson, "Cybill Shepherd: Breaking the Ice," p. 54.
388   *"She was not in love"*: Confidential source.
388   *"She was totally" and following*: Colleen Camp, AI, 10/29/97.
388   *"Look, somebody's making"*: Henry, AI, 12/7/94.
388   *"Where's Peter" and following*: Camp, AI, 10/29/97.

389   *"I dropped the phone"*: Bogdanovich, AI, 10/19/95.
389   *"I thought I could"*: Scorsese, AI, 5/7/96.
389   *"We better have"*: Kelly, *Martin Scorsese*, p. 125.
389   *"This picture is written" and following*: Bach, *Final Cut*, pp. 164–66.
390   *"The key thing"*: Scorsese, AI, 5/8/96.
391   *"It had become"*: Tanen, AI, 1/22/93.
391   *"It looks like"*: Bach, *Final Cut*, p. 256.
391   *"They were so"*: Mankiewicz, AI, 6/23/94.
391   *"I was dead serious"*: Scorsese, AI, 5/8/96.
391   *"After New York" and following*: Scorsese, AI, 7/18/97.
392   *"It's more than one side"*: Scorsese, AI, 5/7/96.
392   *"He stuffed himself"*: Martin, AI, 10/14/95.
392   *"A lot of what"*: Towne, AI, 10/28/97.
393   *"So whaddya think" and following*: Anthea Sylbert, AI, 7/22/93.
394   *"I've never seen"*: Payne, AI, 1/10/95.
394   *"He abandoned everything"*: Payne, AI, 2/24/95.
394   *"He was overwhelmed"*: Patty James, AI, 4/27/96.
394   *"He couldn't make"*: Chapman, AI, 3/28/97.
394   *"If he really"*: James, AI, 4/27/96.
395   *"I've made a mess"*: Payne, AI, 6/20/97.
395   *"Let me be very"*: Confidential source.
395   *"It's an absolute"*: Geffen, AI, 1/6/98.
395   *"ol' write a line"*: James, AI, 5/7/96.
395   *"If you were close"*: Smith, AI, 12/13/96.
395   *"In one of"*: James, AI, 11/14/96.
396   *"A lot of terrible"*: Geffen, AI, 4/18/96.
396   *"Bob would go"*: Smith, AI, 12/13/96.
396   *"I remember Geffen"*: Chapman, AI, 3/28/97.
396   *"It went wildly"*: Geffen, AI, 4/18/96.
396   *"Robert had become"*: Payne, AI, 1/10/95.
397   *"I'm a rich'n"*: Towne, AI, 11/6/97.
397   *"Diller said no"*: Confidential source.
397   *"Bert was competitive"*: Monte Hellman, AI, 3/15/95.
397   *"How could you"*: Blauner, AI, 6/7/94.
398   *"I wanted experienced" and following*: Michie Gleason, AI, 5/13/95.
399   *"I didn't achieve"*: Scorsese, AI, 5/8/96.
399   *"The lights came up"*: Bach, *Final Cut*, p. 347.
399   *"The poster with"*: Scorsese, AI, 8/1/91.
399   *"one of the most"*: Ehrenstein, *The Scorsese Picture*, p. 68.
400   *"Heaven's Gate fails"*: Bach, *Final Cut*, p. 363.
400   *"Yes, the director"*: Hellman, AI, 6/20/94.
401   *"Suddenly there was" and following*: Altman, AI, 5/3/96.
401   *"Heaven's Gate undercut"*: Scorsese, AI, 5/8/96.
401   *"There was a kind"*: Coppola, AI, 12/19/94.
401   *"I went to see"*: Boorman, AI, 2/22/95.
401   *"The stuff that"*: Milius, AI, 1/9/92.
401   *"If a person"*: Justin Wyatt, *High Concept*, Austin, Texas, 1994, p. 13.
402   *"Don redesigned"*: Craig Baumgarten, AI, 2/2/96.
402   *"Don would dictate"*: Cohen, AI, n.d.
402   *"Diller would always"*: Yablans, AI, 6/3/96.

402   *"never really cared"*: Simpson, AI, 7/21/93.

402   *"The cinema of"*: Bogdanovich, AI, 10/19/95.

403   *"I had a film"*: Art Linson, AI, 3/10/92.

403   *"Realizing his life"*: Gay Talese, "Francis Coppola," *Esquire*, 7/81, p. 80.

403   *"It used to be"*: Spielberg, AI, 12/9/96.

403   *"In the '70s if"*: Friedkin, AI, 4/19/96.

404   *"It's really about"*: Mike Bygrave, "Inside the Studio," *Sight and Sound*, Winter 83, p. 20.

404   *"Testing changed"*: Bart, AI, 4/17/92.

404   *"In the '70s"*: Michael Phillips, AI, 3/14/92.

404   *"to be kidnapped"*: Sontag, "The Decay of Cinema."

405   *"So much of the '70s"*: Towne, AI, 11/6/97.

405   *"Marty wanted the kind"*: Sandy Weintraub, AI, 7/30/91.

405   *"When I lost"*: Scorsese, AI, 8/1/91.

405   *"We had explored" and following*: Scorsese, AI, 5/7/96.

405   *"he wanted me"*: Cathleen Young, *Isabella Rossellini*, New York, 1989, p. 96.

406   *"Big people in"*: Scorsese, AI, 8/1/91.

406   *"At the beginning"*: Bart, AI, 4/17/92.

406   *"They explained that"*: Scorsese, AI, 5/7/96.

407   *"I had to make up" and following*: Scorsese, AI, 8/1/91.

Chapter 14: "We Blew It"

PAGE

408   *Epigraph*: Coppola, AI, 12/19/94.

408   *"I felt that"*: Bogdanovich, AI, 10/19/95.

409   *"None of us were"*: Kidder, AI, 4/17/93.

409   *"The trick, for me"*: Scorsese, AI, 8/1/91.

409   *"It isn't any fun"*: Richard Schickel, AI, 1/18/96.

410   *"When you could" and following*: Paul Schrader, AI, 12/19/91.

411   *"He would call"*: Smith, AI, 12/13/96.

411   *"When the movie"*: Milius, AI, 1/9/92.

411   *"Nastassja Kinski is" and following*: Tanen, AI, 1/22/93.

412   *"Jerry Hellman asked" and following*: Paul Schrader, AI, 12/19/91.

412   *"The game was up"*: Paul Schrader, AI, 12/13/95.

413   *"Suddenly this pain"*: Friedkin, AI, 4/19/96; Segaloff, *Hurricane Billy*.

413   *"The way it works is"*: Coppola, AI, 6/27/96.

413   *"They hated Billy"*: Green, AI, 12/3/96.

414   *"I burned a lot" and following*: Friedkin, AI, 4/19/96.

414   *"Even the great"*: Coppola, AI, 6/27/96.

415   *"The directors still"*: Yablans, AI, 6/3/96.

415   *"Francis has only"*: Spielberg, AI, 12/9/96.

415   *"Arrogance and pussy"*: Friedkin, 4/20/96.

415   *"We all thought"*: Friedkin, AI, 4/19/96.

415   *"We didn't know"*: Bogdanovich, AI, 10/19/95.

415   *"The auteur theory"*: Martin, AI, 10/14/95.

415   *"I fell apart" and following*: Bogdanovich, AI, 10/19/95.

416   *"When Dorothy got"*: Michael Ventura, "Peter Bogdanovich: 'What Is the Point of Making Pictures?,' " *LA Weekly*, 5/28–6/3/82.

416   *"The day Dorothy"*: Geoff Andrew, "Mourning Has Broken," *Time Out*, 12/5–12/12/90.

416   *"My excuse is"*: Bogdanovich, AI, 6/29/94.
416   *"Remember me?"*: Confidential source.
417   *"I don't do"*: Coppola, AI, 7/31/97.
417   *"It's like your"*: Pollock, *Skywalking*, p. 245.
417   *"Some people have"*: Ibid.
417   *"Francis helped me"*: Ibid., p. 80.
417   *"I thought Francis"*: Ibid., p. 244.
417   *"It's going to be"*: Goodwin and Wise, "On the Edge," p. 278.
417   *"I was excited"*: Robbins, AI, 5/2/97.
418   *"Francis's voice was"*: Dalva, AI, 3/10/97.
418   *"Francis never wanted"*: Skager, AI, 3/4/97.
418   *"Francis was a man"*: Dalva, AI, 3/10/97.
418   "One from the Heart *started"*: Skager, AI, 3/4/97.
418   "One from the Heart *sank"*: Robbins, AI, 5/2/97.
418   *"Spiotta was in"*: Coppola, AI, 7/31/97.
419   *"George couldn't understand"*: Huyck, AI, 6/28/94.
419   *"Every Friday I"*: Skager, AI, 3/4/97.
419   *"With the collapse"*: David Thomson and Lucy Cray, "Idols of the King," *Film Comment*, 10/83, p. 72.
419   *"I'm broke"*: Confidential source.
419   "Apocalypse Now *was"*: Coppola, AI, 6/27/96.
420   *"Before* The Godfather": Ruddy, AI, 3/12/97.
420   *"Steve, if you're" and following*: Confidential source.
420   *"I don't know"*: Confidential source.
420   *"When Steven decided"*: Steven Schiff, "Seriously Spielberg," *New Yorker*, 3/21/94.
421   *"I had a baby"*: Baxter, *Steven Spielberg*, p. 330.
421   *"I started my career"*: Ibid., p. 321.
421   *"Kate outmanipulated"*: Katz, AI, 6/28/94.
421   *"It started out"*: Milius, AI, 1/9/92.
421   *"I said, 'What' "*: Robbins, AI, 5/2/97.
422   *"So John, you"*: Gottlieb, AI, 6/13/97.
422   *"For me, the bottom line" and following*: Marcia Lucas, AI, 3/3/97.
423   *"It violated all"*: Robbins, AI, 5/2/97.
423   *"He just didn't"*: Gomez, AI, 6/15/94.
423   *"I think what Marcia"*: Murch, AI, 4/20/97.
423   *"He was very bitter"*: Marcia Lucas, 3/3/97.
423   *"When he got"*: Coppola, AI, 7/31/97.
424   *"almost a total recluse"*: Aljean Harmetz, "Star Wars Is 10, and Lucas Reflects," *New York Times*, 5/21/87.
424   *"Francis really tried"*: Milius, AI, 1/9/92.
424   *"The same thing"*: George Lucas, AI, 5/2/97.
424   *"You've had your"*: Pollock, *Skywalking*, p. 277.
424   *"It took a long time"*: George Lucas, AI, 5/2/97.
424   "The Godfather *with music"*: Evans, AI, 3/11/97.
424   *"gangsters, music, pussy"*: Evans, *The Kid Stays*, p. 328.
424   *"I really need your help"*: Coppola, AI, 7/31/97.
425   *"the IRS was in"*: Richard Sylbert, AI, 8/25/92.
425   *"I didn't want"*: Coppola, AI, 7/31/97.
425   *"Gee, I'd like"*: Confidential source.
425   *"I want to be him"*: Confidential source.

425 *"I wanted to"*: Evans, AI, 2/27/94.

426 *"Woody Allen sits"*: Coppola, AI, 6/27/96.

426 *"I started warning people."*: Rosenman, AI, 1/28/92.

426 *"If you compare"*: Paul Schrader, AI, 1/8/92.

426 *"I had always" and following*: Paul Schrader, AI, 12/13/95.

427 *"Stephen Sondheim says"*: Rosenman, AI, 1/28/92.

427 *"He's smarter than"*: Kael, AI, 8/5/95.

427 *"My brother finds"*: Leonard Schrader, 11/17/94.

428 *"I checked myself" and following*: Hopper, AI, 7/15/97.

428 *"Robert went ballistic"*: Steve Roth, AI, 2/1/96.

429 *"Evans was that person"*: Confidential source.

430 *"There are more crosses"*: Evans, AI, 3/11/97.

430 *"a Jewish Chinaman"*: Confidential source.

430 *"Bob had always" and following*: Richard Sylbert, AI, 6/16/93.

431 *"I think Towne"*: Ivor Davis, "Can Jack Save Jake," *Los Angeles*, 12/89.

432 *"Towne has really"*: Kael, AI, 8/5/95.

432 *"Jack was one"*: Towne, AI, 11/6/97.

432 *"Bob was a Gatsby-like"*: Bart, interviewed by Terri Minksy, 5/89.

432 *"When Huey went"*: Bob Rafelson, AI, 11/10/93.

432 *"Despite Easy Rider's" and following*: Confidential source.

433 *"Bert was pissed"*: Blauner, AI, 10/30/97.

433 *"The money was not" and following*: Gittes, AI, 12/12/94.

433 *"Whenever you want" and following*: Blauner, AI, 10/30/97.

433 *"Jack is the King" and following*: Gittes, AI, 12/12/94.

434 *"I love Bert"*: Hopper, AI, 7/15/97.

434 *"When the marriages"*: Henry, AI, 12/7/94.

434 *"Fuck you, Jack"*: Confidential source.

434 *"Directors in order"*: Don Devlin, AI, 6/17/94.

434 *"We had the naive"*: Pollock, *Skywalking*, p. 86.

435 *"You know"*: Persky, AI, 2/26/95.

435 *"We finished shooting"*: Mulvehill, AI, 8/25/94.

435 *"I just give up."*: Confidential source.

436 *"Hal said, 'I' "*: Dern, AI, 6/15/95.

436 *"I got this"*: Beatty, AI, 6/28/94.

436 *"I got there"*: Hellman, AI, 6/20/94.

436 *"Is there such a"*: Beatty, AI, 6/28/94.

437 *"The truth is"*: Hellman, AI, 6/20/94.

437 *"He saw Sherri"*: Mulvehill, AI, 8/25/94.

437 *"Well, they're here"*: Berg, AI, 10/20/95.

438 *"Bob, they're calling" and following*: Jones, AI, 10/5/94.

Index

Photo Credits

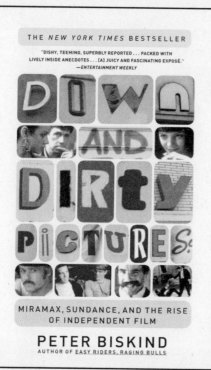

Down and Dirty Pictures

chronicles the rise of independent filmmakers and of the twin engines—Sundance and Miramax— that have powered them. As he did in his acclaimed *Easy Riders, Raging Bulls*, Peter Biskind profiles the people who took the independent movement from obscurity to the Oscars, most notably Sundance founder Robert Redford and Harvey Weinstein, who, with his brother Bob, made Miramax an indie powerhouse. Biskind's incisive account is loaded with vibrant anecdotes and outrageous stories, all of it blended into a fast-moving narrative.

SIMON & SCHUSTER
PAPERBACKS
A VIACOM COMPANY

www.simonsays.com